Handbook of Jealousy

In memory of my grandparents
Sara, Simon, Hannah, Herschel
S.H.

I dedicate this book to my parents
Johanna (Ansje) Koreman and Pieter Legerstee
(The Netherlands),
my children and to all children
M.L.

Handbook of Jealousy

Theory, Research, and Multidisciplinary Approaches

Edited by
Sybil L. Hart and Maria Legerstee

A John Wiley & Sons, Ltd., Publication

Registered Office
John Wiley & Sons, Ltd, The Atrium, Southern Gate, Chichester,
West Sussex, PO19 8SQ, UK

Editorial Offices
350 Main Street, Malden, MA 02148-5020, USA
9600 Garsington Road, Oxford, OX4 2DQ, UK
The Atrium, Southern Gate, Chichester, West Sussex, PO19 8SQ, UK

For details of our global editorial offices, for customer services, and for information about
how to apply for permission to reuse the copyright material in this book please see our
website at www.wiley.com/wiley-blackwell.

Library of Congress Cataloging-in-Publication Data has been applied for this title

ISBN 978-1-4051-8579-0 (hardback) – ISBN 978-1-118-57187-3 (paperback)

A catalogue record for this book is available from the British Library.

Cover image: Johan August Strindberg, Night of Jealousy, Berlin, 1893.
Photo: The Art Archive / Strindberg Museum Stockholm / Alfredo Dagli Orti.
Cover design by Nicki Averill Design & Illustration

Set in 11/13pt Dante by SPi Publisher Services, Pondicherry, India

Printed in Malaysia by Ho Printing (M) Sdn Bhd

1   2013

Contents

Contributors

Julie Wargo Aikins, University of Connecticut, USA
Marian J. Bakermans-Kranenburg, Leiden University, Leiden, The Netherlands
Nirit Bauminger, Bar-Ilan University, Ramat Gan, Israel
Aaron Ben-Ze'ev, University of Haifa, Haifa, Israel
Ben S. Bradley, Charles Stuart University, Bathurst, Australia
Joseph J. Campos, University of California, Berkeley, CA, USA
Audun Dahl, University of California, Berkeley, CA, USA
Ryan S. Darby, University of California, San Diego, CA, USA
Riccardo Draghi-Lorenz, University of Surrey, Surrey, UK
Noel Dyck, Simon Fraser University, Burnaby, BC, Canada
Baila Ellenbogen, York University, Toronto, Ontario, Canada
Nicolas Favez, University of Geneva, Geneva, Switzerland
R. M. Pasco Fearon, University of Reading, UK
Elisabeth Fivaz-Depeursinge, Unité de Recherche-CEF, Prilly, Switzerland
Scott Forbes, University of Winnipeg, Manitoba, Canada
Christine R. Harris, University of California, San Diego, CA, USA
Sybil L. Hart, Texas Tech University, Lubbock, TX, USA
R. Peter Hobson, Tavistock Clinic and University College, London, UK
Lisa M. H. Jackey, University of Michigan, Ann Arbor, MI, USA
Heidi Keller, University of Osnabrück, Osnabrück, Germany
Denise E. Kennedy, University of Michigan, Ann Arbor, MI, USA
Sara A. Kruse, University of Alabama, Tuscaloosa, AL, USA
Bettina Lamm, University of Osnabrück, Osnabrück, Germany
Maria Legerstee, York University, Toronto, Ontario, Canada
Michael Lewis, University of Medicine and Dentistry of New Jersey—Robert Wood Johnson Medical School, New Brunswick, NJ, USA
Francesco Lopes, University of Geneva, Geneva, Switzerland

Gabriela Markova, York University, Toronto, Ontario, Canada

Heidi Marsh, York University, Toronto, Ontario, Canada

Tom Nienhuis, York University, Toronto, Ontario, Canada

Jaak Panksepp, College of Veterinary Medicine, Washington State University, Pullman, WA, USA

Jeffrey G. Parker, University of Alabama, Tuscaloosa, AL, USA

Vasudevi Reddy, University of Portsmouth, Portsmouth, UK

Chloé Lavanchy Scaiola, Unité de Recherche-CEF, Prilly, Switzerland

Peter N. Stearns, George Mason University, Fairfax, VA, USA

James Stieben, York University, Toronto, Ontario, Canada

Marinus H. van IJzendoorn, Leiden University, Leiden, The Netherlands

Brenda L. Volling, University of Michigan, Ann Arbor, MI, USA

Eric A. Walle, University of California, Berkeley, CA, USA

Preface

According to an Old Russian proverb, "jealousy and love are sisters." This seems to suggest that both come from the same brain regions, and because love exists early in life, so might jealousy. Although accounts of infant jealousy date back many centuries, the scientific study of jealousy only started in the mid 1990s, generating but a paucity of information. The idea to address this shortcoming in a volume on Jealousy was sparked by very stimulating discussions I had with Joseph Campos and Sybil Hart at the International Conference of Infant Studies in Kyoto (2006), and again with Sybil at the biennial meeting of the Society for Research in Child Development in 2007. The SRCD symposium was especially revealing. It suggested two important things, namely (1) that the preconditions for the emergence of human jealousy could be elicited during the first months of life; and also in older children with autism; and (2) that there was little systematic knowledge about its development and the factors which influenced its expression. While at SRCD, Nirit Bauminger, Sybil Hart, and I discussed what might be the socio-cognitive and socio-biological foundations of jealousy. How do environmental factors such as parental rearing practices affect the expression of jealousy and how does the age of the person and her culture affect the presentation of jealousy?

What we ultimately discovered was that because little scientific data was available on the *development of jealousy,* few people actually *believed* that jealousy could present itself during infancy as a normal expression against exclusion by a loved one. However, infants have an innate desire to form social bonds and jealousy could be seen as a reaction to the presence of one who threatens this social bond. Would infants be able to perceive such a threat? If so, at what age and more importantly, in what context would infants express jealousy, and what would this reveal about the socio-cognitive underpinnings of jealousy? Another difficulty was that jealousy is not a single emotion. Jealousy is more appropriately labeled "a state" that one experiences and that, depending on the context, may conjure up emotions such as sadness (loss), anger (betrayal), fear/anxiety (loneliness), etc. Consequently, jealousy per se does not have accompanying coherent infrastructures in the brain and thus mapping jealousy onto a specific region is not possible.

It became clear that there was a lot of unpublished work out there that could inform about the development of jealousy in infants and children. I suggested to Sybil that we publish an edited book that focuses on the *development* of jealousy. We created the *Handbook of Jealousy: Theory, Research, and Multidisciplinary Approaches* to provide a comprehensive picture of jealousy, dealing with its functions, origins, and differentiation from infancy to its subsequent development. Twenty-one chapters and two commentaries chart how jealousy unfolds while also looking at the familial, cultural, cognitive, and biological factors that drive its development.

The *Handbook* is organized into five parts.

Part I: *Background*. In order to see how current understanding of jealousy has been formulated, it is important to put jealousy into context. Chapter 1 discusses social, cultural, and political trends during the twentieth century which gave rise to current thought on the topic of jealousy. Chapter 2 discusses issues which pertain to the interpretation of infants' responses that may indicate jealousy and distinctions between these and similar ones involving loss within social contexts that include attachment figures. Chapter 3 clarifies the importance of exclusivity in adult romantic jealousy by distinguishing between jealousy and envy, and examining the sense of belonging and concerns over comparisons with a rival that are key components of jealousy.

Part II: *Socio-Biological Foundations*. The development of jealousy has a starting point and this section provides an account of the socio-biological foundations of jealousy. Chapter 4 explores facial affects associated with the presentation of nascent jealousy during the first year, and proposes a model in which jealousy is conceptualized as an independently organized dimension of temperament. Chapter 5 speculates on the type of neural structures that might be activated when infants experience social exclusion among loved ones and peers, thereby delivering a unique report on the integration of neuroscience and infant behaviors. Chapter 6 provides insight into the evolutionary sources of jealousy by suggesting that jealousy relies on learning and socio-cognitive abilities, but may have a head start as well, in that it is more clearly "prepared" to take on its core form. Chapter 7 examines sibling rivalries in non-human species, and modes of responses to intra-familial competition that may underpin human behavior among siblings. Chapter 8 provides a detailed commentary of the above works and reflects what a world without jealousy would be like—a world without an overriding desire for an exclusive relationship.

Part III: *Cognitive Underpinnings*. It has often been argued that because jealousy is a complex emotion, it cannot have its onset until certain cognitive prerequisites are in place. Chapter 9 establishes the existence of socio-cognitive prerequisites in the development of jealousy in infants, such as social bonds, perception of triadic relationships, and awareness of goals, and with a creative experiment shows that emotions of jealousy are observable early in the first year. Chapter 10 is suggestive of jealousy among infant–peer trios, where vocalizations and gestures are being used in a seeming attempt to elicit or maintain the attention of a favored partner while in competition with a rival infant. Chapter 11 details rich parental reports on sibling interactions showing thwarting or open hostility toward a rival. Finally, Chapters 12 and 13 shed light on whether jealousy is a complex emotion with research on jealousy in people with autistic spectrum disorder (ASD) who have emotional deficits but often only minor cognitive impairments to highlight what capacities are necessary for experiencing jealousy. Chapter 14 provides commentary on the previous chapters and highlights issues in need of attention and elaboration in order to shed light on the processes responsible for the development of jealousy.

Part IV: *Social-Emotional Foundations within the Parent–Child–Sibling Context.* Early presentations of jealousy often take place within the parent–child–sibling context. This section explores the manner in which these are presented, and how they differ with child characteristics, family dynamics, and parental attitudes. Chapter 15 proposes a model of jealousy's development through the integration of theoretical and empirical works on jealousy's presentation in different eliciting conditions, its functions and individual differences. Chapter 16 explores variation among twins in terms of attachment security, and reports findings which lead to suggesting that quality of attachment may be shaped by processes akin to jealousy that reflect sibling competition. Chapter 17 examines family correlates of children's responses to differential treatment and findings of research on sibling jealousy in a sample of toddler and preschool siblings during a triadic laboratory paradigm. Chapter 18 examines parental attitudes toward sibling conflict, how these are distinguished from those toward child misbehavior in other settings, and how they are shaped by concepts of jealousy as an expression of love.

Part V: *Socio-Emotional Foundations within Other Eliciting Contexts.* Chapter 19 details the young infant's awareness and involvement in social exchanges between mother and father, and the challenges of being faced by social exclusion. Chapter 20 sheds light on the evolutionary basis of jealousy before turning to a discussion of cultural conditions that influence the manner in which jealousy is expressed in Western and non-Western caregiving settings. Chapter 21 presents an ethnographic account and anthropological analysis of jealousy as it is encountered among children and youths involved in sports in Canadian cities. Chapter 22 examines friendship jealousy among children and young adolescents, as well vulnerability to jealousy in relation to child characteristics, including age and gender. Chapter 23 focuses on jealousy in adult romantic relationships through attention to factors that impact its elicitation, experience, and expression, including adult attachment styles, relationship variables, attribution processes, rival characteristics, and gender.

1

Jealousy in Western History
From Past toward Present

Peter N. Stearns

Jealousy has a past—that is, it has been subject to significant change over time, which means it's a proper topic for historical study. Amid change, it also displays some interesting continuities within particular cultures—a common complexity which again means it's a proper topic for historical study.

Some stark contrasts are involved. Several of the most famous American trials of the later 19th century involved men who had killed either a wife or a wife's lover, and who argued (in several cases successfully, when they also could afford a high-priced attorney) that they suffered from a legitimate jealousy that simply overcame their will. Just a half-century later (we move to the 1930s), while a number of spousal murderers may have wanted to mount this argument (think of the possibilities, even later on, for O. J. Simpson), they got nowhere with it. Jealousy—in its legitimate power to overwhelm rational controls—had been reassessed, and effective law changed accordingly. We need emotions history to understand this kind of change and, through this in turn, to assess contemporary emotional formulations in terms of a trajectory from past to present. Jealous rage is not the only facet of this particular emotion to warrant historical analysis—it's not even the most significant element in point of fact; but it does demonstrate the kind of dramatic shifts that invite entry to a historical project.

Emotions history, still a fairly new and somewhat tentative entrant, fills several needs. It helps explain why former behaviors often differed from contemporary expectations—when people defined grief, or anger, or jealousy by standards different from those of the present, it is hardly surprising that their patterns of action, even some of their basic institutions, differed as well. Emotions history, in other words, helps historians do their job of exploring the past. Emotions history can generate some good stories, providing some of the wonder that good emotions anthropology offers as to the amazing range of human responses in what might seem to be basic characteristics of the species. Above all, however, emotions history, particularly but not exclusively applied to the past century or so, illuminates current emotional responses and issues directly. By showing the

Handbook of Jealousy: Theory, Research and Multidisciplinary Approaches, First Edition.
Edited by Sybil L. Hart and Maria Legerstee.

immediate antecedents of a contemporary emotional pattern, there is a chance to seek causal explanations that purely presentist evidence would not permit; where significant recent change is involved, complexities may also be identified that might be difficult to discern, or certainly to account for, by using current data alone. Seeing certain emotional formulations in movement, from a prior point in time, adds a vital ingredient to emotions analysis, whether or not there is explicit interest in the past per se.[1]

At its best, emotions history also helps relate emotional standards and experience to wider developments in society. Examination of recent shifts in jealousy certainly requires attention to broader changes in family patterns and gender relationships. Emotional change responds to more general social currents, and adds new components to social patterns in turn. Contemporary jealousy is a revealing case in point.

Obviously, historical analysis faces some limitations, particularly around a topic as elusive as emotion. Evidence is much stronger for cultural standards than for actual emotions experiences or internal perceptions. But the standards themselves matter. They normally shape public translations of emotional expectations, as in matters of law. History here helps explore the wider consequences of emotional criteria, in social and even political areas, beyond the more individualized preoccupations of many more conventional emotions researchers. And the standards do influence personal evaluations and responses, for which there is often a certain amount of independent evidence as well.

Emotions history has value even for emotions commonly regarded as basic—that is, to some degree innate. Changes in anger standards, including concerted efforts to reduce anger at work in the United States for the past several decades, have real impact on work itself but also on personal perceptions and expressions even off the job. A history of fear, including changes in childhood socialization toward the emotion that began to take hold in the 1920s, helps explain why elements of the American public have become increasingly manipulable through political scare tactics. And the list can be expanded.[2]

A more composite emotion such as jealousy, however, is if anything even more open to historical conditioning. Comparative contemporary studies have already shown how jealousy-inducing situations can generate very different amalgams of anger or sadness or embarrassment, depending on particular national cultures.[3] Amalgams can vary at least as much over time, which is where the opportunity to use history to explore the emotion more fully comes into play. Jealousy also has a complex, sometimes confusing relationship with envy, and history sheds light on this relationship, at least in contemporary society, as well.

The target, again, is not primarily the past for its own sake, though going back to jealousy from several centuries ago actually generates a few useful findings. The key goal involves improving contemporary self-understanding (personal and social alike), and in the process convincing other practitioners in disciplines associated with emotions study that adding a significant historical component to the interdisciplinary mix is more than a diversion, but potentially a key element in thorough analysis.

Two related comparative findings can help orient this kind of historical exploration of jealousy. Both suggest that many Americans are unusually uncomfortable with jealousy, not able always to shake it off but often forced to confront an emotion that they reprove. One response, suggested in a rich if brief comparative effort some years ago comparing polled American responses to those of Chinese, Greeks, Jamaicans, and others, is simply to conceal: Americans were more likely than many other cultures to believe that jealous feelings had to be kept secret. The other, perfectly compatible but from a slightly more recent and certainly richer comparative study, shows Americans (in contrast to the French and Dutch) particularly eager, when assailed with jealousy, to check with other people to find out if they had revealed the emotion or behaved unacceptably under its sway. These conclusions suggest an interesting jealousy issue in the United States that recent historical analysis will also highlight.[4] But the historical analysis, beyond confirming, expands the field to probe the causes of this contemporary discomfort, among other things by identifying approximately when and in what circumstances it began; and it facilitates as well a wider discussion of consequences, beyond what may be revealed to zealous pollsters.

We will begin the historical discussion a bit more diffusely, toward identifying some interesting earlier ingredients and issues; but the target, ultimately, is contemporary American discomfort, and how history helps illuminate and explain it.

***

Etymology, even a basic English dictionary, quickly reveals one important aspect of jealousy: that it long had at least two basic meanings in Western culture, only one of which survives very clearly in the present day. Jealousy, in the Middle Ages or in early modern Europe, could of course mean an emotion attached to love and (implicitly at least) sex, but it could also mean an emotion spurred in defense of power or honor, a powerful motivator that could win strong approval. Jealousy, in this second sense, was directly connected with the kindred word zeal (both words derive from the same Greek stem), spurring vigor to safeguard legitimate, though not always completely tangible, assets, a goad to honorable behavior. Jealousy in this sense could support behaviors, such as dueling, seen as essential to manliness or defense of family broadly construed. Intriguingly, though not surprisingly given a more recent history in which notions of honor have yielded to other goals, from commercial success (with which too much fussing about honor might interfere) to fuller definition of individual personality, jealousy as legitimate zeal has tended to fade from view.[5]

For Western society, including the United States, began to pull back from privileging codes of honor by the 18th and 19th centuries. Dueling came under direct attack, and more generally public discussion began to focus on the need to restrain the kinds of emotions that would promote affronts to honor.[6] A few

European and, by the early 20th century, Latin American countries even established committees to regulate affronts to honor, seeking to acknowledge jealous response but quickly smother it with compromise; but this was a transitional measure that soon yielded to the assumption that any balanced individual could keep the emotions associated with honor under control on his own. Only a trickle of commentary kept alive the notion that jealousy could do any good in male–male relations. Thus one aberrant note in the American child advice literature of the 1940s argued that jealousy could have "character-building and creative uses," the idea being not that it supported honor—now hopelessly out of date—but that it could be transformed into competitive motivation that did still fit the needs of a contemporary society. But this interesting argument was decidedly atypical in what had become, as we will shortly see, a pattern of blanket disapproval.

Traditionally, of course, ideas about jealous defense of honor could closely link to more precise discussions of the role of jealousy in love, and in male–female relationships. Here, however, the Western cultural tradition, at least by the later Middle Ages when troubadours began to heap praise on the idea of courtly love, surfaced considerable disagreement and, though inconsistently with ideals of honor, some interesting gender disparities as well. Romantic jealousy could easily be attacked because it produced cruel behaviors, adulterated real love with baser passion, and led jealous individuals to a tragic loss of control. Classically, of course, Shakespeare thus represented jealousy in *Othello*, describing the "venom" and "misery" of the emotion. Seventeenth-century Jesuits blasted jealousy as a "monstrous" passion, the antithesis of real, spiritual love; a jealous husband might incite his wife to sin simply in retaliation for his rantings, and the emotion could lead directly to crime.[7] La Rochefoucauld saw no relationship between jealousy and real love, though he implicitly recognized that the linkage was common: "If (jealous) love is judged by its effects, it resembles hate more than friendship."[8]

There was, however, another view, that jealousy was not only inevitable but actually desirable, in enhancing love. A French courtly love writer of the 12th century argued that "He who is not jealous cannot love ... Real jealousy always increases the feelings of love ... Jealousy, and therefore love, are increased when one suspects his beloved." Jealous men could be literary heroes, defending the honor of their faithful wives. Theater fare of the 17th and 18th centuries often urged the importance of a certain amount of jealousy in flirtation, so long as it did not get out of control. Marriage advice might try, similarly, to distinguish between useful, moderate jealousy and an emotion that could drive couples apart through unfair accusations or obsession: "There is a just and an unjust jealousy. Just, is with married partners who mutually love each other; there is with them a just and prudent zeal lest their conjugal love be violated and therefore just grief if it is violated ... That zeal is a just protection against adultery is plain. Hence it is as a fire flaming against violation, and defending against it."[9]

All of this chatter operated as part of European high culture, sending out mixed signals of warning and acknowledgment. The mixed legacy has some significance. It shows that more contemporary concerns about jealousy as a distortion of valid emotion and a potential hazard are by no means entirely new, though this is unsurprising. The legacy also shows, however, that ideas of honor could get wrapped up in some masculine definitions of love; though this association would later encounter more uniform disapproval, it certainly could survive at least for certain personalities and in certain subcultures (some historians have pointed to a particular Southern attachment to ideas of honor, for example) even against the mainstream. Most interesting, however, before modern times, was an apparent tendency to try to resolve the contradictory signals through gender distinctions, however inconsistently with broader ideas about honor and a disproportionate emphasis on women's responsibility for sexual fidelity. An intriguing investigation into French court records in the 17th century, by historian Natalie Davis, shows that men rarely used a jealousy argument when trying to explain why they committed a disruptive act, preferring instead to claim that they were motivated by righteous anger. Women, however, though obviously less commonly involved in accusations of crime, frequently claimed that they were spurred by jealousy to attack or insult other women or assault their own husbands. Jealousy, in this rendering, was a legitimate but baser emotion, acceptable for the gender widely regarded as less capable of living up to high standards. This rendering at the popular level would also emerge in later formulas, with all its incompatibilities with residual beliefs in legitimate male defense of sexual honor.[10]

There is ample room for additional work on cultural traditions involving jealousy, and how they worked into popular calculations, and a pressing need for more comparative works; but a few points are already clear. Jealousy was a frequent and rather complex subject of discussion, with some deeply held but also inconsistent beliefs. The idea of jealousy as motivational, for men—an idea that would not travel well into the more modern period—struggled against the notion that this was a petty emotion more suited to women, and all within a framework in which some purists disapproved of jealousy altogether, either because it sullied the purity of love or because it could generate obsession or violence.

***

Against this backdrop, discussions of jealousy in the 19th century, at least in the United States, were surprisingly muted. This was a strange preamble to what became an unprecedentedly ardent concern in the early 20th century. Apparently— and one speculates largely in terms of what is meant by absence of evidence, rather than on the basis of elaborate data—Victorian standard-setters implicitly agreed that jealousy-fueled honor was not worth much attention because of general recognition that the goals were inappropriate; while at the same time a new and decidedly ethereal praise for true love involved far too much purity for jealousy to intrude—again, a reason for lack of much attention. Love was a frequently explored topic, but jealous entanglements did not figure into the 19th-century standards, as transmitted in family advice literature. Only on the margins did the older idea of petty female jealousy crop up in much formal discussion. Marital advice literature contained a few cautionary tales about wives who unjustifiably burdened their husbands with jealousy, though interestingly now directed at intense work interests outside the home more than against female rivals. One protagonist's happy home life was thus briefly "clouded" by jealousy, because her lawyer husband sometimes brought work home, until she realized, like a good wife, that she could share his professional ambitions so that his intensity would no longer seem to exclude her emotionally. A few stories and personal diaries evoked jealousies among adult sisters, for example when one found a match yet the other was still nervously single, confirming the femaleness but also the minor inconvenience of the emotion.[11]

The huge exception to this substantial neglect involved the throwback appeals to a jealousy of honor when husbands were directly confronted with wives' indiscretion and responded violently in the heat of the moment. "For jealousy is the rage of a man; therefore he will not spare in the day of vengeance . . . Those who dishonor husbands are here warned of their doom . . . Jealousy, which defies and tears down all restraint, whether it be what we technically call insanity or not, is akin to it. It enslaves the injured husband, and vents itself in one result, which seems to be inevitable and unavoidable." So argued the successful attorney for one Daniel McFarland in 1870, winning acquittal for his wealthy defendant (who had killed his wife's lover in flagrante delicato) amid the open adulation of hundreds of public well-wishers. The McFarland defense built on the pioneering argument in the Daniel Sikles trial of 1859 (another lover-killer) which had also successfully cited the "deep, ineffaceable consuming fire of jealousy." Overall, between 1859 and the early 20th century, about 30 high-profile trials, all involving well-heeled male defendants, had invoked this defense. Intriguingly, an effort to do the same for a woman (who had killed her husband's lover) failed before a court which insisted that women could not possibly be stirred by such a deep and righteous form of jealousy.[12]

The argument for a few men, however, and its apparent resonance both with legal experts and a wider public, was fascinating, a seeming exception to the general disdain for, and feminization of, jealousy in the 19th century. The shift was considerable, though there was an obvious link to older anger arguments that men had used, in Western culture, to justify defense of honor or of spousal fidelity. Changes in the legal niceties of claiming insanity played a role in the change, but so did the increased currency of ideas about romantic love, which allowed new emphasis to be placed on jealousy in relationship to this emotion, rather than to more abstract concepts of honor. The link between jealousy and heightened expectation of love set the stage for ongoing discussions, spilling into the 20th century. But the association of jealousy and loss of control, even temporary insanity, also suggested drawbacks to jealousy that would soon feed a very different kind of evaluation, in which jealousy had to be seen as a deep flaw in character.

Traditional elements were obvious: the new, 19th-century courtroom use of jealousy harked back directly, though not explicitly, to older ideas about emotions legitimate in the defense of male honor. This was not, again implicitly, a petty, female type of jealousy, but an overriding emotion befitting the seriousness of the offense. Double standards, another patriarchal tradition, were fully deployed, for men had a right to emotional responses to infidelity that women did not; and in fact, for many in the middle and upper classes, the later 19th century was a double-standard heyday. But the novel note was vital as well, even aside from the heightened linkage with romantic love: jealousy's surge was equivalent to insanity in its temporary but blinding qualities. The legal reasons for the addition to standard defenses of male honor were obvious: only brief insanity would get the defendant off the hook. Yet while this was a temporarily successful line of argument, it conceded a huge amount to jealousy's downside, to the essential illegitimacy of the emotion in a reasonable society. The very success of the ploy may have contributed to a larger reassessment of jealousy which prepared, in fact, the more contemporary lines of response.

One final feature of 19th-century American society warrants attention, in explaining why comments about jealousy were so infrequent aside from the fascinating but atypical show trials. Men and women, particularly in the standard-setting middle classes, operated in rather separate spheres during the century as a whole, with respectable women confined in or around the home while men were increasingly away at work. Inter-gender contact, of the sort that might provoke adult jealousy, was fairly limited. Courtship could of course provoke conflicting emotion, but even this was a rather private, home-based activity, not springing from an abundance of public socializing among young people. And again, the fashionable statements concerning love, emphasizing pure and ethereal passion, would have been spoiled by too much admission of jealousy in any event.

The 20th century would differ from this pattern, among other things because social interactions between the genders began to change considerably. More respectable women worked outside the home, at least for a period before marriage. Co-education increasingly extended to high school and even college. Dating practices replaced home-based courtship. Even among married couples, social activities expanded and involved both spouses—the older pattern of men heading off to clubs and lodges faded in the middle class. Opportunities for jealousy arguably expanded, which is why new and more explicit commentary and cautionary advice emerged so strongly.

***

For new battle lines against jealousy were drawn in the early 20th century, far from courtrooms and nearer the cribs of young children, who had never before figured significantly in jealousy discussions of any sort. The issue, a crucial 20th-century invention, was of course sibling rivalry. From as early as 1893 (interestingly, in a revised edition of what was then the best-selling childrearing manual), advisors began to warn about the dangers of intense jealousy among young children. Parents should be aware, Felix Adler trumpeted, of the "incipient hatred" that could develop among brothers, at a very early age, which could poison the loving affection that should serve as the core of family life.[13] This early salvo turned into a veritable flood of concern by the 1920s, with Children's Bureau manuals and virtually every commercial handbook addressing systematic attention to sibling rivalry. Research, at centers like Smith College, seemed to confirm the virtually inevitable onset of sibling rivalry when a toddler had to confront a newborn brother or sister. The dangers were twofold: first, an immediate physical threat to the baby, from a jealousy-wracked 3-year-old, something that parents should guard against with great vigilance. But second, the possible emotional perversion of the toddler him- or herself (gender was not a factor in this new campaign) from the poison of sibling jealousy. The verb insistently used was "festering": if parents did not actively intervene to set the toddler on the right track, jealousy might take over permanently, distorting adult opportunities both for successful marriage and for healthy relationships at work. Parental intervention was vital, and at the same time the ubiquity of children's jealousy made this essentially a standard obligation. The message might be stated in various ways: "Children who quarrel because of jealousy are in a serious state ... This type of quarreling should be treated at once by getting at and doing away with the cause of it." Parents who let their children rival each other "may be wrecking their chance of present and future happiness." "Unless parents recognize that jealousy will normally appear, and are prepared for it, strong feelings of hostility often develop which continue to make life miserable for both children over many years." Even worse, according to this new and dire expertise, jealousy incompletely expressed might be worse than overt emotion: "The child whose jealousy is not as easy to recognize suffers more and has greater need for help."[14]

And on it went. Popularizers in the childrearing field were at least dimly aware that they were identifying something that had not previously been highlighted, on which they could therefore assume parental ignorance and the need for external guidance. Even Dr. Spock, later on, widely and inaccurately known for his laidback reassurances to parents, would insist that "a lot of effort" was essential in curbing children's jealous emotion.[15]

The messages, including of course the new term itself (sibling rivalry as a formal concept dates from the 1920s), were systematically disseminated, not only in widely purchased handbooks but also from the pages of new family publications like *Parents' Magazine*. By the 1940s and 1950s, in turn (it takes a while for even a systematic campaign of this sort to take full hold), many parents had clearly internalized the concern, writing frequent letters about manifestations of jealousy among their own children and what they had done, or whom they had consulted, to deal with the problem. A poll in the late 1940s, focused on middle-class parents, found 53% claiming significant problems with sibling rivalry, and overall listing this as the third most pressing parental concern, and at the top of the list in terms of emotional and personality issues. We will turn momentarily to some of the wider consequences of the whole sibling rivalry scare, but it is clear that its proponents reached their immediate goal: to make the concept and the concern part of the standard arsenal of responsible parents.[16]

The result, correspondingly, was a major shift in the status of jealousy in American culture. The key innovations involved were obvious, even while admitting that concerns about jealousy can be found in earlier periods as well. First, jealousy was hauled out for a degree of attention it had certainly never before received in American discussions of emotion, more attention than it had usually received in any prior context. Second, it was now treated with a degree of hostility that was at least unusual if not unprecedented. This was an emotion with no merit whatsoever, indeed an emotion that carried great danger, high on the list of things to be worried about. And third, of course—and this was the most striking feature of all—it had to be encountered and handled in dealing with very young children. The attack on sibling rivalry was a key element in a new sense of parental responsibility for the explicit emotional socialization of the young, for the kind of guidance that would allow them to grow into emotionally healthy, functional adults, in turn a huge expansion of expectations attached to responsible parenthood.

The obvious question, important both historically and in terms of understanding more about the contemporary dynamics of jealousy, focuses on causation. Why did sibling rivalry become such a concern in the second quarter of the 20th century, when siblings had been around as long as the species itself with few indications of significant anxiety? Tensions between adult siblings have a historical record, from Cain and Abel onward. Diary evidence from the 19th century shows how parents occasionally grew a bit annoyed at childish bickering among siblings, but with no sense of a systematic problem and with it a focus on early childhood. The idea that jealousy among young children merited great attention was an innovation, and it begs for explanation.

Explanation, in turn, comes in three parts, granting that there is always a partially speculative element in this aspect of historical analysis, when developments that coexist in time are assigned weight in causation.

First, and most directly, a variety of psychologists began to turn more attention to children's emotions, including jealousy; the results were new at least to the extent that this kind of psychology had not existed before. Already in the later 19th century G. Stanley Hall and colleagues were conducting observations of children, and Hall was already commenting on the role of extreme adult jealousy in motivating crimes. New types of experts thought they knew things about children that had not been adequately explored before, and on this basis they thought they had an obligation to guide parents toward new responsibilities, responsibilities that had not been part of traditional parenting. The sense that scientific expertise was superior to conventional wisdom ran very strong by the early 20th century. It also turned out, of course, that persuading parents that they needed expert help was a great way to sell books and magazines and even therapy visits, which added to the motivation. The new experts (who replaced older popularizers who had relied primarily on their qualifications as moralists) obviously believed they had discovered new problems with jealousy, including its wide and early intrusion into childhood, and this became part of what they sold to the general public. The formal research into sibling rivalry, which extended initial concerns, only added to the sense of scientific discovery.

But why did parents—whose own parents had managed to do their job without knowing that sibling rivalry was a formal concept—buy into the new expertise, however fervently advocated? Clearly, something of a general pattern began to emerge in the 1920s, in which growing numbers of parents thought they needed new kinds of advice. This was a decade, not coincidentally, in which three-generational households began to decline, with grandparents maintaining separate residences more commonly than in the past; so intergenerational advice may have become either less available or seemingly less relevant. More broadly, the sense that modern life required new socialization goals may also have played a role; it was at this point, after all, that government agencies began to get into the parental guidance game, through the publications of the Children's Bureau, steadily branching out from an initial focus on purely physical health to a wider array of psychological criteria. But while factors of this sort explain a general receptivity to new and more detailed advice literature, they hardly explain the special concern about jealousy.[17]

This then moves us to phase two of the explanation: some very real changes in parent–child dynamics that had been emerging gradually since the later 19th century but now became inescapable. Several factors were converging for middle-class families. Use of live-in domestic servants was declining rapidly, which reduced non-parental help in dealing with young children within the household; in some cases, the new trend for older relatives to live separately added to a situation where parent–child interaction was less commonly mediated by other adults, until school age intervened. Most important, the rapid decline in birth rate reduced the availability of assistance from older children and, perhaps ironically, enhanced children's rivalry for adult affection. We know that larger clusters of siblings tend to diffuse jealousy, but this was now the pattern that was becoming exceptional.[18] Siblings grouped together less (a trend also encouraged by growing emphasis on same-age contacts among children), and competed for interaction with parents more. Here is a factor impossible to prove definitively (though more historical work on the neglected topic of changes in sibling relations over time would help), but plausible and perhaps even probable nevertheless, as it builds on a number of concomitant developments of real importance. Jealousy among young children may have been singled out for new attention because in fact it was cropping up more commonly, or at the least because parents were likely to perceive it more acutely. Again, the new attention occurred within a framework where parental responsibility for emotional intervention in general was gaining new emphasis, where beliefs in the necessity of monitoring young children's emotional lives acquired new urgency because of concerns about the relationship between early impulses and later adult personalities. But there were good reasons for the role of jealousy in centering this sense of concern.[19]

Finally—the third layer—the focus on sibling rivalry occurred in a situation where adult jealousy itself was being reevaluated. It is possible that adult tensions encouraged some displacement onto the childish emotional arena, definite that new beliefs in the inappropriateness and danger of adult emotion in this area fostered much of the urgency about trying to create children who would grow up jealousy-free. The result was a causal circuit, in which larger warnings promoted the new signals in children's socialization, which in turn helped publicize and internalize the constraints on adults.

Changes in setting were gradual but cumulative, focusing on new public roles for women and new levels of gender contact in various settings. By the 1920s a majority of Americans could count on going to coeducational institutions for primary and secondary schooling, and a growing number also went on to coeducational colleges. The new practice of dating was gaining ground in these same schools, with considerable emphasis on the importance of "playing the field" for a while rather than forming intense attachments that might legitimately be informed by jealousy. For middle-class adolescents, for whom dating did emphasize multiple or sequential relationships rather than explicit courtship, these recommendations had real influence. At work, in the white collar sector, growing numbers of women shared office space (if often in subordinate roles). To be sure, most middle-class women did end their careers after marriage, but far more gender mixing was beginning to develop in public, as opposed to household-based, work space than had ever previously occurred. Finally, more and more middle-class couples participated in new kinds of entertainment and socializing outside the home. Observers, including perceptive social scientists like the Lynds in "Middletown" (Muncie, Indiana), noted that parties included not only mixed-company card games, and often smoking and drinking, but also frequently flirtatious exchanges of partners for part of an evening. While the new norms did not condone non-marital sex, and there is no indication that this became a more common part of middle-class marriage, the Lynds noted that by the 1930s even extramarital liaisons did not draw the heated condemnation that had once been the case in small-town America.[20] Admittedly at an extreme, a spate of "modernist" marital advice began to emerge as well, that explicitly attacked jealousy for its constraints on freedom. The literature set a tone for a wider, if more moderate, commentary.[21]

All of these changes in middle-class circles, which brought males and females into far more relatively unsupervised contact than had been widely permitted in the 19th century, depended on more explicit constraints on jealousy than had been necessary previously. Whether this contributed to the forces promoting more rigorous emotional socialization of children, or simply built on the changes encouraged by new expertise and new parent–child dynamics within the family, cannot be definitively determined. Certainly, however, a relationship was reflected in the frequent comments, in popularized manuals, on the results of unchecked childish jealousy on adult interactions. It was no surprise, as well, that recommendations similar to those directed toward children began to show up, by the 1930s, in marital and dating advice as well, pruned of course of the specific references to sibling tensions. The new genre of magazines for teenagers (teenaged girls, particularly) repeated warnings about how the green-eyed monster could poison both reputations and relationships. By the 1950s, advice literature offered extensive warnings about the dangers of jealousy in romance. One exception, the widely hailed authority Paul Popenoe who thought the emotion was fundamental to family stability and therefore to civilization, actually proved the rule, for his efforts at insistence so clearly swam against the tide.[22] For most popularizers, the standards were clear and stark. Jealousy revealed personal disorientation: "We may even blight and blacken our happiness by jealousy, which is really an admission of our own inferiority, of our own cowardice and conceit." Implicit connections with childhood socialization were common as well: "The jealous lover is a child hugging his toy so closely that no one else can see it. Jealousy is almost always a mark of immaturity and insecurity. As we grow confident of love and of our loved one, we are not jealous … we need not cling in desperation." The attack on sibling rivalry, in fact, made it increasingly logical to associate adult jealousy with uncorrected childishness, an indictment of the jealous individual and his or her upbringing alike.[23]

The transformation showed clearly in the legal arena, where modernist thinking about the unacceptability of jealous constraints on individual freedom, even within marriage, clearly gained ground. As early as the 1890s, state supreme courts were beginning to find the contention that jealousy could legitimately excuse loss of control and resultant violence unacceptable. There were intriguing hesitations. Some states remained willing to reduce jealousy-based killings to manslaughter, even when rejecting exoneration outright. A Texas statute, reconfirmed in 1925, legitimized killing by a husband confronting adultery directly providing it occurred before formal separation (and always with the insistence that wives did not have similar rights). Georgia similarly referred to "righteous and justifiable indignation," but extended the same thinking to wives with specific reference to sauce for the gander being sauce for the goose. But these Southern holdouts were unusual and also ultimately transient. By the 1970s all the Southern states had specifically withdrawn the justifiable homicide defense, with the Georgia Supreme Court explicitly noting that in these changing times uncontrolled jealousy had become "uncivilized." Other legal shifts, beginning in the 1920s and reaching completion by the 1970s, showed similar thinking: the movement toward no-fault divorce reduced the need to invoke jealousy as part of the termination of marriage (and the widespread decriminalization of adultery moved in the same direction). Opportunities to sue for breach of promise or alienation of affections, a notorious avenue for jealous as well as mercenary actions in the early 20th century, also ended.[24]

In sum: a significant new level of hostility was directed against jealousy in the United States, from early in the 20th century through the 1970s. Reasons for this shift, beyond obvious and influential new expertise, are not entirely clear, but they combined a variety of family concerns with important new settings for hetero-sexual contact. Of course, the hostility built on more traditional antipathies to jealousy, but in largely eliminating any positive evaluation, any ambiguity, it marked a new chapter in approaches to this emotion. Not surprisingly, the resulting shift in standards was not only widely publicized, but affected various public forums including that provided by the legal system.

Actual impacts of the new standards, again not surprisingly, were more complicated than the uncompromising standards themselves. First, given the vigor and insistence of the explicit attacks on jealousy, it was hardly surprising that the message was picked up and internalized at several levels. From the 1930s onward, various studies and polls suggested a widespread desire to seem free from jealousy. Arnold Gesell's evaluation of teenagers revealed a general desire to claim lack of jealousy and an interesting effort to point to the emotion as part of a discarded childhood. Teenagers, in other words, were reflecting the sibling campaign as a source of knowledge of the standards and an association between lack of jealousy and growing up—exactly the terms of the larger campaign.[25] Both boys and girls were eager to claim that jealousy was something they had experienced as young children but had now—by age 13 or so—definitively outgrown. It is vital to note, as a qualification to this claim, that American teenagers were also busily creating procedures that would help them minimize jealousy in fact, working against adult recommendations in the process. Dating was approved by parents and adults alike as a chance for young people to get to know a variety of partners of the opposite sex, in order to gain experiences that would ultimately, much later, help in selecting an appropriate mate. It was supposed to be casual, with neither deep passion nor sex involved. In fact, however, and particularly by the 1930s, many teenagers subverted this process by introducing "steady" dating, an exclusive arrangement that could involve considerable emotion and at least sexual overtones, but in which possible rivals were supposed to play by the rules and not poach on the reserved partner. It was easier to live up to the jealousy-free or at least reduced-jealousy claim when teenage culture fenced the couple off. Adults bemoaned this perversion—hoping obviously that teenagers could manage a more open environment free from jealousy—but teenagers insisted, continuing to seek steady arrangements until the decline of the whole institution of private dating in the 1960s.

For adults themselves, normally aided of course by the more clearly recognized institution of marriage, similar efforts were devoted to claiming, at least, mastery of the jealous emotion. Marriage surveys indicated similar awareness that jealousy was not an appropriate emotion, that it could be subject to legitimate complaint. One California study showed that men's resentment of their wives' jealous nagging ranked quite high in the list of complaints (a sign as well, of course, that jealousy, real or perceived, was still around), far above worries about infidelity.[26] This kind of resentment was not new, of course, but it now received more systematic sanction, which could elevate it as a marital issue and make both partners more eager to claim, at least, that they had risen above the emotion. A classic, though admittedly fleeting and atypical, example of how far the new standards could penetrate came with the open marriage movement of the 1960s, where couples involved were virtually compelled to exhibit no signs of jealousy when one partner openly engaged in a sexual liaison with someone else. The new code encouraged admissions of shame or guilt when jealousy intruded amid open infidelity: as one not-quite-up-to-date spouse admitted, "I think (my reaction) came from possessiveness and I'm trying to get over that." This bled into a jealousy workshop movement, particularly on some college campuses, during the 1970s, where gurus like Larry Constantine helped jealous partners overcome their emotion, for example by watching a stranger massage their mate.[27] On a less extreme level, polls of college students revealed a growing percentage eager to disclose or claim freedom from jealousy. The standards counted, certainly in self-presentation, probably also for many in accepted personal criteria.[28]

The shift of adolescents and college students away from more formal dating and toward more group-based socializing, with brief rather than committed sexual forays, may also have reflected, or at least coincided with, a further internalization of the anti-jealousy standards. Group dynamics were not meant to be disturbed by one-night stands or prior sexual involvements.

Of course, jealousy did not in fact go away. Indeed, though this is a huge claim that requires careful assessment, it seems likely that sexual habits changed more rapidly than the jealousy standards could accommodate. Older traditions (including the longstanding belief that women were more likely than men to suffer from the emotion, despite considerable evidence to the contrary) and the vagaries of individual personalities both played a role in gaps between standards and emotional realities. There are many indications—including, of course, the claim about nagging wives in California—that many people continued to harbor jealousy, even if they often strove to conceal the fact. Another mid-century poll, for example, showed that almost a third of all spouses, though men slightly more commonly than women, experienced jealousy over a partner's previous relationships (whether sexual or not). Aside from a minority of open-marriage adepts, sensitivities to infidelity did not clearly cool. The attacks on jealousy did promote a situation in which disparities in emotional reactions placed a special burden on the more jealous individual, now often called to apologize or even face threats of retaliation along lines of "I'll give you something to be jealous about." But disparities between aspirations and emotional experience did not disappear even with this probable shift in the emotional balance of power.[29]

Another anomaly is harder to interpret. Emotions researchers have noted for some time common popular confusions between jealousy and envy in American culture. The new attacks on jealousy, and particularly their influence on childhood socialization, help explain the intermixing. Even in the 1930s, teenagers commented on being jealous of a schoolmate's beautiful hair or (probably more rarely) academic achievements, when in fact they meant feeling envious. The desire not to seem jealous might spill over into this kind of personal envy, creating a common sense that emotions about someone else's gains or attributes were signs of childishness and should be reproved along with jealousy itself. At the same time, however, envy about material possessions gained new legitimacy, as historian Susan Matt has shown. Long criticized as revealing a distorted sense of values, as contradicting Christian priorities and virtues, consumer envy began to be praised by the 1920s as a legitimate spur to acquisitions and material improvements. To be sure, the idea of motivation in terms of "keeping up with the Joneses" still sometimes seemed shallow, but there was no fundamental flaw implied.[30] Many people used the new legitimization to become fairly open in their desire to keep pace with the consumer gains of a neighbor or colleague. Clearly, this kind of envy had nothing to do with jealousy or with the reproof it now commanded. Indeed—though here we are on speculative ground; the different versions of envy in recent history warrant more attention—it is possible that consumer adjustments might provide a legitimate outlet for emotions about others that might otherwise veer toward jealousy. Many Americans were trained to think of shopping as an emotional outlet and balm.[31]

The main point is, however, the new level of tension between the widely accepted standards and the emotions many people might still encounter in the realm of jealousy. It became harder to admit jealousy to oneself, certainly riskier to manifest it in any public way, even in front of a spouse. Here was the context in which the temptation to conceal jealousy became particularly strong in the United States, as comparison with other emotional cultures suggested. Here was the context in which Americans became unusually interested in checking with other people to make sure their jealousy had not shown through in any blatant fashion. It was the intensity of the new hostility to jealousy juxtaposed with some ongoing impulses that created new divisions in emotional reactions, with those who could claim relative immunity clearly carving an easier path than their more afflicted peers. But it was the intensity, plus the new divisions, plus the fact that some people could not shake jealousy off amid significant changes in gender relations and sexuality in the United States that created the desire to mask and then to make sure that the real emotion had not somehow slipped out from behind the mask.

Tensions may have eased somewhat after the 1970s. Certainly the most explicit campaign against jealousy operated in the half-century after the 1920s. By the 1980s, greater internalization of the new standards made explicit references less necessary. At the same time, however, reactions against the apparent sexual license of the 1960s made jealousy somewhat more acceptable in certain quarters. A few comments now openly admitted the experience of jealousy without self-recrimination. It was also discovered that the worst fears about sibling rivalry had been exaggerated, that the fabled research of the 1920s had been off the mark: certainly the vivid focus on the dangers and ubiquity of sibling jealousies eased. Other changes may have helped, though they often reflected the applicability of jealousy concerns. The decline of dating among teenagers, in favor of group activities, reduced some of the invitations to jealousy during adolescence. At the same time, as we have seen, harmony in the group, along with often temporary sexual pairings, assumed substantial jealousy control, so the standards may in fact have been confirmed even as intense adolescent romance was downplayed.[32]

On balance, the most important developments suggested not a reversal of the campaign against jealousy, but an assumption that the main points were well established and fairly familiar, from childhood socialization onward. This permitted a slight relaxation of anxiety levels, but no massive shift toward greater approval, either in laws, or public reactions, or—insofar as we can determine—personal evaluations. It was precisely because of an assumption that the standards were set and widely understood that the level of discussion and preaching could drop in volume. What had been pages about sibling jealousies in a child guidance handbook thus could become a paragraph or two, because the problem seemed contained and because parents, veterans of sibling controls in their own childhoods, already knew the rules. This only slightly modified framework, then, continues to explain dominant American approaches to jealousy in comparative context. The same framework, the product of a powerful if unfamiliar recent history, invites the linkage between historical analysis and other disciplines concerned with jealousy manifestations and jealousy problems in contemporary life.

Jealousy has never been a comfortable emotion, and both history and contemporary evaluation demonstrate this fact readily enough. The stripping away of any positive components was nevertheless an important development in American emotions history, as was the elevation of the emotion to a position of unusual attention and concern. The new focus on jealousy was almost inevitable given broader changes in gender relationships, for this was an emotion at the center of some sweeping shifts in social patterns.

And this point moves us to a larger, potentially even global setting. Far less is known about the history of jealousy in other societies, particularly non-Western societies, than is desirable. As indicated earlier, we do know that some other societies are more candid than American society is in admitting that jealousy exists or even in finding it constructive in helping to promote or cement a relationship. The French, more open to expressing anger when they experience jealousy, clearly have experienced a different kind of historical evolution from Americans, making them less eager to conceal. Societies closer to traditions of honor, like Greece or Jamaica, are more willing to admit and act upon jealousy as a motivation, for better or worse. It is clear, even absent adequately detailed history, that different cultural traditions produce different expressions of jealousy even in the modern context.

But the American experience, while not providing a global model save insofar as Hollywood film and television fare projects the validity of emotionally casual relationships, may be instructive in one respect. A wide range of societies, in recent decades, have been undergoing some of the same kinds of change that the United States experienced earlier in the 20th century, in moving away from gender seclusion toward more varied and public heterosexual interactions. Growing levels of employment of women outside the home, in China for example, or even the Middle East, or growing rates of involvement in higher education (with 55% of Iranian university students now women), clearly create new opportunities for romantic jealousies or needs for emotional control or both. Obviously, some societies try to counter by insisting on gender segregation even at the university level, or by requiring concealing costumes for women; and some of the counter-attacks on gender change in certain societies might well reflect jealousy outright, along with more purely religious concerns. But the modern era does see the progressive breakdown of some of the devices that many societies long employed to maintain control over women and over female sexuality, and the emotional challenge here, with jealousy on the center stage, may be considerable. Here is an area where historically sensitive comparative analysis will be both exciting and fruitful. Pending ongoing study, jealousy could turn out to be a pivotal emotion at a time of global transitions in gender relations.

In the United States, where at least some of the contemporary history is already clear, the campaign against jealousy has not been entirely successful, though it certainly has changed evaluations and prompted new efforts to measure up, to apologize, or to conceal. Even as anxiety about jealousy has diminished in the past three decades, the emotion and its new associations with childish selfishness and immaturity still carry the possibility of adverse impact in romantic relationships, when one partner cannot adequately control or conceal, and a sense of personal inadequacy when one's own reactions do not measure up to widely known, and rather demanding, standards.

Notes

1   William M. Reddy, *The navigation of feeling: A framework for the history of emotions* (New York: Cambridge University Press, 2001); Jan Lewis and Peter N. Stearns, eds., *An emotional history of the U.S.* (The History of Emotions Series) (New York: NYU Press, 1998).

2   Carol Zisowitz Stearns and Peter N. Stearns, *Anger: The struggle for emotional control in America's history* (Chicago: University of Chicago Press, 1989); Peter N. Stearns, *American fear: The causes and consequences of high anxiety* (New York: Routledge, 2006).

3   Peter Salovey, *The psychology of jealousy and envy* (New York: Guilford Press, 1991).

4   Salovey, *The psychology of jealousy and envy*; Shula Sommers, "Adults evaluating their emotions: A cross-cultural perspective," in *Emotion in Adult Development*, ed. Carol Zander Malatesta & Carroll E. Izard (Beverly Hills, CA: Sage, 1984), 319–338; Janice L. Francis, "Towards the management of heterosexual jealousy," *Journal of Marriage and Family Counseling* 3 (1977): 61–69.

5   Robert A. Nye, *Masculinity and male codes of honor in modern France* (New York: Oxford University Press, 1993).

6   Peter N. Stearns, *Revolutions in sorrow: The American experience of death in global perspective* (Boulder, CO: Paradigm Publishers, 2007).

7   Madeleine Bertrand, *La jalousie dans la littérature au temps de Louis XIII* (Geneva, 1981), 407–418; Peter N. Stearns, *Jealousy: The evolutions of an emotion in American history* (New York: NYU Press, 1989).

8   Bertrand, *Jalousie*, 145; Theodor Reik, *A psychologist looks at love* (New York: Rinehart and Company, 1944).

9   Bertrand, *Jalousie*, passim; Edmund Leites, *The Puritan conscience and modern sexuality* (New Haven: Yale University Press, 1985), 109–110.

10   Natalie Davis, *Fiction in the archives: Pardon tales and their tellers in sixteenth-century France* (Stanford, CA: Stanford University Press, 1990).

11   Mrs. Clarissa Packard [Caroline Howard Gilman], *Recollections of a housekeeper* (New York: Harper and Brothers, 1836), 53, 54–58; Stearns, *Jealousy.*

12   *Summing up of John Graham, Esq., to the Jury, on the part of the Defense, on the trial of Daniel McFarland ... May 6th and 9th, 1870* (New York, 1870), 13; Robert M. Ireland, "The libertine must die: Sexual dishonor and the unwritten law in the nineteenth-century United States," *Journal of Social History* 23 (1989).

13   Felix Adler, *The moral instruction of children* (New York: D. Appleton and Co., 1895) 213–214.

14   Sybil Foster, "A study of the personality makeup and social setting of fifty jealous children," *Mental Hygiene* 11 (1927); 533–571; Mabel Sewall, "Some causes of jealousy in young children," *Smith College Studies in Social Work* 1 (1930–31): 6–22; Ruth E. Smalley, "The influence of differences in age, sex and intelligence in determining the attitudes of siblings toward each other," *Smith College Studies in Social Work* 1 (1930–31): 23–44; D. M. Levy, "Studies in sibling rivalry," *American Orthopsychiatry Research Monograph*, No. 2 (1937); D. M. Levy, "Rivalry Between children of the same family," *Child Study* 22 (1934): 233–261; A. Adler, "Characteristics of the first, second and third child," *Children* 3, no. 5 (1938): 14–39. Only one of these studies, but an interesting one, ran counter to the pessimistic findings about jealousy, noting the diversity of reactions among the children and the frequency of intense affection: M. B. MacFarland, "Relationship between young sisters as revealed on their overt responses," *Journal of Experimental Education* 6 (1937): 73–79. But MacFarland's conclusions were ignored amid the welter of findings that jealousy was a major problem and that its resolution depended on careful parental policy, in what was almost certainly an exaggerated perception of a common (though decidedly not

uniform) childhood response. See Judy Dunn and Carl Kendrick, *Siblings: Love, envy and understanding* (Cambridge, MA: Harvard University Press, 1982), passim. See also D. A. Thom, *Child management* (Washington, DC: Children's Bureau, 1925), 9–12; U.S. Department of Labor, Children's Bureau, *Are you training your child to be happy?* (Washington, DC, 1930), 31; Stearns, *Jealousy.*

15   Benjamin Spock, *The common sense book of baby and child care* (New York: Duell Sloan & Pearce, 1946), 272.

16   Arthur T. Jersild et al., *Joys and problems of childrearing* (New York: Bureau of Publications, Teachers College, Columbia University, 1949), 28–30, 87, 94.

17   Stephanie A. Shields, *Speaking from the heart: Gender and the social meaning of emotion* (New York: Cambridge University Press, 2002); Christopher Lasch, *Haven in a heartless world: The family besieged* (New York: Norton, 1995).

18   Judy Dunn, *Sisters and brothers* (Cambridge, MA: Harvard University Press, 1985), 98–99; Jane S. Brossard and E. S. Boll, *The large family system: An original study in the sociology of family behavior* (Philadelphia, 1956), 186–187.

19   Richard Sennett, *Families against the city* (Cambridge, MA: Harvard University Press, 1984).

20   Stearns, *Jealousy,* chapter 3; Willard Waller, *The family* (New York: Holt, Rinehart and Winston, 1951), 586.

21   Mrs. Havelock Ellis, *The new horizon in love and life* (London, 1921), 27; see also Bertrand Russell, *Marriage and morals* (New York: George Allen & Unwin, 1929); Mikhail Arttzybasheff, *Jealousy* (New York: Boni and Liveright, 1923); Ben B. Lindsey and Wainright Evans, *The companionate marriage* (New York: Arno Press, 1927), 72.

22   Paul Popenoe, *Marriage is what you make it* (New York: Macmillan Company, 1959), 17 et passim; Paul Popenoe, *Marriage: Before and after* (New York: Wilfred Funk, Inc., 1945), passim.

23   Alexander Magoun, *Love and marriage* (New York: Harper, 1948), 301, 304, 306; see also Judson T. Landis and Mary G. Landis, *A successful marriage* (Englewood Cliffs, NJ: Prentice Hall, 1958), 82; Evelyn M. Duval and Dora S. Lewis, "Education for Family Life in the Community," in *Marriage and Family Living*, Vol. 10, No. 2 (Minneapolis: National Council on Family Relations, May 1948), 28.31; Leslie Farber, *Lying, despair, jealousy, envy, sex, suicide and the good life* (New York: HarperCollins, 1978), 182, 194, 200, 202; Robert L. Barker, *The green-eyed marriage: Surviving jealous relationships* (New York: Free Press, 1988); Willard Gaylin, *Feelings: Our vital signs* (New York: HarperCollins, 1988).

24   Joshua Dressler, "Rethinking Heat of Passion: A Defense in Search of a Rationale," *Journal of Criminal Law and Criminology* 73 (1982): 421–434; Rex v. Greening (1913) 23 Cox Crim. C. 601, 603; Scroggs v. State, 94 Ga. App. 28, 93 S.E. 2d 583 (1956).

25   Arnold Gesell, *Youth: The years from ten to sixteen* (New York: HarperCollins, 1956).

26   Gary Schwartz and Don Merten, *Love and Commitment* (Beverly Hills, CA: Sage Publications, 1980), passim.

27   Nena O'Neill and George O'Neill, *Open marriage: A new life style for couples* (New York: M. Evans, 1972), 239, 240.

28   Shula Somers, "Reported Emotions and Conventions of Emotionality among College Students," *Journal of Personality and Social Psychology* 46 (1984): 214.

29   P. M. Spielman, "Envy and jealousy: An attempt at clarification," *Psychoanalytic Quarterly* 40 (1971): 59–82.

30   Susan J. Matt, *Keeping up with the Joneses: Envy in American consumer society, 1890–1930* (Philadelphia: University of Pennsylvania Press, 2003).

31   Ayala Pines and Eliot Aronson, "Antecedents, Correlates and Consequences," *Psychology Today* 18 (1984): 126–140.

32   Clanton Gordon, *Jealousy* (Lanham, MD: University Press of America, 1997); Stearns, *Jealousy.*

2

Loss, Protest, and Emotional Development

Michael Lewis

I approach the topic of jealousy in a rather unusual way. Since I am interested in the question of the development of jealousy, I need to address some basic underlying assumptions that characterize the issue of its development. These issues include the idea of jealousy as growing out of the unique and particular relationship between the child and its mother. For example, I wish to consider whether or not a unique relationship between the child and its mother can be supported by theory and data. I will argue that the monotropic idea of attachment, which underlies most of the work on the child's unique relationship with its mother, may in fact be a too simple understanding of the basic biological mechanisms that place the child in its social world. I shall argue, rather, for a view of a polytropic attachment idea, one in which the child can form relationships with multiple others. If, indeed, the child can form multiple attachment relationships, given the opportunity to do so, then the idea of jealousy as a consequence of the child's protest over the attention withdrawal from the single significant other may need to be reconsidered. For example, if the child can form multiple attachment relationships, it can easily move from one person to another, depending upon the context in which the child finds itself. The mother's withdrawal of attention from the child is more likely to cause upset only if there are not others with whom the child has an attachment relationship. If multiple attachments are possible, the origin of jealousy may have more to do with how we measure it rather than a unique relationship.

The second part of this chapter is devoted to the model of emotional development that I have proposed (Lewis, 1992). In this model, the major transformational event, which gives rise to more complex emotions, emotions which I have called self-conscious emotions, and in particular self-conscious evaluative emotions, requires that the child develop a mental representation of itself. Thus, embarrassment which occurs only after the child has built up this representation of itself occurs when the child becomes the object of another's attention (Lewis, Sullivan, Stanger, & Weiss, 1989). Likewise, empathy becomes possible only

Handbook of Jealousy: Theory, Research and Multidisciplinary Approaches, First Edition.
Edited by Sybil L. Hart and Maria Legerstee.
© 2010 Michael Lewis. Published 2013 by Blackwell Publishing Ltd.

when the child is able to place itself in the role of another. Empathy, therefore, requires the child having a representation of itself which can be actively used in relation to others. Jealousy, too, requires that the child have a self-representation. This being the case, a developmental model requires that jealousy, as we come to understand the term, can occur only after this self-representation has developed. The literature makes clear that this representation occurs between 15 and 24 months of age (Lewis, 2003). If this is the case, then what is it that we witness when the mother–child relationship is disrupted because the mother pays attention to other social objects rather than the child itself? Here we will deal with what I will call proto-jealousy responses, which may become the material of the adult-like jealousy we subsequently see, but which is related more to the withdrawal of attention than to the emotion of jealousy itself. In order to address this issue, it is necessary for me to do two things: in the first case, and before we can even suggest the idea of development, we must confront the general problem that similar behaviors, especially those which appear early as well as later in development, are not necessarily motivated by or determined by the same process (Lewis, 1967). We need to deal with the model of emotional development which is currently understood in order to see how early sets of behavior called jealousy may not be the same as jealousy seen in children once a self-representation is present. Secondly, we need to examine studies which look at the disruption of interaction of the child with others, in particular its mother, in order to see how we can understand these proto-jealousy behaviors. Here we make use of studies of separation and studies of interruption in order to see that these behaviors, as well as attention paid to others, are likely to elicit behaviors of distress and discomfort which, given their context, may be interpreted as jealousy.

Attachment as a Monotropic or Polytropic System

While one might be able to find some doubt in the writings of Bowlby and Ainsworth concerning a monotropic view of attachment, I believe their views are quite clear. Bowlby wrote, "Understanding of the response of a child to separation or loss of this mother-figure turns on understanding of the bond that ties him to that figure. Thus, in any description of traditional theory the terminology of object relations must often be used; in the presentation of a new theory, however, terms such as 'attachment' and 'attachment figure' are preferred" (Bowlby, 1969, p. 177). Thus, we can see that from Bowlby's training and tradition, attachment theory is a continuation of object relation theory. As such, the emphasis on the mother remains. Nevertheless, Bowlby does raise important questions. For example, he asked, "Do children commonly direct their attachment behavior towards more than one person? If they do so, do attachments to a number of figures develop simultaneously, or does one attachment always precede the others? When a child has more than one figure to whom he is attached does he treat all figures alike or does he show a preference for one of them? Can a woman other than a child's natural mother fill adequately the role of principal attachment figure?" (Bowlby, 1969, pp. 303–304). Bowlby's answer to these questions is quite clear: "... By 12 months a plurality of attachment figures is probably the rule; these attachment-figures are *not treated as the equivalents of one another*" (p. 304). "There can be no doubt that in virtually every culture the people in question are most likely to be his natural mother, father, older siblings and perhaps grandparents, and that it is from amongst these figures that a child is most likely to select both his *principal attachment-figure* and his subsidiary figures" (Bowlby, 1969, p. 308). "Such evidence as is at present available supports a hypothesis advanced in an earlier paper (Bowlby, 1958), namely that there is a strong bias for attachment behavior to become directed mainly towards one particular person and for a child to become strongly possessive of that person" (Bowlby, 1969, p. 308).

Moreover, while Bowlby raised some important issues in Volume 1 (1969), it is always the mother who is talked about and is referred to as the attachment figure in the subsequent volumes. Mary Ainsworth is even clearer: "There is nothing in my observations to contradict the hypothesis that, given an opportunity to do so, an infant will seek attachment with one figure ... even though there are several persons available as caretakers" (Ainsworth, 1964).

Even given these writings, it might be argued that attachment theory is not dependent on such a monotropic view. One way to determine whether attachment theory took up the challenge of mono versus polytropism is to look at the research literature generated over the past 40 years. One interesting case is the NICHD study of over 1,300 children in multiple sites across the country. Here the role of infant day care, attachment, and subsequent development was measured. While two attachment scores were obtained for the mother–child dyad, none was taken with the fathers, grandparents, or older siblings. Even more important, none was taken with the key caregivers, even though all children were in day care!

While a count is very difficult, overwhelmingly, articles that refer to attachment study just the mother. Fathers are rarely studied, siblings and grandparents even less. Some time ago, Fox and colleagues (1991) reported on only 11 samples where data were collected on both fathers and mothers. This, as well as more recent studies, found that attachment classification differed between children and their mothers or fathers. That attachments of the child toward parents differ for mothers and fathers suggests that multiple attachments exist and that the child itself cannot be characterized as secure or insecure. Rather, it is in the particular relationship where the security lies.

The upholding of monotropic views of attachment can also be found in the nonhuman primates work. This work had important implications for attachment theory. For example, Bowlby's (1969) belief that primate infants preferred cloth surrogate mothers to milk-giving wire mothers was the basis of his rejection of

Dollard and Miller's secondary reinforcement theory (1950); a theory which held to the belief that mothers derived their importance because they were associated with food giving. Even though this early work was used by Bowlby, it was not supported by Harlow himself in his own later work. Although the early, well-referenced study by Harlow and Zimmerman (1959) reported on the infant primates' preferences for cloth over wire milk-giving surrogates, when Harlow and Suomi (1970) later heated the (the cold) wire mothers, they found that the baby monkeys' preference switched from the cloth surrogate to the wire milk-giving surrogate.

Harlow's monkey babies were raised, not only without mothers, but also without any social contact with conspecifics, as was pointed out by Ruppenthal and associates (1976) in work on peer contact and social isolation. The primates' developmental problems were not just due to the absence of their mothers but to their social isolation. Further studies have revealed that peer contact, even without mothers, ameliorated the major developmental problems.

Figure 2.1 presents the data from the Ruppenthal et al. study, which utilized all the social isolation groups of monkeys, 50 in total.

Notice that infant monkeys raised alone in wire cages become less than adequate (the highest rating of maternal ability). Only 24% were adequate, which was no different from the monkeys raised with cloth mother surrogates. However, monkeys raised with other monkeys were significantly higher in their maternal behavior (75% adequate). Moreover, Suomi's most recent work, looking at genes and environment interactions, appears to support the view that peer-rearing (rather than maternal-rearing) causes few problems over time (Suomi, 2005).

Perhaps the most frequently referenced finding of Harlow's lab was that female monkeys raised without mothers make terrible mothers. The reported intergenerational effects were used as the basis of studies of child abuse (Widom, 1989). Again, look at the Ruppenthal et al. data. Figure 2.1 shows the adequacy of mothering over repeated child rearing of these 50 infants, all of whom were reared without mothers. Notice that adequate mothering on the first child was about 20% while indifferent and abusive was about 80%. By the 5th child, the motherless monkeys had become good mothers with 80% adequate and only 20% indifferent or abusive. The idea of monotropic versus polytropic attachments makes little sense when viewed in light of these data. Harlow and Harlow (1965) talked about the affectional *systems*, as their work showed that infant monkeys could be attached to others as well as their mothers (Lewis & Suomi, in prep.). Thus, polytropism is more likely, and the idea of monotropism is a function of a world view (Popper, 1963) and an outcome of the types of studies done, i.e., only studying the mother–infant relationships.

What then can we conclude about polytropism and jealousy as a function of a unique relationship between mother and child? To begin with, jealousy is not likely a function of a unique relationship but rather a function of

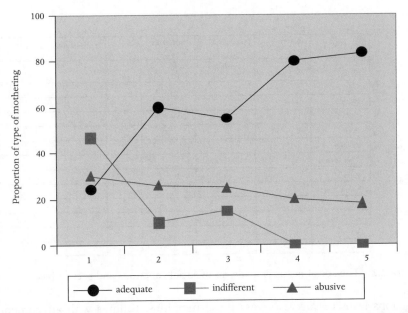

Figure 2.1 Mothering competence as a function of the birth order of the child. *Source*: Ruppenthal et al. (1976)

wanting something that another has. In fact, in a social network made up of many different people performing many different functions, such as protection, education, play, and nurturance, the absence or lack of attention from one person (any person, not only the mother) is likely to result in distress to the extent that there is no one else present to satisfy the infant/child needs (Feinman & Lewis, 1984; Lewis, 1984; Lewis, Feiring, & Kotsonis, 1984; Lewis & Takahashi, 2005). What would happen to the origins of jealousy if we allowed for a polytropic view? Consider first only the mother and father attachments. If we measured attachment to both of them we would generate 16 possible groups, 4 for the mother, 4 for the father. Moreover, if we follow Harlow and Harlow's idea, a matrix can be constructed which includes multiple attachments and multiple functions; for example, peer attachment leads to reproductive success while attachment to each parent may lead to success relative to other females or males. What would happen in the absence of the mother, either doing something else or attending to someone else, if the infant was attended to by another "attached" person? Would there be more or less protest? Such studies have yet to be done.

Figure 2.2 presents the social space created when we take a polytropic view and at the same time consider multiple functions. If we allow for multiple attachments and consider a wider range of needs or functions, then it is possible to reconsider attachment as a socio-emotional and cognitive model within social networks. Success with attachments to specific people with specific

		Social functions					
		F_1	F_2	F_3	F_4	F_5	...F_m
		Protection $B_{11}B_{12}B_{13}$	Care-giving $B_{21}B_{22}B_{23}$	Nurturance $B_{31}B_{32}...$	Play	Exploration/learning	B_{f0}
			Feeding, changing	Rock, Kiss			
	P_1 Self						
	P_2 Mother						
	P_3 Father						
	P_4 Peer						
Social objects	P_5 Sibling						
	P_6 Grandparent						
	P_7 Aunt						
	·						
	·						
	·						
	P_N						

Figure 2.2   The social nexus is made up of social functions and social objects

functions leads to success across those functions. Failures with attachments to specific people with specific functions lead to pathologies in those domains in which the failures occur.

Emotional Development

I have proposed a model of emotional development much as depicted in Figure 2.3 (Lewis, 1992). For our interest, the important point is that for the emergence of the self-conscious emotions, including jealousy, it is necessary that an important maturational event occur, namely the emergence, through brain maturation, of the mental state of the idea of me or consciousness. This mental state emerges in the period of 15–24 months as measured by self-recognition in mirrors, personal pronoun usage such as "me" or "mine," and by pretend play (Lewis & Ramsay, 2004a). In a recent study we have shown a relation between brain maturation of the left temporal parietal function and self-recognition (Lewis & Carmody, 2008). The emergence of consciousness in the second half of the second year of life has important implications for the emergence of jealousy rather than protest. Protest can require only absence of a desired goal; jealousy is more relational. I have argued that relationships require consciousness, taking Hinde's (1979) analysis of the requirements for a relationship into account. Hinde suggests that eight features characterize relationships: (1) goal structures, (2) diversity of interactions, (3) degree of reciprocity, (4) meshing of interactions, (5) frequency, and (6) patterning and multidimensional qualities of interactions, as well as (7) cognitive functions, or those mental processes that allow members of an interaction to think of the other member or themselves, as well as the

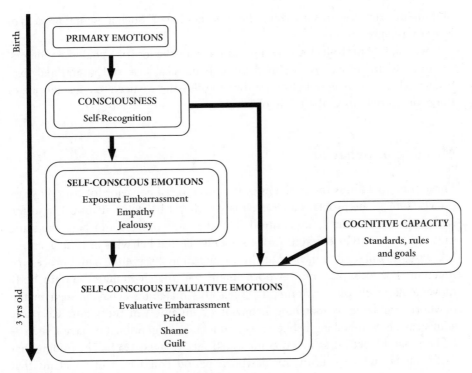

Figure 2.3   A model of emotional development
Source: Lewis (1992)

interactions of others and themselves, and (8) something Hinde calls penetration, which I interpret as something having to do with ego boundaries.

Notice that interactions alone (features 1–6) are insufficient to describe a higher-level human relationship. Thus the infant is unlikely to have a relationship with another if we characterize relationships in terms of adult relationships since the infant does not have the mental processes that allow it to think of itself or the self's interaction with other members. Support for this model of development comes from many sources including the relation between self-referential behavior and brain maturation (Lewis & Carmody, 2008). Relevant is the relationships between self-recognition and the emergence of the more complex emotions, those I have called the self-conscious emotions (Lewis, 1992). While the earlier emotions, joy, fear, sadness, disgust, anger, and interest, do not require a mental representation of self or consciousness, the self-conscious emotions such as embarrassment, empathy, and jealousy and the self-conscious evaluative emotions such as pride and shame, embarrassment and guilt, do. Many studies have shown that empathy and embarrassment require the emergence of consciousness (Bischof-Kohler, 1991; Borke, 1971; Lewis et al., 1989; Zahn-Waxler & Radke-Yarrow, 1990), which suggests that not until 15–24 months will infants be able to show jealousy; and by jealousy we mean that the infant is capable of thinking "that I want something that I do not have." Such a mental process of jealousy requires an "I."

If we think of proto-jealousy as a protest against the loss of a goal, then infants' reactions to maternal loss, defined as both physical loss and attentional loss, become clearer. However, before we turn to this issue we need to consider one of the major problems in the study of development.

Meaning of Behavior

I have tried to address the problem of the meaning of behavior for over 40 years (Lewis, 1967). The problem addressed is whether a behavior at time 1, and the same behavior at time 2, are controlled by the same processes or have the same meaning, or whether different processes underlie the behavior at time 1 and 2. Likewise, do different behaviors at time 1 and time 2 serve the same process or function? For example, the newborn infant will match (imitate) certain body movements (Meltzoff & Moore, 1977). Is this matching behavior seen in the newborn the same as matching behavior or imitation in the adult? Certainly adults can show matching behavior as a function of intentional behavior such as "if I do that, I'll get the same outcome as did she" (Piaget, 1954). The finding that matching behavior exists in the newborn period could lead us to claim that intentional behavior exists in the newborn, thus imitation. Alternatively, the same behavior can be said to have different causes. If we called newborn behavior matching, and the 3-year-old's behavior imitation, then we avoid the nativistic position of giving all capacities to the newborn, allowing for a very limited idea of development.

This problem exists across a wide range of social and emotional behaviors, jealousy being just one. Specifically, I would propose that matching behavior, a function of intersensory processes, and imitation are quite different. Anger at a blockage of a goal and persistence in completing a difficult task are quite different but related to the same developmental path (Lewis, in press). Likewise, protest over loss and jealousy are different but may not be developmentally related.

Protest over Loss

Loss has generally been considered in two ways in the infant research literature. In the first, loss is defined by the departure of the mother, as in her leaving the child alone in a strange environment (Ainsworth & Bell, 1970; Brooks & Lewis, 1974). A second loss of the mother is when the mother is present but is separated from her child by a barrier. In these studies the mother places her child over the barrier and then returns to her seat, this after 15 minutes of play with the mother and toys (Feiring & Lewis, 1979; Goldberg & Lewis, 1969). Also in this category of loss is the still-face situation where the mother, facing her infant, engages in social interaction for a certain length of time, usually 3 minutes, then she suddenly drops her head and ceases to interact with her child. After 1 minute of this non-interaction she again begins to engage the child (Hart, Carrington, Tronick, & Carroll 2004; Lewis & Ramsay, 2005; Tronick et al., 1978; Weinberg & Tronick, 1996). In these two types of situation, the loss of the mother is not a physical loss but a loss of interaction with her.

The results of the attachment-like situation where the mother leaves the child alone in the room are well known. While the "A" babies showed little reaction to their mothers' departure or return, the "B" and "C" babies showed considerable responses of protest. Careful measurement of the protest indicated that they show sadness and crying as well as anger and they also show actions designed to get to their mothers, like trying to open the door (Weinraub & Lewis, 1977). While attachment characterization is obtained by the reaction of the child when its mother is reunited with it, the data when available as to the child's response to her departure show the types of protest to her physical absence. It is interesting to note that the types of protest against the removal of the mother can be characterized as approach as well as withdrawal. The approach reaction is characterized by attempts to reach the door and try to open it while the withdrawal response is characterized by crying and bodily collapse. As we shall shortly see, these types of response can be seen in the other loss of mother paradigms.

Now let us consider cases where the mother is present but is unavailable. The barrier paradigm is considered first. In the Goldberg and Lewis (1969) study, "mother-loss" through a barrier frustration resulted in behavior similar to that seen in the mother departure–attachment situation. Thirteen-month-old children showed the same protest pattern; some cried and were passive, not trying to get through the barrier, while others tried to climb over the barrier or get around it while protesting. We report sex differences in this active approach versus the passive withdrawal approach, with boys showing more active approach behavior.

Feiring and Lewis (1979) looked at this same sample at 24 months of age and compared behaviors seen at 24 months with those seen at 13 months. At both ages, crying and fretting, and looking at the mother were most prevalent, while next most prevalent were pushing, touching, and, at 24 months, trying to undo the latch. Age changes were noted; increased age was associated with decreases in crying, fretting, self-stimulation, and passive touching of the barrier, all withdrawal behaviors. There were significant age-related increases in approach responses, including climbing up the barrier, manipulating the latch, or getting around it to reach the mother. From this longitudinal study it appears as if protest behavior over the mother's loss, while present, changes with age. Initially, protest has many withdrawal elements and few approach responses, but, with age, approach types of protest increase. Finally, Wasserman and Lewis (1985) looked at two play situations, one in which the mother interacted normally with her 12-month-old child, and another in which she did not interact. In the non-interaction situation as compared to the interaction condition, the infant showed significant increases in touch and vocalization, especially the boys, indicating that her non-availability resulted in infant behaviors thought to regain her attention.

In all these studies, careful measurements of facial expressions were not obtained so that the exact nature of the infant's/child's protest could not be examined. This is especially important when we consider the relationship between protest and jealousy since the measurement of jealousy has not been determined. Certainly the difference between jealousy and protest, both of which contain anger and/or sadness facial expressions, has not been well established.

Lewis and colleagues (Lewis, Hitchcock, & Sullivan, 2004; Lewis, Sullivan, Ramsay, & Alessandri, 1992; Sullivan & Lewis, 1989; Sullivan, Lewis, & Alessandri, 1992) have been studying infants' facial and bodily action responses to the loss of a learned response–goal outcome connection. In particular, infants are taught to pull a string in order to obtain the appearance of a picture and sound, a response which they can learn easily (Lewis, Sullivan, & Brooks-Gunn, 1985). After reaching criteria for learning this response, it ceases to produce the picture. Then, approach and withdrawal responses are observed. The majority of infants as young as 2 months of age show predominantly anger faces, although some sadness is shown as well, an increase in arm pulling as if they are trying to regain the pictures, and no increases in the stress hormone cortisol. Although the majority of infants show these approach responses, there are some who show predominantly sadness rather than anger in their faces, do not increase their arm pull responses, and show significant increases in the stress hormone cortisol.

The still-face procedure has been considered by many to elicit the infant's attempt to regain the interaction with its mother (Tronick et al., 1978). We see this as more akin to frustration, and the responses serve as a reference to an attempt to restore the interaction. Lewis and Ramsay (2004b) studied this problem by looking at the 6-month-olds' response to their mothers' withdrawal of attention and we found behaviors exactly parallel to the arm pull–picture outcome paradigm. The protest to her withdrawal was predominantly anger and/or sadness and loss of joy in their faces and changes in cortisol levels such that the angry infants showed no cortisol increase but the sad infants did.

What we see from all these studies of the loss of the mother, either those where the mother disappears or those where in one way or another the mother becomes non-available, is protest which is marked by a complex set of behaviors. We have, in all cases, determined that these protest behaviors can be classified as either approach, that is, an active attempt to overcome the loss including facial expressions of anger and behavior designed to overcome the loss and regain it, or withdrawal behaviors including facial expressions of sadness accompanying passive behaviors that do not appear designed to overcome her loss.

The loss of the mother's attention, measured by her non-availability, as behind a barrier, or disappearance, as in the attachment paradigm, or in her lack of interaction, as in the still-face procedure, appears similar regardless of the type. These are proto-responses to loss. The protest behaviors seen early on are likely to interact with the development of the mental state of the idea of me. These then are likely to become the material of the self-conscious emotion of jealousy as we understand it in the human adult.

References

Ainsworth, M. D. S. (1964). Patterns of attachment behavior shown by the infant in interaction with his mother. *Merrill-Palmer Quarterly, 10*, 51–58.

Ainsworth, M. D. S., & Bell, S. M. (1970). Attachment, exploration, and separation: Illustrated by the behavior of one-year-olds in a strange situation. *Child Development, 41*, 49–67.

Bischof-Kohler, D. (1991). The development of empathy in infants. In M. E. Lamb & H. Keller (Eds.), *Infant development: Perspectives from German-speaking countries* (pp. 245–273). Hillsdale, NJ: Erlbaum.

Borke, H. (1971). Interpersonal perception of young children: Ego-centrism or empathy? *Developmental Psychology, 5*, 263–269.

Bowlby, J. (1958). The nature of the child's tie to his mother. *International Journal of Psychoanalysis, 39*, 350–373.

Bowlby, J. (1969). *Attachment and loss: Vol. 1. Attachment*. New York: Basic Books.

Brooks, J., & Lewis, M. (1974). The effect of time on attachment as measured in a free-play situation. *Child Development, 45*, 311–316.

Dollard, J., & Miller, N. E. (1950). *Personality and psychotherapy: An analysis in terms of learning, thinking, and culture*. New York: McGraw-Hill.

Feinman, S., & Lewis, M. (1984). Is there social life beyond the dyad? A social-psychological view of social connections in infancy. In M. Lewis (Ed.), *Beyond the dyad* (pp. 13–41). New York: Plenum.

Feiring, C., & Lewis, M. (1979). Sex and age differences in young children's reactions to frustration: A further look at the Goldberg and Lewis (1969) subjects. *Child Development, 50*, 848–853.

Fox, N., Kimmerly, N. L., & Schafer, W. D. (1991). Attachment to mother, attachment to father: A meta-analysis. *Child Development, 62*, 210–225.

Goldberg, S., & Lewis, M. (1969). Play behavior in the year-old infant: Early sex differences. *Child Development, 40*, 21–31.

Harlow, H. F., & Harlow, M. K. (1965). The affectional systems. In A. M. Schrier, H. F. Harlow, & F. Stollnitz (Eds.), *Behavior of nonhuman primates* (Vol. 2). New York: Academic Press.

Harlow, H. F., & Suomi, S. J. (1970). Nature of love—simplified. *American Psychologist, 25*, 161–166.

Harlow, H. F., & Zimmerman, R. R. (1959). Affectional responses in the infant monkey. *Science, 130*, 421–432.

Hart, S. L., Carrington, H. A., Tronick, E. Z., & Carroll, S. R. (2004). When infants lose exclusive maternal attention: Is it jealousy? *Infancy, 6*, 57–78.

Hinde, R. A. (1979). *Towards understanding relationships.* London: Academic Press.

Lewis, M. (1967). The meaning of a response or why researchers in infant behavior should be oriental metaphysicians. *Merrill-Palmer Quarterly, 13*, 7–18.

Lewis, M. (1984). Social influences in development. In M. Lewis (Ed.), *Beyond the dyad: The genesis of behavior* (pp. 1–12). New York: Plenum.

Lewis, M. (1992). *Shame, the exposed self.* New York: The Free Press.

Lewis, M. (2003). The emergence of consciousness and its role in human development. In J. LeDoux, J. Debiec, & H. Moss (Eds.), *The self: From soul to brain* (Vol. 1001, pp. 1–29). New York: Annals of the New York Academy of Sciences. Also appearing on the ANNALS ONLINE (www.annalsnyas.org).

Lewis, M. (in press). The development of anger. In M. Potegal, G. Stemmler, & C. D. Spielberger (Eds.), *Handbook of anger.* New York: Springer.

Lewis, M., & Carmody, D. (2008). Self representation and brain development. *Developmental Psychology, 44*, 1329–1334.

Lewis, M., Feiring, C., & Kotsonis, M. (1984). The social network of the young child: A developmental perspective. In M. Lewis (Ed.), *Beyond the dyad: The genesis of behavior* (pp. 129–160). New York: Plenum.

Lewis, M., Hitchcock, D. F. A., & Sullivan, M. W. (2004). Physiological and emotional reactivity to learning and frustration. *Infancy, 6*, 121–143.

Lewis, M., & Ramsay, D. (2004a). Development of self-recognition, personal pronoun use, and pretend play in the second year. *Child Development, 75*, 1821–1831.

Lewis, M., & Ramsay, D. (2004b). Infant emotional response to goal blockage, control, and cortisol response. *Emotion Researcher, 19*(2), 8–9.

Lewis, M., & Ramsay, D. (2005). Infant emotional and cortisol responses to goal blockage. *Child Development, 76*, 518–530.

Lewis, M., Sullivan, M., & Brooks-Gunn, J. (1985). Emotional behavior during the learning of a contingency in early infancy. *British Journal of Developmental Psychology, 3*, 307–316.

Lewis, M., Sullivan, M. W., Ramsay, D. S., & Alessandri, S. M. (1992). Individual differences in anger and sad expressions during extinction: Antecedents and consequences. *Infant Behavior and Development, 15*, 443–452.

Lewis, M., Sullivan, M. W., Stanger, C., & Weiss, M. (1989). Self-development and self-conscious emotions. *Child Development, 60*, 146–156.

Lewis, M., & Suomi, S. (in prep.). *A case study in selective referencing: Monkey infant and mother relations and their effect on subsequent development.*

Lewis, M., & Takahashi, K. (2005). Introduction: Beyond the dyad: Conceptualization of social networks. In M. Lewis & K. Takahashi (Eds.), *Human Development Special Issue, Beyond the Dyad: Conceptualization of Social Networks* (pp. 5–7). Switzerland: Karger.

Meltzoff, A. N., & Moore, M. K. (1977). Imitation of facial and manual gestures by human neonates. *Science, 198*, 75–78.

Piaget, J. (1954). *The origins of intelligence in children* (M. Cook, Trans.). New York: W. W. Norton.

Popper, K. R. (1963). *Conjectures and refutations: The growth of scientific knowledge.* London: Routledge and Kegan Paul.

Ruppenthal, G. C., Arling, G. L., Harlow, H. F., Sackett, G. P., & Suomi, S. J. (1976). A 10-year perspective of motherless-mother monkey behavior. *Journal of Abnormal Psychology, 85,* 341–349.

Sullivan, M., & Lewis, M. (1989). Emotion and cognition in infancy: Facial expressions during contingency learning. *International Journal of Behavioral Development, 12,* 221–237.

Sullivan, M. W., Lewis, M., & Alessandri, S. (1992). Cross-age stability in emotional expressions during learning and extinction. *Developmental Psychology, 28,* 58–63.

Suomi, S. J. (2005). How gene–environment interactions shape the development of impulsive aggression in rhesus monkeys. In D. M. Stoff & E. J. Sussman (Eds.), *Developmental psychobiology of aggression* (pp. 252–268). New York: Cambridge University Press.

Tronick, E., Als, H., Adamson, L., Wise, S., & Brazelton, T. B. (1978). The infant's response to entrapment between contradictory messages in face-to-face interaction. *Journal of the American Academy of Child Psychiatry, 17,* 1–13.

Wasserman, G. A., & Lewis, M. (1985). Infant sex differences: Ecological effects. *Sex Roles, 12,* 665–675.

Weinberg, K. M., & Tronick, E. Z. (1996). Infant affective reactions to the resumption of maternal interaction after the still-face. *Child Development, 67,* 905–914.

Weinraub, M., & Lewis, M. (1977). The determinants of children's responses to separation. *Monographs of the Society for Research in Child Development, 42*(4), 1–78.

Widom, C. S. (1989). The cycle of violence. *Science, 244,* 163.

Zahn-Waxler, C., & Radke-Yarrow, M. (1990). The origins of empathic concern. *Motivation and Emotion, 14,* 107–130.

3

Jealousy and Romantic Love

Aaron Ben-Ze'ev

Romantic jealousy is often perceived to express our fear of losing an important human being that belongs to us; accordingly, jealousy is criticized for regarding another person as one's property. Although both claims have more than a grain of truth in them, jealousy is more complex. Most people do not consider their beloved to be their property, but nevertheless are jealous when they are about to lose her to someone else. It is more appropriate to characterize the central concern of jealousy as that of exclusivity.

In this chapter, I clarify the role of this concern in jealousy. I begin by distinguishing between jealousy and envy, as the two emotions are often confused. Then I briefly discuss the personal comparative concern, which is highly crucial in jealousy, and describe major components of typical jealousy. Next I discuss the central problematic issue of jealousy—the assumption that the partner belongs in some way to the lover. I indicate that although in its crudest mechanical interpretation this assumption is obviously wrong, it has some credence in a more complex psychological sense. As in parental love, the beloved is considered to be part of one's extended-self. However, unlike in parental love, in romantic love the happiness of the beloved is closely connected to the lover. These discussions about various aspects of jealousy pave the way for understanding the main issue in jealousy—that of exclusivity. The chapter ends by briefly discussing some future developments concerning jealousy.

Jealousy and Envy

People often confuse the emotions of jealousy and envy, although a clear distinction can be drawn between the two. Envy involves a negative evaluation of our undeserved inferiority, whereas jealousy involves a negative evaluation of the possibility of losing something—typically, a unique human relationship—to someone else. Envy and jealousy would seem to address a similar concern related

Handbook of Jealousy: Theory, Research and Multidisciplinary Approaches, First Edition.
Edited by Sybil L. Hart and Maria Legerstee.
© 2013 Blackwell Publishing Ltd. Published 2013 by Blackwell Publishing Ltd.

to possessing something: in envy we wish to obtain something that the other has and in jealousy we fear losing something that we already have to someone else. This is not a minor distinction: the wish to obtain something is notably different from the wish not to lose it. In contrast to envy, which is essentially a two-party relationship, jealousy is basically a three-party relationship. It concerns the partner's relationship with another person, since it may threaten one's favorable and exclusive relationship with one's partner.

Jealousy is more personal and generates greater vulnerability than envy; it is more likely to cause profound injury to our self-image since it touches on far more significant aspects of our self-image. The threat it carries is posed by a person who has intimate and reliable information about us. The severity of the threat may explain why jealousy is so intense despite the prevalence of sexual infidelity. The intense pain generated by jealousy is not because something extraordinary has happened, but because we may lose something of crucial importance to us to someone else. The pain here is related to our belief that something to which we consider ourselves entitled is in danger of being breached.

Like envy, jealousy also involves competition—specific, not general, competition with a third party. Jealousy stems from the desire to be "favored" in some respect and the suspicion that one is not. The sense that someone else is chosen over us contributes to the painful nature of jealousy. The competitive concern in jealousy does not refer to social comparison regarding a higher or lower status; rather, it presupposes personal rivalry—someone else may obtain what I have. This is a zero-sum game: the other's loss, or gain, leads to a change in my own situation. In envy, the other's loss, or gain, need not lead to a change in my objective situation but merely in my subjective one—for instance, an alteration in my relative status (Ben-Ze'ev, 2000, chapter 19; Foster, 1965, p. 26; 1972; Friday, 1985, pp. 105–106).

The Personal Comparative Concern

Comparison is crucial for our intellectual and emotional understanding. Understanding something implies grasping its alternative. In emotional experiences, comparisons are made from a personal perspective; hence, the personal comparative concern is at the basis of emotional experiences.

In jealousy the personal comparative concern is most pronounced as it refers to losing something very personal to another person who obtains what we once had. Jealousy stems from the desire to be "favored" in some respect and the suspicion that it is not merely the case that one is not favored, but that another person is being favored more. In jealousy, we are afraid of losing our present favorable position to someone else and of ending up in an inferior position.

The comparative concern is clearly expressed in the manner in which jealousy is generated. Generally, jealousy increases when the domain of the rival's achievements is comparable, and hence relevant, to our self-image. Thus, a jealous reaction is more likely with individuals who place great importance on physical attractiveness when their rival is unusually attractive (Salovey & Rodin, 1989). In jealousy, the significance of the rival's achievements depends not only on their relevance to how we desire to be ourselves, but also to what we believe our partner finds desirable. Jealousy would be intense if we knew that our partner likes clever people and our rival is clever. The threat to our relationship increases when the rival is compatible with our partner's desires (DeSteno & Salovey, 1996).

The personal comparative concern in jealousy is complex and its direction is not always predictable. Consider, for example, the case of a man whose wife has a loving relationship with another woman. It might be plausible to assume that he would be less jealous in this case than if his wife were involved in a similar relationship with another man. The comparative concern is less profound in the first case, and hence the damage to the husband's self-image would usually be less. Moreover, the first case might also be perceived as involving matters beyond the man's control and lesser personal control is typically associated with lesser emotional intensity (Ben-Ze'ev, 2000). However, as emotional intensity also depends upon personality, gender, and contextual features, more intense—or at least different—emotions may be aroused when the rival is the same gender as the partner. Moreover, other factors of emotional intensity, besides that of controllability, are likely to play a role here and could also generate even greater emotional intensity. One such factor might be readiness—that is, the extent to which we have anticipated the occurrence of such a situation. It seems to me that the first considerations would typically carry greater weight.

The empirical studies on this issue are scant. The only two studies I know of agree that men report less intense jealousy in response to same-sex infidelity. However, while one found a similar trend among women (Sagarin et al., 2003), the results of the earlier study are more ambiguous—while it also found that female–female sexual infidelity is considered to be less upsetting than heterosexual infidelity, it was unable to clarify whether male–male infidelity is more upsetting than male–female infidelity (Wiederman & LaMar, 1998). The gender difference is explained by reference to evolutionary considerations: same-sex infidelity does not entail the asymmetrical threats of mistaken paternity (in the case of a female same-sex infidelity) or of resources being diverted to another woman's children (in the case of male same-sex infidelity) (Sagarin et al., 2003; Wiederman & LaMar, 1998). Another suggestion as to why men might be less bothered than women when their partner engages in same-gender sexual contact includes men's relatively greater eroticization of such contact; indeed, research shows that men are much more likely to eroticize female–female sexual contact than women are to eroticize male–male sexual contact (Louderback & Whitley, 1997; Wiederman & LaMar, 1998).

Like other emotions, romantic jealousy is complex and typically consists of a cluster of emotions and not merely a single one. Three major components of typical romantic jealousy are fear of losing a partner to another person, love of the partner, and anger or sorrow at being in such a negative situation.

At the basis of jealousy there is a threat to a valued relationship or to its quality (Pines, 1998). We fear losing this relationship to someone else and ending up in a situation that is worse than our current one. Jealousy is generated not merely because of the negative content associated with losing a favorable relationship to someone else, but also in light of the probability that such an event will actually take place. In this sense, jealousy is similar to other types of fear. Indeed, someone may be in love with her partner and be extremely sad if the relationship ends, but if she trusts her partner and his love for her, she may not consider the possibility of losing him to another person as a reasonable option and hence will not be jealous of him.

The fear in jealousy is often imaginary, as it refers to a future change. Our jealousy does not usually die when we realize our error; any pretext whatsoever is sufficient to revive this emotion. Indeed, the most frequent event eliciting jealousy among married people is not actual infidelity, but involves the partner paying attention, or giving time and support to, a member of the opposite sex (Fitness & Fletcher, 1993). People may also be jealous of their lover even after the lover has ended the relationship and lives with another person. Such people still see themselves as having a relationship with their lover and may even consider the lover as part of their extended-self.

Jealousy typically involves sorrow, which is an expression of our negative evaluation of our circumstances. In jealousy there is an interrupted positive situation that previously had a fair chance of enduring. The sorrow in jealousy may be associated with anger, discontent, humiliation, shame, embarrassment, frustration, grief, as well as feelings of insecurity, helplessness, and of being unlucky. Sorrow is usually not associated with putting up resistance but with passivity and resignation in the face of events over which we have no control. When such control is possible, anger is often more natural (Cunningham, 1988; Stearns, 1993). Indeed, anger, which is a type of reaction to perceived injustice, is often associated with jealousy. In light of the profound damage to one's self-image caused in jealousy, people often connect jealousy with a kind of struggle against potential loss and as containing a retributive desire for revenge on the betraying partner.

Jealousy is frequently interpreted as a sign of caring and love, and many instances show a positive correlation between jealousy and romantic love. Like love, jealousy typically presupposes some type of commitment underlying the relationship, and it cannot arise if our attitude is utter indifference. The characteristics underlying our love are those that we most fear to lose and they are thus at the basis of our jealousy. In this sense it has been claimed that jealousy is "the shadow of love." Thus, a woman who fell in love with her husband because he made her the center of his world, or because he made her "finally come home," will be most jealous if these aspects begin to disappear when her relationship with her spouse is undermined by another person and she begins to feel insecure, abandoned, and alone (Pines, 1998).

Although the elements of fear, love, and sorrow are present in typical jealousy, in less typical cases, which are usually less intense, one or several of these elements may be absent. For example, jealousy does not necessarily involve love. Augustine claimed, "He that is not jealous, is not in love." It may be better to say that wherever there is intense love, there is the possibility of jealousy, once the lover estimates the prospects of losing the beloved to another person as high. Jealousy may arise even in the absence of love and caring, but also when a possible blow to one's self-image is in sight. A man who despises his wife may nevertheless become jealous when someone else looks covetously at her. Here the central feature is losing to a rival. In this case, jealousy is more germane to selfishness than to love. Similarly, although fear and sorrow seem to be necessary components in jealousy, those may not be fear and sorrow over losing one's partner to someone else, which is characteristic of jealousy, but may be related to the damage to one's self-image. Thus, a woman who does not fear losing her spouse may not be sad if this happens, as she does not love him very much; nevertheless, she may be jealous of him when she discovers that he is having a serious affair with another woman, as this affair may hurt her self-image. Likewise, a man who is in a loving relationship with a married woman may be sad when imagining her with her spouse, but his sorrow is not part of jealousy since he does not fear losing her to another man—first, since he trusts that she will continue to love him, and second, because he is not in danger of losing something that he currently has.

Does My Partner Belong to Me?

At the very foundation of romantic jealousy lies the concept of entitlement: we fear the loss of something or someone that we feel entitled to have. Jealousy reflects our fear that someone else will unjustly take possession of something that belongs to us. Hence, romantic jealousy implies some kind of entitlement over another person: our assumed right to exert control. Asserting sexual exclusivity, for example, is in fact asserting the right to control the spouse's sex life. Indeed, the very perception of belonging (*"we belong to one another"*), as it is reflected in popular culture (*"she was my woman"*), carries a sense of belonging (and owner-ship). Although belonging refers to property, it appears in jealousy as part of commitment and intimacy. The function of belonging in this context is clear: when spouses "belong" to each other, the risk of any third party captivating one of them is reduced.

The term "belong" has various meanings; the major ones are: "be the property of, be owned by" (*this book belongs to Laura*), "be a member of" (*belongs to a bridge club*), "be suitable or acceptable" (*after 2 years in this organization,*

I finally feel as if I belong here), "be part of" (*belonging to the assembly mechanism*). When someone says to her partner, in the words of several songs, "*You belong to me*" she probably refers to the first meaning, although the other meanings might also apply. The three other meanings appear to be unproblematic. The partner is indeed a member of a family or another social group, and in many cases he may feel acceptable in and suitable to this group. The fourth meaning of "being part of" is also unproblematic in its symbolic sense, which is close to the second meaning, as the partner is indeed part of a given social group. Needless to say, part of a social group is different from part of a psychological, biological, or physical system.

The most problematic sense of "belong" is that which refers to being the property of and being owned by; this is also the sense that seems to underlie most cases of jealousy. When I speak about owning somebody, I emphasize possession, indicating that this person belongs to me and not to somebody else. The meaning of possession in this case does not have to be physical as much as psychological. It does not have to carry the negative meaning, in which one possesses a car and can do anything one wants with the car; rather it implies that one personally deserves to have something. This feeling may not have moral justification but it can be justified from the personal, comparative concern of the subject, which is so central in emotions. Consider the following statement of Susan, who has a long-term loving relationship with another married man:

> I never felt that he belongs to me in the sense that I own him, this is a feeling I have never had. But I felt that he wants to belong to me, and this gives me the trust in him, and if I will suspect that this is no longer the case, I may become jealous. When I love somebody I want to belong to him, and hope he lets me in; but I do not want somebody to believe he owns me.

The psychological sense of belonging, rather than the mechanistic sense of having something in my possession, is further emphasized by the fact that the loss in jealousy is not accidental and not beyond human control; it is rather an expression of a clear preference for, and free choice of, the other over me. The issue of preference suggests that jealous people do not treat their mates as inanimate objects, but as free responsible people able to make reasonable choices (Farrell, 1980; van Sommers, 1988, p. 19). It hurts much more when we lose something because we are freely considered by our intimate partner as being worth less, than if we lose something due to forces beyond our partner's control. The crucial element in jealousy is the partner's free choice. Accordingly, our jealousy would be weaker were our partner's behavior to be forced upon him or her.

The negative aspect of the feeling of possession does not merely exist from the viewpoint of the person who is being possessed but also from that of the person who has the feeling of possessing the other person. Such a feeling may generate various worries about one's possession and may lead to the destruction of the relationship. Possession entails responsibility and when that responsibility lacks authority, it causes great distress. The constant effort and tension needed to maintain the control involved in possession can be harmful to the possessor. Typically, the possessor's self-confidence is low, and so he is likely to be constantly searching for signs to confirm his authority; when he does not receive such signs, his desperation and inadequacy might lead him to react disturbingly. Moreover, it is self-deceptive to believe that you can possess your partner, as the other person is not an inanimate object but typically a free agent (at least as far as her emotional attitudes are concerned). The partner who is being possessed does not behave and feel like an inanimate object, and this can generate profound psychological dissonance in the would-be possessor, leading to expressions of distress, hostility, and despair. (In this discussion, I am not addressing the cases of possessiveness that result in criminal actions such as violent abuse or murder, which have different, more extreme negative aspects.)

The association with belonging in jealousy is further explained by noting that while emotions are indeed personal, their concern also includes considerations about those related to me. These people are like extensions of my self. As Maccoby argued: "the self is not just a physical entity bounded by the skin, it is a psychological construct in which the concept of *me* and the concept of *my* are blended" (1980, p. 252). As James already said: when members of our family are insulted, "our anger lashes forth as readily as if we stood in their place" (1890, p. 292; see also Wong & Bagozzi, 2005).

The notion of the extended-self is complex, as there are various types of relationship within it. One obvious relation within such a self is the psychological distance from the center, that is, from the subject that constitutes the literal self. Children and spouses are quite near to the center of this self, as they are psychologically very close to the subject. Siblings and friends are a bit further away from the center. In a sense, celebrities may also be regarded as part of our extended-self as we feel some psychological closeness to them. Thus, we may be jealous of a certain person who is romantically engaged with a celebrity. The jealousy will be stronger if this person is comparable to us—for example, if he is an ordinary person, rather than a celebrity with whom we cannot compete. In this case, envy will have a greater role in the complex attitude of jealousy, making the jealousy more intense.

Psychological distance is a complex notion (see, e.g., Cooking et al., 1993; Liberman et al., 2007). For our purposes it may be characterized by the feature of caring—we care more about those who are psychologically closer to us. Psychological distance and caring express our emotional weight regarding people around us. Psychological distance also generally correlates with commitment and reciprocity—the closer the person is to us, the more we are usually committed to this person and the greater is the role of reciprocity in our relationship. Thus, there is a significant distance between me and a celebrity who doesn't even know I exist and since there is no caring, commitment, or reciprocity on one side of the relation, these cannot be profound on the other end. Moreover, even at a similar psychological distance, the nature of caring, commitment, and reciprocity may differ, as it is, for example, in the case of parental and romantic love. Accordingly, a similar psychological distance does not ensure similar attitudes and activities toward a certain person.

If other people are perceived to be an extension of our self, then describing them as psychologically belonging to us makes some sense. If my partner is part of my extended-self, then losing this part may hurt me, and losing her to another person may humiliate me and thus increase my pain.

Parental and Romantic Love

Although my discussion is focused upon romantic love, I would like to briefly indicate some differences between this love and parental love in order to better understand the nature of romantic jealousy.

Both parental and romantic love express close emotional relationships; in both cases, we can often find the claim that the beloved is considered to somehow belong to the lover. This claim seems to be more adequate in parental love since such love involves the biological aspect of creating the child and the psychological aspect of raising and shaping the child to be what she is actually now. At the center of parental care there is the wish to raise the child to be an independent person who will usually live many years without her parents, when having her own family or when living years after her parents' death. There is no expectation in parental love that we have profound common activities, such as living together and being with each other a considerable amount of time every day. It is expected that parents and children will have close warm relationships involving caring and help. At different ages these relationships may take different directions: in child-hood the direction is from the parents to the children while in old age the direction is reversed.

Romantic love is different in this respect. Its claim to belonging has no biological aspect of creation and a much weaker aspect of raising and shaping the person to the point at which she is now. The claim is not based on retrospective past features, but rather on present ongoing features combined with expectations of a common future. At the center of romantic love there is the wish to continue the relationship as much as possible in its current state, where common activities are at the center of the relationship. In both parental and romantic love there is a claim to commitment, but these are different types— the beloved's commitment, which essentially does not have to differ from that of the lover, remains more or less similar throughout the relationship, while the child's commitment changes as time passes.

The issue of reciprocity is also crucial for the emergence of jealousy. If there is no claim or expectation of reciprocity, the legitimacy of jealousy is considerably reduced. Parental love involves reciprocity, but this is not one between equal partners, but rather between people who support each other—first the parents support the children and then vice versa. Unlike parental love and admiration, reciprocity in romantic love is between more or less equal partners, and this is expected to continue in the future. Nevertheless, jealousy (as well as envy) can occur in parents. Thus, mothers are often jealous of their baby's affection for the nanny. Similarly, one woman said that she once felt jealous of her young son who announced that he could not come to a New Year party as he wanted to spend it with his new girlfriend. After this incident she no longer felt jealous of him, either because she adapted to the situation or because she was afraid to lose him. In parental love, exclusivity is less unconditional and a parent can become accustomed to a more flexible exclusivity, as the circumstances of their children will change throughout their lives.

Parental and romantic love also differ in the sense that in parental love the happiness of the beloved is less dependent on the happiness of the lover. The typical wish in parental love is that the children will be happy wherever they are, as they are raised with the expectation that they will one day be independent. The typical wish in romantic love connects, in one way or another, the beloved's happiness to that of the lover. The claim of the Beatles, in their song, "Run for Your Life," "I'd rather see you dead, little girl, than to be with another man," is common among romantic lovers, but seldom occurs among parents.

Jealousy and Exclusivity

Having briefly discussed various types and characteristics of jealousy, I turn now to the heart of the issue—the demand for exclusivity.

The focus of concern in jealousy is the threat to our exclusive position and, in particular, to a certain unique human relationship. The demand for the exclusivity of the beloved stems from the partial nature of emotions. Emotions are partial in that they focus on a narrow target, such as one person or very few people, and express a personal and interested perspective. We cannot assume an emotional state toward everyone. The intensity of emotions is possible due to their focus upon a limited group of objects. Emotions express our values and preferences. Emotions cannot be indiscriminate, as this is tantamount to having no preferences or values. The intensity of emotions is achieved by their focus upon a limited group of objects, just as a laser beam focuses upon a very narrow area and consequently achieves high intensity at that point. As an emotion necessitates limiting parameters, such as time, attention, and other types of "mental energy," the number of its objects must be limited as well. We have greater resources to offer when we limit the number of emotional objects to which we are committed (Ben-Ze'ev, 2000, pp. 35–40; Ben-Ze'ev, 2004, pp. 181–187).

Accordingly, the loss associated with sexual jealousy is often described as a loss of the attention, time, or sexual energy of the partner. Jealousy is aroused in people if they assume that when their partner is having sex with another person, they are losing something. But this is not necessarily the case. There are situations in which the mate, for reasons of guilt, personal considerations, or a better emotional state in general, lavishes extra loving attention on a partner when developing an outside attachment. In line with this view, it has been claimed that people should share their sexuality "the way a philanthropist shares her money—because they have a lot of it to share, because it makes them happy to share it, because sharing makes the world a better place" (Easton & Liszt, 1997). It is obvious, however, that in many other cases an extramarital affair reduces sexual desire and activity within the primary relationship, as resources and attention are directed away from the primary partner.

Even if loss of resources does exist in extramarital affairs, it is not certain whether it is this loss, rather than the loss of exclusivity, that is the focus of concern here. In these cases, too, the spouse may develop negative emotional attitudes, such as jealousy and hostility. In light of the exclusive nature of emotions, romantic intimacy with someone is likely to impair such intimacy with another. This suggests that the value of certain activities is enhanced if people engage in them only with each other, despite the fact that they may reap some benefit in violating such exclusivity. Certain rewards may lose much of their value if they are not exclusive (Ben-Ze'ev, 2000, p. 294).

Analyzing the postulated exclusivity of the beloved from an economic point of view, we may speak of two seemingly opposed effects. One is the consumer effect, in light of which a product becomes more desirable when perceived as desired by others. The second is the rarity effect, in light of which the rarer the product is the more desirable it becomes. The price of a flawed coin is often much higher than that of otherwise identical coins that were minted in large quantities. The two effects are compatible in the sense that we more greatly desire what is desired by others, but for exactly this comparative reason, we value it more if it is ours alone. Thus, a man may desire a woman more if other men desire her as well (accordingly, demonstrating that others are interested is a good way of increasing the interest of your partner), but this man will value her more if she remains exclusively his romantic partner. She is a kind of trophy he has won while the others did not (Ben-Ze'ev, 2000, p. 410; Ben-Ze'ev & Goussinsky, 2008; Buss, 1994, pp. 59–60, 112).

Exclusivity does not necessarily mean the exclusion of all people. There are various types and degrees of exclusivity. A very strict jealousy in this respect forbids all types of social relationships between a married person and an unmarried one. Thus, in some very religious communities, a married woman is not allowed to be in any type of social contact with a man other than her husband. A less strict jealousy may refer only to sexual relationships. There can even be some flexibility in the sexual context. Some people may allow their mate to have one short affair, say once every year, or to have an affair with people they do not know, without considering it as an abrogation of their exclusive relationship, and hence without giving any cause for jealousy, at least not of an intense kind (Ben-Ze'ev, 2000). Consider, for example, the following attitude of Lynn, a divorcee: "If I loved someone and wanted to be with him, and he wanted to be sexual with others, since I couldn't change his desire then I think I could simply allow it and see what it truly means. I don't have now the same need to protect myself from jealousy (like I did back then)" (Ben-Ze'ev & Goussinsky, 2008, p. 203).

People who accept a limited type of exclusivity may nevertheless be somewhat jealous of keeping this exclusivity intact. A woman in a polygamous marriage may not be jealous of any of the other women married to her husband, but she may be jealous of women outside the marriage. Similarly, a woman having an affair with a married man may not be so jealous of his wife, but be highly jealous if he engaged in an affair with a third woman. Thus, Sarah, a married woman having an affair with a married man, says, "Although I am a very jealous woman, I am not stupid. Because I realize rationally that I cannot change my lover's situation, I do not feel jealous." Similarly, Susan, a married woman who is in love with a married man, says: "I cannot come into somebody's life and say, now you belong to me and I am not going to share you with anybody else. I have no right to do so, although certain aspects of sharing hurt me. And the problem of (in) fidelity is doubled here." Limited exclusivity takes into account existing circumstances and limitations, and although these may hurt, they cannot be ignored. Realizing such limitations may reduce jealousy. It may also make the notion of fidelity more complex. On the one hand, violating fidelity (at least total fidelity) will become more prevalent, and in this sense infidelity will acquire justification by virtue of practice—in the sense that "if everyone does it, it cannot be such a profound sin." On the other hand, a greater prevalence of infidelity might make it more of a central insecurity for many people. Infidelity will probably become more common and less criticized.

In this regard, a distinction between formal and genuine fidelity can be made. Formal infidelity does not take into account existing circumstances and limitations. Genuine fidelity considers these limitations. Thus, a married person could claim that while his relationship with his married lover flouts the formal rules of fidelity, he is certainly being true to his heart, and this is the most genuine fidelity. Such an attitude casts doubt on the validity of rules that require one to renounce one's genuine love. Once people make the formal–genuine distinction, they can cope better with their own behavior and may be more understanding of the whole issue of fidelity; this in turn will help to decrease their jealousy. Jealousy is likely to be more intense when genuine, rather than formal, fidelity is breached. With people who lack any formal–genuine distinction, jealousy is generally more frequent and intense. These people are more likely to consider boundaries as absolute and to acknowledge no mitigation or degree, whereas those who make the allowances required by genuine fidelity find it possible to countenance the complexity that enables them to see that fidelity might have been breached only to some degree.

It is obvious that exclusivity in modern life should be limited. The assumption that one person can and should satisfy all the needs of another person is obviously problematic, particularly concerning certain types of needs—for example, intellectual stimulation, psychological support, and social connections. Nevertheless, many people still believe that from a normative point of view, it is better to have most of the beloved's needs satisfied by one person, or at least by very few. It is obvious that a person's intellectual needs can and should be satisfied by various people. It would be hard to defend the claim that a person should satisfy her intellectual needs by talking with only one single person or reading the writings of a single author. Exclusivity is of no relevance to intellectual needs. On the contrary, underlying our intellectual needs is the curiosity to enlarge our knowledge and be aware of novel perspectives and phenomena. Unlike emotions, which are quite focused, curiosity is expansive.

In the realm of social needs, the issue of exclusivity is of some relevance, but not to a very significant extent. A man may be jealous of the time his wife spends with her associates, but the objection is typically related to the issue of the quantity and the quality of these relationships, not to the idea of having social relationships with others. It is clear that one cannot have social relationships with everyone, as these relations require limited resources, such as time. Moreover, social relations may also require some preferential treatment, which cannot be given to everyone. Thus, we really should care more for those with whom we have social relationships (particularly those who are near and dear to us) than we do for strangers, yet this should not be an exclusive concern that violates the rights of strangers. Having close social relationships with several people should not preclude having a more profound relationship with one person. Nevertheless, jealousy can arise in social relations as well. A married woman at her early fifties said that she was never jealous of her husband when he met other women as she did not consider these women as a threat to her and being apart from her husband was not such a negative matter for her. But when her married lover had a business lunch with an 87-year-old lady, she was jealous of him. The presence of intense romantic jealousy in so many people, even those who reject monogamy, is another indication of the profound psychological basis of romantic exclusivity.

What Comes Next?

There is no doubt that jealousy will stay with us for a long time, as it expresses profound aspects of our emotional system. However, it is less easy to predict whether its intensity and frequency will remain the same. One indication of future developments may be found in what is occurring in cyberspace.

In cyberspace, major obstacles to the non-exclusive nature of romantic love—that is, practical limitations, the partner's attitude, and moral norms—are of lesser weight. Accordingly, jealousy may be less intense in the case of online relationships. Another reason for this is that the cost of ending an online relationship is smaller and hence the pain of that event is less intense as well. Moreover, the great availability of online alternatives makes it easier and more common to have several online relationships with various people at the same time. These considerations do not eliminate the presence of jealousy online. The profound degree of intimacy developed in online affairs may generate intense jealousy. Consider the following description by a woman having an online relationship that later developed into a successful marriage: "My feelings for him began to grow stronger and I could tell he felt the same about me. I began to get jealous if he talked to others in the chat room and he was doing the same with me. He finally told me he didn't want me to talk to any other men because they did not know me as he did. He didn't want his lady to be talked down to. I respected his wish and refrained from talking to other men" (cited in Ben-Ze'ev, 2004, p. 184). It seems that because the lines are not clearly defined in cyberspace, and the desired alternative is readily available, it is important for people to draw their own lines. Thus, many people make a choice to be a cybercouple and may even announce this to their online friends.

One major characteristic of online romantic relationships is the decreased weight of exclusivity, in the sense that the boundaries of such relationships are often violated. I believe this is also true of contemporary offline romantic relationships, which are also more flexible than they once were. In light of such developments the value of uniqueness, rather than exclusivity, becomes more significant.

Exclusivity is characterized in negative terms that establish rigid boundaries: it entails "not permitting," "restricting," "not dividing or sharing with others," "excluding some or most, as from membership or participation." Unique is characterized in positive terms that establish distinctiveness: "being one of a kind," "different from others in a way that makes somebody or something special and worthy of note" (Ben-Ze'ev & Goussinsky, 2008). The preference for uniqueness over exclusivity is clear in Internet dating sites where there are so many options for everyone and it is easier to have several relationships at the same time, and where people are asked to give a detailed description of their own uniqueness. Whereas the former reduces exclusivity, the latter emphasizes the role of uniqueness in romantic relationships and requires a deep look inward at the uniqueness of one's self.

The need for uniqueness is indeed a basic emotional need; we need to consider ourselves as very special: "We don't always see ourselves as *superior*, but we almost always see ourselves as *unique*" (Gilbert, 2007, p. 252). No wonder we want to see our beloved, who in a sense is part of our extended-self, as unique as well. Being unique is being different and it expresses a kind of change that, like other changes, excites our emotional system. Consequently, emphasizing our uniqueness is compatible with greater emotional satisfaction. We need to see ourselves as unique, just as we need to see our beloved as unique. And to a certain extent, this is a true perception.

The notion that one person cannot meet all one's needs does not contradict the idea that there are, however, needs that are best fulfilled by one or a few particular people. Emotional meaning acquires its significance by exclusivity. Some activities, not unlike certain merchandise, are cherished for being exclusive. Our wish to spread the fulfillment of our needs among various people does not imply that all people are of equal emotional significance to us. On the contrary, emotional significance is by its very nature partial and discriminative. We should expect some boundaries in the sexual and romantic realms to continue to exist. Sex is an emotional experience and, as such, has its own structure and boundaries. Accordingly, jealousy, which expresses a certain perceived violation of romantic boundaries, will continue to exist (Ben-Ze'ev & Goussinsky, 2008).

The greater flexibility of romantic relationships is bound to have some impact upon romantic jealousy. I believe this impact will be in the direction of more frequent cases of jealousy with typically reduced intensity. Jealousy will become more frequent as opportunities to break a relationship and establish new ones continue to increase. We must remember that jealousy is usually generated by the mere presence of threatening options, and not in the actual presence of infidelity. However, as jealousy prevails more often, and as the prospects of establishing new relationships increase, it is likely that people will become more accustomed to the circumstances associated with jealousy and that its intensity will decrease.

Despite various challenges to the requirement for exclusivity in love, this constraint does have a basis, as it expresses a genuine psychological concern. Moral norms have changed and will change in the future—so we can expect to have such changes affect romantic and sexual exclusivity as well. Indeed, many people gossip about the extramarital affairs of others without any negative moral connotation. It seems that in light of their increase, a growing number of people do not consider such behavior to be morally wrong. It appears then that a more pressing problem in this regard concerns the psychological aspect of the partners of the people involved in extramarital affairs. Non-exclusive love may be accepted on a normative level, yet be quite painful on the emotional one. Married people who are having an extramarital affair may still feel intense jealousy if they suspect their lovers of having an additional affair. The bad news for our future is that jealousy will be part of romantic relationships for a long time; the good news is that people will gradually give less weight to it.

Acknowledgments

I am grateful to Ronald de Sousa and Christine Harris for most helpful comments.

References

Ben-Ze'ev, A. (2000). *The subtlety of emotions.* Cambridge, MA: MIT Press.

Ben-Ze'ev, A. (2004). *Love online: Emotions on the Internet.* Cambridge: Cambridge University Press.

Ben-Ze'ev, A., & Goussinsky, R. (2008). *In the name of love: Romantic ideology and its victims.* Oxford: Oxford University Press.

Buss, D. (1994). *The evolution of desire: Strategies of human mating.* New York: Basic Books.

Cooking, R. R., Renninger, K. A., & Renninger, A. (Eds.). (1993). *The development and meaning of psychological distance.* Hillsdale, NJ: Erlbaum.

Cunningham, M. R. (1988). What do you do when you're happy or blue? Mood, expectancies, and behavioral interest. *Motivation and Emotion, 12,* 309–331.

DeSteno, D. A., & Salovey, P. (1996). Jealousy and the characteristics of one's rival: A self-evaluation maintenance perspective. *Personality and Social Psychology Bulletin, 22,* 920–932.

Easton, D., & Liszt, C. A. (1997). *The ethical slut.* San Francisco: Greenery Press.

Farrell, D. M. (1980). Jealousy. *The Philosophical Review, 89,* 527–559.

Fitness, J., & Fletcher, G. J. O. (1993). Love, hate, anger and jealousy in close relationships: A prototype and cognitive appraisal analysis. *Journal of Personality and Social Psychology, 65,* 942–958.

Foster, G. M. (1965). Cultural responses to expressions of envy in Tzintzuntzan. *Southwestern Journal of Anthropology, 21,* 24–35.

Friday, N. (1985). *Jealousy.* New York: Perigord Press.

Gilbert, D. (2007). *Stumbling on happiness.* New York: Vintage.

James, W. (1890/1950). *The principles of psychology* (Vol. 1). New York: Dover.

Louderback, L. A., & Whitley, B. E. (1997). Perceived erotic value of homosexuality and sex-role attitudes as mediators of sex differences in heterosexual college students' attitudes toward lesbians and gay men. *The Journal of Sex Research, 34,* 175–182.

Liberman, N., Trope, Y., & Stephan, E. (2007). Psychological distance. In A. W. Kruglanski & E. T. Higgins (Eds.), *Social psychology: Handbook of basic principles* (Vol. 2, pp. 353–383). New York: Guilford Press.

Maccoby, E. E. (1980). *Social development: Psychological growth and the parent–child relationship.* New York: Harcourt Brace Jovanovich.

Pines, A. M. (1998). *Romantic jealousy: Causes, symptoms and cures.* New York: Routledge.

Sagarin, B. J., Becker, D. V., Guadagno, R. E., Nicastle, L. D., & Millevoi, A. (2003). Sex differences (and similarities) in jealousy: The moderating influence of infidelity experience and sexual orientation of the infidelity. *Evolution and Human Behavior, 24,* 17–23.

Salovey, P., & Rodin, J. (1989). Envy and jealousy in close relationship. In C. Hendrick (Ed.), *Close relationships.* Newbury Park, CA: Sage.

Stearns, C. Z. (1993). Sadness. In M. Lewis & J. M. Haviland (Eds.), *Handbook of emotions.* New York: Guilford Press.

Van Sommers, P. (1988). *Jealousy.* London: Penguin.

Wiederman, M. W., & LaMar, L. (1998). Not with him you don't!: Gender and emotional reactions to sexual infidelity during courtship. *Journal of Sex Research, 35,* 288–297.

Wong, N. Y., & Bagozzi, R. P. (2005). Emotional intensity as a function of psychological distance and cultural orientation. *Journal of Business Research, 58,* 533–542.

Part II

Socio-Biological Foundations

4

The Ontogenesis of Jealousy in the First Year of Life

A Theory of Jealousy as a Biologically-Based Dimension of Temperament

Sybil L. Hart

Definitions of jealousy have been formulated on the basis of a wide range of factors. In addition to involving social cognitive processes toward the appraisal of antecedent events, jealousy has been interpreted in terms of cultural norms and motives toward various action tendencies (Bryson, 1991; Clanton, 1981; Hupka, 1984; Salovey, 1991; White & Mullen, 1989). Theorists have also considered it in terms of functionality, regarding it as a mechanism involving vulnerabilities and the protection of valued relationships, social status, material resources, identity, and self-esteem (Bringle & Buunk, 1985; Clanton, 1981; Hupka, 1991; Mathes, Roter, & Joerger, 1982). A key element of almost all definitions of jealousy includes some reference to affect (Bringle & Buunk, 1986; Parrott, 1991; Salovey, 1991; White & Mullen, 1989). Jealousy has been operationally defined as "the emotion that people experience when control over valued resources that flow through an attachment to another person is perceived to be in jeopardy because their partner might want or might actually give and/or receive some of these resources from a third party" (Ellis & Weinstein, 1986, p. 341). Similarly, Parrott (1991) has described jealousy as an emotion experienced when a person is threatened by the loss of an important relationship with another person to a rival. He notes too that the precise nature of this emotion is not easily discerned, and describes the experience of jealousy as including a "bewildering" array of emotions (Parrott, 1991). Consequently, jealousy is often conceptualized as a composite of several different emotions (Hupka, 1984; Sharpsteen, 1991), including some that are basic or irreducible, such as anger, sadness, and fear, as well as others, such as love, hatred, anxiety, self-pity, narcissism, guilt, panic, and distrust (Arnold, 1960; Fenichel, 1935; Freud, 1922/1955; Gesell, 1906; Horney, 1937; Panksepp, 1982; Panksepp, this volume, Chapter 6), that are considered more complex. In light of the multiplicity of emotions associated with jealousy, it has been defined as a complex emotion or blend of constituent emotions

Handbook of Jealousy: Theory, Research and Multidisciplinary Approaches, First Edition.
Edited by Sybil L. Hart and Maria Legerstee.
© 2013 Blackwell Publishing Ltd. Published 2013 by Blackwell Publishing Ltd.

(Arnold, 1960; Plutchik, 1980; Sharpsteen, 1991). In a similar vein, jealousy in toddlers has been described as a mixed emotion (Fogel, 2001), or jealousy complex (Volling, McElwain, & Miller, 2002). Still, jealousy is occasionally construed as a distinct and irreducible emotion in its own right (Lazarus, 1966; Mandler, 1984).

These conflicting perspectives on jealousy's affective nucleus call for fresh approaches as may be afforded through research which focuses on the issue of development during infancy. Attention to this early age stage stands to be exceptionally profitable. In addition to pursuing an uncharted area of development, research with infants overcomes several obstacles that have been problematic in research with adults. Infant jealousy can be evoked using experimental procedures that are valid, yet ethical, and yield outcome measures that may be more authentic than those generated by adult self-reports. To emotion researchers, the infant's response to jealousy evocation represents a window for gleaning insight into affective experience. Clinicians and theorists from a wide range of perspectives would agree that the emotional experience of jealousy is pervasive, and that the affects which lie at its root serve as a profound and driving force in the development of personality and the formation of intimate relationships (Buss, 2000, 2004; Freud, 1922/1955; C. R. Harris, 2004; Pines, 1998).

In this chapter, we explore emotions associated with jealousy. We ask how they originate during infancy, and how inquiry into this issue might help inform definitions of jealousy. We begin by reflecting on past works on prototypic features of jealousy and constructions of jealousy using hierarchical models of its affective differentiation. After reviewing models of this type, we turn to focus on developmental approaches and summarize a longitudinal study of our own which explores the nature of jealousy's ontogenesis across the first year of life. In a concluding section, we draw on our empirical work with infants toward proposing a model of jealousy as a constitutionally based feature of temperament.

Differentiation models of jealousy's development have approached the issue of jealousy's hedonistic origins from two opposing positions. According to one, jealousy emerges as a derivative of negative emotionality, usually anger. This view arose from research which assessed prototypic features of emotions in adults by asking college students to rate a large number of emotion labels for prototypicality or "emotionness" (Shaver, Schwartz, Kirson, & O'Connor, 1987). Cluster analysis then condensed the numerous terms into six emotion categories: *love, anger, sadness, fear, joy,* and *surprise.* Within this framework, *jealousy* became subcategorized within the *anger* cluster along with negative affects, including hostility, contempt, and hatred. Building on this process of derivation, theorists have inferred a hierarchy representing the developmental pathway through which emotions unfold during childhood. Fischer and associates (Fischer, Shaver, & Carnochan, 1989) implicitly conveyed their interpretation of jealousy as a derivative of anger within a section called "development from anger to resentment and jealousy." Parallel types of models, in which children's jealousy is viewed as rooted in negatively valenced emotion, had been suggested earlier by Bridges (1932). In her classic work on the genesis of emotions, she reported jealousy among toddlers living in a residential setting as being displayed in situations where a peer had received a caregiver's coveted attention. According to the differentiation theory of emotion which she put forth, jealousy was construed as a derivative of *distress*.

According to a second and contrasting stance, jealousy is interpreted as a derivative of positive emotionality (Darwin, 1877). In an informal sketch of emotional, behavioral, and cognitive markers of development during infancy and early childhood, Darwin provided an account of affects that were displayed by his son, Doddy. Its content was organized so as to include sections on negative affects of *anger* and *fear*, as well as positive affects of *pleasurable sensations* and *affection*. Whereas accounts of Doddy's misbehavior and frustration were discussed within the section on *anger*, instances of jealousy were recounted within the section on *affection* where it was included among positively valenced responses such as hugs, kisses, and sympathy. It would seem that despite its greater structural congruity with frustration, jealousy was classified in line with what Darwin perceived as jealousy's tender underlying meaning and prosocial function.

Developmental research on jealousy's emergence has been rare. Following numerous anecdotal accounts and naturalistic studies, a few experimental studies manipulated a parent's attention among toddler and preschooler age siblings. These revealed that a target child was more disturbed during the experimental condition, in which parental attention was directed toward a sibling, than during a control condition in which it is directed toward the self (Miller, Volling, & McElwain, 2000; Teti & Ablard, 1989; Volling, Kennedy, & Jackey, this volume, Chapter 17). To help rule out the possibility that findings on a target child's behavior were confounded by differences in characteristics of the rival child or to parent behavior toward that child, subsequent research (Hart, Field, del Valle, & Letourneau, 1998a) held parent behavior constant across all conditions and reduced variability in the rival child's characteristics by using a doll (which is described in greater detail in the Procedure section below) to represent a real infant. Because of its lifelike characteristics and the tender manner in which it is handled, this type of doll has been referred to as a "toy baby" (Fearon et al., 2006) and is henceforth referred to as such. In this study, 12-month-olds were exposed to four conditions, two in which their mother and a stranger, in turn, held and attended positively toward the toy baby, and two in which the women behaved comparably toward a story book. Despite being excluded to the same degree in all four episodes, the episode in which the toy baby was held by the mother was more disturbing to infants than that in which it was held by the stranger. It was also found more disturbing than the condition in which the mother attended to a story book. In line with Darwin's interpretation of an apparently similar situation, "jealousy was plainly exhibited when I fondled a large doll" (1877, p. 289), we have proposed that infants' heightened negativity in the mother–toy baby condition indicates that a rudimentary form of jealousy is discernible within the first year of life.

As infants age and acquire enhanced cognitive capacities, the experience and expression of jealousy is likely to become increasingly complex (Draghi-Lorenz, Reddy, & Costall, 2001; Masciuch & Kienapple, 1993; also cited in Case, Hayward, Lewis, & Hurst, 1988; Fischer, Shaver, & Carnochan, 1990; Hobson, this volume, Chapter 13; Lewis, this volume, Chapter 2), but it is also possible that in some rudimentary form, jealousy is evident at even earlier stages of development. To address this question, we exposed 6-month-olds to two conditions, an experimental one in which mother directed positive attention and elicited sounds from a toy baby and a control condition in which she behaved comparably toward a musical story book (Hart & Carrington, 2002). Comparisons of durations of infants' positive affect, negative affect, and visual gaze revealed that durations of negative affect were greater in the toy baby condition. Again, it seems unlikely that disturbances in the experimental condition could be due to being subjected to maternal unresponsiveness since infants were excluded to the same degree in both conditions. Nor does it seem as though it could be attributed to the toy baby's greater desirability since the duration of infants' visual gaze toward the toy baby was no greater than that toward the musical story book. Thus, in line with interpretations of findings in similar conditions with 1-year-olds (Darwin, 1877; Hart et al., 1998a), and empirical reports of research with infants in this age range (Draghi-Lorenz, 1998; Draghi-Lorenz, this volume, Chapter 11; Masciuch & Kienapple, 1993), we concluded that an attachment figure's inattention is especially disturbing if the object of her attention is an infant because this is a context that elicits jealousy.

Following this work in which we had asked "if" evidence of jealousy could be uncovered at the 6-month age stage, our next goal was to examine "how" it is expressed (Hart, Carrington, Tronick, & Carroll, 2004). Evidence of sensitivity to loss of exclusivity at such an early stage opens opportunity to address jealousy's affective origins since the young infant's limited range of mobility facilitates observation and coding of facial affect expressions. With this reasoning in mind, Affex (Izard, Dougherty, & Hembree, 1980) coding was used to explore facial affect expressions in detail. We also quantified behavioral responses, and included a measure of emotional intensity which tapped the integration of affect and behavior. To further highlight features of response that are unique to jealousy evocation, these measures of affect and behavior were explored against a backdrop of infant responses in two episodes known for evoking contrasting types of responses. One consisted of face-to-face play, a context known for eliciting approach behavior and positive affect (see Figure 4.1). In the other, mothers adopted a still-face, a frozen expression known for eliciting infants' negative affect and avoidance behavior. Comparisons across the three interaction episodes revealed that in response to jealousy evocation, 6-month-olds display a pattern of heightened approach responses and negative affectivity. The approach responses consisted of gaze toward mother, approach posture, and facial affect of interest. Findings revealed that durations of approach posture and interest expressions matched those displayed in face-to-face play, while durations of gaze actually exceeded those in play. Negative affectivity was indicated by reduced durations of expressing joy, heightened durations of sadness and anger (see Figures 4.2 and 4.3), and greater intensity of negative emotionality. Findings on these measures matched those displayed in the still-face condition except for sadness which actually exceeded levels exhibited in the still-face situation. Overall, infants appeared distressed and highly agitated despite having shown joy only moments earlier.

The configuration in which infants' negative affectivity corresponds with approach rather than avoidance behavior is unique and peculiar (Camras et al., 2002; Frijda, 1986; Rothbart & Bates, 2006). Avoidance behavior has been interpreted as functioning to reduce input of negative-emotion information and for self-regulation of emotion arousal (Gianino & Tronick, 1988; Stern, 2000; Termine & Izard, 1988). It seems feasible that in response to jealousy evocation, mother-directed approach behaviors too may serve a regulatory function, possibly to solicit comfort, much as has been shown with older infants and toddlers (Bowlby, 1969). It is also interesting to speculate on the reason why

Figure 4.1

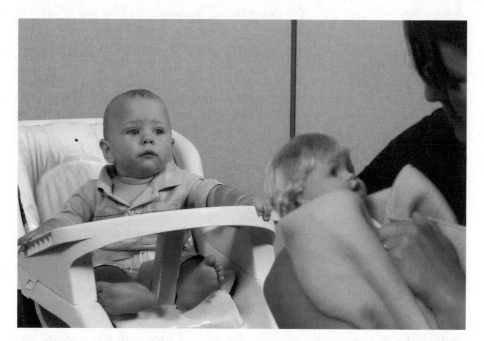

Figure 4.2

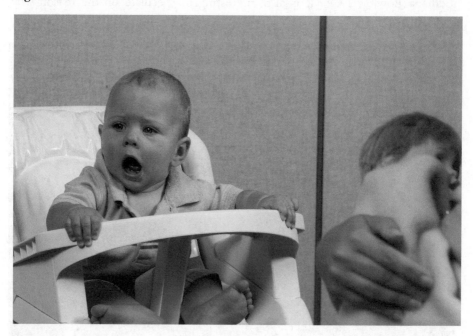

Figure 4.3

Caption for Figures 4.1–4.3 A 6-month-old infant's facial expression of *joy* (Figure 4.1) during mother–infant face-to-face play interaction is followed by expressions of *sadness* (Figure 4.2) and *anger* (Figure 4.3) when his mother turns her positive attention exclusively toward a toy baby.

Source: Photos by Kenny Braun, courtesy of Sybil L. Hart, Texas Tech University

infants respond distinctively to the two perturbation conditions. Why does a mother's disturbing behavior in the still-face situation elicit her infant's avoidance response, whereas in the context of jealousy evocation, mother's upsetting behavior elicits an opposite pattern of approach behavior? One might postulate that the two conditions of maternal unresponsiveness represent contrasting conditions with respect to child perceptions of mother's potential ability to provide resources. Perhaps, as she exhibits affection and positive affect, albeit toward another child, the jealousy-evoking mother demonstrates that she is in possession of valuable resources and that she is able to distribute them, a perception that warrants the child's assertive efforts to attract those resources. The still-faced mother, on the other hand, may be registered as a caregiver with limited resources, which, in turn, calls for an opposite pattern of response that suggests resignation. Though illusive, the distinctive patterns of response in the two perturbation conditions appear to suggest that even in its nascent form, jealousy is more specific than mere distress.

Having unveiled some evidence of jealousy at 6 months, and having also touched on its affective and behavioral content at this particular age stage, the following study was designed with two main objectives. First, we sought to chart the course of jealousy's development by exploring where along this pathway lies the 6-month-old's rudimentary expression of jealousy. The second goal was spawned by differentiation models of jealousy's affective development which led us to seek evidence that might help shed light on whether jealousy's affective roots suggest negative (Bridges, 1932; Fischer et al., 1989, 1990; Shaver et al., 1987) or positive (Darwin, 1877) emotionality. Toward an additional interest in advancing methodology for deriving evidence of jealousy, and in hopes of generating converging lines of evidence, the study was designed using a novel criterion for indexing jealousy. Since jealousy is not linked with a specific facial affect expression (Bringle & Buunk, 1986; Hart et al., 2004; Parrott, 1991; Salovey, 1991; Volling et al., 2002; White & Mullen, 1989), our past work has relied on manipulating elements of jealousy-evoking contexts, that is, situations that involve loss of an attachment figure's exclusive attention to a rival, and then documenting whether infants' responses are differentiated by this manipulation. We have, for example, compared infant reactions during episodes in which mothers direct exclusive attention toward a toy baby with those displayed during other conditions of maternal unresponsiveness, as in episodes where mothers present a still-face or direct attention fully toward a book (Hart et al., 2004, 1998a). We have also explored whether infant reactions during episodes in which adults attend to a toy baby or book depend on whether the adult is the mother or a stranger (Hart et al., 1998a). To identify yet another interactive pattern that is associated with jealousy evocation, the present study drew from earlier work (Hart et al., 1998a) which had reported that infants' responses to jealousy evocation differed with the degree to which mothers spontaneously complied with instructions to express positive vocal-affect toward the toy baby. Surprisingly, we discovered that infants displayed heightened levels of *negative* affect and protest if their mothers had expressed heightened levels of *positive* vocal-affect. Importantly, the inverse association between maternal and infant affective tone was not apparent when the object of maternal attention was a book. Further, the inverse association was limited to contexts in which loss of exclusivity occurred at the hands of the mother. If the adult was a stranger, effects of variation in vocal-affect did not depend on whether the object of attention was a toy baby or book. These observations lead to conjecture that the interactive phenomenon, which we refer to as *inversed affect sharing*, is heightened in contexts involving loss of mother's exclusive attention to a rival.

In the longitudinal study which is described in greater detail below (see shaded area), each infant was exposed at three age stages to a condition in which he was ignored briefly by his mother as she directed neutral or positive vocal-affect exclusively toward a toy baby. By exposing infants to conditions in which the quality of maternal vocal-affect toward a rival was manipulated, we sought to verify the phenomenon of inversed affect sharing. Furthermore, doing so at three age stages allowed us to ascertain whether the phenomenon differs across affects, and when it might change with age. Given that infant facial affects can be coded using Affex in similar contexts at the 3-, 6-, and 9-month age stages and that it seemed unlikely that even by 9 months facial affects can be masked, dissembled, or controlled, this dynamic period of affective development (Frijda, 1986; Lewis, 2008) was thought to provide a promising opportunity to extend earlier work with 6-month-olds. Through this manner of tracking of the emergence of inversed affect sharing among pre-locomotor infants we sought to explore the course of jealousy's ontogenesis during the first year of life.

Participants

Participants were $N = 43$ mother–infant dyads. The mothers were recruited from records of a university hospital, and initially contacted by nursing staff following uncomplicated delivery of healthy full-term infants. These volunteers were paid for their participation and treated in accordance with the ethical standards of the American Psychological Association (Bersoff, 2008). The mothers were (57%) White, (29%) Latina, and (14%) African American 18- to 31-year-olds ($M = 23.14$, $SD = 2.74$) of middle to lower socioeconomic status (Hollingshead four-factor socioeconomic status index $M = 3.31$, $SD = .84$) with $M = 12.38$ ($SD = 1.62$) years of schooling. The infants (22 males, 21 firstborn) and their mothers visited the laboratory at three age stages, when the infants were 14.29 ($SD = 2.02$), 25.15 ($SD = 1.35$), and 38.24 ($SD = 1.08$) weeks of age. The 43 dyads that participated at all three time points were derived from a sample that had consisted originally of 53 dyads. Attrition among the 11 infants

(7 male, 5 firstborn) who were unable to participate at all three time points was due to illness ($N = 6$) and logistical problems such as moving, transportation, or babysitting ($N = 4$), and 1 could not be reached. None were dropped from the sample due to crying or fussiness.

The dyads were randomly assigned to two groups: Maternal-Neutral ($N = 22$) and Positive ($N = 21$) Vocal-Affect, that were approximately equivalent in terms of infant gender and proportion of infants who were firstborn. Preliminary analyses to establish comparability between infants in each of the two groups confirmed that the infants did not differ in terms of distribution by age at each of the three visits to the laboratory, gender, or firstborn status. Nor did the mothers differ on demographic factors, including age, education, socioeconomic status, and ethnicity, suggesting that the two groups of dyads were comparable to each other. Preliminary analyses also found no association between any of the infant outcomes measures and any of the demographic variables pertaining to mothers or infants.

Procedure

The laboratory setting consisted of a video room located in a pediatric clinic of a university hospital. It was equipped with a high chair with an adjustable reclining seat, a swivel stool for the mother, and two cameras, one focused on the infant and the other on the mother. Signals from the two cameras were transmitted through a digital timer and split-screen generator into a video recorder to yield a single image. The image included the time stamp, and a frontal view of the mother's face, hands, and upper torso. The videotape was then viewed on a large-screen monitor to permit viewing facial affect in adequate detail. Appointments for the laboratory visits were scheduled to fit times when the mothers expected their infants to be alert. Upon arrival at the laboratory, mothers expressed verbal consent and signed an informed consent form which explained the study as work on babies' needs for exclusive attention.

After a mother indicated that her infant was comfortably settled in the high chair, a toy baby was placed on her lap. This type of doll (commercially available under the name "True-to-Life Baby Talk Newborn") has natural-looking hair, and when its torso is pressed it emits cooing sounds, such as "ma-ma," with exceptionally high-quality sound. When wrapped in a receiving blanket and held tenderly and attentively, the doll was determined to be a realistic replica of a real baby on the basis of pilot data which found that medical staff on a hospital pediatric unit, including residents and nurses, expressed alarm and distress when the cooing doll was suddenly treated in a manner that is inappropriate for a live infant (Hart et al., 1998a). It has been our experience that in addition to providing a level of control that isimpossible to achieve with a real infant, use of a toy baby precludes potential harm in situations where a target child who is mobile becomes aggressive toward the rival (Hart & Carrington, 2002; Hart et al., 1998a).

The interaction episode commenced when the infant was comfortably settled in the high chair. For a period lasting 90 seconds, mothers turned their attention exclusively toward the doll and ignored their infants. During this period, mothers in the Neutral Vocal-Affect group addressed the doll using a neutral tone of voice and presenting neutral facial affect. They also elicited cooing sounds from the doll only three to four times. Mothers in the Positive Vocal-Affect group smiled at the doll, vocalized using "motherese," and continuously elicited sounds from the doll. In order to confirm mothers' understanding of instructions and ability to comply, each mother was briefly instructed prior to participating and then asked to role-play proper handling of the doll. Episodes were terminated if an infant became overly distressed.

Coding

Infant responses

Infants' responses during the jealousy episode were analyzed by obtaining measures of visual gaze, facial affect expressions, as well as latency and intensity of emotionality. Visual gaze toward the mother was coded as *Looks at mother* using second-by-second coding to yield scores which were expressed as percentages of total time. Affect expressions of: *Joy, Interest, Anger*, and *Sadness* were coded continuously using the Affex system (Izard, Dougherty, & Hembree, 1980). These affects, which included partial expressions, were selected on the basis of earlier work (Hart et al., 2004) which recorded these affects at rates which are amenable to statistical manipulation. Since some of the episodes were shortened due to infant distress, real-time scores were reported as percentages of total time. Coders were trained using videotapes of jealousy evocation interactions which had been obtained in earlier research, and using Izard and associates' (Izard et al., 1980) training tapes and manuals. To measure reliability of coding the research data, each rater independently coded approximately one-third of the videotapes. Reliability checks were conducted frequently to maintain this level of reliability. The Kappa value (Cohen, 1960) for the infant behavior *Looks at mother* was .83. For Affex facial expressions of *Joy, Interest, Anger*, and *Sadness*, Kappa values were .82, .80, .81, and .82 respectively. To help prevent biases, coding was done by several independent coders, with infant and maternal variables coded by different teams of individuals, all of whom were unaware of the study's aims.

Intensity of Negative Emotionality

Intensity of Negative Emotionality was assessed globally on a single instance of videotaped behavior. The instance was selected as representing the most intense instance of negative emotionality, independent of emotion content, by two independent coders. If the two coders could not agree on a selection of videotape, a third coder, who was unfamiliar with the study's goals or hypotheses, rated the two pre-selected segments of videotape, and her judgment was the basis for selecting between the two. Intensity of Negative Emotionality of the selected segment of videotape was coded on the basis of evaluating three expressive components: facial, vocal, and gestural, using Likert scales from 1 to 4, and then summing the three sub-scores. This yielded a total score ranging from 3 to 12. The infant's negative facial expression was scored by observing three regions of the face: forehead/eyebrows, eyes/nose, and mouth/chin. The infant received a score of 1 if there was no sign of negativity in any region of the face, resulting in a flat response; 2 if only one region of the face expressed negativity; 3 if two regions expressed negativity; and 4 if all three expressed negativity. Negative vocalization was coded on the basis of affective tone and volume. The infant received a score of 1 if there was no instance of negative vocalization; 2 if the vocalization was mild; 3 if it was moderately negative; and 4 if the infant was screaming or crying. Negative gesture was scored by observing movement in three regions of the body: head, torso, and limbs. An infant received a score of 1 if he displayed no movement; 2 if one region was in motion; 3 if two regions were in motion; and 4 if all three were active. *Latency* to display negativity was quantified by simply calculating the number of seconds that elapsed between an episode's start and the selected segment's occurrence. Reliability was established for *Latency* scores, Pearson r was .83, and for Intensity of Negativity scores, Gamma was .82.

Maternal Vocal-Affect
In order to assess maternal compliance with instructions, maternal behavior toward the doll was coded on three 4-point Likert scales. These assessed qualities of vocal-affect, facial affect, and physical contact with the doll. Frequency of eliciting sound from the doll was also quantified. The four measures were then summed. For the summed score, Gamma values were .85. Reliability checks were conducted periodically to maintain this level of reliability. Independent sample t-tests revealed that mothers in each group differed on the extent to which they directed positivity toward the doll, suggesting that they had complied with instructions.

Results

Course of jealousy
Toward our primary aim of identifying and tracking inversed affect sharing, we conducted a mixed model multivariate analysis of variance (MANOVA) to evaluate the effects of one within-subjects variable, Infant Age (3-/6-/9-months) and one between-subjects variable, Group (Maternal Neutral/Positive

Vocal-Affect). The dependent measures consisted of the four facial affects: *Joy, Interest, Anger,* and *Sadness.* Scores were first subjected to log 10 transformations in order to normalize their distribution. Significant main effects were found for Age $F(8, 34) = 12.70$, $p < .001$, $\eta^2 = .75$, and Group $F(4, 38) = 5.21$, $p < .001$, $\eta^2 = .35$, and for the Age by Group interaction $F(8, 34) = 2.29$, $p < .05$, $\eta^2 = .35$. These results were followed by univariate tests using a 2 by 3 mixed model ANOVA for each of the four infant affects.

Analyses on *Joy* yielded a significant main effect for Age $F(2, 40) = 15.01$, $p < .001$, $\eta^2 = .43$. This analysis was followed by post hoc tests in which the critical p value was adjusted with the Tukey correction to control for multiple tests. These revealed that mean durations for this measure increased between the 3- and 6-month stages, and did not change between 6 and 9 months. Analyses of the affect expression of *Interest* also yielded a significant main effect for Age $F(2, 40) = 4.68$, $p < .05$, $\eta^2 = .19$. Post hoc comparisons again revealed that means increased between the 3- and 6-month stages. The main effect of Group was also significant $F(1, 41) = 6.65$, $p < .05$, $\eta^2 = .14$. Post hoc comparisons revealed that durations of *Interest* expressions were greater among infants exposed to Positive Maternal Vocal-Affect. Analyses of data on *Anger* yielded a significant main effect for Age $F(2, 40) = 3.51$, $p < .05$, $\eta^2 = .15$. Post hoc comparisons revealed that mean durations at the 9-month stage were greater than those at the 3-month stage. Analyses on *Sadness* yielded significant main effects for both Age $F(2, 40) = 35.36$, $p < .001$, $\eta^2 = .64$ and Group $F(1, 41) = 12.63$, $p < .01$, $\eta^2 = .24$. Post hoc tests revealed that durations of *Sadness* increased between 3 and 6 months and that *Sadness* was displayed for greater durations among infants exposed to Positive Maternal Vocal-Affect. In addition, the Age by Group interaction was significant $F(2, 40) = 9.93$, $p < .001$, $\eta^2 = .33$. To identify the age stages when *Sadness* differed by group, independent samples t-tests compared means for *Sadness* among infants in the Neutral versus Positive Maternal Vocal-Affect groups at each of the three age stages using Bonferonni adjustments to control for family-wise Type I error. These comparisons revealed that *Sadness* was exhibited for greater durations by infants in the Positive group than those in the Neutral group at both the 6-month $t(41) = 2.59$, $p < .05$ and 9-month stages $t(41) = 3.09$, $p < .01$. (See Figure 4.4.)

In order to evaluate *Looks at mother,* an additional univariate test was conducted using a 2 by 3 mixed model ANOVA. The main effect of Age was significant $F(2, 40) = 8.63$, $p < .001$, $\eta^2 = .30$. Post hoc tests revealed that the increase occurred between 6 and 9 months.

To evaluate effects of response *Latency* and *Intensity* a second MANOVA was conducted to evaluate the effects of one within-subjects variable, infant Age (3-/6-/9-months) and one between-subjects variable, Group (Maternal Neutral/Positive Vocal-Affect) on these two measures. A significant main effect was found for Age $F(4, 38) = 7.40$, $p < .001$, $\eta^2 = .44$. Follow-up univariate tests

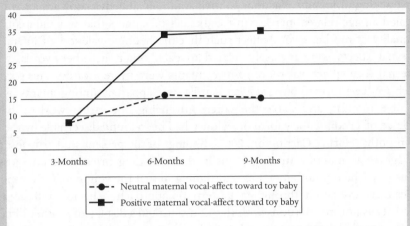

Figure 4.4 Mean durations of facial affect expressions of Sadness of infants at three age-stages as their mothers demonstrated Neutral or Positive vocal-affect toward a toy baby.

using a 2 by 3 mixed model ANOVA for each measure revealed that the main effect of Age was significant for *Latency* $F(2, 40) = 10.61$, $p < .001$, $\eta^2 = .35$. Post hoc comparisons revealed that 3-month-olds displayed negative emotionality more quickly than both 6- and 9-month-olds.

On the basis of these analyses of four facial affect expressions, mother-directed gaze, response intensity and latency among two groups of infants at three age stages we identified evidence of inversed affect sharing on a single outcome variable—sadness. Findings revealed that durations of Affex sadness increased between 3 and 6 months at which point infants who were exposed to mothers' Positive Vocal-Affect were found exhibiting greater durations of sadness than infants who had been exposed to mothers' Neutral Vocal-Affect.

Affective origins of jealousy

Toward our second goal of exploring affective precursors to jealousy's emergence, correlations were conducted only on *Sadness* since no other affect was found linked with evidence of jealousy. The first set explored interrelationships across domain within age. These revealed an association between 6-month *Sadness* and *Interest* $r = .45$, $p < .05$. The next set explored interrelationships within domain across age. These revealed a significant correlation between *Sadness* at the 3- and 6-month stages $r = .61$, $p < .001$. The next set explored associations across age stage and domain. Partial correlations between 6-month *Sadness* and 3-month affects which controlled for 3-month *Sadness* revealed a significant inter-correlation with *Interest* $r = .31$, $p < .05$. Similarly, 9-month *Sadness* was found inter-correlated with 6-month *Interest* $r = .32$, $p < .05$.

Our tracking of infants' reactions to their mothers' affectivity toward a toy baby revealed an age-related increase in facial affect of sadness that was differentiated by quality of mother's vocal-affect such that the hedonic valences of infant and maternal affects were inversely related to each other. In other words, when maternal vocal-affect was more *positive*, infants were more *negative*. This pattern, which we have termed *inversed affect sharing*, was apparent among infants by the age of 6 months, and stable thereafter. Advancing our earlier work in which evidence of a rudimentary form of jealousy had been found discernible by the age of 6 months (Hart & Carrington, 2002), findings of the present study suggest that this age stage marks a turning point in the unfolding of sensitivity to loss of exclusivity. The 6-month juncture is intriguing in that the young infant's response to jealousy evocation through a pattern of approach behavior and negative affectivity is not incongruous with the 12-month-old's display of mother-directed proximity seeking and protest under similar conditions (Hart et al., 1998a). Nor is it incompatible with reports of distress and efforts toward social entry among infants and toddlers in contexts where maternal attention has been directed toward a sibling (Fearon, Bakermans-Kranenburg, & van IJzendoorn, this volume, Chapter 16; Miller, Volling, & McElwain, 2000; Teti & Ablard, 1989; Touris, Kromelow, & Harding, 1995; Volling et al., this volume, Chapter 17) a peer (Bauminger, this volume, Chapter 12; Bauminger, Chomsky-Smolkin, Orbach-Caspi, Zachor, & Levy-Shiff, 2007; Draghi-Lorenz, this volume; Masciuch & Kienapple, 1993), and a father (Cummings, Zahn-Waxler, & Radke-Yarrow, 1981). Evidence of even further continuity of this manner of expressing jealousy may be drawn from work (Cummings, Zahn-Waxler, & Radke-Yarrow, 1981) which found that 10-month-old to 3-year-old children's reactions to jealousy evocation did not differ with age.

The phenomenon of inversed affect sharing is provocative. Infants' greater sadness in the positive vocal-affect condition is reminiscent of distinctions between infants' responses to jealousy evocation versus still-face conditions (Hart et al., 2004). In both of these studies, mothers' positive affect may have served as a stronger stimulus of jealousy due to signaling the presence of a caregiver who is in greater possession of desired resources or, as Bradley (this volume, Chapter 10) suggests, this is a context that is more appealing due to being more obviously relational. The phenomenon also deserves closer attention toward understanding of fundamental capacities in the general area of social cognition and communicative acts, such as those involving intentionality, animicity, intersubjectivity, joint attention, and social referencing (Bauminger & Kasari, 2000; Boccia & Campos, 1989; Draghi-Lorenz et al., 2001; Flavell & Miller, 1998; Hobson, 2004; Markova & Legerstee, 2006), and also more specifically toward the goals of the present study, toward formulation of a basis for an interpretation of jealousy. In addition to its heightened presentation in the context of jealousy evocation, this interactive pattern is rather unique. Notably, it contrasts with the matching of infant and maternal positively valenced facial displays that have frequently been observed (P. Harris, 1989; Hertenstein & Campos, 2004; Termine & Izard, 1988;

Yale, Messinger, Cobo-Lewis, & Delgado, 2003), as in Termine and Izard's work (1988) where investigators found that mothers' displays of joy induced greater smiling in their infants. Given that works from a broad range of perspectives, including learning, imitation, affect sharing, affect contagion, socially induced affect, attunement, and social referencing (Cohn & Tronick, 1988; Crockenberg & Leerkes, 2000; Druckman & Bjork, 1994; Feinman, 1992; Field & Fogel, 1982; Gewirtz & Pelaez-Nogueras, 1992; Haviland & Lelwica, 1987; Izard, 1978; Jaffe, Beebe, Feldstein, Crown, & Jasnow, 2001; Meltzoff & Moore, 1997; Reddy, Hay, Murray, & Trevarthen, 1997; Stern, 1985; Termine & Izard, 1988; Tronick, 1989; Yale et al., 2003) have regularly documented the infant's mirroring of mother's positive affect, and although there is considerable consensus that if an infant is impacted by her mother's positive affect the direction of effects is positive, an infant's dampened positivity as a consequence of exposure to mother's heightened positivity *if it is directed toward another child* represents an exception that is difficult to reconcile without attributing it to the infant's internally organized sensitivity to loss of exclusivity, or what may considered a rudimentary form of jealousy. We would submit that without an interpretation of jealousy, it is difficult to explain why infants are disturbed by an adult's positive affectivity toward a social object, but only if the adult is an attachment figure (Hart et al., 1998a). It would appear that even a simple, emergent form of jealousy could, to some extent, attest to the presence of cognitive prerequisites which underlie the infant's ability to distinguish among contextual stimuli and appraise social cues in a manner that precipitates a self-organized response.

Findings on antecedents of the 6-month transition are also informed by this study. Our findings on infants' facial affects at the 3-month stage did not lend support to the notion that jealousy's appearance at this point is normative. Nevertheless, in line with early anecdotal accounts (Darwin, 1877; Gesell, 1906), as well as recent empirical reports (Draghi-Lorenz, this volume), some infants at this age stage seemed clearly disturbed by their mother's heightened positivity toward a child rival. More definitive findings on the timing of jealousy's early onset may emerge from cross-sectional studies that include attention to a broader range of infant responses than those addressed in the present study which focused narrowly on facial affect expressions. Increased understanding of jealousy in different types of eliciting conditions would also be of benefit. A limitation of the present study was the inclusion of a control condition of neutral maternal vocal-affect which may too may have evoked jealousy, though perhaps to a lesser degree, or what may be better understood as a sense of social exclusion that may be inherent in all triadic interactions. Indeed, it can be argued that until more is known about jealousy all experimental work in this area will be challenged by difficulty arriving at a triadic context that can be upheld as a proper control. The love triangle is surely the most provocative type of triangle (Buss, 2000; Parrott, 1991), but it is not the only one that provokes jealousy, and the precise nature of the context that is triadic, yet absent of jealousy, has yet to be defined.

Toward our aim of exploring jealousy's affective differentiation and core, we discovered that displays of sadness at 6 months were preceded by expressions of interest at 3 months, and correspondingly, presentations of sadness at 9 months were preceded by interest at 6 months. These data do not appear to lend support for views of jealousy as a derivative of anger (Fischer et al., 1990; Shaver et al., 1987). Our uncovering facial affect of interest as an antecedent to sadness may be explained through at least two different types of mechanism. One possibility is that facial affect of interest actually serves as a marker of cognitive capacity rather than emotion. It may be, as we have already argued, that social cognitive processes are involved in appraising the jealousy-evoking context and are then responsible for triggering jealousy. Enthusiasm for this interpretation is some-what dampened, however, by the fact that cognitive abilities are not typically inferred on the basis of facial affect of interest. Rather, they are inferred on the basis of the structurally similar but conceptually distinct phenomenon of visual gaze (Butterworth & Jarrett, 1991), and all associations between sadness and gaze were nonsignificant. A second interpretation of the infant's facial expression of interest stems from the notion that it denotes the affective experience of love. Without a unique facial expression, this emotion has generally been sidestepped in developmental work on emotion despite its resonance among theorists, especially attachment theorists, as well as clinicians, parenting experts, and parents themselves. Nevertheless, it is notable that when approached by social scientists working with adults, love is often indexed by measures of deep interest, which in romantic contexts is sometimes referred to using the related term, *desire* (Hendrick & Hendrick, 2003; Sternberg & Barnes, 1988). The term *desire* has sometimes received treatment within the developmental literature where cognitive scientists have noted its overlap with emotions relating to love. Flavell and Miller (1998) noted, for example, that "mental states, such as that of liking or disliking something, seem to be mixtures of desires and emotions" (p. 863). Thus, we call for asking whether an infant's expression of deep interest can be construed as an expression of love.

An interpretation of interest as signifying the affective experience of desire or love is not incompatible with differentiation models of jealousy in which it has been presented as an outgrowth of *affection* (Darwin, 1877). A model of nascent jealousy as rooted in interest, suggesting desire or love, is also consistent with traditional and more benign conceptualizations of adult jealousy. Suggesting a long history of positive connotations, it may be worth noting that the term jealousy itself is derived from the Latin word *zelus*, meaning zeal or passion. Older views, in which jealousy was considered synonymous with passion and deemed an appropriate mechanism for conveying "proof of love," underwent a major transition during the late 19th century (Clanton, 1981; Stearns, 1989, 2000). By the 20th century, a radical transition in Western views had taken place, leading to currently popular disease models of jealousy in which it is associated with intrapersonal flaws, such as insecurity, low self-esteem, and neurosis, and with deficits in

interpersonal functioning which suggest failure to attain newly heightened standards of selflessness in love (Ben-Ze'ev, this volume, Chapter 3; Mathes, 1992;
Stearns, this volume, Chapter 1). Investigative attention to jealousy's development
in relation to the emotions of love, liking, and desire are much needed,
and potentially crucial to unraveling the under-researched enigma of diminished
jealousy (Hart, Field, Letourneau, & del Valle, 1998b). The age stages and conditions under which its presentation marks affect regulation suggesting optimal
social adjustment, or inhibited effort to protect a valued relationship, or simply
the absence of love, are unknown.

Jealousy as a Dimension of Temperament

Returning to the issue of definition, we now turn to considering how formulating
a definition of jealousy may be advanced by findings of infancy research. To begin,
we can offer some support for views that jealousy is expressed as an amalgam, or
mixed emotion. In addition to facial affects that reflect sadness and anger, links
between sadness and the earlier expression of interest suggest origins that relate
to the emotion of desire or love. Thus, it may be possible to conclude that even in
its nascent form, jealousy is a hybrid of sadness, anger, and love.

Yet, it may be equally important to note that the full array of affects is quite
stunning. Facial affect coding showed that interspersed among the various prominent affect expressions are some, such as fear and surprise, that can be fleeting, and
others, such as contempt, that are both fleeting and rare. Still others are rare and
complex, such as the propitiatory smile. Sometimes referred to as the smile of
appeasement, this expression consists of furrowed eyes / eyebrow region, suggesting
distress, much as in the upper region of the face of the infant illustrated in Figure 4.2,
but accompanied by upturned corners of the mouth, as in smiling. Findings on
older, more mobile and less constrained infants reveal a highly predictable pattern
of protest and parent-directed proximity seeking, but again, individual differences
are striking. Whereas most children, upon contacting mother, will tap or thump
mother's lap, some of the more nimble ones have tried to climb onto mother's
lap using her skirt for scaffolding. One stood by and kissed her mother's thigh,
another bit it until she shrieked (Hart et al., 1998b; Hart, Jones, & Field, 2003). In
other types of cases, infants fail to display mother-directed proximity seeking and
instead exhibit a variety of distal responses. In one case, a child approached
his mother by walking backwards and then stopping short of actually touching
her. In another case, a child threw a temper tantrum in the middle of the room.
Yet another child retreated to the furthest corner of the room and then buried
her head in some pillows, and still another child never moved except to turn his
back to his mother, shred a magazine to pieces, and start to eat it.

Though less prominent in terms of frequency or duration, it is far from clear that
any of these atypical responses are of lesser significance to the intrapersonal

experience of jealousy. In fact, atypical responses are frequently exhibited by an infant whose predominant response is typical. Atypical responses that are intense, such as those marked by anger, may be especially noteworthy. Inquiry into individual differences between infants as well as differences in the organization of typical and atypical responses within an infant may hold potential for informing clinical decisions as to whether a particular response pattern is within or beyond normal boundaries. Thus, findings on infants' modal affects and behaviors, and efforts to draw distinctions between typical versus atypical presentations and organizations, may be crucial to identifying the *kind* of jealousy that is being exhibited. They may also help guide interventions if interpreted as clues in the communication of intra-individual experience or goals that are registered by exposure to jealousy evocation (Campos, Frankel, & Camras, 2004; Tomkins, 1991). Inquiry of this nature stands to yield progress in areas of psychopathology which have stymied social scientists working with adults (Freud, 1922/1955; Pines, 1998).

However relevant such endeavors may be to various clinical issues, query into morphological differences among the various constellations of jealousy affects and behaviors may be of somewhat peripheral importance to actually defining jealousy itself. Once again returning to the issue of definition, we find that there may be little reason to hold that the irregularity of a response should detract from an interpretation of jealousy. We would argue that among infants, as some have argued with respect to adults (Bringle & Buunk, 1985; Ellis & Weinstein, 1986; Parrott, 1991), responses that have negative hedonic value but happen to be atypical can contribute nonetheless to interpretations of jealousy. This might lead to asking, if *any* constellation of negative affects or actions can be labeled jealousy, why use the term? Of course, the term is not meaningless. Though it may apply among infants, as it does among adults (Hupka, 1984), to almost any type of response, the term does *not* apply to responses in any type of context. Rather, it is linked specifically with situations having particular contextual parameters. Hence, much as adult jealousy has operationally been defined as any aversive emotional reaction that occurs as the result of a valued person's extra-dyadic relationship, we propose that infant jealousy can be defined as any negatively valenced emotional reaction that occurs in response to loss of a valued person's exclusive attention to a rival—a definition that holds, regardless of quantitative or qualitative differences in reactivity to that eliciting stimulus. In line with opinions on adult jealousy (Hupka, 1984), we find that the most meaningful and parsimonious definition of infant jealousy may be applied in terms of the eliciting stimulus, and independently of emotional content. This being the case, the construct of temperament may provide a useful framework for research in this area (Hart & Carrington, 2002). Temperament has sometimes been construed in terms of susceptibility to a specific type of eliciting context (Allport, 1961). The term inhibition, for example, refers to sensitivity to novelty, and it is applied regardless of whether an individual's response is marked by affects as contrasting as fear and exuberance, or by behavioral responses with valences as disparate as approach and avoidance (Kagan, Snidman, Kahn, & Towsley, 2007). We propose that the wide array of reactions to jealousy evocation can be treated in a comparable manner.

A model of jealousy as temperament rests on assumptions with respect to its constitutional foundation. Evidence of an inherited mechanism has traditionally been drawn from observations of adult jealousy's universality across culture and species, and upheld by theoretical treatments that emphasize its adaptive function which is generally framed as protection of a valued relationship (Buss, 2004; Darwin, 1877; Forbes, this volume, Chapter 7; Hupka, 1991; Panksepp, this volume; Trivers, 1974). We would add that further support may now be derived from infancy research which points to a constitutional basis via findings which imply that direct experience is not essential to the acquisition of sensitivity to loss of exclusivity. Jealousy arises early in infancy, and it does so even among infants who do not have siblings, suggesting that it emerges even under conditions that afford limited opportunity for learning that loss of an attachment figure's exclusive attention to a rival is an aversive event (Adler, 1931; Dunn, 1992; Stewart, Mobley, Van Tuyl, & Salvador, 1987; Taylor & Kogan, 1973). Additional support may be gleaned from findings on inversed affect sharing. Had we found that mothers' positive affectivity toward the toy baby drew a parallel pattern of affectivity in their infants, we would have been led to conclude that infant reactivity is learned directly through mechanisms such as modeling. Finding an opposite pattern of response, in which infants instead display negative affect, lends credence to the notion that an endogenously organized mechanism plays a role in sparking sensitivity to loss of exclusivity. Certainly, external events play an important role in the socialization of jealousy, but the type of influence necessary toward shaping the infant's expression of jealousy is less direct than that provided by modeling, and the type of exposure need not entail aversive stimuli. Past work which identified dampened jealousy in infants of depressed and insensitive mothers led to speculation on the importance of early histories of dyadic interaction and contexts in which infants develop expectancies of receiving preferential treatment from caregivers. Extending those results, findings of the present study lead us to elaborate that the nature of these early experiences entail aspects which engender love.

The construction of jealousy as a dimension of temperament should provide a useful heuristic to future research on mechanisms that underlie the early sculpting of jealousy. We believe that theory and established methodologies in the area of temperament (Kagan et al., 2007; Rothbart & Bates, 2006) can be applied productively toward informing understanding of both the nature and nurture of jealousy. Following his landmark cross-cultural work on the universality of adult jealousy, Hupka (1991) conveyed this point eloquently by noting, "our genetic heritage enables us to experience jealousy, but all else is learned ... The biological heritage provides the physiological fire, but it is ignited by a psychological spark" (p. 254). In line with this position, we feel that insight into jealousy's development will be unveiled by considering the separate and interrelated roles of both endogenous and environmental influences as they contribute to stability and change in jealousy's unfolding with age, across relationships, and within relationships as they become increasingly complex and intimate. The feasibility of this ambitious endeavor surely depends on a range of factors, but a central one will involve inquiry into the largely uncharted issue of jealousy's endogenous elements. Disentangling the exquisiteness of temperamental jealousy from more diffuse biophysiological dispositions, such as those involving proneness toward reactivity, arousability, and regulation, as well as proclivities for hedonic tone and intensity of emotionality, may be important and profitably pursued by contrasting biobehavioral responses to jealousy evocation with those evoked by exposure to other types of evocative stimuli (Eisenberg, Fabes, Nyman, & Bernzweig, 1994; Fox, Hane, & Perez-Edgar, 2006). Psychophysiological approaches that have been productive in developmental research on children's responses to other types of stimuli (Fox, Schmidt, Henderson, & Marshall, 2007; Jones & Gagnon, 2007) may be especially appealing for their potential to unlock meaning in quantitative and qualitative differences in presentations of jealousy, and, more generally, toward illuminating an intrapersonal experience that is too multifaceted to be articulated by the young child. Thus, psychophysiological measures offer potential to shed light on the significance of affect expressions that are atypical, on affective displays that are lacking in expressivity, and possibly on discrete emotions, such as love, where affective experiences do not correspond in one-to-one fashion with any known facial expression (Aviezer et al., 2008; Barrett, Mesquita, Ochsner, & Gross, 2007; Camras et al., 2007; Camras & Shutter, under review; Eysenck, 1967; Field, 1996). Based on our observations of wide individual differences in the presentation of nascent jealousy, as well as the exquisite sensitivity and sheer intensity of what appears as raw passion in some infants, we would hazard to predict that efforts to unravel the socialization of jealousy and to comprehend conditions under which it goes awry will not be fully productive without deeper insight into the "physiological fire" that is jealousy's constitutional foundation.

References

Adler, A. (1931). *What life should mean to you.* Boston: Little, Brown.

Allport, G. W. (1961). *Pattern and growth in personality.* New York: Holt, Rinehart and Winston.

Arnold, M. B. (1960). *Emotion and personality* (Vols. 1 & 2). New York: Columbia University Press.

Aviezer, H., Hassin, R. R., Ryan, J., Grady, C., Susskind, J., Anderson, A., Moscovitch, M., & Bentin, S. (2008). Angry, disgusted, or afraid? Studies on the malleability of emotion perception. *Psychological Science, 19,* 1467–9280.

Barrett, L. F., Mesquita, B., Ochsner, K. N., & Gross, J. J. (2007). The experience of emotion. *Annual Review of Psychology, 58*, 373–403.

Bauminger, N. (this volume). Jealousy in children with autism spectrum disorder (ASD). In S. L. Hart & M. Legerstee (Eds.), *Handbook of jealousy: Theory, research, and multidisciplinary approaches*. Malden, MA: Wiley-Blackwell.

Bauminger, N., Chomsky-Smolkin, L., Orbach-Caspi, E., Zachor, D., & Levy-Shiff, R. (2007). Jealousy and emotional responsiveness in young children with ASD. *Cognition and Emotion, 22*, 595–619.

Bauminger, N., & Kasari, C. (2000). Loneliness and friendship in high-functioning children with autism. *Child Development, 71*, 447–456.

Ben-Ze'ev, A. (this volume). Jealousy and romantic love. In S. L. Hart & M. Legerstee (Eds.), *Handbook of jealousy: Theory, research, and multidisciplinary approaches*. Malden, MA: Wiley-Blackwell.

Bersoff, D. N. (2008). *Ethical conflicts in psychology* (4th ed.). Washington, DC: American Psychological Association.

Boccia, M., & Campos, J. J. (1989). Maternal emotional signals, social referencing, and infants' reactions to strangers. *New Directions for Child Development, 44*, 25–49.

Bowlby, J. (1969). *Attachment and loss: Vol 1. Attachment* (1st ed.). New York: Basic Books.

Bradley, B. S. (this volume). Jealousy in infant–peer trios: From narcissism to culture. In S. L. Hart & M. Legerstee (Eds.), *Handbook of jealousy: Theory, research, and multidisciplinary approaches*. Malden, MA: Wiley-Blackwell.

Bridges, K. M. B. (1932). Emotional development in early infancy. *Child Development, 3*, 324–341.

Bringle, R. G., & Buunk, B. (1985). Jealousy and social behavior. A review of person, relationship, and situational determinants. In P. Shaver (Ed.), *Review of personality and social psychology: Vol. 6. Self, situations, and social behavior* (pp. 241–264). Beverly Hills, CA: Sage.

Bringle, R. G., & Buunk, B. (1986). Examining the causes and consequences of jealousy: Some recent findings and issues. In R. Gilmour & S. Duck (Eds.), *The emerging field of personal relationships* (pp. 225–240). Hillsdale, NJ: Erlbaum.

Bryson, J. B. (1991). Modes of response to jealousy-evoking situations. In P. Salovey (Ed.), *The psychology of jealousy and envy* (pp. 178–207). New York: Guilford Press.

Buss, D. M. (2000). *The dangerous passion: Why jealousy is as necessary as love and sex*. New York: Free Press.

Buss, D. M. (2004). *Evolutionary psychology*. Boston: Pearson.

Butterworth, G., & Jarrett, N. (1991). What minds have in common space: Spatial mechanisms serving joint visual attention in infancy. *British Journal of Developmental Psychology, 9*, 55–72.

Campos, J. J., Frankel, C. B., & Camras, L. (2004). On the nature of emotion regulation. *Child Development, 75*, 377–394.

Camras, L. A., Meng, Z., Ujiie, T., Dharamsi, S., Miyake, K., Oster, H., et al. (2002). Observing emotion in infants: Facial expression, body behavior, and rater judgments of responses to an expectancy-violating event. *Emotion, 2*, 179–193.

Camras, L. A., Oster, H., Bakeman, R., Meng, Z., Ujiie, T., & Campos, J. J. (2007). Do infants show distinct negative facial expressions for fear and anger? Emotional expression in 11-month-old European American, Chinese, and Japanese Infants. *Infancy, 11*, 131–155.

Camras, L. A., & Shutter, J. M. (under review). Emotional facial expressions in infancy.

Case, R., Hayward, S., Lewis, M., & Hurst, P. (1988). Toward a neo-Piagetian theory of cognitive and emotional development. *Developmental Review, 8,* 1–51.

Clanton, G. (1981). Frontiers of jealousy research: Introduction to the special issue on jealousy. *Alternative Lifestyles, 4,* 259–273.

Cohen, J. (1960). A coefficient of agreement for nominal scales. *Educational and Psychological Measurement, 20,* 37–46.

Cohn, J. F., & Tronick, E. Z. (1988). Mother–infant face-to-face interaction: Influence is bi-directional and unrelated to periodic cycles in either partner's behavior. *Developmental Psychology, 24,* 386–392.

Crockenberg, S., & Leerkes, E. (2000). Infant social and emotional development in family context. In C. Zeanah (Ed.), *Handbook of infant mental health* (pp. 60– 90). New York: Guilford Press.

Cummings, E. M., Zahn-Waxler, C., & Radke-Yarrow, M. (1981). Young children's responses to expressions of anger and affection by others in the family. *Child Development, 52,* 1274–1282.

Darwin, C. (1877). A biographical sketch of an infant. *Mind, 7,* 285–294.

Draghi-Lorenz, R. (1998, April). *Young infants can be jealous.* Paper presented at the 11th Biennial International Conference on Infant Studies (ICIS), Atlanta, GA.

Draghi-Lorenz, R. (this volume). Parental reports of jealousy in early infancy: Growing tensions between evidence and theory. In S. L. Hart & M. Legerstee (Eds.), *Handbook of jealousy: Theory, research, and multidisciplinary approaches.* Malden, MA: Wiley-Blackwell.

Draghi-Lorenz, R., Reddy, V., & Costall, A. (2001). Rethinking the development of "nonbasic" emotions: A critical review of existing theories. *Developmental Review, 21,* 263–304.

Druckman, D., & Bjork, R. A. (1994). *Learning, remembering, believing: Enhancing human performance.* Washington, DC: National Academy Press.

Dunn, J. (1992). Sisters and brothers: Current issues in developmental research. In F. Boer & J. Dunn (Eds.), *Children's sibling relationships: Developmental and clinical issues* (pp. 1–17). Hillsdale, NJ: Erlbaum.

Eisenberg, N., Fabes, R. A., Nyman, M., & Bernzweig, J. (1994). The relations of emotionality and regulation to children's anger-related reactions. *Child Development, 65,* 109–128.

Ellis, C., & Weinstein, E. (1986). Jealousy and the social psychology of emotional experience. *Journal of Social and Personal Relationships, 3,* 337–357.

Eysenck, H. J. (1967). *The biological basis of personality.* Springfield, IL: Thomas.

Fearon, R. M. P., Bakermans-Kranenburg, M. J., & van IJzendoorn, M. H. (this volume). Jealousy and attachment: The case of twins. In S. L. Hart & M. Legerstee (Eds.), *Handbook of jealousy: Theory, research, and multidisciplinary approaches.* Malden, MA: Wiley-Blackwell.

Fearon, R. M. P., Van Ijzendoorn, M. H., Fonagy, P., Bakermans-Kranenburg, M. J., Schuengel, C., & Bokhorst, C. L. (2006). In search of shared and nonshared environmental factors in security of attachment: A behavior-genetic study of the association between sensitivity and attachment security. *Developmental Psychology, 42,* 1026–1040.

Feinman, S. (1992). *Social referencing and the social construction of reality in infancy.* New York: Plenum.

Fenichel, O. (1935). A contribution to the psychology of jealousy. *Imago, 21,* 143–157.

Field, T. M. (1996). Expressivity in physically and emotionally handicapped children. In M. Lewis & M. W. Sullivan (Eds.), *Emotional development in atypical children* (pp. 1–27). Hillsdale, NJ: Erlbaum.

Field, T. M., & Fogel, A. (1982). *Emotion and early interaction.* Hillsdale, NJ: Erlbaum.

Fischer, K. W., Shaver, P. R., & Carnochan, P. (1989). A skill approach to emotional development: From basic- to subordinate-category emotions. In W. Damon (Ed.), *Child development today and tomorrow* (pp. 107–136). San Francisco: Jossey-Bass.

Fischer, K. W., Shaver, P. R., & Carnochan, P. (1990). How emotions develop and how they organize development. *Cognition and Emotion, 4,* 81–127.

Flavell, J. H., & Miller, P. H. (1998). Social cognition. In W. Damon, D. Kuhn, & R. S. Seigler (Eds.), *Handbook of child psychology* (5th ed., pp. 851–898). New York: Wiley.

Fogel, A. (2001). *Infancy: Infant, family, and society* (4th ed.). Minneapolis/St. Paul, MN: West.

Forbes, S. (this volume). Sibling rivalry in the birds and bees. In S. L. Hart & M. Legerstee (Eds.), *Handbook of jealousy: Theory, research, and multidisciplinary approaches.* Malden, MA: Wiley-Blackwell.

Fox, N. A., Hane, A. A., & Perez-Edgar, K. (2006). Psychophysiological methods for the study of developmental psychopathology. In D. Cicchetti & D. J. Cohen (Eds.), *Developmental psychopathology: Vol. 2. Developmental neuroscience* (2nd ed., pp. 381–426). Hoboken, NJ: John Wiley & Sons.

Fox, N. A., Schmidt, L. A., Henderson, H. A., & Marshall, P. J. (2007). Developmental psychophysiology: Conceptual and methodological issues. In J. T. Cacioppo, L. G. Tassinary, & G. G. Berntson (Eds.), *Handbook of psychophysiology* (3rd ed., pp. 453–481). New York: Cambridge University Press.

Freud, S. (1922/1955). Some neurotic mechanisms in jealousy, paranoia, and homosexuality. In J. Trachey (Ed.), *The standard edition of the complete psychological works of Sigmund Freud* (Vol. 18, pp. 221–232). London: Hogarth.

Frijda, N. H. (1986). *The emotions.* New York: Cambridge University Press.

Gesell, A. L. (1906). Jealousy. *American Journal of Psychology, 17,* 437–496.

Gewirtz, J. L., & Pelaez-Nogueras, M. (1992). Social referencing as a learned process. In S. Feinman (Ed.), *Social referencing and the social construction of reality in infancy* (pp. 151–173). New York: Plenum.

Gianino, A., & Tronick, E. Z. (1988). The mutual regulation model: The infant's self and interactive regulation and coping and defensive capacities. In T. M. Field, P. M. McCabe, & N. Schneiderman (Eds.), *Stress and coping across development* (pp. 47–68). Hillsdale, NJ: Erlbaum.

Harris, C. R. (2004). The evolution of jealousy. *American Scientist, 92,* 62–71.

Harris, P. (1989). *Children and emotion.* Oxford: Blackwell.

Hart, S. L., & Carrington, H. (2002). Jealousy in 6-month-old infants. *Infancy, 3,* 395–402.

Hart, S. L., Carrington, H. A., Tronick, E. Z., & Carroll, S. R. (2004). When infants lose exclusive maternal attention: Is it jealousy? *Infancy, 6,* 57–78.

Hart, S. L., Field, T., del Valle, C., & Letourneau, M. (1998a). Infants protest their mothers' attending to an infant-size doll. *Social Development, 7,* 54–61.

Hart, S. L., Field, T., Letourneau, M., & del Valle, C. (1998b). Jealousy protests in infants of depressed mothers. *Infant Behavior and Development, 21,* 137–148.

Hart, S. L., Jones, N. A., & Field, T. (2003). Atypical expressions of jealousy in infants of intrusive- and withdraw-depressed mothers. *Child Psychiatry and Human Development, 33,* 193–207.

Haviland, J. M., & Lelwica, M. (1987). The induced affect response: 10-week-old infants' responses to three emotion expressions. *Developmental Psychology, 23,* 97–104.

Hendrick, C., & Hendrick, S. (2003). Romantic love: Measuring cupid's arrow. In S. J. Lopez & C. R. Snyder (Eds.), *Positive psychological assessment: A handbook of models and measures.* Washington, DC: American Psychological Association.

Hertenstein, M. J., & Campos, J. J. (2004). The retention effects of an adult's emotional displays on infant behavior. *Child Development, 75,* 595–613.

Hobson, P. (2004). *The cradle of thought: Exploring the origins of thinking.* New York: Oxford University Press.

Hobson, R. P. (this volume). Is jealousy a complex emotion? In S. L. Hart & M. Legerstee (Eds.), *Handbook of jealousy: Theory, research, and multidisciplinary approaches.* Malden, MA: Wiley-Blackwell.

Horney, K. (1937). *The neurotic personality of our time.* New York: Norton.

Hupka, R. (1984). Jealousy: Compound emotion or label for a particular situation? *Motivation and Emotion, 8,* 141–155.

Hupka, R. (1991). The motive for the arousal of romantic jealousy: Its cultural origin. In P. Salovey (Ed.), *The psychology of jealousy and envy* (pp. 252–270). New York: Guilford Press.

Izard, C. E. (1978). Emotions as motivations: An evolutionary-developmental perspective. *Nebraska Symposium on Motivation, 26,* 163–200.

Izard, C. E., Dougherty, L. M., & Hembree, E. A. (1980). *A system for identifying affect expressions by holistic judgments (Affex).* Newark, DE: University of Delaware.

Jaffe, J., Beebe, B., Feldstein, S., Crown, C. L., & Jasnow, M. (2001). Rhythms of dialogue in infancy. *Monographs of the Society for Research in Child Development, 66*(2, Serial No. 265), 1–132.

Jones, N. A., & Gagnon, C. M. (2007). The neurophysiology of empathy. In T. Farrow & P. Woodruff (Eds.), *Empathy in mental illness* (pp. 217–238). New York: Cambridge University Press.

Kagan, J., Snidman, N., Kahn, V., & Towsley, S. (2007). The preservation of two infant temperaments into adolescence. *Monographs of the Society for Research in Child Development 287, 72*(2, Serial No. 287), 1–75.

Lazarus, R. S. (1966). *Psychological stress and the coping process.* New York: McGraw-Hill.

Lewis, M. (2008). The emergence of human emotions. In M. Lewis, J. M. Haviland-Jones, & L. F. Barrett (Eds.), *Handbook of emotions* (3rd ed., pp. 265–280). New York: Guilford Press.

Lewis, M. (this volume). Loss, protest and emotional development. In S. L. Hart & M. Legerstee (Eds.), *Handbook of jealousy: Theory, research, and multidisciplinary approaches.* Malden, MA: Wiley-Blackwell.

Mandler, G. (1984). *Mind and body.* New York: Norton.

Markova, G., & Legerstee, M. (2006). Contingency, imitation, and affect sharing: Foundations of infants' social awareness. *Development Psychology, 42,* 132–141.

Masciuch, S., & Kienapple, K. (1993). The emergence of jealousy in children 4 months to 7 years of age. *Journal of Social and Personal Relationships, 10,* 421–435.

Mathes, E. W. (1992). *Jealousy: The psychological data*. London: University of America.

Mathes, E. W., Roter, P. M., & Joerger, S. M. (1982). A convergent validity study of six jealousy scales. *Psychological Reports, 50*, 1143–1147.

Meltzoff, A. N., & Moore, M. K. (1997). Explaining facial imitation: A theoretical model. *Early Development and Parenting, 6*, 170–192.

Miller, A. L., Volling, B. L., & McElwain, N. L. (2000). Sibling jealousy in a triadic context with mothers and fathers. *Social Development, 9*, 433–457.

Panksepp, J. (1982). Toward a general psychobiological theory of emotions. *Behavioral and Brain Sciences, 5*, 407–467.

Panksepp, J. (this volume). The evolutionary sources of jealousy: Cross-species approaches to fundamental issues. In S. L. Hart & M. Legerstee (Eds.), *Handbook of jealousy: Theory, research, and multidisciplinary approaches*. Malden, MA: Wiley-Blackwell.

Parrott, W. G. (1991). The emotional experiences of envy and jealousy. In P. Salovey (Ed.), *The psychology of jealousy and envy* (pp. 3–30). New York: Guilford Press.

Pines, A. M. (1998). *Romantic Jealousy*. New York: Routledge.

Plutchik, R. (1980). *Emotion*. New York: Harper & Row.

Reddy, V., Hay, D., Murray, L., & Trevarthen, C. (1997). Communication in infancy: Mutual regulation of affect and attention. In G. Bremner, A. Slater, & G. Butterworth (Eds.), *Infant development: Recent advances* (pp. 247–273). Hove, England: Psychology Press.

Rothbart, M. K., & Bates, J. E. (2006). Temperament. In N. Eisenberg, W. Damon, & R. M. Lerner (Eds.), *Handbook of child psychology: Vol. 3. Social, emotional, and personality development* (6th ed., pp. 99–166). Hoboken, NJ: Wiley.

Salovey, P. (1991). *The psychology of jealousy and envy*. New York: Guilford Press.

Sharpsteen, D. J. (1991). The organization of jealousy knowledge: Romantic jealousy as blended emotion. In P. Salovey (Ed.), *The psychology of jealousy and envy* (pp. 31–48). New York: Guilford Press.

Shaver, P., Schwartz, J., Kirson, D., & O'Connor, C. (1987). Emotion knowledge: Further exploration of a prototype approach. *Journal of Personality and Social Psychology, 52*, 1061–1086.

Stearns, P. (1989). *Jealousy: The evolution of an emotion in American history*. New York: New York University Press.

Stearns, P. (2000). History of emotions: Issues of change and impact. In M. Lewis & J. Haviland-Jones (Eds.), *Handbook of emotions* (pp. 16–29). New York: Guilford Press.

Stearns, P. N. (this volume). Jealousy in western history: From past toward present. In S. L. Hart & M. Legerstee (Eds.), *Handbook of jealousy: Theory, research, and multidisciplinary approaches*. Malden, MA: Wiley-Blackwell.

Stern, D. N. (1985). Affect attunement. In J. D. Call, E. Galenson, & R. L. Tyson (Eds.), *Frontiers of infant psychiatry* (Vol. 2, pp. 3–14). New York: Basic Books.

Stern, D. N. (2000). *The interpersonal world of the infant: A view from psychoanalysis and developmental psychology*. New York: Perseus.

Sternberg, R. J., & Barnes, M. L. (1988). *The psychology of love*. New Haven, CT: Yale University Press.

Stewart, R. B., Mobley, L. A., Van Tuyl, S. S., & Salvador, M. A. (1987). The firstborn's adjustment to the birth of a sibling: A longitudinal assessment. *Child Development, 58*, 341–355.

Taylor, M., & Kogan, K. (1973). Effects of birth of a sibling on mother–child interactions. *Child Psychiatry and Human Development, 4,* 53–58.

Termine, N. T., & Izard, C. E. (1988). Infants' responses to their mothers' expressions of joy and sadness. *Developmental Psychology, 24,* 223–229.

Teti, D. M., & Ablard, K. E. (1989). Security of attachment and infant–sibling relationships: A laboratory study. *Child Development, 60,* 1519–1528.

Tomkins, S. S. (1991). *Affect, imagery, consciousness: Vol. 3. The negative affects: Anger and fear.* New York: Springer.

Touris, M., Kromelow, S., & Harding, C. (1995). Mother–firstborn attachment and the birth of a sibling. *American Journal of Orthopsychiatry, 65,* 293–297.

Trivers, R. L. (1974). Parent–offspring conflict. *American Zoologist, 14,* 249–264.

Tronick, E. Z. (1989). Emotions and emotional communication in infants. *American Psychologist, 44,* 112–119.

Volling, B. L., Kennedy, D. E., & Jackey, L. M. H. (this volume). The development of sibling jealousy. In S. L. Hart & M. Legerstee (Eds.), *Handbook of jealousy: Theory, research, and multidisciplinary approaches.* Malden, MA: Wiley-Blackwell.

Volling, B. L., McElwain, N. L., & Miller, A. L. (2002). Emotion regulation in context: The jealousy complex between young siblings and its relations with child and family characteristics. *Child Development, 73,* 581–600.

White, G. L., & Mullen, P. E. (1989). *Jealousy: Theory, research, and clinical strategies.* New York: Guilford Press.

Yale, M. E., Messinger, D. S., Cobo-Lewis, A. B., & Delgado, C. F. (2003). The temporal coordination of early infant communication. *Developmental Psychology, 39,* 815–824.

5

Neural Structures of Jealousy
Infants' Experience of Social Exclusion with Caregivers and Peers

Gabriela Markova, James Stieben, and Maria Legerstee

Infants are faced with situations of social exclusion from early on. In its simplest form, when infants are separated from their caregivers, they experience social exclusion to which they react with negative emotions such as sadness and panic. This universal infant reaction is referred to as separation distress, and may be viewed as an evolutionary mechanism which functions to preserve closeness with the caregiver who provides all basic needs. For this reason, emotions that arise during these separate situations are argued to be prewired in the brain (Panksepp, 1998). A more complex social exclusion occurs when infants' close relationships with caregivers are threatened by a third person. In this case the exclusivity with caregivers is at stake and, consequently, infants react with negative emotions and approach behaviors that are interpreted by some authors as jealousy. Both jealousy-evoking and separation distress-evoking situations rely on separation from the caregiver with whom infants have established a close relationship. However, an awareness of social exclusion from the caregiver due to the presence of a rival (i.e., triadic social exclusion) requires more sophisticated socio-cognitive abilities than during simple separation from the caregiver (i.e., dyadic social exclusion). Jealousy-evoking situations thus necessitate both the presence of a close love relationship and cognitive skills to comprehend the situational constraints (see Legerstee, Ellenbogen, Nienhuis, & Marsh, this volume, Chapter 9). Like separation distress, which is conceptualized only through the presence of close bonds with caregivers, there may be other situations of social exclusion that require a certain socio-cognitive level of understanding, but do not presuppose a love relationship. Thus, the question arises whether infants experience social exclusion with partners with whom they do not have a close relationship. For instance, infants may feel social exclusion when playing with same-age peers during the first year of life in a similar way as they experience when they are excluded by their caregivers

Handbook of Jealousy: Theory, Research and Multidisciplinary Approaches, First Edition.
Edited by Sybil L. Hart and Maria Legerstee.
© 2013 Blackwell Publishing Ltd. Published 2013 by Blackwell Publishing Ltd.

(see, e.g., Fivaz-Depeursinge, Favez, Lavanchy Scaiola, & Lopes, this volume, Chapter 19; Legerstee et al., this volume).

The aim of this chapter is to propose a neural model of jealousy that is based on two aspects necessary to understand jealousy-evoking situations: (1) infant inborn tendency to establish and maintain close relationships with caregivers, and (2) socio-cognitive processes linked to emotion regulation and reward-based approach. We will then introduce a study showing that very young infants are sensitive to being excluded from an infant group, even though they might not as yet have developed a close relationship with these peers. We will elaborate on how infant responses to this kind of social exclusion can be explained and propose neural systems that may be at work during such situations.

Social Bonds and Separation Distress

Social bonds are fundamental for human beings because social connections with others ensure the availability of not only basic physiological (e.g., food, shelter) but also social (e.g., relationships, communication, emotional availability) needs. Consequently, the protection of social relationships may have great adaptive value and is regarded as an innate human predisposition (MacDonald & Leary, 2005). This view is supported by evidence indicating that infants' social orientation, such as face and eye gaze processing, perception of emotion, perception of biological motion, and perception of human attention and action, has biological correlates and is already available in the brain of very young infants (see Grossman & Johnson, 2007, for a review). Studies have also shown that biological rhythms (e.g., heart rate), hormonal levels, and activation in specific brain regions (i.e., superior temporal gyrus, anterior cingulate cortex, thalamus, and midbrain) underlie temporally matched interactions between mothers and infants (see Feldman, 2007, for a review; Moore & Calkins, 2004). Additionally, Panksepp (1998) postulates emotion reaction systems in the brain that are linked to caretaking, establishment of social bonds and seeking of social connections, and those that are implicated when becoming separated from the caregiver. Because, in general, emotion reaction systems generate a sense of well-being with regard to the most important physiological and social needs of life (Panksepp, 1998), we would expect that emotions arising within relationships are essential and thus appear early in life.

As suggested by Panksepp (1998), when infants are separated from their caregivers, biologically predetermined neural networks are at work that reestablish the usually close exclusive relations infants have with their caregivers. Animal studies have shown that regions activated during separation distress in guinea pigs include, among others, the periaqueductal gray (PAG: pain and defensive behaviors), amygdala (AM: assesses whether something is pleasurable or aversive), and anterior cingulate cortex (ACC: selective attention and response selection during stressful situations; Panksepp, 1998). Panksepp suggests that the interplay between these neural structures is manifested as negative emotions, such as panic and sadness, and these circuits are major forces that guide the construction of social bonds.

Human infants are rather helpless, and rely on their caregivers to provide them with food, shelter, and security. Therefore, long-lasting separation from caregivers can have detrimental effects. For this reason, MacDonald and Leary (2005; see also Panksepp, 2005) propose that threats to social connections must be processed at a very primitive level. In fact, negative emotions arising during social exclusion may share common neural pathways with affect qualities of physical pain (Eisenberger, Lieberman, & Williams, 2003; Panksepp, 2003). The PAG is an interesting brain structure in this context, because besides processing pain it is also an important structure for affect (Panksepp, 2005), and panic in particular (Graeff, 2004). Thus, the PAG may play a role in both physical pain and emotional distress arising from threats to social bonding. Moreover, Panksepp (2003, 2005) suggests that the same neurochemicals which control separation distress (i.e., corticotrophin-releasing hormone, β-endorphine, oxytocin, and prolactin) also regulate physical pain. Because aversive feelings of social exclusion and physical pain engage the same brain regions, separation distress is also experienced as emotionally painful (Panksepp, 2005). Most importantly, the panic, sadness, and pain circuits operate independently of cognition (Panksepp, 1998), and thus constitute very basic biological reactions that are available even to animals and very young infants.

In summary, from birth infants' brains are prepared to orient toward and process social information. Moreover, specific neural networks are activated when infants are separated from their caregivers (i.e., emotion and pain systems), and these systems are also responsible for perception of separation situations as emotionally painful. Infants' reactions to separation from the caregiver (i.e., separation distress) are essential for the strengthening of social bonds and are void of higher cognitive processes.

From Separation Distress to Jealousy

Because infants are endowed with innate physiological systems that allow them to establish and protect exclusive relationships with their caregivers (i.e., infant separation distress), it is likely that they are also sensitive to social exclusion situations where these relationships are threatened by the presence of a third person (i.e., rival). Behavioral studies show that already during the first year of life infants are sensitive to such triadic social exclusions (see Draghi-Lorenz, Reddy, & Costall, 2001, for a review; see also the various chapters in this volume). For example, research indicates that 4-month-old infants experience loss of exclusivity when their mothers pay exclusive attention to another child (Masciuch & Kienapple, 1993), and 6-month-olds are sensitive to being excluded when their mothers turn their attention to a doll (Hart, Carrington, Tronick, & Carroll, 2004). Moreover, Legerstee et al. (this volume) found that 3- and 6-month-old infants were sensitive to social exclusion in a triadic situation where an experimenter engaged in a lively dialogue with their mothers, as opposed to when the experimenter was the one initiating and sustaining inter-action with the mother in the form of a monologue. That is, infants became upset when they perceived the experimenter as a rival (i.e., mothers showed interest in the experimenter in the dialogue condition), but did not react when mothers did not participate in the interaction initiated and sustained by the experimenter in the monologue condition (i.e., experimenter was not perceived as a threat to the mother–infant relationship). Together, these findings indicate that infants are sensitive to triadic social exclusion, where the social bond the infant has with a loved one is threatened by the presence of a rival. Consequently, authors investigating infant sensitivity to these situations have interpreted infants' responses as jealousy.

Separation distress and jealousy may be conceptually related in that both rely on the presence of exclusive love relationships. However, although jealousy may get its 'affective impact' from feelings of separation distress (Panksepp, 2005), specific socio-cognitive skills are needed to understand triadic social exclusion situations resulting in jealousy. Thus, neural systems involved in separation distress are necessary but not sufficient for jealousy to arise. In line with this argument, Legerstee et al. (this volume) propose that even very young infants possess specific prerequisite abilities that enable them to understand jealousy-evoking situations. Specifically, these authors argue that considering infant innate predispositions for social contact as well as their abilities to understand goal-directed behaviors and triadic social structures, infant reactions to triadic social exclusion situations can be interpreted as jealousy. Accordingly, jealousy may be understood as the result of infant innate predispositions and socio-cognitive advances that make this emotion complex and yet available to infants already during the first year of life (Legerstee et al., this volume).

Previous studies have shown that infant reactions to triadic social exclusion include a combination of different behaviors. On the one hand, infants display negative emotionality such as when experiencing separation distress, and, on the other, infants exhibit behaviors to regain exclusivity with their caregivers (i.e., approach behaviors, such as gaze and calling vocalizations). Thus, our proposed neural model of jealousy must address the interplay between neural circuits implicated in negative emotions and approach behaviors.

Negative emotionality

The experience of social exclusion from a loved one due to the presence of a rival is a stressful event, and thus associated with negative feelings and emotional pain. Studies with infants and adults suggest that experiences of a lack of social exchange with others are associated with emotional distress and underlying physiological mechanisms. For example, infants' behavioral responses when adults stop communicating with them for no apparent reason (i.e., still-face; Tronick, Als, & Adamson, 1979) is correlated with increased heart rate and cortisol secretion (Feldman, 2007; Thompson & Trevathan, 2008), indicating that infants perceive such situations as stressful. Moreover, studies by Eisenberger and colleagues (Eisenberger, Gable, & Lieberman, 2007; Eisenberger et al., 2003) have shown that the experience of social exclusion is associated with self-reports of emotional distress in adults. Thus, it could be hypothesized that the hypothalamic–pituitary–adrenal (HPA) axis, which controls the stress response, is activated during triadic social exclusion. The HPA axis involves a set of direct influences and feedback loops between the hypothalamus (HTh), the pituitary gland, and adrenal glands (Vander, Sherman, & Luciano, 1993). More specifically, the paraventricular nucleus (PVN) of the HTh receives fear signaling impulses from the AM, and consequently releases corticotrophin-releasing hormone (CRH). CRH stimulates the pituitary which then releases adrenocorticotropic hormones that further stimulate the adrenals. This triggers the release of cortisol, which in turn acts in a negative feedback loop on the HTh and pituitary to suppress CRH production and thus inhibits the activity of the HPA axis. In this way, the limbic system appraises the salience of a stressor (e.g., threat to exclusive bond with the caregiver) without conscious awareness, and subsequently initiates and organizes a psychobiological response (Shore, 2001).

However, the HPA axis does not operate in isolation. As in the case of separation distress, neural response systems underlying negative emotions (i.e., fear, panic, sadness, and pain) are also likely to be activated during triadic social exclusion. Research has shown that momentary experience of social exclusion in adults during a virtual ball-tossing game with two other individuals is associated with activation in the dorsal ACC, AM, and PAG (Eisenberger et al., 2007); namely, structures which are all involved in panic and sadness (i.e., separation distress), but also the perception of threat resulting in fear and pain processing. These networks are related and enhanced by the stress circuit, particularly CRH (Panksepp, 1998). Thus, it can be hypothesized that negative emotion response systems interact with and are intensified by the HPA stress axis.

In summary, because separation distress and jealousy have some conceptual similarities, the neural structures involved also likely overlap. In both situations social bonds are at stake (i.e., separation or presence of a rival) and thus both involve negative emotional reactions (i.e., panic, sadness, and pain) which support the reestablishment of these close relationships. Additionally, because of the threat to their exclusive relationship with caregivers, which occurs as the result of the presence of a third person (a rival) who threatens the close bond infants have with their parents, infants may experience fear of losing this relationship. These basic emotion response systems are further exacerbated by the involvement of stress hormones originating in the HPA system.

Approach

In addition to experiencing negative emotionality, infants also display approach behaviors during triadic social exclusion in order to attract back the attention of their caregivers, increase their social appeal, and consequently regain exclusivity (e.g., Legerstee et al., this volume). It could be hypothesized that neural processes and mechanisms that are associated with such positive social approaches have a homeostatic function, which counteracts negative emotionality and stress experienced during triadic social exclusion. That is, negativity alone may not be helpful in triadic social exclusion situations, because infants have to "compete" with the rival for the caregiver's attention; it would seem that the better strategy is to increase their appeal as social partners, rather than display negative emotionality.

Such arguments would support Esch and Stefano's (2005) general idea that stress and love are biologically interconnected. These authors suggest that threatening or challenging situations (e.g., social exclusion) encourage social interactions which, in turn, have anxiety- and stress-relieving effects. Additionally, Panksepp (2005) argues that particular neurochemicals, such as exogeneous opiates, endogenous opioids, and oxytocin, not only establish feelings of social connectedness, but also alleviate pain and regulate negative affect during separation distress. Thus, infants' approach behaviors during episodes of triadic social exclusion may serve the purpose of reestablishing close bonds with their caregivers as well as relieving the stress and negative emotionality during such situations (i.e., emotion regulation).

At the neural level, the dopamine system may be part of the regulatory mechanism for stress, particularly through its connection to the nucleus accumbens (NA), which is activated by stressful and aversive stimuli (Panksepp, 1998; Salamone, 1993). The NA receives its main inputs from the prefrontal cortex, AM, and dopamine neurons of the ventral tegmental area (VTA), and plays a role in reward, laughter, and pleasure. In particular, dopamine, which can motivate behaviors in order to bring about pleasure (i.e., appetitive motivation), or to get away from a situation (i.e., aversive motivation; Esch & Stefano, 2005), modulates the activity of the NA. Salamone (1993) argues that the connection between dopamine and the NA is important for aspects of goal-directed behaviors, because this link is involved in behavioral activation produced by motivational stimuli. That is, during episodes of triadic social exclusion infants produce approach behaviors because their past experience of close love bonds motivates them to reestablish exclusivity with their caregivers, which brings about pleasure. Moreover, the activation of dopamine and its projections to the NA has a pain suppression function via the release of endogenous opioids and substance P within the VTA (Wood, 2004), which can act to suppress negative emotionality and stress during triadic social exclusion situations (see also Panksepp, 2003, 2005). Thus, the dopamine network initiates approach behaviors in the anticipation of pleasure (i.e., exclusivity), and in this way may have an emotion regulation function that counteracts negative emotionality.

The question arises how the approach pathways are activated in the brain. We propose that there are two possible ways: (1) the release of oxytocin and (2) the activation of the ACC. Because both mechanisms mainly affect the VTA that releases dopamine, both are possible vehicles that initiate approach.

The first mechanism that may trigger approach behaviors is the release of oxytocin in the HTh, primarily by sensory stimulation. Oxytocin is implicated in bonding and allows positive social interactions to develop, but it also plays a role in strengthening and consolidating memories of positive social experiences (Kirsch et al., 2005; Panksepp, 1998). Thus, purely psychological processes, such as thoughts, associations, and memories, may also trigger oxytocin release (Petersson & Uvnäss-Moberg, 2003). Because some stimuli are innately pleasurable (e.g., close bonds with caregivers) and pleasure and reward are remembered more easily than negative events (Esch & Stefano, 2004), it could be hypothesized that positive social memories trigger the release of oxytocin and thus are readily available to motivate social interactions. The two neural structures likely involved in this process are the hippocampus (HC) and the AM. According to Phelps (2004), these two structures interact to facilitate the consolidation of emotional memories. That is, the AM activates the HPA axis and stress hormones activate adrenergic receptors of the AM in a feedback loop (Akirav & Richter-Levin, 1999), which then modulates the effect of the stress hormones on the consolidation of HC-dependent memories. Thus, the HC forms representations of emotional significance and can influence the AM response when emotional stimuli are encountered (Phelps, 2004). It seems, then, that the stress infants experience during triadic social exclusion situations facilitates the retrieval of strongly emotional positive social memories of the love relationships with their caregivers, which trigger the release of oxytocin. Oxytocin, in turn, deactivates areas mediating negative emotions, avoidance behaviors, and stress, while, at the same time, it allows for positive social interactions to develop through the activation of the dopamine system.

A complementary way in which approach behaviors may arise during triadic social exclusion situations is through the involvement of the ACC, which may initiate appetitive motivation for the purpose of emotion regulation (Lewis & Stieben, 2004). The ACC is associated with the processing of emotional information, formation of long-term attachments, and regulation of endocrine activities, and damage in the ACC results in abnormalities in social and emotional behaviors (Joseph, 2000). Moreover, this structure has also long been implicated in the experience of physical and psychological pain, because it integrates motor, tactile, autonomic, and emotional stimuli, and it has strong connections with AM, HTh, HC, and PAG, among others (Joseph, 2000). Most importantly, the activation of the ACC may be crucial for controlling negative emotions as well as the stress response through its connections to the dopamine system. Thus, together with oxytocin, the ACC activates the dopamine system to motivate approach behaviors.

In summary, triadic social exclusion and the resulting negative emotionality and stress are counteracted by oxytocin and dopamine systems that trigger a search for pleasure and closeness and, consequently, motivate infants to restore exclusivity with their caregivers.

The complete model of jealousy

As argued thus far, infants' predisposition for establishing and maintaining exclusive social relationships with their caregivers together with their ability to engage in triadic interactions (see Fivaz-Depeursinge et al., this volume) and goal-directed actions (see Legerstee et al., this volume) makes them sensitive to triadic social exclusion situations where a rival threatens the exclusive bonds infants have with their caregivers. In such situations, infants react with jealousy which is manifested as negative emotionality and approach behaviors. At a neural level, this reaction is associated with activation of the panic, sadness, pain, and fear networks (i.e., AM, PAG, ACC), which are related to and enhanced by the HPA stress circuit. Paradoxically, stress also increases social motivation through the activation of the dopamine system via oxytocin and the ACC, while oxytocin and opioids work to reduce stress and negative emotions, and consequently restore neural networks associated with love and bonding.

The idea that the jealousy response is an adaptive mechanism which restores balance in the organism and helps infants to strengthen exclusive social relationships with their caregivers is supported by Weinstock's (1997, p. 1) theorizing: "The survival of living organisms depends upon the maintenance of a harmonious equilibrium or homeostasis in the face of constant challenge by intrinsic or extrinsic forces or stressors. They [behavioral and neurochemical reactions to stress] are designed to promote adaptive response to the physical and psychological stimuli and preserve homeostasis ... Successful equilibrium is reflected by a rapid neurochemical response to these stimuli which is terminated at the appropriate time, or gives way to counter-regulatory measures to prevent an excessive reaction."

Social Exclusion from Peer Groups

Jealousy arises as a function of infant predisposition to maintain close relationships with their caregivers and specific socio-cognitive abilities that facilitate their understanding of triadic social exclusion. If infants are able to engage in triadic social situations and perceive when they are excluded by their mother, because of the presence of a rival (see Legerstee et al., this volume), then they may be able to perceive when they are excluded in other triadic settings. One way to examine this question is to observe infants in groups with social partners with whom they have not yet established close relationships, such as same-age peers.

Peer study

We have recently conducted a study to investigate whether infants establish dyadic preferences for particular peers to the exclusion of others during the first year of life (Markova, 2008). In this longitudinal study, 60 infants visited the Centre for Infancy Studies at York University when they were 7, 9, and 12 months old. Infants were randomly assigned to groups of three same-age and same-gender peers to form 20 groups (11 female groups). We chose to observe infants in triads to be able to examine whether they might react to being excluded by their peers and whether these responses were similar to those exhibited when they found themselves in triadic social exclusion situations with their mothers (see Legerstee et al., this volume). In other words, we examined (1) whether infants would form preferences for a particular peer over another and (2) the behaviors of excluded infants. The same peer groups were observed during free-play interactions at all three ages. The following infant behaviors were coded: gazes at peers, positive and negative affect (i.e., facial expressions and vocalizations), initiations to interact and responses to these initiations, communicative (i. e., point, give, show) and non-communicative (reach, touch) gestures, and play. Dyadic preferences were identified according to mutual gazes, mutual positive affect, initiations, positive responses to initiations, and time spent in play between two infants. For each infant pair within a group (i.e., three possible infant pairs), the average of these five behaviors was calculated at all ages, and infant pairs within each group who ranked highest on the majority of these behaviors were classified as preferred dyads.

We hypothesized that infants will display preferences for particular peers over others by means of interest (i.e., gazes), reciprocity (i.e., initiations and responses to initiations, play), and enjoyment (i.e., positive affect). Moreover, we expected that if infants assign meaning and importance to establishing and maintaining social connections with peers, then they will be sensitive to being excluded from the peer group. However, we did not expect infants to react with a jealousy-like response to this kind of triadic social exclusion, for two important reasons. First, studies examining triadic social exclusion to evoke jealousy have been based upon the assumption that a close exclusive bond already exists between infants and their caregivers. In the present study, infants were observed in groups with unfamiliar peers and although the groups were kept the same across the three ages, it is unlikely that they had enough opportunities and time to establish close bonds with peers that would be comparable to their bonds with caregivers. Accordingly, we argued that triadic social exclusion has different meaning for infants depending on whether they have created a close social bond with the one they are excluded by. Thus, we should expect different behaviors when infants are excluded by their peers. Second, in previous studies the inclusion–exclusion pattern was determined by infants' relationships with caregivers (i.e., the infant was always the excluded one; Legerstee et al., this volume). In contrast, the inclusion–exclusion pattern between infants in the peer study was determined by naturally evolving group dynamics that may be a function of factors such as the infants' temperament, socio-cognitive skills, and family relations. In summary, in the peer study we created a situation that enabled us to observe social exclusion among unfamiliar social partners, which we may call "shunning." Because there was no strong social bond in this situation, we expected to find reactions different from a jealousy response.

Behavioral results

Results of the peer study revealed that dyadic preferences existed at all ages. Dyadic preferences were identified in 17 groups at 7 and 9 months and in 16 groups at 12 months of age. The stability of preferences across age was computed using the Friedman test for related samples. Results of this analysis did not reveal significant differences in the preference pattern between the different ages, suggesting that the classification of preferred dyads was stable.

To examine the reactions of excluded infants, a three-level mixed model was formulated where preference pattern at each age was modeled as a fixed effect to analyze its influence on infant mean production of gazes at infant, positive and negative affect, initiations and responses to initiations, communicative and non-communicative gestures, and play. Variance–covariance components were estimated to model differences within and between infants and between groups in the level and change in production of the various behaviors, accounting for the influence of the preference pattern. No significant results were found at 7 months. However, at 9 months, these analyses revealed that infants who were included in the preferred dyad displayed more positive affect, Estimate $= .430$, $SE = .169$, $t(18.492) = 2.541$, $p = .020$; initiated interactions and responded to others' initiations more often, Estimate $= .940$, $SE = .410$, $t(54.641) = 2.293$, $p = .026$; produced more communicative gestures, Estimate $= .529$, $SE = .248$, $t(103) = 2.129$, $p = .036$; and engaged in significantly more play with their peers, Estimate $= 1.007$, $SE = .234$, $t(33.906) = 4.298$, $p < .001$, than excluded infants. At 12 months, infants who were included in the preferred dyad displayed more positive affect, Estimate $= .372$, $SE = .167$, $t(18.342) = 2.219$, $p = .039$; and used more communicative, Estimate $= .449$, $SE = .246$, $t(103) = 1.829$, $p = .070$, and non-communicative gestures, Estimate $= .681$, $SE = .275$, $t(35.377) = 2.481$, $p = .018$, than excluded infants.

In summary, infants who experienced social exclusion from the group (i.e., were not included in the preferred dyad) displayed different behaviors than included infants. Specifically, in comparison to included infants, infants who were excluded from the group displayed less positive affect, initiated fewer interactions and responded less to others' initiations, produced fewer communicative and non-communicative gestures, and engaged in less play with others. We did, however, observe that excluded infants increased their gaze behavior directed to peers.[1] That is, while excluded infants failed to engage with their peers, they sustained interest in the ongoing interactions of the group. These findings suggest that from a very early age infants are selective with respect to whom they interact with, and are sensitive to being shunned by others, as indicated by their passivity and low positive affect.

Neural structures

Because infants in the peer study reacted to being shunned, we hypothesize that there might be similarities among the neural structures that are activated during jealousy evocation (e.g., Legerstee et al., this volume) and during shunning. However, we suggest that neural systems that are implicated in social bonds and close relationships do not play a role during social exclusion from peer groups.

As discussed earlier, Eisenberger and colleagues (Eisenberger et al., 2007, 2003) examined adults in an fMRI scanner during a so-called cyberball social exclusion task. In that task, participants played a virtual ball-tossing game with allegedly two other individuals, and they were either included or excluded from the game. The authors found that increased distress after being excluded was associated with activation of the dorsal ACC, while diminished distress after social exclusion was associated with activation of the ventromedial prefrontal cortex (VMPFC). Moreover, increased activation of the dorsal ACC, AM, and PAG were related to momentary social distress during social interactions. The activation of these particular neural structures indicates that social exclusion from social groups, regardless of whether it includes a "love object," involves negative response systems such as fear and pain, and is perceived as a stressful event (i.e., HPA axis).

However, the behavioral results of the peer study showed that while excluded infants vigilantly monitored the ongoing peer interactions, they did not display negative emotions nor did they attempt to regain access to the group. Similarly, Legerstee et al. (this volume) found that when infants were excluded by their mothers and a female stranger, in situations where the stranger did not appear to be a rival, infants did not react to being excluded, but simply observed the interaction between the two women. In contrast, when mothers actively conversed with the stranger, infants became terribly upset; they covered their eyes, kicked their legs, and produced odd vocalizations. If infants perceive social exclusion as negative and stressful (i.e., see neural structures activated during social exclusion in the Eisenberger et al., 2003, study), then the question arises why this was not manifested in their overt behavior when being shunned.

One possible explanation may be the novelty of peers as social partners. Novel stimuli, such as unfamiliar peers, may evoke insecurity and be perceived as aversive and stressful (Esch & Stefano, 2004), and this distress may be exacerbated by being shunned. However, it could be argued that in a situation with peers, excluded infants were unsure of the social consequences of their behaviors, which may have resulted in their overall decreased reactivity to social exclusion. Infants' display of negative emotionality may be a learned adaptation; that is, when caregivers are sensitive to infants' signals and respond to them promptly and appropriately, then infants perceive their close relationships with them as pleasurable and rewarding (Markova & Legerstee, 2006), and social exclusion might cause emotional distress and approach to regain exclusivity. Arguably, negative affect and protest triggered by maternal separation is coded strongly in the AM (basic emotional conditioning or long-term potentiation of neural structures) as a result of repeated separation–protest–reunion episodes. When social partners (e.g., peers) are not sensitive to the infants' signals and infants are unsure of the social consequences their behavior may have, then infant reactions will reflect their sensitivity to this novel situation. Thus, infants' insecurity in the peer group may have led to a passive aversive reaction (i.e., freezing; Jhou, 2005) rather than active protest aimed at reestablishing exclusive social contact. While we did not directly measure passive aversion, the lack of responsivity from the excluded infants in general may be indicative of their negative emotionality and stress. This argument also seems supported by the finding that excluded infants displayed significantly less positive affect than included infants.

According to a review by Jhou (2005), the anatomic pathways involved during the production of passive aversive behaviors include the AM and bed nucleus (i.e., freezing), PAG (i.e., passive defense), and the median raphé nucleus (MRN; i.e., anxiety and freezing). These structures overlap nicely with the activation patterns in the studies of Eisenberger and colleagues (Eisenberger et al., 2007, 2003); there, the activation of AM and PAG was associated with distress and negative emotions during social exclusion. Thus, it may be that infants experienced negative emotionality and stress when being shunned by their peers, but their overt expressions were covered by passivity.

Jhou (2005) argues that structures implicated in passive aversive behaviors also activate GABAergic neurons, residing caudal to the VTA and lateral to the MRN, which project preferentially to dopamine neurons. He suggests that these GABAergic neurons inhibit dopamine released from the VTA, resulting in passivity and freezing. Thus, it seems that during passive aversive behaviors the pathway from the VTA to NA via dopamine is inhibited. This proposition would support our arguments as well as findings that infant passive aversive reaction to loss of social access is manifested in overall passivity, including less social behaviors toward peers. Additionally, because this pathway is inhibited, the VTA does not release opioids and substance P, and consequently there is no relief from negative emotions and stress.

It is important to note that GABAergic inhibition of dopamine underlying passivity and freezing may also help to explain the results of Eisenberger et al. (2003) who showed increased ACC activity in socially excluded adults in their cyberball task. The ACC is strongly associated with motivation, attention (particularly for action), and conflict monitoring under conditions of novelty and uncertainty (Tucker et al., 2003). Mesolimbic dopamine is related to phasic activation of the ACC. Increased ACC activity is associated with a decrease in dopamine (Holroyd & Coles, 2002). Thus, GABA inhibition of dopamine during social exclusion may account for the increased ACC activity in Eisenberger et al.'s study, while at the same time help to explain the increased attentional vigilance (gaze) in our excluded infants. Eisenberger et al. (2003) have also reported increased activity in the area of the VMPFC during the social exclusion condition with adults. This may help to explain the inhibition of the panic-related fight–flight systems characteristic of maternal separation and would account for the fact that we did not see negative protest behaviors in infants who were excluded from the peer group. The VMPFC is known to be reciprocally coupled with the AM to exert "top-down" inhibitory control or suppression of limbic areas activated during heightened emotional reactions (Urry et al., 2006). This is consistent with Eisenberger et al.'s (2003) proposal that activation of the right VMPFC region may be related to regulating negative emotions in their task.

It is also possible that infants actively suppressed their display of negative emotions during social exclusion from the peer group. Goldin, McRae, Ramel, and Gross (2008) define suppression as a mechanism for emotion regulation that inhibits ongoing emotional expressive behaviors. This mechanism is associated with increased physiological responding and decreased well-being (Goldin et al., 2008), suggesting that it is not a very effective way to regulate emotions (Braw et al., 2008). In their study, Goldin et al. (2008) found that in adults, suppression for the purpose of emotion regulation resulted in increased activity of the AM and insula, which play a role in emotion processing and are related to the limbic HPA system. These findings indicate that despite the regulation attempt, the stress and negative emotionality remains. Because suppression is not a very effective strategy and keeps the HPA axis active, accompanied by activation of the AM and insula, excluded infants may have been in a state of constant stress. In high-stress situations, such as during social exclusion, physiological measures show increased heart rate and a high level of cortisol secretion (Feldman, 2007; Moore & Calkins, 2004; Thompson & Trevathan, 2008). Although we may not have observed overt signs of stress and negative emotionality during social exclusion in the peer study, measuring heart rate and cortisol levels could confirm the notion that infants perceived this kind of social exclusion as stressful and negative.

Infants' reaction to triadic social exclusion from peer groups in our study may be a function of infant individual characteristics. As previously mentioned, social exclusion in the peer study arose from group dynamics, suggesting that particular infants were more likely to be excluded than others. Specifically, we examined with logistic regressions whether infant temperament, socio-cognitive skills, and relationship quality with their mothers affected whether infants were included in preferred dyads. At 7 months, no significant effects were found. At 9 months, results revealed that infants who were rated high on negative affectivity were more likely to be excluded from a preferred dyad, $B = -2.020$, $SE = .966$, Wald $= 4.375$, $p = .036$. At 12 months, infants who were rated as extraverted by their mothers were more likely to be included in a preferred dyad, $B = 1.238$, $SE = .663$, Wald $= 3.483$, $p = .062$. Thus, only infant temperament, assessed with the Infant Behavior Questionnaire (Garstein & Rothbart, 2003), which was filled out by mothers, predicted exclusion from the peer group. Personality traits of excluded infants may further corroborate their behavioral responses and corresponding neural activations, and therefore influence the proposed neural model. For example, in a recent study, Stein, Simmons, Feinstein, and Paulus (2007) found that increased AM and insula activation (i.e., structures also implicated during suppression of negative emotional experiences; Goldin et al., 2008) during emotional processing in adults was associated with increased anxiety-related temperamental traits. Consequently, we may argue that infant experience of, and behavioral and neural responses to, social exclusion from peer groups can be seen as a result of an interaction between situational constraints and infants' temperamental characteristics.

In summary, we hypothesize that the activation of neural systems associated with the experience of triadic social exclusion from peer groups is the result of infant novelty with the situation and inexperience with new social partners, both of which lead to infant insecurity with the situation. Specifically, we propose that infants experience stress and negative emotionality when they are being shunned by other peers in a group, but the relative lack of emotional displays as well as approach behaviors to regain access may be explained by a passive aversive reaction. Such passive response deactivates pleasure-oriented approach networks and thus brings no relief to negative emotionality and stress, which results in a state of constant negativity. It seems as if infants tried to adapt to the situation (i.e., passive aversion), but were not quite successful (i.e., no release of stress or negative emotionality). Maybe with age, once infants become more accustomed to being with peers and establish stable close relationships outside the mother–infant dyad (i.e., friends), the jealousy model could be applied to social exclusion with peers.

Conclusions

In the present chapter we have introduced neural frameworks to explain infant reactions to different triadic social exclusion situations. When infants perceive a rival who threatens their exclusive relationships with caregivers, their reactions are interpreted as jealousy and are characterized by negative emotions and approach behaviors. It was hypothesized that at the neural level, infant reactions to such triadic social exclusion are associated with activation of negative emotion response systems (i.e., fear, panic, sadness, pain) which are mediated by the workings of the HPA stress axis. Through positive social memories of their close relationships with caregivers as well as the activation of structures associated with basic emotion regulation (i.e., ACC), negative emotionality and stress are counteracted. The neuropeptide oxytocin, involved in bonding, and the pleasure-oriented dopamine system play an important role in restoring homeostasis by shutting down the stress response. In a further step, we have presented evidence for a different triadic social exclusion situation where infants were shunned by playmates with whom they have not yet established exclusive relationships. We have proposed that infants experience negative emotionality and stress which are associated with the loss of social connections in general (see also Eisenberger et al., 2003), while they might suppress these emotions due to their insecurity with the social situation. It is possible that this resulted in a passive aversive reaction at the neural and, consequently, the behavioral level. It appears that infants have the necessary neural substrate as well as the socio-cognitive abilities that allow them to conceptualize different social exclusion situations and react appropriately.

The aim of the present chapter was to show through behavioral evidence and speculations about concurrent neural systems that jealousy may also be observable in infants during the first year of life. Do infants need advanced cognitive abilities to experience jealousy? If one is to differentiate between what moves us (i.e., emotions) and how we reflect about it (i.e., feelings), then one would argue that complex cognitive abilities (e.g., meta-representational abilities) are a necessary prerequisite for the latter and thus not available to very young infants. In contrast, we argue that jealousy is an expression of both basic emotion networks that operate beyond consciousness as well as socio-cognitive appraisal processes that allow infants to understand social exclusion situations. Specifically, if the goal is to establish or maintain social connections with others and social exclusion brings about fear of losing access to established relationships or access to social groups in general for the purpose of establishing new relationships, then one could argue that basic emotion networks are initiated in these processes, because they represent elemental social needs. Moreover, theoretical analyses of Legerstee et al. (this volume) suggest that factors facilitating infants' experience of jealousy include their predisposition to engage with the social world in general (Legerstee, 2005) as well as their basic socio-cognitive abilities (i.e., understanding of others' goals and triadic interactions) that are present from very early on in life. These arguments seem supported by our findings that infants are sensitive to exclusion from peer groups. Thus, jealousy arises from the interplay between infant predisposition to establish and maintain close relationships with their caregivers, innate basic emotion systems, and socio-cognitive abilities that allow them to perceive and understand different social situations.

Social contact is fundamental for humans, especially early on in life. As argued by Darwin, emotions affect the chances of survival of an individual expressing them, because expressive behavior creates an interaction between the individual and the environment that triggered the emotion (as cited in Plutchik, 2001). Thus, it would be evolutionarily disadvantageous if social emotions such as jealousy only came "on-line" late in development, because of their foundation within social relationships and their function to establish and maintain a relationship with others. Emotions allow infants to connect with people from birth, and emotions arising within such early interactions sensitize infants to others' emotional and behavioral acts as contingent to their own.

Note

1   The increase in gaze behavior was consistent at all ages; however, the effect was only at the level of a statistical trend ($p = .09$).

References

Akirav, I., & Richter-Levin, G. (1999). Biphasic modulation of hippocampal plasticity by behavioral stress and basolateral amygdala stimulation in the rat. *Journal of Neuroscience, 19*, 10530–10535.

Braw, Y., Malkesman, O., Merenlender, A., Bercovich, A., Dagan, M., Overstreet, D. H., & Weller, A. (2008). Withdrawal emotional-regulation in infant rats from genetic animal models of depression. *Behavioral Brain Research, 193*, 94–100.

Draghi-Lorenz, R., Reddy, V., & Costall, A. (2001). Rethinking the development of "nonbasic" emotions: A critical review of existing theories. *Developmental Review, 21*, 263–304.

Eisenberger, N. I., Gable, S. L., & Lieberman, M. D. (2007). Functional magnetic resonance imaging responses related to differences in real-world social experience. *Emotion, 7*, 745–754.

Eisenberger, N. I., Lieberman, M. D., & Williams, K. D. (2003). Does rejection hurt? An fMRI study of social exclusion. *Science, 302*, 290–292.

Esch, T., & Stefano, G. B. (2004). The neurobiology of pleasure, reward processes, addiction and their health implications. *Neuroendocrinology Letters, 25*, 235–251.

Esch, T., & Stefano, G. B. (2005). The neurobiology of love. *Neuroendocrinology Letters, 26*, 175–192.

Feldman, R. (2007). Parent–infant synchrony: Biological foundations and developmental outcomes. *Current Directions in Psychological Science, 16*, 340–345.

Fivaz-Depeursinge, E., Favez, C., Lavanchy Scaiola, C., & Lopes, F. (this volume). Family triangular interactions in infancy: A context for the development of jealousy? In S. L. Hart & M. Legerstee (Eds.), *Handbook of jealousy: Theories, principles and multidisciplinary approaches*. Malden, MA: Wiley-Blackwell.

Garstein, M. A., & Rothbart, M. K. (2003). Studying infant temperament via the Revised Infant Behavior Questionnaire. *Infant Behavior and Development, 26*, 64–86.

Goldin, P., McRae, K., Ramel, W., & Gross, J. (2008). The neural bases of emotion regulation: Reappraisal and suppression of negative emotion. *Biological Psychiatry, 63*, 577–586.

Graeff, F. G. (2004). Serotonin, the periaqueductal gray and panic. *Neuroscience and Biobehavioral Reviews, 28*, 239–259.

Grossman, T., & Johnson, M. H. (2007). The development of the social brain in human infancy. *European Journal of Neuroscience, 25*, 909–919.

Hart, S., Carrington, H., Tronick, E. Z., & Carroll, S. R. (2004). When infants lose exclusive maternal attention: Is it jealousy? *Infancy, 6*, 57–78.

Holroyd, C. B., & Coles, M. G. H. (2002). The basis of human error processing: Reinforcement learning, dopamine, and the error-related negativity. *Psychological Review, 109*, 679–709.

Jhou, T. (2005). Neural mechanisms of freezing and passive aversive behaviors. *Journal of Comparative Neurology, 493*, 111–114.

Joseph, R. (2000). *Neuropsychiatry, neuropsychology, clinical neuroscience.* New York: Academic Press.

Kirsch, P., Esslinger, C., Chen, Q., Mier, D., Lis, S., Siddhanti, S., et al. (2005). Oxytocin modulates neural circuitry for social cognition and fear in humans. *Journal of Neuroscience, 25*, 11489–11493.

Legerstee, M. (2005). *Infants' sense of people: Precursors to a theory of mind.* Cambridge: Cambridge University Press.

Legerstee, M., Ellenbogen, B., Nienhuis, T., & Marsh, H. (this volume). Social bonds, triadic relationships, and goals: Preconditions for the emergence of human jealousy. In S. L. Hart & M. Legerstee (Eds.), *Handbook of jealousy: Theories, principles and multidisciplinary approaches.* Malden, MA: Wiley-Blackwell.

Lewis, M. D., & Stieben, J. (2004). Emotion regulation in the brain: Conceptual issues and directions for developmental research. *Child Development, 75*, 371–376.

MacDonald, G., & Leary, M. R. (2005). Why does social exclusion hurt? The relationship between social and physical pain. *Psychological Bulletin, 131*, 202–223.

Markova, G. (2008). *Interactions among infant peers: Examining individual differences in social competence.* Unpublished doctoral dissertation, York University, Toronto, Canada.

Markova, G., & Legerstee, M. (2006). Contingency, imitation, and affect sharing: Foundations of infants' social awareness. *Developmental Psychology, 42*, 132–141.

Masciuch, S., & Kienapple, K. (1993). The emergence of jealousy in children 4 months to 7 years of age. *Journal of Social and Personal Relationships, 10*, 421–435.

Moore, G. A., & Calkins, S. D. (2004). Infants' vagal regulation in the still-face paradigm is related to dyadic coordination of mother–infant interaction. *Developmental Psychology, 40*, 1068–1080.

Panksepp, J. (1998). *Affective neuroscience: The foundations of human and animal emotions.* New York: Oxford University Press.

Panksepp, J. (2003). Feeling the pain of social loss. *Science, 302*, 237–239.

Panksepp, J. (2005). Why does separation distress hurt? Comment on MacDonald and Leary (2005). *Psychological Bulletin, 131*, 224–230.

Petersson, M., & Uvnäss-Moberg, K. (2003). Systemic oxytocin treatment modulates glucocorticoid and mineralocorticoid receptor mRNA in the rat. *Neuroscience Letters, 343*, 97–100.

Phelps, E. A. (2004). Human emotion and memory: Interactions of the amygdala and hippocampal complex. *Current Opinions in Neurobiology, 14*, 198–202.

Plutchik, R. (2001). The nature of emotions. *American Scientist, 89*, 344.

Salamone, J. D. (1993). The involvement of nucleus accumbens dopamine in appetitive and aversive motivation. *Behavioral Brain Research, 61*, 117–133.

Shore, A. N. (2001). The effects of early relational trauma on right brain development, affect regulation, and infant mental health. *Infant Mental Health Journal, 22*, 201–269.

Stein, M. B., Simmons, A. N., Feinstein, J. S., & Paulus, M. P. (2007). Increased amygdala and insula activation during emotion processing in anxiety-prone subjects. *American Journal of Psychiatry, 164*, 318–327.

Thompson, L. A., & Trevathan, W. R. (2008). Cortisol reactivity, maternal sensitivity, and learning in 3-month-old infants. *Infant Behavior and Development, 31*, 92–106.

Tronick, E. Z., Als, H., & Adamson, L. (1979). The communicative structure of face-to-face interactions. In M. Bullowa (Ed.), *Before speech: The beginnings of interpersonal communication* (pp. 349–372). New York: Cambridge University Press.

Tucker, D. M., Luu, P., Desmond, R. E., Jr., Hartry-Speiser, A., Davey, C., & Flaisch, T. (2003). Corticolimbic mechanisms in emotional decisions. *Emotion, 3*, 127–149.

Urry, H., van Reekum, C., Johnstone, T., Kalin, N. H., Thurow, M. E., Schaefer, H. S., et al. (2006). Amygdala and ventromedial prefrontal cortex are inversely coupled during regulation of negative affect and predict the diurnal pattern of cortisol secretion among older adults. *Journal of Neuroscience, 26*, 4415–4425.

Vander, A., Sherman, J., & Luciano, D. (1993). *Human physiology: The mechanisms of body functions* (8th ed.). New York: McGraw-Hill.

Weinstock, M. (1997). Does prenatal stress impair coping and regulation of hypothalamic–pituitary–adrenal axis? *Neuroscience and Biobehavioral Reviews, 21*, 1–10.

Wood, P. (2004). Stress and dopamine: Implications for the pathophysiology of chronic widespread pain. *Medical Hypotheses, 62*, 420–424.

6

The Evolutionary Sources of Jealousy

Cross-Species Approaches to Fundamental Issues

Jaak Panksepp

It is no understatement to say that jealousy is one of the least studied emotions in the field of affective science, with very little relevant neuroscientific data. If one scans major treatises on emotions, one finds few references to jealousy: The 2nd edition of the *Handbook of Emotions* (Lewis & Haviland-Jones, 2000) has five passing mentions to the topic in the index. The 3rd edition (Lewis, Haviland-Jones, & Barrett, 2008) has even fewer. The massive *Handbook of Affective Sciences* (Davidson, Scherer, & Goldsmith, 2003) has three, only one of them (pp. 776–778) of any substance. None of these address neurological issues.

This chapter will summarize the little we know about jealousy across mammalian species. Jealousy is rarely considered to be a primary emotion, since it requires certain types of social relationships, for instance triadic conflicts of some kind, in order to be fully expressed. This does not mean that jealousy is not based on a variety of primary, genetically ingrained, emotional processes. It surely is. The primary feelings experienced at the loss of a valued social relationship, as might be triggered by the conviction of a spouse's infidelity, can vary enormously among different people. As Salovey and Rodin (1986, 1989) noted, in some individuals anxiety prevails, others primarily manifest anger, and yet others sorrow. Are any of these feelings more foundational than others? Perhaps a basic social emotion such as separation-distress/PANIC,[1] one of the foundational processes for human sadness and loneliness (Panksepp, 2003a), is most influential developmentally because it is of foremost importance in the regulation of prosocial feelings in early emergence of social attachments (Panksepp, 1981). In any event, jealousy ultimately becomes that affectively complex emotion whose adaptive value is to counteract severance of existing social bonds.

I would advocate the common view that an affective precondition for the emergence of human jealousy is the existence of an established social bond that is threatened by the perceived intervention of a third party—a witting or unwitting

Handbook of Jealousy: Theory, Research and Multidisciplinary Approaches, First Edition.
Edited by Sybil L. Hart and Maria Legerstee.

interloper. Although jealousy is not a basic emotion, it is certainly evolutionarily prepared to emerge developmentally from the types of MindBrain dynamics that can defensibly be deemed basic emotions.

Jealousy, just like the many other secondary/tertiary emotions that rely on learning and higher cognitive activities, becomes manifest through existential experiences of living in social worlds. By contrast, the basic emotions are fundamentally "gifts of nature" handed down from ancestral selection pressures, even though subsequent living experiences surely fine-tune even those evolution-arily ingrained networks through epigenetic influences. Because of its secondary nature, jealousy is bound to take on a larger variety of affective dynamics than is generated by any single one of the various emotional primes that can be aroused during jealousy, such as RAGE, FEAR, separation-distress/PANIC, and desire/SEEKING. Also, certain affective preconditions for jealousy may arise from LUST and CARE systems of the brain. Although all these primary emotional processes can participate in jealousy, the specific symphony of jealous feelings experienced by a person is dependent not only on an individual's life history but also the specifics of the relationship that is challenged. There is neither a single genetically pre-ordained evolutionary brain network nor a single emotional feeling that can define jealousy.

Still, of all the socially constructed emotions, jealousy may be especially closely tethered to the basic emotional systems—more clearly "prepared" to take on its core form than other social emotions such as embarrassment, guilt, and shame, not to mention the yet higher-level social emotions such as empathy, envy, and social disgust. The intimate proximity of jealousy to several basic emotional processes may eventually allow animal models to provide robust empirical strat-egies to inform us about the neural underpinnings of jealousy, comparable to those that have already illuminated various basic emotions (Panksepp, 1998a, 2005a).

Utility of Animal Models

It should be self-evident that there are no effective strategies for detailed causal studies of neural underpinnings of emotions in the human brain. All human brain imaging technologies, from electroencephalograms (EEGs) to functional mag-netic resonance imaging (fMRI), only provide some *correlates* of brain emotional processing. They are not well suited to permit *causal* studies of the underlying neural infrastructures. That is why animal models of proto-jealousy are so desperately needed to make progress on the evolutionary underpinnings of the human mind. I use the term "proto-jealousy" advisedly to highlight the difficulty science has of illuminating the specific psychological contents of animal minds, a task that is much easier for basic emotions than secondary or tertiary emotions: Abundant evidence indicates that raw affects are part and parcel of the instinctual emotional action systems of the brain (Panksepp, 1998a, 1998b, 2005a).

In any event, the scientific utility of animal models of basic emotions in psychology is substantial, and much underutilized. Only animal models can provide robust causal evidence about underlying brain processes of basic psychological functions shared by all mammals, which could be a foundation pillar for a neurobiologically coherent evolutionary psychology (Panksepp & Panksepp, 2000, 2001; Panksepp, 2007a). In other words, the underlying neural principles that generate raw affective experiences are most readily deciphered through the study of animal models where relevant affective neuroscientific issues can be addressed in a depth of detail that may never be achieved in either experimental psychology or human cognitive neuroscience. Animal models allow us to pursue systematic research on the following topics with great rigor:

1   Epigenetic influences and genetic vulnerabilities can be studied in detail.
2   Developmental processes can be isolated and systematically studied.
3   Underlying brain and body systems can be studied in detail, even down to single gene levels within the brain.
4   Specific environmental influences—physical, emotional and social—can be independently manipulated.
5   New endophenotype processes and biological therapies for emotional problems (and psychiatric disorders) can be evaluated in model systems (Panksepp, 2006a).
6   Basic affects—sensory, homeostatic and emotional—can finally be understood for the first time (Panksepp, 1998a, 2005a, 2005b) even as the associated cognitions remain neuroscientifically less tractable.

Systematic work along these lines finally provides us with a coherent strategy to empirically unravel how primary-process affective experiences are constructed within the brain and how they influence brain development (Panksepp, 2008). By triangulating between a neural, behavioral, and mental analysis of the intrinsic, evolutionarily homologous emotional systems of the mammalian brain, a cross-species affective neuroscience may be able to provide a basic science foundation for addressing such issues.

Can the nature of jealousy be illuminated through animal models? Surely to some extent, especially the underlying affective substrates. Can all aspects of human jealousy be clarified through animal models? Surely not, especially the psychologically subtle cognitive aspects. The perennial problem with animal models is that they have very poor resolution for cognitive mentation. However, this is an equally great problem in preverbal human infants and children, where one must also rely completely on behavioral indicators of affective states rather than propositional self-reports. In this contribution I only seek to show how the basic neuro-affective substrates of jealousy—the primary-process underpinnings—can be illuminated through the study of our fellow mammals.

Basic Emotional Substrates of Jealousy

Here I will develop the idea that jealousy is a multidimensional process, socially constructed through basic forms of learning as well as higher cortico-cognitive processes, that ultimately relies on a variety of more basic emotional systems we share with all other mammals (Panksepp, 1998a, 2005a), such as those devoted to FEAR, RAGE, and separation-distress/PANIC which arise from evolutionarily ancient subcortical regions of the brain. Because of the developmentally emergent and sexually dimorphic nature of these substrates, it is easier to envision why it might take somewhat different manifestations in males than females, as well as infants and young children compared to adults. As I will seek to show, work with animal models suggests that one of the key neuropeptide regulators of jealous rage in males may be vasopressin, but there are bound to be many other participants, especially the various neurochemical controls of the other basic emotional systems that contribute to patterns of jealous feelings. For instance, reduction of brain opioid activity with pharmacological agents such as naloxone and naltrexone (opiate receptor antagonists) would be expected to facilitate jealous feelings because they should promote socially insecure feelings and the psychic pain of separation distress/PANIC (Panksepp, Herman, Vilberg, Bishop, & DeEskinazi, 1980; Panksepp, 2005c, 2005d; Panksepp, 2006b). Conversely, neurochemistries that may reduce the impact of jealousy may be found among those that strengthen social bonds such as endogenous opioids and oxytocin, as well as those that reduce anxiety/FEAR in addition to the aggressiveness/RAGE already noted. Thus, this essay will discuss whether higher-level emotional concepts such as jealousy, when applied to other animals, can be scientifically useful. I think it can, especially if we wish to get a clear idea of how the primary-process emotional networks contribute to the emergence of jealousy.

I will also summarize some recent evidence relevant for understanding the brain substrates of human and animal jealousies as well as strategies on how we can understand this complex feeling more clearly from a psychobiological perspective. Although jealousy is surely not a "primary emotion" in the sense that there are ancient evolutionarily dedicated circuits that generate this as a uniquely primal feeling, still there is something fundamentally coherent about this socially constructed emotion. It requires strong affiliative bonds before it can be aroused, but it may be manifested in several distinct forms, since it may be constructed from various cognitive perceptions interacting with several primal feelings such as those generated by RAGE (anger), FEAR (anxiety), and PANIC (loneliness). This affective complexity means that jealousy could readily take different forms depending on gender dispositions, individual learning, and temperament as well as cultural features. Since the resulting complex spectrum of feelings can take several forms that can fluctuate affectively during single episodes, it will be very difficult to capture the underlying brain networks in action. Although there are likely to be several routes to jealousy, surely one of the main paths is from the "social pain" one experiences when one's social and sexual attachment bonds are threatened. As far as we currently understand it, social pain is engendered substantially by separation-distress/PANIC systems of the brain (Panksepp, 2003a, 2003b, 2005c, 2005d).

Once More: Is Jealousy Initially an "Objectless" Primary-Emotional Process?

Although some have considered jealousy to be a primary emotion, that seems unlikely from an affective neuroscience perspective, where the basic emotions are conceived to be initially "objectless" in the sense that they have a coherence that is based upon evolved brain mechanisms that are initially minimally connected to environmental events.[2] The manner in which the experientially constructed social emotions may arise from the power of more fundamental (primary-process) emotional urges when combined with developmentally emerging cognitive processes has been discussed by Draghi-Lorenz, Reddy, and Costall (2001) as well as Hobson, Chidambi, Lee, and Meyer (2006) and Legerstee, Ellenbogen, Nienhuis, and Marsh (this volume, Chapter 9). Primary-processes are those that are built into the nervous system, and hence the neuro-mental apparatus, by the genetic heritage of animals. There is no evidence that jealousy has such privileged status in the functional architecture of the social brain, but it comes closer than most. Thus, of all the prominent social-moral emotions besides jealousy—for instance, envy, shame, guilt, pride, arrogance, pity, scorn, contempt, embarrassment, sympathy, and empathy—jealousy stands out as being the most "prepared" in terms of its likelihood of being exhibited by practically everyone, at some stage of life, if the correct precipitating circumstances are present. The most important is the perceived weakening and severance of social bonds.

Evidence strongly indicates that most mammalian species come into the world prepared to make social bonds.[3] All mammals are social by nature, so jealousy could be understood as a function of the underlying neuropsychological processes. The main environmental factor is the social presence of others who might threaten the strength of existing social and sexual bonds. This suggests that the more cognitive aspects of the nervous system rapidly become highly tuned to precipitate jealousy when one's social resources are compromised. However, feelings of jealousy do not necessarily arise from cortical processes that mediate social cognitions. Indeed, the minimal cognitions necessary to trigger jealous feelings need not be cortically mediated at all. This scenario suggests that jealousy is not simply a creation of human culture, but its roots go back into deeper ancestral regions of brain and mind. The fact that autistic children readily exhibit jealous tendencies (Bauminger, this volume, Chapter 12; Bauminger et al., 2007), although they exhibit deficiencies in expressions of pity, concern, guilt, and pride (see Hobson, this volume, Chapter 13) further highlights the more primal, even "primitive," nature of jealousy among the non-primary social emotions.

Indeed, very young children tend to exhibit jealousy—perhaps earlier than the other social emotions, and the data stream has recently become enriched through direct experimental analyses of developmental patterns, covered in detail in other chapters of this volume (see Hart, this volume, Chapter 4; Legerstee et al., this volume; Markova, Stieben, & Lergerstee, this volume, Chapter 5). The maturation of jealousy may arise from even earlier social-emotional abilities such as the capacity for coyness (Reddy, 2000) and the mood changes that occur when a socially engaged infant loses exclusive "possession" of maternal attentions (Hart, Carrington, Tronick, & Carroll, 2004).

Rather than repeating materials covered elsewhere, let me reflect on an example from my own life—a display of jealousy by my first child, Tiina, when she was little more than a year old. Tiina's mother and I had divorced when she was only a year old. By no-fault agreement, Tiina remained with me, while my wife departed with her young lover (which had, of course, been a matter of intense distress and jealousy for me). When I finally started dating again, I was confronted by a striking instance of infantile jealousy: Following the first night my first new female companion (let's call her Jane) stayed over for the evening, Tiina exhibited a striking bout of jealousy when she realized this potential threat to her security—our primary social-bond. Even though Tiina was familiar with her, Jane had not yet stayed over for the evening. In the morning, when Tiina woke in her crib, I went to attend to her; I picked her up and carried her to my bedroom where Jane was sitting in a bathrobe. As I approached, and Jane stood up to greet my daughter with a smile, Tiina briskly pushed her away, clearly conveying that Jane was an unwelcome person. What a display of parent-guarding! Was it jealousy? Perhaps even "mate"-guarding in some deeper recesses of Tiina's mind? Or was it simply incipient anger?

Tiina's relatively short-lived response certainly had all the outward indications of jealousy, suggesting that very young children may evaluate the potential social-investment threats in their lives before they can speak. This should be no surprise, for the social attachment bonds are among the most precious affective resources they possess, and any potential threat to the integrity of their bonds should be viewed with profound affective concern. But is such covetousness built into their nervous system? Not if one considers that all the basic primary-process emotional systems of the mammalian brain are initially born "objectless"—without robust connections to most events in the outside world that eventually become major provocations to emotional arousal.

This almost Freudian notion of basic emotions initially being largely "objectless" may cause consternation to many emotion researchers who assume that all emotions must be strongly bound to outward stimuli. I am sympathetic to this view, since emotional systems learn to be associated with a wide array of external events very rapidly. However, we must consider that it may have been unwise for evolution to try to build too many object relations into the raw, primary emotional processes that can be evoked simply by electrically and chemically stimulating specific subcortical regions of all mammalian brains (Panksepp, 1982, 1998a, 2005a). It is certainly appropriate to question whether the coherent emotional behavior patterns evoked by such activations can be considered to be emotional, as opposed to mere behavioral displays (Barrett, 2006), but in considering this dilemma, one must not forget that there is abundant affective evidence that these displays are accompanied by strong feelings. Animals are not neutral about such artificially induced emotional brain arousals. They readily demonstrate simple approach or avoidance behaviors (e.g., self-stimulation or escape) of such aroused states, and also more sophisticated affect-based choices such as conditioned place preferences or place avoidances for locations in which they were thus aroused.

Thus, it is easy to demonstrate that psychological urgencies accompany such brain stimulation. The difficulty is distinguishing among the various positive and negative affects engendered in these ways, but that task is also empirically workable (Panksepp, 2007a, 2007b; Panksepp & Burgdorf, 2003). Indeed, the mass of evidence indicating that affect is a property of various inbuilt instinctual-emotional systems of the brain provides the first empirically robust strategy for decoding how basic emotional affects are generated in the brain (Panksepp, 2005b, 2008).

By definition, the feelings of jealousy require the developmental acquisition of object relations. Considering that jealousy is the affective response to the perceived potential loss of a specific love object, we are wise to envision jealousy as a rapidly integrated secondary, as opposed to a primary, emotional process—with evolutionarily well-prepared brain affective substrates, but not unique ones that are genetically ingrained in our inherited neural circuitry. The potential for RAGE, FEAR, and PANIC, on the other hand, are innate. They are minimally connected to the world before birth, but there always have to be some primal connections. For instance, FEAR can be evoked in all species by pain, and certain other stimuli that are more species specific. Thus, rats become intrinsically fearful when in the presence of the smell of certain predators, and such stimuli enter the brain via intrinsic vomeronasal inputs to FEAR processing networks of the amygdala, with no need for learning (Panksepp & Crepeau, 1990; also see Panksepp, 1998a, figure 6.1). To our knowledge, jealousy has no such infrastructure in the brain. However, the feelings that accompany jealousy can readily arise from the spectrum of primary-processes already discussed. In this scenario, the varieties of jealousy are about as innate as the languages we so readily learn to speak.

Jealousy: From Primary Process to Tertiary Process Levels of Analysis

So let me reemphasize, it is useful to conceptualize brain emotional networks at several levels of complexity. At the foundational level we find a variety of primary-process systems that are built into the mammalian brain, in rough form, as a function of ancestral inheritance. To the best of our knowledge, all mammals share resource SEEKING, danger-anticipating FEAR, irritable anger-generating

RAGE, sexual LUST, maternal CARE, separation-distress PANIC, and social-joy PLAY systems (Panksepp, 1998a). The evidential base for the existence of such ingrained systems comes largely from the fact that distinct instinctual behavior patterns can be evoked with localized electrical stimulation of the brain (ESB) from homologous neural regions in all mammalian species that have been studied (Panksepp, 1982, 1998a, 2005a). The operations of all these neurologically ingrained systems are refined by experiences, and throughout development they interact with higher brain processes—from basic learning to complex thoughtful deliberative cognitive mechanisms—to generate a variety of secondary (learning-based) and tertiary (thought-based) emotional processes. Where does jealousy lie on this gradient of complexity?

Again, let me emphasize a seemingly subtle point: The primary-process emotions are born largely "objectless"—initially they have minimal stimuli in the environment that can activate them. As already noted, the smell of predators, for instance the odor of cats for rats, yields an unconditional form of fearfulness. However, the visual image of a cat as a scary creature is learned. And it does not take much experience. A single experience with threat from a cat is sufficient to generate apparent flash-bulb memories that make the specter of a cat very scary on future occasions. As soon as basic emotional systems develop learned object-relationships with worldly objects and events, we are entering the realm of secondary (learning-related) and eventually, at least in humans, tertiary (thought-related) emotional manifestations.

Jealousy clearly belongs in both of these categories. It is an emotion that is dependent on certain types of object- and subject-relations in the world, which is initially constituted of, and eventually recruits, patterned arousals in a variety of more basic brain emotional processes to yield a derivative emotion. How might this occur through social learning? Perhaps a few experiences with separation-distress/PANIC are enough? Since mothers have to make a living (e.g., hunting and foraging) in the world, they often leave their infants alone, and there are many other opportunities for the psychic pain of separation-distress to have been aroused. Repeated experiences of this sort may developmentally prepare neural ground for adult jealousies. Thus, jealousy can become an anticipatory mood in various social situations where the comfort of the social-bond is compromised and strained by various social events. Indeed, there may be various types of jealousy depending on the patterns of basic emotions aroused, and they may be somewhat different in males and females.

Neurological and Gender Aspects of Jealousy

Evolutionary psychologists have provided evidence that males are more likely to become jealous in response to sexual transgression while females are more sensitive to perceived flaws in emotional commitments (Salovey, 1991). However, such effects are typically significant with more forced-choice questionnaires (Buss & Haselton, 2005; Schutzwohl, 2005) but not typically with more open-ended measures of jealousy (DeSteno, Bartlett, Braverman, & Salovey, 2002). Still, the one human fMRI study of jealousy in a Japanese sample has yielded different brain arousal patterns in males and females as a function of imagined jealousy-provoking scenarios (Takahashi et al., 2006). Males tend to exhibit more lower-brain, primary-process brain arousal (e.g., amygdala and hypothalamus) while females exhibit more neocortical arousal by the posterior STS (Superior Temporal Sulcus or angular gyrus), suggesting that women's minds take a more cognitive, deliberative stance in such pretend situations. Whether such patterns generalize across cultures remains to be seen.

The neuroscience of jealousy remains in its infancy, and the only extensive case-study database comes from accidental brain damage, where amplification of delusional jealousy is often seen. Indeed, such delusional jealousy has been given the name Othello's Syndrome, and it was first described following brain damage by Richardson, Malloy, and Grace (1991); such morbid jealousies are also seen in various psychiatric disorders. Across neurological case studies, the most robust pattern of results appears to be the finding that intensification of jealousy reactions typically results from right hemisphere damage (for a few key recent examples from the past decade see: Blasco-Fontecilla, Jimenez, Santos, & Romero, 2005; Chae & Kang, 2006; Narumoto, Nakamura, Kitabayashi, & Fukui, 2006; and Westlake & Weeks, 1999). Following diffuse stroke-induced brain damage (but sometimes delimited to specific regions such as the right orbito-frontal cortex), individuals exhibited sustained beliefs and accusations that their spouses or sexual partners were being unfaithful, although they had exhibited no jealous or paranoid personality traits prior to brain damage. This suggests that prosocial psychological balance, and realistic perspective taking, is supported better by the typically non-speaking right hemisphere, while jealousy may be amplified by the linguistic-conceptual abilities of the left hemisphere.

Even though most variants of human jealousy may require higher-order mentation, the affective intensity of the aroused feelings may be linked to the arousal of subcortical emotional networks. If the affective power of jealousy obtains its affective intensity from the homologous subcortical infrastructure of mammalian brains, there should eventually be a role for animal brain research in deciphering what is happening in jealous minds.

Jealousy in Animals

So far only a tangential case has been made for the possibility of jealousy in other mammals, and owing to the difficulty of studying higher emotions in nonhuman mammals, there is hardly any sustained neuroscientific data showing evidence for such a contention. This is not to say, though, that other mammals do not have

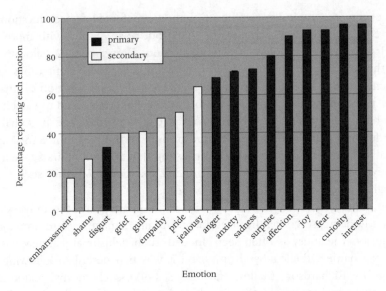

Figure 6.1 Percentage of animals reported to have a particular emotion (*N* = 907) arranged in ascending order. Published with the permission of the author

secondary and perhaps even tertiary emotions. Observers since Darwin have noted jealousy-type reactions in animals, but no systematic research program on the topic has ever been initiated. Still, there are relevant strands of thought.

At the descriptive-belief level, Paul Morris and colleagues recently published an extensive survey of 907 animal owners' beliefs about the existence of potential secondary emotions, including jealousy, in their animal (Morris, Doe, & Godsell, 2008). Animal lovers commonly believe that many of our companion animals experience quite a few secondary emotions, and Morris documented existing beliefs about "self-conscious" emotions, including jealousy and pride and various "self-conscious evaluative emotions" such as guilt and shame, and several other higher-order social emotions. Specifically, they evaluated perceived existence of the potential primary emotions of anger, fear, surprise, joy/happiness, sadness, anxiety, disgust, interest, love/affection, and curiosity, and the secondary emotions of empathy, shame, pride, grief, guilt, jealousy, and embarrassment (Lewis, 2002; Tangney & Fischer, 1995). Owners of birds, cats, dogs, horses, and various rodents or lagomorphs (i.e., guinea pigs, hamsters, rabbits, and rats) were included in the survey. The overall findings are summarized in Figure 6.1.

With respect to jealousy, the highest percentage of reports was for dogs (81% of respondents), followed by horses (79%), cats (66%), birds (67%), rats (47%), rabbits (37%), guinea pigs (27%), and hamsters (17%). Thus, for the major categories of large companion animals as well as birds, more than two-thirds of owners believed they had observed indices of jealousy. Indeed, even in lowly rats, almost half the owners had detected what they took to be indications of jealousy. If even our most common species (of convenience) in animal behavior laboratories, rodents, are commonly perceived to be capable of jealousy, might it be possible to generate a psychobiological laboratory model of this secondary emotion? I ask this question in all seriousness. As already emphasized, only through animal models could we ever have a detailed science of the underlying neural processes. In my review of the relevant databases in Pubmed, it seems that no one has tried. When the key words "jealousy" and "rats" were inserted, "jealousy" alone yielded only 754 hits, "rats" yielded 1,240,037 hits, and the combo yielded none. It was gratifying that the "jealousy" and "dog" combo yielded 5 hits, including a gem from *Science* (1892, pp. 20, 305–306) entitled "Jealousy of a Dog." Many dog owners believe that their emotionally sensitive pack-creatures are quite sensitive to being socially slighted.

Can animals really experience jealousy? How could one ever tell? If they do, can it outlast the immediate perception of threat to their socio-sexual resources? We may never know. Above the primary-process level (*vide supra*), where instinct-ual emotional behaviors appear to be veridical, proxy readouts of affective states (Panksepp, 2005a, 2005b, 2008), it is increasingly difficult to fathom higher aspects of animal minds, most especially when precipitating circumstances are long past. As one commentator noted: "It seems doubtful, for example, that animals worry about the security of their nests or burrows while they are away from home or feel happy things about their 'loved ones' when they are not physically present. In contrast, human beings regularly experience emotions thinking about these appendages of themselves" (Leary, 2004, p. 776). I would personally withhold such judgments, especially when ongoing work, even in birds, suggests that they can partake of mental "time travel"—envisioning potential future events in their "mind's eye": For instance, scrub-jays who have cached food for future use in the presence of another jay who may rob them will take an opportunity to re-cache their food if given another chance without an observer being present; this suggests that they are worried about future loss of resources (Clayton, Bussey, & Dickinson, 2003). In any event, it would seem that the possibility of secondary and even tertiary process emotions should remain an open question, and certainly there are processes in animals that resemble jealousy sufficiently well that they deserve our attention, especially since animal models are the optimal way to really get *detailed* information about underlying neural processes.

It seems that there is an underutilized opportunity for developing relevant animal models here. So, how might one generate a model of jealousy for widely used laboratory rodents? One reasonable starting point would be to have a male and female rat couple living together, so they might perceive each other (impli-citly, presumably) as a major social resource, and to then concoct a situation where the "ownership" of that resource was threatened. Since evolutionary psychologists have argued that males value sexual resources more than females, it would be most appropriate to threaten the common-law "husband's" sole proprietary rights over his female companion. This is easily done simply by placing an unwary "intruder" rat into the established "love-nest" and observing what jealousies—as indexed by agonistic interactions—might emerge. Abundant research shows that the aggressive consequences in such situations are robust and clear-cut. This is not simply territorial behavior, since the aggression is substantially more intense than that observed when an intruder is placed into the living space of a singly-housed male.

The most interesting aspect of this *ménage a trois*, at least initially for the intruder, is that there is a female about. This leads to the high probability of putting his nose in someone else's business, which is not well received by the resident autocrat. Indeed, it is well known that this is an ideal way to provoke intense aggression and fear, with the resident serving up the aggression and the intruder getting the full measure of a fearsome defeat which, if sustained, can promote a depressive syndrome, with distinct brain neurochemical changes (Panksepp, Burgdorf, Beinfeld, Kroes, & Moskal, 2007). It works like clockwork— the resident wins, the intruder loses (showing many 22 kHz ultrasonic complaints), and the female stands by observing the activities. However, we have preliminary data indicating that the female becomes aggressive if the effects of a female intruder are evaluated. Might all this reflect the fruits of a jealous rage on the part of the resident? Could this be an animal model of primal jealousy? I suspect this is about as good as it can get with rodent models of jealousy.

Perhaps this model would be more compelling if it could be demonstrated that the female took a special interest in the intruder male, but aggression is typically so fast that this aspect remains to be evaluated. An increase in aggression could potentially be seen if the resident male were forced to experience some "infidelities" as might be done by restricting the resident male to an observation chamber where it is exposed to different levels of socio-sexual activity by the female and the intruder male. To my knowledge, such an experiment has not yet been done.

Toward a Neurochemistry of Jealousy

The best evidence that the above animal models may provide some insight for the neurochemical substrates of jealousy has come from such mate-guarding studies. There are a variety of neurochemical changes in the intruders that result from such depression-promoting social encounters (Panksepp, 2007c; Watt & Panksepp, 2009), but there are currently no studies of comparable changes in the resident animals. Presumably, future studies along those lines may help reveal brain system changes that may be candidates for mediating jealousy-type tendencies.

However, there is one such neurochemical study that may be especially relevant for modeling and understanding jealousy: Using a resident-intruder model in monogamous prairie voles, Winslow and colleagues (1993) first evaluated the role of vasopressin in the emergence of sexually mediated pair-bonds

(Winslow, Hastings, Carter, Harbaugh, & Insel, 1993). It is clear that a single sexual episode is enough to develop a defensive–offensive attitude in a male prairie vole. In other words, one sexual escapade was enough to promote an aggressive attitude toward potential interlopers. However, if a vasopressin antagonist was infused into the brain just prior to the initial bond-solidifying sexual encounter, a neurochemical manipulation that in itself does not reduce sexual performance, the resident males failed to become aggressive toward male intruders. It seemed that the experience of possessiveness did not develop in the prairie vole mind if they did not experience the sexual episode with the full psychobiological effects of vasopressin, a neuropeptide that is released during sexual arousal, even in humans (Murphy, Seckl, Buron, Checkley, & Lightman, 1990).

Also, to the extent that vasopressin was a social memory aid in such a study, which has been demonstrated (Dantzer, 1998), the above work may indicate that social relationships established under the influence of high brain vasopressin levels may become more "worthwhile" and hence worthy of being protected when threatened.

Thus, a remarkable empirical corollary of the above finding was that the sexual experience itself was not necessary for the emergence of a jealousy-type mate-guarding. Simply infusing the vasopressin into the brain of the male in the presence of a receptive female was sufficient to allow the defensive–possessive attitude to emerge. In other words, it was the vasopressin released within the brain of the male during the sexual activity that was sufficient to induce males to respond to potential interlopers in highly aggressive ways.

Although the authors interpreted these findings only in the context of how socio-sexual bonds form, with no mention of jealousy, they can as readily be interpreted in the context of jealousy. If this interpretation has substance, a prediction would be that a future vasopressin antagonist would possess anti-jealousy properties in humans. Currently none exist that can be used in humans. Further, would such maneuvers reduce symptoms of the morbid jealousy manifested as Othello's Syndrome? So far, only modest symptom reductions have been observed following serotonin-modulating antidepressants (Blasco-Fontecilla et al., 2005) and the antipsychotic pimozide which blocks dopamine receptors (Munro, 1984). Indeed, more recent work implicating brain dopamine on adult socio-sexual attachments of prairie voles (Aragona et al., 2006) may be relevant for future work on jealousy-related processes in this convenient laboratory species.

With regard to other possible neurochemical predictions, if one accepts that one affective aspect of human jealousy is enraged feelings, it might be predicted that all anti-anger drugs would tend to moderate the intensity of jealous feelings. Unfortunately, there are no drugs that have been shown to have specific effects on human anger. However, analysis of RAGE circuits in animal models clearly indicates that the neuropeptide Substance P is present at all major subcortical way-stations of such circuits—in amygdala, medial hypothalamus, and periaque-ductal gray—and that it facilitates aggressiveness in various animal models (Gregg & Siegel, 2003). Conversely, Substance P antagonists reduce irritable aggression (Halasz et al., 2008). One Substance P receptor anatagonist, aprepi-tant, originally developed as a potential antidepressant (which failed miserably), has been subsequently developed as an anti-nausea agent, and approved for human use. From the above perspective, we might anticipate that not only would aprepitant be a fairly robust anti-anger medication, but that it would also ameliorate the rage that often accompanies jealousy, perhaps with sufficient strength to dampen the passionate intensity of jealousy. As noted earlier, a similar logic can be applied for opioid and oxytocinergic modulators of social bonds, since both are quite effective anti-anger agents (Panksepp, 1998a).

Such studies may eventually be able to dissect the degree to which jealous feelings are dependent on anger, and to what extent on the other basic affects discussed above. If anti-anger agents dissolve the affective force of jealousy, leaving only the residue of cognitive contents in comparatively untroubled minds, it would be very informative. Perhaps the other primary emotions are not able, by themselves, to sustain the affective edge of jealousy. In any event, this is the way animal models may eventually inform our neuroscientific understand-ing of the causes of human jealousies.

Evolutionary Reflections

Thus, it seems that jealousy would probably not exist if human brains were not so capable of making social and sexual bonds, along with the capacity for paranoid thinking. Neuroscience suggests differences in these two types of bonding . . . and one must wonder if there are several distinct types of jealousy, for instance mate-guarding forms (more prominent in males) and social investment-guarding forms (more prominent in females). These are, of course, the two strategies highlighted by evolutionary psychologists, and different brain patterns were evident in the Takahashi et al. (2006) brain-imaging study, with males showing more arousal in lower brain regions strongly linked to primal sexual and aggressive urges, while females exhibited more abundant higher cerebral, cognitive arousal, especially in the superior temporal gyrus.

In this context, it is most interesting that a single study (Rilling, Winslow, & Kilts, 2004) has sought to evaluate mate-guarding strategies in primates, and it phrased its findings in terms of a male "sexual jealousy" framework. Just as in other species, dominant male rhesus macaques are known to respond aggressively when their sexual rights (exclusivity) are threatened by potential interlopers. To evaluate what was happening in their brain, 9 dominant males were intravenously injected with the positron-emitting sugar (18)F]-FDG ([(18)F]-fluorodeoxyglucose) typically used in positron emission tomography

(PET) studies that evaluate the effects of psychological challenges on changes in brain metabolism. The monkeys were confronted by a mate-possessiveness challenge to estimate the localization of emergent jealousies within their brains: During one condition, only their female consort was visible, while in the other mate-guarding or jealousy "challenge" condition, the dominant monkeys witnessed a potential sexual encounter between their consort and a rival male that was sufficient to raise their plasma testosterone levels along with threatening displays. Brain PET images showed greater activation in the periaqueductal gray (PAG) of the midbrain, a brain area known to mediate aggression (Panksepp, 1998a) but also one that is rich in androgen receptors. The jealousy challenge also aroused the right amygdala and right superior temporal sulcus, the former of which mediates both anger and fear, while the latter is probably related to increased social vigilance. Let us recall that a comparable cortical brain change was observed only in females in the Takahashi et al. (2006) human study. Considering that the monkeys were evaluated during a real-life challenge as opposed to the simulated one, such as that used to study human jealousy, one is tempted to conclude, as did the authors, that sexual jealousy in male humans might recruit similar neural networks to those evident in the monkeys.

Still, the laterality results are a bit puzzling if we consider the fact that neurological damage inducing Othello's Syndrome is typically restricted to the right hemisphere. How can one reconcile this with the increased metabolism found in the right hemisphere of the above monkey work? It is impossible to say, but we should recall that human brain imaging only provides loci of interest, and it is not well suited to tell us even if the aroused brain regions elaborate mainly excitatory or inhibitory processes related to the psychological function being studied. The generation of both excitatory and inhibitory functions requires action potentials. Although most are eager to interpret increased brain-tissue metabolism and regional blood oxygenation signals as indicative of active excitatory processing of a psychological function, we have very little basis for reaching such conclusions.

Conclusions

The neuroscientific analysis of jealousy remains in its infancy. However, our understanding of subcortically concentrated basic emotional networks provides novel ways to approach the affectively multidimensional nature of jealousy in novel conceptual and empirical ways. Thus, the increasing future use of animal models, as described, may yield neurochemical and neuropharmacological findings that can be evaluated psychologically in humans. Also, by clearly distinguishing primary-process foundational issues, secondary-learning, and tertiary-thought processes in the genesis of jealousy, we can begin to better envision the developmental landscapes that lead to the affective, temperamental, and gender-based varieties of jealousy.

With respect to advancing animal brain research, the topic of jealousy may allow us to penetrate slightly into the so-far forbidding territory of higher-order social emotions. How far we can proceed into this unexplored territory remains to be seen. However, if substantive models do emerge, we can be confident that they will enrich our scientific understanding of what it means to have jealousy percolating in the human BrainMind.

With respect to exploring the dynamics of the human mind, more work needs to be done on the affective and temporal dynamics of the obsessive thoughts and feelings that characterize jealousy states. In discussing gender differences in jealousy, we do not know whether males and females consistently exhibit different emotional spectrums during feelings of jealousy. We do not even know how frequently such feelings of jealousy reflect unshakable but false convictions of another's infidelity as opposed to veridical evaluations of changing social commitments. We do not know which aspects of personality, whether evaluated by traditional scales or recent neuroscience-based basic emotion scales (Davis, Panksepp, & Normansell, 2003), predispose individuals to jealousy and how patterns of early developmental social and nonsocial vicissitudes predispose one to attacks of jealousy. We have no reliable evidence-based psychiatric medicines to control pathological jealousy and the associated rage. The wider use of animal models may eventually facilitate acquisition of substantive evidence on some of these remaining questions.

Notes

1   Capitalizations are used to (i) avoid part–whole confusions, (ii) to alert readers to the claim that these may be *necessary* brain systems for those types of emotional behaviors and feelings although by no means *sufficient* for all the emotional manifestations that may arise from those systems in real-world activities, and (iii) to highlight that *specific psychobehavioral brain systems* are the referents of these labels.

2   I have found that the concept of "objectless" emotional arousals is a difficult concept for many human psychologists to envision. The assumption that all emotions have object relations with occurrences in the outside world is heavily ingrained since that is a self-evident aspect of human psychological life. However, from the perspective of what evolution actually built into the brain, it seems unlikely that the specific types of emotional arousal that can be evoked with localized brain stimulation are initially strongly coupled to any specific environmental events. They are more tightly coupled to bodily needs and events such as hunger, pain, and discomfort. These instinctual systems are tightly coupled to learning systems that can rapidly develop object relations. A better recognition of this type of organization can facilitate various levels of understanding, especially how social emotions emerge during development.

3   The neural mechanisms of social bonding were first outlined in Panksepp et al. (1980) and Panksepp (1981), with the introduction of an understanding of the separation-distress mechanisms of the brain and the brain opioid social-addiction model. The

work was first conducted in dogs, guinea pigs, and domestic chicks, and subsequently in primates and other species. Most of this work was done in infant animals. More recent work on adult-pair bonding in prairie voles has focused more on the role of oxytocin to the exclusion of brain opioids (for recent review, see Hammock & Young, 2006). It should be noted that there are certain laboratory species, such as rats, which have become popular in separation-distress research (for critical review, see Blumberg & Sokoloff, 2001), but there is little evidence that rat-pups born with little sensory or motor competence develop social bonds with their mothers; they are more bonded to the smell of their nests. Thus, it is difficult to argue that such animals exhibit true social bonds, and that may explain many of the peculiar neuropharmacological findings in rats as compared to species that exhibit robust social bonds (Panksepp, 2003b). Thus, it is dubious if work on such rats truly highlights the nature of mammalian social bonds, where mutual recognition between mother and infant is a critical aspect of the social bond.

References

Aragona, B. J., Liu, Y., Yu, Y. J., Curtis, J. T., Detwiller, J. M., Insel, T. R. & Wang, Z. (2006). Nucleus accumbens dopamine differentially mediates the formation and maintenance of monogamous pair bonds. *Nature Neuroscience, 9,* 132–139.

Barrett, L. F. (2006). Are emotions natural kinds? *Perspectives on Psychological Science, 1,* 28–58.

Bauminger, N. (this volume). Jealousy in autism spectrum disorders (ASD). In S. L. Hart & M. Legerstee (Eds.), *Handbook of jealousy: Theory, research, and multidisciplinary approaches.* Malden, MA: Wiley-Blackwell.

Bauminger, N., Chomsky-Smolkin, L., Orbach-Caspi, E., Zahor, D., & Levy-Shiff, R. (2007). Jealousy and emotional responsiveness in young children with ASD. *Cognition and Emotion, 22,* 556–619.

Blasco-Fontecilla, H., Jimenez, M. D. B., Santos, L. M. G., & Romero, J. M. B. (2005). Delusional disorder with delusions of parasitosis and jealousy after stroke. *Journal of Clinical Psychopharmacology, 25,* 615–617.

Blumberg, M. S., & Sokoloff, G. (2001). Do infant rats cry? *Psychological Review, 108,* 83–95.

Buss, D. M., & Haselton, M. (2005). The evolution of jealousy. *Trends in Cognitive Sciences, 20,* 1–2.

Chae, B., & Kang, B. (2006). Quetiapine for hypersexuality and delusional jealousy after stroke. *Journal of Clinical Psychopharmacology, 26,* 331–332.

Clayton, N. S., Bussey, T. J., & Dickinson, A. (2003). Can animals recall the past and plan for the future? *Nature Reviews Neuroscience, 4,* 685–691.

Dantzer, R. (1998). Vasopressin, gonadal steroids and social recognition. *Progress in Brain Research, 119,* 409–414.

Davidson, R. J., Scherer, K. R., & Goldsmith, H. H. (Eds.). (2003). *Handbook of affective sciences.* New York: Oxford University Press.

Davis, K. L., Panksepp, J., & Normansell, L. (2003). The affective neuroscience personality scales: Normative data and implications. *Neuro-Psychoanalysis, 5,* 21–29.

DeSteno, D. A., Bartlett, M. Y., Braverman, J., & Salovey, P. (2002). Sex differences in jealousy: Evolutionary mechanism of artifact of measurement? *Journal of Personality and Social Psychology, 83*, 1103–1116.

Draghi-Lorenz, R., Reddy, V., & Costall, A. (2001). Rethinking the development of "non-basic" emotions: A critical review of existing theories. *Developmental Review, 21*, 263–304.

Gregg, T. R., & Siegel, A. (2003). Differential effects of NK1 receptors in the midbrain Periaqueductal gray upon defensive rage and predatory attack in the cat. *Brain Research, 994*, 55–66.

Halasz, J., Toth, M., Hrabovzky, E., Barsy, B., Barsvari, B., & Haller, J. (2008). The effect of neurokinin 1 receptor blockade on territorial aggression and in a model of violent aggression. *Biological Psychiatry, 633*, 271–278.

Hammock, E. A. D., & Young, L. J. (2006). Oxytocin, vasopressin and pair bonding: Implications for autism. *Philosophical Transactions of the Royal Society, B, 361*, 2187–2198.

Hart, S. L. (this volume). The ontogenesis of jealousy in the first year of life: A theory of jealousy as a biologically-based dimension of temperament. In S. L. Hart & M. Legerstee (Eds.), *Handbook of jealousy: Theory, research, and multidisciplinary approaches*. Malden, MA: Wiley-Blackwell.

Hart, S. L., Carrington, H. A., Tronick, E. Z., & Carroll, S. R. (2004). When infants lose exclusive maternal attention: Is it jealousy? *Infancy, 6*, 57–78.

Hobson, R. P. (this volume). Is jealousy a complex emotion? In S. L. Hart & M. Legerstee (Eds.), *Handbook of jealousy: Theory, research, and multidisciplinary approaches*. Malden, MA: Wiley-Blackwell.

Hobson, R. P., Chidambi, G., Lee, A., & Meyer, J. (2006). Foundations for self- awareness: An exploration through autism. *Monographs of the Society for Research in Child Development, 71*(Serial No. 284).

Leary, M. R. (2004). *The curse of the self: Self-awareness, egotism, and the quality of human life.* New York: Oxford University Press.

Legerstee, M., Ellenbogen, B., Nienhuis, T., & Marsh, H. (this volume). Social bonds, triadic relationships, and goals: Preconditions for the emergence of human Jealousy. In S. L. Hart, & M. Legerstee (Eds.), *Handbook of jealousy: Theory, research, and multidisciplinary approaches*. Malden, MA: Wiley-Blackwell.

Lewis, M. (2002). Early emotional development. In A. Slater & M. Lewis (Eds.), *Introduction to infant development* (pp. 192–209). Oxford: Oxford University Press.

Lewis, M., & Haviland-Jones, J. M. (Eds.). (2000). *Handbook of emotions* (2nd ed.). New York: Guilford Press.

Lewis, M., Haviland-Jones, J. M., & Barrett, L. F. (Eds.). (2008). *Handbook of emotions* (3rd ed.). New York: Guilford Press.

Markova, G., Stieben, J., & Legerstee, M. (this volume). Neural structures of jealousy: Infants' experience of social exclusion with caregivers and peers. In S. L. Hart & M. Legerstee (Eds.), *Handbook of jealousy: Theory, research, and multidisciplinary approaches*. Malden, MA: Wiley-Blackwell.

Morris, P. H., Doe, C., & Godsell, E. (2008). Secondary emotions in non-primate species? Behavioural reports and subjective claims by animal owners. *Cognition and Emotion, 22*, 3–20.

Munro, A. (1984). Excellent response of pathologic jealousy to pimozide. *Canadian Medical Association Journal, 131*, 852–853.

Murphy, M. R., Seckl, J. R., Buron, S., Checkley, S. A., & Lightman, S. L. (1990). Changes in oxytocin and vasopressin secretion during sexual activity in men. *Journal of Clinical Endocrinology and Metabolism, 65*, 738–741.

Narumoto, J., Nakamura, K., Kitabayashi, Y., & Fukui, K. (2006). Othello syndrome secondary to right orbitofrontal lobe excision. *Journal of Neuropsychiatry and Clinical Neuroscience, 18*, 560–561.

Panksepp, J. (1981). Brain opioids: A neurochemical substrate for narcotic and social dependence. In S. Cooper (Ed.), *Progress in theory in psychopharmacology* (pp. 149–175). London: Academic Press.

Panksepp, J. (1982). Toward a general psychobiological theory of emotions. *The Behavioral and Brain Sciences, 5*, 407–467.

Panksepp, J. (1998a). *Affective neuroscience: The foundations of human and animal emotions*. New York: Oxford University Press.

Panksepp, J. (1998b). The periconscious substrates of consciousness: Affective states and the evolutionary origins of the SELF. *Journal of Consciousness Studies, 5*, 566–582.

Panksepp, J. (2001). The long-term psychobiological consequences of infant emotions: Prescriptions for the twenty-first century. *Infant Mental Health Journal, 22*, 132–173.

Panksepp, J. (2003a). Feeling the pain of social loss. *Science, 302*, 237–239.

Panksepp, J. (2003b). Can anthropomorphic analyses of "separation cries" in other animals inform us about the emotional nature of social loss in humans? *Psychological Review, 110*, 376–388.

Panksepp, J. (2005a). Affective consciousness: Core emotional feelings in animals and humans. *Consciousness and Cognition, 14*, 30–80.

Panksepp, J. (2005b). On the embodied neural nature of core emotional affects. *Journal of Consciousness Studies, 12*, 161–187.

Panksepp, J. (2005c). Why does separation-distress hurt? A comment on MacDonald and Leary. *Psychological Bulletin, 131*, 224–230.

Panksepp, J. (2005d). Social support and pain: How does the brain feel the ache of a broke heart? *Journal of Cancer Pain and Symptom Palliation, 1*, 59–65.

Panksepp, J. (2006a). Emotional endophenotypes in evolutionary psychiatry. *Progress in Neuro-Psychopharmacology and Biological Psychiatry, 30*, 778–784.

Panksepp, J. (2006b). On the neuro-evolutionary nature of social pain, support, and empathy. In M. Aydede (Ed.), *Pain: New essays on its nature and the methodology of its study* (pp. 367–387). Cambridge, MA: MIT Press.

Panksepp J. (2007a). The neuroevolutionary and neuroaffective psychobiology of the prosocial brain. In R. I. M. Dunbar & L. Barrett (Eds.), *The Oxford handbook of evolutionary psychology* (pp. 145–162). Oxford: Oxford University Press.

Panksepp, J. (2007b). Neurologizing the psychology of affects: How appraisal-based constructivism and basic emotion theory can coexist. *Perspectives on Psychological Science, 2*, 281–296.

Panksepp, J. (2007c). Neuroevolutionary sources of laughter and social joy: Modeling primal human laughter in laboratory rats. *Behavioral Brain Research, 182*, 231–244.

Panksepp, J. (2008). The affective brain and core-consciousness: How does neural activity generate emotional feelings? In M. Lewis, J. M. Haviland, & L. F. Barrett, (Eds.), *Handbook of emotions*. New York: Guilford Press.

Panksepp, J., & Burgdorf, J. (2003). "Laughing" rats and the evolutionary antecedents of human joy? *Physiology and Behavior, 79,* 533–547.

Panksepp, J., Burgdorf, J., Beinfeld, M. C., Kroes, R., & Moskal, J. (2007). Brain regional neuropeptide changes resulting from social defeat. *Behavioral Neuroscience, 121,* 1364–1371.

Panksepp, J., & Crepeau, L. (1990). Selective lesions of the dual olfactory system and cat smell-attenuated play fighting among juvenile rats. *Aggressive Behavior, 16,* 130–131.

Panksepp, J., Herman, B. H., Vilberg, T., Bishop, P., & DeEskinazi, F. G. (1980). Endogenous opioids and social behavior. *Neuroscience and Biobehavioral Reviews, 4,* 473–487.

Panksepp, J., & Panksepp, J. B. (2000). The seven sins of evolutionary psychology. *Evolution and Cognition, 6,* 108–131.

Panksepp, J., & Panksepp, J. B. (2001). A continuing critique of evolutionary psychology: Seven sins for seven sinners, plus or minus two. *Evolution and Cognition, 7,* 56–80.

Reddy, V. (2000). Coyness in early infancy. *Developmental Science, 3,* 186–192.

Richardson, E. D., Malloy, P. F., & Grace, J. (1991). Othello syndrome secondary to right cerebrovascular infarction. *Journal of Geriatric Psychiatry and Neurology, 4,* 160–165.

Rilling, J. K., Winslow, J. T., & Kilts, C. D. (2004). The neural correlates of mate competition in dominant male rhesus macaques. *Biological Psychiatry, 56,* 364–375.

Salovey, P. (1991). *The psychology of jealousy and envy.* New York: Guilford Press.

Salovey, P., & Rodin, J. (1986). Differentiation of social-comparison jealousy and romantic jealousy. *Journal of Personality and Social Psychology, 50,* 1100–1112.

Salovey, P., & Rodin, J. (1989). Envy and jealousy in close relationships. *Review of Personality and Social Psychology, 10,* 221–246.

Schutzwohl, A. (2005). Sex differences in jealousy: The processing of cues to infidelity. *Evolution and Human Behavior, 26,* 288–299.

Takahashi, H., Matsuura, M., Yahata, N., Koeda, M., Suhara, T., & Okubo Y. (2006). Men and women show distinct brain activations during imagery of sexual and emotional infidelity. *NeuroImage, 32,* 1299–1307.

Tangney, J. P., & Fischer, K. W. (1995). *Self-conscious emotions: The psychology of shame, guilt, embarrassment, and pride.* New York: Guilford Press.

Watt, D. F., & Panksepp, J. (2009). Depression: An evolutionarily conserved mechanism to terminate separation-distress? A review of aminergic, peptidergic, and neural network perspectives. *Neuropsychoanalysis, 11,* 5–48; with commentaries and responses, pp. 49–105.

Westlake, R. J., & Weeks, S. M. (1999). Pathological jealousy appearing after cerebrovascular infarction in a 25-year-old woman. *Australian and New Zealand Journal of Psychiatry, 33,* 105–107.

Winslow, J. T., Hastings, N., Carter, C. S., Harbaugh, C. R., & Insel, T. R. (1993). A role for central vasopressin in pair bonding in monogamous prairie voles, *Nature, 365,* 545–548.

7

Sibling Rivalry in the Birds and Bees

Scott Forbes

Families are complex social structures that are forums for often-spectacular cooperation and altruism among close kin. We find myriad examples of self-sacrificial behavior across the full spectrum of nature, from simple social insects where sisters forgo their own reproduction, and sometimes forfeit their lives to aid their close relatives, to mother hippos, bears, and crocodiles that are both fearless and lethal in the protection of their progeny. Nurturing parents and affectionate siblings match our expectations of family harmony, and biologists on the basis of shared genetic interests expect cooperation and altruism among close relatives.

Inclusive fitness theory, first proposed by biologist William D. Hamilton (Hamilton, 1964a, 1964b), provides the conceptual framework for understanding interactions among kin. Close relatives have a high probability of sharing identical copies of genes by recent common ancestry, and promoting the interests of relatives also promotes one's own (shared) genetic interest; the closer the relationship, the higher the probability of sharing identical genes. Thus from a genetic perspective, altruism within the family is easy to understand. But families are also venues for extremes of violence and selfishness, and Robert Trivers (1974), building upon Hamilton's work, showed how parents and offspring might disagree over how resources within the family should be shared, defining the concept of parent–offspring conflict (Trivers, 1974).

Examples of selfishness within animal families are not hard to find. Baby eaglets and pelicans murder siblings with a ruthless efficiency (Gargett, 1977; Cash & Evans, 1986). Shark embryos slaughter brothers and sisters in utero (Gilmore, Dodrill, & Linley, 1983; Joung & Hsu, 2005) and spadefoot toad tadpoles cannibalize sibs when their pond dries too quickly, developing huge predatory jaws to accomplish the task (Pfennig, 1992). The obvious question is why? If we expect relatives with shared genetic interests to behave altruistically, how can we explain selfishness and violence within families?

Handbook of Jealousy: Theory, Research and Multidisciplinary Approaches, First Edition.
Edited by Sybil L. Hart and Maria Legerstee.
© 2013 Blackwell Publishing Ltd. Published 2013 by Blackwell Publishing Ltd.

Table 7.1   Glossary of biological terms

Altricial	Offspring that are born helpless, requiring both nourishment and protection by parents
Androgens	Male hormones such as testosterone
Antioxidants	Molecules that prevent the cellular damage that arises during oxidative reactions. Includes such things as vitamin c, e and carotenoids that may have beneficial health effects
Asymmetric sibling competition	Competition between core and marginal offspring usually decided by the developmental advantage initially conferred by the parents to core offspring
Brood reduction	The death of one or more brood members as a result of sibling competition
Core offspring	In species that provide extended care for their offspring, offspring that are favored by their parents, usually by birth or hatching asynchrony. Core off-spring are often older, stronger and developmentally advanced compared to their marginal brood-mates, and as a consequence enjoy higher expected growth and survival
Developmental uncertainty	Unpredictable developmental fate of offspring; off-spring may be afflicted by genetic defects, disease, parasites or injury
Dizygotic twins	Twins arising from separate fertilized eggs. Also known as fraternal twins, with a coefficient of relationship of ½ the same as ordinary brothers and sisters. Monozygotic twins arise from cleavage of the same egg and are genetically identical
Eusocial	Term applied to ants, bees, and wasps among invertebrates, and mole rats among vertebrates to denote social systems where reproductive individuals are accompanied by sterile workers and soldiers
Facilitation	Where the production of surplus offspring benefits other family members, e.g., through the production of trophic eggs
Follicle stimulating hormone	A peptide hormone produced by the anterior pituitary that stimulates the development of egg foll-icles into ova (eggs)
Follicle atresia	The attrition of egg follicles
Hatching asynchrony	Where the hatching of eggs is staggered in time; a term usually applied to birds or insects
Inclusive fitness	Fitness of an individual (roughly equivalent to expected survival and reproduction) that takes into account the effects of one's actions on the fitness of close relatives, and vice versa—e.g., assisting a brother or sister to help rear their offspring

Table 7.1   *(Cont.)*

Kin selection	Natural selection favoring altruistic behaviors among genetic kin
Marginal offspring	In a brood or litter of more than one, offspring that are handicapped by their parents, usually by virtue of birth or hatching asynchrony. Marginal offspring typically grow slower and suffer higher mortality than core brood-mates
Oocyte	Egg cell
Parent–offspring conflict	Genetically-based conflict between parents and offspring based upon genetic asymmetries
Parental optimism	In organisms that provide extended care for their offspring, the habit of parents to produce more incipient offspring than can or will be reared to independence
Polyovulation	The production of more than one ova (egg) during a monthly cycle
Polytocous	Mammals with multi-pup litters
Phenotype	Observable characteristics of an organism, including morphology and behavior
Polyphenism	Phenotypic diversity among genetically identical individuals; individuals develop differently due to hormonal or environmental cues. The castes of ants and bees (workers, soldiers) are examples
Precocial	Offspring that are mobile and self-feeding when born
Replacement/insurance	Where marginal offspring replace failed or low quality core offspring
Resource tracking	Where the survival of marginal offspring is conditional upon prevailing resource (usually food) levels
Siblicide	Fatal sibling rivalry involving aggression. It may be *obligatory,* occurring always or nearly so, or *facultative,* with its occurrence being conditional usually upon prevailing food levels
Trophic egg	An egg that serves as food for other family members

Much of the mayhem that occurs within families of animals and even plants can be traced to the initial parental decision to overproduce incipient offspring numbers. This is the first step on the path to conflicts between parents and offspring about how big the family should be, and among siblings over how limited resources should be shared (Mock & Forbes, 1995). Parents often choreograph the rivalries that ensue for their own ends by imposing phenotypic handicaps on certain of their progeny (hatching/birth asynchrony; chemical manipulation), and conferring advantages to others. The handicapped offspring I shall refer to as *marginal* progeny. These may be the last-hatched and hence smallest nestlings in a brood of birds, or the runts in litters of mammals: they typically face uncertain prospects for growth and survival, and suffer the brunt of sibling competition. By comparison, their older, stronger brood or litter-mates— the *core* offspring—enjoy more secure fitness prospects, growing faster and surviving to independence more often than their marginal counterparts.

Why do parents play favorites among their progeny? Part of the answer is that parents use "marginal" offspring as pawns—often to be sacrificed—in an evolutionary game to cope with ecological and developmental uncertainty. They may not know in advance if an offspring will be afflicted by a congenital defect, or how much food will be available to sustain their progeny. The creation of surplus incipient offspring that are relatively cheap to make, and that can be later eliminated if not needed, is a general-purpose strategy to cope with uncertainty.

I shall explore how they do this in greater detail below. But first I must address a basic and important question: If shared genetic interests promote harmony, how then do we explain how close relatives can become rivals? The answer lies in the fact that close kin are, because of propinquity, also one's closest competitors for finite resources—food, warmth, space, shelter. But this begs the question: why are resources limited?

Rivalry and the "Thrifty" Parent

If parental investment is sufficient to meet the needs of all their progeny, the motivation for competition among siblings and hence rivalry is removed. But parents ranging from parrots to pandas routinely create incipient families larger than they are capable and/or willing to rear. Why parents do this is key to understanding the evolutionary origins of sibling rivalry.

There are three broad incentives for the overproduction of incipient offspring numbers (Mock & Forbes, 1995): First, as a hedge against future uncertainty about food or other key resources. This is the *resource-tracking* mechanism. It is easier to start with a large initial family size and trim downward than it is to add more offspring later due mainly to constraints of time. In strongly seasonal environments, adding extra offspring may be limited by the available time for rearing families, or activities such as incubating eggs/gestating offspring may be incompatible with feeding dependent offspring.

Second, as a means to screen out low-quality progeny and/or replace offspring that fail prematurely. This is the *replacement* mechanism. Offspring may be afflicted by a variety of congenital defects, or stricken by pathogens, parasites, or injury during early development. Holding a spare offspring in reserve to replace failed offspring or upgrade defective progeny can be a useful insurance policy.

Third, the presence of the surplus offspring may enhance the fitness of other family members. The most obvious example of this *facilitation* mechanism is to serve as food for other family members, and is sometimes referred to as the icebox hypothesis: Progeny are used as a living food store that stays fresh until needed. The most conspicuous examples occur in ants and bees where during periods of privation, adults consume larvae as a key food source (Elgar & Crespi, 1992). If food is plentiful, offspring cannibalism may not be needed, but if food is short, the consumption of embryos may avert widespread starvation of colony members.

In other species such as certain marine snails and ladybird beetles, the mother packages unfertilized "trophic" eggs alongside fertilized eggs. The trophic eggs serve as food for the developing larvae, and experimental work on ladybird beetles shows that parents use trophic eggs to offset starvation risk (Perry & Roitberg, 2005). In live-bearing sand tiger sharks, cannibalism of siblings and the consumption of trophic eggs are the main food sources for developing pups (Gilmore et al., 1983).

Of these three mechanisms, replacement has the most direct relevance to humans—we are not, for example, in the habit of eating our children, however tempting that may be to contemplate. Examples of the replacement mechanism can be found both prenatally and postnatally. Dizygotic (fraternal) twinning is probably more about replacing embryos with chromosomal defects—the incidence of which rises sharply after maternal age 35, as does the incidence of dizygotic twinning—than about giving birth to twins. Far more twins are present at conception than are ever brought to term, and older mothers appear to have a built-in strategy to polyovulate as a hedge against a rising proportion of defective embryos when the time for additional reproductive opportunities grows short in the shadow of menopause (see Forbes, 2005 for a review).

Postnatally, human demographers have described two patterns that fit the replacement mechanism. First, in human populations where birth interval is regulated largely by lactation (or, more formally, lactational amenorrhea where breastfeeding results in natural postpartum infertility), the death of a lactating offspring is followed by a shorter birth interval (Preston, 1978). Demographically this partially offsets the early death of a child. The second pattern is referred to as "hoarding," where family size is overbuilt in anticipation of some offspring mortality. Over most of human history and still in regions of sub-Saharan Africa and south Asia the rate of infant mortality was and is much higher than experienced over most of the developed world today. Highly prevalent and unpredictable offspring mortality provides the incentive for a hoarding strategy (Preston, 1978); but if offspring mortality does not occur, a larger family is generated.

Antecedents of Sibling Aggression

Sibling rivalry in plants and animals stems chiefly from competition for parentally provided food. In some cases food competition is more or less assured. In certain marsupials (pouched mammals), for example, the litter size routinely exceeds the number of mother's nipples, and offspring that fail to secure a nipple perish.

More often the likelihood and extent of any food shortfall are subject to some uncertainty. Random variation in food levels within or across breeding seasons may leave broods or litters amid conditions of either feast or famine. When food shortfall cannot be known in advance, rivalries may develop, not to meet immediate food needs, but to assure priority access to food (to the winners) by establishing a stable dominance hierarchy in advance of any shortfall. This appears to be the case in a variety of birds exhibiting sibling aggression, such as cattle egrets and blue-footed boobies. When food is short, the marginal sibs that rank low in the brood hierarchy are the first to perish (Drummond & Garcia Chavelas, 1989; Mock & Lamey, 1991).

The art of war is to gain time when your strength is inferior. (Napoleon Bonaparte)

At the extreme in obligate brood-reducing species, siblings may murder siblings while sitting amid a current food surplus. The first-hatched black eagle chick kills its younger sibling as soon as the latter hatches, when the parents can easily meet the modest food demands of both (Gargett, 1977). But those food demands will rise sharply and predictably as the nestlings grow older and much, much larger: the stronger older sibling appears to cut its losses by executing its brood-mate early when it has a maximal size advantage and the risk of injury to itself is low (Stinson, 1979). In accord with Napoleon's maxim about warfare, a delay may be a fatal error, allowing a potentially lethal rival to grow larger and stronger.

Among animals the incidence of sibling aggression has been studied in the greatest detail in birds. It is conspicuously linked to the presence of weaponry—the spear-like bills of egrets and herons; the talons and aquiline bills of hawks and owls; the modified egg-teeth in bee-eaters; the heavy heads and bills of pelicans (Mock, 1984). Aggression is rare among the songbirds that are typically much smaller than siblicidal species, perhaps due to the simple laws of physics: their small heads and weak neck muscles leave them unable to inflict damage on opponents (Gonzalez-Voyer, Székely, & Drummond, 2007).

A recent comparative analysis of 69 species across 7 avian families exhibiting sibling violence revealed three main life history correlates: indirect feeding (where parents do not feed nestlings directly but instead leave food on the nest floor); long periods of nestling development; and small brood sizes (Gonzalez-Voyer et al., 2007). It is probably worth noting that two—long periods for offspring development and small brood sizes—and sometimes all three of these three traits hold for human families.

How is Rivalry Manifest?

Sibling rivalry takes on myriad forms ranging from mild to severe, sublethal to lethal, and is most evident when contemporary offspring compete for parentally provided resources. Most bird and mammals rear offspring with little contact between different broods or litters, though there are exceptions as described below.

In mammals, rivalry begins even before fertilization among cohorts of egg follicles in the ovary. A rise in the level of follicle-stimulating hormone (FSH) early in the menstrual cycle triggers a wave of follicle development, from which one dominant follicle will survive, the remainder undergoing follicle atresia (cell death). The process is a growth race and the first follicle to cross the finish line is able to eliminate its competitors via the production of hormonal signals to mother. The mechanism appears to be the production of the peptide hormone *inhibin* that acts as a developmental switch (Beg & Ginther, 2006; Knight & Glister, 2006). Once the switch is flipped, mother reduces her production of FSH from the pituitary, arresting the development of all other follicles. The surviving dominant follicle has already reached the stage where it no longer needs FSH for survival.

In humans, this follicle selection mechanism appears to break down in older mothers, resulting in a higher frequency of polyovulation (multiple ova during each cycle) and an increased likelihood of dizygotic (two-egg) twins. The breakdown may be linked to declining oocyte quality and the inability of the dominant follicle to suppress the development of subordinate follicles (see Forbes, 2005 for a review).

Sibling interactions in utero

Sibling interactions in mammals begin in utero particularly in polytocous mammals (e.g., mice with multi-pup litters), but perhaps also in monotocous species (e.g., humans giving birth to one offspring at a time). Variation in hormonal exposure during fetal development is known to influence a variety of postnatal traits—aggressiveness, sexual behavior, anatomical and physiological features—and intrauterine position affects mice, other rodents, and pigs (review in Ryan & Vandenbergh, 2002). For example, a female mouse embryo sitting between two brothers in utero is bathed in extra testosterone, and as a consequence is likely to exhibit masculinized genitalia, is more likely to mount other females, is more aggressive, and will defend a larger home range. A male mouse embryo situated between two sisters in utero is less aggressive, defends a smaller home range, exhibits less parental behavior, and has a shorter anogenital distance.

At the extreme, siblicide occurs in utero as in pronghorn antelope, where the anterior-most in the embryo spears its sibling with necrotic (dead) tissue (O'Gara, 1969), and in doing so avoids postnatal competition for milk.

Benign sibling interactions or manipulation?

Sibling interactions in mammals may extend across gestations. In humans, fraternal birth order affects a suite of traits including birth-weight, handedness, and sexual orientation (Blanchard & Klassen, 1997; Blanchard, 2004; Blanchard, Cantora, Bogaert, Breedlove, & Ellis, 2006). One possible though still contentious explanation is that pattern is due to priming of the maternal immune system by the presence of sons (not daughters) in the womb. Blanchard and Bogaert (1996) hypothesize that each succeeding male fetus results in a progressive immunization of mothers to Y-linked antigens resulting in increasing effects of anti-male antibodies on subsequent male fetuses. If this is indeed the case, it might be a genetic quirk resulting from commingling of fetal and maternal cells in mother's bloodstream. But to students of sibling competition this looks suspiciously like a mechanism to regulate competition with future male siblings, making them smaller and perhaps less prone to compete for mates.

Such a sibling ploy is of course entirely conjectural at present, but examples of sibling manipulation via effects on maternal physiology are well known.

Triadic interactions

Triadic interactions often foster conflict in human (Hart, 2001) and nonhuman families, particularly when the triad includes a nursing mother and different-aged offspring. In some cases the third member of the triad is a future and as yet unborn offspring. In red deer (*Cervus elaphus*) the fitness (growth and survival) of a yearling calf is enhanced if suckling is prolonged, but mother's fitness is maximized if her calf is weaned earlier, allowing her to conceive again (Clutton-Brock, Guinness, & Albon, 1982; Clutton-Brock, 1991). More vigorous suckling by the yearling calf may interfere with mother's future reproduction to the benefit of the calf.

In rhesus macaques, behavioral conflict between infant and mother rises at the time when she resumes estrus. Mothers who eventually conceive anew reject their infant's attempts to suckle more, reducing access to milk supplies (reviewed in Maestripieri, 2002). In chimpanzees, infants may harass their mother's mating activities and provoke intense maternal aggression (Clark, 1977; van de Rijt-Plooij & Plooij, 1987). Similarly and in the category of "more than I really wanted to know," a hand-reared chimpanzee harassed her human handlers (putative alloparents) during sexual intercourse (Niemeyer & Anderson, 1983).

Maternal rejections of infants attempting to suckle intensify when mothers resume estrus, and during the process of weaning, infants display elements of depression and infantile behaviors such as whimpering and ventral riding with mother (Clark, 1977). One possible interpretation of this behavior is that infants are jealous of their mother's attempts to mate and become pregnant again. If the infant is successful, it reduces the magnitude of sibling competition with mother's next-born offspring, at a cost to mother's reproductive success.

Even more dramatic examples of this pattern are found in Galapagos fur seals where fatal sibling rivalry is a routine outcome of triadic interactions. In these seals, a pup from the previous year is frequently present alongside a newborn pup. Short inter-birth intervals portend trouble for both the younger offspring and its mother (Trillmich & Wolf, 2008). Pups born without an older sibling present enjoy very high (94%) survival over their first month, but those odds plummet to only 31% if a yearling or 2-year-old sib is present due to a combination of causes—maternal neglect, sibling aggression, suckling competition with the older sibling. Pups born to mothers with an older dependent sibling paid a prenatal cost as well, being born smaller due to the extra costs of lactation during pregnancy. Mothers too pay a reproductive cost; non-reproductive females have a 91% probability of giving birth in a given year, lactating females only 35%.

Shorter inter-birth intervals (1 vs. 2 years) accentuate an asymmetric sibling competition with the burden falling disproportionately on the younger offspring. Galapagos seal mothers initially defend newborns against their older, stronger siblings, but acquiesce to the older sibling's demands if they persist in their demand to continue nursing, with usually fatal consequences for the newborn (Trillmich & Wolf, 2008). Whether the older sibling persists appears to be conditional on whether it is large enough to forage on its own. In extreme cases an older sibling may attempt to drag a newborn away from their mother, resulting in a tug-of-war with the unfortunate younger pup caught fatally between (Trillmich, pers. comm. in Mock & Parker, 1997, p. 322).

Despotism in sibling triads

Parent birds often structure their families into castes of "core" and "marginal" offspring by controlling the timing of hatching of their eggs. Mechanistically this is easily done by varying the onset of incubation. If incubation commences after the last egg is laid, all nestlings hatch more or less simultaneously. If it commences on the penultimate egg, as is often the case, the last egg hatches after the remainder of the clutch, creating a single marginal offspring or "runt" alongside older, even-aged siblings. This last-hatched nestling suffers lower growth and higher mortality than its older brood-mates, especially as brood size grows.

This dynamic is well studied in red-winged blackbirds, an archetypal North American songbird. Nestling blackbirds engage in non-aggressive begging competitions for parentally delivered food and older, stronger nestlings are more successful than their younger nestmates by virtue of their ability to stretch their necks higher, and present themselves as more conspicuous targets for parents with food. Crowding is evident in larger broods as nestlings generally grow more slowly and suffer higher mortality (Forbes, Thornton, Glassey, Forbes, & Buckley, 1997; Forbes & Glassey, 2000; Forbes, Glassey, Thornton, & Earle, 2001). But the costs of crowding do not befall all nestlings equally. It is the last-hatched runts that bear the brunt of any food shortfalls, and the effect of additional core siblings on runt survival is dramatic. In doubleton broods with a single older offspring alongside the runt, the two nestlings fare almost equally well. But if a second "core" offspring is added to the brood (i.e., one matching the age and size of the larger nestmate), the survival of the runt (but not the survival of its core sibling) falls sharply. In this sibling triad, the begging dynamic has changed from the simple competition between older core sib and smaller runt. Now there are two levels of competition at work. The oldest sibling is now competing against an equal, resulting in an escalated begging competition between the two. And the runt now faces the challenge of competing against two older siblings that are begging more intensely, exaggerating the effect of the competitive handicap it faces. As brood size grows, the problem for the runt only grows worse. The begging competition among the core brood grows more intense, leaving the runt in an ever more vulnerable position, and its survival falls sharply while the survival of core offspring changes little. One wonders whether a similar dynamic could hold for human families, where younger children are afflicted by competition among older siblings and/or playmates.

Parental Manipulation of Sibling Rivalry

The most spectacular sibling rivalries occur among contemporary offspring competing in broods or litters for finite parental resources. Curiously, parents effectively choreograph these competitions, and indeed play favorites. Parental control of the process stems from two key decisions: the choice of family size; and establishing competitive handicaps among brood/litter members. Both are primarily maternal decisions in birds and mammals, though both can in principle be influenced indirectly by male partners—e.g., a female bird may lay more eggs if her mate delivers more food during the courtship period. Larger families lead to higher food demands and increase the likelihood of conflict. In some cases the presence of one extra mouth to feed can spell the difference between harmony and discord.

Among nestling cattle egrets the fighting that often leads to siblicidal brood reduction is common in three-chick broods but if a chick is experimentally removed a near cessation of all hostilities ensues. If an experimentally removed chick is restored to brood the fighting begins anew (Mock & Lamey, 1991). The chicks evidently can count to three and obey the simple behavioral rule: fight if in a trio; stop fighting if only two. The immediate trigger for aggression is brood size and from an evolutionary perspective the difference between three and two chicks is the prospect of future food shortfall. Parents can easily provision two chicks, but in some seasons there is not sufficient food for three. But when food levels are adequate for all, the last-hatched chick remains sufficiently strong to withstand the inimical effects of sibling aggression. In this case parents derive a reproductive benefit from its presence, hence the initial choice of the brood size that leads predictably to sibling aggression.

In birds, when one hatches relative to one's siblings is often the single most important determinant of future life prospects. If a nestling hatches before, or at worst at the same time as, its brothers and sisters (core offspring), it typically enjoys good prospects for future growth and survival. But if it has the misfortune to hatch a day or more after its brood-mates (as a marginal offspring), its future prospects wane. This reaches an extreme in species that practice the grim habit of obligate siblicide.

Determining whether a nonhuman animal experiences emotion is a tricky business, as it is in human infants (Hart, Carrington, Tronick, & Carroll, 2004; Legerstee, Ellenbogen, Nienhuis, & Marsh, this volume, Chapter 9). But animals certainly encounter conditions that would evoke fear or jealousy in humans. One wonders, for example, whether a baby black eaglet knows the sensation of fear or experiences foreboding. After a long six-week residency in an egg, it readies itself for life in the nest and its future rests upon the flip of a Darwinian coin. If it hatches from the first of the two eggs laid by its mother, then its future is secure. The eaglet is likely to receive ample food from its parents, and grow to be a large, robust predator that may live for decades. But if it has the misfortune to hatch from the second of the two eggs in the clutch, its expected lifespan is measured in hours not years. Its older brother or sister has a 3- to 7-day head start and a genetically embedded streak of mean. The older eaglet will commence an assault on its younger sibling almost immediately after junior hatches, battering and bludgeoning its nestmate relentlessly until only a bloody corpse is left. And unless its senior sibling is weakened by a congenital handicap, our younger eaglet is doomed. As the day of hatching approaches, it can probably sense its surroundings: it can hear the peeping and rustling of its older, larger sibling. Of course we do not know the internal emotional state of our eaglet, but fear would seem logical in such circumstances and perhaps adaptive if it was coupled to a behavioral response—e.g., hormonal priming for aggression just in case its older sib is one of those rare weaklings.

Chemical brothers

Mothers can also influence the outcome of sibling rivalry by providing certain progeny with a chemical assist. This has been best studied in birds where mothers often fortify certain eggs in the clutch with steroid hormones (Schwabl, Mock, & Gieg, 1997; Sockman & Schwabl, 2000; Groothuis, Müller, von Engelhardt, Carere, & Eising, 2005). A testosterone boost in some species, e.g., canaries, enhances begging effort which can translate into faster growth and higher survival (Schwabl, 1996). Some birds add extra steroids to last-laid eggs, which tends to diminish the handicap of hatching last, whereas in others the opposite is true, exaggerating the effects of hatching asynchrony.

Overall this system of offspring manipulation is complex: mothers appear to be able to manipulate offspring phenotype flexibly in response to environmental conditions using a non-genetic mechanism (Groothuis et al., 2005). And such manipulations may not be without cost. Royle, Surai, and Hartley (2001), for example, suggest that high androgen levels may depress the immune system of nestlings, favoring the addition of antioxidants to eggs to offset this effect.

Hormones have been studied in relation to sibling aggression in birds, and show a hormonal link to social, or perhaps more accurately, antisocial behavior. A comparison of two closely related seabirds—obligately siblicidal Nazca boobies and facultatively siblicidal blue-footed boobies—shows a strong hormonal link to sibling violence. Blue-footed boobies lack lethal aggression as neonates, whereas in Nazca boobies, the elder nestling in the characteristic two-chick brood unconditionally attacks and kills its younger nestmate shortly after hatching (Anderson, 1989; Müller, Brennecke, Porter, Ottinger, & Anderson, 2008); recent work shows that Nazca boobies are primed for aggression, being born with treble the level of circulating androgen of blue-footed boobies (Müller et al., 2008). And androgen levels respond to the likelihood of aggression, as testosterone (T) levels are temporarily elevated around the time of fights (Ferree, Wikelskib, & Anderson, 2004).

An extraordinary by-product of this early hormonal surge is that it apparently affects adult social and sexual behavior. Some adult Nazca boobies visit unrelated nestlings and display a mixture of courtship and parental behavior, aggression, and sexual behavior to varying degrees toward unguarded nestlings (Anderson et al., 2004). Recent work by Müller et al. (2008) shows a link between siblicidal violence as a neonate and the aggressive component of the behavior of these non-parental adult visitors toward the nestlings. It appears that in this species aberrant adult social behavior is conditioned by early androgen exposure as a neonate during a sensitive period of development.

The study of jealousy in nonhuman families is complicated by the fact that we cannot enquire directly about an individual's emotional state—it must be inferred by behavioral or physiological indices. The study of hormonal profiles potentially provides both the objective index and a possible translation system between human and nonhuman families.

Do Parents Interfere in Sibling Aggression?

A curious feature about sibling aggression in birds is that parents most often do nothing to prevent fighting among their offspring. Parental interference in sibling aggression in birds is uncommon, though examples are known. Parent bald eagles intervened in 9% of bouts of fighting between sibs (Wiebe & Bortolotti, 2000), and in egrets the simple presence of parents at the nest seemed to attenuate the intensity of sibling aggression even though parents took no obvious steps to interfere (Mock & Parker, 1997).

In spotted hyenas that routinely raise two-cub litters consisting of a dominant and subordinate offspring, mothers do intervene in bouts of aggression (White, 2008). They are one of the few mammals to practice facultative siblicide and its occurrence appears to reflect prevailing nutritional conditions: siblicide is more likely when food is short (Golla, Hofer, & East, 1999). Fighting is most common when both cubs attempt to suckle, and dominant sibs are more aggressive than subordinates. Similar to siblicidal birds, dominants sibs show higher growth and lower mortality than subordinate cubs (Golla et al., 1999). The often substantial size asymmetries among littermates lead to dominant sibs monopolizing maternal milk supplies and socially enforced starvation of subordinate cubs (Hofer & East, 1997). Mother hyenas use a variety of strategies—punishing, pacifying, physical separation—to modulate sibling aggression and protect the subordinate pup (White, 2008). Maternal behavior was influenced by a mother's dominance status: high-ranking mothers tended to punish both cubs during bouts of aggression; low-ranking mothers select-ively punished the dominant cub, which may relate to a greater likelihood of food stress in these families.

Conflict Resolution over Sibling Rivalry in Mammals and Birds

Evolutionary biologists have devoted considerable attention to the resolution of evolutionary (genetic) conflict among siblings and parents and offspring (reviews in Mock & Parker, 1997; Mock, 2004; Forbes, 2005). Much less attention has been focused on the mechanisms to resolve behavioral conflicts among siblings. Wiebe and Bortolotti (2000) present a taxonomy of parental responses to sibling aggres-sion in birds and their work can be applied more broadly. They describe both general remedial behaviors and acute responses to aggression and I present a modified version of their taxonomy here. The mechanisms of conflict resolution for contemporary siblings in mammals and birds can be usefully divided into five categories:

1 *Physical separation.* Overt conflict may be avoided by physically separating the offending parties. In a variety of birds brood division occurs after fledging: the brood is divided after the offspring leave the nest, allowing parents to reduce or eliminate the potential for sibling conflict (Slagsvold, 1997). And in hyenas, as described above, mothers may separate pups to minimize aggressive interactions among contemporary siblings.
2 *Intimidation/Subordination.* In the minority of vertebrate species that employ aggression in sibling interactions, intimidation/subordination is a nonlethal means to resolve conflict (Drummond, 2006). Drummond divides dominance relationships into six categories:
  a) *Aggression–submission*, where one offspring is habitually aggressive and the other responds submissively. Such behavior occurs in blue-footed boo-bies, osprey, and western grebes.

b) *Aggression–aggression*, where both brood-mates are aggressive. Here the dominant individual will overwhelm the other and the subordinate may attempt to evade the aggression of the dominant by crouching or hiding. Such behavior occurs in brown and Nazca boobies and black eagles.

c) *Aggression resistance*, where there are repeated fights between individuals reluctant to adopt the subordinate role. Such behavior occurs in cattle egrets where the nestling hierarchy is established by violent pecking. In three-chick broods, fighting is most intense between the youngest dyad, and the subordinate chick retaliates when attacked.

d) *Aggression avoidance*, where there are dominant and subordinate roles, but the subordinate offspring learns to avoid its dominant sibling. Such behavior occurs in precocial American oystercatchers (a large shorebird) where subordinate chicks flee and hide when in the presence of a dominant sibling.

e) *Rotating dominance*, where there are aggressive dominant and submissive subordinate roles among offspring, but these are not permanent and rotate among members of the group. Such behavior occurs in crested ibis where in older broods, the first chick to peck at its brood-mates is dominant when a parent arrives at the nest with food, and the remaining chicks adopt submissive postures (Li, Li, Ma, Zhai, & Drummond, 2004). The dominant chick remains so until another chick rises up and pecks it, supplanting the until-now dominant chick, which now adopts a submissive posture. The dominant role rotates among brood members.

f) *Flock dominance*, where self-feeding offspring associate in mobile flocks. In aggressive encounters, one offspring assumes the dominant role, the other the submissive role. This kind of behavior is common in ducks, geese and chickens.

Which form of dominance is employed is a function of the feeding mode (whether food is defendable or not; whether offspring are fed by parents as in altricial species or are self-feeding as in precocial species; fighting ability of the participants and the cost of subordination. Flock dominance occurs among self-feeding offspring, whereas aggression is most likely when the brood or litter is found in a confined space. When the cost of subordination is low, aggression submission or rotating dominance is more likely; aggression–aggression or aggression resistance is more likely when the cost of subordination is high—e.g., a subordinate faces a much increased likelihood of death (Drummond, 2006).

3 *Punishment.* Parents may punish aggressive or selfish siblings. Horned grebes are aquatic birds that feed their swimming chicks on ponds, lakes, and sloughs. Parents often chase away older siblings when attempting to feed younger chicks (Ferguson & Sealy, 1983). Parent moorhens that similarly feed swimming young on marshes and ponds often "tousle" chicks that approach for food. They grab their head or neck and shake the chick from side to side.

Leonard, Horn, and Eden (1988) observed that all chicks in most broods were "tousled" by their parents at some time. This behavior appears to serve to reduce food demands by individual chicks, potentially reducing sibling competition. In skuas (large gull-like birds) parents often intervene aggressively in chick fights, discouraging the dominant chick from feeding from the same parent as the subordinate chick (Young, 1963). And as described above, mother hyenas and fur seals often punish aggressive offspring.

4   *Distraction or deception.* Parents sometimes manipulate the occurrence of sibling aggression by either distracting or deceiving their progeny. Parent skuas, for example, sometimes interrupt sibling aggression by calling alarm in the absence of a predator (Spellerberg, 1971). Bald eagles and ospreys appear to use false-feeding to stop nestlings from fighting: parents adopt a posture indistinguishable from the normal feeding of nestlings, but do not present any real food, either offering nothing at all, or presenting an inedible stick (Wiebe & Bortolotti, 2000; personal observation). Eagles and ospreys may also use genuine feeding to interrupt sibling aggression, either by resuming the presentation of a partially eaten food item, or by picking scraps of food from the bottom of the nest (Wiebe & Bortolotti, 2000; personal observation).

5   *Bribery.* Parents may manage the opportunity for sibling aggression by manipulating the size and/or schedule of meals. Where hunger is a proximate trigger for aggression, as in ospreys, bald eagles, great blue herons, and blue-footed boobies, parents may avert aggression in three ways: by simply bringing more food (Ellis, 1979; Collopy, 1984; Wiebe & Bortolotti, 2000); by clumping food deliveries so that weaker sibs may feed when stronger sibs are sated (Mock, 1987; Viñuela, 1999); or by bringing back food in large packages that cannot be easily monopolized by individual offspring (Mock, 1985).

Conflict Resolution over Sibling Rivalry at an Evolutionary Level

What I have described above are behavioral mechanisms of conflict resolution—the proximate level of causation—over sibling rivalry which have received only modest attention from biologists. Conflict resolution at the ultimate (evolutionary) level has received much more attention (O'Connor, 1978; Parker & Macnair, 1979; Parker, 1985; Parker, Mock, & Lamey, 1989; Forbes & Ydenberg, 1992; Forbes, 1993; Godfray, 1995; Johnstone 1996; Mock & Parker, 1997; Parker, Royle, & Hartley, 2002a, 2002b).

In sexually reproducing species, genetic conflict is expected among siblings and between parents and offspring (review in Mock & Parker, 1997). How these conflicts are resolved will depend on which party has the power to affect the behavioral outcome (Mock & Forbes, 1992). For example, salmon fry may "prefer" to hatch from a larger egg, but since its mother is long dead when it hatches, the offspring has no power to influence its parent's decision. Where offspring cannot influence how parents allocate critical resources such as food, "parent wins" is the default outcome. But where siblings can influence how resources are shared, e.g., via psychological or other physical manipulation, the offspring can potentially move the behavioral outcome in their preferred direction.

Examples of such conflict between parents and offspring are evident in human pregnancy as well. Hormones produced by the embryo that cross the placental barrier trigger both gestational diabetes and pre-eclampsia (high blood pressure) in pregnant women (Haig, 1993). Both serve to increase nutrient flow to the developing embryo at a cost to mother. More generally, where both parties (contemporary siblings; parents and offspring) can potentially affect the behavioral outcome, a pro rata compromise balanced by the costs to each party is the expected result: neither party gets its ideal outcome, with parents providing more than they desire, offspring getting less than they want (Mock & Parker, 1997).

Sibling Harmony and the Cost of Selfishness

Human sibs closer in age are more likely to develop friendships and share interests and activities (Hart, 2001). Among birds and (other) mammals, there are sibling synergies and mutualisms that are key to growth and survival. Conversely, selfish behavior limits the potential of cooperation, and at the extreme, killing a sibling may eliminate a potential competitor for resources but also a potential partner and ally in future social interactions.

Many of the most spectacular examples of sibling harmony are found among the eusocial insects, the ants, bees, termites, and wasps, where all-female castes of workers assist their mother to raise more sisters while forgoing their own reproduction; in the honey ants sterile "replete" or honeypot workers serve as food storage organs for other colony members, their abdomens ballooning to the size of small grapes (Wilson, 1971; Børgesen, 2000).

Some of this caste differentiation occurs through the process of "polyphenism" where individuals with identical genotypes can develop radically different architectures based upon developmental switches that are turned on or off by environmental or hormonal cues. For example, an external hormone secreted at a sensitive time in development can suppress the development of wings in the worker caste of ants and bees, or trigger the development of oversized mandibles in the soldier caste of ants and termites. This is not an example of nature versus nurture—it is nurture coupled intimately with nature. A common genetic program creates the potential for multiple discrete pathways and which pathway is followed is affected by the local environment.

In vertebrates, examples of sibling symbiosis are perhaps less dramatic than in the eusocial insects but are nonetheless widespread (Forbes, 2007). For example, brood- and litter-mates in birds and mammals share warmth to mutual benefit; ospreys with surviving brood-mates learn foraging skills faster when they leave the nest (Edwards, 1989). In wild turkeys, brothers assist brothers in attracting mates in cooperative courtship. Even though subordinates do not themselves reproduce, they benefit indirectly by enhancing the reproductive success of their brothers (Krakauer, 2005). For dominant siblings there is an obvious and powerful incentive for keeping subordinate siblings around.

Birds, Bees, and Humans?

How does the study of sibling rivalry in birds and bees help us to understand sibling rivalry in humans? Serious work in this area is still nascent. For a parallel, consider that as recently as the 1970s the default assumption for the study of infanticide among animals was that such behavior was pathological (Hausfater & Hrdy, 1984), largely because infanticide seemed unlikely to be adaptive. Only when this behavior was studied systematically did it dawn upon herpetologists, ornithologists, and mammalogists that infanticide—including siblicide—was a routine feature of family life in many species. But if such behavior were pathological, it became increasingly difficult to explain its frequency: whole species were exhibiting apparently maladaptive behavior! As the documentation of such behavior grew, so did the possibility that this widespread mayhem was not merely an aberration which led to a fairer consideration of the biological alternative: it soon became clear that parent and offspring interests were not always congruent (Hamilton, 1964a, 1964b; Trivers, 1974), and that some parental actions led directly to sibling conflict—e.g., parent pelicans, eagles, and boobies lay a second egg not because they intend to raise two offspring—they do not—but rather to insure against failure of their first egg to hatch. If both hatch, the second chick is redundant to the parents, and a potentially lethal competitor to the first-hatched progeny.

Obligate siblicide represents an extreme, and such behavior does not translate obviously to any human equivalent. But the more modest forms of sibling rivalry that are ubiquitous in species with extensive parental care—the scrambles for food and begging competitions—resemble more closely the dynamics that occur in human families. Understanding the rules that govern these competitions has the potential to help us better understand ourselves. But progress in this area requires that we dismiss the myth that all conflict within human families is a symptom of dysfunction. Conflict in families in general and sibling rivalry in particular is a normal part of our behavioral repertoire and likely subject to similar rules that govern other organisms. A useful starting point for such investigations is not to assume that we are exempt from the rules that govern the rest of nature and that have been honed by a long history of natural selection. This is the first hurdle that must be overcome before we can apply animal behavior to human behavior.

A second hurdle is the widespread misunderstanding about "biological" origins of behavior. An unfortunate etymological accident has resulted in the term "biological" becoming a shorthand term for genetic determinism. Biologists study both the genetic and environmental antecedents of behavior, and the myriad ways in which they intertwine, including cultural (non-genetic) transmission.

Animal behaviorists operate from the premise that behavior is subject to natural selection no differently than the fin of a fish or the wing of a bird. Some selection of behavior results in instinctive and reflexive outcomes. Examples would include textbook cases of fixed action patterns and sign stimuli: incubating geese rolling displaced eggs back into the nest, or spawning stickleback fish responding not to fish-shaped models, but to non-fish-shaped models colored red, the signature of another male and potential rival. These simple rules were derived from the pioneering work of early ethologists such as Tinbergen, von Frisch, and Lorenz who quite justly shared a Nobel Prize for this work in 1972. But this represents only a starting point for the study of animal behavior, not a finished product. Such simple examples are useful entry points to the discipline but do not capture the complex underpinnings of most interesting behaviors in nature. There is an obvious parallel to the early study of transmission genetics. The Bavarian monk Gregor Mendel, working with the simple traits of garden pea plants, deciphered the fundamental laws of how genes are transmitted from generation to generation. Part of Mendel's genius was to focus on simple traits—one gene, two alleles, one dominant and one recessive. The results obtained were neat, clean, and now feature prominently in every introduction to genetics.

But if we wish to understand most interesting human traits, Mendel's laws, though necessary, are not sufficient. Most traits are affected by multiple—often many—genes of differing effect. The expression of one gene may be affected by the presence or absence of a second or third gene. Simple dominant–recessive relationships may not hold. In some cases the expression of a gene depends upon whether it came from mother or father. Mendel was not wrong—just incomplete. The work of the early ethologists was not wrong—just incomplete. Most interesting behaviors are more than simple and inflexible stimulus–response rules. Behavioral ecology is a field that has grown out of classical ethology: it integrates ecological conditions and learning (=environment) with evolved behavioral programs.

Behaviors with a genetic basis are often plastic in relation to ecological context, as the best response (that maximizing fitness) may differ dramatically in different contexts. Facultative brood reduction, which is normally a by-product of sibling rivalry, is an archetypal example. When food is short, the best response for an older, stronger sibling may well be to eliminate its younger sibling, a potential competitor for food. But when food is plentiful, such behavior is wasteful and an inappropriate response. Red-winged blackbirds practice facultative brood reduction via a sometimes fatal sibling rivalry. When food is short, older, stronger siblings outcompete younger nestmates for food, and the latter perish due to socially enforced starvation.

Spadefoot toad tadpoles have a built-in genetic program that contains a developmental switch: If conditions are benign they grow slowly and large as peaceful herbivores grazing on algae in their natal pond. But if the pond begins to dry too quickly, a switch is flipped triggering the development of huge predatory jaws that enable them to cannibalize other tadpoles, often including siblings (Pfennig, 1992). This developmental pathway allows the tadpoles to develop more quickly and escape the pond before it and they dry out. But this program lies dormant unless needed in exigent circumstances, and often is not invoked at all. Both the genetic program and the ecological circumstances determine the outcome. Thus, plentiful resources curb selfish tendencies; scarcity accentuates them. A complex blend of genes and environment governs the expression of sibling rivalry in animals as diverse as blackbirds and bonobos. One wonders if the same is true in humans.

References

Anderson, D. J. (1989). The role of hatching asynchrony in siblicidal brood reduction of two booby species. *Behavioral Ecology and Sociobiology, 25*, 363–368.

Anderson, D. J., Porter, E. T., & Ferree, E. D. (2004). Non-breeding Nazca boobies (Sula granti) show social and sexual interest in chicks: Behavioral and ecological aspects. *Behaviour, 141*, 959–977.

Beg, M. A., & Ginther, O. J. (2006). Follicle selection in cattle and horses: Role of intrafollicular factors. *Reproduction, 132*, 365–377.

Blanchard, R. (2004). Quantitative and theoretical analyses of the relation between older brothers and homosexuality in men. *Journal of Theoretical Biology, 230*, 173–187.

Blanchard, R., & Bogaert, A. F. (1996). Homosexuality in men and number of older brothers. *American Journal of Psychiatry, 153*, 27–31.

Blanchard, R., Cantora, J. M., Bogaert, A. F., Breedlove, S. M., & Ellis, L. (2006). Interaction of fraternal birth order and handedness in the development of male homosexuality. *Hormones and Behavior, 49*, 405–414.

Blanchard, R., & Klassen, P. (1997). H-Y antigen and homosexuality in men. *Journal of Theoretical Biology, 185*, 373–378.

Børgesen, L. W. (2000). Nutritional function of replete workers in the pharaoh's ant, Monomorium pharaonis (L.). *Insectes Sociaux, 47*, 141–146.

Cash, K. J., & Evans, R. M. (1986). Brood reduction in the American white pelican (Pelecanus erythrohynchos). *Behavioral Ecology and Sociobiology, 18*, 413–418.

Clark, C. B. (1977). A preliminary report on weaning among chimpanzees of the Gombe National Park, Tanzania. In S. Chevalier-Skolnikoff & F. E. Poirier (Eds.), *Primate biosocial development* (pp. 235–260). New York: Garland.

Clutton-Brock, T. H. (1991). *The evolution of parental care*. Princeton, NJ: Princeton University Press.

Clutton-Brock, T. H., Guinness, F. E., & Albon, S. D. (1982). *Red deer. Behavior and ecology of the two sexes.* Chicago: University of Chicago Press.

Collopy, M. W. (1984). Parental care and feeding ecology of golden eagle nestlings. *Auk, 101,* 753–760.

Drummond, H. (2006). Dominance in vertebrate broods and litters. *Quarterly Review of Biology, 81,* 3–32.

Drummond, H., & Garcia Chavelas, C. (1989). Food shortage influences sibling aggression in the blue-footed booby. *Animal Behaviour, 37,* 806–820.

Edwards, T. C. (1989). The ontogeny of diet selection in fledgling ospreys. *Ecology, 70,* 881–889.

Elgar, M. A., & Crespi, B. J. (1992). *Cannibalism: Ecology and evolution among diverse taxa.* New York: Oxford University Press.

Ellis, D. H. (1979). Development of behavior in the golden eagle. *Wildlife Monographs, 70,* 1–94.

Ferguson, R. S., & Sealy, S. G. (1983). Breeding ecology of the horned grebe, Podiceps auritus, in Southwestern Manitoba. *Canadian Field Naturalist, 97,* 401–408.

Ferree, E. D., Wikelskib, M. C., & Anderson D. J. (2004). Hormonal correlates of siblicide in Nazca boobies: Support for the Challenge Hypothesis. *Hormones and Behavior, 46,* 655–662.

Forbes, L. S. (1993). Avian brood reduction and parent–offspring "conflict." *American Naturalist, 142,* 82–117.

Forbes, L. S., & Ydenberg, R. C. (1992). Sibling rivalry in a variable environment. *Theoretical Population Biology, 41,* 135–160.

Forbes, S. (2005). *A natural history of families.* Princeton, NJ: Princeton University Press.

Forbes, S. (2007). Sibling symbiosis in nestling birds. *Auk, 124,* 1–10.

Forbes, S., & Glassey, B. (2000). Asymmetric sibling rivalry and nestling growth in red-winged blackbirds. *Behavioral Ecology and Sociobiology, 48,* 413–417.

Forbes, S., Glassey, B., Thornton, S., & Earle, L. (2001). The secondary adjustment of clutch size in red-winged blackbirds (Agelaius phoeniceus). *Behavioral Ecology and Sociobiology, 50,* 37–44.

Forbes, S., Thornton, S., Glassey, B, Forbes, M., & Buckley, N. (1997). Why parent birds play favourites. *Nature, 390,* 351–352.

Gargett, V. (1977). Sibling aggression in the Black Eagle in the Matopos, Rhodesia. *Ostrich, 49,* 57–63.

Gilmore, R. G., Dodrill, J. W., & Linley, P. A. (1983). Reproductive and embryonic development of the sandtiger shark, *Odontaspis taurus* (Rafinesque). *Fish Bulletin, 81,* 201–225.

Godfray, H. C. J. (1995). Signaling of need between parents and young: Parent–offspring conflict and sibling rivalry. *American Naturalist, 146,* 1–24.

Golla, W., Hofer, H., & East, M. L. (1999). Within-litter sibling aggression in spotted hyenas: Effect of maternal nursing, sex and age. *Animal Behaviour, 58,* 715–726.

Gonzalez-Voyer, A., Székely, T., & Drummond, H. (2007). Why do some siblings attack each other? Comparative analysis of aggression in avian broods. *Evolution, 61,* 1946–1955.

Groothuis, T. G. G., Müller, W., von Engelhardt, N., Carere, C., & Eising, C. (2005). Maternal hormones as a tool to adjust offspring phenotype in avian species. *Neuroscience and Biobehavioral Reviews, 29,* 329–352.

Haig, D. (1993). Genetic conflicts in human pregnancy. *Quarterly Review of Biology, 68*, 495–532.

Hamilton, W. D. (1964a). The genetical evolution of social behaviour I. *Journal of Theoretical Biology, 7*, 1–16.

Hamilton, W. D. (1964b). The genetical evolution of social behaviour II. *Journal of Theoretical Biology, 7*, 17–52.

Hart, S. (2001). *Preventing sibling rivalry.* New York: Free Press.

Hart, S. L., Carrington, H. A., Tronick, E. Z., & Carroll, S. R. (2004). When infants lose exclusive maternal attention: Is it jealousy? *Infancy, 6*, 57–78.

Hausfater, G., & Hrdy, S. B. (1984). *Infanticide: Comparative and evolutionary perspectives.* New York: Aldine.

Hofer, H., & East, M. L. (1997). Skewed offspring sex ratios and sex composition of twin litters in Serengeti spotted hyenas (Crocuta crocuta) are a consequence of siblicide. *Applied Animal Behaviour Science, 51*, 307–316.

Johnstone, R. A. (1996). Begging signals and parent–offspring conflict: Do parents always win? *Proceedings of the Royal Society of London Series B, 263*, 1677–1681.

Joung, S.-J., & Hsu, H.-H. (2005). Reproduction and embryonic development of the Shortfin Mako, Isurus oxyrinchus Rafinesque, 1810, in the Northwestern Pacific. *Zoological Studies, 44*, 487–496.

Knight, P. G., & Glister, C. (2006). TGF-β superfamily members and ovarian follicle development. *Reproduction, 132*, 191–206.

Krakauer, A. H. (2005). Kin selection and cooperative courtship in wild turkeys. *Nature, 434*, 69–72.

Legerstee, M., Ellenbogen, B., Nienhuis, T., & Marsh, H. (this volume). Social bonds, triadic relationships, and goals: Preconditions for the emergence of human jealousy. In S. L. Hart & M. Legerstee (Eds.), *Handbook of jealousy: Theory, research, and multidisciplinary approaches.* Malden, MA: Wiley-Blackwell.

Leonard, M. L., Horn, A. G., & Eden, S. F. (1988). Parent–offspring aggression in moorhens. *Behavioral Ecology and Sociobiology, 23*, 265–270.

Li, X., Li, D., Ma, Z., Zhai, T., & Drummond, H. (2004). Ritualized aggression and unstable dominance in broods of the crested ibis (Niponia nippon). *Wilson Bulletin, 116*, 172–176.

Maestripieri, D. (2002). Parent–offspring conflict in primates. *International Journal of Primatology, 23*, 923–951.

Mock, D. W. (1984). Infanticide, siblicide, and avian nestling mortality. In G. Hausfater & S. B. Hrdy (Eds.), *Infanticide: Comparative and evolutionary perspectives* (pp. 3–30). New York: Aldine.

Mock, D. W. (1985). Siblicidal brood reduction: The prey-size hypothesis. *American Naturalist, 125*, 327–343.

Mock, D. W. (1987). Siblicide, parent–offspring conflict, and unequal parental investment. *Behavioral Ecology and Sociobiology, 20*, 247–256.

Mock, D. W. (2004). *More than kin and less than kind.* Cambridge, MA: Belknap Press.

Mock, D. W., & Forbes, L. S. (1992). Parent–offspring conflict: A case of arrested development. *Trends in Ecology and Evolution, 7*, 409–413.

Mock, D. W., & Forbes, L. S. (1995). The evolution of parental optimism. *Trends in Ecology and Evolution, 10*, 130–134.

Mock, D. W., & Lamey, T. C. (1991). The role of brood size in regulating egret sibling aggression. *American Naturalist, 138*, 1015–1026.

Mock, D. W., & Parker, G. A. (1997). *The evolution of sibling rivalry.* Oxford: Oxford University Press.

Müller, M. S., Brennecke, J. F., Porter, E. T., Ottinger, M. A., & Anderson, D. J. (2008). Perinatal androgens and adult behavior vary with nestling social system in siblicidal boobies. *PLoS ONE 3*(6): e2460. doi:10.1371/journal.pone.0002460.

Niemeyer, C. L., & Anderson, J. R. (1983). Primate harassment of matings. *Ethology and Sociobiology, 4*, 205–220.

O'Connor, R. J. (1978). Brood reduction in birds: Selection for fratricide, infanticide and suicide? *Animal Behaviour, 26*, 79–96.

O'Gara, B. W. (1969). Unique aspects of reproduction in the female pronghorn (Antilocapra americana Ord.). *American Journal of Anatomy, 125*, 217–259.

Parker, G. A. (1985). Models of parent–offspring conflict. V. Effects of the behaviour of the two parents. *Animal Behavior, 33*, 519–533.

Parker, G. A., & Macnair, M. R. (1979). Models of parent–offspring conflict. IV. Suppression: Evolutionary retaliation by the parent. *Animal Behaviour, 27*, 1210–1235.

Parker, G. A., Mock, D. W., & Lamey, T. C. (1989). How selfish should stronger sibs be? *American Naturalist, 133*, 846–868.

Parker, G. A., Royle, N. J., & Hartley, I. R. (2002a). Begging scrambles with unequal chicks: Interactions between need and competitive ability. *Ecology Letters, 5*, 206–215.

Parker, G. A., Royle, N. J., & Hartley, I. R. (2002b). Intrafamilial conflict and parental investment: A synthesis. *Philosophical Transactions of the Royal Society B: Biological Sciences, 357*, 295–307.

Perry, J. C., & Roitberg, B. D. (2005). Ladybird mothers mitigate offspring starvation risk by laying trophic eggs. *Behavioral Ecology and Sociobiology, 58*, 578–586.

Pfennig, D. W. (1992). Polyphenism in spadefoot toad tadpoles as a logically adjusted evolutionarily stable strategy. *Evolution, 46*, 1408–1420.

Preston, S. H. (1978). *The effect of infant and child mortality on fertility.* New York: Academic Press.

Royle, N. J., Surai, P. F., & Hartley, I. R. (2001). Maternal derived androgens and antioxidants in bird eggs: Complementary but opposing effects? *Behavioral Ecology, 12*, 381–385.

Ryan, B. C., & Vandenbergh, J. G. (2002). Intrauterine position effects. *Neuroscience and Biobehavioral Reviews, 26*, 665–678.

Schwabl, H. (1996). Maternal testosterone in the egg enhances postnatal growth. *Comparative Biochemistry and Physiology, 114*, 271–276.

Schwabl, H., Mock, D. W., & Gieg, J. A. (1997). A hormonal mechanism for parental favouritism. *Nature, 386*, 231.

Slagsvold, T. (1997). Brood division in birds in relation to offspring size: Sibling rivalry and parental control. *Animal Behaviour, 54*, 1357–1368.

Sockman, K. W., & Schwabl, H. (2000). Yolk androgens reduce offspring survival. *Proceedings of the Royal Society of London, Series B, 267*, 1451–1456.

Spellerberg, I. F. (1971). Breeding behaviour of the McCormick skua Catharacta maccormicki in Antarctica. *Ardea, 59*, 189–230.

Stinson, C. H. (1979). On the selective advantage of fratricide in raptors. *Evolution, 33*, 1219–1225.

Trillmich, F., & Wolf, J. B. W. (2008). Parent–offspring and sibling conflict in Galapagos fur seals and sea lions. *Behavioral Ecology and Sociobiology, 62*, 363–375.

Trivers, R. L. (1974). Parent–offspring conflict. *American Zoologist, 14*, 249–264.

van de Rijt-Plooij, H. H. C., & Plooij, F. X. (1987). Growing independence, conflict and learning in mother–infant relations in free-ranging chimpanzees. *Behaviour, 101*, 1–86.

Viñuela, J. (1999). Sibling aggression, hatching asynchrony, and nestling mortality in the black kite (Milvus migrans). *Behavioral Ecology and Sociobiology, 45*, 33–45.

White, P. P. (2008). Maternal response to neonatal sibling conflict in the spotted hyena, Crocuta crocuta. *Behavioral Ecology and Sociobiology, 62*, 353–361.

Wiebe, K. L., & Bortolotti, G. R. (2000). Parental interference in sibling aggression in birds: What should we look for? *Ecoscience, 7*, 1–9.

Wilson, E. O. (1971). *The insect societies.* Cambridge, MA: Belknap Press.

Young, E. C. (1963). The breeding behaviour of the South Polar Skua. *Ibis, 105*, 203–233.

8

Green Eyes in Bio-Cultural Frames

Vasudevi Reddy

In this commentary I explore issues that emerge from looking at jealousy with bio-cultural spectacles. Taking a biological perspective forces us to adopt a broad-brush look at this phenomenon, setting human jealousy in the context of similar behavior in species as wide ranging in this case as bald eagles, hyenas, and rats. It forces us to address our preoccupations with exclusivity in general and in particular with our experience of this complex emotion. It requires us to directly address the categorical hurdles often used to separate us from other animals, and older children from infants. Contrary to notions of biology as genetic or neuro-logical determinism or as implying nativism, however, these chapters have shown us that what is key to the biological underpinnings of jealousy (and emotion in general) is in fact its openness to experiential contexts, and hence culture, in its broadest sense. In conclusion I ask also one specific question in relation to jealousy—just how it is influenced by love.

I remember the most favorite uncle of my childhood in India sometimes teasingly using the phrase "Someone's feeling J . . ." with that typically rising teasing intonation inviting a response. The unspoken word attracted to itself much more significance, and a tantalizing sense of charm and of things unknown, than if it were simply a word uttered. The sense I had of this mysterious "J" (always imagined as a capital letter) was of something forbidden, an almost adult thing, something out of the ordinary, to be remarked upon with affection and amuse-ment. I didn't really know what it meant. I sensed it was something to be a little embarrassed about feeling—a feeling which I never was able to identify but only knew from a distance—but not to be really ashamed about. Not at that age anyway. I am not really sure I understand it much better now!

The topic opens up a fascinating set of as yet unanswered questions and these questions may well be the most striking contribution of the chapters in this book. Overtly the chapters focus on patterns of expressions of jealousy, its emergence across ages, across cultures, and in various species. But subtly, throughout these chapters, there are questions being posed which are profoundly

Handbook of Jealousy: Theory, Research and Multidisciplinary Approaches, First Edition.
Edited by Sybil L. Hart and Maria Legerstee.
© 2013 Blackwell Publishing Ltd. Published 2013 by Blackwell Publishing Ltd.

important for the human condition. One such question is the simple—perhaps even obvious—one of whether jealousy is a pathology or a valuable and adaptive capacity. Hart (this volume, Chapter 4) raises this issue using Darwin's classification (in terms of the chapters of his book) of jealousy among emotions of affection rather than among emotions of anger and rage. Tracing the historical course of the classification of jealousy as a negative emotion, Hart contrasts its modern roots in factor analysis with its 19th-century roots in participant observation. Although she does not focus on the methodological differences that give rise to different ways of thinking about this emotion, the link is intriguing. When involved with his son, fully sensitive to the affection that fueled his son's anxiety and anger, Darwin saw the latter as a corollary of love. In the context of an affectionate relationship, similarly, the teasing I describe at the start of this chapter was also embedded firmly within the warmth of an avuncular affection, and was perceived as such by the young recipient. Classifications deriving from more detached factor analyses of questionnaire data, however, are entirely free to choose their emphases independent of the origins or background of the phenomenon in question. The negativism that is dominant in the culmination of jealous feelings becomes, logically in this more detached method, the feature to focus upon.

But the question goes deeper than that. For every saying of cultural wisdom suggesting that the measure of jealousy is the measure of love, there is a cultural saying that claims the opposite. For instance, St. Augustine is believed to say that "he that is not jealous is not in love" while, attributed to the famous François, Duc de La Rochefoucauld (to whom, incidentally, is also attributed the thought that if we hadn't heard about being in love, no one would fall in love!) is the saying "In jealousy there is more self-love than love." Ultimately, the issue is one of possession and ownership. Do we—*should* we—own the love or attention or praise or touch that is given to us by another person? It is the owning or possessing that calls up Shakespeare's green-eyed monster, not upon the loss of the thing owned and felt as simple pain, but upon the perception of its possession by another person. Where does the sense of "mine-ness" come from? Another such question is that of equality—about the acceptance of inequality, about whether equality is even possible, and about how it might be defined for various animals and various situations. Still hinging on the issue of possession and ownership, jealous reactions seem to sit side by side with notions of fairness. Which is more fundamental: A sense of fair distribution of resources (for example, that one's rival should receive a fair share of attention or reward or recognition too)? Or a sense of the rights of ownership that come from possession (for example, that any attention or reward or recognition one has received should remain one's own)?

This book seems to be bringing down all sorts of walls. Approaching this dark and dramatic topic from a number of different directions, it seems to disregard boundaries—between ages, species, disciplines, and different conceptualizations of jealousy. Perhaps all it lacks is a perspective on jealousy from a totally alien culture.

Cultures of Jealousy?

What would a world without jealousy be like—a world without ownership, possession, and an overriding desire for exclusive relation? I cast my mind back along fragments of remembered anthropology and science fiction. I find an image of Ursula Le Guin's *The Dispossessed*—a story of an experiment with a non-hierarchical, non-totalitarian, and deeply anti-propertarian society, where material possessions are trivial and impermanent and social relationships unforced and largely unbound; where children are persuaded to share all things and to refer to all close adults as mother and father (Le Guin, 1974). This is fantasy. But then anthropology doesn't lag too far behind either. Ruth Benedict's description of the similarly Appollonian Zunis (the Pueblos of New Mexico) reveals a determinedly non-egoistical society in which both goods and attachment figures are shared, seemingly unproblematically. Adultery is reported to be no crime at all in this matrilineal society where it is the man who has the double family allegiance. Unfaithfulness is largely ignored on both sides, although women can "beat" the "other woman" ritually and can decide to end a marriage, and although this is not common, it is, according to Benedict, always done peacefully (Benedict, 1961).

I have often shared with students their disbelief when watching anthropological interviews with (often the last remaining) practitioner members of polyandrous societies where they talk of not getting jealous or upset or bothered at all by the presence of the "other" husband or when they see the signs of the other lover at the front door (see, for instance, Rivers, 1906, on the polyandrous Todas of South India and television programs showing interviews with contemporary Todas). It is impossible (from where we stand today) to believe that their sense of being—or at least a sense of well-being—isn't threatened or wounded by rivals for affection. After all, in polygamous communities the women are hardly innocent of turbulence and feelings of rejection. The harem might survive in general harmony, but not without its rivalries and attempted coups. Even Tikkana, a 13th-century Telugu poet in the south of India, depicting the poem as a bride, advises the husband—the poet—to protect the new bride from the jealous eyes of his other consorts. Even if the practices are of polygamy and a lack of possessiveness, the possibilities of jealous reactions seem no stranger to them, and jealousy has been reported in every culture studied (Buss, 2000). Nonetheless, whether these fictional worlds are ever achievable or these tribal dreams still realizable, there is no doubt that attitudes toward the possessing of things and people differ deeply, even amongst modern-day cultures. Stanley Kurtz's *All the Mothers Are One* paints a striking picture of Indian (even urban Indian) childhoods in which that seemingly most exclusive and inimitable of relationships—that of a child and its primary significant "other"—is also shareable (Kurtz, 1992). The multiplicity of mothers and children living in close proximity and sharing caregiving as well as authority and obedience promises significant implications for the forms and frequencies of jealousy.

Culture and the conceptualizations of differing cultures can be useful for our understanding of jealousy in a number of ways. The idea of a "problem space" (Leavens, Hopkins, & Bard, 2005) could be useful here for tracing the emergence of specific behaviors. This idea has been used to explore the local factors that influence the occurrence and forms of communicative behavior, such as pointing in infants and in apes. In other words, treating culture as crucial stresses a situational psychology where biological patterns can also be seen as "situated," emerging and meaningful only in their particular eco-cultural contexts. Jealousy then becomes thought of as a situated pattern of reactions—an approach which could help us ask more appropriate questions about its presence, forms, and development. Another sense in which culture is useful is of course to look at how jealousy is more directly valued and treated in typical interactions. Cultures of jealousy then become a conceptual option, like cultures of infancy (Keller, 2007), and understanding the situational factors that lead to the predominance of jealousy then becomes more possible to unravel—as for instance in the Spain of Cervantes (Wagschal, 2007). So we come to the focus of this section on the biological bases of jealousy. Something born in relation—and existing only in and because of relation—cannot but be affected by variations in relation and in the structures within which relations thrive. Is there, across many animal species, a common problem space that gives rise to jealousy? Or perhaps different problem spaces that give rise to different cultures of jealousy?

Scott Forbes (this volume, Chapter 7) takes us on a fascinating journey through examples of the most extreme forms of sibling rivalry in nonhuman species. His chapter acts not only as a sharp reminder of the fragility—perhaps even triviality—of psychological arguments about jealousy when seen against the backdrop of jealous actions and patterns in various species in ways we would be horrified to endure in humans. It reminds us that we do need to ground our discussions in the behavior, as he puts it, of the birds and bees. We end his chapter with the strong feeling that what we need first of all is a broad-brush picture of this gloomy phenomenon. Until we know the bigger picture we cannot sensibly begin to define jealousy or differentiate between levels and contexts of motives and understanding in humans.

Forbes describes gruesome occurrences of siblicide, in many different species of animal, where, even in embryo, young birds and mammals attack, kill, and even eat siblings. And worse, siblicide is often encouraged by parents who use surplus offspring as pawns in a larger game of the survival of offspring, where they may be useful as replacements for future deaths of other infants or valuable as food for stronger siblings or as a hedge against future resource needs for the family. The presence of such patterns particularly in embryo is blood-curdling. In some species of birds, known as "obligate brood-reducing species," Forbes describes how "siblings may murder siblings while sitting amid a current food surplus." The first-hatched chick of black eagles kills its younger sibling as soon as it hatches. The reason? Although the parents can meet the current food demands of both chicks, the demand will rise sharply as they grow. Killing the younger chick now not only ensures that food in times of shortage will be secured for itself, but also capitalizes on the weakness of the new chick and the reduced risk of injury as a result of the aggression. If we are talking of ecological "problem spaces" and neat solutions, we couldn't get much neater than this.

There are, intriguingly, some species of birds which are siblicidal and some which aren't. Why? Forbes links sibling aggression to the presence of weaponry and to certain life-history correlates. Birds which have sharp or very heavy bills and talons and egg teeth are more often siblicidal. Those which are smaller—like songbirds—aren't. Avian families display more sibling aggression if they have indirect feeding, where parents leave the food on the floor for chicks to take, have long periods of development in the nest, and have small brood sizes.

To add to the picture of cultural patterns conducive to jealousy, there appear also to be differences among animal species in cultures of parenting! Most birds do nothing at all to handle sibling aggression, but in a small percentage of cases even the presence of the parent serves to reduce the intensity of sibling aggression. In a few species—like moorhens—parents appear to rough up (or "tousle") their chicks when they rush for food, thus indirectly reducing sibling competitiveness. More directly, parent skuas intervene by trying to discourage dominant chicks from feeding from the same parent as the subordinate chick. Even more striking are attempts by bald eagles and ospreys where false feeding is used to trick fighting nestlings, and bribery too—several bird species are reported to use food to break up fights or stealthily feed more to subordinates to protect them. The strategies are frighteningly indistinguishable from those of human parents. Mammalian parental management of sibling aggression is even more complex. Hyena mothers, for instance (routinely raising two-cub litters with one dominant and one subordinate), interfere in bouts of aggression with a variety of strategies. These include punishing, pacifying, and physically separating the squabbling siblings in order to protect the subordinate. More intriguing, mothers who are high-ranking tend to punish both cubs for squabbling, while the lower-ranking mothers punish the dominant cub more. Thoughts run wild here, with memories of parenting literature (for humans) advising parents to punish all participation in sibling conflicts, to not interfere in the details, to not take sides, to let them sort out the rights and wrongs themselves, the parent's role recommended only for clamping down on the whole phenomenon. I am filled with respect for these lower-ranking mothers who are doing the "right" thing, nonetheless, in defending the weaker child. But I am brought to earth very quickly when I remember these are hyenas we are talking about. The answer to the question of animal cultures of jealousy appears to be a yes. That is, among different species there seem to be not only different biological strategies for the management of competition between siblings, such that even embryos are already preparing for strategic aggression, but there appear to be different maternal management practices which lead to different patterns of sibling rivalry and different eco-cultural factors which affect its presence and intensity. The similarity between these life-history correlates of sibling rivalry, situational spurs to aggression, and parental management strategies and those in humans is deeply impressive. And thought provoking.

Continuities in Jealousy?

Forbes certainly manages to test our complacent human assumption of a clear difference between biological survival strategies on the one hand and psychological feelings of jealousy on the other. Although he mentions, more than once, that the trouble with dealing with animals is that we don't know—and can't know—what they are feeling, the data he presents challenge the boundary between sibling rivalry as mere biology and sibling rivalry as jealousy. The answer to the thorny question of whether we really know what an organism feels, and of what we are basing our knowledge on when we think we do, lies in action. All the chapters in this section of the book focus on jealous actions and base their knowledge on what the various species (or infants at different ages) *do* in various jealousy-evoking contexts. Especially when it comes to the more complex behavior of mammals the possibility of a clear animal–human divide is implausible. Can we talk, for instance, about jealousy in human infants but of sibling rivalry in hyenas? Whether Forbes intends it or not, the categorical distinction becomes, at best, questionable.

The literature on emotions often speaks in terms of categorical differences in development, in the presence versus absence of, or levels of, manifestation of various emotions. Two categorical hurdles are commonly invoked. One is that of primary versus secondary (or basic versus non-basic) emotions, and another is that of the presence or absence of a mental representation of the self or a concept or idea of "me." Although these two dimensions are not necessarily parallel, and are certainly not identical, they are sometimes used in an overlapping or interchangeable way. For instance, jealousy is often seen as a secondary emotion, and also seen as requiring a conceptualization of the self. From this perspective jealousy would not be possible in animals (or in young infants) and we would have to explain the behavior of animals and young infants in other ways. Michael Lewis, for example (this volume, Chapter 2), classifies early manifestations of jealousy as proto-jealousy, revealing only a protest at loss of desired resources, not genuine jealousy. The latter would require an awareness of the "I" that feels the loss. Lewis argues convincingly for the similarities between protests in jealousy-evoking situations and other situations of simpler loss occurring early in development—a still-face condition, for instance—showing that we could not claim a reaction of jealousy in all of them. On the basis of early reactions of protest across a range of such situations, Lewis argues that until there is a conceptualization of self, these are protest-at-loss reactions, not jealousy. However, it is not very clear how we could ever argue for a clear case of jealousy other than from a situational and contextual basis (such as the presence of a rival for a mother's affections). The reactions that even adults show in a range of situations (such as when criticized by a superior, when facing the anger of a parent, or when watching a partner flirt with another person) are so mixed in terms of the characteristic anger, sadness, and fear of loss or jealousy, that most often it is only the contextual information that clarifies its nature as jealousy. In all of these reactions there could also be protest at loss. But only some of them would we call jealousy. With nonverbal creatures, therefore, unless we are to rule out jealousy a priori on theoretical grounds, the contextual evidence needs to be taken seriously (Legerstee, Ellenbogen, Nienhuis, & Marsh, this volume, Chapter 9).

Can animal rivalries be called jealousies? There are different ways of tackling this question, and different issues that need to be dealt with. One key issue is that of the extent to which the organism is seeking to protect material resources (or bonds) versus psychological resources (or bonds). This issue is often bound up with the issue of whether one can label as jealousy any rivalries that involve only two organisms (that is, whether jealousy necessarily requires a three-organism situation or can also occur when there are only two organisms and an object).[1] Both these issues are probably red herrings: it is actually impossible to separate the materiality of a resource from its psychological attributes (a parent's gift to a sibling and the loss of a job to a rival are psychological as well as material losses), and it is possible to be jealous of a loved organism's relationship with a physical object as well as with a person (a husband's devotion to his job, or a wife's to her laptop, might both arouse feelings of jealousy). The sibling rivalries in animals may be principally about access to food but inevitably involve access to parental attention and care, and mate-protection rivalries may be principally about protecting one's offspring but also involve protection of the pair bond. The materiality of the resource is difficult to separate entirely from its implicit sociality (in terms of status or recognition or even, when we are talking of inheritance, love). So, using the sociality of the threatening object to define jealousy is problematic, as is insisting that a purely psychological bond (i.e., without resource implications) needs to be protected in order to give it a label of jealousy. A more fruitful analysis of the evidence comes from looking at gradations of difference in what sorts of bonds are being protected and what sorts of actions are involved in the protection, or perhaps even at the balance of psychological–material emphases in the protection.

Forbes only talks of sibling rivalry, but there is much evidence about the protection of mates in birds and certainly much in mammals. Here are two intriguing studies: some male birds protect their females during nesting for longer than needed for ensuring parentage and the protection of the offspring—leading to speculation that they might be aiming at some protection of the pair bond (Martin, 1984), and some female birds show aggression to other females and seek to prevent the males from displaying to other females during the brooding season

(Kilpimaa et al., 1995). Every social bond, in humans too, must carry some degree of resource implication. In the light of mate-protection studies in birds, the fact that sibling rivalries are often about food becomes less dramatically different and Forbes' data as evidence for continuities between humans and animals becomes more compelling. There is, in addition, a vast literature on the protection of social bonds in nonhuman primates (de Waal, 2000) even beyond mates and parents—to friendships and alliances. This suggests that what is changing between species may be the complexity of the social bond that is being protected. Seeking to protect the bond with friends (although also involving material benefits such as power or access to other resources) is a step more impressive than protecting relationships with parents and with mates (although equally vulnerable to criticism that it is the material resource rather than the bond that is being protected).

Asking whether animals can ever really experience jealousy may point as much to human detachment from animal lives as to our lack of knowledge about the neurochemistry of jealous reactions. Jaak Panksepp (this volume, Chapter 6) has long worked toward a theoretical approach which does not divide the animal kingdom into human versus nonhuman camps and points to multiple sources of evidence for continuities between animal and human emotional systems. First, there is considerable recent evidence pointing to common neural pathways for negative emotions arising during social exclusion and the affective qualities of physical pain. The PAG (periacqueductal gray) is not only seriously involved in pain, but also in many affects, and particularly in PANIC—which according to Panksepp's theory is key to jealousy. Second, Markova, Stieben, and Legerstee (this volume, Chapter 5) make a strong argument for the similarity between loss of, or threat to, serious bonds of love in triadic situations and simpler social exclusion or lack of social exchange. They trace a complex and persuasive path between the HPA (hypothalamic–pituitary–adrenal) axis and the PAG and infants' social behavior in triadic situations with peers. They argue on the basis of previous evidence that a lack of social exchange leads to fear and stress, which, bypassing conscious awareness, leads directly to distress, increases in heart rate, and cortisol secretion. In situations with close social love bonds and the presence of a rival—e.g., with the parent—infant reactions to exclusion also involve approach behavior, an effect that can not only be explained through the activation of other neural systems, but in turn leads to the release of dopamine which, in addition to increasing the attractiveness of approach behavior, provides a neural relief from stress and anxiety and the suppression of pain. As with the chapters by Forbes and Panskepp, we are left with a picture of jealousy which has strong biological roots, is deeply underpinned by neural reactions, and is fundamentally adaptive. Both Panskepp and Markova and colleagues argue that conscious awareness is not necessary for jealousy—that emotions such as this can be felt at a pre-reflective level.

Nonetheless, there is a lay perception as well as a scientific presumption that only the primary emotions are experienced by species other than humans

(Demoulin et al., 1994, cited in Ogarkova, 2007). Challenging this, Panksepp cites a study of animal owners' beliefs about the jealous (and other emotional) reactions of their pets (Morris, Doe, & Godsell, 2008). The finding from behavioral reports and subjective judgments of pet owners that 67% of pet owners reported jealousy in pet birds strongly supports the complex and extensive data of sibling rivalry in birds reported by Forbes. This is in contrast, for instance, to only 17% of the participants who reported jealousy in hamsters. However, reports of jealousy in rats, that common laboratory animal, were also frequent—47% of rat owners reported jealousy (a finding that should not surprise us given Panksepp's previous studies of laughter and play in rats). The consistency of these reports across different species is perhaps the most impressive finding in these data. Dogs and horses were, unsurprisingly, reported to show the most jealousy—about 80% in each case. The pattern here is not a simple one of mammalian advance in secondary emotions: hamsters and guinea pigs are both mammals and both rear their young in similar ways to other higher-order mammals but are not frequently observed to be jealous, while birds, which are not mammals at all, are. There could, of course, be another reason for this—that pet owners can't engage with hamsters and guinea pigs as well as they do with birds and the rather more intelligent rats, and that therefore their ability to detect and understand jealous reactions may be more limited in these species.

Panksepp resolves the apparent contradiction between, on the one hand, the status of jealousy as a secondary emotion and, on the other, its apparent universality and early ontogenetic emergence in two ways. One, he emphasizes an experiential logic—the organism needs social bonds and needs to feel threatened by their reallocation. And two, he disconnects the secondary emotions, or this one in particular, from alleged cognitive and meta-cognitive roots. In keeping with his general theoretical approach—emphasizing analogic rather than symbolic modes of thought, and emphasizing the primacy of affective consciousness over cognitive consciousness—Panksepp argues that while cognitions are necessary to trigger jealous feelings, these minimal cognitions need not even be cortically mediated. The neural roots of jealousy, he suggests, lie prior to the evolution of the cortex.

All the chapters in this section present a problem for claims that on the grounds of a lack of conceptual ability, animals cannot be jealous or that jealousy is delayed until the second year of life in human infants. They point both to a more differentiated and to a more continuous picture of the emergence of jealousy in ontogeny and across species. Nonetheless, they present puzzles and unresolved contradictions in relation to the emergence of jealousy in human infancy. While Legerstee and colleagues (this volume) show continuities between 3 and 6 months in manifestations of jealous reactions, Hart (this volume) points to a categorical shift at 6 months. There are various procedural differences between the studies which could explain the contradictions—for instance in the study by Legerstee and colleagues, there is a two-way engagement between the mother and the rival, while in Hart's study the toy baby is simply being spoken to by the mother. Certainly the studies of Fivaz-Depeursinge and colleagues in Lausanne (Fivaz-Depeursinge & Favez, 2006; Fivaz-Depeursinge, Favez, Lavanchy, de Noni, & Frascarolo, 2005; Frascarolo, Favez, Carneiro, & Fivaz-Depeursinge, 2004) show a much earlier sensitivity to triadic attentional engagements. All the chapters, nonetheless, point to the problems (both evolutionary and ontogenetic) that come from a theory predicting late-onset jealousy. Survival as a species and attempts to regain attention as an individual would be threatened without some form of jealousy. Both sensitivity to exclusion and the attempts to counteract it appear to be necessary for social well-being.

Biological Openness and Experiential Chains

To what extent does biology chain us? Was Rousseau's vision of freedom at birth curtailed by experiential chains really a myth? The answer from all the chapters in this section points to an openness to experience of whatever biological underpinnings we bring to our lives. In fact, it would seem, it may be cumulative experiences that bind humans more than does biology.

Forbes explicitly raises the confusions that arise when biology is confounded with genetic transmission, with behavior being seen as somehow different from physical features of the body and not subject to similar laws of natural selection. This is probably a remnant dualist separation of the psychological from the physical to which psychologists may be particularly prey. What we need to do to understand human complexity, argues Forbes, is not to reject the rest of nature but add to it. His fascinating examples of the relation between food shortages and family size and parent behavior point to the likely openness of human "being" to ecological contexts.

Accepting that jealousy is not a primary emotion, Panksepp argues that it is nonetheless one of the most fundamentally coherent of the complex emotions, almost inescapable in social life for mammals—that is, for any animal which is involved in social bonds. It "comes closer than most" of the other social-moral emotions—such as envy, shame, guilt, contempt, embarrassment—in terms of being universally exhibitable, Panksepp argues. Something in the nervous systems of such animals becomes highly tuned, he suggests, to precipitate jealousy when social resources are compromised. Emerging only with the development of social relationships and in the right sort of contexts, jealousy is an experientially emerging social emotion. It has no specified neural architecture but can nonetheless arise easily from a spectrum of primary processes and in this sense jealousy is about as innate, Panksepp argues, as the languages we so readily learn to speak! This may seem an oddly anti-Chomskyan position for a neuropsychologist to adopt—but it is an intriguing one.

Panksepp's consideration of the commonly assumed "objectlessness" of the primary emotions, with clear brain mechanisms but minimal connections to environmental events, is a deeply contextual perspective. He suggests that evolution may have wisely refrained from trying to specify too many "objects" for too many raw primary emotional processes, leaving doors open for experience to create its own objects. Notwithstanding the frustrated question of whether it makes sense to ever talk about objectless emotions, the openness of jealousy to experience is the most interesting aspect of Panksepp's neurological stance. It goes like this. Experience gives emotion its objects. This can happen very rapidly. For jealousy, situations of separation-distress/PANIC are pretty common in early life. And repeated experiences not only give rise to emotion, but to longer-term anticipatory moods—repeated separations, therefore, developmentally prepare neural ground, as it were, for adult jealousies. Given the relative openness of jealous feelings to a variety of basic emotional patterns, experience allows there to develop varieties of jealousy, depending on gender, situations, and culture. The reactions to these genetically ingrained emotional processes are, however, hugely varied amongst people: sometimes it is anxiety and fear that dominate, sometimes anger, sometimes sorrow. As it is a secondary emotion, jealousy reveals a larger variety of affective dynamics (RAGE, FEAR, PANIC, SEEKING—even a bit of LUST) with "the specific symphony of jealous feelings experienced by a person" dependent on specific life histories and specific challenges to specific relationships. No genetically pre-ordained evolutionary brain network or single emotional feeling can define jealousy. Cultures of jealousy, then, seem a particularly apt possibility.

Markova and colleagues, similarly, point to the fascinating—if frightening— possibility that infants may learn, very early on, to anticipate rejection and exclusion. They paint a picture in neurological terms of the possible longer-term effects, not just on particular relationships, but also on the individuals themselves and suggest that in response to exclusion by peers, infant passive responses which deactivate pleasure-oriented approach networks can result in a state of constant negativity. Couple this with their finding that the only thing that predicts exclusion (in these natural if impermanent situations) is infant temperament. From as early as 7 months, maternal ratings of infant negativity of temperament predict whether their infants are going to be the excluded ones in these little social groups. Ouch! The sadness that is inherent in nature cannot be more powerfully demonstrated. It is not nature red in tooth and claw that makes us want to throw up our hands in philosophical distress (if not quite despair), but rather nature filled with tears.

This evidence lends support to Hart's suggestion that temperament must be a serious factor—both contributory and inhibitory in manifestations of jealousy. Hart's argument for the role of temperament is based on indirect evidence. She reports both from findings in her own longitudinal study and from other research that there is no increase in expressions of sadness between 6 and 9 months of age in jealousy-evoking situations. Nor does there appear to be an increase in the components of jealousy in older infants and toddlers. However, whatever the role of temperament, conclusions of the lifelong continuity of jealous reactions need more data and more explication. Perhaps indeed the training of the neural circuits is set from experience early on (as Markova et al. suggest), or perhaps there are other physiological differences in individual infants which are independent of experience (as the notion of temperament usually implies). The story is still sketchy, however, and needs much more exploration to fill out.

Similar to the distinction between infants' passive / sad reactions to exclusion by peers versus the more approach-oriented mixture of emotional reactions in response to exclusion by a parent is Hart's conclusion that in contrast to still-face or neutral affect situations, situations where the desired "other" is actually expressing positive affect to a rival evoke more sadness and also more approach attempts and attempts to regain the attention of the mother. Hart suggests a persuasive explanation of the different types of reaction in the dyadic still-face and the triadic jealousy-evoking situations. Whereas in the former, the infant may see the mother as a weak source of care and affection, in the latter the mother is evidently rich in psychological resources which are being given away to a third person. The crucial conclusion here is not only, as Hart points out, that jealousy is already more specific than a generalized global distress even at 6 months, but that its emergence must depend on the kind of experience that infants—of any species perhaps—have of being cared for by others. Even more, the specific kind of jealous reaction that any infant exhibits varies—perhaps dependent on differing experiences, and perhaps signifying different emotional aspects of jealousy. If this conclusion is right, biology leaves an experiential door open, and to add to Forbes' list of life-history correlates we must add another one—the greater the affectional resources a parent has, the greater the likelihood that infants will mind their reallocation. Although this may not quite work empirically, the issue of experiential openness is very well made.

How Much Love Does Jealousy Need?

The chapters in this section tackle this question in two interesting ways. The first is by asking the question of what kinds of love could give rise to jealousy, and the second by asking whether the depth of love relates to the depths of jealousy.

In how many ways can we be jealous? Panksepp raised the possibility that sexual jealousy may be fundamentally neurologically different from other social forms of jealousy. Markova and colleagues take this question further. Within even the category of social jealousy, they ask, is it only intense love bonds—such as between a child and parent—that arouse jealous reactions when threatened, or is it also less intense social bonds such as with friends, or even with mere acquaintances? Does the protective function of jealousy extend also to mild social bonds, transient exclusions in situations where it doesn't—one could argue—*really* matter? If we follow Trevarthen's argument against Psychology's passionate attachment to attachment theory, and in favor of the importance of companionship for human infants (Trevarthen, 2001), this question would have to be answered in the affirmative. Perhaps the human and mammalian search for connection—rather than just physical form of survival—can best be understood in terms of intersubjective encounters of all kinds. We know that in adults social exclusion doesn't in fact need a love bond. The exquisite—if depressing—studies by Williams have shown that even when forewarned about an action that is going to exclude them in a group of acquaintances, individuals react with pain (Williams, 2007).

Is this the case with infants too? Markova and her colleagues explore naturally occurring social exclusions in triads of human infants in the second half of the first year of life. In situations where three infants have only just met and two of them turn to each other, they find that the excluded infants react with what might be described as a freezing of social reactions—less positive affect, fewer interaction initiations, fewer responses to others' initiations, but an increase in gaze to the excluding peers. They draw a fascinating conclusion: that in cases of exclusion in the absence of serious love bonds infants may simply not be showing the negativity they feel, but engaging in a kind of passive aversion. The lack of expression plus the lack of actual repair attempts or approach behaviors, they argue, could lead to an absence of relief from this negativity.

This argument makes sense. In adult life, we can point to the many occasions when small misunderstandings or small hurts occur. They are too small to mention. Too trivial to attempt to resolve. They remain like little thorns under the skin, often not felt, but always there and accruing pain, waiting for a second and a third thorn to add to their now incomprehensible and undealable-with threat to trust in relationships. The answer to the question therefore is yes—even non-intense relationships can cause problems—sometimes more pernicious problems—if threatened.

The more you love, the more you grieve? Jaak Panksepp once began a talk with this quote from Jane Austen's memorial stone in Winchester Cathedral in Hampshire, written about her mourners: "Their grief is in proportion to their affection." Hart's empirical report (this volume) of what she calls "inversed affect sharing" is an important attempt to explore the co-relations of different kinds of feeling in relationships. She finds, in a longitudinal study, that infants who are exposed at 3, 6, and 9 months to mothers who show lots of positive vocal affect to a toy baby show, at 6 and 9 months, more reactions of sadness to the mother's interactions with the toy baby than those infants who, at 3, 6, and 9 months, are exposed to their mother engaging in neutral affective vocal interactions with the toy baby. Basically, the finding suggests that the nature of the mother's "affection" for the rival influences the extent of the infant's sadness at encountering the rival. This is strikingly similar to the finding by Legerstee and others. (this volume) where triadic interactions between mother and experimenter lead to infant "jealous" reactions only when it is the mother that engages positively with the experimenter, not the other way around. Further, Hart finds significant correlations between the degree of the infant's interest in the mother and in the encounter and the degree of sadness shown. Interestingly, these correlations occur at single points in time—at 3 months and at 6 months—as well as over time. So the degree of interest shown at an earlier age—3 months and 6 months—is significantly correlated to sadness at a later age—6 months and 9 months, respectively.

At first sight, the notion of any inversed affective reactions is unsurprising. The deeper the wound, one could simply argue, the greater the hurt. What is interesting in Hart's data is, however, the confirmation that this sadness indicates jealousy—it is the degree of the mother's positiveness to the rival that is related to infant sadness, not a direct wound to the infant. That is crucial here for conclusions about jealousy—the degree of loss is neatly specified by the degree of positiveness. In a sense, it is not the inversion that is fascinating about this, but something about the characterization of the nature of jealousy. Notions of inversed affective relations in infancy are not, in fact, new. About 30 years ago Trevarthen described subtle and complex shifts in the direct expressions between infants and mothers in proto-conversations: the boldness or teasing voice of one would lead to shyness in the other and the silence or shyness of one to boldness and approach in the other (Trevarthen, 1979). The claim of a conversation of reciprocal affects is a strong and older one. However, what is interesting about these data is their illustration of the perversity of jealousy. They suggest that it isn't resources *per se* that determine sibling rivalry. It really isn't how poor you are that determines whether you mind resources going elsewhere. It is how good those other-directed resources are that may be key. What really needs to be shown now is whether that factor of the quality of those other-directed resources is indeed independent of the wealth the infant already has. Maria Legerstee's previous studies of classifying mother–infant dyads in terms of their affective mirroring and mutual sensitivity come to mind and offer serious questions for future research (Legerstee & Varghese, 2001; Markova & Legerstee, 2006). The major hitch in this, of course, is that once one has already established for science that such situations arouse sadness, one is limited in the extent to which one can experiment with perturbations in relations unless further gains from such experimentation in terms of social care and respect for infant capacities are clear.

Conclusions

All authors in this section share a focus on jealousy as action. Forbes' depiction of sibling rivalries in the animal kingdom is, of course, entirely focused on actions in response to the threat of clear and present danger. The range and diversity of reactions as well as the range and diversity of parental management of these reactions all serve a very evident functional end—attempts to regain something precious that is threatened—or to use Panksepp's words to "counteract the severance of a social bond." They all point to similarities between jealousy in various nonhuman species and that in humans, and between jealousy in early infancy and that occurring later.

And in an interesting twist to their biological explorations, all of them emphasize the openness of biology to context and experience. A key strength of their chapters lies in their dispelling of 19th-century notions of biology and leaving us instead with a much subtler set of leads about the origins and manifestations of jealousy. In opening up issues of different eco-cultures of jealousy, biology gives us, instead, a commitment to the use of a wide-angled lens for a picture of multiple developmental narratives of jealousy. We, as humans, are really not alone in this story.

Their leads, however, leave us with many questions: How do infants deal with naturally occurring social exclusions? Do such exclusions actually occur in the forced way that we are driven to set up in experiments? Do they occur among naturally occurring infant peer groups? And if so, how do they fare and develop? Does the distance and involvement of the third party with the self and with the partner make a difference to the infant's experience of jealousy? Does it matter, in other words, whether you also really like your rival?

Can we go forward in our understanding of this phenomenon in humans by listing contributory factors? Or is all such listing bound to fail given the complex interplay of factors in social situations? For instance, does it ever make sense to list factors such as large family size and competition for resources, or inter-sibling gaps or maternal control strategies as jealousy-enhancing factors? Or should we always talk of complex cultural patterns?

Is competition over material resources derivative (in a Pavlovian sense of primary and secondary reinforcers) of the need for social bonds, as is suggested from Panksepp's emphasis on separation-distress as a main contributor to jealousy? Or is it in fact the reverse as suggested by Forbes—that resources for physical survival are the primary feature, from which psychological bonds and protection are merely one significant offshoot?

Forbes' chapter concludes with what seems at first to be a simple and reassuring argument—plentiful resources curb selfish tendencies, scarcity accentuates them. This is the case in as wide a range of species as blackbirds and bonobos. So: are human political problems solved? Perhaps not! Compare different classes in industrialized societies and at a higher level of analysis the selfishness of different political ideologies suggests that this doesn't quite work! Yet, the openness that the chapters emphasize suggests that something in the way we show and experience this emotion can yet be influenced by our cultures. Reflective awareness may not be necessary for experiencing jealousy, but it may well be necessary to take us away from it.

Note

1   Sometimes this distinction is expressed as that between envy and jealousy—with envy represented as being a simple desire for a resource that another organism has (and thus requiring only two organisms) and jealousy represented as being a desire to

protect a social bond from a rival, thus always requiring three organisms. Others would see the distinction between envy and jealousy as being a more complex one with variations in intensity and negativeness being more salient than a material–physical or two-organism versus three-organism divide. In many languages it is linguistically acceptable to use both words as referring to identical or very similar situations, e.g., "Perhaps he is jealous of the players who were offered huge sums of money to tour, while he wasn't" (Ogarkova, 2007). Another slant on this comes from Van Sommers: "Envy concerns what you would like to have but don't possess, whereas jealousy concerns what you have and don't wish to lose" (Van Sommers, 1988, cited in Ogarkova, 2007).

References

Benedict, R. (1935). *Patterns of culture*. London: Routledge and Kegan Paul.

Buss, D. M. (2000). *The dangerous passion: Why jealousy is as necessary as love and sex*. New York: The Free Press.

De Waal, F. (2000). *Chimpanzee politics: Power and sex among apes*. Baltimore: Johns Hopkins University Press.

Fivaz-Depeursinge, E., & Favez, N. (2006). Exploring triangulation in infancy: Two contrasted cases. *Family Process, 45*, 3–18.

Fivaz-Depeursinge, E., Favez, N., Lavanchy, C., de Noni, S., & Frascarolo, F. (2005). Four-month-olds make triangular bids to father and mother during trilogue play with still-face. *Social Development, 14*, 361–378.

Forbes, S. (this volume). Sibling rivalry in the birds and bees. In S. L. Hart & M. Legerstee (Eds.), *Handbook of jealousy: Theory, research, and multidisciplinary approaches*. Malden, MA: Wiley-Blackwell.

François, Duc de La Rochefoucauld, (1665). *Maxims*.

Frascarolo, F., Favez, N., Carneiro, C., & Fivaz-Depeursinge, E. (2004). Hierarchy of interactive functions in father–mother–baby three-way games. *Infant and Child Development, 13*, 301–322.

Hart, S. (this volume). The ontogenesis of jealousy in the first year of life: A theory of jealousy as a biologically-based dimension of temperament. In S. L. Hart & M. Legerstee (Eds.), *Handbook of jealousy: Theory, research, and multidisciplinary approaches*. Malden, MA: Wiley-Blackwell.

Keller, H. (2007). *Cultures of infancy*. New York: Psychology Press.

Kilpimaa, J., Alatalo, R. V., Raetti, O., & Siikimaeki, P. (1995). Do pied flycatcher females guard their monogamous status? *Animal Behavior, 50*, 573–578.

Kurtz, S. (1992). *All the mothers are one*. New York: Columbia University Press.

Le Guin, U. (1974). *The dispossessed*. London: Gollancz.

Leavens, D., Hopkins, W., & Bard, K. (2005). Understanding the point of chimpanzee pointing. *Current Directions in Psychological Science, 14*, 185–189.

Legerstee, M., Ellenbogen, B., Nienhuis, T., & Marsh, H. (this volume). Social bonds, triadic relationships, and goals: Preconditions for the emergence of human jealousy. In S. L. Hart & M. Legerstee (Eds.), *Handbook of jealousy: Theory, research, and multidisciplinary approaches*. Malden, MA: Wiley-Blackwell.

Legerstee, M., & Varghese, J. (2001). The role of maternal affect mirroring on social expectancies in 3-month-old infants. *Child Development, 72,* 1301–1313.

Lewis, M. (this volume). Loss, protest, and emotional development. In S. L. Hart & M. Legerstee (Eds.), *Handbook of jealousy: Theory, research, and multidisciplinary approaches.* Malden, MA: Wiley-Blackwell.

Markova, G., & Legerstee, M. (2006). Contingency, imitation, and affect sharing: Foundations of infants' social awareness. *Developmental Psychology, 42,* 132–141.

Markova, G., Stieben, J., & Legerstee, M. (this volume). Neural structures of jealousy: Infants' experience of social exclusion with caregivers and peers. In S. L. Hart & M. Legerstee (Eds.), *Handbook of jealousy: Theory, research, and multidisciplinary approaches.* Malden, MA: Wiley-Blackwell.

Martin, K. (1984). Reproductive defence priorities of male willow ptarmigan (*Lagopus lagopus*): Enhancing mate survival or extending paternity options? *Behavioral Ecology and Sociobiology, 16,* 57–63.

Morris, P., Doe, C., & Godsell, E. (2008). Secondary emotions in non-primate species? Behavioural reports and subjective claims by animal owners. *Cognition and Emotion, 22,* 3–20.

Ogarkova, A. (2007). "Green-eyed monsters": A corpus-based study of metaphoric conceptualisations of jealousy and envy in modern English. *Metaphorik.de, 13,* 87–147.

Panksepp, J. (this volume). The evolutionary sources of jealousy: Cross-species approaches to fundamental issues. In S. L. Hart & M. Legerstee (Eds.), *Handbook of jealousy: Theory, research, and multidisciplinary approaches.* Malden, MA: Wiley-Blackwell.

Rivers, W. H. (1906). Report on the psychology and sociology of the Todas and other Indian tribes. *Proceedings of the Royal Society of London, B, 77,* 239–241.

Trevarthen, C. (1979). Communication and cooperation in early infancy: A description of primary intersubjectivity. In M. Bullowa (Ed.), *Before speech: The beginning of interpersonal communication* (pp. 321–347). New York: Cambridge University Press.

Trevarthen, C. (2001). Intrinsic motives for companionship in understanding: Their origin, development and significance for infant mental health. *Infant Mental Health Journal, 22,* 95–131.

Wagschal, S. (2007). *The literature of jealousy in the age of Cervantes.* Columbia, MO: University of Missouri Press.

Williams, K. (2007). Ostracism. *Annual Review of Psychology, 58,* 425–452.

Part III
Cognitive Underpinnings

9

Social Bonds, Triadic Relationships, and Goals

Preconditions for the Emergence of Human Jealousy

Maria Legerstee, Baila Ellenbogen, Tom Nienhuis, and Heidi Marsh

One way to examine the meaning infants assign to their relationships with others is to observe their reactions when faced with a possible loss of these relationships. Research has revealed that infants as young as 5 months (Draghi-Lorenz, 1997) get upset when their mothers pay exclusive attention to another child. This finding has since been replicated by other authors with 6-month-olds in paradigms where mothers pay exclusive attention to a doll (Hart, Carrington, Tronick, & Carroll, 2004; see Draghi-Lorenz, Reddy, & Costall, 2001, for a review). The authors argued that they found evidence for the precocious existence of jealousy. If confirmed, these findings are interesting for various reasons. First, jealousy is defined as the fear of losing a loved one to a third party, a rival. As a consequence, jealousy has been called a "complex" or self-conscious emotion (Mahler, Pine, & Bergman, 1975; Piaget, 1932), because of the hypothesized need for the presence of foundational socio-cognitive capacities such as self–other differentiation and attachment which traditionally are believed to develop gradually during the second year of life. Another reason the findings of jealous reactions in such young infants was questioned is because jealousy involves a minimum of three people. That is, jealousy involves an awareness of "thirdness, the capacity to see a relationship between two other entities—as when C is jealous of a perceived relationship between A and B" (Bradley, this volume, Chapter 10). Researchers examining infant abilities to engage in triadic relationships have traditionally focused on the *end* of the first year of life, because it was believed that the ability to share attention over an interesting object (social or nonsocial) was not possible until infants became goal-directed agents (i.e., demonstrated means–end behavior), which was supposed to occur between 9 and 12 months (Carpenter, Nagell, & Tomasello, 1998; Piaget, 1954). However, not only

Handbook of Jealousy: Theory, Research and Multidisciplinary Approaches, First Edition.
Edited by Sybil L. Hart and Maria Legerstee.
© 2013 Blackwell Publishing Ltd. Published 2013 by Blackwell Publishing Ltd.

should *the infant* be a goal-directed agent, but in order to ascertain that infant distress is the result of an awareness of being "excluded" infants also need to be aware of the goals underlying the actions of *others*. That is, infants need to be aware of the reason why people break contact with them. Perceiving others as goal-directed agents has been suggested not to occur before the end of the second year of life (Carpendale & Lewis, 2004; Piaget, 1954).

How can these discrepancies between theory and data be reconciled? Stearns (this volume, Chapter 1) suggests that identifying jealousy as a complex (i.e., self-conscious) emotion may be a scientific mistake. He feels that the data from children with autism, such as reported by Bauminger (this volume, Chapter 12), who have jealous reactions when they perceive the exclusiveness of the relation-ship between a loved one and a third party, might suggest that there are neural structures underlying these social emotions. According to the neuroscientist Panksepp (this volume, Chapter 6), infants have an innate desire to form social bonds and jealousy could be seen as a reaction to the presence of one who threatens this social bond. If true, this would suggest that jealousy is not purely a creation of human culture, but goes back into deeper ancestral regions of brain and mind. The difficulty is that jealousy is not a single emotion. Jealousy is more appropriately labeled "a state" that one experiences, which, depending on the context, may conjure up emotions such as sadness (loss), anger (betrayal), fear/anxiety (loneliness), etc. Consequently, jealousy per se does not have accompany-ing coherent infrastructures in the brain and thus mapping jealousy onto a specific region is not possible (Panksepp, this volume). As a result, speculations about the origin of jealousy are primarily drawn from secondary sources. For instance, according to Panksepp (this volume), neurochemicals that reduce the impact of jealousy (because they reduce the painful feelings of being excluded) may be found among those that strengthen social bonds such as endogenous opioids (endorphins—substances in the brain that attach to the same cell recep-tors that morphine does) and the pituitary hormone oxytocin, which regulates separation distress in animals, as well as those chemicals that reduce anxiety/FEAR, an emotion commonly associated with the feelings of jealousy. Although Panksepp (this volume) proposes that variations in human jealousy may be a function of different cognitive capacities and environmental situations, the inten-sity of the feeling may be linked to subcortical emotional networks (see also Markova, Stieben, & Legerstee, this volume, Chapter 5).

If some foundational aspects of jealousy are instinctual then research involving animal models may shed light on what is happening during jealousy in the human mind. For instance, Forbes (this volume, Chapter 7) describes sibling rivalry in the lives of animals, as follows: "families are venues for extremes of violence and selfishness. Baby eaglets and pelicans murder siblings with ruthless efficiency. Shark embryos slaughter brothers and sisters in utero, and spadefoot toad tadpoles cannibalize sibs when their pond dries too quickly, developing huge predatory jaws to accomplish this task." However, these behaviors are primarily elicited as a result of competition for food, shelter, and warmth, and do not really address the affective preconditions for the emergence of human jealousy, namely the existence of a social bond that is threatened by the perceived intervention of a third party.

In human animals, sibling rivalry refers to the feelings of envy, jealousy, and competitiveness that exist between brothers and sisters within a family, and the expression can take many forms, from playful competition to intense feelings of hatred and envy at the other sibling's achievements (Volling, Kennedy, & Jackey, this volume, Chapter 17). However, although animal models can potentially allow investigators to study the neural underpinnings of various affective and emotional feelings that may underlie a state of jealousy, and thus have important implications for our understanding of the mammalian brain, we need to be careful not to explain away the socio-cognitive underpinnings of jealousy, such as infants' social awareness, existence of a social bond, awareness of triadic relationships, and an awareness of why they are excluded (i.e., of the goals underlying people's actions).

Infants' Social Awareness During the First Year of Life

If jealousy involves the fear of losing a loved one to a third party, then we need to show that infants have the necessary preconditions to apprehend such a situation. That is, we need to show that young infants (1) are able to distinguish between people and objects, as well as between self and other people, (2) have created a primary or social bond with a special person (whom the baby fears to lose), and (3) are able to perceive *and react to* the other two relationships of the social triad (i.e., the one between the beloved and the rival, and the one the infant has with the rival). Although research has found that infants react to being shunned or excluded (Draghi-Lorenz, 1998; Hart et al., 2004), not all such reactions are the result of feelings of jealousy. In order to make sure that infants are not reacting to lack of attention, stimulation, etc., when being excluded, infants need to be assessed in an experimental paradigm where their responses to the exclusion by a loved one are contrasted with their responses to someone with whom the infant does not have a social bond. Only if the infant reacts with upset when excluded by the loved one in favor of a rival can one propose that the infant's reactions are the result of jealousy. That is, that the infant is reacting, as Panksepp (this volume) calls it, "as the result of the existence of a social bond that is threatened by the perceived intervention of a third party." If one fails to show this, then the interpretation of the infant's reaction toward maternal exclusions as being primitive reactions of jealousy needs to be revised. In the end, as Hobson (this volume, Chapter 13) argues, we can do one of two things. If we find that babies display particular reactions when excluded by a loved one, who appears to favor another, we may assume that jealousy is too complex a cognitive ability for the young infant and thus throw out the facts, or we may choose to examine our assumptions instead. However, before exploring whether infants have the necessary prerequisites to experience jealousy, the concept of jealousy needs to be examined.

The Concept of Jealousy

Bringle and Buunk (1991, p. 135) define jealousy as "any aversive reaction that occurs as the result of a partner's extra-dyadic relationships that is real, imagined, or considered likely to occur." Thus jealousy is expressed when we have a social bond (an exclusive, dyadic relationship) that we are afraid of losing to someone else. Hence, jealousy involves a triangle, and is different from envy, which is dyadic because it is about destroying the other's pleasures.

Although many researchers have provided definitions of jealousy, to give a precise operational definition of jealousy is not easy. Jealousy has often been called a blended or mixed emotion (Plutchik, 1980), and has been suggested to include "a bewildering" array of emotions (Parrot, 1991, p. 15). In fact, jealousy is not really a distinct emotion such as anger, sadness, fear, disgust, and happiness. Most people believe that they recognize anger or fear when they see it expressed. That is because these emotions are presumed to be hardwired in the brain and to have perceptual features that are expressed facially and with other parts of the body, and thus can be identified objectively as basic emotions that "exist independent of our perception of them" (Barrett, 2006, p. 1).

There is also little consensus among emotion theorists about the basis of jealousy. Some developmental models propose that jealousy is founded in negative emotions (Fischer, Shaver, & Carnochan, 1989), whereas others discuss jealousy in the context of positive affective behaviors—because one has to love people to feel jealous of them (Darwin, 1877). Barrett and Campos (1987) provide a more functional definition of emotions, namely, they refer to "concurrent-goal/desire" emotions, which are connected to the realization of an end state. These kinds of emotion seem more appropriately associated with jealousy in very young infants, because it would seem that infant distress reactions are goal-directed such that their aim is to reinstate the social interaction in order to restore the social bond (see also Markova et al., this volume). According to Panksepp (this volume), jealousy stands out as being the most "prepared" among the social-moral emotions (such as envy, shame, guilt, pride, arrogance, pity, scorn, contempt, embarrassment, sympathy, and empathy) in terms of their likelihood of being exhibited by practically everyone, at some stage of life, if the correct precipitating circumstances are present. The most important precipitating circumstance is the perceived weakening and severance of social bonds.

Volling and her colleagues (this volume) argue that rather than searching for *the only* definition, jealousy should be defined and measured depending on the context in which it occurs. The authors deal with jealousy as it is provoked among children in a specific *interpersonal context*; namely the *social triangle* which includes the jealous individual, the beloved, and the rival. Drawing on the work by White and Mullen (1989) in their presentation of romantic jealousy, Volling et al. (this volume) propose that three dyadic relationships make up the social triad, namely: the *primary relationship* which exists between the jealous individual and the beloved, the *secondary relationship* which exists between the beloved and the rival, and the *adverse* or third relationship which exists between the jealous person and the rival. These relationships make up the interpersonal system of jealousy. Each person in the triad has their own behavioral affective and cognitive experiences and reacts as a result of the perceived loss of exclusivity which may influence the dynamics of the social triangle (e.g., if the loss of a relationship is perceived, sadness and withdrawal may be expressed, but if betrayal is perceived, anger may be felt).

Thus in order for infants to feel jealous, they need to distinguish among the three people in the social triangle; even though infants do not need to *represent* these relationships, they need to perceive and respond to the interpersonal dynamics of this social triad. According to Fogel (1993), infants come to know themselves and other people through ongoing relationships: "Infants are participants in these relationships from the beginning of life and they share with significant others in the creation of meaning" (p. 85). Thus, meaning is created jointly; infant and caregiver regulate each other's attention and cognitive interests with the social and nonsocial world, and bring together, in increasingly complex ways, their subjectivity and the history of their relationships. Variations in the co-construction of these relationships not only are the result of the unique characteristics of each partner, but are also created by the history of their relationship (Hsu & Fogel, 2003). It is through relationships that infants self-organize and construct new forms of interactions and an elaborated awareness of the other's mental states. This theoretical account suggests that infants early in life construct meaningful relationships with those they frequently socially encounter, such as their caregivers, and discriminate between these relationships and other less important ones.

Prerequisites for Jealousy

We will now examine empirical evidence that suggests that infants have the prerequisite abilities to experience a primitive form of jealousy. This evidence shows that infants differentiate between self and the environment, form social bonds, engage in triadic relationships, and are aware of people's goals during the first 6 months of life.

Person–object and self–other differentiation

An important prerequisite for meaningful triadic relationships is that infants separate the self from surrounding environments. According to Piaget (1954; see also Mahler et al., 1975), it is only when infants understand that people and things continue to exist when not perceptually discernible, at the end of the sensori-motor period (18–24 months), that infants begin to separate themselves from the external world and to place themselves within a common space with other objects. The end of the sensori-motor period, then, marks the beginning of thought. According to Piaget, infants at this period (concrete-operational) are becoming social and their responses intentional. However, numerous studies have demonstrated that infants at a much earlier stage not only are aware of their surroundings but also perceive themselves as independent agents. Consciousness of the bodily self would refute the notion that infants begin life unable to separate self from others. For instance, it appears that infants perceive themselves as distinct physical agents, because they become distressed when hearing a recording of the cries of another infant but not of their own (Dondi, Simion, & Caltran, 1999). Infants also engage in visually guided reaching (Hofsten, 1980). The fact that infants only reach for three-dimensional objects rather than two-dimensional representations of them (Rader & Stern, 1982) indicates that this behavior is not unconscious or reflexive, but that infants perceive the distance of the object relative to the self. Similarly, when infants respond with avoidant reactions to looming objects and not to objects approaching on a "miss" path (Ball & Tronick, 1971; Yonas et al., 1979), they reveal that they are aware that object knowledge and self-knowledge are related. Further knowledge of the self is evidenced when infants augment non-nutritive sucking to bring a picture into focus (Kalins & Bruner, 1973) and increase the movement of a leg, attached to a rotating mobile, in order to make it move (Rovee-Collier & Fagen, 1981). Thus, by 2 months, infants show some sense of personal agency, revealing awareness that they can control the environment in the physical realm. By 5 months, infants in a preferential looking paradigm discriminate the moving images and sounds they themselves make from those of peers and dolls (Legerstee, Anderson, & Schaffer, 1998). Interestingly, when neural mechanisms underlying the perception of biological motion are assessed, 8-month-olds appear to process biological motion similarly to adults (Slaughter & Heron, 2004). Combined, these studies show that soon after birth, infants perceive themselves as separate from the environment, and that this ability develops rapidly into a mature form before the end of the first year of life.

Social bonds—relationships between self and others

Thus, infants show that they differentiate between self and the social and non-social environment, but when do infants form relationships with people? It has been suggested that from birth infants show a strong desire to connect with the social world (Legerstee, 2005; Stern, 1985; Trevarthen, 1979), and are sensitive to the exchange of social signals such as emotions (Campos, Mumme, Kermoian, & Campos, 1994). In particular, it is argued that very young infants perceive their interactions with adults as a mutually regulated system, where each participant engages in affective exchanges, and during which the emotional meaning of the other's expressive behavior is appreciated (Campos, Frankel, & Camras, 2004; Legerstee & Varghese, 2001; Fogel, 1993). "Prima facie, they appear to relate to that other embodied person as the source of the special, sharing form of experience" (Hobson, 2007, p. 270).

That infants might have an inborn capacity for intersubjectivity is plausible when one considers research that shows that infants become upset when adults in face-to-face interactions suddenly stop communicating with them for no apparent reason, a phenomenon which has been called the still-face response (Legerstee, Corter, & Kienapple, 1990; Legerstee & Markova, 2007; Legerstee, Pomerleau, Malcuit, & Feider, 1987; Tronick, Als, Adamson, Wise, & Brazelton, 1978), but not when mothers stop communicating for some salient reason, such as drinking a refreshment (Legerstee & Markova, 2007).

It should be noted that the classic still-face response occurs primarily in infants whose primary caretakers are systematically attuned to their signals, which they show through sensitive sharing of emotions with them. If these caretakers are not attuned, or are depressed, infants do not get upset, revealing that they have not developed expectations of affect sharing with others (Legerstee & Varghese, 2001; Markova & Legerstee, 2006). Thus it appears that affective sharing is a pivotal mechanism that connects the infant with the social world, and which is responsible for the formation of social bonds in infants.

There are different opinions about the way infants set up interpersonal relationships with people. For example, some theorists argue that intersubjectivity is a result of infant perception of social contingencies. Specifically, these authors propose that from birth infants are only able to detect the effect their own actions have in the world, which is important for the development of an awareness of the self (e.g., by kicking the sides of the crib I become aware of my feet), but it is not until 3 months of age that infants begin to be sensitive to the type of contingent interactions provided by people (Gergely & Watson, 1999). Thus, according to these theorists, infants for the first few months of life are not capable of connecting with their caregivers in a meaningful way.

Other theorists propose that infants establish intersubjective connections with people by detecting similarities between own and others' actions (Meltzoff & Moore, 1983). According to Meltzoff and Moore (1983), infants are born with multimodal coordination, which allows them to operate with multimodal information, thereby recognizing equivalences in information across different sensory modalities. Intermodal coordination enables infants to imitate, early on, people's communicative facial gestures. For example, even newborn babies are able to imitate simple actions they see others perform, such as opening the mouth or sticking the tongue out (Meltzoff & Moore, 1977). The imitative games infants play with people are exciting for infants. Imitation is an "attention getter" and through it infants begin to perceive others to be "like me." Thus infants' ability for multimodal coordination allows them to recognize people as physically similar through imitation. This process lays the foundation for a later-developing reciprocal communication system that allows infants to understand and sympathize with others (Meltzoff & Moore, 1983).

Legerstee (2005, 2009) provides a framework to explain how infants connect with the social world by relying on innate predispositions and attuned social relationships. Accordingly, infants are born with three important predispositions that allow them to learn about the minds of others: (a) the ability to recognize people as similar to themselves, (b) the awareness of their own and others' emotions, and (c) the recognition of the caregivers' attunement to the infant's emotions and needs. The interplay between these three predispositions results in affectively attuned relationships that are important mechanisms for infants' socio-cognitive development (Legerstee & Varghese, 2001; Markova & Legerstee, 2006). Thus, Legerstee (2005, 2009) postulates that infants' connections with the social world develop through sharing emotional experiences with attuned adults, who reciprocate the infants' communicative behaviors. As a result, infants not only begin to perceive others to be "like me," but more importantly "with me." It is through this recognition that infants develop social bonds with others.

We have recently conducted a study that tested these different theoretical approaches (Markova & Legerstee, 2006). We observed infants in three conditions at 5 and 13 weeks of age: (1) a natural interaction where mothers interacted with their babies as they usually did at home; (2) an imitatively/contingent interaction where mothers were asked to imitate all behaviors of their infants; and (3) a random interaction where mothers listened to the previous interaction with their babies through headphones, and were asked to repeat what they had said and reenact how they may have acted in that interaction. We further used the 3-minute interactions at 4 and 11 months to assess mothers on their affect attunement. Maternal affect attunement was defined as maintaining infant attention, warm sensitivity, and social responsiveness (see Landry, Smith, Millar-Loncar, & Swank, 1998; Legerstee & Varghese, 2001). *Maintaining attention* was defined as a maternal request or comment that related to or elaborated on the activity the infant was currently visually engaged with, physically engaged with, or both. Maintaining could also be a maternal request, question, or comment that was in direct response to the infant's attempt to attract the mother's attention to an object or activity. *Warm sensitivity* was a composite assessment of the degree of sensitivity that mothers display to infants' affective cues, including promptness and appropriateness of reactions, acceptance of the infants' interest, amount of physical affection, positive affect, and tone of voice. *Social responsiveness* was defined as maternal imitative responses to infants' smiles and vocalizations, and as modulations of infants' negative affect. Based on these measures, mothers and infants were divided into high- and low-attuned groups. To determine whether infants enjoyed their mothers' interactions, infant smiles, vocalizations, negative face, and gazes were coded. This allowed for the assessment of "goodness of fit" of the interaction.

Results showed that at both ages, infants of highly attuned mothers gazed, smiled, and vocalized more during the natural interaction than during imitative and random interactions. Overall, infants of low-attuned mothers did not behave differently in the three interactions. These findings suggest that by 3 months infants have developed a social bond with their mothers, and have developed particular expectations about face-to-face interactions. When these expectations are violated infants become distressed (Legerstee & Varghese, 2001; Legerstee et al., 1987, 1990; Legerstee & Markova, 2007).

According to Bowlby (1980), the deepest emotions surface during changes to the social bond. Changes that endanger the social bond engender anxiety and fear, whereas those that leave the bond uncontested elicit joy and security. In a seminal article, titled "Feeling the pain of social loss," Panksepp (2003) argues that two key brain areas are implicated in psychological pain in humans. Whereas the anterior cingulate cortex has been implicated in physical pain, the prefrontal cortex showed an opposite pattern of activity, becoming more active when the distress was least. Thus both brain areas *regulate* the pain of social loss, suggesting that feelings of social exclusion might come from the same brain regions. He concludes, "Given the dependence of the mammalian young on their caregivers, it is not hard to comprehend the strong survival value conferred by common neural pathways that elaborate both social attachment and the affective qualities of physical pain" (Panksepp, 2003, p. 238). The implications for the onset of jealousy are interesting. According to an old Russian proverb, "jealousy and love are sisters." This seems to suggest that both come from the same brain regions and because love exists early in life, so might jealousy. However, within the interpersonal jealousy system, the social bond is the primary relationship. At what age do infants become aware of the secondary relationship (the one between their mother and the rival) and the tertiary relationship (the aversive relationship the infants have with the rival)?

The social triad—awareness of secondary and tertiary relationships

It has been shown that as early as 2–3 months, infants coordinate three-person interactions cognitively and socially, revealing the beginnings of intersubjectivity in this context. The Lausanne Trilogue Play (LTP) observational paradigm

(Fivaz-Depeursinge, & Corboz-Warnery, 1999; Fivaz-Depeursinge, Favez, Lavanchy Scaiola, & Lopes, this volume, Chapter 19) has allowed researchers to document infants' three-way distribution of attention with their parents and to identify their bids to share an experience with them. For instance, Fivaz-Depeursinge and her colleagues (this volume) report that during these triadic interactions, "infants will rapidly shift positive signals of pleasure or interest between their parents ... they will signal their need to change the interaction through shifting negative signals of distress or protest and visually check with both parents when uncertain. For infants, triangular interactions create a dynamic exchange, not present in dyadic ones, given the social feedback provided by the third party and the increased number of possible interactive contexts for interaction." The authors further noticed that infants react with distress to their parents' inattention. Infants want the fullest attention of both parents, and if this fails, they engage in actions that will restore the social triad or trilogue.

These are wonderful episodes because they not only illustrate the infants' awareness of the other two loved ones, but the trilogue method also affords the infants an active influence on the context, which allows them to change the roles of the other two people. Invaluable to the present chapter is the description of the infant's construction of the *aversive relation* between herself and one of her parents, namely the one who takes away attention from the infant and directs it to the other parent. When this occurs, the infant responds with negative signals of distress or protest, and visually checks with both parents. The awareness of the relationship/attention between her mother and the other parent (i.e., the secondary relationship), and the tertiary or aversive relationship the infant develops at the moment when one of the parents becomes a rival, fulfills the preconditions of the interpersonal jealousy system.

Similar dynamics are at play between twins and their mother. Fearon, Bakermans-Kranenburg, and van IJzendoorn (this volume, Chapter 16) found that 1-year-old twins who see maternal resources (attention and affect) being preferentially allocated to the co-twin shift toward expressing greater, or stronger, attachment behavior (e.g., from avoidance to security) to the mother, and infants who are the recipients of maternal attention and affect shift toward resistance as a means of maintaining those resources and out-competing their sibling. The authors argued "that insecure attachment behavior, in this case, represents a strategy to secure those resources," and that "insecure resistant behavior, characterized as it is by intense crying, anger, and an apparent active attempt to maintain a prolonged state of distress, might be 'designed' to maintain maternal attention and other resources" (Fearon et al., this volume).

Further evidence that infants during the first year of life are sensitive to what happens between two other people is reported by Selby and Bradley (2003) who showed in a qualitative analysis that infants between 7 and 10 months are able to interact with two other peers simultaneously without parental support. A peer triad allows spatial symmetry between its group members, which may be crucial to obtain a realistic picture of infant abilities to coordinate their behaviors with others and to reveal their possible relationships. According to Markova et al. (this volume), there is some indication that infants react to social exclusion by their peers. The authors studied social competence in 60 same-aged, same-sex peers at 7, 9, and 12 months. Social competence was operationalized as infants' social interaction skills and preferences for particular peers to the exclusion of other infants in the group. Evidence showed that infants from early on directed meaningful social signals to peers; that is, they responded appropriately to the peers' social signals, preferred some peers over others, and seemed to react with anxiety and panic when excluded by the other infants, because they appeared to freeze, while their eyes moved rapidly.

Taken together, the existence of the social bond (i.e., the primary relationship), the ability to participate in a social triangle, the evidence of sensitivity to social exclusion, and the revelation that infants develop an aversive feeling toward a rival provide the basis for the existence of the interpersonal jealousy system in infants during the first year of life. However, in order to provide evidence that the three dyadic relationships (i.e., the primary, secondary, and tertiary or aversive relationships) are meaningful for infants, infants need to be able to differentiate between the various communicative goals of those that comprise the social triangle. That is, infants need to differentiate not only between different social partners but also the goals underlying their actions.

Discriminating between different people and their goals

When do infants understand the goal-directedness of an action and to what extent does this understanding represent an appreciation of an actor's internal goals? Understanding failed intentional actions—when the goal of the action is unfulfilled and thus non-apparent in the actor's movements—critically addresses these questions. Imitation of incomplete actions is generally viewed as the most definitive test of goal-directed understanding because these paradigms separate an actor's goal from the outcome. Meltzoff (1995) showed that 18-month-old infants imitated the goal-directed actions of people when the demonstration was completed successfully (i.e., pulling apart a dumbbell), but completed the action when the demonstration failed. This finding was replicated by Legerstee and Markova (2008) with 10-month-olds. However, infants younger than 9–12 months cannot be tested on imitation because they do not imitate such novel and combined action sequences (Bjorklund, 1987; Killen & Uzgiris, 1981; Want & Harris, 2002; Piaget, 1954). Recently a new paradigm was developed to assess infants' appreciation of internal goals. Infants were presented with a social partner who was sometimes unwilling (teased) and sometimes unable (dropped) to share a toy (Behne, Carpenter, Call, & Tomasello, 2005). This method is more amenable to a range of infant ages as various infants' behavioral responses can be used as a measure of discrimination. Behne et al., found that only 9-month-olds, but not 6-month-olds discriminated between the unwilling and unable persons. To shed light on why the 6-month-old infants in the Behne et al. (2005) study did not discriminate between the unable and unwilling conditions we replicated and extended their findings with 6- and 9-months-olds, using a similar methodology, but an expanded repertoire of behavioral measures (Marsh, Stavropoulos, Nienhuis, & Legerstee, 2009). Specifically, to assess discrimination, we used, like Behne et al., banging, reaching, and looking away, as well as measures that younger infants use when people are unwilling to interact with them, such as gaze aversions and negative and positive affect (Legerstee & Varghese, 2001; Legerstee & Markova, 2007; Tronick et al., 1978). The results showed that infants in both age groups systematically discriminated between the unwilling and unable conditions through different constellations of behavioral measures. Importantly, in all cases of systematic discrimination, infants not only showed differentiation, but also behaved in socially appropriate manners, suggestive of an understanding of the experimenter's goals. That is, infants showed more patient behavior (positive affect, reaching to receive) in the unable conditions, and more frustrated behavior (negative affect, banging, and gaze aversion) in the unwilling conditions. Thus, infants at 6 months, and perhaps earlier, perceive others as independent and goal-directed agents (see also Legerstee, Barna, & Di Adamo, 2000).

Infant Reactions to Social Exclusion

Given that between 3 and 6 months infants discriminate between social and nonsocial objects, self and other, have formed social bonds with their primary caregivers, and perceive the goals of the actions of their partners during various interactions, it becomes possible to pose the question whether infants at this age may respond to jealousy-evoking situations. Pioneering research by Draghi-Lorenz (1997) showed that 5-month-old infants reacted with distress when mothers paid exclusive attention to another infant. The author studied 24 five-month-old infants and found that more than half of the infants became distressed when mothers expressed love for another infant (the rival). If the rival was another adult, only 10% of the infants got upset. It is not exactly clear why the subject's aversive relationship with the infant rival should be more profound than the one with the adult rival.

In subsequent work by Hart and colleagues (Hart et al., 2004), 6-month-old infants were tested in two dyadic interactions, namely a natural interaction during which infants responded with smiles and vocalizations and a classic still-face during which infants reacted with gaze aversions and sadness. The third interaction was triadic, where mothers paid attention to a life-size doll to the exclusion of their infants. This time, infants responded with agitation and re-proach to the jealousy-evoking situation. The authors asked whether this could be jealousy.

Although the Hart et al. (2004) findings are highly suggestive, it should be noted that in this study mothers interacted with an inanimate object, namely a doll. Given that infants differentiate between animate and inanimate objects soon after birth (Wellman, 1990; see Legerstee, 1992, for a review; Legerstee et al., 1998, 1987; Legerstee, 1991; Legerstee & Markova, 2007) and discriminate robustly between the faces of self and peers as early as 3 months (Bahrick, Moss, & Fadil, 1996) and also between faces and sounds of self, peers, and dolls between 5 and 8 months (Legerstee et al., 1998), the possibility remains that infants did not perceive their mother's behavior as a threat to their primary relationship, nor did they perceive their relationship to the rival doll as aversive. In contrast, the infants might have emitted approach behaviors and sad facial expressions because they desired the doll but were not permitted access.

There are anecdotal reports of jealousy in infants as young as 3 months (Gesell, 1906; Darwin, 1877) and observational reports of anger and fussing in 10-month-old infants when they viewed affective exchanges between family members (Cummings, Zahn-Waxler, & Radke-Yarrow, 1981). Furthermore, Masciuch and Kienapple (1993) reported studies of children aged 4.5 months to 4.5 years where mothers paid exclusive attention to another child, and in children aged 4.9 to 7.3 years where mothers praised another child's drawing. The authors argued that jealousy was not observed until the age of 13 months (Masciuch & Kienapple, 1993).

Taken together, the evidence suggests the possibility of jealousy in infants during the first year of life. This is in line with the ability to produce and experience other types of social emotions (e.g., Baldwin, 1902; Barrett & Campos, 1987; see Draghi-Lorenz et al., 2001, for a review). For instance, Reddy (2000) found that infants between 7 and 20 weeks displayed shyness, and were also perceived as coy by adults (Draghi-Lorenz, Reddy, & Morris, 2005). Additionally, Zahn-Waxler and Radke-Yarrow (1982) reported that 12-month-old infants provided physical comfort and offered objects to another person in distress, suggesting empathetic concern. The data concur with proposals of emotion theorists such as Izard (1978, p. 188) that shame and shyness can occur at any time after the infant's ability to discriminate between self and other and between familiar persons and strange persons, and with that of Barrett and Campos (1987, p. 558) who perceive emotions as bidirectional processes of establishing, maintaining, and/or disrupting relationships between an organism and the external or internal environment.

The Interpersonal Jealousy System

As indicated above, although revealing, little *systematic* study has been conducted to assess the existence of the interpersonal jealousy system in infants. According to the definition of jealousy, three relationships make up the interpersonal jealousy system. In order to determine whether young infants are able to experience jealousy, they need to be studied in such a context. In addition, controls need to be implemented that preclude alternative interpretations. To do that, infant reactions to their exclusion by a loved one in favor of a rival should be contrasted to infant reactions to exclusion by a loved one in favor of a third person whom the infant might not perceive as a rival. These two conditions should be pitted against each other in one experimental paradigm.

In 1985, Murray and Trevarthen (1985) conducted a study in order to clarify why young infants became upset when mothers refused to communicate with them during a dyadic interaction (i.e., still-face paradigm). Research addressing this question often focuses on infant sensitivity to various perceptual features such as the face, voice, or numerous combinations of face, gaze, and voice (Gusella, Muir, & Tronick, 1988). However, by manipulating the face, voice, or gaze independently from each other, the interactive format with which infants' communicative competence is being investigated is being modified. As a consequence, the process underlying infants' differential responsiveness is not revealed. Addressing these methodological problems, Murray and Trevarthen (1985) presented 2–3-month-old infants with three conditions: a face-to-face, a still-face, and a condition during which mothers tried to communicate with their infants, but for some obvious reason (i.e., a third person interrupted the mother) were not able to continue to do so. The authors found that infants responded as if they were evaluating *the reason* why contact was broken, because they displayed more negative affect and withdrawal during the still-face when mothers were unwilling to communicate, but they responded with "quiet interest" during the interrupted episode when mothers were unable to communicate.

It should be noted that these findings contrast sharply with those of Draghi-Lorenz (1998) and Hart et al. (2004), who found that rather than "quiet interest," 5- and 6-month-old infants became very upset in the condition in which mother broke off communication with them, and began to attend to another infant or a life-like doll in a playful and affectionate manner. Thus, the studies by Murray and Trevarthen (1985), Draghi-Lorenz (1998), and Hart et al. (2004) provide inconsistent results about infant abilities to infer why contact is broken, and also about infant expressions of jealousy. It is possible that the differences in infant age (2–3 months versus 5–6 months) and the persons who excluded them (mother versus stranger) as well as a different rival (doll versus infant) may have resulted in differences between the studies.

The Emergence of Human Jealousy

To shed light on these issues, we conducted a study with 3- and 6-month-old infants during *triadic social interactions*, namely the infant, their mother, and a female stranger (the experimenter). To find out whether infants distinguished between the three dyadic relationships in the social triad (i.e., the interpersonal jealousy system), namely the one between them and mother (primary relationship), the one between the mother and the rival (secondary relationship), and the one between self and the rival (the aversive condition), infants were presented with a female stranger during a natural, still-face, and two modified still-face conditions; in one modified still-face condition, the experimenter, while looking at the infant, drank from a water bottle, and in the other modified still-face the experimenter who was talking to the infant was interrupted by the mother, at which time the experimenter either talked to the mother about the experiment while the mother listened (monologue condition), or she would engage the mother in an active discussion about her baby (dialogue condition). During these interrupted conditions both women excluded the baby. With the bottle and interrupted conditions, we controlled for the possibility that a discrepancy between eye contact and subsequent lack of stimulation between the conditions might be the reason for the increased negative response to the classic still-face condition. We reasoned that an adult who drinks and an adult who talks with another person in the presence of the infant would be perceived fully by the infant as having a reason why they did not engage the infant. However, we anticipated that the infants would respond differentially to the two interrupted still-face conditions as a function of who did the talking. It was hypothesized that in the monologue condition, where the mother did not show an interest in the experimenter, infants would not get upset. However, we felt that the dialogue condition, where the experimenter and mother engaged in an exciting verbal exchange, might create the affective precondition for the emergence of human jealousy, namely the existence of a social bond that is threatened by the perceived intervention of a third party.

Based on evidence from the classic still-face conditions (Tronick et al., 1978), we expected 3-month-old infants to respond with more negative affect (sadness, gaze aversions) during the still-face condition, where no reason for a break was given, than during the normal, bottle, and interrupted conditions. In addition, if infants were experiencing the modified still-face conditions as instances where people for some apparent reason were unable to communicate with them because they either drank a refreshment or were interrupted by someone, then we expected fewer smiles and vocalizations, compared to the normal interaction. That is, we expected to replicate the findings of "quiet interest" (Murray & Trevarthen, 1985). However, we hypothesized that if we had mothers engage with the experimenter in a joyful and exciting dialogue while excluding the infants, we might produce a jealousy evocation situation to which infants should react with intense agitation.

Seventeen 3-month-olds and twenty 6-month-olds participated in the study. All infants were presented with six conditions, including three natural interactions, and three "break in contact" conditions: still-face, bottle still-face, and interrupted still-face. These conditions were randomly distributed between the first,

Table 9.1   Description of social triadic conditions embedded within the flow of events

Conditions	Time	Description
Natural Interaction (1, 2, 3)	40s	Experimenter talks to infant
	5s	Experimenter talks to mother
Still-face (SF)	40s	Experimenter still-face
	5s	Experimenter talks to mother
Bottle Still-face (BSF)	5s	Experimenter says: "I'm so thirsty" to infant
	40s	Experimenter still-face with bottle
Interrupted Still-face (ISF) to exclusion of infants	5s	Experimenter looks at infant as if beginning to speak
	40s	Mother says: "Hi" to experimenter
ISF-Monologue		○ Experiment 1: experimenter talks to mother
ISF-Dialogue		○ Experiment 2: experimenter and mother engage

Note: The order of SF, BSF, and ISF was randomized across infants and separated by a natural interaction.

second, and third natural interactions. In order to optimize infant awareness of the various breaks in contact, we not only ensured that infants were able to make sense out of the constellation of the various behaviors of the social partner, but we presented infants with more naturalistic contact episodes that could potentially be shared or jointly attended to. That is, we presented the infants with social triadic conditions embedded within the flow of events.

Thus, a session with an infant might proceed in the following way. There was a 40 s natural interaction during which the experimenter talked with the infant as she naturally would when meeting infants. Each natural interaction was then followed by a 5 s activity, and then one of the 40 s still-face conditions as follows. For the classic still-face condition the experimenter spoke for 5 s to the mother, and then assumed a neutral, unresponsive facial expression. In the bottle condition, the experimenter spoke for 5 s to the infants, saying she was very thirsty; then, while maintaining eye contact with the infant, she proceeded to drink from a water bottle held against her lips, while maintaining a neutral, unresponsive facial expression. In the interrupted condition, the experimenter established eye contact for 5 s while portraying a facial expression as if she was going to communicate with the infant (eyes wide open and mouth in a speaking position), but before she could do so, the mother (responding to a cue) interrupted the experimenter, by saying "hi," whereupon the experimenter engaged the mother in either a dialogue or a monologue to the exclusion of the infant (see Table 9.1).

During the monologue condition, the experimenter, after being interrupted, began to explain to the mother, with few interruptions, what the goal of the experiment was. During the dialogue condition, however, the experimenter would engage the mother in talking about her baby, through questioning, laughing, and speaking in a very animated fashion. A dialogue condition was subsequently defined as one where mothers responded to the experimenter for more than 30% of the duration of the condition. In the monologue condition they responded for less than 30% of the duration of the condition. Given that jealousy is an expression that is made up of various types of emotions, cognitions, and behaviors, we coded 9 behaviors. Affective expressions were coded as (1) joy and (2) sadness using the Affex system (Izard, Dougherty, & Hembree, 1980). Vocalizations were coded as (3) positive, (4) negative, and (5) forceful. These vocalizations were defined as vocalizations accompanied by positive or negative facial expressions, or loudness and force, respectively. The infants' attention patterns or gaze orientations are also revealing indicators of the infant states. Infants will look intently at interesting stimuli, but will avert their gazes from people when they stare at the infant impassively. Consequently, we coded *gazing*, which was defined as (6) any gaze at the experimenter's or (7) mother's face, (8) *gaze aversion*, which was defined as infants lowering the eyelids, without closing the eyes, and a subsequent diversion of gaze, and (9) intense interest, coded when an infant showed interest in a stimulus (Izard et al., 1980), but with an intense frown. These measures reflected the approach of previous still-face and modified still-face and jealousy evocation research (Hart et al., 2004; Hsu, Fogel, & Messinger, 2001; Legerstee et al., 1987; Legerstee & Markova, 2007; Legerstee & Varghese, 2001; Toda & Fogel, 1993; Weinberg & Tronick, 1996).

The results confirmed our hypotheses. Infants at both ages reacted with significantly more sadness and gaze aversions and less joy to the still-face than to the natural interactions, but with prolonged gazes and neutral facial expressions when the experimenter drank water from a bottle. In contrast, infant reactions during the interrupted still-face condition depended on who spoke. If the experimenter spoke primarily (monologue group), infants reacted with "quiet interest" (prolonged gazes, lack of smiling and vocalizations) (see Figure 9.1) but if the mother actively engaged with her (dialogue group), infants reacted with much agitation (forceful vocalizations and intense interest). Videotapes further showed that infants might also cover their faces with their arms (see Figure 9.2), or kick their legs and put their feet in their mouths (see Figure 9.3).

The findings support classic still-face studies, in that they provided evidence that by 3 months, infants expect people to engage in communicative exchanges with them when they look at them (Tronick et al., 1978; Murray & Trevarthen, 1985). The similarity of infant responses in the bottle and interrupted-monologue conditions indicated that infants were not simply responding to variations in affective stimulation. If infants relied on perceptual differences between the two conditions only, such as affective stimulation rather than the reason why contact was broken, then they should have been upset in the bottle condition, because except for the bottle, the stranger's eye contact, her impassive face, and lack of an interactive voice were similar to the still-face condition. Instead, the bottle appeared to provide a salient reason to infants why the person was not communicating, reasons that were not provided in the classic still-face condition. Thus, infants' responses revealed that they did not interpret the stranger's lack of communication in both the bottle and interrupted conditions as a refusal to communicate, but rather showed interest in the person's behavior, and watched intently. Interestingly, an examination of the videotapes showed that by 6 months, infants often began to reach for the stranger's bottle, which appears to be the result of developing meaning structures that allow for increasingly complex evaluations of the situation.

The reactions of the infants in the dialogue condition versus the monologue condition can be seen to contribute to the discussion of jealousy described by others (Draghi-Lorenz, 1998; Hart et al., 2004; Masciuch & Kienapple, 1993). In the monologue group, in which the experimenter essentially talked to the mother about the study and received very little input from her, infant reactions mirrored those described by Murray and Trevarthen (1985) in regard to their condition of the mother interrupting the experimenter. According to Murray and Trevarthen (1985, p. 1902), "quiet interest" was observed, with less sadness than in the still-face condition, and less vocalizing than in the normal interaction. In the dialogue group, however, the results were quite different. Most importantly, the infants were not quiet. Compared to the monologue group, there were higher levels of negative and neutral vocalizations, with an urgent or insistent tone to them.

Figure 9.1   Infant reactions in the Monologue condition—quiet interest (Copyright @ Maria Legerstee)

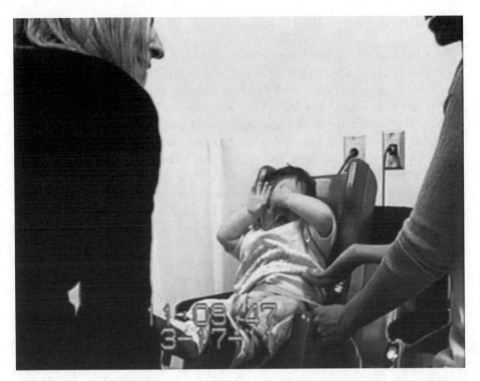

Figure 9.2 Infant reactions in the Dialogue condition—covering face (Copyright @ Maria Legerstee)

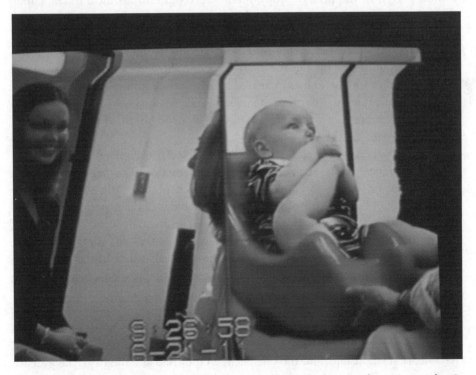

Figure 9.3 Infant reactions in the Dialogue condition—kicking up legs (Copyright @ Maria Legerstee)

The infants often displayed intense facial expressions, with brows straight, and held low. Gazes at the mother increased in the dialogue group, as compared to the monologue group. The combination of the various responses was unique and unlike anything observed in the other conditions.

Note that in both the monologue and the dialogue conditions the infants were excluded by the mother, but only in the dialogue condition did mothers show an active interest in a third party. The finding that infants reacted negatively in the dialogue, but not the monologue condition, suggests that the infants perceived the third party as a rival. These responses demonstrated that "an affective precondition for the emergence of human jealousy is the existence of an established social bond that is threatened by the perceived intervention of a third party" (Panksepp, this volume).

In Hart's review of the literature on jealousy, she noted that young infants had been observed to be sensitive to "instances of social exclusion" (Hart et al., 2004, p. 59), and that the infants' responses, like those to the classic still-face "exclusion," were likely to be negative and sad, but also, unlike the still-face, involved approach behaviors such as increased gaze and interest. It should be noted that the conditions in the Hart study and the present study are different. Hart et al. (2004) studied infants' reaction to mothers hugging dolls. No controls to measure alternative responses to triadic social relations were included (the natural interaction and still-face conditions were dyadic interactions, and thus did not include a third party). In the present study, infants received two identical *triadic* conditions. Only when the mother entered into a happy and engaging dialogue with the experimenter did infants become upset, but not when mother simply listened to the experimenter. That is, infants in both the monologue and dialogue groups displayed reduced smiling, but the dialogue group showed increased negative and neutral vocalizations as well as increased gazing at the mother. Upon viewing the videotapes one is led to infer that the infants' vocalizations were the embodiment of a "negative approach": the infants seem to be saying both "don't talk to her!" *and* "talk to me!" at the same time.

Most important was the way a condition of social exclusion highlighted the infant's awareness of the social nature of the interaction. The negative reproach response did not seem to result from too much or too little stimulation, or differences in eye contact, or other perceptual qualities of the experimental condition. It seemed to reflect the infant's awareness of the uniquely social implication of "exclusion," that is, the goals underlying the experimenter's and mother's actions, as compared to the lack of such implication in the "exclusion" of the classic still-face condition. In particular, our results showed that infants do not mind being excluded by the mother as long as she does not show interest in the interloper. These findings reveal that infants distinguish between the three dyadic relationships in the social triad (i.e., the interpersonal jealousy system), namely, the one between them and mother (primary relationship), the one between the mother and the rival (secondary relationship), and the one between the child and the rival (the aversive or tertiary relationship). In conclusion, the present study used two unique modifications of the still-face paradigm in order to investigate 3- and 6-month-old infants' awareness of the reason why people excluded them. Both the condition in which the experimenter drank a refreshment and the condition in which the experimenter interrupted contact with the infant to talk to the mother resulted in infants' responses that supported the prediction that infants will differentiate interruptions in contact when the goal underlying these interruptions differs.

As discussed earlier, to make the present design as natural as possible, the changes between conditions were not abrupt; rather, to enhance perception of the social triad, each condition was followed by a 5 s interval, during which the experimenter talked with the mother very briefly, and then went on to engage in the next condition with the infant. This led to an interesting observation which may lead to further investigations into the area of infant social cognitive awareness in early communicative interactions, social exclusions, and early indices of jealousy. The 5 s intervals revealed that most infants did not gaze at the experimenter. Instead, the 6-month-old infants were likely to play intently with their shoes, or the chair, or the belt on the chair, and the 3-month-old infants were likely to fuss mildly and squirm impatiently. While these responses seemed to indicate disinterest in the interactive experimenter, it was intriguing to note that as soon as the experimenter turned her focus away from the infant, to the mother, almost all of these "distracted" infants looked up instantly to the experimenter. This reaction not only indicated an awareness that the condition had changed, but it also showed that the infant's behavior prior to looking up was not necessarily indicative of lack of awareness of the social context of this 5 s natural interaction, but a particular kind of response *to it*. Interestingly, such "fractional glancing" was also found in a longitudinal study by Sylvester-Bradley (1981, pp. 9–17), when 4-month-old infants were avoiding their mothers' overtures, but would look at their mothers' face if mother looked away, and then away again before she could look back. The author suggested that these displacement activities imply conflict in infant motivation for not getting involved with other people. In all, it appears that infants respond to social contexts in a variety of ways. In this case, they seemed to demonstrate awareness of the attentions of an adult by fussing, or fidgeting, which they stopped as soon as the attentions stopped. These subtle and unexpected responses, in addition to the unique reproach/negative reactions observed when mothers excluded infants in favor of a third party, give impetus for more sensitive and varied research into the ontogeny of infant social cognitive awareness and preconditions for the emergence of human jealousy in young infants.

Preconditions for the Emergence of Human Jealousy

What are the underlying capacities of infant jealousy responses? Hobson (this volume) proposes that on the one hand, we need to provide a complex description of the settings within which jealousy is expressed and experienced, in that these entail one person having an emotional response to the relation between two other people. On the other hand, the state of being jealous might be simple in the sense that it arises not through cognitive elaboration of supposedly more basic emotions, but rather as one among several primitive states of emotional relatedness.

According to Panksepp (this volume), jealousy, like many other socially constructed emotions, relies on learning and socio-cognitive abilities such as those discussed above (awareness of thirdness and goals). However, jealousy may have a head start as well, in that it is more clearly "prepared" to take on its core form, as opposed to other social emotions such as embarrassment, guilt, and shame. Recent research has shown that the human infant is born with the ability to perceive others "like me" physically (Meltzoff, 2007), but through interactions with sympathetic adults quickly begins to perceive others to be "with me" psychologically (Legerstee, 2005; Markova & Legerstee, 2006). These predispositions enable infants not only to identify with others (Meltzoff, 2007) and to perceive whether the interactions are attuned (Legerstee, 2005; Markova & Legerstee, 2006), but more importantly to form social bonds. According to Panksepp (this volume), the main environmental factor that may disturb the social bond is a person who threatens it. Initially such a threat is posed by the mothers' absence, to which infants react with sadness and, if prolonged, panic: "The correspondence between the brain regions activated during human sadness and those activated during animal separation distress suggests that human feelings may arise from the instinctual emotional action systems of ancient regions of the mammalian brain" (Panksepp, 2003, p. 237). Thus both the ability to form social bonds and the fear of losing this bond (separation distress) seem wired in the human brain. However, separation distress is dyadic rather than triadic, and does not require an awareness of thirdness. In contrast, jealousy requires, in addition to the existence of the primary relation between mother and child and the awareness that she might leave (separation anxiety), a perception of the reason *why* mothers exclude them, which evokes the third relationship, namely the aversive relation between the infant and the rival. Thus, whereas separation anxiety and jealousy may have similar roots, in order for infants to feel jealous, they not only need to be aware of others, but also of the goals underlying their actions.

Summary and Future Directions

In the present study infants between 3 and 6 months perceive the actions of people who engage in exciting dialogues with their mothers as a threat to the social bond they have with their mothers. Infants do not have these feelings when mothers simply listen to others. Infants in these situations do not feel excluded in the psychological sense. The present findings are in sharp contrast to the idea that infants do not distinguish between self and other and thus do not develop social bonds until later in the first year. The present findings also refute the idea that infants are not aware of the goals underlying the actions of people until the end of the sensori-motor period and therefore could not play a determining role in development. Our findings support recent theorizing and empirical findings that have accumulated over the past 20 years. Infancy researchers have begun to address the ontogeny of socio-cognitive development and to describe its function and developmental trajectory. This has been done through examining core abilities of the very young infant (Legerstee, 2005; Meltzoff, 2007). In particular, findings from dyadic and triadic communicative interactions suggest that soon after birth infants engage in intersubjective relations with others, have particular expectations from people in such settings, and react with appropriate responses when their expectations are violated (Legerstee, Markova, & Fisher, 2007). They do so before the onset of more advanced socio-cognitive abilities such as the use of language and meta-representational abilities. The finding that infants reacted with distress when the relationship with their mother appears threatened by a third party (dialogue condition) and not when mother does not show interest in the third party (monologue condition) "suggests that the more cognitive aspects of the nervous system rapidly become highly attuned to precipitate jealousy when one's social resources are compromised" (Panksepp, this volume). Social or moral emotions such as jealousy, shame, guilt, and embarrassment only have meaning within a social context and may have their foundation in the infants' feel of being with the other (Trevarthen & Aitken, 2001). Although we provided behavioral evidence for the existence of the affective precondition for the emergence of human jealousy in 3–6-month-old infants, apart from very informative and stimulating theoretical models (see the various chapters in this volume) there are no studies that have examined what is happening in the human infant brain. Future research should focus on collaborations between traditional socio-cognitive developmental theory and developmental social neuroscience in order to provide a more detailed account of the relative contributions that innate and environmental components make to social emotional development. Given that jealousy is not a single emotion, mapping jealousy onto a specific brain region is not possible (Panksepp, this volume). Future research may reveal whether infants feel the pain of social loss that adults speak of, when being excluded. Functional magnetic resonance imaging has shown that when adult participants were excluded from a virtual tossing video-game (the other players stopped throwing the ball to them) while blood flow was monitored by fMRI, they experienced emotional distress as measured by substantial blood flow in the anterior cingulate cortex, an area associated with physical pain (Eisenberg, Lieberman, & Williams, 2003; see also Panksepp, 2003).

Studies need to be conducted that shed light on whether the ability to perceive thirdness, which enables the affective precondition for the emergence of human jealousy, is the result of cortical processes that mediate social cognition. Research by Mundy and Newell (2007; see also Markova et al., this volume) suggests that this too may *not* be exclusively molded by the environment (as suggested by Piaget, 1954; Mahler et al., 1975), but that its foundation may reflect neurobiological structures of the brain and mind of the human infant (Panksepp, this volume).

Acknowledgments

The editing of the *Handbook on Jealousy*, the preparation of this paper, and the various research projects discussed in it have been funded by the Social Sciences and Humanities Research Council (Canada), and York University, Funds of the Deans of the Faculty of Arts and Faculty of Health, Toronto, Canada, to Maria Legerstee. We are most grateful to the mothers and babies who participated in this research. The Jealousy study discussed in this chapter has been presented at the Society for Research in Child Development (Boston, MA, 2007), Canadian Broadcast Corporation, Sunday News, February 15, 2009, York University Magazine, November 15, 2008, New York Public Radio Interview: *The Leonard Lopate Show*, October 24, 2008, and various outlets of the international and Canadian press.

References

Bahrick, L. E., Moss, L., & Fadil, C. (1996). Development of visual self-recognition in infancy. *Ecological Psychology, 8*, 189–208.

Baldwin, J. M. (1902). *Social and ethical interpretations in mental development*. New York: MacMillan.

Ball, W., & Tronick, E. (1971). Infant responses to impending collision: Optical and real. *Science, 171*, 818–820.

Barrett, K. C., & Campos, J. J. (1987). Perspectives on emotional development II: A functionalist approach to emotions. In J. Osofsky (Ed.), *Handbook of infant development* (2nd ed., pp. 555–578). New York: Wiley.

Barrett, L. F. (2006). Are all emotions natural kinds? *Perspectives on Psychological Science, 1*, 28–58.

Bauminger, N. (this volume). Jealousy in autism spectrum disorders (ASD). In S. L. Hart & M. Legerstee (Eds.), *Handbook of jealousy: Theory, research, and multidisciplinary approaches*. Malden, MA: Wiley-Blackwell.

Behne, T., Carpenter, M., Call, J., & Tomasello, M. (2005). Unwilling versus unable: Infants' understanding of intentional action. *Developmental Psychology, 41*, 328–337.

Bjorklund, D. F. (1987). A note on neonatal imitation. *Developmental Review, 7*, 86–92.

Bowlby, J. (1980). *Attachment and loss*. New York: Basic Books.

Bradley, B. S. (this volume). Jealousy in infant–peer trios: From narcissism to culture. In S. L. Hart & M. Legerstee (Eds.), *Handbook of jealousy: Theory, research, and multidisciplinary approaches*. Malden, MA: Wiley-Blackwell.

Bringle, R. G., & Buunk, B. P. (1991). Extradyadic relationships and sexual jealousy. In K. McKinney & S. Sprecher (Eds.), *Sexuality in close relationships* (pp. 135–153). Hillsdale, NJ: Erlbaum.

Campos, J., Frankel, C., & Camras, L. (2004). On the nature of emotion regulation. *Child Development, 75*, 377–394.

Campos, J., Mumme, D., Kermoian, R., & Campos, R. (1994). A functionalist perspective on the nature of emotion. In N. Fox (Ed.), The development of emotion regulation: Biological and behavioral considerations. *Monographs of the Society for research in Child Development, 59*(2–3, Serial No. 240), 284–303.

Carpendale, J., & Lewis, M. (2004). Constructing an understanding of mind: The development of children's social understanding within social interaction. *Behavioral and Brain Sciences, 27*, 79–151.

Carpenter, M., Nagell, L., & Tomasello, M. (1998). Social cognition, joint attention, and communicative competence from 9 to 15 months of age. *Monographs of the Society for Research in Child Development, 63*(4, Serial No. 255).

Cummings, E. M., Zahn-Waxler, C., & Radke-Yarrow, M. (1981). Young children's responses to expressions of anger and affection by others in the family. *Child Development, 52*, 1274–1282.

Darwin, C. (1877). A biographical sketch of an infant. *Mind, 7*, 285–294.

Dondi, M., Simion, F., & Caltran, G. (1999). Can newborns discriminate between their own cry and the cry of another newborn infant? *Developmental Psychology, 35*, 418–426.

Draghi-Lorenz, R. (1997). *Jealousy in the first year: Evidence of interpersonal awareness*. Paper presented at the BPS Annual Conference of the Developmental Psychology Section, September 12–15, Oxford, UK.

Draghi-Lorenz, R. (1998, April). *Jealousy in the first year: Evidence of early interpersonal awareness*. Paper presented at the 11th Biennial International Conference on Infant Studies, Atlanta, GA.

Draghi-Lorenz, R., Reddy, V., & Costall, A. (2001). Rethinking the development of "nonbasic" emotions: A critical review of existing theories. *Developmental Review, 21*, 263–304.

Draghi-Lorenz, R., Reddy, V., & Morris, P. (2005). Young infants can be perceived as shy, coy, bashful and embarrassed. *Infant and Child Development, 14*, 63–83.

Eisenberg, N. I., Lieberman, K. D., & Williams, K. D. (2003). Does rejection hurt? An fMRI study of social exclusion. *Science, 302*, 290–292.

Fearon, P., Bakermans-Kranenburg, M. J., & van IJzendoorn, M. H. (this volume). Jealousy and attachment: The case of twins. In S. L. Hart & M. Legerstee (Eds.), *Handbook of jealousy: Theory, research, and multidisciplinary approaches*. Malden, MA: Wiley-Blackwell.

Fischer, K. W., Shaver, P. R., & Carnochan, P. (1989). A skill approach to emotional development: From basic- to subordinate-category emotions. In W. Damon (Ed.), *Child development today and tomorrow* (pp. 107–136). San Francisco: Jossey-Bass.

Fivaz-Depeursinge, E., & Corboz-Warnery, A. (1999). *The primary triangle. A developmental systems view of mothers, fathers and infants.* New York: Basic Books.

Fivaz-Depeursinge, E., Favez, N., Lavanchy Scaiola, C., & Lopes, F. (this volume). Family triangular interactions in infancy: A context for the development of jealousy? In S. L. Hart & M. Legerstee (Eds.), *Handbook of jealousy: Theory, research, and multidisciplinary approaches.* Malden, MA: Wiley-Blackwell.

Fogel, A. (1993). *Developing through relationships: Origins of communication, self and culture.* Chicago: University of Chicago Press.

Forbes, S. (this volume). Sibling rivalry in the birds and bees. In S. L. Hart & M. Legerstee (Eds.), *Handbook of jealousy: Theory, research, and multidisciplinary approaches.* Malden, MA: Wiley-Blackwell.

Gergely, G., & Watson, J. S. (1999). Early socio-emotional development: Contingency perception and the social biofeedback model. In P. Rochat (Ed.), *Early social cognition: Understanding others in the first months of life* (pp. 101–136).Mahwah, NJ: Erlbaum.

Gesell, A. L. (1906). Jealousy. *American Journal of Psychology, 17,* 437–496.

Gusella, J., Muir, D., & Tronick, E. (1988). The effect of manipulating maternal behaviour during an interaction on three- and six-month-olds' affect and attention. *Child Development, 59,* 1111–1124.

Hart, S., Carrington, H., Tronick, E. Z., & Carroll, S. (2004). When infants lose exclusive maternal attention: Is it jealousy? *Infancy, 6,* 57–78.

Hobson, R. P. (2007). Communicative depth: Soundings from developmental psychopathology. In M. Legerstee & V. Reddy (Eds.), What does it mean to communicate for infants? [Special edition]. *Infant Behavior and Development, 30,* 267–277.

Hobson, R. P. (this volume). Is jealousy a complex emotion? In S. L. Hart & M. Legerstee (Eds.), *Handbook of jealousy: Theory, research, and multidisciplinary approaches.* Malden, MA: Wiley-Blackwell.

Hofsten, C. von (1980). Predictive reaching for moving objects by human infants. *Journal of Experimental Child Psychology, 30,* 369–382.

Hsu, H. C., & Fogel, A. (2003). Stability and transitions in mother–infant face-to-face communication during the first 6 months: A micro-historical approach. *Developmental Psychology, 39,* 1061–1082.

Hsu, H. C., Fogel, A., & Messinger, D. (2001). Infant non-distress vocalizations during mother–infant face-to-face interaction: Factors associated with quantitative and qualitative differences. *Infant Behavior and Development, 24,* 107–128.

Izard, C. E. (1978). Emotions as motivations: An evolutionary-developmental perspective. *Nebraska Symposium on Motivation, 26,* 163–200.

Izard, C. E., Dougherty, L. M., & Hembree, E. A. (1980). *A system for identifying affect expressions by holistic judgments (Affex).* Newark, DE: University of Delaware.

Kalins, I. V., & Bruner, J. S. (1973). The coordination of visual observation and instrumental behaviour in early infancy. *Perception, 2,* 307–314.

Killen, M., & Uzgiris, I. C. (1981). Imitation of actions with objects: The role of social meaning. *Journal of Genetic Psychology, 138,* 219–229.

Landry, S. H., Smith, K. E., Millar-Loncar, C. L., & Swank, P. R. (1998). The relation of change in maternal interactive styles to the developing social competence in full-term and pre-term children. *Child Development, 69,* 105–123.

Legerstee, M. (1991). The role of person and object in eliciting early imitation. *Journal of Experimental Child Psychology, 51*, 423–433.

Legerstee, M. (1992). A review of the animate–inanimate distinction in infancy: Implications for models of social and cognitive knowing. *Early Development and Parenting, 1*, 57–67.

Legerstee, M. (2005). *Infants' sense of people: Precursors to a theory of mind.* Cambridge: Cambridge University Press.

Legerstee, M. (2009). The role of dyadic communication in infant social cognitive development. In P. Bauer (Ed.), *Advances in child development and behavior* (Vol. 37, pp. 1–53.). Amsterdam: Elsevier.

Legerstee, M., Anderson, D., & Schaffer, M. (1998). Five- and eight-month-old infants recognize their faces and voices as familiar and social stimuli. *Child Development, 69*, 37–50.

Legerstee, M., Barna, J., & Di Adamo, C. (2000). Precursors to the development of intention: Understanding people and their actions at 6-months. *Developmental Psychology, 36*, 627–634.

Legerstee, M. Corter, C., & Kienapple, K. (1990). Hand, arm and facial actions of young infants to a social and nonsocial stimulus. *Child Development, 61*, 774–784.

Legerstee, M., & Markova, G. (2007). Intentions make a difference: Infant responses to still-face and modified still-face conditions. *Infant Behavior and Development, 30*, 232–250.

Legerstee, M., & Markova, G. (2008). Variations in imitation: Ten-month-old infant awareness of intentional action. *Infant Behavior and Development, 31*, 81–91.

Legerstee, M., Markova, G., & Fisher, T. (2007). The role of maternal affect attunement in dyadic and triadic communication. *Infant Behavior and Development, 2*, 296–306.

Legerstee, M., Pomerleau, A., Malcuit, G., & Feider, H. (1987). The development of infants' responses to people and a doll: Implications for research in communication. *Infant Behavior and Development, 10*, 81–95.

Legerstee, M., & Varghese, J. M. (2001). The role of maternal affect mirroring on social expectancies in 3-month-old infants. *Child Development, 5*, 1301–1313.

Mahler, M. S., Pine, F., & Bergman, A. (1975). *Separation-individuation: The psychological birth of the human infant.* London: Hutchinson.

Markova, G., & Legerstee, M. (2006). Contingency, imitation, and affect sharing: Foundations of infants' social awareness. *Developmental Psychology, 42*, 132–141.

Markova, M., Stieben, J., & Legerstee, M. (this volume). Neural structures of jealousy: Infants' experience of social exclusion with caregivers and peers. In S. L. Hart & M. Legerstee (Eds.), *Handbook of jealousy: Theory, research, and multidisciplinary approaches.* Malden, MA: Wiley-Blackwell.

Marsh, H., Stavropoulos, J. Nienhuis, T., & Legerstee, M. (2009). *Six- and nine-month-olds discriminate between unwilling and unable social partner.* Poster presented at Biennial Conference of the Society for Research in Child Development, Denver, CO.

Masciuch, S., & Kienapple, K. (1993). The emergence of jealousy in children 4 months to 7 years of age. *Journal of Social and Personal Relationships, 10*, 421–435.

Meltzoff, A. N. (1995). Understanding the intentions of others: Reenactment of intended acts by 18-month-old children. *Developmental Psychology, 31*, 838–850.

Meltzoff, A. N. (2007). "Like me" a foundation for social cognition. *Developmental Science, 10*, 126–134.

Meltzoff, A. N., & Moore, M. K. (1977). Imitation of facial and manual gestures of human neonates. *Science, 198*, 75–78.

Meltzoff, A. N., & Moore, M. K. (1983). The origins of imitation in infancy: Paradigm, phenomena, and theories. In L. P. Lipsitt & C. Rovee-Collier (Eds.), *Advances in infancy research*. Norwood, NJ: Ablex.

Mundy, P., & Newell, L. (2007). Attention, joint attention, and social cognition. *Current Directions in Psychological Science, 16*, 269–274.

Murray, L., & Trevarthen, C. (1985). Emotional regulations of interactions between two-month-olds and their mothers. In T. M. Field & N. Fox (Eds.), *Social perception in infants* (pp. 177–199). Norwood, NJ: Ablex.

Panksepp, J. (2003). Feeling the pain of social loss. *Science, 302*, 237–239.

Panksepp, J. (this volume). The evolutionary sources of jealousy: Cross-species approaches to fundamental issues. In S. L. Hart & M. Legerstee (Eds.), *Handbook of jealousy: Theory, research, and multidisciplinary approaches*. Malden, MA: Wiley-Blackwell.

Parrot, W. G. (1991). The emotional experience of envy and jealousy. In P. Salovey (Ed.), *The psychology of jealousy and envy* (pp. 3–28). New York: Guilford Press.

Piaget, J. (1932). *Le jugement morale chez l'enfant*. Paris: Puf.

Piaget, J. (1954). *The origins of intelligence in children*. New York: Norton.

Plutchik, R. (1980). *Emotion*. New York: Harper & Row.

Rader, N., & Stern, J. D. (1982). Visually elicited reaching in neonates. *Child Development, 53*, 1004–1007.

Reddy, V. (2000). Coyness in early infancy. *Developmental Science, 3*, 186–192.

Rovee-Collier, C. K., & Fagen, J. W. (1981). The retrieval of memory in early infancy. *Advances in Infancy Research, 1*, 225–254.

Selby, J. M., & Bradley, B. S. (2003). Infants in groups: A paradigm for the study of early social experience. *Human Development, 46*, 197–221.

Slaughter, V., & Heron, M. (2004). Origins and early development of human body knowledge. *Monograph Society for Research in Child Development, 69*, 103–113.

Stearns, P. N. (this volume). Jealousy in Western history: From past toward present. In S. L. Hart & M. Legerstee (Eds.), *Handbook of jealousy: Theory, research and multidisciplinary approaches*. Malden, MA: Wiley-Blackwell.

Stern, D. N. (1985). *The interpersonal world of the infant*. New York: Basic Books.

Sylvester-Bradley, B. (1981). Negativity in early infant–adult exchanges and its developmental significance. In W. P. Robinson (Ed.), *Communication in development* (pp. 1–37). London: Academic Press.

Toda, S., & Fogel, A. (1993). Infant response to still-face situation at 3 and 6 months. *Developmental Psychology, 29*, 532–538.

Trevarthen, C. (1979). Communication and cooperation in early infancy. A description of primary intersubjectivity. In M. Bullowa (Ed.), *Before speech: The beginning of human communication* (pp. 321–347). London: Cambridge University Press.

Trevarthen, C., & Aitken, K. J. (2001). Infant intersubjectivity: Research, theory, and clinical applications. *Journal of Child Psychology and Psychiatry, 42*, 3–48.

Tronick, E. Z., Als, H., Adamson, L., Wise, S., & Brazelton, T. B. (1978). The infant's response to entrapment between contradictory messages in face-to-face interaction. *Journal of the American Academy of Child Psychiatry, 17*, 1–13.

Volling, B. L., Kennedy, D. E., & Jackey, L. M. H. (this volume). The development of sibling jealousy. In S. L. Hart & M. Legerstee (Eds.), *Handbook of jealousy: Theory, research, and multidisciplinary approaches*. Malden, MA: Wiley-Blackwell.

Want, S. C., & Harris, P. L. (2002). Social learning: Compounding some problems and dissolving others. *Developmental Science, 5*, 39–41.

Weinberg, M. K., & Tronick, E. Z. (1996). Infant affective reactions to the resumption of maternal interaction after the still-face. *Child Development, 67*, 905–914.

Wellman, H. M. (1990). *The child's theory of mind*. Cambridge, MA: MIT Press.

White, G. L., & Mullen, P. E. (1989). *Jealousy: Theory, research and clinical strategies*. New York: Guilford Press.

Yonas, A., Petterson, L., & Lockman, J. J. (1979). Young infants' sensitivity to optical information for collision. *Canadian Journal of Psychology, 33*, 268–276.

Zahn-Waxler, C., & Radke-Yarrow, M. (1982). The development of altruism: Alternative research strategies. In N. Eisenberg (Ed.), *The development of pro-social behaviour* (pp. 109–137). New York: Academic Press.

10

Jealousy in Infant–Peer Trios
From Narcissism to Culture

Ben S. Bradley

Jealousy involves a minimum of three people. A *Handbook of Jealousy* might thus justly lament that the past 40 years of scientific thinking about social and emotional life in infancy have mostly imagined and hence focused on two people, the baby and the mother. Even when psychologists' interest has veered away from the infant's relationship to mother, the two-person or "dyadic" format of infant–mother research has been preserved.

The reasons for this dyadic focus are not just those of convenience or techno-logical simplicity. They are methodological and theoretical and even, some would argue, ideological (Riley, 1977a, 1978, 1983; Steedman, 1982). Hence to look for jealousy in the first year of life does not just require the invention of new protocols for recording infants. We must also resolve beforehand what the occurrence of jealousy in infancy might mean existentially and theoretically about newborns and about development. Only then can we begin to plan research.

The first sections of this chapter rework the dyadic framework of infancy research in terms of a theory of "thirdness," the capacity for relating as a "third party" to relationships between two (or more) others, a capacity which is argued by some cultural theorists to underpin humans' accession to culture. We will then be in a position to examine the recent surge of research on "triadic interaction," to assess its implications for conceptualizing the early stages of human enculturation. Central to my discussion is previously published empirical case-based research on infants in groups, in particular, all-infant trios (Selby & Bradley, 2003a, 2003b; Bradley & Selby, 2004).

The Dyadic Framework and Its Limitations

When Rudolph Schaffer (1971, p. 1) opened his book on *The Growth of Sociability* with the confident words "at birth, an infant is essentially an asocial being," he was encapsulating an approach to early social development that was ripe for

Handbook of Jealousy: Theory, Research and Multidisciplinary Approaches, First Edition.
Edited by Sybil L. Hart and Maria Legerstee.
© 2013 Blackwell Publishing Ltd. Published 2013 by Blackwell Publishing Ltd.

eclipse. It was true that neo-behaviorists (e.g., Watson, 1972) and cognitive psychologists working in the tradition of Piaget (e.g., 1955; Brennan, Ames, & Moore, 1966) had for decades shared an assumption that babies started life without a social orientation. But, just as Schaffer's book hit the shops, three innovations, two theoretical, one technological, were about to render his starting-point far more controversial than he probably hoped.

The first of these emerged from moves in the school of psychoanalytic thinking known as "object relations" in which, rather than others being thought of as ungendered and physical, these "objects" were conceived emotio-relationally. Drawing on an innovative female tradition of scholarship, direct observation of infants, and inventive therapeutic work with toddlers using play with simple toys to uncover their symbolic life, analysts like Fairbairn and Klein argued that babies must have a far more complex emotional life than Freudians had previously suspected (Relke, 1993). In particular, Klein (1952a, 1952b) argued that the Oedipus complex, which Freud had thought to come into force around 5 years of age, first manifested itself around 9 months of age.

It first appeared as a "depressive position" in which babies struggle to reconcile their hateful with their loving feelings for their mother, experiencing guilt and gratitude as a result. These emotions are shown in a new possessiveness of the mother (e.g., stranger anxiety) and early attempts at reparation (e.g., early acts of giving) at this age. Explicit in Klein's view was the assumption that babies are born with a strong and immediate liking for, or "emotional involvement with," their mothers, a bond constituted through defenses against the anxieties aroused by their enormous sense of vulnerability: idealization, denial, omnipotence, splitting and projective identification. The basis of Klein's approach was summed up in one of her colleague's (Winnicott, 1940; quoted 1960/1965a, p. 39) aphorisms that, psychologically speaking: "there is no such thing as an infant." This is because the infant's world is both biologically and emotionally constituted from the start through his or her relationships, primarily, with the baby's "mother" (or "the breast").[1]

Klein's main influence on the experimental psychology of infants has come through the work of her student John Bowlby. Bowlby harnessed the idea that babies were "born social" to a theory that reworked psychoanalytic ideas through the medium of animal research in ethology (Lorenz, 1935; Sluckin, 1964) and experimental psychology (Harlow & Harlow, 1965). In the process, and much deplored by other psychoanalysts (e.g., Freud, 1960; Schur, 1960; Spitz, 1960), Bowlby's (1958, 1960, 1969) "attachment theory" dropped all reference to the triadic relationships comprising the mother–father–baby triangle that were thought to generate Oedipal jealousies and anxieties, focusing instead exclusively on the infant–mother dyad (Selby, 1993a). Bowlby argued that the tie between infant and mother is the biological foundation and prototype for all subsequent social relationships, a belief that is still widely promulgated (Cassidy & Shaver, 1999). For example, we get studies predicting that an infant whose attachment to mother is impaired by the mother's postnatal depression will subsequently experience impaired relationships with father, caregivers, and peers (Denham, Renwick, & Holt, 1991; Lamb & Nash, 1989; Murray & Cooper, 1997; Nash & Hay, 1993). This "maternal prototype hypothesis"—or "maternal precursor hypothesis" (Lamb & Nash, 1989)—implies that all social relationships have a dyadic template. Such a formulation makes it impossible to see how babies could be jealous of a relationship between two other people. Yet, as Hart and her colleagues' (Hart, Field, & del Valle, 1998a; Hart, Field, Letourneau, & del Valle, 1998b; Hart & Carrington, 2002; Hart, Carrington, Tronick, & Carroll, 2004) research shows, distress at a relationship between two other people appears precisely to be the form that early jealousy takes.

A second theoretical innovation added impetus to the vision of the "baby born social" bruited by attachment theory. This came from the study of early communication. Building on the ideas of Vygotsky (1978, p. 7; Bradley, 1989a, 2005, pp. 97ff) that babies individuate out of a primary togetherness, an influential group of researchers at Harvard's Center for Cognitive Studies had become interested in the late 1960s in the relational basis of preverbal communication: Berry Brazelton, Jerome Bruner, Martin Richards, Colwyn Trevarthen, and Peter Wolff.[2] Their path-breaking observational research gelled with the critique of Chomskyan linguistics that stressed that early speech has much meaning but little syntax (Donaldson, 1978). This implied that so-called grammatical competence must be preceded by "communicative competence" (Habermas, 1970; Campbell & Wales, 1970). In this vein, Joanna Ryan's (1974) important review argued that the developmental basis for communicative development should be conceptualized as a form of "intersubjectivity" based in a shared understanding of intentions between baby and adult. This word was taken up with alacrity by the Harvard group and has now, with its synonyms (e.g., attunement, empathy, meshing), found a central place in infant psychology's conceptual arsenal (Stern, 1985, 1995, 2000; Bruner, 1975, 1983; Trevarthen, 1974; Trevarthen & Aitken, 2001; Newson, 1979; Richards, 1974; Brazelton, Koslowski, & Main, 1974; Tronick, 1989; Kaye, 1984; Vygotsky, 1978).

Amplifying these two theoretical moves was a technological advance: the sudden availability of relatively cheap video-recorders. At Harvard in 1968, Trevarthen and Richards had filmed pilot observations of 2-month-olds "chatting" face-to-face with their mothers using a single camera and a specially designed baby-chair alongside a mirror to record the facial expressions of the mother (Trevarthen, 1974; Trevarthen, Sheeran, & Hubley, 1975, Trevarthen, 1977; Richards, 1974). These films revealed a host of subtle "pre-speech" behaviors in babies which appeared to be calibrated as turns with the conversational expressions of their mothers. Boosted by the new economies of videotape, there was very soon a proliferation of infant laboratories using the "*en face*" recording paradigm to study early communication (e.g., Schaffer, 1977; Lock, 1978; Bullowa, 1979; Kaye, 1984). Videotape was also a useful tool in the analysis of "the strange situation"

(Ainsworth, Blehar, Waters, & Wall, 1978), the principal means of measuring attachment formation in infancy. Both these recording paradigms are dyadic in conception. Recently the two paradigms have been combined in the push to find ways of measuring attachment in babies too young to be tested in the strange situation. For example, Braungart-Rieker, Garwood, Powers, and Wang (2001; Cohn, Campbell, & Ross, 1991) have proposed that 4-month-olds' reactions to their mothers' freezing their expressions during *en face* "conversation" is indicative of attachment classification.

Backing the focus on the infant–mother dyad is a theoretical assumption derived from reflections on human evolutionary history. Bowlby (1969) goes into this at great length, drawing a vivid picture of the dangers besetting human babies in our "environment of evolutionary adaptedness," especially the danger of falling prey to big cats. He argued that, in such conditions, there would have been a strong selection pressure for humans to evolve a behavioral system promoting a tight infant–mother bond that would serve to protect the vulnerable baby. Main (1999, p. 852) reiterates this argument, saying that for "humans and other ground-living primates, ... only gaining access to a protective older conspecific [singular] can serve as a solution to situations involving danger and fright."

Problems with the dyadic framework

Over the years, many psychologists have argued that scientific thinking about infants needs to move "beyond the dyad" (Bakeman & Brownlee, 1982; Lamb & Nash, 1989; Nash & Hay, 1993; Harris, 1995; Rutter, 1995; Muller, 1996; Cowan, 1997; Thompson, 1997; Berlin & Cassidy, 1999; Lewis, 2005). The main problem which these critics stress is that the social lives of babies demonstrably involve many players other than mothers: siblings, fathers, grandparents, passing strangers, peers, and caregivers. Hence we need a theory of infant social development that can include people other than the mother. I will return to this point in a later section. Suffice it to say here that, while these critiques push the need for a theoretical move beyond the *infant–mother* dyad, the ways they conceive the infant's other social relationships typically remain dyadic. For example, toward the end of his latest treatment of babies' participation in social networks, Lewis (2005, p. 21) ponders the need to theorize what he calls the "indirect effects" of "direct" (dyadic) interactions, namely, "those effects that occur in the presence of the child, but that do not focus on the child." This is the conceptual space that preoccupies theories of thirdness. However, Lewis's examples of "indirect effects" are "identification, observational, vicarious, and incidental learning, imitation, or modelling" (Lewis, 2005, p. 22). Lewis does not elaborate the possibility that babies could interact "directly" with more than one person *at the same time*. But they can, as this *Handbook* demonstrates.

Group processes, as soon as infants can take part in them, depend upon forms of engagement that are *supra*-dyadic (Thibaut & Kelley, 1959;

Paul & Thomson-Salo, 1996). For a group to exist, group members must be aware of and affected by *relationships between* other group members, as in a status organization or the complexities of jealousy. Group-minded babies must be able effectively to "act into" a group of people, all of whom have relationships with each other, as in a family or day care. For instance, a jealous person does not usually "suffer in silence." They act in a jealous way, whether they like it or not, often disrupting a relationship which they feel excludes them—as is to be observed both in experiments on infants (e.g., Hart et al., 1998a, 2004) and in toddlers' interactions with their siblings (e.g., Dunn & Kendrick, 1982; Miller, Volling, & McElwain, 2000). But equally a generous impulse may lead an infant to intervene to help someone they feel is being excluded by a third party (e.g., Tremblay & Rovira, 2007; Tremblay-Leveau & Nadel, 1995; Selby & Bradley, 2003a; see below). Lewis's (2005) formulation is mute on triadic action proper (in the sense of action having the quality of thirdness).

Regarding phylogeny, recent moves in evolutionary psychology have challenged the assumption that the best protection against danger in humans' environment of evolutionary adaptedness would have been a dyadic infant–mother bond. As Bowlby (1969, pp. 89ff) himself argued, the key unit of adaptation to the proto-hominid lifestyle of hunting and gathering was "social groups made up of members of both sexes and all ages." These "var[ied] in size from one or two families to some two hundred members . . . [and remain] stable throughout the year . . . With few exceptions, individuals spen[t] the whole of their lives in close proximity to other familiar individuals." Dunbar (2003), Perry (1997), and their colleagues have now collected impressive evidence from primatology, anthropology, and archaeology that it was primarily the demands of group membership that led to the dispropor-tionate growth of the human neo-cortex: the so-called "social brain hypothesis" (see later section). If humans evolved in a group context, it would have been more adaptive for pre-human infants to form multiple bonds to clan members than a single bond to one parent, as the parent may go missing while the clan lives on (Harris, 1998).

Early Intersubjectivity is a Form of Narcissism

Beyond the evolutionary probability of the mind's group origins, there are significant logical, psychological, and methodological problems with the dyadic framework for research on infant sociability—all of which have implications for how we understand the emergence of infantile jealousy. These problems surround the elision of behavior with subjectivity that dyadic studies typically condone (Tissaw, 2007). The many fascinating results that the study of dyads has produced have largely involved categorizing different kinds of behavioral or cognitive matching between infants and adults. This is most obviously the case in studies of early imitation (e.g., Field, Woodson, Greenberg, & Cohen,

1982; Meltzoff, 1985; Meltzoff & Moore, 1997; Nagy, 2006). The capacity of infants to imitate facial expressions and manual gestures is often argued to provide "a unique channel for early communication" (Meltzoff, 1985, p. 28) or lead to "sharing affect" (Legerstee, 2005, p. 58). Likewise, the finding that babies respond with different kinds of gestures (a) when Mother is actively talking to them, (b) when Mother is instructed to be passive, and (c) Mother is talking to dolls (Fogel & Hannan, 1985; Legerstee, Corter, & Kienapple, 1990) is taken as evidence that infants are "sharing emotional states" with the Other (Legerstee, 2005, p. 31). In this way, dyadic studies tend to conflate infants' changing reactions to the mother's visible *behavior* with infants' reading or "matching" of their mothers' subjectivities—subjectivities which actually hold myriad relational multiplicities and contradictions. This is a mistake in existential realism—there is more to mothers than being the Mother (Riley, 1977b; Selby, 1985). It is also a failure of logic and in the theorization of infantile and maternal subjectivities.

Take for example the well-known finding that little ones get upset and treat Mother as aversive in the so-called "still-face" procedure (cf. Murray & Trevarthen, 1985; Tronick, 2003). This uses the *en face* paradigm. A mother is instructed first to chat normally to her baby. Then, at some prearranged time or signal, the mother is instructed to freeze her expression for a minute or so. Finally she is asked to return to normal conversation. Two-month-olds will typically respond to their mothers' conversation with cheerful "pre-speech" in the first part of the procedure (Trevarthen et al., 1975; Trevarthen & Aitken, 2001). But when the mother goes still-faced babies first try to attract her attention and then turn away from her with expressions of uncertainty, anger, and distress. It takes a little while for babies to "reconnect" with their mothers in the final phase of the experiment when she returns to normal conversation.

Note that there is no evidence that babies are trying to "read" their mothers' mental states during the still-face procedure. Or, at least, if they are, their "readings" do not appear to be particularly insightful. While Legerstee and Markova (2007) have recently shown that babies seem less upset when mothers are obviously prevented from communicating with them (by drinking from a bottle or being made to wear a mask) than by the classic still-faced procedure, what mothers are actually feeling or thinking when they freeze their expressions has not been seriously investigated by psychologists—though anecdotal evidence suggests some mothers find freezing their expressions easier than others. They may be feeling anxious, sad, neutral, amused, or compliant (with the experimenter's instructions). Whatever the mothers are feeling, babies react non-empathetically: they turn away. Even more telling is Murray and Trevarthen's (1985) "double video" procedure that shows babies respond "communicatively" to their mothers when interacting with them "live" through closed circuit television (CCTV). But when babies are exposed to exactly the same behavior in a "replay" condition, they find their mothers disappointing or aversive. This changed response has nothing to do with the babies reading a change in the mother's emotio-mental state—which is identical in both "live" and "playback" conditions. It has to do with whether or not mothers appeared to be actively and therefore contingently "mirroring" their baby's moods back to the baby (Sylvester-Bradley & Trevarthen, 1978). Findings from still-face and double-video procedures also argue that young babies are motivated less by a wish to read others' minds, as proponents of "primary intersubjectivity" propose, than by a wish to find reflections of themselves in others, that is, by a primitive kind of "narcissism" (Lacan, 1949; Winnicott, 1967/1974b; Bradley, 1982). That this is also true for at least some "spontaneous" infant–adult conversations (Trevarthen, 1974) has been demon-strated in detail by case-analyses of infant–adult exchanges (e.g., Bradley, 1989a, chapter 8). Vasudevi Reddy's work is relevant here. Reddy (e.g., 2000, 2003) documents the "coyness" and "pride" evident early in infant–mother exchanges, and in infants' early views of themselves in mirrors. Reddy (2003, p. 397) empha-sizes that 2-month-olds' social behavior is centered around their sensitivity and responsiveness of "attention to self" (and, as in still-face and double-video procedures, loss of attention to self).[3] Her research has carefully documented how this early sometimes-complicated pleasure in the attention of others develops into "attention-seeking, clowning and showing off" and actions which effect the "re-eliciting of positive attention or praise" in the second 6 months of life (Reddy, 2003, 2005, pp. 100–101).

So what are we to understand when babies as young as 2 months old are described by a substantial sub-section of infancy researchers as manifesting a primary intersubjectivity that is synonymous with "affect sharing," "communi-cation," or, at greater length, "affective engagement with the attitudes of another in such a way that the otherness of the embodied other is encompassed within the experience" (Hobson, 2007, p. 275)? Is there truly the same subjective symmetry between mother and baby that obtains between two adults who are conversing (Nakano, Kondo-Ikemura, & Kusanagi, 2007, p. 213)? We can only accept this conclusion for as long as we ignore the need to account for mothers' and babies' motivations for their engagement with each other.

The few studies that have tried to establish what a mother aims to do when asked to "chat as they would at home" with their very young baby have hit upon the metaphor of the mirror—which goes back via Winnicott (1967/1974b) to Lacan (1949; see Sylvester-Bradley & Trevarthen, 1978). A host of authors have since argued the importance of maternal "affect mirroring" for infant develop-ment (Uzgiris, 1984; Gergely & Watson, 1996; Legerstee & Varghese, 2001; Kernberg, 2006; Nakano et al., 2007). Indeed, even where "affect mirroring" is not mentioned as such, the most effective form of "natural" mothering is tacitly equated with affect mirroring (e.g., Markova & Legerstee, 2006). The irony here is that affect mirroring (i) implies a highly *asymmetrical* form of interaction in which (ii) the mother's face, actions, and babytalk reflect, *not her own mood*, but her interpretation of *her baby's mood* (Winnicott, 1967/1974b, p. 131;

Sylvester-Bradley & Trevarthen, 1978, pp. 85–89). Hence, for Winnicott, "good-enough" mothering requires the mother of a small baby *not* to communicate what *she* is feeling but to reflect what her baby is feeling. If this is "affect sharing" it is a peculiar form of sharing, because what is "shared" by the mother is not originally hers but her baby's.

If one now goes on to ask why this kind of reflective behavior might have become "natural" (Winnicott, 1967/1974b, p. 131) or "species-specific" and hence "instinctive" (Gergely & Watson, 1996, p. 1186) in mothers, one plausible answer would be that it matches what mothers perceive to be the "natural" enjoyment young babies find in being mirrored. From a Lacanian point of view mirroring removes the challenge of difference from the baby's world "reflecting back the illusion of sameness . . . it is almost always found in the dual relationship wherein one seeks to be affirmed as idealized by the other; to be found in the conscious-ness of the other just as one is found in one's own narcissistic consciousness" (Muller, 1985, p. 234).[4] Hence what Lacan (1949) calls the baby's "jubilation" when she catches sight of her own image in the mirror. In line with Gergely and Watson (1996) we can argue that mirroring gives the baby pleasure because it flatters the baby's wish for power in that the mother's mirroring makes her behavior contingent upon what the baby does. But maternal mirroring offers the baby more than contingency: it also proffers an affectively enhanced "flattering" formal similarity to the baby's currently expressed subjective state (viz. what Gergely and Watson call "affect modulation"; Legerstee & Varghese, 2001).[5] In Virginia Woolf's (1929, p. 41; my italics) words: "Women have served all these centuries as looking-glasses possessing the magic and delicious power of reflect-ing the figure of man *at twice his natural size.*"[6] While Gergely and Watson's analysis proposes that there are long-term developmental gains from the "like me" aspect of mirroring (in setting up a "secondary" representational system over the first 9 months of life), they give no explanation for what immediate infantile desires mirroring might satisfy to make it as bewitching for young babies as it is. This is where the theory of narcissism comes in. It proposes that young babies are motivated to seek out a sense of enhanced control (omnipotence) *and coherence* (giving them a sense of "sameness" or identity) to offset the constant threat of feeling vulnerable and confused by difference and "otherness." This is what maternal mirroring offers infants.

The observation that "mirroring" is not veridical but "flatters" the baby underlines the fact that the way mothers mirror will have characteristic nuances that vary from individual to individual. Mirroring comes with an interpretation. Hence babies will not simply "internalize" themselves when they identify with their mother's mirroring. They will identify with themselves-as-seen-by-their-mothers. This may be crucial in the way they later come to understand them-selves, as has been argued in the long tradition of symbolic interactionist social psychology that stretches back to Cooley's (1902; Shaffer, 2005) theory of "the looking-glass self."

The idea that babies may be interested in reading others' expressions, not to read them "realistically"[7] but to satisfy their own narcissistic wish for power and coherence, introduces the possibility that babies' socio-emotional lives have an imaginative dimension. But do babies have imagination? Yes, according to studies of infants' responses to people versus things. It is often assumed that adults treat people and things in categorically different ways: "they communicate with people but act on objects" (Legerstee, 2005, p. 47; cf. Hobson, 2007, p. 270). The idea is that we impute thoughts and feelings to people, thoughts and feelings like our own. But we take a purely instrumental attitude to things. This implies that we never treat people as things, nor things as people. It was Winnicott (1953/1974a) who most famously refuted this dichotomy, arguing that there is a category of things which we treat like people, what he called "transitional objects." He argued that "transitional phenomena" were particularly important in infancy, where play gives babies a way of exploring their thoughts and feelings about their "significant others" through acting out fantasies about them with cherished objects (e.g., cuddly toys; cf. the "Fort! Da!" game in Freud, 1920, pp. 14ff).

When we look in detail at studies that aim to discover whether young babies treat people differently from things, results are equivocal. There are a number of studies that are said to show that even very young babies distinguish people from things (Brazelton et al., 1974; Bruner, 1975; Trevarthen, 1974; Sylvester-Bradley, 1985; Legerstee, Pomerlau, Malacuit, & Feidler, 1987; Legerstee et al., 1990; Legerstee, 1997). However, when the details of these studies are examined, we find that the differences, while statistically significant, are not categorical, as for example Bruner (1975) and Hobson (2007) have claimed. They only obtain "on average." Thus Frye, Rawling, Moore, and Myers (1983), Sylvester-Bradley (1985), and Legerstee (1997) all report that the "person-related" behaviors that babies predominantly direct toward people (e.g., smiling; vocalizing; gesturing; greeting; withdrawal) are all also, if less frequently, directed toward things. Likewise, the thing-directed behaviors that babies direct toward toys (e.g., reaching) are also all sometimes directed toward people. In my study of 10-week-olds, I was able to show that the frequencies of some "social" behaviors were significantly higher with people than things. But I was also able to distinguish a subset of "sociable behaviors" (mouth-opening; tongue protrusion; eyebrow raising; smiling) that were positively inter-correlated with each other (while correlating negatively with staring and eyebrow lowering) across *both* the "person" and "thing" conditions of my experiment (Sylvester-Bradley, 1985). Further analysis showed that some babies tended to stay in a "sociable mood" across both conditions; that is, they would smile, greet, and make "pre-speech" movements to both their chatting mothers *and* the moving reachable ball that provided the stimuli for the study. Hence, while babies significantly more often act sociably with people than with things, their perception of people cannot be assumed to be unremittingly veridical, because they sometimes act sociably toward things too.

Peter Hobson (2007, p. 270) may seem to be refuting the argument that these observations imply babies have an imaginative or fantastical capacity when he writes:

> We can fool infants into engaging with clever stimuli as if they were humans, of course, just as we can fool adults with holograms, but that does not detract from the fact that there is a categorical distinction between personal and non-personal forms of relatedness from early in life.

The question is: in whose mind does this categorical distinction reside? In Peter Hobson's, with his professional psychologist's hat on? Or in the 8-week-old baby's? (See Sylvester-Bradley, 1985 for an extensive treatment of this point.) To me, the word "categorical" means "all or none." Babies certainly do not show an all-or-none difference between their responses to people and to things. Neither do adults. The very idea that, categorically, "objects are objects and people are people and never the twain shall meet" blinds us to the existence of symbols, signs, and hence cultural life: because symbols and signs are precisely "things (signifiers: sounds, letters, pictures, toys) that have (interpersonal, socio-emotional) meanings" (Bradley, in press). As thinkers like Winnicott—not to mention Freud and the host of other authors stretching back through Shakespeare, Cervantes, and Erasmus—have long insisted, human beings have a profound capacity for imagination and fantasy or what we might call "folly," following Hobson's linguistic cue.[8] The fact is that human creativity and culture constantly exploit this human capacity for "folly": novels, toys, gardening, sculpture, pornography, painting, alcohol, recreational drugs, music, fashion, TV, film, religious artifacts—all have effects in what Winnicott (1967/1974c, p. 120) calls the "third area" of transitional phenomena that exists in between pure subjectivity and pure objectivity. Culture aside, we all, from time to time, treat people as objects and objects as people. Why should babies be any different? The evidence I have reviewed here shows that they are not. (Note that the "clever stimulus" I "fooled" the babies with in my experiment was not a hologram. It was a ball on a string.)

As soon as we entertain the possibility that babies' mental lives are imaginative—and that they may therefore "misconstrue" the people and things they meet—we realize the methodological flaw in assuming that babies are sharing mental states with adults solely because they affect, and are affected in correlated ways by, others' expressive displays. Hence we can never assume without evidence that there is a one-to-one correspondence between facial expression and subjectivity, whether we are observing infants or adults. Neither can we assume that babies are from birth motivated to understand others. A theory of primitive narcissism fits better with the facts: babies are motivated to find images of themselves in the behavior of others (cf. Gergely & Watson, 1996; Tomasello, 1995; Meltzoff & Brooks, 2001), experiences that adults frequently provide for them by adopting a "mirror-role" in early *en face* interactions. But if the mirror "breaks"—as in still-face or double-video "playback" procedures—the baby finds the adult distressing and aversive. In fact, as babies get older, they may begin to find the mother's mirror-role aversive, frustrating, or "empty" in any case (Papousek & Papousek, 1977). Thus around 4 or 5 months of age we find the dynamics of mother–infant couples changing as person–person games are introduced (Sylvester-Bradley & Trevarthen, 1978; Trevarthen & Hubley, 1978; Trevarthen, 1978, 1979; Trevarthen & Reddy, 2007; Sylvester-Bradley, 1981; Trevarthen & Aitken, 2001; Nakano et al., 2007).

The theory of infant narcissism proposes a close relationship between attraction (desire, love) and repulsion (negativity, anxiety, aggression) in early social life (Lacan, 1948, 1949; Laplanche & Pontalis, 1977; Wilden, 1981; Bradley, 1989b). It argues that babies are predisposed to see themselves in the behavior of their (M)others. Once found, the baby tries to accentuate the similarities between themselves and what is seen in the Other—as evinced by demonstrations of imitation and behavioral matching by young babies (e.g., Nagy, 2006) and the "depression" of babies by their postnatally depressed mothers (but see Hart, Jones, Field, & Lundy, 1999). But if the "mirror" provided by the other proves ineffective for any reason, frustration, disappointment, and even aggression (anger) can result (Hart et al., 2004). Hence, in the Grimms' tale of Snow White, when the Mirror told the Evil Queen that she was *not* "the fairest in the land" (because Snow White was "fairer a thousandfold"), "the Queen was horror-struck and turned green and yellow with jealousy" (Grimm & Grimm, 1822/1996, p. 162).

There is not much discussion in the literature of "normal" frustration with Mother in early *en face* recordings (Bradley, 1983; though see Reddy, 2001). This is largely because researchers strive to record infant–mother exchanges that are positive by ensuring that babies reach their laboratories well-fed, healthy, alert, and happy. If babies do get angry or frustrated, recording is often terminated (Bradley, 1991). Moreover, the main theory that deals with crying is attachment theory. Here crying is coded as "positive" (Bowlby, 1958) because it tends to promote proximity between mother and baby. This hides the possibility that crying has subjective significance for the baby which is negative rather than positive, manifesting anger, anxiety, or fear. Once we accept the possibility that babies normally experience negativity with their mothers and that this has theoretical relevance, we should note that, in everyday interaction, Tronick (1986) estimates that less than a third of early infant–mother exchanges are harmonious (Bradley, 1989b). My longitudinal case-studies of baby–mother dyads recorded in the *en face* paradigm from 2 to 6 months confirmed a rise in anger with (frustration with and aversion from) the mother from 2 to 4 months of age (Sylvester-Bradley, 1981).

While the work of Lacan (see Figure 10.1) shows that the concepts of narcissism and intersubjectivity are perfectly compatible, the concept of narcissism implies a more complicated and nuanced understanding of infant–mother

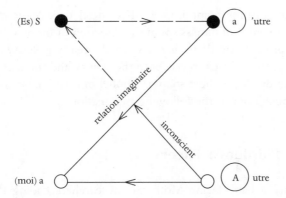

Figure 10.1 "S" refers to the baby's "ineffable" subjective existence. "(a)'utre" refers to the mother as perceived by the baby. "(moi) a" refers to the image of the self the baby identifies with in the mother's expressiveness. "(A)utre" refers to the mother as a true counterpart of communication. The line a ← a' refers to the narcissistic dimension of the baby's imagination. The line S ← A refers to the unexperienced possibility of true communication.
Source: Adapted from Lacan, 1981, pp. 106ff

dyads than that promulgated under the rubric of attachment or, more particularly, of emotional attunement, affect sharing, or "primary intersubjectivity" (Trevarthen, 1979; Tronick, 2003; Legerstee, 2005; Hobson, 2007)—and therefore a different approach to the significance of early jealousy. The metaphor of attunement implies that baby and mother "tune in" to each other's feelings or states of consciousness such that there is a simple correspondence between maternal and infant subjectivity. In contrast, narcissism implies that the baby's expressive behavior is not generated by a desire to understand the mother's thoughts and feelings. Rather the baby looks for him- or herself in the mother's expressiveness. Hence, while the mother's mood/behavioral style (e.g., colored by the need to comply with the experimenter's instructions, or by postnatal depression) should by rights be included in the description of early infant–mother exchanges, that style does not apparently equate to what the mother reflects back to the baby or to what the baby imagines about or "finds in" the mother's expressiveness. Equally, how the baby responds to the mother's "mirroring," for example, by imitating what she or he "sees" in it, does not necessarily represent everything about the baby's subjectivity (temperament, style, mood, personality). So we arrive at a picture of the intersubjective dynamics of early infant–mother exchanges where the baby's observable behavior is organized along an apparently dyadic narcissistic dimension, but one that is actually orthogonal to a deeper, more inclusive but as-yet-unrealized dimension representing the real communication that would take place if the baby were mature and conversing in an ideal speech-situation (Bradley, 2005; Lacan, 1981; Habermas, 1970; Figure 10.1). This other dimension represents the "thirdness" that is hidden from the young baby.

A narcissistic starting point implies that social development comprises an eventual transcendence of narcissism in the direction of more authentic communication. If we are empirically to discover whether early jealousy is an important step along this path, we must revise both the theory and the methods underpinning the pseudo-dyadic,[9] "affect sharing" model of early infant sociability. These revisions are spelled out in the following two sections.

Inescapable Thirdness: Theory

Whether we are a baby facing Mother or researchers coding the behavior of mother or baby, the signs we must interpret have a triadic structure: *signifier* (e.g., the mother's smile), its *object* (the baby's behavior), and its *context* (the train of thought or discourse which gives this signifier–object equation meaning: e.g., the mother's loving feelings for and/or amusement at her baby and/or her desire to be a "good mother" for the psychologist). This triadic structure prevails whether one recognizes it or not—and I contend that initially neither babies nor, sometimes, the researchers who study them in the dyadic paradigm, do recognize it. The significance of early jealousy is that it would show that babies have taken a step out of a context dominated by their own narcissism toward a recognition of others' interests.

Any comprehensive psychological account of social development needs to link what newborn babies can do socially with what we adults are required to do socially as members of our cultures. One way of understanding culture is that it provides what Bhabha (1994, p. 37) calls a "third space" which, while being "unrepresentable in itself," constitutes "the discursive conditions of enunciation," the indispensable background to the use of signs which results in their meaning one thing rather than another. Culture, like language, "is a drama in which three characters participate (it is not a duet, but a trio)," speaker, listener, and "third space" or tradition (Bakhtin, 1979/1986, p. 122). Peirce (1931) seminally conceptualized these three characters as the Sign, its Object, and the Interpretant (the person, tradition, or discourse in which the Sign equates to its Object). Peirce argued that all the semiotic processes upon which culture—and human cognition—are based have this triune or "triadic" character. He used "triadic" in a theoretically specified sense for relations that had the defining quality of what he called "thirdness," a quality which he distinguished from "monadic" firstness (e.g., disembodied qualities like blueness, sadness, tightness, hardness) and "dyadic" secondness (e.g., transitive effortful actions like pushing, cutting, breaking, throwing):

> Firstly come "firstnesses," or positive internal characters of the subject in itself;
> secondly come "secondnesses," or brute actions of one subject or substance on
> another, regardless of law or of any third subject; thirdly comes *"thirdnesses,"* or the

mental or quasi-mental influence of one subject on another relatively to a third. (Peirce, 1931, p. 469)

One way of understanding the thirdness of triadic relations, according to Peirce, is that thirdness involves a recognition of relationships or "a capacity to make relational judgements" (Hookway, 1985, p. 92).[10] One of Peirce's examples of thirdness is the act of giving. In behavioral terms a man's (A) gift of a vase (B) to his wife (C) might be summarized as "merely one dyadic relation followed by another" (Peirce, 1931, p. 176): A put B down; C picked B up. However, triadic relations, if genuine, tie together three entities "in a way that does not consist in any complexus of dyadic relations" (Peirce, 1903/1931, p. 272). The same is true of giving. Hence for any sequence of events to count as an episode of giving, something beyond secondness is needed: the concept of thirdness. In our example, C has *to recognize A's intention* to give her B. Only in this way can the ownership of the vase "legally" be transferred from husband to wife and only in this way will the vase gain a unique sentimental significance for the couple (Bradley, in press). In this chapter I will follow Peirce in using the word "triadic" to refer to the capacity to recognize a subjective relationship between two other entities (the husband's intention to give the vase), whether these be a person and an object or between two (or more) other people.

Thirdness, the capacity to see a relationship between two other entities—as when C is jealous of a perceived relationship between A and B—is the capacity which is necessary for participation in culture. More than one significant theory of socialization invokes this sort of thirdness. Thus, while the extent of Peirce's influence on Mead is controversial (Diggins, 1994; Joas, 1997), there are undoubted parallels between their formulations of cultural participation. Mead's (1934) "symbolic interactionism" proposed that the process of becoming a member of society involved children learning how to take on the perspectives of others, particularly through playing with peers. Role playing or perspective taking was the basis of meaning-making. "Meaning as such, i.e., the object of thought, arises in experience through the individual stimulating himself to take the attitude of the other in his reaction toward the object" (Mead, 1934, p. 89). Through playing (e.g., as doctor and nurse) and other occasions for role taking, the child learns to take on different attitudes when communicating with others and this enables children to take the attitudes of others toward themselves.

In Freud, the concept of the super-ego or what Lacan calls "the name of the father" was developed to show that any access to a community of others brings with it rules of communication and restrictions of our desires (Bradley, in press). Thus, even the simplest symbolic communication between two people requires both to be participating in something that exists independently of them, a "symbolic order" (cf. Muller, 1996). For this reason Lacan (1988, p. 227; cf. Green, 2004) argued that a two-body psychology is impossible: "With a two-body psychology, we come upon the famous problem, which is unresolved in physics, of two bodies. In fact, if you restrict yourselves to the level of two bodies, there is no satisfactory symbolism available." Within psychoanalytic theories of development, the child's accession to the symbolic order is represented through the myth of Oedipus (Selby, 1993a). That this accession is theoretically equivalent to what Peirce calls thirdness has been canvassed at length in an issue of *Psychoanalytic Quarterly* in 2004 by Jessica Benjamin, Thomas Ogden, Ronald Britton, and others. These psychoanalysts stress that thirdness does not just underpin important intellectual and cultural achievements, such as our capacities for group membership and objectivity, but requires a certain degree of emotional maturity (Winnicott, 1941/1975a):

> If the link between the parents perceived in love and hate can be tolerated in the child's mind ... this provides us with a capacity for seeing ourselves in interaction with others and for entertaining another point of view whilst retaining our own, for reflecting on ourselves whilst being ourselves. (Britton, 2004, p. 47; Britton, 1989)

Britton concludes that the achievement of thirdness creates what he dubs "tri-angular space," a space in which we can appreciate events from more than one perspective. This is equivalent to the "potential space" for play and reflection that Winnicott (1967/1974c) argued furnishes the location for cultural experience.

Hence the capacity for jealousy represents a step away from a narcissistic involve-ment with the (m)other (which always phenomenologically presents itself as dyadic to the narcissist—where object seems to mimic subject in an unmediated fashion—even though it is not), in which the baby does not recognize the mother as genuinely other (i.e., as part of another—"third"—world that is "beyond" the baby). It is a step toward a recognition and acceptance of the (m)other as having relationships of her own that do not include the baby. According to this formulation, jealousy would share with narcissism the baby's sense of frustration at the "failure" of the mother to fulfill the mirror-role and so provide the infant with an image of him or herself. But it would represent an advance over narcissism in that it would constitute a recognition—but not yet an acceptance—of the (m)other's independence in having other relationships. As such, jealousy would provide early evidence that the baby was capable of representing and so responding to interpersonal relationships and hence, potentially, of recognizing the quality of its own relationships. Jealousy therefore represents an escape from entrapment in the here and now of the imaginary dimension of intersubjectivity and the beginnings of the capacity to represent symbolically the relationships that really constitute the baby's social world.

Toward Triadic Measures: Method

The idea that, to be jealous, infants must be aware not just of others' social *behavior*, but of others' social *relationships*—which is the essence of thirdness—implies that an awareness of the meanings of what they and others are doing is not just something to be "read into" it by external interpreters but is guiding the actions of babies themselves. This means that existing procedures for observing and coding infant behavior according to interpretive categories decided before-hand by observers need rethinking. This section undertakes that task.

Observational researchers in developmental psychology use the term "triadic" in at least two different ways. Most studies of babies' "triadic" relations use the term to refer to tasks which expect the baby and an adult to coordinate their attention to a nearby object or event, something thing-like which Bates, Camaioni, and Volterra (1976; see Reddy, 2005) called the "third element." This is the person–person–object paradigm (e.g., Moll & Tomasello, 2007; Striano & Stahl, 2005; Legerstee, 2005; Legerstee, Markova, & Fisher, 2007; Tomasello, Carpenter, Call, Behne, & Moll, 2005; Butterworth, 2001). A minority use the term "triadic" to refer to studies which position babies for interaction with two other people: the person–person–person paradigm.[11] Examples include a baby observed with his or her parents (Parke, Power, & Bottman, 1979; Barrett & Hinde, 1988; Hedenbro, Shapiro, & Gottman, 2006), with a parent and a sibling (Dunn & Kendrick, 1982), with an adult and a same-age peer (Fivaz-Depeursinge & Corboz-Warnery, 1999), with two adults (Tremblay & Rovira, 2007), or with two same-age peers (Selby & Bradley, 2003a; Ishikawa & Hay, 2006). Until now the term triadic has been used indiscriminately in the developmental literature to apply to either or both of these situations. What both usages assume is that babies are studied "triadically" when in situations which include two significant entities other than the baby. This promotes a purely descriptive understanding of the term. Following this logic, if psychologists studied babies in company with three or four significant other entities, they would presumably call their studies "tetradic" or "pentadic."

This chapter attaches a more precise theoretical signification to the term "triadic," such that it signals solely those states of affairs where a baby can be shown to have relationships that involve thirdness: viz. a subjective orientation to a relationship between (at least) two other entities (whether just people or people and things). This is in accordance with Peirce's (1931, p. 177) observation that "any analysis will show that every relation which is *tetradic, pentadic*, or any greater number of correlates is nothing but a compound of triadic relations ... beyond the three elements of Firstness, Secondness, and Thirdness, there is nothing else to be found in the phenomenon." If we use the term "triadic" in a purely descriptive way, it is likely to be used indiscriminately to denote a variety of phenomena, some of which do and some of which do not involve the crucial theoretical attribute of thirdness (crucial because it underpins the infant's inte-gration into culture). Perhaps unsurprisingly, given this untheorized understand-ing of "triadic," most research on so-called "triadic" relations in infancy uses behavioral measures that are actually dyadic.

One of the most widely used conceptualizations of "triadic" relations was devised by Parke et al. (1979) for the analysis of "influence" within family triads (mother, father, child). Parke et al. argue that "triadic interaction" can be represented as a concatenation of two or three dyadic interactions or "moves." Hence if A (the "influence source") influences B (the "primary recipient") and then B ("secondary influence source") influences C ("secondary recipient"), this is a triadic "influence pattern." Three kinds of influence source are distinguished: *transitive* (i.e., A → B; B → C; e.g., father kisses mother who then nuzzles baby); *circular* (i.e., A → B; B → C; C → A; e.g., father tickles infant; infant vocalizes; mother smiles at father); and *parallel* (i.e., A → C; B → C; e.g., mother tickles baby; father tickles baby). However, as Parke et al. (1979, p. 235) note:

> This scheme cannot classify all influences. Family members' perceptions of the family as a unit and perceptions of relationships between two family members (for example, the father's perception of the mother–infant relationship) do not fit well into this scheme. This weakness is a function of the classification scheme's emphasis on pairs of dyads within the triad.

Ironically, "this weakness" means that Parke et al.'s scheme excludes any genuinely triadic interactions, that is, ones that have the quality of thirdness. Nevertheless, most studies of infants in groups of three (or more) adopt a dyadic form of analysis akin to Parke et al.'s scheme. Thus Dunn and Kendrick's (1982) analysis of the effects of a new sibling on the mother–child relationship is conceived dyadically, as is Barrett and Hinde's (1988) study of the "triadic interactions" between mothers and their first- and second-born children. Stern et al.'s (1975) analysis of a mother interacting simultaneously with her two 4-month-old twins is also entirely dyadic. Most recently, Ishikawa and Hay (2006) claim the existence of "triadic interaction among newly acquainted 2-year-olds" entirely on the basis of a sequential dyadic analysis developed from Parke et al.'s (1979) scheme. Indeed, Ishikawa and Hay's analysis was so sequential that they "decided to disallow co-occurrence ... if two children were acting simultaneously, the observer had to judge who began to act first, and then code a separate move for each child" (Ishikawa & Hay, 2006, pp. 159–160).

Another dyadic conceptualization is to be found in the widespread use of "socially directed behaviors" (SDBs) as a measure of infant communication, whether in dyads or trios. An SDB is defined as "any behavior accompanied by or immediately preceded or followed by looking at another person" (Mueller & Brenner, 1977, p. 856; cf. Tremblay-Leveau & Nadel, 1995, 1996). This definition makes SDBs intrinsically dyadic because, for an action to register as "socially directed," it must be accompanied by a look. It is impossible to look at two people at once, so SDBs can only be coded as occurring between two people. Thus Nadel and Tremblay-Leveau (1999, p. 205) report with surprise that, in baby–baby–adult trios, 11-month-olds would sometimes direct their actions not to one but to both of the other participants. They have suggested that the definition of SDB needs to be broadened to accommodate "behavior directed at *two* persons" by coding as triadic any behavior accompanied by "at least one discrete look at each of the two persons or to-and-fro gazing between both persons." Yet, with few exceptions, SDBs continue to be coded in a way that can only accommodate dyadic behavior.

Another problem with traditional methods of analyzing infant behavior where thirdness is at issue is that researchers use predefined categories for coding behavior (e.g., Ishikawa & Hay, 2006). Thus SDBs are typically defined as *"any behavior* accompanied by or immediately preceded or followed by looking at another person" (Mueller & Brenner, 1977, p. 856; emphasis added). Now, if infants are capable of creating and sharing meanings (Trevarthen & Aitken, 2001; Mueller, 1991; Halliday, 1975), new meanings could well arise in infant groups. Such significance-making activities would potentially count as triadic in Peirce's sense. Yet, if we ask what would be behavioral indices of meaning-sharing in a group, the candidates can never emerge from an analysis in terms of SDBs that necessarily fails to distinguish between the meanings of, say, a "cry + look" versus a "point + look" versus a "cough + look." If babies are to be shown to put their "communicative competence" to work in any social context, the meanings they create must be shown to be specific to their context and hence not capable of predefinition. Whether it be in a long-term group like the baby's family or in a more ephemeral group such as an experimental trio of infants running over 15 minutes for scientific purposes, meaning-sharing will depend on the babies' participation in the idiosyncratic history and traditions of that particular group. Depending on the group's history and the babies' intentions, what looks superficially to be "the same" gesture (e.g., toe-holding or staccato cooing) may mean quite different things in one group than in another and even on different occasions in the same group (Selby & Bradley, 2003a; see next section). Inevitably, therefore, "behaviors of young children which take into account more than one person . . . do not fit with one-to-one behavioral definitions" (Tremblay-Leveau & Nadel, 1995, p. 228).

Clearly, in order to discover whether babies are capable of triadic behavior such as jealousy, we need to devise measures and procedures that do not entrench dyadic assumptions in our research. In particular, we need to find a way of uncovering what infants themselves mean by what they do. And we need to detect exchanges where infants respond as a "third party" to relationships between two or more others. Selby and Bradley's (2003a) "babies in groups" paradigm attempts to fulfill both these desiderata.

The "Babies in Groups" Paradigm

Ryan's (1974) introduction of the term "intersubjectivity" to the study of infant communication was taken from Habermas's (1970) critique of Chomsky. According to Habermas, the communicative competence which intersubjectivity affords is at its most fluent in conditions approximating an "ideal speech situation" where relationships between the communicators are at their most symmetrical with regards to the capacity for self-representation, criticism, and expression. We (Selby & Bradley, 2003a) observed that the *en face* paradigm for the study of infant–adult communication was inevitably "distorted" by asymmetries in that adults are far more powerful, knowledgeable, and skilled in communication than babies. Hence, skeptics are given license to argue that "proto-conversations" and turn taking between mothers and babies do not betoken intersubjectivity. They are rather the product of a semi-conscious form of puppetry or "scaffolding" by the mother, who, under pressure to perform from the demand characteristics of the experimental set-up, and far more powerful as a communicator, fits her expressions to the baby's endogenous behavioral cadences. By acting *as if* what the baby does is communicative, she gives the observers the false impression she is exchanging meanings with her charge, like a ventriloquist with a dummy (e.g., Newson, 1979; Shotter & Gregory, 1976; Kaye, 1984). Like Mueller (1991), we argued that a stronger test of the infant's capacity to communicate and understand meanings would be a more symmetrical "speech situation" involving same-aged peers.

Aware of moves in evolutionary psychology (e.g., Perry, 1997; Dunbar, 2003) which suggested that humans are psychologically pre-adapted for group living, we were surprised to find that there had been few tests of babies' capacity to take part in group relations and none involving solely peers (see Hart et al., 1998a, 1998b; Tremblay-Leveau & Nadel, 1995; 1996; Fivaz-Depeursinge & Corboz-Warnery, 1999; Paul & Thomson-Salo, 1996). So we created a set situation in which a trio of infants of approximately 9 months of age were sat in three equidistant strollers that had been immobilized but were placed close enough together for babies to be able to touch each other (see Figure 10.2). Our protocol ensured that babies had not met prior to their meeting in the recording studio. They could be observed through CCTV from an adjoining "control" room by parents and researchers. Once the babies had been secured in the strollers by their guardians, all adults left the studio and the babies' actions were recorded on two digital TV cameras. Recording only stopped when babies became too frustrated to continue, according to the judgment of parents or researchers. In the five trios we recorded, sessions lasted for between 5 and 25 minutes with a mean duration of 12 minutes.[12]

We adopted a two-step case-based approach to the analysis of the action we recorded. We argued that, if babies were capable of communicating meanings, these would not be discoverable by frequency counts of generic categories defined a priori by adult researchers because the meanings would be specific to the context in which any given communication was taking place. Hence the first step in our analysis was a prima facie "thick" description of each group session, focusing on meanings and feelings and contexts (cf. Geertz, 1973). This was subsequently tested by a second analytic step in which fine-grained numerical

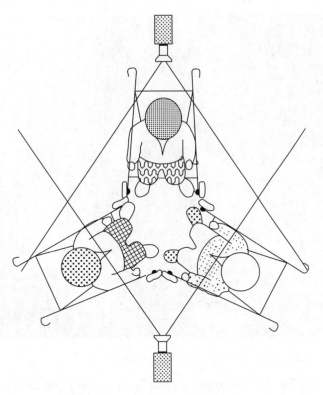

Figure 10.2   Set-up for Selby and Bradley's "babies in groups" paradigm

evidence was sought that might bear out or refute the "thick" description. The behavioral categories used in this second step were defined so as to allow for the establishment of inter-observer reliability and replicability.

The need to take a two-step case-based approach to infant communication is illustrated by our demonstration that a given infant action can change its meaning as a result of a trio's communicative process. One of our prima facie descriptions suggested that an 8-month-old girl, Paula, grabbed onto her left foot in order to "contain" (cf. Bion, 1962) or "hold" (cf. Winnicott, 1965b) anxieties aroused by her mother's departure from the recording studio. We initially arrived at this interpretation from noting that Paula first grabbed her foot as she looked with dismay at her mother disappearing through the studio door and that she appeared to be more engaged with the other two babies in the trio when holding her foot than when not holding it. The idea that Paula's foot-holding provided her with a sense of a having a "secure base" for (visuo-social) exploration (Bowlby, 1988) was subsequently tested by calculating the proportion of the session for which she held her foot (48%) and the proportion of her looking at her peers that occurred while she was foot-holding (twice as much as when she wasn't). This supported the interpretation that Paula's foot-holding signified security in the face of her mother's absence. However, during the course of the group-process, this meaning

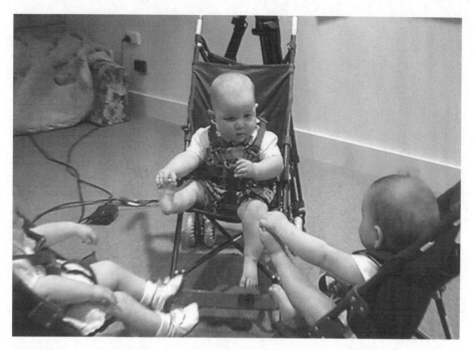

Figure 10.3   Paula imitating Esther imitating Paula

was augmented by the actions of a second baby, 7-month-old Esther. Esther soon became fascinated by Paula's foot-holding and began to imitate it, making a series of "initiations" (Tremblay-Leveau & Nadel, 1996, p. 149: i.e., foot-holding plus looking) back both to Paula and one to Ethel (the third baby in the trio). A minute and a half into the group-process, Esther's 4th foot-holding initiation attracted Paula and she responded to it by imitating Esther's foot-holding back to Esther (see Figure 10.3). From this point on, Paula's foot-holding formed part of an imitative game with Esther such that she looked three times as much at Esther as at the third baby (Ethel) in the remainder of the group's interaction. In sum, Paula's foot-holding gained a new meaning that emerged from the communicative process specific to this group and could not have been guessed at a priori.

Ethel's response to the imitative game played by her two peers Paula and Esther was one of relaxed curiosity. That this is not always the case in baby trios was illustrated by a different group made up of two 9-month-olds, Joe and Ann, and a 6-month-old, Mona. The session lasted 12 minutes. The first 3 minutes of the session featured a great many short looks by Ann at both Mona and Joe, the glue-like "gripped" attention of Mona to both Joe and Ann (but increasingly to Joe), and smiling overtures by Joe to both Ann and Mona.

By the 4th minute, both Ann and Mona were looking predominately at Joe (Mona looked for 54 s at Joe and 5 s at Ann during minute 4; Ann looked at Joe for 39 s and at Mona for 6 s during the same period), whilst Joe looked relatively little at

Figure 10.4   Ann plays "footsie" with Joe

either of them (12 s at each). This pattern characterized the whole interaction, with Joe looking at the others least (total 410 s = 57%) but being looked at most (713 s). Mona looked at the others most (640 s or 89%) but was looked at least by the others (total = 248 s); and Ann being in the middle on both counts (looking at others = 488 s or 68%; looked at = 580 s). Whilst both Ann and Mona seemed to prefer Joe to each other, this was far more the case with Ann than Mona. Thus Ann spent three times as much time (365 s or 75%) looking at Joe as she did at Mona, whereas Mona spent only slightly more time looking at Joe than at Ann (348 s or 54%). Joe looked more at Ann than at Mona (Ann tot = 285 s or 70%).

Ann and Joe's interest in each other increased as their conversation progressed, largely because Ann found two ways to keep his attention: frequent vocalizing and "playing footsie" by reaching out with her foot to touch his foot (Figure 10.4). To begin with, looking was the main form of interaction for all three, though both Ann and particularly Joe made brief smiling overtures to both the other babies during the 1st minute—overtures which soon fade out (Mona did not smile throughout the recording). During the 5th minute, Ann began to make frequent staccato vocalizations, predominantly whilst looking at Joe (she made 25 brief vocalizations in the 5th minute and a further 104 over the next 3 minutes; 73% while looking at Joe and only 6% while looking at Mona). The rate at which she made these increased markedly after Joe made one brief vocalization to her (from 2 sounds in 20 seconds prior to his vocalization, to 10 in 10 seconds after; throughout all this Mona was mute; see Bradley, 2009). After watching Ann make this flurry of vocalizations, Joe then turned to Mona to make an expansive initiation, as if "bringing her in" to the conversation: he reoriented his body towards her, leant towards her, waved both his arms up and down, all accompanied by an 8-second-long wide-open smile and raised eyebrows.

This attracted Mona's attention, who had also been watching Ann vocalize. In contrast, as Ann saw Mona and Joe make mutual gaze, her legs, which had been stretched out towards the other two, drop down and she looks down at herself, seemingly deflated. Joe looks briefly back at her, still smiling and they make mutual gaze. But then he turns back to Mona, still smiling. After this, 30 seconds pass before Ann and Joe make mutual gaze again. Five seconds after Joe's big initiation to Mona, Ann turns and scowls at Mona—an expression which she never made to Joe. Ann also reached out and briefly touched Joe's left foot with her own right foot during this period of the interaction (immediately thereafter bringing her right foot to touch her own left foot). Mona watches this sequence and then rubs her own feet together.

In the 8th minute, Ann begins an intense game of footsie with Joe that lasts until the interaction breaks down 4 minutes later. Twenty seconds into this game, Mona once again holds her own feet out, rubbing them together, looking at Ann. After a minute she stretches her own feet out even further, now towards Ann, still rubbing them together, apparently trying to touch Ann's left foot (which is symmetrically stretched out, at the same angle as her right foot that is touching Joe's foot, and hence is close to Mona). At this point, Mona whines loudly (as if to say "what about me?"; Mona's first vocalization). Both Joe and Ann briefly look at her and then back at each other. In the 10th minute, Mona finally manages to touch Ann's left foot with her own right foot. Ann looks at her, in contact through her feet with both Joe and Mona simultaneously. Ann then withdraws both her feet, clutches her right foot in her right hand and her left foot with her left hand and deliberately brings her two feet together with her hands until they touch in front of her face. She then looks at Joe and reaches her right foot to make contact with his foot while tucking her left foot under her stroller, bending it as far as possible away from contact with Mona.

Whereas hitherto both Ann's feet were stretching out symmetrically, she now sits asymmetrically, apparently to avoid contact ("contamination"?) by Mona's attempts to touch her. During the 11th minute she is not only looking at Joe, vocalizing frequently and playing footsie with him but points at him with both index fingers. (Both Ann and Mona point at Joe but never at each other.) Finally, in the 12th minute Ann turns simultaneously to sneer towards and make a gesture with the back of her hand, index finger raised, towards Mona, who was looking straight at Ann (Ann drew her foot back from Joe whilst making this gesture). She then turned back to Joe, stretched out her foot towards him and gave him a brief smile. Joe, who had been watching Ann throughout this sequence, then turned away to Mona with big smiling initiation similar to those 6 minutes earlier, described above (as if to comfort Mona by saying "Don't mind about her"). Mona turned to look at him. Ann, watching Joe "deserting" her for mutual gaze with Mona, immediately pouts and begins to cry (the first crying in the session). Her crying builds up and within thirty seconds the session ends. (Selby & Bradley, 2003a, pp. 213–216).

The suggestion here is of powerful feelings circulating in the group, even though these babies had never met before. Joe is interested in both the other babies, smiles at both of them throughout the interaction, and also seems to have a "sense of fair play" in that, twice, when it seems Ann gets too exclusively pro-Joe, he turns away in a friendly fashion to make compensating overtures to Mona. Mona mainly watches, though she does prefer Joe (despite Ann's greater activity) and acts "left out" when Ann engages Joe in prolonged games of footsie: making a complaining vocalization, rubbing her own feet together when their feet are in contact, and stretching out to "join in" by touching Ann's foot at the same time as Ann's foot is touching Joe's. The most active is Ann, who appears increasingly pro-Joe and increasingly uninterested in or even anti-Mona—and resentful of Joe's even-handed interest in Mona, a resentment which ultimately leads to the breakdown of the group.

Experimental studies of infants' jealousy typically code as jealous any reaction to social exclusion that involves negative affect (crying, distress, negative vocalizations; Hart et al., 2004). A description of infant trios such as that given above shows an interplay of inclusion and exclusion in the spontaneous behavior of the three participants that is more complex than can be caught by the term jealousy, so defined. According to the usual global definition (negative affect caused by social exclusion), three obvious instances of jealousy occurred: twice when Ann seems to "deflate" after Joe has made an overture to Mona (the second time bursting into tears and ending the interaction) and once when Mona stretches out her feet toward where Ann and Joe's feet are touching, rubs them together (self-comforting), and whines. But we can also see the kinds of jealousy observed in this trio as parts of a larger picture. An important factor is Ann's increasing attraction to Joe, shown by her looking at him three times as much as at Mona, making 12 times as many vocalizations to Joe as to Mona, pointing at him, smiling at him, and playing footsie with him. There is a sense of possessiveness about this attraction as Ann does not point at Mona, smiles at her only once at the start of the interaction, removes her foot from Mona once touched, tucking it under her seat, and makes three ambivalent gestures toward Mona with a scowling facial expression. But Ann's expressions of jealousy would not have come about if Joe had not had a very different attitude to Ann than she had toward him. Joe clearly enjoyed and engaged with Ann's overtures, but his actions toward Mona were inclusive rather than exclusive. He made three expansive smiling initiations to Mona: once near the beginning of the interaction, once after Ann had begun to vocalize frequently and pointedly at him, and once after Ann had directed the last of her ambivalent scowling gestures toward Mona. Meanwhile, though Mona seemed to want to be included in the footsie game Ann began with Joe, she was content (like Ethel in the Paula–Esther–Ethel trio described earlier) to watch Joe and Ann's interchanges for much of the interaction, her head flicking back from one to the other, like a girl watching a tennis final.

According to the earlier theoretical discussion, the three expressions of jealousy I have just documented gain their meaning from a wider context that suggests a variety of different responses manifesting "thirdness" (a subjective orientation to others' relationships). While Ann's preference for Joe over Mona is not necessarily triadic in this strict sense, her distress at Joe's smiling initiations at Mona is. Likewise with Mona's whining at Ann's and Joe's game of footsie. Further, given the timing of Joe's last initiation to Mona (just after Ann had made the back-of-the-hand gesture described above), it seems to be an attempt to "bring her in" to the conversation or condole with her after Ann's apparent rejection of her; this also manifests thirdness. Finally, the frequent to-and-fro looking that all babies showed in the first 4 minutes of the recording, and that Mona, in particular, continued to show throughout the session, implies that each baby was constantly "making connections" between the actions of both their peers in a manner that is likely to be part of the thirdness we observed.

Theoretical Implications: Jealousy and the Development of Thirdness

It has been widely claimed that infants undergo a revolution in their orientation to other people at around 9 months of age. It is usually forgotten that this idea was put forward by Klein over half a century ago (1952a), though Klein was careful not to confuse chronology with process (Selby, 1993b). A rather different 9-months revolution has since been (re)discovered by Trevarthen and Hubley (1978). Their claim has been taken up and elaborated by various developmentalists, all along similar lines.[13] Though this new revolution has turned out to be nebulous chronologically, theoretically, and descriptively (Legerstee, 2005), most theorists argue that a crucial element in it is the incorporation of things into what was formerly a "contentless" dyadic sharing:

> At 9 months there is attainment of functional control, of intrinsic origin, for the use of innate and practiced communicative abilities so they can be related to physical objects that have been brought inside the field of shared experience and shared knowledge. (Trevarthen & Hubley, 1978, p. 223; Braten & Trevarthen, 2007)

> At around 9 to 12 months of age, infants begin to engage in interactions that are triadic in the sense that they involve the referential triangle of child, adult, and some outside entity to which they share attention. (Tomasello, 1999, p. 302)

Tomasello (1999, p. 302) sees all these "triadic" achievements as forms of "joint attention" which are underpinned by the birth of the ability "to understand other persons as intentional agents." Yet joint attention may appear at any time between 2 months of age (Butterworth, 2001; Scaife & Bruner, 1975; Striano & Rochat, 1999; Racine & Carpendale, 2007) and the baby's second year (cf. Tomasello et al., 2005). What this chronological imprecision implies is that there is conceptual confusion about the radical change which babies' social understanding is supposed to undergo in the second 6 months of life. Some of the claimed achievements are socio-cognitive (joint attention), some are emotional (the advent of negation; Schaffer, 1984; or of "non-basic" emotions such as jealousy and shame; Draghi-Lorenz, Reddy, & Costall, 2001), and some are semiotic (the first use of conventional signs: words, gestures; Halliday, 1975). (See Table 10.1.)

The concept of thirdness potentially integrates semiosis, joint attention, and emotionality—and also 9-month-olds' success in solving Piaget's (1955) test of object permanence (which depends on a baby recognizing that an adult's actions are inspired by an intention to hide an object from the baby). Thirdness is intrinsic to the structure of all meaning-making. More significantly for my argument, thirdness relates as easily to person–person–object relations (e.g., joint attention, social referencing) as it does to the mentally more demanding multi-person relations in trios and other groups, *provided that the baby's actions are informed by an interpretation of the subjective orientation of another person to a third entity* (sign, object, or person). Under this rubric, certain instances of joint attention and gaze-following do not necessarily entail thirdness. For example, if a mother looks at an attractive object like a teddy, her baby may mimic her movement or be attracted to follow her line of sight and so also catch sight of and look at the teddy, but without any interpretation of how the mother is feeling or thinking about it (Tremblay & Rovira, 2007). Of course, babies do sometimes act on their interpretation of the adult's subjective orientation to an object, as in social referencing. But the kinds of *object-directed behavior* cited by Tomasello, Trevarthen, and Schaffer (Table 10.1) do not necessarily involve any emotional tone (viz. requesting, declaring, obeying, cooperating, imitating, performing a task, using an object appropriately, looking at an object). This is quite otherwise in *multi-person situations* where attraction, gratitude, dislike, jealousy, envy, violence, impatience, preference, yearning, generosity may all color the way the baby's thirdness is manifested. This means that there is a much broader range of types of thirdness potentially present in a three-person trio or larger group than with two people and an object.

Let me develop this point in more detail. Thirdness is the subjective relationship one forms to others' relationships. Within a person–person–person (**A-B-C**) setting, thirdness is the resultant of three different kinds of variable (see Figure 10.5). From **A**'s perspective, **A** will

1 observe the individual behaviors that **B** directs at **C** (**bc**) and **C** directs at **B** (**cb**);
2 interpret **bc** and **cb** as constituting some kind (**y**) of relationship between **B** and **C**;
3 come up with their own subjective orientation/response (**x**) to this perceived relationship **y** (the orientation of their response being what allows researchers to interpret the value of **y**).

Table 10.1   Capacities potentially relevant to the "nine months revolution" in infants' social understanding

Emotional	
1.	First signs of gratitude, guilt and reparation (e.g., giving: Klein, 1952a, 1952b)
2.	Demonstrates affection by hugging and kissing * +
3.	Shows jealousy and other "non-basic" emotions (Hart et al., 1998a; 1998b; Selby & Bradley, 2003a; Draghi-Lorenz et al., 2001)
4.	Fear of rejection, quest for approbation %
5.	Onset of stranger anxiety (Spitz, 1960; Ainsworth et al., 1978) %
6.	First attachments form (Bowlby, 1969)
Social	
7.	Deixis: shifting roles between recipient and agent (Bruner, 1975) #
8.	Initiates/plays give-and-take games, peek-a-boo # + *
9.	Imitates demonstrated actions on objects *@
10.	Follows adult gaze, joint attention to objects *@ %
11.	Preoccupied by others' attention %
12.	Shows social referencing @ %
Communication/ Semiotic	
13.	Pretend play (holds cup to doll's mouth) * +
14.	Makes vocal and gestural commands and declarations (e.g. pointing) #*
15.	Co-operates with non-verbal requests # + *
16.	Obeys learnt instructions to select or manipulate objects #
17.	Appropriate use of artifacts (toy phone; toy car; mop; cup; spoon; book: Zelazo & Kearsley, 1980) #*
18.	Use of "protolanguage" and symbolic communication, incl. by gestures (Halliday, 1975) # %
19.	Requests help in performing task with object* +
20.	Shakes head or says "No" appropriately * +
21.	Conventional manners e.g. waves good bye +
22.	Begins to use conventional labels for objects. Names people and pets * +
Cognitive	
23.	Beginnings of object permanence (Piaget, 1955) #
24.	Beginnings of intentional action (secondary circular reactions; Piaget, 1953) #
Motor	
25.	Onset of locomotion %

Source: Condensed from #Trevarthen & Hubley, 1978; +Bretherton et al., 1981; *Schaffer, 1996, p.115; @Tomasello, 1999; %Rochat, 2004; and other sources cited in the text.

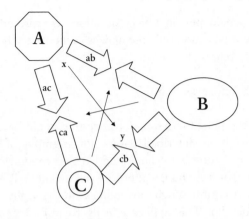

Figure 10.5 Schematic representation of thirdness in a person–person–person setting (see text for explanation)

In a person–person–object (**A-B-o**) setting, as typically described, there appears to be a far less complex set of relationships and far smaller range of variation under (1) than with three people. For example, a person **B** and an object **o** are unlikely to be perceived by **A** as conversing, fighting, agreeing, disagreeing, teasing, or mutually attracted to each other. This means there is assumed to be correspondingly less variation in (2) and (3) in the **A-B-o** situation than with **A-B-C**. Thus there is every possibility of a discordance between how **B** and **C** relate to each other (**bc/cb**), on the one hand, and, on the other, **A**'s interpretation and orientation/response to the relationship s/he perceives between **B** and **C** (**x-y**). For example, **B** may behave in an alluring fashion toward **C** (**bc**); **C** may watch **B**'s overtures with mild interest (**cb**); **A** may perceive the **B-C** relationship as excluding her (**y**) and protest vociferously (**x**). Here:

$$\textbf{x-y} \neq \textbf{B-C}$$

hence

$$\textbf{ab} \neq \textbf{bc} \text{ and } \textbf{ac} \neq \textbf{cb}$$

Furthermore, **x** is not predictable from **y**. For example, **A** might not protest at her perceived exclusion by **B** and **C**. She might look on curiously. Or she might get bored and prefer to examine the lights on the ceiling above her.

In the kind of person–person–object situation, as represented by Tomasello, however, his conceptualization only recognizes as theoretically relevant occasions where concordance reigns:

$$Xy = \mathbf{bo} \text{ and therefore } \mathbf{ao} = \mathbf{bo}$$

While, in theory, the person–person–object setting could be conceived as more complicated than I have described it—as, for example, if there were some contrasting emotional tone between A's and B's perception of the object (e.g., A likes it, B doesn't), or if A and B's interpersonal dynamic (A ← → B) were seen as affecting joint attention—such possibilities are typically not canvassed by theorists like Tomasello. This applies equally to imitation, social referencing, and joint attention, for all of which it is assumed that triadic interaction requires baby to do and perceive as adult does. Hence, whereas misrecognition and a host of subjective orientations other than the empathetic can be comprehended under the rubric of thirdness, the kinds of triadic relationship proposed by Tomasello, Schaffer, and Trevarthen and Hubley predominantly assume veridical interpersonal perception and identical or complementary motivations. Consequently, the kinds of relationship their theories theorize are few, symmetrical, and culturally non-specific (e.g., looking, giving, showing, asking, telling). Yet, thirdness, the fact that an infant **A** can construe **B–C** relationships in diverse ways, is their key to their culture: it is by identifying and entering into how other people treat each other that babies glean the necessary foothold in the idiosyncratic patterns of power and subordination, action and resistance, discourse and practice, that will, in 18 months or so, have begun to make them recognizably members of the culture into which they have been born (e.g., on early gender identity, see Urwin, 1984, p. 274). At its simplest, therefore, thirdness constitutes the left-hand side of Lacan's Schema L as pictured in Figure 10.1.

A theory of the infant's accession to culture which builds in the concept thirdness would thus posit there to be a three-stranded progression toward cultural membership through development of:

(a) the complexity of social experience babies manifest with others;
(b) the ways this implies babies at first construe others' social actions and relationships, which will become increasingly culture-specific over time (Urwin, 1984; Selby & Bradley, 2005);
(c) the kinds of response invoked by these constructions, which will also become increasingly culture-specific over time.

Apropos (b), I have proposed that babies initially construe others' social actions narcissistically, citing evidence from the ubiquity of maternal "mirroring" (which seems naturally designed to complement a narcissistic orientation), the structure of spontaneous *en face* conversations (e.g., Bradley, 1989a, chapter 8), and babies' aversive reactions to still-face and double-video procedures.

The key question posed by my analysis is why and how do babies escape their early narcissism? One well-developed answer is to be found in psychoanalytic writings. Freud's (1914) introductory article on narcissism equates the baby's initial orientation with an egg-like state from which the baby needs to hatch if it is to get to grips with reality. Narcissism serves to subdue the baby's immediate anxieties and as such is dominated by the pleasure principle. But it is a here-and-now solution which has no future. Moreover, the scant "content" of narcissistic inter-action is provided largely by the baby: the baby's expressions being reflected back by the (m)other. Subjectively, this kind of intersubjectivity quickly proves empty and hence frustrating, as evinced by the growing infant's increasing flight from face-to-face interactions after 3 months (e.g., Papousek & Papousek, 1977). Fur-thermore, as the baby's interests in and capacities for the manipulation and comprehension of its physical and social world increase, the rewards offered by the proportionately brief periods of maternal "affect mirroring" will decline in salience: the baby will begin to develop and want to extend his or her more reality-based forms of control over the environment (cf. what Freud, 1911, calls the rise of the "reality principle") which is necessary for survival. Added to this is Winnicott's (1956/1975b; cf. Uzgiris, 1984) observation that, as the baby grows older and the mother's "primary maternal preoccupation" fades, she invests less and less time in "mirroring" and more time playing person–person and person–person–object games (a progressive dynamic that authors like Bruner, 1983, call "scaffolding").

In this context, jealousy provides a crucial index of when the baby gains the capacity to integrate this new sense of realism into its social relations.[14] As Lacan (1949, p. 5) puts it: "This moment in which the mirror-stage comes to an end inaugurates, by the identification with the *imago* of the counterpart and the drama of primordial jealousy ..., the dialectic that will henceforth link the *I* to socially elaborated situations." It is interesting to note, therefore, that there are significant overlaps, but also signal differences, between infantile jealousy and infants' responses to stilled faces. Babies in both conditions show a reduction in enjoyment, more anger, and more intense negative emotions than in normal conversation. However, babies' jealousy differs from their response to frozen faces in involving less distancing and more interest in the (m)other (Hart et al., 2004). Indubitably a (m)other addressing a life-sized doll is more obviously relational than a (m)other with a stilled face. Hart's jealousy procedure will therefore signally engage (and hence manifest) the baby's capacity for thirdness in that the mother's "failure" to attend to her baby can only be understood by a baby who continues to attend to and interpret (i.e., maintain an interest in) what the mother is doing (attending to the doll).

Conclusion

Piaget (1981) famously compared his vision of the infant's mind to the blueprint of an engine, a blueprint that did not include drivers or fuel. I have argued that what drives early development can be conceived on analogy with the hypothesis that the demands of group membership drove the evolutionary development of human language and culture. This proposal has been backed by an increasing weight of evidence and argument over recent years. Previously it had been assumed that primates had relatively large brains (or more precisely, neocortices; Finlay & Darlington, 1995) compared to their body-size as a consequence of their need to solve ecological problems. But Byrne and Whiten (1988) proposed that what differentiated primates from non-primates was their social skills or "Machiavellian intelligence," not their survival skills: primates solve ecological problems by social aggregation. Hence it was the demands of living in groups that led to accelerated evolution of the neocortex in primates.[15]

A parallel case can be built for ontogeny: it is the psycho-social demands of group-living that drive the infant toward a sign-based (symbolic) understanding of others from a starting position of narcissistic intersubjectivity. The fuel for this drive must be the need to gain more diverse sources of pleasure and experience and a more effective control over the environment than can be gained from the seductions of maternal mirroring (Urwin, 1984). Hence jealousy marks a crucial way-station in the baby's drive away from narcissism toward thirdness, that is, the development of a subjective orientation toward, and recognition of, other–other relationships. Interestingly, the baby's growing awareness of group relations shows other continuities with early narcissism as, for example, when a 10-month-old repeatedly "shows off" to her delighted family (Reddy, 1991, 2003, 2005).[16] So, while jealousy in infant–peer trios gains its significance from the light it sheds on this intersubjective transformation, it is not the only evidence of the baby's growing thirdness.

Acknowledgments

This work draws substantially on my collaboration with Jane Selby, who has also carefully read and strengthened my argument. Thanks also to an anonymous reviewer and to Colwyn Trevarthen, Vasudevi Reddy, and Lynne Murray for so willingly giving me illustrative materials.

Notes

1   "Whenever one finds an infant one finds maternal care, and without maternal care there would be no infant" (Winnicott, 1960/1965a, p. 39).
2   Colwyn Trevarthen tells me that he adapted the technique of using a mirror to ensure mothers' and babies' expressions were recorded simultaneously on the film from one he had earlier used in France with baboons. He adds: "What we did not know until years later was that Dan Stern was beginning his study of a mother playing with twins in New York, and that Mary Catherine Bateson was looking at films of a mother chatting to

her 9-week-old in the phonetics lab at MIT where Margaret Bullowa was researching preverbal communication" (pers. comm., May 20, 2008).

3 The word "attend" has interesting resonances in this context. When we say that babies are aware of when others are "attending" to them, we use a word that implies the other is "waiting upon" them as an "inferior waits on a superior . . . in readiness of service" (Simpson & Weiner, 1989, p. 765). The word "attend" thus underlines a special kind of asymmetry in infant–mother interaction.

4 Hence, in the tale of Snow White, the wicked queen does not look in her "mirror, mirror on the wall" for an objective assessment of how she looks. She looks in her mirror to be reassured that she is "the fairest one of all." She flies into a murderous fury when the mirror does not fulfill her narcissistic wishes.

5 This means that mothers "give a twist" to what they perceive their babies to be feeling or thinking when they mirror. They may exaggerate some positive expressions and minimize negative expressions. Hence it is not literally accurate to say that mirroring offers babies a slavishly "like me" reflection, as Gergely and Watson propose. Mothers reflect back an "improved" version of the baby to the baby—as Woolf underlines in the subsequent quote (see next endnote). Hence it is to be expected that some babies prefer "natural" interaction (i.e., affect mirroring) to straight imitation (Markova & Legerstee, 2006; Reddy, Chisholm, Forrester, Conforti, & Maniatopoulou, 2007).

6 Albeit satirically, Woolf's quote goes on to add that mirroring is the basis of human enculturation phylogenetically as I do ontogenetically: "Without that power probably the earth would still be a swamp and a jungle. The glories of all our wars would be unknown. We should still be scratching the outlines of deer on the remains of mutton bones and bartering flints for sheep skins or whatever simple ornament took our unsophisticated taste. Supermen and Fingers of Destiny would be never have existed. The Czar and the Kaiser would never have worn crowns or lost them. Whatever may be their use in civilized societies, mirrors are essential to all violent and heroic action. That is why Napoleon and Mussolini both insist so emphatically on the inferiority of women, for if they were not inferior, they would cease to enlarge. That serves to explain in part the necessity that women so often are to men."

7 Gergely and Watson (1996, p. 1199) claim that babies have the option of reading others' expressions (i) "realistically," as expressing the (m)other's emotions, or as (ii) "mirroring" their own emotions. (NB they advance no evidence that babies can read the "real" meaning of others' emotional expressions.) In fact, they argue (p. 1187) that this kind of "realistic" perception of adults' emotions is "pre-wired" from birth. They do not seem to have noticed that this implies adults have exactly the same emotional expressions as babies and that these are "anchored" to exactly the same internal states as they are in babies. So their theory of "emotional development" assumes that human emotional life does not develop at all. It also assumes that we have a "direct line" to what others are feeling. The theory I am proposing does not make these assumptions. I argue that understanding others' (and our own) emotions is the goal, not the starting point, of emotional development.

8 The psychoanalytic terms "object" and "cathexis" would make no sense if people and things were categorically distinct in the human mind.

9 Because there is no such thing as a dyad—the (infant–mother) dyad always exists in a context, e.g., of experimental investigation or family history that gives it thirdness (Walkerdine, 1982). Hence a two-body psychology is impossible (Lacan, 1988). Cf. "There is no such thing as a mother–infant relationship" (Green, 2004, p. 101).

10 Interestingly, Green (2004, p. 110) glosses what Freud calls "secondary process" (i.e., the processes dominated by the reality principle) as "the relationship of relationships."

11 Note that Tremblay and Rovira (2007) call person–person–object settings "triadic" and person–person–person settings "triangular." But this remains a purely descriptive distinction which misses the theoretical point being made here.

12 Since 2003, a number of other studies have been undertaken using the BiG paradigm or are in train (e.g., Helliesen, 2006; Malloch, Crncec, Adam, & Bradley, 2005; Markova, 2008).

13 Bretherton, McNew, and Beeghly-Smith (1981) refer to it as "the eight months blossoming" and Schaffer (1984, 1996), drawing on these earlier authors, has tabulated a set of findings that persuade him that "some of the most profound changes to be found in children's development occur at around 8 or 9 months."

14 Following Lacanian thinking and the observations of Trevarthen (e.g., 1978), I conceive babies' capacities for dealing with different aspects of their reality—as for example, their physical reality and their social reality—as not all progressing "in synch," but constantly requiring reintegration, somewhat along the lines of Piagetian *décalages*.

15 This proposal has become the cornerstone of "the social brain hypothesis." Dunbar demonstrated a significant positive correlation between various indices of social complexity and skill—for example, the size of group in which different species of primate and proto-hominid live—and the average size of their neocortices. In contrast, neocortex size does not have a predictable relationship with indices of ecological demand like home range size or foraging style (Dunbar, 2003). This implies that some aspect of neocortex volume acts as a constraint on social aggregation or, more precisely, on the capacity to maintain a cohesive and ecologically effective social group. Dunbar (2003) observes that the chief method of binding primates into groups is social grooming. However, there is a limit to the amount of time an animal can invest in social grooming if it is to have time to do everything else it needs to do (Dunbar reports this to be 20% from research on extant primate groups).

Dunbar argues that the functional size-limit for human groups (i.e., the maximum size of a group that can be bound by personalized bonds) both today and in our environment of evolutionary adaptedness was 150, which is far too large to be maintained by social grooming (he estimates members would need to spend 43% of their day grooming to cohere in groups of 150). He therefore proposed that language evolved to maintain cohesion in large groups: it "bridges the gap in bonding time requirement because it allows time to be used more efficiently" (Dunbar, 2003, p. 174). This proposal has been supported by fossil evidence which shows that two anatomical indices of hominid language-use appear at historically the same time (500,000 years ago) as average group size swelled beyond the number that could be maintained by social grooming or vocal chorusing (choral singing is a halfway house to grammatical language, according to Dunbar). These are widening of the thoracic vertebral canal (required for fine control over breathing when articulating words) and of the hypoglossal canal at the base of the skull (required for control of the tongue).

These steps toward the evolution of language are accompanied by what Dunbar (2003) calls cognitive changes in our ancestors' understanding of others.

16 These continuities do not end in childhood. See Lasch (1979).

References

Ainsworth, M. D. S., Blehar, M., Waters, E., & Wall, E. (1978). *Patterns of attachment: A psychological study of the strange situation*. Hillsdale, NJ: Erlbaum.

Bakeman, R., & Brownlee, J. (1982). Social rules governing object conflicts in toddlers and preschoolers. In K. H. Rubin & H. S. Ross (Eds.), *Peer relations and social skills in childhood*. New York: Springer-Verlag.

Bakhtin, M. M. (1986). *Speech genres and other late essays* (V. W. McGee, Trans.). Austin, TX: University of Texas Press. (Original work published 1979).

Barrett, J., & Hinde, R. A. (1988). Triadic interactions: Mother–first-born–second-born. In R. A. Hinde & J. Stevenson-Hinde (Eds.), *Relationships within families: Mutual influences* (pp. 181–192). Oxford: Clarendon Press.

Bates, E., Camaioni, L., & Volterra, V. (1976). Sensori-motor performatives. In E. Bates (Ed.), *Language and context: The acquisition of pragmatics* (pp. 49–71). New York: Academic Press.

Benjamin, J. (2004). Beyond doer and done to: An intersubjective view of thirdness. *Psychoanalytic Quarterly, 73*, 5–46.

Berlin, L. J., & Cassidy, J. (1999). Relations among relationships: Contributions from attachment theory and research. In J. Cassidy & P. R. Shaver (Eds.), *Handbook of attachment: Theory, research, and clinical applications* (pp. 688–712). New York: Guilford Press.

Bhabha, H. (1994). *The location of culture*. New York: Routledge.

Bion, W. R. (1962). *Learning from experience*. New York: Basic Books.

Bowlby, J. (1958). The nature of the child's tie to his mother. *International Journal of Psycho-Analysis, 390*, 350–373.

Bowlby, J. (1960). Grief and mourning in infancy and early childhood. *The Psychoanalytic Study of the Child, 15*, 3–39.

Bowlby, J. (1969). *Attachment*. Harmondsworth: Penguin (2nd ed., 1982).

Bowlby, J. (1988). *A secure base: Clinical applications of attachment theory*. London: Routledge.

Bradley, B. S. (1982). *Narcissism and the myth of inter-subjectivity*. Paper delivered to the Annual Conference of the BPS (Developmental Section). Durham University, September.

Bradley, B. S. (1983). The neglect of hatefulness in psychological studies of early infancy. Manuscript in SPS Library, Cambridge University, Free School Lane, Cambridge, UK.

Bradley, B. S. (1989a). *Visions of infancy: A critical introduction to child psychology*. Cambridge: Polity Press.

Bradley, B. S. (1989b). The asymmetric involvement of infants in social life: Consequences for theory. *Revue Internationale de Psychologie Sociale, 2,* 61–81.

Bradley, B. S. (1991). Infancy as paradise. *Human Development, 34,* 35–54.

Bradley, B. S. (2005). *Psychology and experience.* Cambridge: Cambridge University Press.

Bradley, B. S. (2009). Early trios: Patterns of sound and movement in the genesis of meaning between infants. In S. Malloch & C. B. Trevarthen (Eds.), *Communicative musicality: Narratives of expressive gesture and being human* (pp. 263–280). Oxford: Oxford University Press.

Bradley, B. S. (in press). Experiencing symbols. In B. Wagoner (Ed.), *Symbolic transformation: Toward an interdisciplinary science of symbols.* London: Routledge.

Bradley, B. S., & Selby, J. M. (2004). Observing infants in groups: The clan revisited. *The International Journal of Infant Observation* [C. Urwin & K. Arnold, Eds. Special Issue on Developmental Psychology and Psycho-Analysis], *7,* 107–122.

Braten, S., & Trevarthen, C. B. (2007). Prologue: From infant intersubjectivity and participant movements to simulation and conversation in cultural common sense. In S. Braten (Ed.), *On being moved: From mirror neurons to empathy* (pp. 21–34). Amsterdam: John Benjamins.

Braungart-Rieker, J. M., Garwood, M. M., Powers, B. P., & Wang, X. (2001). Parental sensitivity, infant affect, and affect regulation: Predictors of later attachment. *Child Development, 72,* 252–270.

Brazelton, T. B., Koslowski, B., & Main, M. (1974). The origins of reciprocity. In M. Lewis & L. A. Rosenblum (Eds.), *The effect of the infant on its caregiver.* New York: Wiley.

Brennan, W. M., Ames, E. W., & Moore, R. W. (1966). Age differences in infants' attention to patterns of different complexities. *Science, 151,* 354–355.

Bretherton, I., McNew, S., & Beeghly-Smith, M. (1981). Early person knowledge as expressed in gestural and verbal communication: When do infants acquire a "theory of mind"? In M. E. Lamb & L. R. Sherrod (Eds.), *Infant social cognition.* Hillsdale, NJ: Erlbaum.

Britton, R. (1989). The missing link: Parental sexuality in the Oedipus complex. In R. Britton, M. Feldman, & E. O'Shaughnessy (Eds.), *The Oedipus complex today* (pp. 83–101). London: Karnac.

Britton R. (2004). Subjectivity, objectivity, and triangular space. *Psychoanalytic Quarterly, 73,* 47–61.

Bruner, J. S. (1975). The ontogenesis of speech acts. *Journal of Child Language, 2,* 1–19.

Bruner, J. S. (1983). *Child's talk: Learning to use language.* New York: Norton.

Bullowa, M. (Ed.). (1979). *Before speech: The beginnings of human communication.* Cambridge: Cambridge University Press.

Butterworth, G. (2001). Joint visual attention. In G. Bremner & A. Fogel (Eds.), *Blackwell handbook of infant development* (pp. 213–224). Oxford: Blackwell.

Byrne, R. W., & Whiten, A. (Eds.). (1988). *Machiavellian intelligence: Social expertise and the evolution of intellect in monkeys, apes, and humans.* New York: Clarendon Press/ Oxford University Press.

Campbell, R. N., & Wales, R. J. (1970). The study of language acquisition. In J. Lyons (Ed.), *New horizons in linguistics.* Harmondsworth: Penguin.

Cassidy, J., & Shaver, P. R. (Eds.). (1999). *Handbook of attachment: Theory, research, and clinical applications.* New York: Guilford Press.

Cohn, J. F., Campbell, S. B., & Ross, S. (1991). Infant response in the still-face paradigm at 6 months predicts avoidant and secure attachment at 12 months. *Development and Psychopathology, 3,* 367–376.

Cooley, C. H. (1902). *Human nature and the social order.* New York: Scribner's.

Cowan, P. A. (1997). Beyond meta-analysis. A plea for a family systems view of attachment. *Child Development, 68,* 601–603.

Denham, S. A., Renwick, S. M., & Holt, R. W. (1991). Working and playing together: Prediction of preschool socio-emotional competence from mother–child interaction. *Child Development, 62,* 242–249.

Diggins, J. P. (1994). *The promise of pragmatism: Modernism and the crisis of knowledge and authority.* Chicago: University of Chicago Press.

Donaldson, M. (1978). *Children's minds.* Glasgow, Scotland: Fontana/Open Books.

Draghi-Lorenz, R., Reddy, V., & Costall, A. (2001). Rethinking the development of "nonbasic" emotions: A critical review of existing theories. *Developmental Review, 21,* 261–304.

Dunbar, R. I. M. (2003). The social brain: Mind, language, and society in evolutionary perspective. *Annual Review of Anthropology, 32,* 163–181.

Dunn, J., & Kendrick, C. (1982). Social behavior of young siblings in the family context: Differences between same-sex and different-sex dyads. *Annual Progress in Child Psychiatry and Child Development,* 166–181.

Field, T., Woodson, R., Greenberg, R., & Cohen, D. (1982). Discrimination and imitation of facial expressions of neonates. *Science, 218,* 179–181.

Finlay, B. L., & Darlington, R. B. (1995). Linked regularities in the development and evolution of mammalian brains. *Science, 268,* 1678–1684.

Fivaz-Depeursinge, E., & Corboz-Warnery, A. (1999). *The primary triangle: A developmental systems view of mothers, fathers and infants.* New York: Basic Books.

Fogel, A., & Hannan, T. E. (1985). Manual actions of nine to fifteen-week-old human infants during face-to-face interactions with their mothers. *Child Development, 56,* 1271–1279.

Freud, A. (1960). Discussion of Dr. John Bowlby's paper. *Psychoanalytic Study of the Child, 15,* 53–62.

Freud, S. (1911). Formulations on the two principles of mental functioning. In J. Strachey (Ed.), *The standard edition of the complete psychological works of Sigmund Freud* (Vol. 12, pp. 213–226). London: Hogarth Press (1953–1974).

Freud, S. (1914). On narcissism: An introduction. In J. Strachey (Ed.), *The standard edition of the complete psychological works of Sigmund Freud* (Vol. 14, pp. 73–107). London: Hogarth Press (1953–1974).

Freud, S. (1920). *Beyond the pleasure principle.* London: Hogarth Press.

Frye, D., Rawling, P., Moore, C., & Myers, I. (1983). Object–person discrimination and communication at 3 and 10 months. *Developmental Psychology, 19,* 303–309.

Geertz, C. (1973). *The interpretation of cultures: Selected essays.* London: Hutchinson.

Gergely, G., & Watson, J. S. (1996). The social biofeedback theory of parental affect-mirroring: The development of emotional self-awareness and self-control in infancy. *International Journal of Psycho-Analysis, 77,* 1181–1212.

Green, A. (2004). Thirdness and psychoanalytic concepts. *Psychoanalytic Quarterly, 73,* 99–135.

Grimm, J. L., & Grimm, W. K. (1996). Snowdrop. In *The fairy tales of the brothers Grimm* (E. Lucas, Trans.; A. Rackham, Illust.) (pp. 158–167). London: Folio Society. (First published circa 1822).

Habermas, J. (1970). Towards a theory of communicative competence. In H. P. Dreitzel (Ed.), *Recent sociology* (No. 2, pp. 115–148). London: Macmillan.

Halliday, M. A. K. (1975). *Learning how to mean: Explorations in the development of language*. London: Edward Arnold.

Harlow, H. F., & Harlow, M. K. (1965). The affectional systems. In A. M. Schrier, H. F. Harlow, & F. Stollnitz (Eds.), *Behavior of nonhuman primates* (Vol. 2). New York: Academic Press.

Harris, J. R. (1995). Where is the child's environment? A group socialization theory of development. *Psychological Review, 102*, 458–489.

Harris, J. R. (1998). *The nurture assumption: Why children turn out the way they do*. New York: Free Press.

Hart, S. L., & Carrington, H. A. (2002). Jealousy in six-month-old infants. *Infancy, 3*, 395–402.

Hart, S. L., Carrington, H. A., Tronick, E. Z., & Carroll, S. R. (2004). When infants lose exclusive maternal attention: Is it jealousy? *Infancy, 6*, 57–78.

Hart, S., Field, T., & del Valle, C. (1998a). Infants protest their mothers' attending to an infant-size doll. *Social Development, 7*, 54–61.

Hart, S., Field, T., Letourneau, M., & del Valle, C. (1998b). Jealousy protests in infants of depressed mothers. *Infant Behavior and Development, 21*, 137–148.

Hart, S., Jones, N. A., Field, T., & Lundy, B. (1999). One-year-old infants of intrusive and withdrawn depressed mothers. *Child Psychiatry and Human Development. 30*, 111–120.

Hedenbro, M., Shapiro, A. F., & Gottman, J. M. (2006). Play with me at my speed: Describing differences in the tempo of parent–infant interactions in the Lausanne Triadic Play paradigm in two cultures. *Family Process, 45*, 485–498.

Helliesen, M. (2006). *From buzzing confusion to jealousy and empathic concern: Re-examining emotional and social development in infancy.* Bachelors Thesis, Bates College, Lewiston, Maine, USA.

Hobson, R. P. (2007). Communicative depth: Soundings from developmental psychopathology. *Infant Behavior and Development, 30*, 267–277.

Hookway, C. (1985). *Peirce*. London: Routledge.

Ishikawa, F., & Hay, D. F. (2006). Triadic interaction among newly acquainted 2-year-olds. *Social Development, 15*, 145–168.

Joas, H. (1997). *G. H. Mead: A contemporary re-examination of his thought*. Cambridge, MA: MIT Press.

Kaye, K. (1984). *The mental and social life of babies: How parents create persons*. Brighton, UK: Harvester.

Kernberg, P. (2006). *Beyond reflection: The role of the mirror paradigm in clinical practice*. New York: Other Press.

Klein, M. (1952a). On observing the behaviour of young infants. In *Envy and gratitude and other works, 1946–1963* (pp. 94–121). London: Hogarth Press.

Klein, M. (1952b). Some theoretical conclusions regarding the emotional life of the infant. In *Envy and gratitude and other works, 1946–1963* (pp. 122–140). London: Hogarth Press.

Lacan, J. (1948). Aggressivity in psychoanalysis. In *Écrits: A selection* (A. Sheridan, Ed. & Trans.) (pp. 8–29). London: Tavistock.

Lacan, J. (1949). The mirror stage as formative of the function of the I. In *Écrits: A selection* (A. Sheridan, Ed. & Trans.) (pp. 1–7). London: Tavistock.

Lacan, J. (1981). *Speech and language in psychoanalysis* (A. Wilden, Ed. & Trans.). Baltimore: Johns Hopkins University Press.

Lacan, J. (1988). *The seminar of Jacques Lacan* (J. Forrester, Ed. & Trans.). Cambridge: Cambridge University Press.

Lamb, M. E., & Nash, A. (1989). Infant–mother attachment sociability, and peer competence. In T. J. Berndt & G. W. Ladd (Eds.), *Peer relationships in child development*. New York: Wiley.

Laplanche, J., & Pontalis, J.-B. (1977). *The language of psycho-analysis*. London: Hogarth Press.

Lasch, C. (1979). *The culture of narcissism: American life in an age of diminishing expectations*. New York: Norton.

Legerstee, M. (1997). Contingency effects of people and objects on subsequent cognitive functioning in three-month-old infants. *Social Development, 6*, 307–321.

Legerstee, M. (2005). *Infants' sense of people: Precursors to a theory of mind*. Cambridge: Cambridge University Press.

Legerstee, M., Corter, C., & Kienapple, K. (1990). Hand, arm and facial actions of young infants to a social and non-social stimulus. *Child Development, 61*, 774–784.

Legerstee, M., & Markova, G. (2007). Intentions make a difference: Infant responses to still-face and modified still-face conditions. *Infant Behavior and Development, 30*, 232–250.

Legerstee, M., Markova, G., & Fisher, T. (2007). The role of maternal affect attunement in dyadic and triadic communication. *Infant Behavior and Development, 30*, 296–306.

Legerstee, M., Pomerlau, A., Malacuit, G., & Feidler, H. (1987). The development of infants' responses to people and a doll: Implications for research in communication. *Infant Behavior and Development, 10*, 81–95.

Legerstee, M., & Varghese, M. (2001). The role of maternal affect mirroring on social expectancies in 3-month-old infants. *Child Development, 72*, 1301–1313.

Lewis, M. (2005). The child and its family: The social network model. *Human Development, 48*, 8–27.

Lock, A. (Ed.). (1978). *Action, gesture and symbol: The emergence of language*. New York: Academic Press.

Lorenz, K. Z. (1935). Der Kumpan in der Umwelt des Vogels. In C. H. Schiller (Ed.), *Instinctive behaviour*. New York: International Universities Press (1957).

Main, M. (1999). Attachment theory: Eighteen points with suggestions for future studies. In J. Cassidy & P. R. Shaver (Eds.), *Handbook of attachment: Theory, research, and clinical applications* (pp. 845–888). New York: Guilford Press.

Malloch, S., Crncec, R., Adam, B., & Bradley, B. S. (2005). Infants interacting with infants. In M. Atherton (Ed.), *Proceedings of the University of Western Sydney's College of Arts, Education and Social Sciences Conference: Scholarship and Community*. Sydney: UWS.

Markova, G. (2008). *Interactions among infant peers: Examining individual differences in social competence*. PhD Dissertation, York University, Toronto, Canada.

Markova, G., & Legerstee, M. (2006). Contingency, imitation, and affect sharing: Foundations of infants' social awareness. *Developmental Psychology, 42*, 132–141.

Mead, G. H. (1934). *Mind, self and society: From the standpoint of a social behaviourist*. Chicago: University of Chicago Press.

Meltzoff, A. N. (1985). Immediate and deferred imitation in fourteen- and twenty-four-month-old infants. *Child Development, 59*, 217–225.

Meltzoff, A. N., & Brooks, R. (2001). "Like me" as a building block for understanding other minds: Bodily acts, attention, and intention. In B. F. Malle & L. J. Bertram (Eds.), *Intentions and intentionality: Foundations of social cognition* (pp. 171–195). Cambridge, MA: MIT Press.

Meltzoff, A. N., & Moore, M. K. (1997). Explaining facial imitation: A theoretical model. *Early Development and Parenting, 6*, 179–192.

Miller, A-L., Volling, B. L., & McElwain, N. L. (2000). Sibling jealousy in a triadic context with mothers and fathers. *Social Development, 9*, 433–457.

Moll, H., & Tomasello, M. (2007). How 14- and 18-month-olds know what others have experienced. *Developmental Psychology, 43*, 309–317.

Mueller, E. (1991). Toddlers' peer relations: Shared meaning and semantics. In W. Damon (Ed.), *Child development today and tomorrow.* San Francisco: Jossey-Bass.

Mueller, E., & Brenner, J. (1977). The origins of social skills and interaction among playgroup toddlers. *Child Development, 48*, 854–861.

Muller, J. P. (1985). Lacan's mirror stage. *Psychoanalytic Inquiry, 5*, 233–252.

Muller, J. P. (1996). *Beyond the psychoanalytic dyad: Developmental semiotics in Freud, Peirce, and Lacan.* New York: Routledge.

Murray, L., & Cooper, P. J. (Eds.). (1997). *Postpartum depression and child development.* London: Guilford Press.

Murray, L., & Trevarthen, C. (1985). Emotional regulation of interactions between two-month-olds and their mothers. In T. M. Field & N. A. Fox (Eds.), *Social perception in infants.* Norwood, NJ: Ablex.

Nadel, J., & Tremblay-Leveau, H. (1999). Early perception of social contingencies and interpersonal intentionality: Dyadic and triadic paradigms. In P. Rochat (Ed.), *Early social cognition: Understanding others in the first months of life* (pp. 189–212). Mahwah, NJ: Erlbaum.

Nagy, E. (2006). From imitation to conversation: The first dialogues with human neonates. *Infant and Child Development, 15*, 223–232.

Nakano, S., Kondo-Ikemura, K., & Kusanagi, E. (2007). Perturbation of Japanese mother–infant habitual interactions in the double video paradigm and relationship to maternal playfulness. *Infant Behavior and Development, 30*, 213–231.

Nash, A., & Hay, D. F. (1993). Relationships in infancy as precursors and causes of later relationships and psychopathology. In D. F. Hay & A. Angold (Eds.), *Precursors, causes and psychopathology.* Chichester: Wiley.

Newson, J. (1979). The growth of shared understandings between infant and caregiver. In M. Bullowa (Ed.), *Before speech: The beginning of interpersonal communication.* Cambridge: Cambridge University Press.

Ogden, T. H. (2004). The analytic third: Implications for psychoanalytic theory and technique. *Psychoanalytic Quarterly, 73*, 167–195.

Papousek, H., & Papousek, M. (1977). Mothering and the cognitive headstart: Psycho-biological considerations. In H. R. Schaffer (Ed.) *Studies in mother–infant interaction* (pp. 63–88). London: Academic Press.

Parke, R. D., Power, T. G., & Bottman, J. M. (1979). Conceptualizing and quantifying influence patterns in the family triad. In M. E. Lamb, S. J. Suomi, & G. R.

Richardson (Eds.), *Social interaction analysis: Methodological issues* (pp. 231–252). Madison, WI: University of Wisconsin Press.

Paul, C., & Thomson-Salo, F. (1996). Infant-led psychotherapy with groups. *Journal of Child Psychotherapy, 6*, 118–136.

Peirce, C. S. (1931). Thirdness. In C. Hartshorne, P. Weiss, & A. W. Burks (Eds.), *Collected papers of Charles Sanders Peirce* (Vol. 5, pp. 104ff). Cambridge: Cambridge University Press.

Perry, B. D. (1997). Incubated in terror: Neurodevelopmental factors in the "cycle of violence." In J. D. Osofsky (Ed.), *Children in a violent society.* New York: Guilford Press.

Piaget, J. (1953). *The origin of intelligence in the child.* London: Routledge & Kegan Paul.

Piaget, J. (1955). *The child's construction of reality.* London: Routledge & Kegan Paul.

Piaget, J. (1981). *Intelligence and affectivity.* Palo Alto, CA: Annual Review Press.

Racine, T. P., & Carpendale, J. I. M. (2007). Shared practices, understanding, language and joint attention. *British Journal of Developmental Psychology, 25*, 45–54.

Reddy, V. (1991). Playing with others' expectations: Teasing and mucking about in the first year. In A. Whiten (Ed.), *Natural theories of mind* (pp. 143–158). Oxford: Blackwell.

Reddy, V. (2000). Coyness in early infancy. *Developmental Science, 3*, 186–192.

Reddy, V. (2001). Positively shy! Developmental continuities in the expression of shyness, coyness, and embarrassment. In W. R. Crozier & L. E. Alden (Eds.), *International handbook of social anxiety: Research and interventions relating to the self and shyness* (pp. 77–99). London: Wiley.

Reddy, V. (2003). On being the object of attention: Implications for self–other consciousness. *Trends in Cognitive Sciences, 7*, 397–402.

Reddy, V. (2005). Before the "third element": Understanding attention to self. In N. Eilan, C. Hoerl, T. McCormack, & J. Roessler (Eds.), *Joint attention: Communication and other minds* (pp. 85–109). Issues in Philosophy and Psychology. Oxford: Clarendon Press.

Reddy, V., Chisholm, V., Forrester, D., Conforti, M., & Maniatopoulou, D. (2007). Facing the perfect contingency: Interactions with the self at 2 and 3 months. *Infant Behavior and Development, 30*, 195–212.

Relke, D. M. A. (1993). Foremothers who cared: Paula Heimann, Margaret Little and the female tradition in psychoanalysis. *Feminism and Psychology, 3*, 89–109.

Richards, M. P. M. (1974). First steps in becoming social. In M. P. M. Richards (Ed.), *The integration of a child into a social world.* Cambridge: Cambridge University Press.

Riley, D. (1977a). Marxism for infants. In *Dry air* (pp. 1–22). London: Virago (1985).

Riley, D. (1977b). An infant. In *Dry air* (p. 18). London: Virago (1985).

Riley, D. (1978). Developmental psychology, biology and Marxism. *Ideology and Consciousness, 4*, 73–92.

Riley, D. (1983). *War in the nursery: Theories of child and mother.* London: Virago.

Rochat, P. (2004). The emergence of self-awareness as co-awareness in early child development. In D. Zahavi, T. Grunbaum, & J. Parnas (Eds.), *The structure and development of self-consciousness: Interdisciplinary perspectives* (pp. 1–20). Amsterdam: John Benjamins.

Rutter, M. (1995). Clinical implications of attachment concepts: Retrospect and prospect. *Journal of Child Psychology and Psychiatry, 36*, 549–571.

Ryan, J. (1974). Early language development: Towards a communicational analysis. In M. P. M. Richards (Ed.), *The integration of a child into a social world*. Cambridge: Cambridge University Press.

Scaife, M., & Bruner, J. (1975). The capacity for joint visual attention in the infant. *Nature, 253*, 265–266.

Schaffer, H. R. (1971). *The growth of sociability*. Harmondsworth: Penguin.

Schaffer, H. R. (Ed.). (1977). *Studies in mother–infant interaction*. London: Academic Press.

Schaffer, H. R. (1984). *The child's entry into a social world*. London: Academic Press.

Schaffer, H. R. (1996). *Social development*. Oxford: Blackwell.

Schur, M. (1960). Discussion of Dr. John Bowlby's paper. *Psychoanalytic Study of the Child, 15*, 63–84.

Selby, J. M. (1985). *Feminine identity and contradiction: Women research students at Cambridge University*. Ph.D. Thesis, Darwin College, Cambridge University.

Selby, J. M. (1993a). Psychoanalysis as a critical theory of gender. In L. Mos, W. Thorngate, B. Kaplan, & H. Stam (Eds.), *Recent trends in theoretical psychology* (Vol. III). New York: Springer-Verlag.

Selby, J. M. (1993b). Primary processes: Developing infants as adults. *Theory and Psychology, 3*, 523–544.

Selby, J. M., & Bradley, B. S. (2003a). Infants in groups: A paradigm for the study of early social experience. *Human Development, 46*, 197–221.

Selby, J. M., & Bradley, B. S. (2003b). Infants in groups: Extending the debate. *Human Development, 46*, 247–249.

Selby, J. M., & Bradley, B. S. (2005). Psychologist as moral agent: Negotiating praxis-oriented knowledge in infancy. In A. Gulerce, A. Hofmeister, I. Staeuble, G. Saunders, & J. Kaye (Eds.), *Contemporary theorizing in psychology: Global perspectives* (pp. 242–250). New York: Captus Press.

Shaffer, L. S. (2005). From mirror self-recognition to the looking-glass self: Exploring the justification hypothesis. *Journal of Clinical Psychology, 61*, 47–65.

Shotter, J., & Gregory, S. (1976). On first gaining the idea of oneself as a person. In R. Harré (Ed.), *Life sentences: Aspects of the social role of language*. New York: Wiley.

Simpson, J. A., & Weiner, E. S. C. (1989). *The Oxford English dictionary: Vol. 1. A-Bazouki* (2nd ed.). Oxford: Clarendon Press.

Sluckin, W. (1964). *Imprinting and early learning*. London: Methuen.

Spitz, R. A. (1960). Discussion of Dr. John Bowlby's paper. *Psychoanalytic Study of the Child, 15*, 85–208.

Steedman, C. (1982). *The tidy house. Little girls writing*. London: Virago.

Stern, D. N. (1985). *The interpersonal world of the infant*. New York: Basic Books.

Stern, D. N. (1995). *The motherhood constellation: A unified view of parent–infant therapy*. New York: Basic Books.

Stern, D. N. (2000). Putting time back into our considerations of infant experience: A micro-diachronic view. *Infant Mental Health Journal, 21*, 21–28.

Stern, D. N., Jaffe, J., Beebe, B., & Bennett, S. L. (1975). Vocalising in unison and in alternation: Two modes of communicating within the mother–infant dyad. In D. Aronson and R. W. Rieber (Eds.), *Developmental psycholinguistics and communication disorders*. New York: New York Academy of Sciences.

Striano, T., & Rochat, P. (1999). Developmental link between dyadic and triadic social competence in infancy. *British Journal of Developmental Psychology, 17*, 551–562.

Striano, T., & Stahl, D. (2005). Sensitivity to triadic attention in early infancy. *Developmental Science, 8*, 333–343.

Sylvester-Bradley, B. (1981). Negativity in early infant–adult exchanges and its developmental significance. In W. P. Robinson (Ed.), *Communication in development*. London: Academic Press.

Sylvester-Bradley, B. (1985). Failure to distinguish between people and things in early infancy. *British Journal of Developmental Psychology, 3*, 281–92.

Sylvester-Bradley, B., & Trevarthen, C. B. (1978). Babytalk as an adaptation to the infant's communication. In C. Snow & N. Waterson (Eds.), *The development of communication*. London: Wiley.

Thibaut, J. W., & Kelley, H. H. (1959). *The social psychology of groups*. New York: Wiley.

Thompson, R. A. (1997). Sensitivity and security: New questions to ponder. *Child Development, 68*, 595–597.

Tissaw, M. A. (2007). Making sense of neonatal imitation. *Theory and Psychology, 17*, 217–242.

Tomasello, M. (1995). Joint attention as social cognition. In C. Moore & P. Dunham (Eds.), *Joint attention: Its origins and role in development* (pp. 319–346). New York: Academic Press.

Tomasello, M. (1999). Early social cognition: Understanding others in the first months of life. In P. Rochat (Ed.), *Social cognition before the revolution* (pp. 301–314). Mahwah, NJ: Erlbaum.

Tomasello, M., Carpenter, M., Call, J., Behne, T., & Moll, H. (2005). Understanding and sharing intentions: The origins of cultural cognition. *Behavioral and Brain Sciences, 28*, 675–735.

Tremblay, H., & Rovira, K. (2007). Joint visual attention and social triangular engagement at 3 and 6 months. *Infant Behavior and Development, 30*, 366–379.

Tremblay-Leveau, H., & Nadel, J. (1995). Young children's communicative skills in triads. *International Journal of Behavioral Development, 18*, 227–242.

Tremblay-Leveau, H., & Nadel, J. (1996). Exclusion in triads: Can it serve "metacommunicative" knowledge in 11- and 23-month-old children? *British Journal of Developmental Psychology, 14*, 145–158.

Trevarthen, C. B. (1974). Conversations with a two-month-old. *New Scientist*, May 2, 230–235.

Trevarthen, C. B. (1977). Descriptive analyses of infant communicative behaviour. In H. R. Schaffer (Ed.), *Studies in mother–infant interaction*. London: Academic Press.

Trevarthen, C. B. (1978). Basic patterns of psychogenetic change in infancy. In T. G. Bever & J. Mehler (Eds.), *Dips in learning and development curves*. Hillsdale, NJ: Erlbaum.

Trevarthen, C. B. (1979). Communication and cooperation in early infancy: A description of primary intersubjectivity. In M. Bullowa (Ed.), *Before speech: The beginnings of human communication*. Cambridge: Cambridge University Press.

Trevarthen, C. B., & Aitken, K. J. (2001). Infant intersubjectivity: Research, theory and clinical applications. *Journal of Child Psychology and Psychiatry, 42*, 3–48.

Trevarthen, C. B., & Hubley, P. A. (1978). Secondary intersubjectivity: Confidence, confiding and acts of meaning in the second year. In A. Lock (Ed.), *Action, gesture and symbol: The emergence of language* (pp. 183–229). New York: Academic Press.

Trevarthen, C. B., & Reddy, V. (2007). Consciousness in infants. In M. Velmans & S. Schneider (Eds.), *The Blackwell companion to consciousness* (pp. 41–57). Malden, MA: Wiley-Blackwell.

Trevarthen, C. B., Sheeran, L., & Hubley, P. A. (1975). Psychological actions in early infancy. *La Recherche, 6,* 447–458.

Tronick, E. Z. (1986). Interactive mismatch and repair: Challenges to the coping infant. *Zero to Three, 6,* 1–6.

Tronick, E. Z. (1989). Emotions and emotional communication in infants. *American Psychologist, 44,* 112–126.

Tronick, E. Z. (2003). Things still to be done on the still-face effect. *Infancy, 4,* 475–482.

Urwin, C. (1984). Power relations and the emergence of language. In J. Henriques, W. Hollway, C. Urwin, C. Venn, & V. Walkerdine, *Changing the subject: Psychology, social regulation and subjectivity* (pp. 264–322). London: Routledge. (2nd ed., 1998).

Uzgiris, I. C. (1984). Imitation in infancy: Its interpersonal aspects. In M. Perlmutter (Ed.), *Parent–infant interaction and parent–child relations in child development. The Minnesota Symposia on Child Psychology* (Vol. 17, pp. 1–32). Hillsdale, NJ: Erlbaum.

Vygotsky, L. S. (1978). *Mind and society: The development of higher psychological processes.* Cambridge, MA: Harvard University Press.

Walkerdine, V. (1982). From context to text: A psycho-semiotic approach to abstract thought. In M. Beveridge (Ed.), *Children thinking through language.* London: Arnold.

Watson, J. S. (1972). Smiling, cooing and "the game." *Merrill-Palmer Quarterly, 18,* 323–339.

Wilden, A. (1981). Lacan and the discourse of the Other. In J. Lacan, *Speech and language in psychoanalysis* (A. Wilden, Ed. & Trans.) (pp. 157–312). Baltimore: Johns Hopkins University Press.

Winnicott, D. W. (1965a). The theory of the parent–infant relationship. In *The maturational processes and the facilitating environment: Studies in the theory of emotional development* (pp. 37–55). London: Hogarth Press. (Original work published 1960).

Winnicott, D. W. (1965b). *The maturational processes and the facilitating environment: Studies in the theory of emotional development.* London: Hogarth Press.

Winnicott, D. W. (1974a). Transitional objects and transitional phenomena. In *Playing and reality* (pp. 1–30). Harmondsworth: Penguin. (Original work published 1953).

Winnicott, D. W. (1974b). Mirror-role of mother and family in child development. In *Playing and reality* (pp. 130–138). Harmondsworth: Penguin. (Original work published 1967).

Winnicott, D. W. (1974c). The location of cultural experience. In *Playing and reality* (pp. 112–121). Harmondsworth: Penguin. (Original work published 1967).

Winnicott, D. W. (1975a). The observation of infants in a set situation. In *Collected papers: Through paediatrics to psycho-analysis* (pp. 52–69). London: Hogarth Press (1975). (Original work published 1941).

Winnicott, D. W. (1975b). Primary maternal preoccupation. In *Collected papers: Through paediatrics to psycho-analysis* (pp. 300–305). London: Hogarth Press. (Original work published 1956).

Woolf, V. (1929). *A room of one's own.* London: Hogarth Press.

Zelazo, P. R., & Kearsley, R. B. (1980). The emergence of functional play in infants: Evidence for a major cognitive transition. *Journal of Applied Developmental Psychology, 1,* 95–117.

11

Parental Reports of Jealousy in Early Infancy

Growing Tensions between Evidence and Theory

Riccardo Draghi-Lorenz

For crying out loud . . .
At Surrey University, boffins (scientists) wanted to prove that young babies feel jealousy: "[They] asked mothers of five-month-olds to show affection to another baby. The exuberant boss boffin was delighted to have his thesis proved: Within five minutes, he announced . . . , more than half of their babies cried. Question: why even MIGHT a mother have volunteered her baby for this, uh, research?"
(The People, London, July 23, 2000)

Introduction

Albeit provocatively and giving little information on the experimental procedure, the above comment on a study by this author asks a legitimate question. For psychologists, if not for mothers, the answer lies with the potential implications that evidence of early jealousy has for how we understand young infants' capacity to relate to others, that is, for how we understand the very origins and foundations of human sociality.

It is now widely recognized that young infants and even newborns must be social to some extent. Newborns' preference for face-like stimuli (Goren, Sarty, & Wu, 1975), their imitation of facial movements (Maratos, 1973), and differentiation between own and other's cry (Sagi & Hoffman, 1976), as well as very young infants' capacity for proto-conversations (Trevarthen, 1974) and distress when mothers hold a still-face (Tronick, Als, Adamson, Wise, & Brazelton, 1978), are all well-established phenomena. It is also agreed that in the first 6 months or so infants come to recognize others' expressed emotions (for a review see Walker-Andrews, 1997), that 6-month-olds can be distressed by a lack of maternal attunement (Murray & Trevarthen, 1985), and that by the end of the first year at the latest

Handbook of Jealousy: Theory, Research and Multidisciplinary Approaches, First Edition.
Edited by Sybil L. Hart and Maria Legerstee.
© 2013 Blackwell Publishing Ltd. Published 2013 by Blackwell Publishing Ltd.

infants also become capable of joint attention, social/emotional referencing, and declarative pointing (e.g., Bretherton, McNew, & Beeghly-Smith, 1981; Klinnert, Campos, Sorce, Emde, & Svejda, 1983; Butterworth & Grover, 1988).

Nonetheless, not only are theorists still debating exactly how much awareness of others is really required for these early interactive phenomena but the levels of social awareness typically associated with jealousy are also deemed unequivocally superior. Jealous emotions, including jealousy over people or over material objects, envy, possessiveness, and rivalry, are indeed part of a larger group of emotions thought to imply comparatively high levels of social understanding. This group also includes emotions such as empathic concern, shyness and embarrassment, guilt, pride, and other highly social affects (here referred to as "non-basic" emotions). Views may again differ on exactly how much or which kind of social awareness is needed for different forms of jealousy, let alone for other non-basic emotions (e.g., Hobson, this volume, Chapter 13; Bradley, this volume, Chapter 10). However, mainstream theorists of social and emotional development typically agree that these are beyond young infants' social capacity anyhow (for a review see Draghi-Lorenz, Reddy, & Costall, 2001). Importantly, this position is often accompanied by the argument that the level of self and other awareness implied in these emotions is underpinned by representational capacities of which there is little evidence before the second year of life, such as a concept of self, multi- or meta-representational skills, imagery, etc. (e.g., Lewis, 1995; Harris, 1989; Perner, 1991; Izard, 1994; Sroufe, 1996). Only a few theorists, with a rather different view of both young infants' social capacity and its cognitive underpinnings, have ever considered the development of non-basic emotions before the second year of life (e.g., Baldwin, 1902; Klein, 1921–1945, 1946–1963; Trevarthen, 1984, 1993; Barrett, 1995; Draghi-Lorenz et al., 2001).

In this context, the available experimental evidence of jealousy of positive maternal attention in 4/5- and 8/9-month-olds (Masciuch, 1988),[1] 5-month-olds (Draghi-Lorenz, 1997, 1998, 2001), 6-month-olds (Hart & Carrington, 2002; Hart et al., 2004), and now even 3-month-olds (Legerstee, Ellenboge, Nienhuis, & Marsh, this volume, Chapter 9) deserves serious attention. Confirming old anecdotal and more recent parental reports of this emotion in infants as young as 3 (Gesell, 1906) and 10 months (Cummings, Zahn-Waxler, & Radke-Yarrow, 1981), this evidence suggests the possibility of jealousy of maternal attention throughout the first year and immediately raises two fundamental questions regarding the ontogenesis of social awareness. The question of description: *When and in which forms does this awareness actually emerge?* And that of explanation: *Which are the cognitive processes that underpin it?*

In fact, further data on early jealousy could actually also help us answer these questions. In particular, it would be important to know whether early jealousy is restricted to positive attention from primary attachment figures or if it also includes other jealous emotions, like in later development, such as jealousy over the attention of less significant others, over material possessions and/or activities, feelings of rivalry, competition, and envy. We also need to clearly establish how socially sophisticated early jealous behaviors actually are, how they develop, and why. As mentioned above, not all authors agree on exactly how much social awareness is really signaled by jealousy, especially jealousy over maternal attention, and one can also envisage specific ad hoc explanations emerging that call upon lower levels of sociality than previously deemed necessary. In particular, this form of jealousy may be "explained away" as an instinctive reaction that is part of the attachment system, manifests itself and develops somewhat uniformly across infants, and really implies comparatively little social awareness. Jealousy over significant others has also been reported in non-primate mammals such as dogs and horses (e.g., Morris, Doe, & Godsell, 2008) and while to some authors this might suggest good social awareness in these animals too, to others it may suggest the possibility of instinctive "automatic" jealousy. In brief, it would be useful to know how many and how fixed and predetermined, or alternatively varied, complex, or even creative, early manifestations and developmental pathways of jealousy can be. If they are limited in number and form we may be able to explain them without calling upon particularly differentiated levels of social awareness. The more they vary and resemble older children's and adults' manifestations of jealous emotions, instead, the more social awareness we may need to grant to young infants too.

Additional experimental work, for instance on the exact conditions of early jealousy (see Legerstee et al., this volume), is thus particularly welcome. At the same time, to fully understand young infants' emotional capacity we can also profit from their parents' natural observations and understanding. Parental reports are often considered overly subjective and interpretative but while parents may be biased by their personal involvement with infants, researchers may be biased by their professional involvement with theory. In our review (Draghi-Lorenz et al., 2001) we found that when it did not fit with their theory some researchers simply dismissed in various ways the possibility of early non-basic emotions, even against their own studies' results (for the case of jealousy see Masciuch & Kienapple, 1993). In addition, parents spend great amounts of time interacting with infants in ways that are beyond researchers' possibilities, and are likely to witness instances of non-basic emotions that are otherwise difficult to access. As a result, they are also particularly well placed to report on both these emotions' development and the contextual factors that seem to shape it, which would be difficult to track for an external observer let alone to monitor in a laboratory. It is also worth noting that, so far, experimental data have only confirmed previous anecdotal and parental reports of early jealousy, and that there is evidence that lay adults are fairly reliable judges of other early non-basic emotions, such as shyness, coyness, and embarrassment (Draghi-Lorenz, Reddy, & Morris, 2005). Indeed, when taken seriously and systematically, parental reports have proved very useful for our understanding of early socio-emotional development (e.g., Zahn-Waxler, Radke-Yarrow, & King, 1979).

The data presented here, namely verbal reports from caregivers used as key informants and videotaped observations by this author, were collected in the mid-90s as part of a naturalistic longitudinal investigation into the early development of social awareness as manifested in a variety of non-basic emotions. Its original research questions were: (i) What is the full range of non-basic emotions that emerge in the first year? (ii) What are their developmental paths? (iii) What are the determinants of these paths? Results concerned many emotions, including also shyness, pride, empathic concern, sadism, guilt, etc. (Draghi-Lorenz, 2001). For obvious reasons this contribution will summarize and discuss only those related to early jealous emotions. It will be argued that even by themselves these results are difficult to reconcile with current accounts of the development of social awareness, which tend to hinge on inner representational and/or empathic processes as mediating the relation between self and others. It will be proposed instead that social awareness is underpinned throughout the lifespan by the immediate perception of the relational functions specified in interactive behavior.

Method

Participants and data collection

Nine Caucasian infants and their families were recruited in the south of England. Infants were visited for 30–60 min every week/several weeks, starting at ages ranging from 2 to 7 months and ending around their first birthday (see later tables). Their mothers, one professional nanny, and occasionally other family members acted as key informants. Caregivers knew that the research aimed to explore the early possibility of non-basic emotions and other phenomena implying social awareness, and were asked to "keep their eyes open" between visits.

The study collected videotapes of: (i) semi-structured interviews with caregivers, and (ii) relevant infant behavior either naturally occurring or intentionally provoked in visits. Interviews started with a general prompt: "Have you noticed anything of interest since the last visit?" Questions were then asked about the reported phenomena's manifestations and context of occurrence, and about phenomena that had not been spontaneously mentioned yet (e.g., "Any envy?"; "Pride?"; etc.). The list of possibly relevant phenomena grew as unexpected events were reported and/or videotaped, and a preliminary analysis showed that of the original 9 infants, 6 (4 boys of whom 2 are identical twins) yielded sufficient material to explore the research questions.

Data analysis

Visits to these 6 infants yielded 58 hours of videotaped interviews and interactions. Reports were subjected to: (i) a thematic analysis; (ii) simple frequency counts; (iii) comparison with videotaped interactions. For the thematic analysis both interviewees' reports and the videotaped observations were transcribed with notes on interviewees' and the interviewer's interpretations. Transcripts were then read and reread and parts that grouped in clusters of either similar emotions or dissimilar ones which occurred in similar contexts were extracted. This process was reiterated to identify possible subgroupings, developmental and contextual themes across infants, and individual differences. By this stage the analysis was turning into key findings like those summarized below for jealousy.

Most groupings/subgroupings were termed with expressions used by interviewees. Tables of reported frequencies of the relevant behaviors across infants and ages are presented for groupings/subgroupings that are not excessively overlapping. For these (201 reports in total, of which almost half related to jealousy), inter-coder agreement was 98% (these reports often used the label in question and/or were sufficiently detailed). The reader can gain a further sense of reliability by considering consistencies/inconsistencies across the interviewees' reports below. Several authors note how, in the evaluation of qualitative data, validity also needs to be redefined as transparency of the original data set, persuasiveness of its interpretation, and internal coherence of both (e.g., Elliott, Fischer, & Rennie, 1999). About a third of observations and reports relevant to jealousy are reported here, so these criteria should be easy to apply throughout.

Terms such as "says" are used to indicate spontaneous reports, "adds" and "explains" for expansions on reports, and "replies" for answers to specific questions. "(. . .)" indicates the exclusion of words, and ."..." indicates a pause. Pseudonyms are used and ages are indicated in months;days. As the data were collected by this author the pronoun "I" will be used instead of "the researcher."

Key Findings

Sections of interviews related to jealousy typically revolved around the following themes: jealousy about people, wanting what others have (because they have it), rivalry/antagonism, wanting to join in expressions of affection or activities, how all these were expressed, the situations in which they were noticed, and their developmental courses and determinants.

Jealousy about people

All interviewees at some point reported jealousy about people, mainly mothers, but also fathers and occasionally other persons to whom the infants appeared attracted. Table 11.1 shows reported frequencies of such observations since the last visit across infants, and specifies whether the report described only "simple" emotion expressions (e.g., crying or shouting), or also expressions involving actual actions (e.g., moving toward or between, pushing away, etc.).

Table 11.1   Reported frequency of observations of interpersonal jealousy since the last visit

	Infant					
Age (months)	Daisy	Richard	Arthur	Erica	Harry	Andrew
2						
	0					
	0					
	SomeE					
3	0					
	0					
	SomeE					
4						SomeE
						0
					0	
5					0	
	ManyAE					
	0				0	0
6	0					0
					0	0
	1/2E	SomeE	SomeE		1/2E	0
7	0					
		0	0	0		0
		0	0			SomeE
		0	0	1/2E		
8		0	0			0
	0	0	0		0	
		0	0	0	ManyAE	0
	SomeAE					
9		1/2AE	1/2AE	0	ManyAE	0
	0					
				0	0	0
		SomeE	SomeE			
10						0
		0	0			0
				0		SomeAE
	0	SomeAE	ManyAE		ManyAE	
11		0	0	1/2AE		
		0	0			ManyAE
				SomeAE		
12						
						0

Note: 0 = not observed since last visit; 1/2 = observed once/twice; Some = observed "sometimes" (more than once/twice but not often); Many = observed "many times." E = only involving "simple" emotion Expressions; AE = involving Actions as well as "simple" Expressions.

Jealousy over people was identified in infants' anger/aggression, seeking reassurance and/or crying, and, occasionally, in both "offended" avoidance and some complex attention-seeking behaviors.

Anger and aggression

Jealous anger/aggression was reported fairly frequently, with physical aggression toward the third party reported in 5 of the 6 infants. For instance, asked about jealousy in Harry at 8;15 his mother replies:

> Yes very much, with his brothers. If I pick them up then I'll cuddle them, sometimes he'll get quite cross, he'll try to climb up and try and do like that to Charles or Irvin [she mimics Harry pushing his brothers away].

Similarly at 9;01 the twins' nanny replies:

> They have started pushing each other away when you hold them both. Richard was trying to push Arthur off the other day. It has happened a couple of times with Beth as well [Beth being their mother].

At 10;25, she also spontaneously reports how, some days before, Richard "shoved" a little girl off her nanny's lap ("he didn't want her there"), and explains how he seemed particularly keen on this young woman (Penny)—so much so that "Richard only wanted Penny." The earliest example of actual aggression was spontaneously reported in Daisy at 6;21 and involved a kitten:

> I picked up this new kitten we had and cuddled it and Daisy cried (. . .) she was jealous (. . .) she was happy when I held them both but very brutal to the kitten [I ask: Has this happened often?] Two or three times (. . .) and she was happy playing alone before I picked up the kitten.

Naturally, often young infants were unable or not close enough to reach and push/hit the other. However, parents still detected jealousy in angry protests. Such expressions were reported with various degrees of frequency in all infants. At 8;25 Daisy's mother replies:

> Yes, with her dad holding Alison (middle sister) . . . Daisy has gone deeply into her dad—if I was sitting next to Daisy and her dad goes out of the room Daisy would cry (. . .) If her dad picks up or carries Alison she screams!

She adds how she noticed this reaction more than once and her au-pair, also present, spontaneously nods saying "yes, yes." The mother explains:

> Her dad didn't believe me so I said "put Alison down" and she was like "coo-coo" [meaning Daisy was happy now]. Then I said "now pick her up again, [and she was like] "Grrrr!" [meaning that she was angry again].

Seeking reassurance and crying

According to parents, jealousy over people could also be expressed in ways other than aggression and/or anger. At 10;27 Erica's mother replies:

> She has started coming over—I noticed one day at the weekend when I was cuddling Rose [eldest sister]. I think Rose had hurt herself and she [Erica] came over just to be cuddled. It was the first time that it wasn't really "joining in"—it was *she* (Erica) *wanted* a cuddle.... She didn't touch Rose, she wanted me, she wanted me to cuddle her. [I ask: Did she look concerned?] She didn't look upset or distressed by Rose's crying.

At 11;11 Erica's mother reports again "some jealousy" expressed by wanting to be comforted: "like when I was dancing with Hazel (older sister) before, Erica wanted a cuddle." Similarly, at 10;15 Andrew's mother spontaneously reports having noticed "bits of jealousy" expressed in searches for reassurance, and that if she holds another baby Andrew would come for a cuddle but not push the other baby away. As she puts it, this jealousy is a case of "I want to go to my mummy, that's my mummy, that's where I want to be."

In similar reports infants did not express strong overt distress but rather sought immediate comfort by approaching the caregiver. Again, often young infants were not able to do so and jealousy was also reportedly expressed with simple and clear distress. The earliest reports of jealousy naturally tended to involve similar expressions. For instance, asked about jealousy at 3;23 Daisy's mother answers for the first time with a definite "Yes!" and adds:

> Yesterday I had a friend's child over, and as I went to pick him up Daisy cried. She had cried before, because the other child cried, but I had consoled her and I put her down and went to pick up the other child [still crying]. But I had a clear feeling she was jealous—she followed me with her eyes and cried when I picked him up.

Similarly, on the first visit at 4;1 Andrew's mother replies that "sometimes" he is jealous of his brother John and cries:

> For instance if I have to calm him down because he's upset [John], Andrew may start whimpering.

She replies that she has noticed this since a month at least and spontaneously adds: "It may be coincidental [rather than jealousy], but I don't think so." Under my suggestion she puts down Andrew and picks up John, and the following occurs:

> Andrew looks at John on his mother's lap, gazes from one to the other a few times and becomes progressively upset.

Avoidance / rejection

A couple of intriguing reports described jealous reactions actually involving avoidance / rejection of the caregiver's attention. At 6;20 Harry's mother spontaneously starts the interview as follows:

> The other day Irvin [middle brother] and Harry were playing and Charles [oldest brother] came along (. . .) and it was bedtime so I was giving Charles lots of cuddles and lots of—and Harry looked and then he just looked away, he wouldn't look towards me ... he *completely* avoided looking at him [Charles] because I was cuddling Charles and I had been cuddling him. There were *lots* of opportunities where he could have looked and yet he looked very quickly and looked away. It wasn't like an angry face it was just a ... "no" expression and he just looked at Irvin and the toys. (. . .) It could have been interpreted as a kind of jealousy, couldn't it. . . . Kind of "Mmph!" you know.

Similar observations were rare and Harry's mother added that she would not have noticed this event had she not purposefully observed him. Avoidant behavior may naturally attract little attention. Open rejection, instead, may notably impact caregivers. At 9 months the twins' nanny spontaneously starts the interview saying: "The other day something really interesting happened!" She then explains how Arthur was crying and, for the first time, when his mother (Beth) tried to pass him over to her he actually rejected her. She reasons that Arthur behaved as if "offended" by her "possibly because" she had attended to Richard and not to him. The nanny reports having felt guilty and "awful ... all night," "but what could I do?" and that she was afraid that the next day he would reject her again. She also reports that Beth felt sorry for being preferred over the nanny.[2]

Complex attention seeking / disruptive behaviors

Reportedly, all infants also expressed jealousy over people by means of comparatively complex behaviors openly intended to attract attention to the self, disrupt others' games / activities, or somehow exclude another from them. At 8;15 Harry's mother spontaneously reports:

> He gets cross if the others get more attention (. . .) but if I am sitting on the floor he will quite often get over it by coming and sitting on my knees (. . .) or he will go— let's say they are playing with their trains—he will go and go like this on the track [she mimics him hitting the track] so that they immediately say "Oh no, Harry!" and then he will start laughing [mother imitates a little "ha-ha" laugh] and he might even take something and go off with it ... a piece or a toy ... I've noticed him do that quite a lot.

Similarly, on my last visit I asked if Erica would try to attract her attention if she is doing something else; the mother replied "Yes!" adding "for instance" that when she reads a book to Erica's sisters:

That's her favorite time to go over there [a *forbidden* corner of the room, with mains plugs and TV and hi-fi sets]. [I ask: Can you give me an example?] She did this morning, as soon as Rose and I sat down with a book she went straight to the door of the hi-fi cabinet. [I ask: When did this start?] She has been doing that for a couple of months now [i.e., since she was 9 months].

Maybe precisely because more noticeable, these complex behaviors were reported more frequently than simple avoidance.

Wanting what others have, rivalry, and joining in

Reports like the last two, where infants' reaction appeared to be provoked by being excluded from some appealing interaction/activity other than affectionate exchanges, lead to the identification of several other phenomena of relevance toward understanding early jealousy. Consider the following exchange with Harry's parents at 8;5. I was explaining to the father my interest in infants' emotions when the latter interjects: "Anger!" The mother immediately adds:

We are getting lots of anger, when he [Harry] doesn't get it his own way or if you take something away from him (. . .) he shouts and he screams and he [she mimics Harry banging his fists]. This afternoon Irvin had a Calippo [ice-cream] and he [Harry] wanted one and was going [she mimics slurping] and he was trying to get it off Irvin and Irvin did not let him so he was getting *really cross* and shouting (. . .) Irvin wouldn't share it, so in the end I had to get one for him and he was very pleased.

She also spontaneously reports that:

He was trying to crawl into the swimming pool today. He was trying to join his brothers.

Then, asked about jealousy she replies:

Oh yes. Oh well, jealousy often with food, like this thing with the Calippo was pure, I mean partly—

And her husband interjects:

If his brothers get something he doesn't get he gets very cross. (. . .) he wants what they have! (. . .) and other food will not do . . . He's always been a bit like that, hasn't he.

Then, asked about joining in, she replies that when she cuddles his brothers: "Yeah, he does—he does." Her husband agrees and adds: "On the bed." A little later she spontaneously reports:

I've noticed that if I'm sitting with the boys on the sofa reading a story, he will get *very-very* angry if he is not sitting with us. . . . He won't have it if he is not part of a little circle.

And then adds:

(. . .) he will play next to them. (. . .) but he also, it's very-very noticeable that he's got it in him to start to disrupt what they are doing [e.g., destroy their Lego constructions].

Overall, similar reports of "wanting what others have," "wanting to do what others do," "joining in" and "wanting to be part of," or coping strategies such as "disrupting" others' activities or somehow trying to attract their attention were quite frequent. For clarity here they are separated but they were often reported as overlapping such as in the above exchange.

Wanting what others have
All interviewees reported how infants very often manifested a strong preference for what others have *because* they have it. Interestingly, interviewees never used the term "envy." Providing a definitional clue, Andrew's mother explains that while he shows this "all the time" she would not call it envy because "if he were envious he would not try to get it, whereas he tries to get it straight away." However, "wanting what others have" was considered a form of jealousy by most if not all interviewees and was reported more often than any other form of jealousy (see Table 11.2).

"Wanting what others have" was identified in reaching, grabbing, and generally trying to get what others have, and/or in expressions of distress, anger, or frustration (often quite intense) for not having it. For instance, asked about jealousy at 10;14 Erica's mother first replies negatively ("not with the girls, she joins in if we have a cuddle") but then spontaneously adds:

With toys now, like if there is a toy and she pulls it and the other child would take it, then she'll take it back regardless of what else is around.

She also replies that this would also happen if the other child had the toy first, and clearly because they had it. Indeed, some of the most striking examples involved infants wanting the identical copy of an object already in their possession. For instance, at 7;18 the twins' nanny spontaneously reports:

They have started to want what the other one's got (. . .) They did it on Monday. . . or Tuesday . . . I gave them both a rusk (baby-biscuit), they both had one but right from the beginning Arthur was looking at Richard's, he didn't want to eat, he didn't even taste it, he let go of his and he was trying to get hold of Richard's but

Table 11.2   Reported frequency of observations of wanting what others have since the last visit

	Infant					
Age (months)	Daisy	Richard	Arthur	Erica	Harry	Andrew
2						
	0					
	0					
	SomeE					
3	SomeE					
	0					
	0					
4						0
						0
	0					SomeE
5					ManyAE	
	ManyE					
	0				ManyAE	ManyAE
6	ManyE					ManyAE
					ManyAE	ManyAE
	ManyE	0	ManyAE		0	ManyAE
7	0					
		0	0	ManyE		ManyAE
		0	0			ManyAE
		ManyE	ManyE	1/2AE		
8		ManyAE	ManyAE			0
	ManyE	0	ManyAE		ManyAE	
		0	ManyAE	0	0	ManyAE
	0					
9		ManyAE	ManyAE	0	0	ManyAE
	ManyE					
				SomeE	0	0
		ManyAE	ManyAE			
10						0
		ManyAE	0			
				SomeAE		ManyAE
	ManyE	0	ManyAE		ManyAE	
11		ManyAE	ManyAE	ManyAE		
		ManyAE	ManyAE			0
				ManyAE		
12						
						0

Note: 0 = not observed since last visit; 1/2 = observed once/twice; Some = observed "sometimes" (more than once/twice but not often); Many = observed "many times." E = only involving "simple" emotion Expressions; AE = involving Actions as well as "simple" Expressions.

obviously Richard was eating his, and he got Richard's and I took it off him and I picked his own biscuit up at the same time, and he looked at the biscuit and he took Richard's! It could have been a fluke, but I think he kept his eyes on Richard's and he followed the biscuit, and when I had it then in my hand he took Richard's biscuit! And he was really happy! He looked really pleased with himself!!

The twins had two identical pink foam octopuses and she also reports how:

(. . .) both wanted the other one! Both wanted the other one's pink thing!! [she laughs] It's really funny!!

In fact, at 7;12, the following event was videotaped:

Arthur has a dummy in his hand and with the other he gets hold of Richard's dummy and kind of puts them both in his mouth. Richard turns around and after a little while whimpers a bit. The nanny gives him a dummy back. Shortly after, Arthur takes it out of Richard's mouth again (even if he still has the other one in his mouth).

As they grew older the twins also fought over toys. At 8;10 their nanny reports that Arthur "pulled a fight" with Richard and "All they wanted was what the other had." At 9 months she reports how the twins' mother had to buy another copy of the same Jack-in-the-box "because they kept fighting over it." However, she adds, "quite often they would still have a fight over the same one." Indeed, later the following occurred:

Arthur leans toward and tries to get Richard's copy of the "wanted" toy. I attract his attention to the copy lying next to him [pointing at it and saying: "Look, you have one here!"]. He looks at it and then at me, with one side of his lip rising slightly (as in an expression of contempt), and then returns his attention to Richard's copy. The nanny, as if she was Arthur, jokingly says in an impatient tone: "I know this Riccardo, I saw that half an hour ago! I just want the one that Richard's got—Thank-you!" We both laugh.

The twins provided most such examples as they had several toy "doubles." However, examples with some kind of internal control, e.g., where "substitutes won't work" or where infants leave what they just got to go "for the next thing you have," were provided by all caregivers. At 8;10 the twins' nanny reports: "Today, everything that Richard got, Arthur took, every single thing!" At 6;25 Daisy's mother replies: "She goes for the newspaper I read, not the others, even if I give her another." Daisy's father, when she was 10;26, reports: "She would quite happily eat her food until you start eating something—then she wants what you're having." When Erica was 7;11, on my first visit, her mother replies:

> Every day we go to the park (. . .) with Tom [another baby]. When Tom takes a toy
> Erica wants it as well.

This "wanting whatever the other has" was rarely considered to be about the
object in question. Sometimes it was described as an expression of wanting to
"be" like others (e.g., like an older sibling), and other times it was reported as
part of relational dynamics characterized by feelings of competition, rivalry, or
antagonism.

Rivalry, competition, antagonism

Parents rarely used these terms (hence a frequency table is not reported here) but
their reports often implied the presence of the feelings they refer to. At 10;25, for
instance, the twins' nanny spontaneously reports that "Arthur didn't want
Richard to play with him and me at speaking over the telephone." Later the
following occurred:

> Arthur goes for an object that Richard has even if he has an identical one in his
> hand. The nanny swaps the two but he still goes for the one Richard has,
> whilst he repeatedly shakes his head as if to say "no!" He ends up hurting
> Richard who cries. They then have a fight over this object, and then another
> over a different one. She spontaneously comments that her friend Penny thinks
> that Arthur is "antagonizing" Richard, but, she adds, "I don't think that Arthur
> is worse than Richard or vice versa."

Besides pushing the other away, or wanting what they have, according to
caregivers similar feelings could be expressed in several other ways. At 5;27
Harry's mother spontaneously reports that he "often wants what his brother
forbids him to have":

> Irvin will say "no-no-no you can't have this," then he will start to cry, even if it's out
> of his reach he will try to crawl toward it—it becomes his goal.

Occasionally, competitive dynamics were also identified in playful interactions.
At 8;15 she spontaneously reports that Harry would "race" with Irvin and is
"aware" of the purpose of the "competition" (crawling faster), and that this had
been happening for at least a month ("he did that a lot last month"). At 8;29 the
following was videotaped:

> A 2-year-old son of a friend teases Harry by repeatedly offering him some food
> and then withdrawing it. Harry gets some food from his mother and then
> shows it to the 2-year-old in a rather demonstrative manner, moving it in front
> of him. His mother puts words to his actions: "I've got some too!" She then
> comments "He's flaunting it!", turns to Harry and says: "You're laughing!"

Playful competitive interactions were also identified in behaviors such as sticking out one's tongue and even shouting louder or gesturing aggressively. At 11;08 Andrew's mother spontaneously reports:

If John goes "prrrrrr!" to Andrew, now he does it back to him, and quite often they end up having a little fight doing "prrrrrr!" to each other.

At 12;06 she spontaneously reports:

Andrew and John argue now. [I ask: What would they do?] If John rows at Andrew, Andrew rows back, or shouts at him.

Interestingly, by this visit similar interactions must have been established enough for Andrew and John to "ritualize" them, and a few seconds later the following was videotaped:

Andrew makes a little shout at John and moves his hand toward him in a little "against" manner. The mother explains that this is similar to what Andrew would do when arguing. In this case, however, both boys end up laughing. This sequence is then repeated, again with laughter at the end.

Most often, however, reports of competitive shouting and fighting had a more serious tone to them. At 10;18 the twins' nanny reports that they can both get very frustrated with each other (especially over toys):

They scream at each other. (. . .) Richard screams so hard at Arthur sometimes that Arthur cries because he gets upset or scared.

Fights between the twins were particularly frequent and, with time, came to involve hitting, biting, scratching, and pulling hair. Nonetheless, all infants were at some point said to have seriously competed with another infant/child, particularly with siblings and sometimes to protect their position within the family or even conquer new ones. At 10;24 Harry's mother spontaneously reports how:

(. . .) he really stands up for his own—he'll fight back with Irvin now! Harry does. He'll fight for his position, you know. They were both in the shower at swimming, and he was making sure that he got what he wanted, as much as Irvin, and he'll do that quite often now, with toys, getting toys. He goes for what he wants, he won't let him [Irvin] swap something over that he doesn't want.

As a matter of fact, according to interviewees some fights were provoked by the infants themselves and, as mentioned before, involved intentional disruption of others' activities. On the same visit Harry's mother spontaneously explains how he would often try to provoke his brothers:

> What he does a lot is—he'll watch what they are playing with, he'll pick it up and kind of shake his head and laugh and run off with it, but really gives them a look before he does. [I ask: How would he do that?] He'll look and see what they are playing with and as soon as they put it down he'll grab it, he'll take it. (...) And he'll check that they have seen him doing it, so he wants them to—to see what he's done. . . . He'll even wave it under their faces if they don't.

However, interviewees also believed that ultimately even the more disruptive forms of jealousy were meant to get some attention (albeit negative) when feeling left out from appealing interactions. In this interview, when asked about jealousy, Harry's mother replies:

> Oh yeah! I've noticed that more with his brothers. I don't know if it's so much jealousy. It's more like being in on the act, like if I'm doing something with them he will *always* want to come over . . . and he will fuss if he cannot.

This brings us to consider examples of "wanting to join in," which parents actually presented as *alternative* to jealous behavior.

Wanting to join in
"Joining in," whether identified in joining affectionate exchanges, games, or activities, was often interpreted as an alternative to jealousy. For example, the month before the above visit, at 9;15, asked about jealousy Harry's mother replies "no, but when I am with the boys he would want to crawl up as well." As an alternative to jealousy, joining in/wanting to join in was reported in 4 of the 6 infants (see Table 11.3).

At times, reports of "wanting to join in" remind one of reports of jealous anger/aggression followed, however, by contentment with being included. For example, at 8:15 asked about "joining in" Harry's mother replies:

> Quite often, I've noticed, if we are reading a story he'll come and sit in as well. Last week, he was a bit cross to begin with but then sat still.

She then specifies that when she cuddles the boys "quite often he'll grab and shake, it's his way, I think, of joining in."

Other times reports seem to point to something between this angry or at best resigned joining in and something more tolerant, eventually even pleased. At 11;03 the twins' mother notes that when she and her husband come back from work:

> (...) if you pick one up the other one will get quite cross, so usually you end up holding both of them, and they are really pleased.

Table 11.3   Reported frequency of observations of wanting to join in since the last visit

Age (months)	Daisy	Richard	Arthur	Erica	Harry	Andrew
				Infant		
2						
	0					
	0					
	0					
3	0					
	0					
	0					
4						0
						0
	0					ManyAE
5					SomeE	
	0					
	0				0	1/2AE
6	0					0
					SomeE	0
	0	0	0		0	0
7	0					
		0	0	0		0
		0	0			SomeAE
		ManyE	ManyE	0		
8		0	0			0
	0	0	0		ManyAE	
	0	0	0	0	ManyAE	0
	0					
9		0	0	0	0	ManyAE
	0					
				0	ManyAE	0
		0	0			
10						1/2AE
		0	0			
				0		0
	0	0	0		0	
11		0	0	0		
		ManyAE	ManyAE			0
				0		
12						
						ManyAE

Note: 0 = not observed since last visit; 1/2 = observed once/twice; Some = observed "sometimes" (more than once/twice but not often); Many = observed "many times." E = only involving "simple" emotion Expressions; AE = involving Actions as well as "simple" Expressions.

He confirms: "Yes, you hold both of them and they go 'hihihi'."

Yet other reports point to affectionate forms of joining in, like in "family cuddles." At 9;10 Erica's mother replies that she has not shown jealousy of her sisters and that when she cuddles them "she just joins in, messing about." On the next visit (10;14) she gives the same answer and later the following occurred:

> The mother cuddles Hazel twice within a few minutes and Erica immediately joins in both times. The second time she kisses Hazel and Erica does the same.

When Andrew was 10;3 the following was videotaped:

> The mother and John are having a cuddle. Andrew joins in and gives a cuddle to John first, and then turns to cuddle his mother.

Finally, some reports of joining in/wanting to join in appeared to involve "wanting to do what others do." At 5;01, for instance, Harry reportedly cried until his mother took him into the swimming pool with his brothers. At 6;13 she looks at him watching his brothers playing in the garden and "tells" him:

> You'll be able to do that quite soon—playing in the sun! ... [turns to me] ... I have noticed quite a lot of frustration—not being able to do things with them—he is sitting quite calmly now but quite often he'll get very restless (...) he wants to join them.

When Andrew was 4;08, asked about joining in his mother replies:

> When Andrew sees his dad and brother playing rough-and-tumble he very much wants to join in. If he is in his walker he'd push himself toward them, otherwise he'll get all excited [the brother later confirmed this].

Joining in/wanting to join in was not reported very frequently but was still held to express good levels of social awareness and strong motivation. At 8;25 Andrew's mother reports that Andrew got so excited about joining his dad and brother playing rough-and-tumble together that he "forgot" he could not walk, ran toward them and fell on his face, twice in a row.

Development and possible determinants

As one would expect, overall the frequency of reported observations of jealousy increased with the age of infants. However, according to parents the same jealous emotions emerged at different ages across infants and then, instead of "staying" as established achievements, often "went" only to reappear after some time. The tables, the reports, and the present observations point to several concurring explanations of these mixed and apparently random developmental patterns.

Motor developments

One evident factor here is motor development. The tables show that the increase in frequency of manifestations involving actual actions as well as simple emotion expressions directly contributed to the increase in frequency of reports. The parental reports and naturalistic observations suggest several different ways in which this occurred.

Firstly, motor development made infants capable of manifesting jealous emotions in more ways and situations. A friend of Erica's mother with a son of the same age (11 months) explains:

> Sometimes (...) he pushes his sister over and says "no-no-no" when he wants mummy and she is on my lap. (...) [This started] a few weeks ago—since he could walk and talk—before, he couldn't do these things. Before then he just pushed if he was on my lap.

Secondly, motor development increased the "noticeability" and "recognizability" of expressions. Many of the earliest and/or simplest expressions of jealous emotions may have passed unnoticed. Andrew's mother reported jealousy in her 6-month-old son's gaze avoidance but, asked if she had noticed this before, she explains:

> These things happen quite fast and it is difficult to tell, that time [the one mentioned above] when I really thought—Oh! This is a perfect moment—so I really watched and made a fuss of Charles [older brother].

At 7;22, Erica's mother spontaneously reports that when she picked up a friend's baby-boy Erica "looked on very intently" until she put the baby down. However, she adds:

> (...) this is the first time I noticed something like jealousy, and that wasn't me, it was his mother! [who first noticed it and then drew her attention to it]

Thirdly, motor development might have increased the frequency of reports because it allowed social interactions that directly affect the intensity and frequency of jealous emotions. Erica's mother, asked when did she start wanting what her sisters have, replies:

> I don't know when it started but it's been more noticeable in the last few weeks because they play together more now.

At 5;21 Andrew's mother makes a similar point when she reports some of the consequences of the recent emergence of better reaching and grabbing: "Yesterday he was chasing John [3-year old brother] around the room [in his walker] because he wanted a cup his brother had that Andrew thinks is great" (John, asked about that, confirms by commenting "naughty person"). She then adds that now Andrew grabs food, cups of coffee "you have," etc. and that "now he definitely prefers things that I or other people have."

The increase in variety, "noticeability," and range of jealousy-provoking inter-actions afforded by motor developments is well exemplified by the development of conflicts over objects between the twins. On the first visit, at 6;29, these two events were recorded:

> Arthur spends 4 minutes unsuccessfully trying to get hold of a toy held by Richard as he cannot move close enough. A few minutes later Arthur shows again the same interest for the toy (a different one) held by Richard, but this time he almost manages to get it, making Richard fall on his back in the process and give a little annoyed scream.

Here, it is not even clear whether Richard is annoyed because he fell or because of his brother's interference with his activity. Compare this with a 6-minute-long conflict recorded at 8;15:

> Their nanny gives them a big toy (jack-in-the-box) and they start a fight over it. This goes on for a while, until Arthur gives up. However, after another little while he goes again for it with an "attacking" scream. The nanny notes that at some point (not visible on video) Arthur had looked at her as if to say "Help me!" In fact he physically attacks Richard by pushing him repeatedly. The fight only ends when she pulls them apart.

Or consider how, at 10;05, the twins engage in an 11-minute-long conflict involving taking toys away from each other, trying to or taking them back, pushing each other, rolling over each other, and pulling hair. When their nanny stops them we laugh a lot and she shouts jokingly: "What am I going to do!" Indeed within another few seconds:

> . . . they go again for the same toy, and Richard tries again to pull Arthur's hair (stopped by the nanny). After a minute they resume the fight over their socks (pulling them off each other). Now Arthur bites Richard, who screams with a very angry face. Arthur puts a toy on his face and the nanny interprets this: "Arthur is saying to shut up!"

Social "opportunities"/dynamics
While motor development contributed directly to the increase in frequency of reports, a much more complex nonlinear effect appeared due to "simple" matters of opportunity for jealousy and evolving family dynamics.

Most mothers, for instance, were largely devoted to their young infants. This promoted the development of attachment and opportunity for later feelings of jealousy over maternal attention yet probably also reduced earlier opportunities for this emotion. While true for all infants, this was particularly clear for Daisy, whose development was followed from very early on. On my first visit, at 2;06, her mother spontaneously reports how Daisy cries immediately if separated from her, can be consoled only by her, wants to be with her all the time, so much that she can never put her down, even if she is sleeping, because she would "immediately cry" (this had indeed just happened before I switched the video-camera on). She also replies that Daisy was left with someone else only twice—once for about 2 hrs and another time for $1\frac{1}{2}$ hrs—and on both occasions Daisy "screamed hysterically until I came back." She also notes that Daisy would find and follow her with her gaze while crying in order to be picked up. In her own words: "She is a little limpet: Cling to a rock, never move!" At 4;15 both her parents also report having observed several instances of stranger's anxiety since about a month. These reports indicate a case of early clear-cut attachment and everybody around Daisy (mother, father, sisters, nanny) described her as extremely possessive. However, possibly because she was so successful in securing her mother's attention she did not often show jealousy. On the first five visits her mother replies negatively to my question on jealousy, explaining that because Daisy "doesn't like the attention taken away from her" and "wants it all the time," "She's always in my arms!" Only on the fourth visit, at 2;21, does she reply that *"maybe"* Daisy showed some jealousy when she was combing her other daughter's hair because, she explains, Daisy cried even though she had her on her lap.

The presence and possibly the age of other children may also have played an important and different role across families. Daisy's sisters are older by 6 and 9 years respectively and this may have contributed to reduce opportunities for jealousy generally. At 6;21 Daisy's mother replied that she is more interested in her mother's food than her own but not in her sisters' toys "because of the age-gap." Daisy's mother's first report of jealousy concerned an unfamiliar child at 3;23 and she explained how "Daisy does not cry when I look after the girls [sisters]." Similarly, at 9;03 Erica's mother first replies that "no," she hasn't observed any jealousy, and that she joins in laughing when she cuddles her other daughters (5 and 8 years old), and adds:

> She [Erica] does not appear to show any jealousy of her sisters. (. . .) When I pick up other babies then she is more concerned. We've spoken about this.[3] [I ask: What would she do?] She would leave what she is doing to come over, if I have another baby, definitely, and would want/would sort of come to climb on me. [I ask: And with her sisters?] With her sisters she would come over and laugh at them, or whatever, and then they would laugh at her. . . . With other babies she does not show this positive attitude.

At 10;14, when asked about when "wanting what others have" first started, she replies:

> (...) it is more noticeable now, I suppose, because she is more with other children of her own age [rather than with her sisters]—but it has been going on for a few months.

With siblings of a similar age, who would naturally share an interest in the same resources, competition might be more prominent. At 9;28 the twins' nanny, for example, reports how a friend had tried to "force them" to share four bricks by giving them two each. Richard reportedly threw his two on the floor and went for the two that Arthur had. She laughed because, as she put it, "I know that's how they are!" Yet, according to some interviewees their infants were less jealous of other babies than their own siblings, even when these were older by several years. At 8;29, asked about jealousy Harris' mother replies:

> Well, what he does, what I've noticed is, that if I am holding another baby he will always climb up me but his expression doesn't change (...) even if I don't pick him up because I've got the other baby... he'll make little noises. (...) But if I'm sitting with the boys [5 and 9 years old]... then sometimes he gets a bit jealous.

In fact, more than age difference or degree of familiarity per se, what appeared to affect infants' responses were the ongoing relational dynamics with the "competitor" and the "competed" (whether object or person), and how these naturally changed over time. Andrew was reportedly showing jealousy of his brother John (over their mother's attention) throughout his third and fourth months but then, as his mother put it, at 4;15: "jealousy seems to be getting better." At 5;21, asked about jealousy over people, she replies:

> He is nowhere near as jealous as he used to [be]. He and John [2.5 years old] are now very close, much closer than before.

She explains that Andrew is not jealous "because he's realized that I will be there for him," that now she can leave the two boys playing alone "for a good half-hour or so!" and that John is very good with Andrew who "follows him around all the time." At 7;13 she shows how when she cuddles John she would actively include Andrew and picks them both up. Andrew not only appears unaffected by his brother's presence but actually eager to go back to play. Instead by then he had started to show jealousy over his father, and she replies:

> Andrew has a whinge if dad pays attention to John first when he comes back from work. It happened tonight and is happening more and more often recently. His dad always pays attention to John first because John comes to the door. [I ask: And what

would Andrew do?] He would want to join in, he would pull his arms out or try to get up. (. . .) He stops whinging as soon as Dad picks him up.

At 10;15, she also spontaneously reports having noticed "bits of jealousy" of another baby whom she had started to look after (to support a friend going through a difficult time). During this visit Andrew also shows jealousy over the father exactly as described above and his mother comments: "He does that only when Roland comes in." At 11;08, she replies "now he's started to push other children away from me. (. . .) It's happening a lot now." These changes in family dynamics, objects of jealousy, and possible "competitors" appeared to have a clear effect on reported frequencies of jealousy.

Caregivers' reactions to infant jealousy

It is important to note that jealousy was not just determined by the ongoing social dynamics but actually also influenced them, often in ways that had a negative feedback effect on its own occurrence. We have already seen the twins' nanny reporting feeling "awful . . . all night" after being rejected by a jealous and offended Arthur. At 8;15 I ask her to try to make the twins jealous by picking up another baby (who was there visiting with his nanny). The baby was crying and she tries to console him, but when the twins turn around and one stretches a hand toward her with a worried face she puts the baby down and says, laughing embarrassedly: "I don't want to be cruel!"

Whether to reduce infants' jealousy and/or their own guilt, caregivers often reacted to jealousy with "reparative" interventions. Occasionally this happened out of their immediate awareness. At 8;01 the twins' nanny had not reported any jealousy yet, but, when she plays with Richard for a couple of minutes and Arthur starts moaning, she turns to him saying "you're getting left out" and proceeds to involve him without further noting any jealousy. We have also seen how at 5;21 Andrew's mother reports that jealousy is diminished since she includes him in cuddles with John. Nonetheless, on the same visit the following occurred:

> The mother is comforting John who has been crying. Andrew looks and smiles at them, then looks away. However, he then looks back and moves toward them with his baby-walker whinging until the mother picks him up as well (ending up with both boys on her lap).

Like the twins' nanny, she failed to notice the dynamic.

Similar reactions to early jealousy are likely to have both immediate and, if repeated, long-term effects on its occurrence. We have seen how Andrew's mother explained that jealousy is diminishing "because he's realized that I will be there for him." Similarly, at 9;10 Erica's mother explains a failed attempt to make her jealous by cuddling her sisters as follows: "(. . .) because she knows that she can have it too if she wants."

Temperamental differences

Variation in frequencies of jealous emotions across infants may be also due to genetic or epigenetic temperamental differences. Arthur and Richard, identical twins, were reportedly showing different inclinations already. Arthur was deemed more active and generally faster but also more troublesome and more likely to try to get something off the other. At 8;10 both their nanny and mother spontaneously note that Arthur "steals" Richard's food more often than the contrary. The nanny explains:

> We were talking about this. Quite often you give something to one of the boys, normally, say, Richard, and when you get back Arthur has got it and is eating it or whatever.

At 10;18, about jealousy she replies:

> It happens quite often that one of the boys moans when you pay attention to the other—especially Arthur.

The videotaped observations of the twins were consistent with this reported difference and the hypothesis that, as a temperamental inclination, jealousy is epigenetic.

Discussion

In summary, besides the expressions of infant jealousy of maternal attention reported also in other studies, this study points to the possible occurrence of further and more complex expressions of jealousy of the mother involving offended rejection, disruptive and/or attention-seeking behaviors, and to the potential for jealousy over other people (e.g., the father but occasionally also unrelated people). Most interestingly, however, the study also points toward the possibility of several other forms of jealous emotions—namely, jealousy over objects and/or activities, feelings of rivalry, competition, and antagonism, and the possibility of alternative behaviors such as "joining in"—that, to this author's knowledge, have not been systematically studied yet. If these results are to be taken seriously, young infants' potential for jealous emotions may not be that different from that of older children and adults.

The variety, complexity, and occasional ingenuity of the infant jealous behaviors reported by caregivers are indeed so remarkable that one may want to question whether they reflect the actual occurrence and development of jealous emotions or, alternatively, something that the interviewees believed/came to believe through the interviewing process. However, there are several reasons to suggest that reports were fairly reliable and valid and, if anything, actually under-rated the occurrence of jealous behaviors in the infants investigated here. Firstly, positive reports of jealousy did not appear to be caused by the interview process, as most caregivers reported jealous behaviors from the first visits and all also replied negatively to the interviewer's questions many times (see tables). Secondly, overall interviewees' reports also appeared sufficiently reliable both between and within infants. Some reports were infrequent or even specific to individual infants (e.g., "going to the plugs" in Erica) but most were notably frequent and consistent across infants and, where different caregivers of the same infant were interviewed, their reports tended to confirm one another. Last but not least, the interactions captured on camera confirm the actual occurrence of many of these behaviors. Here, it should be also noted how some of the videotaped examples of possible jealousy originally passed unnoticed by the interviewees and occasionally this researcher. This confirms interviewees' suggestion that between visits they probably missed several other possible instances of jealous behaviors.

Obviously, this is not to say that interviewees' interpretations of these behaviors were all valid. However, if anything, overall the bias appeared to be again on the conservative side as most interviewees betrayed ambivalent feelings around the possibility of infant jealousy. Consider, for instance, the following report and recorded event. Asked about jealousy at 7;05 the twins' mother replies:

> It's very difficult to know. (. . .) Yes you can sometimes pick up one and the other would cry—but I don't think it's because you haven't got one but because they haven't got you. I don't think it's in relation to the other baby. It's just that they don't want to be on their own.

Asked then if when both on her lap the twins ever push each other away, she first replies negatively but then adds that she rarely holds them together because "it's uncomfortable and they get cross" (sic). When she agrees to try this out the following occurs:

> Arthur—who was on her lap already—immediately turns to look at his brother and quickly grabs/pulls him by the shirt while giving a little "annoyed" cry. Both she and the nanny intervene promptly; she kisses and talks to Arthur (who appears pleased) and the nanny gives them a toy each. A minute later Arthur starts moaning and the mother ends up putting Richard down. When she then picks him up again and passes Arthur to the nanny he moans a lot.

The twins' mother then immediately interjects that while the twins may moan if their parents have a cuddle she does not think it's jealousy—just wanting attention. It's a "slightly different kind of emphasis," although "they do try to catch your attention when you give it to someone else. (. . .) if they haven't got something else to distract them." Later the nanny explained that the twins' mother was particularly reluctant to use the label "jealousy" because she had just read a book saying that jealousy can be a "serious problem" between twins. Possibly as a result of similar ambivalences about infant jealousy, interviewees generally appeared rather cautious in their interpretations, unless they observed something repeatedly or this implied a kind of internal control (e.g., going after whatever the other has, or wanting the same one of two identical objects).

In considering the validity of this study's results it is also important to stress how they predict virtually all manifestations of jealousy reported in later experiments on jealousy of maternal attention. It would be unreasonable to selectively dismiss all (but only) the other forms of jealousy identified here simply because they have not been experimentally investigated yet. Obviously, the results reported here cannot be considered representative of the occurrence and development of all jealous emotions in all infants independently of family dynamics and/or rearing practices. In fact, they clearly point toward the fundamental role of these dynamics and practices. Nonetheless, these results offer a rich taxonomy of many possible early forms of jealousy and related feelings thoroughly grounded in natural experience and (English) language, and an in-depth insight into possible developmental pathways of jealousy and their determinants.

Conclusions

The richness of the taxonomy identified here suggests that young infants' potential for jealous emotions is still seriously underestimated by many psychologists, if not by parents. The early age of emergence, relative immediacy and immediate functionality, variety, complexity, and different developmental courses of the jealous emotions in this taxonomy are also striking. Even more striking is that neither their contexts of occurrence (for data on the context of jealousy of maternal attention see also Legerstee et al.'s study with 3- and 6-month-olds, this volume), nor the behaviors involved, appear to be fundamentally different in their relational dynamics and functions from those that specify similar emotions in older children and adults. Ultimately, all the different jealous behaviors identified here can be explained as ways to involve the self in and/or exclude others from appealing relationships and activities that are functionally similar to the ways in which adults deal with comparable situations. This point has not been stressed enough in the literature on social development, which has tended to focus on change in behavior rather than continuity in its functional aspect. Yet acknowledging this functional continuity is fundamental to answer both the question of description and that of explanation of the ontogenesis of social awareness. To illustrate this point, let us briefly consider the following parallel between adult and infant jealousy.

Say that at a party you saw your romantic partner flirting with an attractive stranger and that later, on the way back home together, you "casually" note how this stranger was dressed a bit like a whore or clearly appeared to be a loser. Your partner will perceive you as jealous because, functionally, you are behaving like Daisy (as discussed earlier) when she attacked the kitten her mother was stroking. Your behavior is verbal and delayed while Daisy's was physical and immediate but the relational function that they both specify is the same (i.e., an attack on someone to whom a significant other showed clear positive attention). Such adult versions could be easily drawn for all the infant manifestations of jealousy identified here, and even some of their "developmental" changes are similar to those that may occur in relationships between adults. Andrew's mother reported that his jealousy toward the brother decreased and their relationship improved when Andrew realized that she would be there for him anyway. Similarly, in romantic relationships and/or intimate friendships between adults initial jealousy toward ex-partners or other friends can be followed by tolerance or even affection after one is reassured that they do not constitute a threat. These and other parallels between infant and adult instances of jealousy show how the taxonomy developed here really is meaningful to us because it identifies invariants in the relational functions of different behaviors across the lifespan. This finding goes some unexpected way toward answering our initial question of description of the ontogenesis of social awareness by suggesting that, with regard to the basic level of the relational functions of behavior, *this awareness does not actually change that much*.

That the taxonomy developed here identifies so many functional and context-ual similarities between infant and adult manifestations of jealousy also brings an unexpected twist to the question of explanation of the ontogenesis of social awareness. For which could be the cognitive capacities that underpin the levels of social awareness signaled by all these manifestations *in both young infants and adults*? The traditional cognitive approach cannot answer this question as it relies on representational skills for which there is very little evidence before the second year. To accommodate the evidence of early sociality that has amassed in the past few decades, many cognitive theorists have turned to consider more infant-friendly forms of representation, such as an early-emerging or innate domain-general representational capacity (e.g., Perner, 1991), domain-specific representa-tions of other people and the self (e.g., Leslie, 1987), or both (e.g., Karmiloff-Smith, 1992). Typically these authors also postulate the presence of innate non-representational sensitivities to certain human characteristics, such as self-propelled movement, the human voice and face, facial/body expression of emo-tion, etc. (see also Harris, 1989). Some even suggest that these and/or other sensitivities are organized in a "theory of mind" module, defined for instance as a social instinct molded by evolution to aid "normally developing children to attend the invisible mental states of others" (Leslie, 2000, p. 61). Since the discovery of "mirror neurons" in the pre-motor cortex of macaques there is also much renewed interest in the old "empathy" solution to the "problem of other minds," according to which social awareness is mediated by (pre-motor) mimicry of others' movements followed by an ensuing "mirror" experience. Nonetheless, with the notable exception of Trevarthen (see Draghi-Lorenz et al., 2001), very few authors have ever referred to these cognitive processes to predict or explain the early presence of social phenomena as complex as the manifestations of jealousy identified here.

It is indeed difficult to imagine how explanations based on the processes listed above could ever account for the required levels of social awareness. Firstly because the causal workings of these cognitive processes are often insufficiently defined (e.g., how do "social instincts" or "innate sensitivities" actually function?) and hence do not really explain anything. Secondly because, when they are causally defined, their explanatory power invariably relies upon the *mediation of representational and/or empathic reproductions* of others' experiences when, instead, *immediate and differentiated perception* appears to occur. That the relational dynamics specifying jealousy in young infants are fundamentally similar to those specifying jealousy in adults makes the latter problem particularly clear. Say that, in the scenario hypothesized above, you saw your beloved partner and his/her flirt casually touching each other's arms while engaging in prolonged eye contact and laughing together, and say that your partner then also rejected your attempts to join the conversation by letting them fall flat. Your experience throughout this interaction would not be one of accessing a series of representations of the meaning of the others' actions somewhere in your head (let alone one of reasoning or theorizing on this meaning). Even less would your experience be one of empathizing with your partner's and their flirt's enjoyment of each other first, and with your partner's rejection of you thereafter. On the contrary, your experience would be one of *immediately seeing and hearing* the relational meaning of the unfolding interaction while you actually experienced something rather *different* from that expressed by either your partner or their flirt. Likewise, an infant may directly perceive loving affection in their mother's caressing or fondling behavior but if this is directed at another and if, say, the mother also fails to respond to the infant's calls, then the infant would also perceive her actions as specifying "preference" for the other and (just like you) would feel "less wanted/loved than" and react accordingly. It is very important to stress that this evaluative aspect, so prominent in the experience of non-basic emotions, is also immediately specified in the here and now of interaction.

Given the predominant role played in the field by representational explanations and the recent revamping of the empathy explanation, the following is thus a critical hypothesis for current understandings of social awareness: *At all ages interpersonal awareness of others' motives, emotions, and attitudes in relation to the self and third parties, including evaluative ones, may be based on the direct perception of the relational functions specified by ongoing interactive vocal, facial, and body behavior.* Similar ecological explanations of the "cognitive" underpinnings of social emotions such as jealousy have been suggested before. Both Frijda (1993, p. 370) and Butterworth (1998), in particular, have argued that early non-basic emotions such as jealousy (but also embarrassment, guilt, etc.) are likely to follow a direct perceptual appraisal of others' intentions and emotions in relation to self, as these are manifested in the interaction with/between these others. In so doing, both authors also referred to two fundamental ideas which underlie much of the reasoning presented here: (i) Michotte's understanding of people's perception of emotions in others as perception of the functional relations specified by recipro-cal movements between individuals (Michotte, 1950), and (ii) Gibson's idea (e.g., 1979) that what is perceived are affordances, i.e., the fit/misfit between perceived environmental features (in our example the others' intimate and exclu-sive behavior) and the opportunity for functional actions (e.g., achieve closeness to significant others and secure their attention).

Obviously, past experience and learning, the formation of specific and progres-sively complex representations, and the empathic reproductions of others' experi-ences *also* play important roles in socio-emotional development. The repeated experience of a mother's preference for a sibling, for instance, could sediment into a learned sense of being "less loved" and eventually "less lovable than" the other/s. Whether even this less transient sense of self needs to be representa-tional is debatable but there is little doubt that a perceptual social awareness would naturally lead to, and be eventually enriched by, increasingly complex representational understandings of self and others. Interviewees, for example, clearly relied on a rather complex representational understanding of their infants when testing their perceptions of jealousy against alternative hypotheses in a careful and detached way. An empathic reaction, instead, could add to the direct social awareness of others a sense of identification with them, and thus play a specific role in the determination of emotions involving closeness to others' experiences such as empathic concern, sympathy, and guilt (see Hobson, this volume). Nonetheless, as pointed out by Solomon Asch already in 1952, learning about, representation of, and empathy with others could only emerge within social interactions that are already perceived as immediately meaningful. The data presented here are consistent with this thesis and suggest that further empirical and theoretical work in this direction could take us surprisingly far in explaining social awareness in adults as well as infants. Research on other early non-basic emotions is particularly needed, but the available research on jealous emotions already calls for explanations based on the direct perception of the relational functions of interactive behavior, rather than on the representational and/or empathic mediation of others' experiences.

Acknowledgments

To the teenagers who as little babies participated in this research, trusting that they are leading their relational lives as skillfully today as they were then—and with thanks from the heart to Alan Costall for his invaluable help with this chapter.

Notes

1 For theoretical reasons Masciuch interpreted jealousy in her 8/9-month-old participants as exceptional and dismissed it altogether in the 4/5-month-olds, yet her data
   clearly point to the possibility of jealousy in both groups.
2 Unexpressed feelings of jealousy between the caregivers may have also affected their
   experience.
3 In fact we had not, as she had mentioned jealousy of other children only as a
   theoretical possibility.

References

Asch, S. E. (1952). *Social psychology.* Englewood Cliffs, NJ: Prentice-Hall.

Baldwin, J. (1902). *Social and ethical interpretations in mental development.* New York:
   The Macmillan Company.

Barrett, K. C. (1995). A functionalist approach to shame and guilt. In J. P. Tangney &
   K. W. Fischer (Eds.), *Self-conscious emotions* (pp. 25–63). New York: Guilford Press.

Bretherton, I., McNew, S., & Beeghly-Smith, M. (1981). Early person knowledge as
   expressed in gestural and verbal communication: When do infants acquire a "theory
   of mind"? In M. Lamb & L. Sherrod (Eds.), *Infant social cognition* (pp. 333–373).
   Hillsdale, NJ: Erlbaum.

Butterworth, G. (1998). *The infant self from a non-conceptual point of view.* Paper presented
   at the XVth Biennial Meetings of the ISSBD (International Society of Social Behaviour and Development), July 1–4, Berne, Switzerland.

Butterworth, G., & Grover, L. (1988). The origins of referential communication in
   human infancy. In L. Weiskrantz (Ed.), *Thought without language* (pp. 5–24). Oxford:
   Clarendon Press.

Cummings, E. M., Zahn-Waxler, C., & Radke-Yarrow, M. (1981). Young children's
   responses to expressions of anger and affection by others in the family. *Child
   Development, 52,* 1274–1282.

Draghi-Lorenz, R. (1997). *Jealousy in the first year: Evidence of interpersonal awareness.* Paper
   presented at the BPS Annual Conference of the Developmental Psychology Section,
   September 12–15, Oxford, UK.

Draghi-Lorenz, R. (1998). *Young infants can be jealous.* Paper presented at the XIth Biennial
   International Conference on Infant Studies (ICIS), April 2–5, Atlanta, Georgia.

Draghi-Lorenz, R. (2001). *Young infants are capable of 'non-basic' emotions.* Unpublished
   PhD thesis, University of Portsmouth, UK.

Draghi-Lorenz, R., Reddy, V., & Costall, A. (2001). Rethinking the development of "non-
   basic" emotions: A critical review of existing theories. *Developmental Review, 21,* 263–304.

Draghi-Lorenz, R., Reddy, V., & Morris, P. (2005). Adult perception of three-months-olds'
   expression of shyness and related emotions. *Infant and Child Psychology, 14,* 63–83.

Elliott, R., Fischer, C. T., & Rennie, D. L. (1999). Evolving guidelines for publication of
   qualitative research studies in psychology and related fields. *British Journal of Clinical
   Psychology, 38,* 215–229.

Frijda, N. H. (1993). The place of appraisal in emotion. *Cognition and Emotion, 7,* 357–387.

Gesell, A. (1906). Jealousy. *The American Journal of Psychology, 17*, 437–96.

Gibson, J. J. (1979). *The ecological approach to visual perception.* Boston: Houghton-Mifflin.

Goren, C. C., Sarty, M., & Wu, P. Y. K. (1975). Visual following and pattern-discrimination of face-like stimuli by newborn infants. *Pediatrics, 56*, 544–549.

Harris, P. L. (1989). *Children and emotion: The development of psychological understanding.* Oxford: Blackwell.

Hart, S. L. & Carrington, H. A. (2002). Jealousy in six-month-old infants. *Infancy, 3*, 395–402.

Hart, S. L., Carrington, H. A., Tronick, E. Z., & Carroll, S. R. (2004). When infants lose exclusive maternal attention: Is it jealousy? *Infancy, 6*, 57–78.

Izard, C.E. (1994). What develops in emotional development? Intersystems connections. In P. Ekman & J. Davidson (Eds.), *The nature of emotions* (pp. 356–361). Oxford: Oxford University Press.

Karmiloff-Smith, A. (1992). *Beyond modularity.* Cambridge, MA: MIT Press.

Klein, M. (1921–1945). *Love, guilt and reparation and other works, 1921–1945.* London: Hogarth Press.

Klein, M. (1946–1963). *Envy and gratitude and other works, 1946–1963.* London: Hogarth Press.

Klinnert, M. D., Campos, J. J., Sorce, J. F., Emde, R. N., & Svejda, M. (1983). Emotions as behavior regulators: Social referencing in infancy. In R. Plutchik & H. Kellerman (Eds.), *Emotions: Theory, research and experience* (Vol. 2, pp. 57–86). New York: Academic Press.

Leslie, A. (1987). Pretence and representation: The origins of a "theory of mind." *Psychological Review, 94*, 412–426.

Leslie, A. (2000). Theory of mind. In A. E. Kazdin (Ed.), *Encyclopedia of psychology* (Vol. 8, pp. 60–61). Washington, DC: American Psychological Association/New York: Oxford University Press.

Lewis, M. (1995). Self-conscious emotions. *American Psychologist, 63*, 68–78.

Maratos, O. (1973). *The origin and development of imitation in the first six months of life.* PhD Thesis, University of Geneva.

Masciuch, S. (1988). Jealousy: The quantitative and qualitative testing of a Kleinian psychoanalytic neo-Piagetian paradigm. *Journal of the Melanie Klein Society, 6*, 14–34.

Masciuch, S., & Kienapple, K. (1993). The emergence of jealousy in children 4 months to 7 years of age. *Journal of Social and Personal Relationships, 10*, 421–435.

Michotte, A. (1950). The emotions regarded as functional connections. In M. L. Reymert (Ed.), *Feelings and emotions: The Mooseheart Symposium* (pp. 114–126). New York: McGraw-Hill. (Also published in A. Costall, G. Thines, & G. Butterworth (1991), *Michotte's experimental psychology* (pp. 103–116). Hillsdale, NJ: Erlbaum.)

Morris, P. H., Doe, C., & Godsell, E. (2008). Secondary emotions in non-primate species? Behavioural reports and subjective claims by animal owners. *Cognition and Emotion, 22*, 3–20.

Murray, L., & Trevarthen, C. (1985). Emotional regulation of interactions between two-month-old infants and their mothers. In T. Field & N. Fox (Eds.), *Social perception in infancy.* Norwood, NJ: Erlbaum.

Perner, J. (1991). *Understanding the representational mind.* Cambridge, MA: MIT Press.

Sagi, A., & Hoffman, M. L. (1976). Empathic distress in newborn. *Developmental Psychology, 12*, 175–176.

Sroufe, A. (1996). *Emotional development*. Cambridge: Cambridge University Press.

Trevarthen, C. (1974). Conversations with a two-month old. *New Scientist, 62,* 230–235.

Trevarthen, C. (1984). Emotions in infancy. In K. R. Scherer & P. Ekman (Eds.), *Approaches to emotions* (pp. 129–157). London: Erlbaum.

Trevarthen, C. (1993). The functions of emotions in early infancy communication and development. In L. Camaioni & J. Nadel (Eds.), *New perspectives in early communicative development* (pp. 48–81). London: Routledge.

Tronick, E. Z., Als, H., Adamson, L., Wise, S., & Brazelton, T. B. (1978). The infant's response to entrapment between contradictory messages in face-to-face interaction. *Journal of the American Academy of Child Psychiatry, 17,* 1–13.

Walker-Andrews, A. S. (1997). Infants' perception of expressive behaviors: Differentiation of multimodal information. *Psychological Bulletin, 121,* pp. 437–456.

Zahn-Waxler, C., Radke-Yarrow, M., & King, R. A. (1979). Child rearing and children's prosocial initiations toward victims of distress. *Child Development, 50,* 319–330.

12

Jealousy in Autism Spectrum Disorders (ASD)

Nirit Bauminger

Introduction

Yuval is a 4-year-old boy with high-functioning autism spectrum disorder (ASD) who participated in our ongoing study of jealousy and other social-emotional capabilities among young children with high-functioning ASD. The following was a spontaneous family interaction that I was fortunate to observe during a home visit:

> "Hey, Mom, look! I can crawl forward!" Yuval shouted as a reaction to his mother's praise of his baby brother's first-time crawling. Immediately, almost simultaneously with his mother's "Great job!!" and clapping to praise her baby son, Yuval got down on all fours to imitate his brother and signaled the mother that he could also crawl. Yuval repeated this behavior several times, smiling each time his mother praised him.

Later, after my home visit, we conducted a laboratory situation in Yuval's preschool, with Yuval, his mother, and Yuval's female friend Roni present in the room:

> Upon instruction, Yuval's mother put Roni on her lap, hugged her, and read her a story, while ignoring her son. Immediately after the mother put Roni on her lap, Yuval stood up, stopped playing, approached his mother, and said: "I want Mom." When his mother started reading the story to his friend, Yuval yelled: "No! Me! You aren't Roni's mom! You're my mom!" At this stage, he also started to climb up on the mother and hug her. A few seconds later he said: "Enough Mom" and threw the book to the floor.

What can we learn about the emotional deficit in ASD based on this child's behavior during these two situations? What conclusions can be drawn about the

Handbook of Jealousy: Theory, Research and Multidisciplinary Approaches, First Edition.
Edited by Sybil L. Hart and Maria Legerstee.

psychological underpinnings of jealousy based on these two situations? And why are such conclusions important for both typical and abnormal emotional development? These are the questions to be explored in the current chapter.

Yuval's reactions definitely lend support to the accepted notion that jealousy is an unpleasant emotion that acquires its meaning based on the social context in which it occurs (e.g., Izard, 1991; Miller, Volling, & McElwain, 2000). But what other conclusions can be drawn? Can we say, for example, that Yuval is attached to his mother and that this attachment explains his behavior? Some will answer, "Yes, Yuval is very clearly attached to his mother," but others will reply: "Attached? Possibly so, but is he affectively related to her? It is not so clear." The answers to these questions remain uncertain, due to both the vagueness of current knowledge about the nature of the emotional deficit in ASD and the existing controversies concerning the conceptualization of jealousy in typical development (e.g., Hobson, 2005; Draghi-Lorenz, Reddy, & Costall, 2001). In this chapter, I will try to touch upon and clarify these complexities.

ASD is a neurobiological disorder that significantly impairs reciprocal social relations, verbal and nonverbal communication, and behavior (*Diagnostic and Statistical Manual of Mental Disorders—DSM-IV-TR*; APA, 2000). It is not yet known why. The boundaries and nature of the emotional deficit in ASD are not well defined, but clearly children with this disorder exhibit a profound emotional deficit. Historically, Kanner (1943) described these children as innately lacking the ability "to form the usual biologically provided affective contact with people" (p. 250). More recent works highlight difficulties and abnormalities in intersubjective sharing, in experiencing, understanding, being sensitive, responding to other's emotions, and reacting emotionally within social contexts, more specifically within interpersonal interactions (e.g., Dissanayake & Sigman, 2001; Hobson, 2005; Rogers & Bennetto, 2001; Rogers & Pennington, 1991). As a consequence, the experience of emotions that have their foundations in the dynamic reactions between people (such as jealousy) should be considered as implausible in ASD.

However, accumulating data support a continuum of emotional capabilities in children with ASD. Thus, the crucial research question (e.g., Hobson, 2005) must focus on identifying who along the spectrum can do what. In this chapter, I will describe the interplay between what can be learned about jealousy from children with ASD and what can be learned about ASD from the understanding of jealousy. I will first discuss the conceptualization of jealousy in typical development, highlighting the debate as to whether jealousy is a basic or a secondary emotion. This will be followed by the presentation of findings on jealousy and its affective and cognitive correlates in children with ASD and in children with typical development. A broader picture about the emotional competence of children with ASD will then be offered, mainly in terms of their understanding and expression of other social emotions such as pride, guilt, and embarrassment. Discussion about the theoretical implications of conceptualizing jealousy as a secondary or as a basic emotion in typical development, as well as its possible significance as an early indicator of children's ability for interpersonal relationships such as attachment in both ASD and typical development, will then conclude the chapter.

Jealousy: Basic or Secondary Emotion?

Despite controversies on the complexity of the experience of jealousy in typical development, there seems to be at least one common denominator for the different views: They all underscore the experience of jealousy in the context of a social triangle (Hansen, 1991; Masciuch & Kienapple, 1993; Miller et al., 2000; Parrott, 1991; Salovey, 1991; Volling, McElwain, & Miller, 2002). The conventional conceptual perception of jealousy describes this emotion as a secondary, socially mediated emotion that is highly dependent on individual awareness and responsiveness within a system of relationships between three participants: the jealous individual, a significant other, and a rival (White & Mullen, 1989).

Unlike primary or basic emotions, like happiness and sadness, which are believed to be present during the first year and built upon primitive cognitive processes such as mean–ends understanding, secondary or complex emotions emerge later in development, during the second and third years of life (Izard & Harris, 1995) and require a blending of cognitive and social skills. The key issue differentiating "basic" from "complex" emotions is that "basic" emotions are considered to be independent of representation (Draghi-Lorenz et al., 2001; Izard & Harris, 1995; Lewis, 2000b). Complex emotions, which are also referred to as self-conscious, social, or secondary emotions, are based on the differentiation of self from other, and particularly on the ability to put oneself in the place of another—the development of interpersonal awareness (Lewis, 2000b). Social emotions are invariably connected with real or imagined social interactions, where experiences with others centrally influence their development (Barrett, 1995).

According to White and Mullen, the experience of jealousy reflects an interplay between the intrapersonal (the jealous individual) and an interpersonal network of three dyadic relationships within this triangle: (1) the primary jealous relationship, a valued close relationship between the jealous individual and the beloved; (2) the secondary or rival relationship between the beloved and the rival; and (3) the adverse relationship between the individual and the rival. According to this perception, to feel jealousy, triggered by the real or perceived loss to a rival of the valued close primary relationship (or loss of "formative" or "exclusive" love and attention, Hansen, 1991; Parrott, 1991), the jealous individual first needs to possess such a close valued relationship with a significant other and, second, probably needs to make multiple inferences regarding interpersonal relationships that involve the self and others, including representations of another person's mental state (the beloved's preference for a rival).

Experimentally, studies have evoked jealousy in children via interpersonal triadic situations like the mother–child–peer rival scenario or the parent and two sibling scenario. In these situations, children provided rich verbal and non-verbal signifiers of jealousy, such as discontinuing their task and focusing attention on the triad, frowning, making attempts to interfere with or enter into the rival interaction, using attention-provoking behaviors, taking the other child's objects, hugging or climbing on the main caregiver, answering questions that were addressed to the other child, attempting to correct the other child, trying to change the situation by complaining, and attempting to do at least as well as (equalization) or better than the rival (e.g., Bers & Rodin, 1984; Masciuch & Kienapple, 1993; Miller et al., 2000; Volling et al., 2002).

The classic perception of jealousy as a secondary emotion has been challenged recently by findings (e.g., Draghi-Lorenz et al., 2001) of jealousy expressions in very young children with typical development (6 to 12 months), who are probably younger than the age when capabilities develop for complex inferences, as required by definitions of complex secondary emotions. Hart and her colleagues defined jealousy as infant disturbance (e.g., negative affect or vocalization) in reaction to a situation where the mother cuddles a lifelike doll (e.g., Hart & Carrington, 2002; Hart, Carrington, Tronick, & Carroll, 2004; Hart, Field, del Valle, & Letourneau, 1998; Hart, Field, Letourneau, & del Valle, 1998; Hart, Jones, & Field, 2003). If Hart's results are interpreted as jealousy, then to experience jealousy at even the lowest developmental level infants should possess some degree of intersubjectivity or interpersonal awareness, because jealousy is the result of loss of exclusive attention from a significant other to a rival. On a higher developmental level and in line with more conservative perceptions of jealousy, the experience of jealousy may involve complex affective and cognitive capabilities (e.g., Volling et al., 2002).

Several conceptual issues should be regarded that add to our conceptual confusion vis-à-vis jealousy. First, jealousy experiences do not necessarily include persons only. For example, a woman may feel jealous about her husband's selective attention to his car. Moreover, examples of "jealousy behaviors" can appear in nonhuman species such as dogs. A dog can protest in a triadic interaction, for example when the husband hugs his wife (although this can be interpreted as pure imitation of the husband). Adding to the conceptual confusion is the differentiation of jealousy from envy. Envy, in contrast to jealousy, may involve only two-person situations, where someone wishes to have another person's possession or success and/or wishes that the other person did not possess this desired characteristic or object (Parrott, 1991). Parrott and Smith (1993) have suggested that in envy one's own appraisal leads to dissatisfaction with oneself, whereas in jealousy the reflected appraisal or attention of another leads to a lack of security and confidence. However, what precludes a distinct differentiation is that both jealousy and envy may be concerned with losses of self-esteem stemming from social comparison, and they demonstrate similar behavioral manifestations (e.g., Bers & Rodin, 1984; Parrott, 1991; Salovey & Rodin, 1984; Silver & Sabini, 1978).

How can we solve this conceptual haziness? Do all these qualify as forms of jealousy, because they appear the same in terms of their behavioral manifestations? Are we talking about the same emotion? Is there one shared schema for the experience of jealousy, which underlies all the types of examples? Or else, as Hobson suggests in Chapter 12 of this book, is jealousy an emotion with multiple forms or with multiple developmental requirements? It is premature to draw clear conclusions, particularly because jealousy has almost never been examined with regard to its potential developmental correlates in children with typical development. I will expand on this later in this chapter, but an exception to this is Hart's work, which has focused on examining the links between attachment and jealousy. Hart and her colleagues found that jealousy protest was greater in a mother condition than in a stranger condition (as a reaction to cuddling the lifelike doll; Hart, Field, del Valle, & Letourneau, 1998) and in infants with non-depressed mothers compared to infants of depressed mothers (e.g., Hart, Field, Letourneau, & del Valle, 1998). Hart's results on the links between attachment and jealousy are described in more detail elsewhere in this book.

The discussion here has thus far focused on individuals' experience of jealousy; however, individuals' own understanding of jealousy must also be investigated in order to explain the emotion's full complexity. According to Lewis (2000a), children may sustain an emotional state but not necessarily experience conscious awareness of that state. For example, children as young as 2–3 years can express pride in the presence of others, but it is not until 7 or 8 years that they recognize the role that others play in the evaluation of their own accomplishments (Kasari, Sigman, Yirmiya, & Mundy, 1993; Seidner, Stipek, & Fesbach, 1988). Furthermore, according to Saarni (1999), the ability to describe emotional experience requires the development of a network of concepts, which are scripts for representing children's own emotional responses within a multidimensional matrix of causes, goals, values, social relations, and beliefs about emotional management. Typically developing children of about age 6–8 have well-defined scripts that reveal such a multidimensional matrix. Thus, the investigation of children's expressions and understanding of jealousy can help clarify whether a gap exists between a more automatic behavioral process of affective expression on the one hand, and a higher-level process of conscious awareness on the other. The latter should entail children's ability to understand the factors eliciting this emotion, including the role of others. The understanding of jealousy may require complex interpersonal projections of self and other. Such an understanding of jealousy among typically developing children will be discussed by analyzing group differences in jealousy between ASD and typical samples.

Taken together, these aspects of the study of jealousy in children with typical development raise important questions about the psychological underpinnings of the emotion. Such questions are meaningful for further investigation of the emotional deficit among children with ASD, which highlights a core lack of intersubjective sharing (e.g., Rogers & Bennetto, 2001; Rogers & Pennington, 1991). In the next section I will talk about the expression and understanding of jealousy in children with ASD.

Jealousy in ASD: Expression and Understanding

Jealousy expression

To scrutinize the ability to express jealousy among individuals with ASD, I will next present three empirical sources of information and then will draw preliminary conclusions. We examined expressions of jealousy in my laboratory in two groups of children with ASD versus with typical development: older children at preadolescence and younger children in preschool (Bauminger, 2004; Bauminger, Chomsky-Smolkin, Orbach-Caspi, Zachor, & Levy-Shiff, 2008). I will also report on Hobson's research on children with ASD versus children with developmental delay. Table 12.1 presents these findings in table form.

Our study that examined jealousy in preadolescents included 16 highfunctioning children with ASD (mean age = 11.14 years) and 17 children with typical development (mean age = 11.51 years) who were matched to the ASD group on IQ, chronological age, gender, and maternal education. To measure children's jealousy expressions, we manipulated two experimental triadic scenarios: the drawing and the playing scenario. Each scenario included a triad consisting of the child in the experimental group (autism or typical), his or her main caregiver, and another familiar child (the rival) who was either the child's friend or a sibling. The drawing scenario had an emphasis on more cognitive processes such as social comparison. In this scenario, each of the 2 children drew a picture of his or her choice and, upon completion, mothers were instructed to praise the rival child's picture while ignoring their child's picture. The playing scenario was rooted in interpersonal, social-affective processes. In this scenario, the 2 children played alone for a while; then upon instruction the mother joined the rival in affectionate and lively play while ignoring her own child.

Based on the difficulties in interpersonal interactions among children with ASD, we hypothesized fewer manifestations of jealousy experience in the playing scenario versus the drawing scenario. Results were surprisingly different. Regarding jealousy explicitness, measured on a hierarchical scale ranging from an absence of explicit jealousy indices to the most explicit indices of jealousy, we found no statistically significant interactions for group (ASD/typical), scenario (drawing/playing), or for group × scenario. The majority of children in both groups expressed explicit jealousy in both scenarios (88% = ASD and 67% = typical for drawing; and 75% = ASD and 73% = typical for playing). Group differences did emerge on the manifestations of jealousy as measured by a

Table 12.1 Jealousy in ASD: Summary of findings

Study objectives	Name of study	Participants	Main findings
	Jealousy expression and understanding		
Jealousy expression	Bauminger, 2004	HFASD; TYP (preadolescents)	1. Nonsignificant group differences on the explicitness of jealousy. 2. Significant group differences on jealousy manifestations: ASD gazed less and acted more toward the parent compared with TYP.
	Bauminger et al., 2008	ASD; TYP (preschoolers)	1. Significant group differences on jealousy explicitness (ASD < TYP). 2. Significant group differences on jealousy manifestations: ASD gazed less at the peer and more at the interaction compared with TYP. ASD displayed fewer actions to attract parents' attention.
	Hobson et al., 2006	ASD; DD ($CA = 7–13$ years, $VMA = 3–9$ years)	Nonsignificant group differences on the expression of jealousy (approximately half of the children in each group showed clear signs of jealousy).
Jealousy understanding	Bauminger, 2004	ASD; TYP (preadolescents)	1. Significant group differences in recognition of jealousy: ASD < TYP. 2a. Significant group differences in examples of affective jealousy: ASD < TYP. 2b. Nonsignificant group differences in examples of social-cognitive jealousy (envy).

Table 12.1   *(Cont.)*

Study objectives	Name of study	Participants	Main findings
	Affective and cognitive correlates of jealousy		
	Affective correlates:		
Emotional responsiveness (ER)	Bauminger et al., 2008	ASD; TYP (preschoolers)	Close, significant links between jealousy and ER in both groups: **ASD**: Higher ER behaviors correlated with higher jealousy gazes and actions and tended to link with more explicitness of jealousy. **TYP**: Higher verbalizations, actions, and levels of concern in ER were related with higher verbal expressions of jealousy; higher verbalization of ER linked also with higher jealousy gazes and behaviors; higher level of concern in ER linked with more explicitness of jealousy.
Social referencing (SR)	Bauminger & Orbach-Caspi, 2005	HFASD; TYP (preschoolers)	**ASD**: Jealousy verbalizations and actions correlated positively with appropriate verbalization in SR; more explicitness of jealousy correlated with more approach behaviors in SR. **TYP**: More explicit jealousy linked with higher levels of appropriate verbalization in SR.
	Cognitive correlates:		
IQ	Bauminger et al., 2008	ASD; TYP (preschoolers)	**In ASD only**: IQ positively correlated with jealousy explicitness.
Mental age (MA)	Bauminger, 2004	ASD; TYP (preadolescents)	**In ASD only**: MA correlated positively with social-comparison examples of jealousy.

Note: ASD = autism spectrum disorder; HFASD = high-functioning ASD; TYP = typical development; DD = developmental disabilities.

behavioral scale, which tapped 10 indices of jealousy comprising three main categories: the child's gaze direction (at parent or at peer/sibling); the child's verbalization (e.g., attention seeking, negative, or interactive comments); and the child's actions (e.g., attention-seeking behaviors and involvement behaviors). Compared to typically developing children, children with ASD were significantly less likely to look at the parent and/or the rival child but were significantly more likely to act toward them, regardless of the scenario. Altogether, these outcomes demonstrated that jealousy was clearly expressed by children in both groups across both scenarios, but the ASD manifestations of jealousy differed in quality.

The study on younger preschoolers with ASD revealed a somewhat similar picture. Participants were 32 preschoolers with ASD and 18 preschoolers with typical development who were matched on mental age, verbal and nonverbal mental age, mother's education, and birth order. The expression of jealousy was measured through the aforementioned jealousy-provoking experimental scenario of storybook reading to a rival. The scenario consisted of the target child (ASD/typical); his or her main caregiver; and a familiar peer attending the child's preschool. The scenario started with 2 children playing separately with their own toys. Upon instruction, the mother placed the rival peer on her lap and embraced the peer while reading a story aloud to that child. Similarly to the findings with the older children, the majority of preschoolers with ASD (68.75%) as well as of preschoolers with typical development (94.5%) demonstrated explicit expressions of jealousy. However, due to the fact that almost all preschoolers with typical development expressed jealousy in an explicit way, group differences here were significant. As for the older children, manifestations of jealousy differed significantly between the preschool groups. Compared to typical controls, children with ASD gazed less at the peer and more at the interaction. Children with ASD also displayed fewer actions to attract the parent's attention, compared with their typical counterparts. In addition, preschoolers with typical development displayed their jealousy responses quicker than the ASD group, whereas response time did not significantly differ between the older groups.

Another source of information on the expression of jealousy in ASD comes from Hobson's laboratory, which has extensively examined the expression of various social-emotions. In their study of jealousy (Hobson, Chidambi, Lee, & Meyer, 2006), parents reported on 10 children with ASD and 9 children with developmental delay, with groups matched on chronological age (7–13 years) and on verbal mental age (3–9 years). Parents were asked if they had observed their child expressing jealousy as a reaction to the attention that the parent or someone else had given to other individuals. Results demonstrated no group differences on the expression of jealousy, with around half of the children in each group showing clear signs of jealousy and very few showing no signs at all. For example, one mother reported that if the child's siblings were seated near the mother, the child with ASD would move his siblings away (even push them) and sit by the mother.

Taking these three sources of information into account, it is clear that a vast majority of the children in the autism spectrum do experience jealousy, but the expression of jealousy is probably manifested differently in ASD versus typical controls. Eye gaze behaviors were found to be significantly impaired in ASD compared with typically developing children. Younger children with ASD revealed less gazing focused on the rival and more diffuse gazes at the interaction, whereas the older children with ASD gazed less at the interaction. These data suggest important methodological implications inasmuch as many studies on these children's responsiveness and emotional functioning focus on the coding of their gaze behaviors as a signifier of their responsiveness. In our studies (Bauminger, 2004; Bauminger et al., 2008), we were able to tap jealousy expression based on a multilevel coding scheme that included actions and verbalizations in addition to eye gazing. This enabled the detection of jealousy. In line with our results and the well-documented deficient eye gaze behavior in children with ASD (*DSM-IV-TR*; APA, 2000; see also extensive review in Nation & Penny, 2008), it may be necessary to expand the empirical coding scales to include other more complex behaviors as indices of emotional response when investigating ASD.

One other interesting result involves children's use of actions to draw the parents' attention. Compared with their typically developing peers, younger children with ASD demonstrated fewer such behaviors, whereas older children with ASD demonstrated more of these attention-seeking actions. This may hint at a developmental trend in the growth of children's "interpersonal self," suggesting the need to further investigate when these children begin to show outward attention-seeking actions, between the preschool and the preadolescent years. Older children's showing behaviors and their direct and indirect spontaneous attempts to share attention with the caregiver regarding a third object (e.g., the child's drawing) (Bauminger, 2004) call for further examination of the possibility of delayed development of secondary intersubjectivity (i.e., person–person–object awareness, Trevarthen, 1979; Trevarthen & Aitken, 2001) in these children (e.g., Nation & Penny, 2008; Mundy & Sigman, 2006). The lack of a spontaneous search for shared experiences is considered a cardinal symptom of ASD, but less is known about this behavior in older high-functioning children with ASD (Clifford & Dissanayake, 2008; Rogers & Bennetto, 2001).

In that regard, it is also worthy to note that expressing jealousy more explicitly through actions, as demonstrated by the preadolescents with ASD, is less developmentally appropriate and resembles jealousy-provoked behaviors reported as characterizing younger typically developing children (e.g., Bers & Rodin, 1984; Masciuch & Kienapple, 1993). In typical development, when children get older (in particular, preadolescents and adolescents), they are socialized to show their negative emotional states (i.e., anger, distress, fear, anxiety) indirectly through more subtle behaviors (e.g., eye gaze) rather than through direct actions. Thus, in typical development, explicit negative affect associated with jealousy diminishes with age, even in the face of higher capacities for social comparison (Bers & Rodin,

1984). The more explicit manifestation of jealousy demonstrated by the preadolescents with ASD compared with their typical age mates may result from a deficit
in the understanding of socially accepted rules for emotional display, which are
typically acquired through socialization (e.g., Barbaro & Dissanayake, 2007).
Support for a deficit in emotional understanding in children with ASD is provided
by the section to follow, describing findings about the ability for understanding
jealousy in these children.

Jealousy understanding

The jealousy study on older children with ASD (Bauminger, 2004) also examined
children's understanding of jealousy (see Table 12.1). Jealousy understanding
was measured through two tasks assessing children's ability to recognize jealousy
in a picture and to elicit examples of different situations that provoke jealousy.
The recognition task comprised a color illustration depicting a typical scenario in
which a mother is hugging her new baby while an older sibling is watching. The
majority of children with typical development ($n = 13$, 76.5%) accurately recognized jealousy in the picture, but only 4 children (25%) in the ASD group did so,
yielding statistically significant group differences. Indeed, it is important to note
that 7 of the children with ASD (43.8%), who could not recognize jealousy in the
picture, were able to identify basic and complex emotions with an accurate
hedonic tone (e.g., sad).

The task of asking children to elicit examples of different situations that
provoke jealousy also provided group differences of interest. Our coding divided
the jealousy examples provided by the children into two main categories: affective
jealousy and social cognitive jealousy. Affective jealousy was coded when participants' examples indicated that jealousy involved negative feelings associated with
a child's response to a social triangle in which the parents, another familiar adult
(e.g., teacher, grandfather), or a peer paid exclusive attention to another peer or a
sibling. This type of jealousy reflected situations threatening the child's exclusivity in a relationship. Social cognitive jealousy was coded when the participants'
example indicated that jealousy arose when one child enjoyed more success
or possessions compared with another child, thus challenging the first child's
superiority or equality.

Results revealed significant differences regarding the types of jealousy examples
provided by the children. Children with ASD provided fewer examples of affective
jealousy (31.2% ASD; 70.5% typical), but not of social cognitive jealousy (75%
ASD; 88.2% typical), compared with the typically developing children. These
outcomes on the understanding of jealousy indicated that children with ASD
presented a major deficiency in the reflection processes that are rooted in interpersonal relationships, whereas their social-comparison capabilities appeared
relatively intact. Reflection on interpersonal relationships seems to be a cardinal
difficulty, even for older children (preadolescents) with ASD who were cognitively

able (high-functioning). Thus, children with ASD exhibit a gap between their relatively intact experience of jealousy (a socially mediated emotion) and their relatively severe deficit in understanding jealousy, particularly jealousy of the affective type, which is highly rooted in interpersonal engagement.

These findings regarding the understanding of jealousy indeed present a pattern of specific impairment in the more affective aspects of jealousy among the ASD group. Yet, it is important to take into account that some difficulties of the children with ASD may arise from deficits in the specific abilities related to completing the task of going beneath the surface description of a picture and inferring about a picture's underlying emotions. In a like manner, even though we matched the group according to verbal IQ, it still may be that the impoverished jealousy examples in the ASD group resulted from pragmatic-semantic deficiencies in language. Another issue to consider is that examples of social cognitive jealousy could have merged with examples of envy ("I want for myself what the other child has"). Inasmuch as jealousy involves complex projections about the self vis-à-vis others whereas envy does not necessarily, the children with autism in the present study could more easily provide the less mature examples of jealousy (or envy). Their difficulties emerged in performing the more complex projections about the self required for the reflection of jealousy. They could more easily furnish examples stemming from their own self-needs or their own appraisal that led to dissatisfaction, rather than examples rooted in interpersonal relationships and dealing with the fear of losing these relationships. Thus, the study of understanding of jealousy in ASD can benefit from an expansion of the means for assessing jealousy, through verbal and nonverbal tasks. In order to tease apart some aspects of the emotional deficit in ASD and some of the complexities in the conceptualization of jealousy, I will now talk about affective and cognitive correlates of jealousy both in ASD and typical development.

Affective and Cognitive Correlates of Jealousy in ASD and Typical Development

If jealousy is indeed a complex social emotion, then the experience of jealousy is built upon certain affective and cognitive resources. Attachment was suggested by Hart et al. (Hart, Field, del Valle, & Letourneau, 1998; Hart, Field, Letourneau, & del Valle, 1998) as one possible affective correlate of jealousy. However, research on the link between attachment and jealousy in children with ASD has yet to be published. We are currently examining this link in my laboratory among pre-schoolers with ASD and with typical development, but this ongoing study is at too preliminary a stage to report any of its results. Meanwhile, I will touch upon other possible affective and cognitive correlates of jealousy in this section, namely, emotional responsiveness, social referencing, IQ, and mental age. Table 12.1 presents these findings for several correlates of jealousy.

Affective correlates

Emotional responsiveness

In the experience of jealousy, the child expresses an emotion with regard to an event that happened to the self (e.g., my mother prefers my friend/sibling over me). In "emotional responsiveness," the child must reflect on another person's mental state but with regard to an event that happened to that other person (e.g., my mother hurt her knee). For typically developing children, the ability to relate to another's emotional state is related to the ability to relate an emotional state to the self (Saarni, 1999). Thus, we may speculate a correlation between jealousy expression and emotional responsiveness—an affective correlate of jealousy— both in typical development and in ASD.

In Bauminger et al. (2008), we examined the child's reactions to an event where his or her main caregiver hurt his or her knee and its correlation with the child's jealousy expressions in the book-reading scenario (described above), among preschoolers with ASD and with typical development. Findings revealed a close link between emotional responsiveness and jealousy expression for both populations. For the ASD group, emotional responsiveness behaviors toward the distressed parents correlated with several of the jealousy measures, namely, with children's gazes and actions on the jealousy behavioral scale, and also tended to correlate with the explicitness of jealousy. Children who demonstrated emotional responsiveness behaviors, such as giving a toy to the distressed parent or comforting the parent by patting the hurt knee or hugging the parent, also tended to reveal more explicit indices of jealousy, gazed more, and demonstrated more actions in the jealousy situation.

In a like manner, though perhaps even more closely, jealousy and emotional responsiveness also correlated for the children with typical development. As for the ASD group, typically developing children who demonstrated emotional responsiveness behaviors tended to express more explicit indices of jealousy. Differently from the ASD group, typically developing children, who demonstrated more verbal expressions of jealousy, also verbalized, acted, and expressed a higher level of concern toward the injured caregiver. In addition, children with typical development who gazed more at the caregiver to express their jealousy also used more verbalizations to express their concern. Thus, in these two groups of typical and atypical preschoolers, jealousy and emotional responsiveness corresponded well: children who exhibited more emotional responsiveness behaviors also demonstrated clearer indices of jealousy. These data may identify a subgroup within the ASD sample that is characterized by coherency between their ability to express their own emotions and their ability to relate to the emotions of another person.

Sigman, Kasari, Kwon, and Yirmiya (1992) have also demonstrated individual differences in emotional responsiveness in children with ASD. Furthermore, children with ASD who were more attentive to negative emotions in others' affects at initial testing (Sigman et al., 1992) were still more attentive to negative emotions in others 5 years later (Dissanayake, Sigman, & Kasari, 1996). In terms of typical development, this supports the close link between self and other's emotional projection and also may hint that jealousy resembles the developmental complexity that is required for prosocial functioning. Prosocial functioning, which is the foundation for emotional expressiveness, develops gradually within the second year of life. It builds upon the capacity for secondary intersubjectivity, and it may be manifested through an empathic response (i.e., an emotional reaction to another's emotional state or condition that is consistent with the other's state or condition, such as feeling sad when viewing a sad person; Denham, 1998; Harris, 1989; Saarni, 1999); or through the more complex sympathetic response (i.e., feelings of concern or sorrow for another in reaction to the other's emotional state or condition, or deliberately performing comforting behaviors; Denham, 1998; Eisenberg, 1992).

Social referencing

Another potential affective correlate for jealousy that is built upon secondary intersubjectivity is social referencing, defined as infants' looking at their parents' emotional-expressive behavior in order to figure out the emotional meaning of an ambiguous situation (e.g., Feinman & Lewis, 1983). Bauminger and Orbach-Caspi (2005) examined the correlation between jealousy and social referencing in high-functioning preschoolers with ASD ($n = 17$; age range 23–60 months, $M = 40.24$, mean mental age $= 37.70$) and typically developing children ($n = 19$; age range 20–60 months, $M = 34.50$, mean mental age $= 37.70$). Jealousy was examined using the aforementioned story-reading scenario. Social referencing was examined by exposing the child to a loud recorded sound (thunder) in the room while he or she was playing with some games in the presence of the caregiver. Jealousy and social referencing correlated very well for children with ASD. That is, their jealousy verbalizations and actions correlated positively with their appropriate verbalizations in the social-referencing scenario (e.g., "Mom, what is it?"). Also, children with ASD who expressed jealousy more explicitly made appropriate efforts to approach the mother during the ambiguous social-referencing situation.

In typically developing children, only one correlation was statistically significant: Children who demonstrated more explicit jealousy also expressed higher levels of appropriate verbalization in the social-referencing scenario (Bauminger & Orbach-Caspi, 2005). Although only one correlation was found significant for the children in the typical group, the overall results between social referencing and jealousy did support the formerly discussed outcomes with regard to jealousy and emotional responsiveness.

Both affective abilities—social referencing and emotional responsiveness—share commonalities. In both, the child is aware of and acknowledges the emotional expression of another person; in one case for the child's own purposes (to figure out a situation—social referencing) and in the other case to be able to help or provide comfort to another person (in a distressing situation—emotional responsiveness). A prerequisite for both capacities is secondary intersubjectivity, or person–person–object awareness. Emotional responsiveness and social referencing are both seriously hampered in children with ASD (APA, 2000; Hobson, 2005). However, the close links between social referencing and jealousy and between emotional responsiveness and jealousy highlight individual differences in emotional functioning in children with ASD, suggesting that a subgroup may be identified that has more resourceful emotional capabilities.

What can be learned about the complexity of jealousy based on these associations? It should first be noted that correlations do not designate causality. It is impossible to determine the chronology of either the skills or their path, based on correlational data. But what we can say is that the three capacities (social referencing, emotional responsiveness, and jealousy) may possibly be closely linked in children with typical development. This may mean that the developmental sophistication needed for both social referencing and emotional responsiveness (i.e., secondary intersubjectivity) may perhaps be needed, too, for the expression of jealousy, lending some support for the perception of jealousy as a secondary rather than basic emotion. Nevertheless, this assumption should be further examined with larger numbers of participants to allow for the examination of causality and also due to the fact that jealousy's links with social referencing and with emotional expressiveness have only been tested separately thus far. Hence, the links between all three variables should be examined further to draw clear conclusions about the nature of these associations.

Cognitive correlates (IQ and mental age)

The logico-affective hypothesis (e.g., Hermelin & O'Connor, 1985) suggests that children with ASD learn strategies to help them recognize the emotions that "come naturally" to individuals with typical development. Thus, a link between jealousy and cognitive capabilities (e.g., IQ, mental age) is expected for this group of children. The correlation between IQ and jealousy expression was examined in Bauminger et al. (2008). Results provided support for the logico-affective hypothesis. IQ correlated positively with jealousy explicitness only for the ASD group, indicating more explicit expressions of jealousy in preschoolers with ASD who had higher IQs. It is important to note that an alternative interpretation is also possible: Children with ASD who have a higher IQ may be those with less severe ASD social symptomatology, thus resulting in more explicit jealousy. Possible implications for typical development are not clear, but these findings might suggest that jealousy may necessitate certain cognitive underpinnings, at least at the average or normative range, corresponding with the typical group's IQ level, thus providing some support for the perception of jealousy as a secondary rather than basic emotion (Salovey, 1991). However, the data thus far are inconclusive because the jealousy expressions did not require any cognitive efforts from the children in the typical group; thus, such expressions may merely be built upon simple cognitive processes such as those required for basic emotions.

Findings regarding the link between cognitive functioning (mental age) and jealousy understanding are even more informative in terms of the compensatory mechanism in ASD (Bauminger, 2004). Only for the group of preadolescents with ASD did mental age correlate with their ability to provide social-comparison examples of jealousy, but not with their ability to provide examples of social-relations jealousy. This implies a more profound deficit in these children's ability to generate examples of jealousy that are rooted in interpersonal relationships and engagement, shown in the small number of such examples provided by the children compared with the typical controls. On one hand, these findings offer support to the view of ASD as a disorder of "interpersonal engagement" (Hobson, 2005). On the other hand, the outcomes point to the boundaries of cognitive compensatory mechanisms, which are not helpful when reflection on one's interpersonal relationships is needed.

Taken altogether, the study of affective and cognitive correlates of jealousy may provide some insights into the emotional deficit of children with ASD and into the complexity of the conceptualization of jealousy. Indeed, causality cannot be inferred; however, jealousy's close links with emotional responsiveness and with social referencing call for further research on the complexity of jealousy expressions. The link with cognitive functioning was more informative regarding the emotional deficit in ASD, emphasizing a deficient capability for interpersonal reflection among these children.

Social versus Nonsocial Examination of Jealousy

Considering that a major component of the definition of jealousy is loss of exclusive attention (Tov-Ruach, 1980), a helpful procedure to elucidate the social nature of jealousy experience is the examination of children's different reactions when they lose exclusive attention in social versus nonsocial scenarios. In Hart and Carrington's study (2002), 6-month-olds exhibited greater negativity in an interaction episode where their mothers directed positive attention toward a lifelike baby doll versus a control condition in which the mothers focused positive attention toward a book. Our research outcomes with preschoolers (Bauminger et al., 2008) corroborate this finding. To control for the possibility that the child's attention toward the parent–rival dyad related to mere interest in the book and to examine the child's reaction to losing attention to a nonsocial stimulus, we implemented a nonsocial book-reading scenario in addition to the jealousy-evoking procedure. In the nonsocial book-reading scenario, the parent read the story aloud to her- or himself. During this scenario, only the parent and the child were present in the room; the child played with his or her toys; and the parent read aloud from a children's book that was used later in the jealousy-provoking scenario. We examined the correlation between the child's interest in the book and the explicitness of jealousy expressions. No significant correlation emerged for the ASD group, and a negative correlation emerged for the typical group, denoting that the jealousy experience in preschoolers with ASD was not related to their interest in the book, whereas preschoolers with typical development who revealed higher degrees of jealousy were less interested in the book.

We also further examined separate within-group correlations between the child's level of interest in the book and the child's level of jealousy explicitness. We transformed the original 7-point hierarchical jealousy explicitness scale to a 3-point scale, to create equivalence between the jealousy scale and the book interest scale. Originally, the scores were 1 = no interest at all in the scenario, 2 and 3 = different levels of gaze behaviors, 4 and 5 = direct and indirect actions and verbalizations to draw parents' attention, and 6 and 7 = direct verbal indication of comparison without negative affect (6) or with negative affect (7). On the 3-point scale, scores of 1–3 were converted to a score of 1, scores of 4–5 were converted to 2, and scores of 6–7 were converted to 3.

Results demonstrated significant within-group differences between the social and nonsocial scenarios. For both groups, the reactions to the social triangle jealousy-provoking scenario were much stronger than reactions to losing attention when the mother only read the story aloud to herself. (For the ASD group: $M = 1.97$; $SD = .78$ on the social-jealousy scenario and $M = .91$; $SD = .81$ for the nonsocial book-reading scenario, $t^{31} = 14.23$, $p < .001$; for the typical group: $M = 2.33$; $SD = .59$ on the social-jealousy scenario and $M = .1.22$; $SD = .65$ for the nonsocial book-reading scenario, $t^{17} = 16.63$, $p < .001$.) Thus, as for the infants in Hart's et al. (2004) study, the preschoolers in our study also revealed much more interest in the mother when she paid attention to a peer rival than to an object. These data provide support for the social nature of jealousy. Jealousy reactions do not simply occur in all cases of losing exclusive attention, but occur more when that attention is lost in a social-interpersonal context, when the attention is given to a peer rival who might put the parent–child relationship in jeopardy. In that vein, we are currently conducting an ongoing study at my laboratory that compares jealousy reactions in a triangle scenario involving a mother versus a stranger. At this time, I can only provide some clinical reflections based on very preliminary evaluations of the data, but it seems that the jealousy situation enacted with the mother elicits higher levels and more explicit indices of jealousy, compared with the situation enacted by the stranger. However, these early reflections need to be supported later when data collection is completed.

A more inclusive picture on the meaningfulness of jealousy to the understanding of the emotional deficit in ASD calls for the examination of jealousy in light of other secondary-social emotions. This will be described in the section to follow.

The Expression and Understanding of Social-Complex Emotions in ASD

Studies that have examined the expression and understanding of social-complex emotions such as pride, embarrassment, guilt, or loneliness are scarce. An exception to this is an extensive recent study by Hobson and his colleagues (Hobson et al., 2006), cited elsewhere in this book, which provided differential examination of a variety of social-complex emotions, such as jealousy, pride, guilt, embarrassment, concern, and pity in children with ASD, using multiple information resources (parents' and children's reports, identification of emotion through observation of scenarios enacted by professional actors, and procedures to evoke emotions in children). Jealousy was examined only in the parent reports. According to these reports, children with ASD were found to show a more intact profile of jealousy expression and a somewhat intact profile of pride (as a result of achievement) but showed very deficient profiles of pity, concern, and guilt (both in form and frequency of expression). Overall, in this extensive project, the data on functioning with regard to social emotions in ASD portrayed a complex picture. Children with ASD were not totally lacking in any of the emotions; in many cases, children's manifestations of emotions differed greatly from the typical profile (e.g., person-directed expressions, person–person gaze, and emotion interplay were missing); and their understanding of emotions often lacked social acknowledgment (e.g., for pride they mostly reacted to an achievement). Based on these data, Hobson implied that not all social emotions should be treated the same, suggesting that a separable typical developmental trajectory may characterize each different social emotion, and that each emotion may affect children with ASD differently.

Hobson viewed jealousy as more intact in ASD but also as a non-complex emotion. Jealousy, according to Hobson, resembles attachment, in which it reflects an intact ability to form relationships (that does not necessarily require complex self/other awareness), but this does not imply an ability to feel related to or intersubjectively engage with another person. Thus, Hobson suggested that jealousy does not necessarily need to involve (but may involve) complex reflections on the self and other, or identification, or affective capabilities (to feel related to someone; Hobson, this volume, Chapter 13). I will return to Hobson's arguments in a moment; however, first I would like to present some additional data on social emotions in ASD.

In another study, Kasari, Sigman, Baumgartner, and Stipek (1993) investigated pride in young children with low-functioning autism (mean mental age = 22.90 months, mean chronological age = 42.40 months) compared to children with mental retardation and to children with typical development. Corresponding with Hobson's results, Kasari et al.'s findings demonstrated that young children with autism expressed pleasure from their success (or mastery) in completing a puzzle as often as typically developing children, but they showed a different pattern of response when given praise by their mothers. These children with ASD failed to look for praise from their mothers, showed fewer attention-seeking behaviors, and even looked away (demonstrating avoidance) when they were given praise. Kasari et al. concluded that the lack of evidence for pride in the form of attention-seeking behaviors implies a deficiency in pride as a self-reflective emotion in these children.

Results regarding attention seeking in our study of jealousy in young pre-schoolers with ASD differed somewhat (Bauminger et al., 2008). Two-thirds of the ASD group demonstrated an explicit indication of jealousy, as demonstrated by at least one attention-seeking action, at different levels of directiveness. In addition, although the ASD group demonstrated less attention-seeking behavior in the form of actions generated by the jealousy-provoking scenario, such as moving closer to the parent, they did not score lower than their typical counter-parts on involvement actions, which in fact comprise more direct attention-seeking behaviors, like physically intervening in the parent–rival interaction, pushing the peer, or trying to climb onto the parent's lap. Moreover, although the ASD group was less focused in the target of their eye gaze (toward either the peer or the parent), they looked more at the mother–rival interaction than did the typical control group. These outcomes imply that the preschoolers with ASD in Bauminger et al. were not uninterested in the mother–rival interaction, and also, like the young infants in Hart et al.'s (2004) study, they used an approach response and not avoidance.

In comparing these two studies on jealousy and on pride in preschoolers with ASD, it is clear that children with ASD lacked what was suggested by Stipek, Recchia, and McClintic (1992) as evidence of self-reflective processes associated with pride, namely attention-seeking behaviors in the pride study. But it is less clear that such behaviors were missing from their expression of jealousy. To the contrary, some of the children's behaviors toward the mother during the jealousy situation, such as approaching and hugging her or caressing her hair, are difficult to interpret as lacking in interpersonal engagement. Also, selective attention given to a book by the mother did not evoke any such behavior in the children. Coming back to Hobson's suggestion, I do not mean to say, based on the jealousy data, that interpersonal engagement is intact in these children. I acknowledge that interpersonal engagement is deeply distorted in children with ASD; however, I am not certain that the lower defining boundary of the experience of jealousy should take no notice at all of connectedness.

The data on the understanding of social emotions provide more clear support for the origin of the affective deficit as a disorder of intersubjective engagement. Accumulative data support that children with ASD have an inherent difficulty in reflecting on emotions that are rooted in interpersonal functioning. For example, when describing their experience of loneliness, high-functioning preadolescents and adolescents with ASD could produce examples of social cognitive loneliness (e.g., "I feel lonely when I have no one to play with") as well as typical controls, but could not do so for examples of social-relations loneliness (e.g., "I feel lonely when I do not have a close friend") (Bauminger & Kasari, 2000). As reported above, preadolescents with high-functioning ASD produced more examples of social-comparison jealousy (e.g., "When kids in school can buy whatever they want whenever they want") versus social-relations jealousy (e.g., "When someone walks with his girlfriend, his other friends feel jealous. They also want to be friends with that kid, who is my friend"). It is important to note that regarding the social-comparison examples, it was hard to differentiate between examples of jealousy and envy. However, only one-third of the children with ASD, versus more than two-thirds of the typical controls, could provide examples of social-relations jealousy (Bauminger, 2004). In the same study, children with ASD had difficulties identifying social-relations jealousy in a picture of a mother hugging her new baby while an older sibling looks on. It seems clearer that children with ASD have a profound deficit in the ability for reflection about interpersonal engagement, but it is less clear whether they have that same profound deficit in the actual experience of such a relationship.

Such an explanation contradicts affective theory (Hobson, 2002, 2005), which asserts that something is profoundly lacking in the orientation toward people among children with autism, mainly in their experience of another person as a person and, perhaps most strikingly, in their emotional engagement. Hobson (2005) suggested an alternative, biological explanation for the experience of jealousy in autism:

> Just in the case of jealousy, there may turn out to be biologically based determinants of interpersonal relationships that are dissociable from aspects of interpersonal relatedness; and we may yet have to revise some of our conventional ideas about which aspects of emotional relatedness do or do not require sophisticated cognitive underpinning. (p. 416)

It may indeed be true that a differentiation exists between biological bases underlying aspects of relationships, which may differ from the bases underlying affective relatedness. For example, most individuals with ASD will differentiate between a stranger and a significant other in a strange situation (e.g., Buitelaar, 1995; Dissanayake & Crossley, 1996; Sigman & Mundy, 1989; Sigman & Ungerer, 1984), but only half of them, presumably those with the higher IQs, will form a secure attachment (Capps, Sigman, & Mundy, 1994; Rogers, Ozonoff, & Masline-Cole, 1991, 1993; Rutgers, Bakermans-Kranenburg, van IJzendoorn, & van Berckelaer-Onnes, 2004; Shapiro, Sherman, Calamari, & Koch, 1987; Willemsen-Swinkels, Bakermans-Kranenburg, Buitelaar, van IJzendoorn, & van Engeland, 2000). However, if jealousy is merely a basic biologically based emotion, then it would be difficult to explain why only two-thirds of the children with ASD expressed it explicitly (in Bauminger et al., 2008) and even harder to explain why those preschoolers within the ASD group who expressed jealousy were those with a higher IQ. The findings that jealousy correlated with cognitive capabilities for the autism sample may possibly hint that there is more to jealousy and the emotional deficit in autism than assumed under the biological-evolutionary explanation.

An alternative theoretical explanation may be that the development of relationships and of relatedness lies on a continuum of gradually developing affective and cognitive resources. This would enable some children with autism to develop internal working models of secure attachment while others remain at the stage of differentiating a significant other from a caregiver (Rutgers et al., 2004). Yet, both situations (attachment and jealousy) raise the possibility that children with ASD may possess some level of interpersonal awareness, at least primary (person–person) intersubjectivity and possibly secondary (person–person–environment) intersubjectivity (Trevarthen & Aitken, 2001), as may be implied based on their attention-seeking behaviors within the interpersonal context. Along such a continuum, perhaps it is possible that jealousy could constitute a signifier for those children with autism who possess higher interpersonal resources.

Summary and Conclusions: The Theoretical Implications of the Understanding of Jealousy as a Secondary or Basic Emotion in Typical Development and in ASD

Is jealousy a complex or a basic emotion? We are still at a premature empirical stage to solve the theoretical puzzle concerning the prerequisites of jealousy. However, several conclusions can be drawn based on the information currently presented. The close links of jealousy with emotional responsiveness and with social referencing support a close link in typical development between emotional understanding in the self and others. It may also offer implications about the complexity of jealousy. Emotional responsiveness and social referencing are both based upon secondary intersubjectivity (person–person–object awareness). Thus, it may be that, similarly to emotional responsiveness and social referencing, jealousy also requires some capacity for self/other awareness, at least at the level of secondary intersubjectivity. This would provide some support for the perception of jealousy as a secondary rather than basic emotion. However, this conclusion should be further examined due to the fact that correlational data (as presented in the current chapter) cannot assume causality. Longitudinal studies with larger numbers of participants should be performed to enable the examination of the chronology of jealousy with regard to representational skills, such as emotional responsiveness, social referencing, and theory of mind. Further collaboration for the social nature of jealousy may be implied by the comparison between the loss of selective attention in the nonsocial (book) scenario and the loss of attention in the social (mother–rival) scenario. Children with typical development demonstrated a more intense emotional response when the mother read the story to a peer compared with reading the story to herself. It was the interaction between the mother and the rival that evoked jealousy in the children, not merely the loss of exclusive attention, attesting to the affective-interpersonal nature of jealousy.

The finding regarding the correlation between jealousy and IQ was not so helpful in determining if jealousy should be perceived as a simple or a complex emotion. Children with typical development who have at least an average IQ level do not need to invest any special cognitive effort in order to experience jealousy. The experience of jealousy may require at least a normative IQ level, or else it may not require any cognitive energy, supporting the perception of the emotion as simple. Nonetheless, this conclusion is very speculative and needs further research.

Altogether, it seems that the perception of the experience of jealousy as merely a basic emotion might fail to take into account its full affective and cognitive complexities. If this is correct, what are the implications of the understanding of jealousy for children with ASD? Is it plausible to assume that the majority of children with ASD possess the complex interpersonal as well as representational capabilities possibly underlying jealousy?

Both the affective and cognitive theories concerning the emotional deficit in autism would suggest it is implausible. The affective view highlights children's disturbance in intersubjective personal engagement with others, which causes a serious disruption in children's ability to experience interpersonal relationships as such (e.g., Hobson, 2002, 2005; Rogers & Pennington, 1991). The cognitive view underscores children's deficits in taking another person's view into account, which leads to difficulties in attributing mental states to others and to oneself with regard to others (e.g., Tager-Flusberg, 2001). So how can we resolve this conflict? On the one hand, intersubjective engagement and representational capabilities are indeed very deficient in children with ASD, and on the other hand the majority of the children in the spectrum do manifest clear emotional responses in an interpersonal situation and react more intensely in the interpersonal situation than in the non-interpersonal situation. It is also important to note that the complete understanding of jealousy in ASD must take into account these children's deep deficit in understanding or in reflecting about affective jealousy, but not in their experience of the emotion.

One way to solve the conceptual dilemma is to say that jealousy is indeed a simple emotion that does not require a high level of representational skill (identification, for example) or the ability to develop relatedness but merely a relationship with others, and this is within the capacity of most of the children in the spectrum (Hobson, this volume). Owing to the fact that the nature of jealousy in typical development is not yet completely understood and we still lack empirical support for the perception of jealousy as either a secondary or a basic emotion, this explanation cannot be declined at present. However, based on the emotionally intense reactions that I have witnessed among at least some of the children with ASD (possibly those with higher IQs) toward their mothers in the interpersonal situation, my sense is that jealousy has the potential to tell us more about these children's interpersonal capacities. Further research on jealousy may pinpoint a subgroup of children who can do more than merely establish a relationship; they may possibly be able to develop relatedness with their significant other, even if in a very distorted way (because the manifestations of jealousy differed for ASD across studies). The differentiation in social functioning between children with Asperger syndrome and children with high-functioning autism is much debated (e.g., Macintosh & Dissanayake, 2004); yet, future studies may also benefit from subgrouping children according to diagnosis within ASD in trying to denote individual differences in jealousy. The expression of jealousy as well as its understanding and reflection are surely distorted, but not necessarily its experience. It is clear that future study is needed to clarify this conceptual dilemma and its obvious implications for the emotional deficit in children with ASD. However, I would like to suggest the possibility of looking at jealousy as a potential very early signifier to identify those children with autism who possess the capacity to establish more complex forms of social relatedness such as secure attachment or friendship with peers.

References

American Psychiatric Association (APA). (2000). *Diagnostic and statistical manual of mental disorders: Text revision* (4th ed., rev.). Washington, DC: Author.

Barbaro, J., & Dissanayake, C. (2007). A comparative study of the use and understanding of self-presentational display rules in children with high functioning autism and Asperger's disorder. *Journal of Autism and Developmental Disorders, 37,* 1235–1246.

Barrett, K. C. (1995). A functionalist approach to shame and guilt. In J. P. Tangney & K. W. Fischer (Eds.), *Self-conscious emotions: The psychology of shame, guilt, embarrassment, and pride* (pp. 25–63). New York: Guilford Press.

Bauminger, N. (2004). The expression and understanding of jealousy in children with autism. *Development and Psychopathology, 16,* 157–177.

Bauminger, N., Chomsky-Smolkin, L., Orbach-Caspi, E., Zachor, D., & Levy-Shiff, R. (2008). Jealousy and emotional responsiveness in young children with ASD. *Cognition and Emotion, 22,* 595–619.

Bauminger, N., & Kasari, C. (2000). Loneliness and friendship in high-functioning children with autism. *Child Development, 71,* 447–456.

Bauminger, N., & Orbach-Caspi, E. (2005). *Jealousy and social referencing in high-functioning children with ASD.* Unpublished master's thesis, Bar-Ilan University.

Bers, S. A., & Rodin, J. (1984). Social comparison jealousy: A developmental and motivational study. *Journal of Personality and Social Psychology, 47,* 766–779.

Buitelaar, J. K. (1995). Attachment and social withdrawal in autism: Hypotheses and findings. *Behavior, 132,* 319–350.

Capps, L., Sigman, M., & Mundy, P. (1994). Attachment security in children with autism. *Developmental Psychopathology, 6,* 249–261.

Clifford, S., & Dissanayake, C. (2008). The early development of joint attention in infants with autistic disorder using home video observations and parental interview. *Journal of Autism and Developmental Disorders, 79,* 791–805.

Denham, S. A. (1998). *Emotional development in young children.* The Guilford Series on Social and Emotional Development. New York: Guilford Press.

Dissanayake, C., & Crossley, S. A. (1996). Proximity and sociable behaviors in autism: Evidence for attachment. *Journal of Child Psychology and Psychiatry, 37,* 149–156.

Dissanayake, C., & Sigman, M. (2001). Attachment and ER in children with autism. *International Review of Research in Mental Retardation, 23,* 239–266.

Dissanayake, C., Sigman, M., & Kasari, C. (1996). Long term stability of individual differences in the emotional responsiveness of children with autism. *Journal of Child Psychology and Psychiatry, 37,* 461–467.

Draghi-Lorenz, R., Reddy, V., & Costall, A. (2001). Rethinking the development of "nonbasic" emotions: A critical review of existing theories. *Developmental Review, 21,* 263–304.

Eisenberg, N. (1992). *The caring child.* The Developing Child Series. Cambridge, MA: Harvard University Press.

Feinman, S., & Lewis, M. (1983). Social referencing at ten months: A second-order effect on infants' responses to strangers. *Child Development, 54,* 878–887.

Hansen, G. L. (1991). Jealousy: Its conceptualization, measurement, and integration with family stress theory. In P. Salovey (Ed.), *The psychology of jealousy and envy* (pp. 211–230). New York: Guilford Press.

Harris, P. L. (1989). *Children and emotion: The development of psychological understanding.* Oxford: Basil Blackwell.

Hart, S., & Carrington, H. (2002). Jealousy in 6-month-old infants. *Infancy, 3,* 395–402.

Hart, S., Carrington, H., Tronick, E. Z., & Carroll, S. R. (2004). When infants lose exclusive maternal attention: Is it jealousy? *Infancy, 6,* 57–78.

Hart, S., Field, T., del Valle, C., & Letourneau, M. (1998). Infants protest their mother's attending to an infant-size doll. *Social Development, 7,* 54–56.

Hart, S., Field, T., Letourneau, M., & del Valle, C. (1998). Jealousy protests in infants of depressed mothers. *Infant Behavior and Development, 21,* 137–148.

Hart, S., Jones, A. N., & Field, T. (2003). Atypical expressions of jealousy in infants of intrusive- and withdrawn-depressed mothers. *Child Psychiatry and Human Development, 33,* 193–207.

Hermelin, B., & O'Connor, N. (1985). The logico-affective disorder in autism. In E. Schopler & G. B. Mesibov (Eds.), *Communication problems in autism* (pp. 283–310). New York: Plenum Press.

Hobson, R. P. (2002). *The cradle of thought: Exploring the origin of thinking.* London: Pan Macmillan Press.

Hobson, R. P. (2005). Autism and emotion. In F. R. Volkmar, R. Paul, A. Klin., & D. Cohen (Eds.), *Handbook of autism and pervasive developmental disorders* (pp. 406–422). Hoboken, NJ: Wiley.

Hobson, R. P. (this volume). Is jealousy a complex emotion? In S. L. Hart & M. Legerstee (Eds.), *Handbook of jealousy: Theory, research, and multidisciplinary approaches*. Malden, MA: Wiley-Blackwell.

Hobson, R. P., Chidambi, G., Lee, A., & Meyer, J. (2006). Foundations of self-awareness: An exploration through autism. *Monographs of the Society for Research in Child Development, 71*(1, Serial No. 284).

Izard, C. E. (1991). *The psychology of emotions*. New York: Plenum Press.

Izard, C. E., & Harris, P. (1995). Emotional development and developmental psychopathology. In D. Cicchetti & D. J. Cohen (Eds.), *Developmental psychopathology: Vol. I. Theories and methods*. New York: Wiley.

Kanner, L. (1943). Autistic disturbance of affective contact. *Nervous Child, 2*, 217–250.

Kasari, C., Sigman, M., Baumgartner, P., & Stipek, D. (1993). Pride and mastery in children with autism. *Journal of Child Psychology and Psychiatry, 34*, 353–362.

Kasari, C., Sigman, M., Yirmiya, N. & Mundy, P. (1993). Affective development and communication in children with autism. In A. Kaiser & D. Gray (Eds.), *Enhancing children's communication: Research foundations for intervention* (pp. 201–222). New York: Brooks.

Lewis, M. (2000a). The emergence of human emotions. In M. Lewis & J. M. Haviland (Eds.), *Handbook of emotions* (pp. 223–235). New York: Guilford Press.

Lewis, M. (2000b). Self-conscious emotions: Embarrassment, pride, shame, and guilt. In M. Lewis, & J. M. Haviland (Eds.), *Handbook of emotions*. New York: Guilford Press.

Macintosh, K. E., & Dissanayake, C. (2004). Annotation: The similarities and differences between autistic disorder and Asperger's disorder: A review of empirical evidence. *Journal of Child Psychology and Psychiatry, 45*, 421–434.

Masciuch, S., & Kienapple, K. (1993). The emergence of jealousy in children 4 months to 7 years of age. *Journal of Social and Personal Relationships, 10*, 421–435.

Miller, A. L., Volling, B. L., & McElwain, N. L. (2000). Sibling jealousy in a triadic context with mothers and fathers. *Social Development, 9*, 433–457.

Mundy, P., & Sigman, M. (2006). Joint attention, social competence and developmental psychopathology. In D. Cicchetti & D. Cohen (Eds.), *Developmental psychopathology: Vol. 1. Theory and methods* (2nd ed.). Hoboken, NJ: Wiley.

Nation, K., & Penny, S. (2008). Sensitivity to eye gaze in autism: Is it normal? Is it automatic? Is it social? *Development and Psychopathology, 20*, 79–97.

Parrott, W. G. (1991). The emotional experience of envy and jealousy. In P. Salovey (Ed.), *The psychology of jealousy and envy* (pp. 3–31). New York: Guilford Press.

Parrott, W. G., & Smith, R. H. (1993). Distinguishing the experiences of envy and jealousy. *Journal of Personality and Social Psychology, 64*, 906–920.

Rogers, S. R., & Bennetto, L. (2001). Intersubjectivity in autism: The role of imitation and executive function. In A. M. Wetherby & B. M. Prizant (Eds.), *Autism spectrum disorders: A transactional developmental perspective* (Vol. 9, pp. 79–107). Baltimore: Paul H. Brooks.

Rogers, S. R, Ozonoff, S., & Masline-Cole, C. (1991). A comparative study of attachment behavior in children with autism and children with other disorders of behavior and development. *Journal of American Academy of Child and Adolescent Psychiatry, 30*, 433–438.

Rogers, S. R., Ozonoff, S., & Masline-Cole, C. (1993). Developmental aspects of attachment behavior in young children with pervasive developmental disorder. *Journal of American Academy of Child and Adolescent Psychiatry, 32*, 1274–1282.

Rogers, S. R., & Pennington, B. F. (1991). A theoretical approach to the deficits in infantile autism. *Development and Psychopathology, 3*, 137–162.

Rutgers, A. H., Bakermans-Kranenburg, M. J., van IJzendoorn, M. H., & van Berckelaer-Onnes, I. A. (2004). Autism and attachment: A meta-analytic review. *Journal of Child Psychology and Psychiatry, 45*, 1123–1134.

Saarni, C. (1999). *The development of emotional competence.* New York: Guilford Press.

Salovey, P. (1991). *The psychology of jealousy and envy.* New York: Guilford Press.

Salovey, P., & Rodin, J. (1984). Some antecedents and consequences of social-comparison jealousy. *Journal of Personality and Social Psychology, 4*, 780–792.

Seidner, L. B., Stipek, D. J., & Fesbach, N. D. (1988). A developmental analysis of elementary school-aged children's concept of pride and embarrassment. *Child Development, 59*, 367–377.

Shapiro, T., Sherman, M., Calamari, G., & Koch, D. (1987). Attachment in autism and other developmental disorders. *Journal of American Academy of Child and Adolescent Psychiatry, 26*, 480–484.

Sigman, M., Kasari, C., Kwon, J., & Yirmiya, N. (1992). Responses to negative emotion of others by autistic, mentally retarded, and normal children. *Child Development, 63*, 796–807.

Sigman, M., & Mundy, P. (1989). Social attachment in autistic children. *Journal of American Academy of Child and Adolescent Psychiatry, 28*, 74–81.

Sigman, M., & Ungerer, J. (1984). Attachment behaviors in autistic children. *Journal of Autism and Developmental Disorders, 14*, 231–243.

Silver, M., & Sabini, J. (1978). The perception of envy. *Social Psychology, 41*, 105–117.

Stipek, D. J., Recchia, S., & McClintic, S. (1992). Self-evaluation in young children. *SRCD Monograph, 57*.

Tager-Flusberg, H. (2001). A reexamination of the theory of mind hypothesis of autism. In J. Burack, T. Charman, N. Yirmiya, & P. Zelazo (Eds.), *Development and autism: Perspectives from theory and research* (pp. 173–193). Hillsdale, NJ: Erlbaum.

Tov-Ruach, L. (1980). Jealousy, attention, and loss. In A. O. Rorty (Ed.), *Explaining emotions* (pp. 465–488). Berkeley, CA: University of California Press.

Trevarthen, C. (1979). Communication and cooperation in early infancy: A description of primary intersubjectivity. In M. Bullowa (Ed.), *Before speech: The beginning of interpersonal communication.* Cambridge: Cambridge University Press.

Trevarthen, C., & Aitken, K. J. (2001). Infant intersubjectivity: Research, theory, and clinical implications. *Journal of Child Psychology and Psychiatry, 42*, 3–48.

Volling, B. L., McElwain, N. L., & Miller, A. (2002). Emotion regulation in context: The jealousy complex between young siblings and its relations with child and family characteristics. *Child Development, 73*, 581–600.

White, G. L., & Mullen, P. E. (1989). *Jealousy: Theory, research, and clinical strategies.* New York: Guilford Press.

Willemsen-Swinkels, S. H. N., Bakermans-Kranenburg, M. J., Buitelaar, J. K, van IJzendoorn, M. H., & van Engeland, H. (2000). Insecure and disorganized attachment in children with pervasive developmental disorder: Relationship with social interaction and heart rate. *Journal of Child Psychology and Psychiatry, 41*, 759–767.

13

Is Jealousy a Complex Emotion?

R. Peter Hobson

Introduction

I doubt whether I shall be the only contributor to this volume to begin with quotations from Act III of Shakespeare's *Othello*. The following comes from Scene IV:

> EMILIA: But jealous souls will not be answer'd so;
> They are not ever jealous for the cause,
> But jealous for they are jealous. 'Tis a monster
> Begot upon it self, born on it self.

Emilia insists that there is something about jealousy that comes from within. For some people, it is a monster that cannot be tamed by logic or reason. As the play conveys all too forcefully, jealousy may be inflamed to the point of madness even when the grounds for discerning a cause for jealousy are highly questionable.

Somewhat earlier in the same Act, in Scene III, we have this from the villain of the piece:

> IAGO: O, beware, my lord, of jealousy;
> It is the green-ey'd monster which doth mock
> The meat it feeds on.

Here it might seem curious that Iago's description seems more applicable to the emotion of envy than jealousy. It is true that jealousy led Othello to despoil the character of Desdemona in acts of denunciation that seem more malign even than her murder. Perhaps it was anticipating such hostile and denigratory attacks that Iago uttered these words of premonition. Yet we might also surmise that Iago's own, monstrous envy colored his experience of jealousy, and his

Handbook of Jealousy: Theory, Research and Multidisciplinary Approaches, First Edition.
Edited by Sybil L. Hart and Maria Legerstee.
© 2013 Blackwell Publishing Ltd. Published 2013 by Blackwell Publishing Ltd.

understanding of what jealousy entails. Whereas envy is mixed up with the wish to spoil, jealousy is roused precisely because of the value attached to a person's attentiveness and love for oneself, and the pain of witnessing or imagining that attentiveness and love being directed to someone else. Embodied in people who are neither as suspicious nor near-delusional as Othello, jealousy can move to desperation and even murder, but this is less because it mocks than that it is all-consuming. Moreover, jealousy admits the existence of a third party, whereas for envy, as Iago bears witness, there need be just one possessor (in this case, Othello) whose attributes or status or power or possessions are both desired and despised, and whose dispossession is longed for or even, as in this tragedy, accomplished.

If jealousy involves a three-person relationship, and envy a two-person relationship—and if the two emotions can become fused in an especially destructive mix—then what is the phylogenetic and ontogenetic relation between the two? Are they equally complex in their psychological structure? For example, does jealousy entail that an individual understands what it means for two people to engage intimately with each other to that individual's exclusion, and does envy require a certain sophistication in an individual's understanding of him- or herself and someone else? Do such considerations determine when and how, in childhood, jealousy and envy come to cast their shadows on a young person's emotional landscape?

In this contribution, I shall be questioning whether jealousy is as complex an emotion as some would believe. True, we need to provide a complex description of the settings within which jealousy is expressed and experienced. As we have seen, jealousy entails that one person has an emotional response to the relation between two other people. Surely, one might think, a child has to have a pretty complex set of cognitions to feel jealous. But if I recall correctly (and it may have been in relation to a different song), the Beatles scorned the pomposity of the complex musicological characterization that was offered for the opening bars of "Ob-la-di, Ob-la-da." The writing and performing of the song did not need such fancy ideas, it was just a song. So, too, jealousy may not need such fancy cognitions, if it is begot upon itself. Or again, if jealous souls are simply jealous for they are jealous, then jealousy should be seen not as the unwelcome side-effect of social cognitive sophistication, but rather as its harbinger. Jealousy may contribute to young children's social cognition, and more specifically to children's attitudes to people, but not depend upon concepts of self and other. This could be the case even if, subsequently, conceptual thought plays an important role in shaping one's experience of jealousy.

I shall develop this argument in three ways. Firstly, I shall try to create a level playing field for combat between two opposing views on the development of jealousy and other supposedly complex emotions. I shall make a specific theoretical proposal to this end, and suggest that we need to distinguish between *aspects* of any psychological function and its putative *components*. Secondly,

I consider how this approach may alter our thinking about the typical early development of social emotions. Here I shall return to the contrasts between jealousy and envy, and to the different contribution that intersubjective engagement—and more specifically, identification—makes in each case. Thirdly, I shall adopt the perspective of developmental psychopathology and consider what children with autism might reveal to us about the development of jealousy and other supposedly complex emotions.

The Development of Social Emotions

A worthwhile preliminary step for any investigation is to identify ideas that may turn out to be assumptions, or supposed "facts" that may turn out to be falsehoods, so that one is partly freed from the restrictions and distortions of prejudice. In these respects, Draghi-Lorenz, Reddy, and Costall (2001) do a fine job in reviewing recent thinking about the nature and ontogeny of complex emotions. One of the important conclusions to be drawn from their survey is that empirical evidence is inconclusive over some commonly held views about the relatively late time in childhood when emotions such as pride, guilt, and jealousy become evident in young children's behavior. For example, there is observational data that emotions such as shyness and coyness may be observed in the first year of an infant's life (Reddy, 2000), and contributors to this volume provide vivid illustration that this is also the case with jealousy (e.g., Hart & Carrington, 2002; Hart, Carrington, Tronick, & Carroll, 2004; Legerstee, Ellenbogen, Nienhuis, & Marsh, this volume, Chapter 9).

Such empirical considerations challenge some very influential theoretical positions about the precedence and role of cognition in social-emotional development. For example, Lewis (2003, p. 286) states: "In the case of jealousy, envy, empathy, embarrassment, shame, pride, and guilt . . . the elicitation of this class of emotions involves elaborate cognitive processes, and these elaborate cognitive processes have, at their heart, the notion of self, agency, and conscious intentions." It is understandable that Lewis arrives at these conclusions, given his view that such emotions do not appear in the developmental timetable of early childhood until after the middle of the second year of life. Yet if the timetable is in error, then we may need to rethink how we explain its construction, and in particular, reconceptualize the place of the "notion" of self in the developmental story.

There is another source of disquiet for contemporary social cognitive views of emotional development. This is evidence that species other than *Homo sapiens* may have feelings such as jealousy. As an internet page of physorg.com declared in August, 2006: "Jilted dogs feel intense jealousy, new study." This was a trailer for the research of Morris, Doe, and Godsell (2008), who report that adults who knew their animals well described jealousy in 81% of dogs and 79% of horses. Moreover, interviews with dog-owners revealed that most instances of jealousy occurred when the carer gave attention to a person or another dog, and often they involved the dog pushing between the carer and the third party. At other times, dogs' attention-seeking behavior might involve barking, growling, or whining, and also aggressiveness toward the rival.

There is an obvious riposte that may be made here: What dogs or human infants feel is not *real* jealousy, but something else. The something else might even have some phylogenetic or ontogenetic link with jealousy proper, and in the case of human infants, it might even be some precursor form of jealousy, but that does not mean that our prototypically human form of jealousy is present either in nonhuman species or in human babies.

This is an argument that has some force. There is every reason to suppose that with progress in conceptual development, including the development of concepts of oneself in relation to other selves in the middle of the second year of life, as well as concepts about relations that can exist among individual people and (in the case of jealousy) more than two people, there are changes in children's experience and expression of emotions (see, for example, Lewis, 2003; Lewis, Sullivan, Stanger, & Weiss, 1989; Hobson, 2007a). Of course it is true that in order to experience and express the full gamut of phenomenological features of human jealousy, such as a sense of betrayal and an insatiable drive to unearth the truth of what is going on (Mullen, 1990), one does need a sophisticated repertoire of cognitive abilities. The question is: How far do such qualities of experience and behavior represent essential ingredients of jealousy, or rather, elaborations of simpler core characteristics of this relational state? If we debar nonhuman species and human infants from having jealousy on the grounds that they do not have the kind of jealousy we see in humans who have reached middle childhood or adulthood, then immediately we face the threat of circularity in argument. If one defines what will count as jealousy in accord with the conditions that are supposed to explain jealousy, then that is the end of that. The position is unassailable, and therefore deeply vulnerable.

Fortunately, there is an alternative position available, even if it is one that has been subject to attack and even derision (especially in its psychoanalytic versions). According to this position, one maintains an open mind about the following: (a) how emotions are structured, (b) whether or not seemingly complex emotions appear early in development, perhaps before much cognitive development has occurred, (c) whether it is appropriate and justified to apply terms that we use for the emotions of grown-ups to infant-level emotions, and if so, with what caveats, and (d) how we should characterize as well as explain the changes that occur with development, including those that depend on social cognitive advances.

The challenges of holding such a position are several, beyond the need to withstand the more-than-usually harsh skepticism of fellow scientists. Among the most important of these are to articulate a theoretical argument that gives plausibility to the position, and then encompasses sufficient evidence to challenge alternative explanations. In framing the argument, one may need to enter philosophical territory in order to examine the concepts we employ to think about and explain emotional development, as well as to ensure that phenomeno-logical considerations are not sidelined. In my own experience, this part of the enterprise is less than welcome to hard-nosed scientists who are unaware of their own philosophical assumptions (a point that Waddington, 1977, crystallized in his critique of the Conventional Wisdom of the Dominant Group, or COWDUNG for short). In mounting an empirical case for the position, moreover, one faces potentially heated disputes over what is to count as evidence, as well as what range of psychological phenomena are to be explained. These issues are especially difficult insofar as the behavioral expressions of emotions alter dramatically over the course of early development, and when it is difficult to be other than speculative over potential continuities in phenomenal experience from infancy to later periods of life.

What is "Complex" about Complex Emotions?

Notwithstanding the challenges I have outlined, writers such as Frijda (1993), Barrett (1995), Draghi-Lorenz et al. (2001), and Hobson, Chidambi, Lee, and Meyer (2006) have articulated reasons why we should not presume whether the structure of "complex" social emotions is derived from the coordination of newfound cognitive capacities with simpler forms of emotion. As Frijda (1993) expresses the view, "even emotions like anger, guilt, and shame, that have cognitively complex definitions, can result from rather elementary stimulus constellations, and through rather elementary appraisal processes" (p. 374). Although we may need a complex *description* of what is involved in emotions like guilt or jealousy, this does not mean that what we describe is constructed from building blocks that correspond with the elements in that description. For example, just because jealousy involves feelings toward the attentions that another person is giving a third party, it does not follow that in order to feel jealousy, one needs to conceptualize what it means to be a self in relation to another self, never mind two selves relating to one another.

Why does it not follow? Here I want to highlight the distinction between *aspects* and *components* of psychological states. I have introduced this distinction in other writings (Hobson, 2008) in order to press the argument that developmental psychologists should beware of making what seems to be a common assumption. The assumption is to suppose that if we think of processes such as those involved in social relations as having cognitive, conative, and affective aspects—we can have thoughts about people, we can be motivated to seek and do things in relation to people, and we can have feelings about people—then it follows that we need to trace where the components of such relations come from, and how they are assembled into the final product. Or if we are trying to understand atypical behavior, the assumption is that it always makes sense to analyze whether the sources of such behavior are cognitive, motivational, *or* affective in nature.

Perhaps it is easiest to see the dangers of making such assumptions by considering the interpersonal relations of infants of, say, 3 months old. Babies of this age can distinguish between people and things (what one might consider a cognitive accomplishment), they are motivated to orient toward others, and they engage in affectively charged interpersonal exchanges. Here it is obvious that we are not making claims about the operation of three distinct components to infants' behavior and experience. Social engagement does not arise from, nor express, a combination of cognitive ability, a motivational urge, and an affective coloring, even if there are certain circumstances in which it makes sense to say that limitations in thinking, or a lack of motivation, or disturbances of feeling, may be responsible for individual differences in such relations. For a 3-month-old infant to make the distinction between persons and things *is* to orient to, and become affectively engaged with, persons in ways that differ from his or her relations toward things; for the infant to be motivated to engage affectively with persons is to make not just any distinction between persons and things, for example by picking up the distinguishing feature of self-propelled movement, but instead to make the very distinction that is needed if the infant is to experience other persons *as* persons.

Just as one can describe the color, temperature, and mass of an object, therefore, so one can highlight cognitive, conative, and affective aspects of social relations. Aspects are not components. Yet there are two important complications to this picture. Firstly, in the course of human development it becomes increasingly possible, and sometimes appropriate, to distinguish among thoughts, motivations, and feelings. Indeed it is a hallmark of human symbolic thinking that one can entertain thoughts that are (relatively) emancipated from action and feeling, as well as applying thoughts generatively and reflexively. So it is that developmental theorists such as Piaget (Piaget & Inhelder, 1969), Werner and Kaplan (1963/1984), and Vygotsky (1962) have dwelt upon the developmental transition *from* modes of engagement with the world *to* modes of thinking about that world. One way of capturing this development would be to say that what had been aspects of relations with the world become partly but never wholly separable from those relations, and to this extent also acquire the potential to become components of mental processes to which they contribute.

Secondly, and connected with this, it is not merely that we should beware of trying to explain early social relations in terms of cognitive, conative, and affective components of mental life. More radically, we need to recognize how qualities of interpersonal relations may *determine* what becomes thinkable, willable, and felt. Specifically human forms of person-with-person relatedness may configure early development in such a way as to forge both the symbolic means to, and the conceptual content of, thinking about human beings (Hobson, 1990, 2002/2004).

The Case of Jealousy

So what has all this to do with jealousy? Perhaps we should consider whether we are assuming that jealousy *has* to be complex because of its sophisticated cognitive components. Yet what makes us think infants would need cognitive, affective, and conative "components" to feel jealousy? At root, jealousy may not require the ability to have particular kinds of thought interacting with particular kinds of affect and particular kinds of desire. Alternatively, we may assume that jealousy *has* to be complex because of its sophisticated intersubjective dimension. One might even presume that jealousy proper needs to be derived from typically human forms of intersubjective engagement, for the reason that it concerns how one person matters to another in relation to a third. I shall consider each assumption in turn.

Firstly, the cognitive sophistication assumption. One way to undermine this position is to cite evidence that the phenomena of development are simply out of keeping with the claims that are being made. I shall leave others in this book to review whether such evidence is decisive—I think it is—but as I have indicated, there are ways to diminish the status of the evidence by re-describing what is being observed as somehow less than jealousy. What I want to do is to question the logic of the assumption—or rather, point out that there is no logical reasoning here. After all, there are many ways of relating to the personal and non-personal world that are complex but not conceptually mediated. There are plenty of examples of complex behavior among nonhuman animal species, and it is highly doubtful whether *any* of this behavior is conceptually mediated. So if one avoids *defining* jealousy in terms of thinking as well as feeling things about the relation between two other people, why should one suppose that toddlers need concepts of self and other people in order to have feelings about, and be motivated to act toward, an attachment figure giving attention to someone else?

I want to turn the argument around. Suppose, instead of confining our attention to just one feeling, jealousy, we consider a range of feelings that feature in our interpersonal relations—anger with someone, distress toward someone, joy with someone, aggressiveness toward someone, possessiveness toward someone, rivalry with someone, and so on. Suppose, now, we imagine a child who felt none of these things. How much of a *concept* of a person, or of a self vis-à-vis other selves, would that child acquire? If, indeed, interpersonal understanding, including "knowledge of other minds," is founded upon experience of *relations with* another person (Hamlyn, 1974; Hobson, 1993a, 1993b), then the answer would be: not much.

It would be difficult to argue that concepts of self and other are necessary for each of these socially directed feelings, because at the peril of an infinite regress, one would need to give an account of what content such concepts would have *prior* to the individual's experience of the relational states. Yet one need not fall into this trap, for an important implication of my argument is that a very young child could have a partial concept of self and other selves, basing this concept upon an initially limited range of interpersonally grounded relations. I think this is what happens, but we are left with the question of *which* relations are present very early in life, and how they are sufficient to serve as foundations for the content of what toddlers come to conceptualize as self and other. And if one approached the matter of self/other awareness and concept development from the opposite direction, one might wonder whether a toddler is helped to recognize the importance of a parent because he feels jealous, just as much as the toddler becomes jealous because the parent is thought or felt to be so important. This raises the possibility that an extensive range of pre-conceptual emotionally configured interpersonal relations contribute to what becomes a toddler's awareness of the special status of persons.

An openness to the latter view is justified by a number of reasons beyond those I have already adumbrated. Firstly, one important facet of conceptual understanding of persons is awareness that other people have states of mind that are comparable to, albeit differentiated from, one's own. However the comparability between self and other is recognized (and I shall come to this shortly), this will depend on there being sufficiently salient respects in which self and other correspond—and so there may need to be a number of relational states perceptible in the expressions and gestures of other people with which infants and toddlers can identify.

Secondly, I cannot see why acquiring concepts of self and other would *lead to* new feelings such as those of jealousy, guilt, or concern. Already I have questioned whether it is necessary to have concepts of self and other in order to *feel for* or *in relation to* others, and now the question arises whether such conceptual equipment would be sufficient. Why should the acquisition of concepts per se lead to these new feelings, and feelings with a phenomenology that seems "born on it self." I have already emphasized that the acquisition of concepts of self and other in the middle of the second year make a big difference to how children relate to others (also Hobson, 2007a). Yet I am in grave doubt whether it suffices to explain how we come to have such deep and distinctive emotional states as that of jealousy. Is it really plausible to suppose that Othello's murderous, wrenching, contorting state of mind originates in supposedly simple emotional states such as anger and whatever else (take your choice!), fused together into the new amalgam of jealousy ... and all of this, by dint of newly arrived concepts?

There is a third reason why I believe there need to be a range of attitudes with which infants and toddlers can identify prior to, and as a precondition for, acquiring the symbolic vehicles that subserve conceptual thought, including thoughts about self and other. This is that according to arguments I have made elsewhere (especially Hobson, 1993a, 2002/2004, 2007b), it is through identifying with other people's attitudes that infants are "moved" to adopt new attitudes to a shared world, as seen most graphically in instances of social referencing. To identify with attitudes one does not have to conceptualize anything, nor does one need to infer anything about anyone else's mental state. On the contrary, it is to engage in a primitive—albeit distinctively human—mode of intersubjective linkage with others. I have suggested that this is the route by which infants come to attribute person-anchored meanings to objects and events, and to grasp how they and others can transpose meanings from one context to another, and anchor those meanings in symbols. If this is so, then infants would need a sufficient range of states *with which to identify* in order not only to derive content for their concepts of self and other, but also to construct the symbolic vehicles to encompass such concepts in the first place.

This brings me to the second form of assumption we might question, namely that jealousy would not be possible without human forms of intersubjectivity. There may be truth in this, but I am unhappy that it should stand as an assumption. Do dogs show jealousy because of their intersubjective engagement with their masters? This is both highly plausible and highly questionable. Here it is worthwhile to consider the phenomenon in the context of attachment relationships. Certainly, dogs become attached, as do very many species of animal. Yet goslings became attached to Konrad Lorenz without much intersubjective experience. In the case of primates, including humans, there is much evidence that infants' experiences with their caregivers shape the form of infant–caregiver attachment, but it would appear that the attachment system is ready to kick in even when there is very little intersubjective engagement (recall Harlow's monkeys attaching themselves to cloth surrogate mothers). If among humans and many species of nonhuman animal, attachment is expressed in a variety of settings such as responses to separation and other forms of "secure base" behavior, why could it not also find expression in jealousy? In other words, even if it is very probable that jealousy can be shaped by intersubjective experience (e.g., Hart, Jones, & Field, 2003), just like other phenomena of attachment, we should not presume that such experience is necessary for all manifestations of jealousy. This is an empirical matter. Even if it turns out that jealousy is not so tightly bound up with attachment, still we have a model for tracing separable developmental lines in the development of social emotions and relations.

Identifying with Others

At this point, it may seem that my argument borders on the nihilistic. What benefit is there to supposing that "anything goes," and that there are no cognitive nor other constraints on emotional organization and experience? My response here is to point out that my mission has been to provide level ground from which the evidence can be viewed without distorting prejudice. I have also alluded to the risks of marginalizing relevant considerations about the phenomenology of those states of mind for which we are seeking origins. Besides this, I do not think that anything goes, but rather, that researchers have been overenthusiastic about a particular individualistic, over-intellectual, rather disembodied form of social cognitive explanation for the emergence of social emotions in particular.

I shall make one positive suggestion about an important factor that may prove to be an alternative way of distinguishing among different developmental lines in the emotional development of human beings. I propose that this factor also provides the key to differences between human and nonhuman intersubjectivity. This is the process to which I have already referred, namely the propensity to identify with the attitudes of others (inspired by Freud, 1955/1921). To oversimplify the account, identification is a natural inclination of humans but not nonhuman animals, through which an individual responds to, and is moved by, another person's attitudes *as* the other's. There is a paradox here, one that can be illustrated by the phenomenon of sharing experiences with someone else. The paradox is that sharing is impossible without the other person's involvement, yet one's own experience of sharing is one's own experience. This means that the other's attitudes are experienced (affectively) oneself, but as the other person's.

Among the first manifestations of the earliest kind of identification—and there are progressively more elaborate forms of identification as development proceeds—are those seen in the responses of 2-month-olds relating face-to-face with another adult. What the tradition of still-face studies reveal is that not only do infants respond with discomfort and agitation when the adult poses a "still-face," but also they are prone to look away and then dart looks back to the adult (originally Tronick, Als, Adamson, Wise, & Brazelton, 1978; also Crandell, Patrick, & Hobson, 2003, in the context of developmental psychopathology). The infant registers that the other person is needed to play a role in the sharing— which is not to say that the infant registers much about the person as a person, beyond this very species of phenomenon. Later in the first year of life, when sharing encompasses objects and events situated in a common environment, the differentiation between self and other within the infant's experience becomes manifest in various forms of joint attention and social referencing (e.g., Bretherton, McNew, & Beeghly-Smith, 1981; Carpenter, Nagell, & Tomasello, 1998).

So my claim is that in order to become engaged in certain forms of relatedness, and to experience certain forms of emotion, a human being needs the kind of intersubjective contact with others that only the process of identifying-with can supply. I do not think that nonhuman primates have more than a minimal ability to identify with others. Although this does not preclude their having jealousy, I do think it means they lack the organization of other-centered feelings that yield human qualities of concern, guilt, and envy. The caveat is that even without identification, animals might still have *some* responsiveness to the manifest distress of others, or even to their own "transgressions." And note that what I am proposing is not a non-cognitive theory, because identification has cognitive as well as conative and affective *aspects*. Because of this, identification has cognitive, conative, and affective developmental implications.

This returns me to the distinction between envy and jealousy. Jealousy looks the more "complex" emotion, but in my view, does not require the ability to identify with someone else. Othello feels jealousy just because … he feels jealousy (and the reasons he feels it in so tragically twisted a way requires a psychoanalytic explanation, not a social cognitive one). Envy looks simpler, but does depend on identification. Iago needs to identify with what Othello has, and he himself does not have, in order to despise him so.

Having said this, if the role of identification in configuring emotional relations is as important, and as early in onset, as I am suggesting, then if a baby *can* identify with someone else in the "primitive" way I explored through the still-face phenomenon, it may not be so outlandish to suppose that the baby can also have feelings akin to envy or concern. If jealousy is such a deeply engrained facet of mental life, and one prone to interweave with other relational states (such as those involved in sexuality), then no wonder the Oedipus complex resurfaces again and again in cultural as well as individual manifestations. It is unlikely that a majority of developmentalists would entertain these notions, not least because they could be prompted to hesitate in their disparagement toward at least certain aspects of Freudian and Kleinian psychoanalytic theory. But this does not make them any less candidates for the way things are.

The Case of Autism

Much of what I have written is thick on theory, and thin on evidence. My excuse is that other chapters of this volume will be rich in evidence, and perhaps more cautious (or not cautious enough) in theoretical exposition. To conclude, however, I do want to refer to some evidence that may lend plausibility to my argument. This evidence comes from developmental psychopathology, and specifically studies of children and adolescents with autism.

The aim of developmental psychopathology is not only to further our understanding of psychopathological conditions, but also to illuminate the pathways and processes of typical development. One way in which it can do so is to highlight dissociations among separable developmental pathways that are inseparably intertwined in typical development. The study of early childhood autism has become a cause célèbre in this respect.

I shall oversimplify and state my own hypothesis that whatever the etiology of their condition, (most) individuals with autism have a weakened or ill-organized propensity to identify with the attitudes of other people (Hobson, 1993a, 2002/2004, 2007b). The strongest evidence comes from studies of imitation (e.g., Hobson & Lee, 1999), verbal and nonverbal communication (Garcia-Perez, Lee, & Hobson, 2007; Hobson & Meyer, 2005; Hobson, Lee, & Hobson, 2007), and socio-emotional relations (Hobson et al, 2006). To give one example: Children with autism were found to be less likely to imitate the self-orientation of another person's actions, for example copying actions that were close-to-the-demonstrator by performing similar actions close-to-themselves (Meyer & Hobson, 2004). Yet those children with autism who *were* observed to imitate the self-orientation of a tester were also those who showed "sharing looks" to that tester within the testing situation (Hobson & Hobson, 2007). Making a certain kind of personal contact with the tester was associated with the propensity to copy self/other-orientation; so the kind of identification manifest in the imitation might have an essential connection with whatever was involved in the personal contact.

Having illustrated what identification can mean, I turn to one of a series of studies on social emotions that were conducted by colleagues and myself (Hobson, Chidambi, Lee, & Meyer, 2006). This involved conducting a semi-structured interview with parents of children with autism, and children without autism of similar age (6–13 years) and verbal mental age (3.5–9 years). The questions concerned whether the children showed particular emotions, with a focus on social emotions such as jealousy, guilt, and concern. (Unfortunately, it was not possible to assess envy effectively, partly because parents tended to respond with examples of jealousy.) We enquired after specific instances of each emotion. For example, the question about jealousy was:

> Have you observed jealousy in your child—that is, resenting the attention you or someone else is giving to other individuals?

Parents of both groups of children reported that their offspring showed feelings such as happiness, distress, and anger (although we did not enquire closely on the person-directedness of the anger). On the other hand, when parents were asked about their children's emotions of pity, concern, and guilt, the numbers of children in each group showing clear, ambiguous, or absent feelings of these kinds are shown in Figure 13.1.

For pity and concern, the group differences arose not so much from an absence of *some* such feelings among the children with autism, but rather, how the features of these emotions were ambiguous or atypical, whereas they were clearly present in the majority of the children without autism. For guilt, the contrast was more stark, because the great majority of children without autism showed guilt, but most of those with autism did not, and even among those who seemed to show some such feelings, the expressions were ambiguous.

Now if jealousy were on the same developmental line as pity, concern, and guilt, or if the constraints on feeling jealousy were similar to those on these other emotions, one would expect the results on jealousy to follow a similar pattern. This was not the case, as Figure 13.2 illustrates.

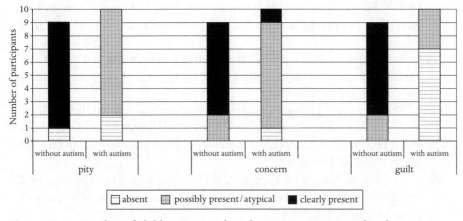

Figure 13.1 Number of children reported to show pity, concern, and guilt

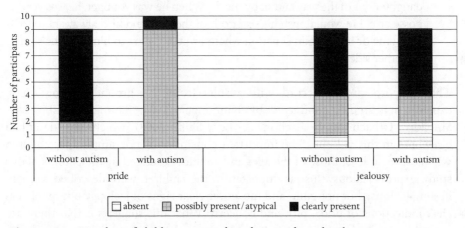

Figure 13.2 Number of children reported to show pride and jealousy

The results concerning pride are complex, for the reason that there are forms of pride in accomplishment that appear dissociable from showing pride toward other people (Kasari, Sigman, Baumgartner, & Stipek, 1993). But the results to do with jealousy (where there was no response to this question for one participant with autism) could hardly be clearer. The two groups were almost identical. Indeed, of the two parents who thought that their children with autism did not show jealousy, one was our only poor respondent, and the other was far from confident about the matter. Here are examples of what parents said about their children with autism:

H: "Yes she's very possessive towards her nanny and her mum. She just blocks others out. She loves spending time with them."

I: "He doesn't like S (partner) and me hugging or holding hands some-times ... When he was very tiny, like two, he was very jealous of us

I think. He didn't like us sitting next to each other or hugging. I remember one occasion when he actually led you [to partner] to the door and shut the door."

A: "He's quite jealous as well. If something simple like if I've got my hands full then obviously I'd give my hands to the little one, but he wants me to give my hands to him."

E: "She hates seeing any togetherness between me and my husband ... there's an obsessive element to her possessiveness of me ... So it's very much person orientated, here are the people that she cares about and she wants them all for herself."

B: "... until he was 6 or 7 I suppose, if I cuddled a child or whatever, he'd come over and just be near me, he wouldn't make a fuss as much as just come and stake his claim."

D: "If I'm sitting here and my daughter's sitting there, he will move my daughter out of the way and sit by me ... When he was younger, he was very possessive. He would push his sister out of the way, and he'd always have to be by me or in a certain situation where I'm there next to him and she's on the other side."

These reports are in accord with results from the groundbreaking quasi-experimental studies conducted by Bauminger (2004; Bauminger, Chomsky-Smolkin, Orbach-Caspi, Zachor, & Levy-Shiff, 2008) which are described elsewhere in this volume. The important conclusion is not simply that children with autism, at least those of the ages and abilities described by the parents of our study, express jealousy. Just as importantly, the children were described as manifesting jealousy but not guilt, and moreover clear signs of jealousy but much less clear indications of pride, pity, and concern. What this suggests is that there are separable developmental lines for social emotions, and that whatever handicaps afflict children with autism, these affect some social emotions more than others. In particular, jealousy appears to be spared when emotions that appear to require identification with someone else—especially those emotions that entail person-centered feelings such as concern and guilt—are conspicuous by their absence or ill-organized form among children with autism.

It is also the case that children with autism form attachments (e.g., Shapiro, Sherman, Calamari, & Koch, 1987; Sigman & Ungerer, 1984; Rogers, Ozonoff, & Maslin-Cole, 1991). Although there is evidence that they are atypical in the patterns of their social relatedness, as for example manifest in their greetings and farewells (Hobson & Lee, 1998) and affective engagement (Garcia-Perez et al., 2007), yet aspects of their relationships are relatively typical in at least certain respects. It is in view of this pattern of results that one might consider how far cognitive sophistication or intersubjective engagement is either necessary or sufficient for the development of attachment on the one hand, and jealousy on the other.

At this point I want to acknowledge how Bauminger (e.g., Bauminger et al., 2008) has taken a different theoretical line from that outlined here. Bauminger et al. (2008) write: "The interpersonal nature of the experience of jealousy requires children to intersubjectively relate to others" (p. 2 of electronic publication). In the study from which this quotation comes, a group of preschoolers with autism spectrum disorder (ASD) were not significantly different from matched typically developing children in mean scores for explicit expressions of jealousy. On the other hand, there was a relative group contrast in *clear* expressions of jealousy: almost 70% of preschoolers with ASD showed actions, verbalizations, and feelings reflecting jealousy, compared with almost 95% of a matched typically developing group. The participants with ASD gazed less at the peer and "more diffusedly at the interaction in general (i.e., a less focused gaze whose exact point of reference could not be determined) than did the typical group. The preschoolers in the ASD group also expressed fewer actions that aimed to attract parental attention, and required a longer response time before exhibiting jealousy behaviours compared with their typically developing peers" (Bauminger et al., 2008, p. 18). In addition, from among many correlations explored, children with ASD who expressed emotional responsiveness in relation to a parent appearing hurt (although a maximum rating for "concern" could be given if the child showed little more than a facial expression of discomfort) tended to show more gazes and actions expressive of jealousy.

I have expressed my skepticism about the *presumption* that all forms and manifestations of jealousy must be founded upon intersubjective engagement, even though I accept that to the extent that the experience of jealousy is truly "interpersonal" (which one might question in relation to nonhuman species), this would require intersubjective relations. What I think the acute observations of Bauminger and colleagues reveal is atypicality in person-centered aspects of the expression of jealousy. The children with autism related more "diffusedly" in their jealous responses. On the other hand, those who had more potential for person-centered feelings, as assessed by responses to someone's hurt, were also those who showed more clearly recognizable signs of relating to the people toward whom jealousy was felt.

Therefore one way of reconciling the seeming opposition between the view of Bauminger and myself is (a) to agree that it is very rare for children with autism to lack *any* intersubjective responsiveness (as also illustrated in the systematic observations of Hobson et al., 2006), and (b) to entertain the hypothesis that only some forms of intersubjectivity (perhaps) may be intrinsic to jealousy, whereas other forms (involving identification) may not, even though all varieties of intersubjective engagement play a part in giving human jealousy its ultimate depth and coloring. Correspondingly, the fact that children with autism show jealousy may indeed reflect the fact that they do not totally lack intersubjectivity, but there are grounds for believing that this does not amount to a typical quality and/or degree of intersubjective engagement. In addition, there is reason to explore how far among children with autism, as indeed among typically developing children and nonhuman animals, the *existence* of jealousy may relate to the potential to form attachments, while the expressive (and experiential) forms that jealousy assumes may depend upon specifically intersubjective aspects of an individual's social relations.

To summarize my proposed scheme: jealousy, like attachment, appears to have its own organizational underpinnings. Only for the more elaborated and refined phenomenological and behavioral expressions of jealousy are processes structured by identification, or mediated by conceptual abilities, a sine qua non.

Conclusion

In this chapter I have considered how the structure and phenomenology of *some* forms of jealousy may not depend upon complex (conceptual) cognitions such as notions of self and other, even if the advent of such concepts alters what it is like to feel jealousy and behave jealously, just as they alter all aspects of self/ other experience in some way. I have also questioned how far intersubjective experience—and more specifically, which *kind* of intersubjectivity—is necessarily implicated in feeling jealousy, even though such experience undoubtedly colors and transforms jealous modes of relatedness. Evidence from nonhuman animals such as dogs and from children with autism suggests that one might see signs of jealousy when intersubjective engagement is relatively (perhaps not absolutely) limited in quality and/or degree.

I have drawn attention to how, in our picture of early development, phenomenologically primitive states of mind—of which states of jealousy may comprise one class—may not only antedate, but also be formative for, concepts of self and other. I have tried to highlight two facts that tend to be downplayed in thinking about the development of concepts of self and other, and that of social emotions. Firstly, we apprehend and subsequently conceptualize other people as having mental states that are much like our own. This is partly because other people, as a matter of fact, do have attitudes akin to ours. If this were not the case, the processes through which we perceive and respond to those attitudes would not gain a purchase on the nature of self–other linkage and differentiation. Although this does not mean that infants and toddlers have to have the full suite of emotions familiar to adults, they do need enough for the business of constructing self/other understanding to get under way. I have not claimed that infants can identify with another person's jealousy, because we simply do not know, but I have suggested that jealousy may add a distinctive quality to infants' and toddlers' experience of certain other people, namely those whose special significance and value we adults can recognize in part through the very signs of jealousy.

Secondly, I have alluded to the importance of phenomenological considerations when we evaluate the sources of jealousy among human beings from infancy onwards. Any theory that appears to neglect the problem of how jealousy has the particular power and qualities that it does is likely to be unsatisfactory. Whatever misgivings readers may have about Freud's suggestions about the Oedipus complex (for a succinct overview of which, see Laplanche & Pontalis, 1973) —and like many psychoanalytic ideas, this is frequently mis-characterized to the point of caricature—at least it should be acknowledged that Freud took jealousy and its embellishments very seriously.

It is with phenomenology and Shakespeare that I began, and it is with these that I end. Not with Othello this time, nor with the prominent Oedipus theme in *Hamlet*, but with another of Shakespeare's jealousy-ridden characters, Leontes, King of Sicilia, in the early part of *The Winter's Tale*. Again we see that although to feel jealousy is to be human—would not emotional life be the poorer without this emotion?—there is something so awful, disturbed, and dangerous about Leontes' state that we must wonder how deeply (and far back) we need to seek for the sources of his diseas'd opinion. Here in Act I, Scene II, he ponders what he imagines to be passing between his innocent Queen Hermione and Polixenes, King of Bohemia:

> LEONTES: Is whispering nothing?
> Is leaning cheek to cheek? Is meeting noses?
> Kissing with inside lip? Stopping the career
> Of laughter with a sigh?—a note infallible
> Of breaking honesty. Horsing foot on foot?
> Skulking in corners? Wishing clocks more swift;
> Hours, minutes; noon, midnight? And all eyes
> Blind with the pin and web but theirs, theirs only,
> That would unseen be wicked—is this nothing?
> Why, then the world and all that's in't is nothing;
> The covering sky is nothing; Bohemia nothing;
> My wife is nothing; nor nothings have these nothings,
> If this be nothing.
>
> CAMILLO: Good my lord, be cur'd
> Of this diseas'd opinion, and betimes;
> For 'tis most dangerous.

References

Barrett, K. C. (1995). A functionalist approach to shame and guilt. In J. P. Tangney & K. W. Fischer (Eds.), *Self-conscious emotions* (pp. 25–63). New York: Guilford Press.

Bauminger, N. (2004). The expression and understanding of jealousy in children with autism. *Development and Psychopathology, 16*, 157–177.

Bauminger, N., Chomsky-Smolkin, L., Orbach-Caspi, E., Zachor, D., & Levy-Shiff, R. (2008). Jealousy and emotional responsiveness in young children with ASD. *Cognition and Emotion, 22*, 595–619.

Bretherton, I., McNew, S., & Beeghly-Smith, M. (1981). Early person knowledge as expressed in gestural and verbal communication: When do infants acquire a "theory of mind"? In M. E. Lamb & L. R. Sherrod (Eds.), *Infant social cognition: Empirical and theoretical considerations* (pp. 333–373). Hillsdale, NJ: Erlbaum.

Carpenter, M., Nagell, K., & Tomasello, M. (1998). Social cognition, joint attention, and communicative competence from 9 to 15 months of age. *Monographs of the Society for Research in Child Development, 63*(4, Serial No. 255).

Crandell, L. E., Patrick, M. P. H., & Hobson, R. P. (2003). "Still-face" interactions between mothers with borderline personality disorder and their 2-month-old infants. *British Journal of Psychiatry, 183*, 239–247.

Draghi-Lorenz, R., Reddy, V., & Costall, A. (2001). Rethinking the development of "non-basic" emotions: A critical review of existing theories. *Developmental Review, 21*, 263–304.

Freud, S. (1955/1921). Identification. In J. Strachey (Ed.), *The standard edition of the complete psychological works of Sigmund Freud* (Vol. xviii, pp. 105–110). London: Hogarth Press.

Frijda, N. H. (1993). The place of appraisal in emotion. *Cognition and Emotion, 7*, 357–387.

Garcia-Perez, R. M., Lee, A., & Hobson, R. P. (2007). On intersubjective engagement in autism: A controlled study of nonverbal aspects of conversation. *Journal of Autism and Developmental Disorders, 37*, 1310–1322.

Hamlyn, D. W. (1974). Person-perception and our understanding of others. In T. Mischel (Ed.), *Understanding other persons* (pp. 1–36). Oxford: Basil Blackwell.

Hart, S. L., & Carrington, H. (2002). Jealousy in 6-month-old infants. *Infancy, 3*, 395–402.

Hart, S. L., Carrington, H. A., Tronick, E. Z., & Carroll, S. R. (2004). When infants lose exclusive maternal attention: Is it jealousy? *Infancy, 6*, 57–78.

Hart, S., Jones, N. A., & Field, T. (2003). Atypical expressions of jealousy in infants of intrusive- and withdrawn-depressed mothers. *Child Psychiatry and Human Development, 33*, 193–207.

Hobson, J. A., & Hobson, R. P. (2007). Identification: The missing link between imitation and joint attention? *Development and Psychopathology, 19*, 411–431.

Hobson, R. P. (1990). On acquiring knowledge about people and the capacity to pretend: Response to Leslie. *Psychological Review, 97*, 114–121.

Hobson, R. P. (1993a). *Autism and the development of mind.* Hove, Sussex: Erlbaum.

Hobson, R. P. (1993b). The emotional origins of social understanding. *Philosophical Psychology, 6*, 227–249.

Hobson, R. P. (2002). *The cradle of thought.* London: Macmillan (and 2004: New York, Oxford University Press).

Hobson, R. P. (2007a). Social relations, self-awareness, and symbolizing: A perspective from autism. In C. A. Brownell & C. B. Kopp (Eds.), *Socioemotional development in the toddler years* (pp. 423–450). New York: Guilford Press.

Hobson, R. P. (2007b). Communicative depth: Soundings from developmental psycho-pathology. In M. Legerstee & V. Reddy (Eds.), "What does it mean to communicate for infants?" [Special edition]. *Infant behavior and development, 30*, 267–277.

Hobson, R. P. (2008). Interpersonally situated cognition. *International Journal of Philosophy, 16*, 377–397.

Hobson, R. P., Chidambi, G., Lee, A., & Meyer, J. (2006). Foundations for self-awareness: An exploration through autism. *Monographs of the Society for Research in Child Development, 71*(2 Serial No 284).

Hobson, R. P., & Lee, A. (1998). "Hello and goodbye: A study of social engagement in autism." *Journal of Autism and Developmental Disorders, 28*, 117–127.

Hobson, R. P., & Lee, A. (1999). Imitation and identification in autism. *Journal of Child Psychology and Psychiatry, 40*, 649–659.

Hobson, R. P., Lee, A., & Hobson, J. A. (2007). Only connect? Communication, identification, and autism. *Social Neuroscience, 2*, 320–335.

Hobson, R. P., & Meyer, J. A. (2005). Foundations for self and other: A study in autism. *Developmental Science, 8*, 481–491.

Kasari, C., Sigman, M. D., Baumgartner, P. & Stipek, D. J. (1993). Pride and mastery in children with autism. *Journal of Child Psychology and Psychiatry, 34*, 352–362.

Laplanche, J., & Pontalis, J-B. (1973). *The language of psycho-analysis*. London: Hogarth Press.

Legerstee, M., Ellenbogen, B., Nienhuis, T., & Marsh, H. (this volume). Social bonds, triadic relationships, and goals: Preconditions for the emergence of human jealousy. In S. L. Hart, & M. Legerstee (Eds.), *Handbook of jealousy: Theory, research, and multidisciplinary approaches*. Malden, MA: Wiley-Blackwell.

Lewis, M. (2003). The development of self-consciousness. In J. Roessler & N. Eilan (Eds.), *Agency and self-awareness* (pp. 275–295). Oxford: Clarendon Press.

Lewis, M., Sullivan, M. W., Stanger, C., & Weiss, M. (1989). Self development and self-conscious emotions. *Child Development, 60*, 146–156.

Meyer, J. A., & Hobson, R. P. (2004). Orientation in relation to self and other: The case of autism. *Interaction Studies, 5*, 221–244.

Morris, P. H., Doe, C., & Godsell, E. (2008). Secondary emotions in non-primate species? Behavioural reports and subjective claims by animal owners. *Cognition and Emotion, 22*, 3–20.

Mullen, P. E. (1990). A phenomenology of jealousy. *Australian and New Zealand Journal of Psychiatry, 24*, 17–28.

Piaget J., & Inhelder, B. (1969). *The psychology of the child* (H. Weaver, Trans.). London: Routledge & Kegan Paul.

Reddy, V. (2000). Coyness in early infancy. *Developmental Science, 3*, 186–192.

Rogers, S. J., Ozonoff, S., & Maslin-Cole, C. (1991). A comparative study of attachment behaviour in young children with autism or other psychiatric disorders. *Journal of the American Academy of Child and Adolescent Psychiatry, 30*, 483–488.

Shapiro, T., Sherman, M., Calamari, G., & Koch, D. (1987). Attachment in autism and other developmental disorders. *Journal of the American Academy of Child and Adolescent Psychiatry, 26*, 485–490.

Sigman, M., & Ungerer, J. A. (1984). Attachment behaviors in autistic children. *Journal of Autism and Developmental Disorders, 14*, 231–243.

Tronick, E., Als, H., Adamson, L., Wise, S., & Brazelton, T. B. (1978). The infant's response to entrapment between contradictory messages in face-to-face interaction. *Journal of the American Academy of Child Psychiatry, 17*, 1–13.

Vygotsky, L. S. (1962). *Thought and language* (E. Hanfmann & G. Vaker, Trans.). Cambridge, MA: MIT Press.

Waddington, C. H. (1977). *Tools for thought*. Paladin.

Werner, H., & Kaplan, B. (1984). *Symbol formation*. Hillsdale, NJ: Erlbaum. (Original work published 1963).

14

What Is Missing in the Study of the Development of Jealousy?

Joseph J. Campos, Eric A. Walle, and Audun Dahl

This commentary will emphasize some aspects of the development of jealousy that the previous chapters did not cover, viz., a more complete consideration of the development of jealousy from infancy to adulthood. It takes as a starting point that recent studies are sufficiently convincing in demonstrating the *existence* of a form or jealousy, perhaps manifested in a very rudimentary way, by the middle of the first year of life, but that this discovery, important as it is, leaves many important issues uncovered. For instance, the discovery has little bearing on the distinction between "basic" and "non-basic" emotions. Moreover, these important findings on early manifestations of jealousy must be extended to the study of development of jealousy into older ages, and to the more complex ways by which jealousy can be manifested. We agree with the various authors that jealousy takes place in a triadic interaction involving a target person (e.g., a young infant), a partner (e.g., a mother), and a rival (e.g., a sibling or another child), but that the identification of structural differences in the social organization of events that result in jealousy does not go far enough to explain the generation of the emotion or the ways by which the emotion is manifested. This commentary accepts the assumption that infants must have a cognitive understanding of social relationships, without which they cannot show jealousy; however, to understand the role of cognition in jealousy, we must also understand the development of different behavioral strategies that are used in jealousy encounters, and how cognition plays into those strategies. In sum, this commentary is designed to supplement, rather than to reiterate or criticize, the chapters on which it is based.

Two questions form the heart of our comments on jealousy: (1) What are the roles and functions of jealousy in the social relationships of the young child? (2) Are these functions at all similar to the functions of jealousy in adults?

We will maintain that jealousy does not serve the same set of functions at each point in life. Furthermore, even if jealousy in a young child plays some of the roles that adult jealousy plays, we cannot assume that a child can exhibit the full range of behaviors associated with jealousy in adults. In what follows, we will

Handbook of Jealousy: Theory, Research and Multidisciplinary Approaches, First Edition.
Edited by Sybil L. Hart and Maria Legerstee.

elaborate on some of the major ways in which jealousy can be expressed—the different *behavioral modes* of jealousy, as we will call them. Clearly, these behavioral modes of jealousy do not all develop simultaneously, nor are they present from birth. Indeed, there is a need for very important research documenting in what sequence, if any, these behavioral modes become manifest, and how factors related to age, experience, and socialization help bring these behavioral modes online. In laying out these behavioral modes, we also highlight useful, but often neglected, principles of emotion. One is the *goal relevance* of emotions and their manifestation; that is, emotions always follow from a person's goals, and cannot be inferred independently of these goals. A second principle is that of *intentionality*; emotions are always *targeted* toward something—they have an "object," which in the case of jealousy is a social one. In concluding, we will argue that only when one considers which among the many manifestations of jealousy are shown at a given point in development can one begin to theorize more precisely about the cognitive prerequisites for jealousy.

Emotional Development: A Principle to Keep in Mind

Emotional development is often conceptualized inadequately. A major misconstrual, seen in the literature on jealousy and elsewhere, relates to the tendency to differentiate a "true" emotion from a "proto-emotion." A classic instance of this misconstrual is in the otherwise-excellent article on the development of disgust by Rozin and Fallon (1987). They delineated a series of steps a child goes through with development to manifest disgust. These steps proceed from the neonate's facial reactions and aversive movements to bitter and sour tastes, continue through avoidance at later ages of ingestion of a fluid within which a child can see floating pieces of plastic feces, and terminate with the child's avoidance of ingestion of a fluid into which the pieces of plastic feces were inserted, but then removed. Although each of these steps produced clear negative reactions in children, Rozin and Fallon stressed that only in the last-described step, at about 7 years of age, is the child's reaction "true" disgust. The authors, in brief, set up an arbitrary criterion—the prior but no longer evident contamination of a foodstuff—to discriminate "proto-disgust" from "true" disgust. A similar categorical division was made by Arnold Buss and colleagues (Buss, Iscoe, & Buss, 1979), who argued that a child could not show "true" embarrassment until the age of 5, because only then did the child have a sense of self sufficiently developed to warrant the attribution of that emotion. Such arbitrary divisions lead investigators to focus on the later-manifested (i.e., "true") emotion to the neglect of the study of developmental antecedents, or to study the developmentally prior manifestations, without considering linkages to later manifestations. We shall note both tendencies in the review of the jealousy literature that follows.

How should we more appropriately view the development of emotion? We view emotional development using Wittgenstein's (1958) metaphor of a rope. There need be no continuity between one end of a rope and the other, yet the rope is a single entity. The overlapping strands of the rope, proceeding systematically along its length, unify it. Similarly, the early manifestations in the development of an emotion need have no similarity with its adult manifestation. However, each step in development overlaps sufficiently with the preceding and the subsequent ones to provide unity. The major proponents of this view of emotional development have been Mascolo and Fischer (e.g., 1995), along with Barrett and Campos (1987).

What Is Jealousy and What Is Its Importance?

It is tempting to skip definitions, and indeed, some of the preceding chapters do so. For us, jealousy is the emotion evoked when we perceive that a significant relationship is challenged by a third person. Jealousy is distinguished from envy on the basis of the social structure of the interaction. In envy, there is a person who wishes for what another has, and the person who has that which is wished-for; there need be no third party. In both jealousy and envy, the principle of goal relevance comes into play, insofar as there is in both cases something that another has and that the first person wants. To see how pervasive jealousy is in our adult relationships, and how it depends on the personal goal relevance of the interactions involved, we should consider the circumstances in which we do *not* feel jealous. For example, no jealousy can arise in a relationship where the attention and affection of the partner are entirely unimportant to us (thus attesting to the motivational principle mentioned above). The audience watching Shakespeare's *Othello* is not jealous of Cassio were it to think that he had an affair with Desdemona, though Desdemona's husband would be. We might be *envious* of Brad Pitt because he is seeing Angelina Jolie, but we are not *jealous* of him (unless Angelina is a former girlfriend of ours). Neither would we have envy if for whatever reason we did not value Angelina's charms. (We will leave it for a later section of this commentary to elaborate on how critical the principle of intentionality, described above, is for a fuller understanding of jealousy.)

Jealousy is important for many reasons. It is a universal experience, a bitter one, and a potentially violent one as well. The phenomenon is universal because we enter numerous relationships that to a lesser or greater extent are significant to us. In fact, the greater the relevance the relationship has for oneself, the more intense (and hence, the more dangerous) the manifestation of jealousy. For instance, participants reporting greater dependency on their partners also thought they would react more strongly to seeing their partner flirting with someone of the opposite sex (Rydell & Bringle, 2007). Furthermore, it is unavoidable that we sometimes compete for the attention and affection of those we love, even when they do love us in return. An illustrative case in point is the jealousy young siblings exhibit when fighting for their mother's attention (Miller, Volling, & McElwain, 2000).

Jealousy is important also for its relevance to the evolution of human psychology. From an evolutionary perspective, situations evoking jealousy are more than unpleasant; they constitute threats to the passing on of our genes. Accordingly, Buss and Haselton (2005) characterize jealousy as "an emotion designed to alert an individual to threats to a valued relationship" (p. 506). It is easy to imagine how naïve, unjealous, males were wiped out of the evolutionary tournament by our more watchful ancestors, because the former unknowingly helped raise the offspring of the latter. To secure the survival of one's genes (and not those of another), it was (and continues to be) essential to keep one's female partner for oneself. David Buss and his colleagues (Buss, Larsen, Westen, & Semmelroth, 1992; Shackelford et al., 2004) have provided support for this idea by finding that men were likely to be most upset by imagining their partner engaging in the reproductive act of sexual intercourse with another person. In contrast, women responded that they felt more distress when imagining their partner forming a deep emotional attachment to someone else; for women there was never any doubt that the child was their own offspring and their major concern was the loss of the mate's commitment and protection to another female.

In brief, jealousy has a large impact on our adult lives. The role and the importance of jealousy in young children's social relationships is less obvious—and is even less so in infants. This subtlety accounts, in part, for the neglect of the study of jealousy in early development; yet, the functions of jealousy in early development, different as they are in many ways from those of adults, may nevertheless be extraordinarily important. Surely, jealousy must have enduring consequences, both for child–parent attachment, as well as sibling–peer relationships. The question is worth posing in the context of this handbook: How similar, then, are the functions of jealousy in childhood to jealousy in adulthood, and what role do they play in the organization of the later social relationships of the child?

The Apparent Paradox of Early Jealousy

There is a paradox about the presence of jealousy in the middle of the first year of life, a presence now confirmed by Draghi-Lorenz (this volume, Chapter 11), Hart (this volume, Chapter 4), and Legerstee, Ellenbogen, Neinhuis, and Marsh (this volume, Chapter 9). The paradox is that jealousy should not exist in the first year of life, yet it evidently does.

Reasons for neglecting the study of early jealousy

There are at least two reasons why it had been thought that jealousy should not exist in the first year. First of all, some influential writers on jealousy, such as White and Mullen (1989), do not talk about jealousy in infancy and childhood, preferring to refer to *developmental antecedents* of jealousy, such as sibling rivalry. Presumably, White and Mullen would consider the experimental operations used by those who investigate jealousy in the first year of life to be too rudimentary to infer jealousy, in the manner that Rozin and Fallon (1987) dismissed distaste in infancy as an indicator of disgust, and Buss et al. (1979) dismissed early embarrassment. The second reason is the widespread distinction in emotional development between basic and non-basic emotions (the basic emotions being joy, fear, sadness, anger, distaste, surprise, and possibly others including pride and shame; see Tracy, Robins, & Tangney, 2007). The second reason has as a corollary the belief that basic emotions should be observable in the first year of life but the non-basic ones only after 15–18 months (Lewis, 2000), despite reports of early manifestations of jealousy by Gesell (1906). Both of these objections have had the undesirable consequence of discouraging investigations into jealousy in the first year of life, or worse, implying that jealousy should not be observable in early infancy at all.

There is reason for not putting too much stock in either basis for believing that jealousy should not be observable in the first year of life. We have already addressed the problems with the first issue, that of developmental antecedents, believing that the approach of Mascolo and Fischer (1995) avoids categorical thinking that discourages investigations of phenomena that are not the full-blown manifestation of an emotion. The groundbreaking work by Hart, Draghi-Lorenz, Legerstee, and others has clearly established that emotions meeting the criteria of jealousy are observable by the beginning of the second half-year of life, and possibly even earlier. Infant jealousy is definitely part of the family of emotions designated as jealousy.

The second basis for the neglect of investigations of jealousy in the first year of life—that based on the distinction between basic and non-basic emotions—is harder to deal with. There are many misconceptions about what a basic emotion is and is not. When properly understood, the conceptualizations of two categories of emotion—basic vs. non-basic—in no way should preclude the observation of jealousy in the first year of life. However, in another sense, what are called basic emotions may indeed condition at what age the manifestation of jealousy is evident in the first year of life. If we are correct in making this assertion, the criticism of basic emotions that is both implicit and explicit in the infant jealousy literature is not apt.

Clarifying the distinction between basic and non-basic emotions

To clarify the misconceptualizations about basic emotions and jealousy, we will deal here with some of the inclusion and exclusion criteria that define basic and non-basic emotions, to ascertain (a) why the basic vs. non-basic distinction should not have delayed the study of infant jealousy, and (b) why there are good ontological reasons for dividing emotions into two rather different sets. We make the second distinction because at times it appears as if research on jealousy blurs a distinction we consider both valid and very relevant for understanding how jealousy is manifest. The inclusion and exclusion criteria we apply to basic emotions are as follows:

1   Basic emotions refer to that subset of emotions that (a) show cross-cultural universality in the recognition of their expression; (b) have cross-modal specification (i.e., can be identified in face and voice, and possibly touch and gesture as well); (c) may be evident in phylogenesis, at least among higher primates (Plutchik, 1982); and (d) can be directed to both physical objects and social ones (whereas the non-basic emotions apply only to social encounters, except when used metaphorically). It is clear that there are some emotions that meet these criteria, as well as some that do not; the latter are the so-called non-basic emotions, with jealousy one such non-basic emotion.

2   The concept of basic emotions was never intended to imply their emergence in the first year of life, and the emergence of the non-basic only after the first year and a half of age. In fact, the emotion of contempt is a basic emotion (Boucher & Brant, 1981), but contempt has not been reported in the first year of life and may not be evident until the late preschool years or afterward. A simplistic equation of basic with emergence in the first year and non-basic at later ages is not warranted.

3   The term basic emotion does not imply that such an emotion is *constitutive* of other emotions, in the fashion that a Mendeleyev chemical element is constitutive of a chemical mixture (as hydrogen, together with oxygen, is constitutive of water). Because they are not constitutive, emotions like fear, joy, anger, sadness, etc., are not necessary to generate jealousy.

4   Basic emotions *do* enter into emotion blends, by which we mean combinations of emotional responses to a situation. These blends can be sequential or simultaneous. Thus, one can express both fear and anger in close temporal proximity in response to the same transaction. Similarly, joy and contempt go together (e.g., in smugness), as well as surprise with any one or more of the other basic emotions. Scrutiny of the responses cited when young infants are said to be jealous leads us to consider jealousy to be a blended emotion (Hart, this volume; Hobson, this volume, Chapter 13; Legerstee et al., this volume; Rydell & Bringle, 2007). When feeling jealous, a person can simultaneously experience several emotions, like sadness, anger, and shame.

In sum, this examination of what constitutes basic and non-basic emotions leads us to conclude that (1) the term "basic" has unfortunate and erroneous connotations of being constitutive of more complex emotions, (2) that the distinction between two different classes of emotions is real, though the distinction requires redesignation to eliminate undesirable implications of the terms basic and non-basic, and (3) that for jealousy to be manifest, the responses of what are currently designated as the basic emotions must be available to the child. If we conceptualize jealousy as a shifting between or among various emotional states, some of them "basic," it becomes less paradoxical that jealousy appears to emerge during the first year of life but yet is somehow secondary to the manifestation of simpler (i.e., basic) emotions. We thus caution against the use of findings on early jealousy to challenge a valid distinction between two classes of emotions.

The Behavioral Modes of Jealousy

The goals, feelings, and behaviors of the jealous person will change drastically as his or her appraisal of the jealousy-evoking situation changes. It is this multifarious character of jealousy that prompted Marcel Proust to say: "jealousy is never a single continuous and indivisible passion. It is composed out of an infinity [. . .] of different jealousies" (Proust, 1989, p. 404). Though Proust's description of an infinite number of jealousies is a bit of poetic license, we do believe that there are multiple and distinct ways by which jealousy can be manifested.

Inspired by Bryson's (1991) notion of "response modes," we define a *behavioral mode* of an emotion as a distinct way in which the emotion is targeted and acted out with the goal of coping with the appraised situation.[1] Importantly, children can show one of the behavioral modes of jealousy without being able to show another. In fact, we argue that the development of jealousy involves describing the developmental order by which the child starts acting out more modes of jealousy and shows a more flexible response to the potentially jealousy-evoking situation (see Masciuch & Kienapple, 1993).

The emphasis on behavioral modes is fruitful in two respects. First, it provides a conceptual framework for studying jealousy in early childhood. Though interesting, we do not find the question of *when* jealousy first emerges to be the most pressing research question. In our view, the answer depends too much on how a particular researcher probes for jealousy, and operationalizes the infant's response as jealous or not. For an incremental science, it is more fruitful to ask in what way jealousy is manifested at different points in development.

Second, knowing the development of behavioral modes in jealousy puts us in a better position for theorizing about the cognitive and emotional capacities present at the different ages. Consider the study by Hobson and his colleagues involving parental reports of a range of emotions in school-aged children with and without autism (Hobson, this volume). For jealousy, but not for other emotions like pity, concern, and guilt, an equal proportion of parents of autistic and non-autistic children reported seeing clear signs of the emotion. All the other social emotions appeared to occur less frequently in children with autism than in other children of similar age. However, it is hard to know from these data alone exactly what kind of jealous behavior the autistic children exhibited, and therefore we do not know precisely what kinds of behavior we are finding the cognitive prerequisites for.

We now turn to highlighting some of the core behavioral modes of jealousy, and the extent to which they have been noted or ignored in research on early childhood jealousy. In delineating these modes, we take into account two essential issues for the evocation of any emotion: First, what is the goal of the behavior expressing the emotion? Is it to reestablish or to sever the relationship with the beloved other? Second, toward whom is the emotion directed? Is it toward the beloved or the rival? A consideration of these two questions as they pertain to the emotion of jealousy leads to the following five core modes: (1) attempts to restore the relationship with the beloved, (2) hostility toward the beloved, (3) thwarting the rival, (4) hostility toward the rival, and (5) fear, sadness and despair in the face of perceived loss of a valued relationship.

(1) Restorative behaviors toward the beloved

One of the earliest responses infants display in jealous contexts is the attempt to reestablish social interaction with the loved one. It is important to separate such behaviors from hostility directed toward the beloved or rival. Though hostile behaviors may have the overarching goal of restoring the lost or threatened relationship, restorative behaviors as we define them are attempts to confirm or reestablish the threatened relationship with the beloved through non-hostile means.

Masciuch and Kienapple (1993) provide longitudinal data on the progressive nature of infant attempts at restoring the threatened social relationship. Early infant attempts to reestablish the social relationship with the parent are quite primitive, relying mainly on distress cries or reaching toward the parent. Anecdotal evidence of these restorative behaviors may be taking place in Bradley's (this volume, Chapter 10) reports on infant–peer trios, where games of "footsie" and vocalizations are prevalent in the effort of orienting or maintaining the attention of a sought-after partner while in competition with a rival infant.

Empirical findings of increased infant displays of sadness in jealousy-evoking situations may be indicative of the infant's attempt to restore the relationship by creating a situation that is likely to elicit caregiving behaviors by the attachment figure, especially when these sad displays are associated with infant gaze to the caregiver (Hart, Carrington, Tronick, & Carroll, 2004). The gaze of the infant is particularly significant here, as it demonstrates the directedness of the emotional display and distinguishes it from the withdrawn sadness associated with the fifth behavioral mode of despair. Additionally, Volling, Kennnedy, and Jackey (this volume, Chapter 17) report that younger infants are more likely than older infants to seek comfort from mothers in jealousy-evoking situations.

These behaviors may be the best available response the child has to regain the affection of the caregiver, particularly at the younger ages at which they are primarily reported.

Although infant crying in these contexts may be expressions of jealousy, crying can also demonstrate any number of other negative emotional states. For infant distress behaviors to be interpreted as jealousy they should co-occur with other goal-directed behaviors indicative of jealousy, as well as be present in jealousy-evoking contexts. One paradigm to investigate the co-occurrence of distress with other behaviors indicative of jealousy is to have the infant become distressed at observing the mother attend to a rival, the mother respond to the infant with a reassuring expression, but then refocus on the rival as before. If the infant calms down, it would help affirm that the distress was in response to the disrupted relationship, rather than merely the disrupted attention itself, and the goal of the distress was to confirm that the dyadic relationship between mother and infant was still intact.

(2) Hostility toward the beloved

Very few reports of hostility directed toward the significant other are reported in the developmental literature. This may indicate either a lack of specificity in coding such behaviors, or a later onset for the response to appear. Based on anecdotal reports, it is difficult to determine which case it is. For example, in Bauminger's (this volume, Chapter 12) report of 4-year-old Yuval's response to his mother's reading a book to a rival child, Yuval yelled "No! Me!" and then threw the book to the floor. Young infants may also show hostile-like behavior. In his parental interview study, Draghi-Lorenz (this volume) reported that at 9 months of age, research participant Daisy growled upon seeing her father lift up older sister Alison. Such responses may be indicative of anger toward the beloved. However, even in these instances, it is difficult to tell whether such vocalizations and actions are in fact angry or hostile, or instead are a more general distress reaction on the part of the infant. Behaviors of hitting, pinching, or tugging a loved one would be more demonstrative of jealous hostility. Many studies report that infants touch their parent more in jealous contexts (Hart, Field, del Valle, & Letourneau, 1998a; Hart, Field, Letourneau, & del Valle, 1998b). However, these studies do not describe and differentiate what type of touching this is, as a gentle tug on the mother's blouse is very different from striking out at her arm.

Many covert aggressive behaviors become evident later in development. Infants have been reported to ignore the competing relationship, complain to the parent, ask for time with the rival child, ask to leave, or even pretend to dial someone on a toy phone to report the parent's undesirable behavior (Masciuch & Kienapple, 1993). Furthermore, more general infant distress reactions at being ignored by a significant other (Legerstee et al., this volume; Bradley, this volume) may also indicate hostile verbalizations (such as a jealous adult yelling profanity at a loved one). However, as discussed with the previous mode evaluating restorative behaviors, such conclusions are entirely speculative without converging evidence for the directedness and goals of such distress displays. Examples of hostile behavior toward the beloved, be they overt or covert, are of great relevance when considering the drastic consequences such behaviors can take in adults, in the forms of spousal abuse or murder.

Hostility directed toward the beloved may also be observed after the rival is removed. The child may demonstrate continued hostility through decreases in warmth, helping behavior, or empathic responding when later interacting with the significant other. We are unaware of any studies that have investigated the lingering impact of jealousy-evoking situations on the child's interactions with the beloved. Considerations from attachment theory suggest that these carryover effects may well result in insecure attachment behaviors.

(3) Hostility toward the rival

In mature jealousy the rival is an equally natural target as the beloved for the anger of a jealous person. Intentionally or not, the rival poses a threat to the person's goal of having a stable and lasting relationship with the beloved. Compared to instances of hostility toward the beloved, instances of hostility toward the rival are relatively frequent in the maternal reports presented in this volume. Draghi-Lorenz (this volume) gives the example of a 6-month-old girl who had seen her mother pick up the family's kitten and cuddle it. The mother says that this had made the girl start crying, and when the girl was picked up, she was brutal to a kitten she had otherwise loved to play with.

Experimental studies have found increased anger in young children when they are in jealousy-evoking situations (Hart, this volume; Hart et al., 2004). However, most studies looking at infants' reactions in these situations do not report toward whom the child's anger is directed. When Volling, McElwain, and Miller (2002) observed toddlers' reactions to seeing a parent play with their older sibling, they coded negativity toward parent, negativity toward a sibling, and rough play all in the same category as "disruptive behavior." In another study, Hart and her colleagues (Hart et al., 2004) compared 6-month-olds' responses to three different conditions. In one the mother was instructed to interact naturally with her child, in another she was instructed to pose a still-face, and in a third she was instructed to ignore her child and engage in a lively conversation with an infant-size doll (jealousy condition). The infants showed more anger in the still-face and jealousy conditions than in the natural condition, but there was no significant difference in anger between the two former conditions. However, in the jealousy-evoking situation there were two possible targets of the hostility, the mother and the rival doll, whereas the still-face condition only contained one. Hence, there is no way of knowing whether the children in the jealousy condition were angry at the mother or the baby doll.

As Draghi-Lorenz (this volume) notes, the target of aggression should become more visible when the child's range of action increases through motoric development and the acquisition of independent locomotion. Consistent with this idea, Hart et al. (1998a) mention that some 12-month-olds aggressed toward the rival doll to whom the mother was exclusively attending. Nevertheless, infants' anger has been shown to have directedness from 4 months of age and perhaps even earlier (Sternberg & Campos, 1990), demonstrating that it may be possible to determine the target of jealous anger in the first third of a year of life.

Also, as said above in the section on hostility toward the beloved, it appears possible to study lingering anger in children after the jealousy-evoking situation has ended. The question can then be whether the child acts with more hostility toward an experimenter who has just challenged the child's relationship to his or her mother. An additional way of studying anger toward the rival is inspired by Masciuch and Kienapple's (1993) report that some children play with the rival's toys when being ignored by their parent. It would be interesting to investigate whether the jealous child would also engage with the rival's parent in response to being ignored by the beloved. Such behaviors would demonstrate intentional elicitation of jealousy in the rival as a means for the child to express anger at the rival, and perhaps even its own, unfaithful, parent. In sum, we encourage researchers to pay closer attention to the directedness of jealous anger, and even to develop paradigms designed specifically to elicit the behavioral mode of showing hostility toward the rival.

(4) Thwarting the rival

Attempts to hinder the rival, be it a sibling or a Don Juan, are easily confounded with aggression toward the rival. Yet, the distinction between them is crucial. Though thwarting may co-occur with anger, the former does not imply the latter, either in cases of jealousy or otherwise. An adult instantiation of the behavioral mode of thwarting would be interrupting the conversation between one's partner and an attractive rival, and gently suggesting that you and the partner go home because you need to get up early the next day. Hobson (this volume) provides a charming story reported by a mother demonstrating non-hostile thwarting of a rival. On one occasion, the mother was hugging her partner while her autistic 2-year-old boy was sitting next to them on the couch. In response to this exclusion, the boy eventually took the partner's hand, led him out of the room and shut the door. By at least temporarily hindering the rival from having access to his mother, the boy was apparently hoping to secure his threatened place in the mother's heart.

Draghi-Lorenz (this volume) presents rich data on similar sibling interactions from an interview study with mothers of 9 infants less than a year old. Parental reports revealed that infants as young as 8.5 months may try to push their sibling away from their mother. These reports need corroboration by more direct measures of behavior to determine whether such actions are examples of thwarting or open hostility toward the rival, but suggest that jealous thwarting does occur in the first year of life. A commonly investigated setting for jealousy early in life is sibling competition for parental attention. Volling et al. (2002) found that jealousy-related distress in 16-month-olds correlated with attempts to interrupt play between a parent and the older sibling. Volling and her colleagues argue that the toddlers' distress was due primarily to jealousy because it was directed at the parent–sibling interaction.

Notably, there also seems to be development in the ways in which the jealous individual thwarts his or her rival. Volling et al. (this volume) found that preschoolers engaged in both attention seeking at a distance and physical intrusion into the play between the mother and the sibling. The 2-year-old siblings, however, were found to engage in interference behavior but not attention seeking. These distal and proximal forms of interfering in the interaction between the rival and the beloved are representative of the behavioral mode of thwarting. Whether they are also expressions of hostility on the part of the jealous child toward the mother or rival child has not yet been studied in sufficient detail. Based on the present research, we see a need to distinguish between the three modes in question, as well as studying the development of each.

(5) Negative emotions over losing a relationship

The fluctuation between sadness and fear at the prospect of losing a significant relationship is one of the most dominant parts of the subjective experience of jealousy (Mullen, 1990). Needless to say, little is more detrimental to one's well-being than having one's bonds with a loved one severed or permanently damaged. If in a given situation one perceives a threat but is unable to remove it, withdrawal and introversion signify the beginning of the grieving process. This withdrawn sadness should be kept apart from the distress discussed as part of the jealous person's attempts to restore the relationship with the beloved. Whereas a person hoping to achieve reunion can do so by seeking compassion from the loved one, a person who does not believe that the relationship can be saved will instead seek to be away from the loved one.

Seemingly, jealous despair has been extensively studied in infancy. Studies consistently report increased distress and sadness by infants in situations where the mother is paying attention to a rival while ignoring her child (e.g. Hart & Carrington, 2002; Hart et al., 2004). Indeed, in a study by Hart et al. (2004), heightened sadness was what most clearly differentiated between the 5-month-olds' emotional reactions to their mother talking to a rival doll and their reactions to the mother posing a still-face. Furthermore, Hart et al. (1998a) describe 12-month-olds who display "disorganized behaviors (such as stilling), evidence of anxiety (such as rocking, pacing, self-clinging, propitiatory smiling, and numerous self-comforting and avoidance responses)..." (p. 60).

To ensure that infants' negative reactions were not merely due to mothers behaving in an unusual way, Legerstee et al. (this volume) investigated the effects of specific characteristics of the conversation with the rival by contrasting a "monologue" with a "dialogue" condition in an experiment with 3- and 6-month-olds. In both conditions, the experimenter was about to communicate with the infant, when the mother interrupted. In the monologue condition, the experimenter explained to the mother, with only a few interruptions, what the goal of the experiment was. In the dialogue condition, the experimenter engaged the mother in a lively conversation about her child. The authors concluded that "(t)he finding that infants reacted negatively in the dialogue, but not in the monologue condition, suggests that the infants perceived the third party as a rival" (p. 182). The results from Legerstee and her colleagues are highly interesting, and we look forward to learning more about the differences between 3- and 6-month-olds.

Elegant as these studies are, they cannot remove one's doubts as to whether a young child can understand what it means to lose a significant relationship. The ability to think of relationships as something that can be wholly or partially lost, and be lost *to* someone else, would seem more cognitively advanced than merely being sad about one's mother being unusually inattentive. Bowlby describes a horrifying case of such a realization in his studies of children separated from their mothers and placed in nurseries (Bowlby, 1973; Robertson & Bowlby, 1952). According to Bowlby, over the span of prolonged separation from their mothers these children go through stages of protest, despair, and, finally, detachment. Studies of children subjected to protracted experiences of jealousy might reveal an analogue of Bowlby's three stages or reaction following separations.

Experiencing the loss of maternal love and attention obviously cannot be induced experimentally. However, even if a threat to the relationship with the mother is likely to be the strongest elicitor of jealousy and jealous despair, this should not lead researchers to exclude the possibility that infants can feel jealous if their relationship to someone else is threatened. On the contrary, it seems that allowing for this possibility when designing further studies opens up the road to a new and informative line of research. As shown in Bradley's studies of infant–peer trios (Bradley, this volume; Selby & Bradley, 2003), relationships that appear sufficiently strong to evoke jealousy may be established within a lab setting. Moreover, it might be possible to test how the child reacts to the experience of losing a relationship to a friendly adult experimenter, and how this affects the child's interpretation of future interactions with adults in a similar setting.

Implications for Empirical Investigations of the Prerequisites for Jealousy

From the above outline of five modes of jealousy, it should be clear that the cognitive and motoric prerequisites of one behavioral mode are different from the prerequisites of another behavioral mode. These behaviors, though partially evident in some infants in some contexts at 7–8 months, are not coordinated with the actions and perceptions of more complete displays of jealousy evident at 12–18 months (Masciuch & Kienapple, 1993). Such discrepancies in behavioral responding by infants may be the result of undeveloped motoric abilities, social understanding, or both. Legerstee and her colleagues (Legerstee et al., this volume) lay out some candidate prerequisites for jealousy early in life with admirable clarity. What we request in addition is greater attention to the range of jealous behavior for which we are postulating cognitive prerequisites. The case of jealousy in autistic spectrum disorder (ASD) illustrates why it is necessary to specify the range of behavioral modes one is trying to explain.

Several authors in this handbook (Bauminger, this volume; Hobson, this volume) argue that the research on jealousy in children with ASD may be helpful in highlighting what capacities are necessary for experiencing jealousy. Children with ASD typically have emotional deficits, but only minor cognitive impairment, leading researchers to think that this population may tell us to what extent cognitive abilities are necessary for a given emotional behavior.

A caveat against drawing too strong conclusions from findings with autistic children is the broad range of characteristics encompassed by this diagnostic label. Not all autistic children are merely normal children with some emotionality subtracted; in fact one may wonder if such a simplistic description fits any children with ASD. For this reason, when we use diagnostic status as a classificatory or blocking variable, we will not know exactly what factors are co-varying with it. Note, for instance, that when Bauminger, Chomsky-Smolkin, Orbach-Caspi, Zachor, and Levy-Shiff (2008) attempted to match normal and autistic preschoolers on mental age, as assessed by the Mullen scales (Mullen, 1997), they ended up with an ASD sample whose average chronological age was 14 months higher than the normal sample (46 vs. 32 months). In this situation, it is hard to say what causes the differences in jealousy manifestation—autism or the child's age.

We strongly agree with Bauminger's (this volume) suggestion that future studies will need to differentiate between subgroups within the autistic spectrum. To understand jealousy in autistic children, we then need to know what modes of jealous behavior the different subgroups of autistic children exhibit. In Bauminger's studies (Bauminger, 2004; Bauminger, this volume; Bauminger et al., 2008), interesting differences emerged between the autistic group and the normative group for both preadolescent and preschool samples. For example, preadolescents with ASD looked less at a rival and parent interacting, but engaged in more attention-seeking and involvement behavior. Yet, only when we know to what extent this pattern is observable in all subgroupings of the autistic spectrum will we be better able to explain the jealous behavior. Hence, we maintain that general conclusions about jealousy based on research with autistic children seem premature.

In uncovering the emergence of jealousy early in life, be it in normal or clinical populations, researchers face a theoretical dilemma (Legerstee et al., this volume). They can either see jealousy as the harbinger of a certain cognitive change, for example interpersonal awareness (Bradley, this volume; Hobson, this volume), or as precluded on logical grounds because the presumed necessary cognitive capacities are not yet in place. If we stop seeing jealousy as an all-or-none phenomenon, but rather as something that takes different forms throughout development, we can also stop seeing these cognitive capacities as all-or-none phenomena. As Hobson argues, it is conceivable, and indeed likely, that only some forms of interpersonal awareness are necessary for experiencing jealousy.

The experience of jealousy should not be assumed to be the same across all stages of development. Nor is jealousy ever an invariant state, be it in the infant or the mature adult. Rather, as Shakespeare may well have understood, the feeling of being jealous is largely determined by the goals of the jealous person and the directedness of the emotion. Like Desdemona's husband Othello, we may feel betrayed by our beloved, we may be angry at and humiliated by our rival, and we may experience fear and even sadness over the prospects of losing a significant other. Each of Othello's possible modes of responding is in the effort at coping with the jealous situation. However, Othello's killing of Desdemona will seem at odds with his great love for her only if one fails to take into account the target and goal of the jealous response. More than anything else, it is this multifarious collection of partly contradicting goals that makes jealousy a complex emotion.

Acknowledgments

The preparation of this paper was made possible by grant HD-39925 from the National Institute of Child Health and Human Development to the first author, and another grant, from the Amini Foundation, to the first and second authors.

Note

1   The notion of behavioral modes is related to, but not identical with, Frijda's term "action tendency." For Frijda, an "action tendency is readiness for different actions having the same intent" (Frijda, 1986, p. 70). In jealousy, the ultimate goal is to cope with the unpleasant state of being jealous, hence all jealousy behavior can be seen as expressing the same action tendency. At the same time, achieving this goal will involve the achievement of one or more sub-goals, for example either breaking up with one's girlfriend or reestablishing one's exclusive position as the one and only boyfriend. In the terminology we are proposing, the action tendency of jealousy can be expressed through multiple behavioral modes.

References

Barrett, K., & Campos, J. (1987). Perspectives on emotional development II: A functionalist approach to emotions. In J. Osofsky (Ed.), *Handbook of infant development* (2nd ed., pp. 555–578). New York: Wiley.

Bauminger, N. (2004). The expression and understanding of jealousy in children with autism. *Development and Psychopathology, 16,* 157–177.

Bauminger, N. (this volume). Jealousy in children with autism spectrum disorder (ASD). In S. L. Hart & M. Legerstee (Eds.), *Handbook of jealousy: Theory, research, and multidisciplinary approaches.* Malden, MA: Wiley-Blackwell.

Bauminger, N., Chomsky-Smolkin, L., Orbach-Caspi, E., Zachor, D., & Levy-Shiff, R. (2008). Jealousy and emotional responsiveness in young children with ASD. *Cognition and Emotion, 22,* 595–619.

Boucher, J. D., & Brant, M. E. (1981). Judgment of emotion: American and Malay antecedents. *Journal of Cross-Cultural Psychology, 12,* 272–283.

Bowlby, J. (1973). *Attachment and loss: Vol. 2. Separation anxiety and anger.* New York: Basic Books.

Bradley, B. S. (this volume). Jealousy in infant–peer trios: From narcissism to culture. In S. L. Hart & M. Legerstee (Eds.), *Handbook of jealousy: Theory, research, and multidisciplinary approaches.* Malden, MA: Wiley-Blackwell.

Bryson, J. B. (1991). Modes of response to jealousy-evoking situations. In P. Salovey (Ed.), *The psychology of jealousy and envy* (pp. 178–205). New York: Guilford Press.

Buss, A. H., Iscoe, I., & Buss, E. H. (1979). The development of embarrassment. *Journal of Psychology: Interdisciplinary and Applied, 103,* 227–230.

Buss, D. M., & Haselton, M. (2005). The evolution of jealousy. *Trends in Cognitive Sciences, 9*(11), 506–507.

Buss, D. M., Larsen, R. J., Westen, D., & Semmelroth, J. (1992). Sex differences in jealousy: Evolution, physiology, and psychology. *Psychological Science, 3,* 251–255.

Draghi-Lorenz, R. (this volume). Parental reports of jealousy in early infancy: Growing tensions between evidence and theory. In S. L. Hart & M. Legerstee (Eds.), *Handbook of jealousy: Theory, research, and multidisciplinary approaches.* Malden, MA: Wiley-Blackwell.

Frijda, N. H. (1986). *The emotions.* Cambridge: Cambridge University Press.

Gesell, A. L. (1906). Jealousy. *The American Journal of Psychology, 17,* 437–496.

Hart, S. L. (this volume). The ontogenesis of jealousy in the first year of life: A theory of jealousy as a biologically-based dimension of temperament. In S. L. Hart & M. Legerstee (Eds.), *Handbook of jealousy: Theory, research, and multidisciplinary approaches.* Malden, MA: Wiley-Blackwell.

Hart, S. L., & Carrington, H. A. (2002). Jealousy in 6-month-old infants. *Infancy, 3,* 395–402.

Hart, S. L., Carrington, H. A., Tronick, E. Z., & Carroll, S. R. (2004). When infants lose exclusive maternal attention: Is it jealousy? *Infancy, 6,* 57–78.

Hart, S. L., Field, T., del Valle, C., & Letourneau, M. (1998a). Infants protest their mothers' attending to an infant-size doll. *Social Development, 7*(1), 54–61.

Hart, S. L., Field, T., Letourneau, M., & del Valle, C. (1998b). Jealousy protests in infants of depressed mothers. *Infant Behavior and Development, 21,* 137–148.

Hobson, R. P. (this volume). Is jealousy a complex emotion? In S. L. Hart & M. Legerstee (Eds.), *Handbook of jealousy: Theory, research, and multidisciplinary approaches.* Malden, MA: Wiley-Blackwell.

Legerstee, M., Ellenbogen, B., Neinhuis, T., & Marsh, H. (this volume). Social bonds, triadic relationships, and goals: Preconditions for the emergence of human jealousy. In S. L. Hart & M. Legerstee (Eds.), *Handbook of jealousy: Theory, research, and multidisciplinary approaches*. Malden, MA: Wiley-Blackwell.

Lewis, M. (2000). Self-conscious emotions: Embarrassment, pride, shame, and guilt. In M. Lewis & J. M. Haviland-Jones (Eds.), *Handbook of emotion* (2nd ed., pp. 623–636). New York: Guilford Press.

Masciuch, S., & Kienapple, K. (1993). The emergence of jealousy in children 4 months to 7 years of age. *Journal of Social and Personal Relationships, 10*, 421–435.

Mascolo, M. F., & Fischer, K. W., (1995). Developmental transformations for appraisals for pride, shame, and guilt. In J. P. Taney & K. W. Fischer (Eds.), *Self-conscious emotions: The psychology of shame, guilt, embarrassment, and pride* (pp. 64–113). New York: Guilford Press.

Miller, A. L., Volling, B. L., & McElwain, N. L. (2000). Sibling jealousy in a triadic context with mothers and fathers. *Social Development, 9*, 433–457.

Mullen, E. M. (1997). *Mullen scales of early learning*. Los Angeles: Western Psychological Service.

Mullen, P. E. (1990). A phenomenology of jealousy. *Australian and New Zealand Journal of Psychiatry, 24*, 17–28.

Plutchik, R. (1982). A psycho evolutionary theory of emotions. *Social Science Information, 21*, 529–553.

Proust, M. (1989). *Swann's way* (C. K. Scott Moncrieff & T. Kilmartin, Trans.). New York: Random House.

Robertson, J., & Bowlby, J. (1952). Responses of young children to separation from their mothers. *Courrier du Centre International de l'Enfance, 2*, 131–142.

Rozin, P., & Fallon, A. E. (1987). A perspective on disgust. *Psychological Review, 94*, 23–41.

Rydell, R. J., & Bringle, R. G. (2007). Differentiating reactive and suspicious jealousy. *Social Behavior and Personality, 35*, 1099–1114.

Selby, J. M., & Bradley, B. S. (2003). Infants in groups: A paradigm for the study of early social experience. *Human Development, 46*, 197–221.

Shackelford, T. K., Voracek, M., Schmitt, D. P., Buss, D. M., Weekes-Shackelford, V. A., & Michalski, R. L. (2004). Romantic jealousy in early adulthood and in later life. *Human Nature, 15*, 283–300.

Sternberg, C. R., & Campos, J. J. (1990). The development of anger expressions in infancy. In N. L. Stein, B. Leventhal, & T. Trabasso (Eds.), *Psychological and biological approaches to emotion* (pp. 247–282). Hillsdale, NJ: Erlbaum.

Tracy, J. L., Robins, R.W., & Tangney, J.P. (2007). *The self-conscious emotions: Theory and research*. New York: Guilford Press.

Volling, B. L., Kennedy, D. E., & Jackey, L. M. H. (this volume). The development of sibling jealousy. In S. L. Hart & M. Legerstee (Eds.), *Handbook of jealousy: Theory, research, and multidisciplinary approaches*. Malden, MA: Wiley-Blackwell.

Volling, B. L., McElwain, N. L., & Miller, A. L. (2002). Emotion regulation in context: The jealousy complex between young siblings and its relations with child and family characteristics. *Child Development, 73*, 581–600.

White, G. L., & Mullen, P. E. (1989). *Jealousy: Theory, research, and clinical strategies*. New York: Guilford Press.

Wittgenstein, L. (1958). *Philosophical investigations*. Oxford: Blackwell.

Part IV

Social-Emotional Foundations within the Parent–Child–Sibling Context

15

A Theoretical Model of the Development of Jealousy
Insight through Inquiry into Jealousy Protest

Sybil L. Hart

Natalie was a pleasant and "easy" 9-month-old. Arriving to pick her up from the childcare center where she spent 2 days per week, I peeked through the window only to find her standing up in her crib, rattling the bars, and screaming. After carrying on in this manner for a few moments, she suddenly stopped screaming, sat down, and started to play. Later, I was to learn that it had been the sight of Linda, the assistant teacher, changing another infant's diaper that had been the focus of Natalie's rage. On the next occasion when Natalie was to spend the day in childcare I was about to leave her, as usual, in the arms of the head teacher when it occurred to me that perhaps I had been misinterpreting my daughter's protests on my departures. Instead of saying "don't leave me," maybe she was saying, "don't leave me *with the wrong caregiver.*" So, this time, instead of placing my baby in the arms of the head teacher, I left her with Linda; and from that day onward, Natalie no longer protested when I departed as she had done regularly in the past.

A second outburst was to take place several months later, when Natalie was 12 months old, and I took her to visit the home of cousins who had invited the extended family to welcome their newborn infant. In full view of Natalie, still strapped into a carrier and cheerfully engaged with a toy, I slowly and deliberately picked up the newborn infant as he began to cry. Instantaneously, Natalie's face contorted into a caricature of anger. Her eyebrows, normally positioned like quotation marks beside her eyes, flashed together into the shape of the letter V. Her lips parted and formed a square, showing the place where canine teeth would be if she had teeth. She thrashed her arms and legs, flushed a dark shade of red and screamed. After a few seconds, I abruptly put the baby down. Equally abruptly, Natalie stopped screaming and resumed playing.

Dumbfounded by this uncharacteristically sharp reaction, and curious as to whether its pairing with my attention to another child could have been

Handbook of Jealousy: Theory, Research and Multidisciplinary Approaches, First Edition.
Edited by Sybil L. Hart and Maria Legerstee.
© 2013 Blackwell Publishing Ltd. Published 2013 by Blackwell Publishing Ltd.

coincidental, I repeated the event that I thought had provoked it. This time Natalie erupted with a level of rage that is indescribable. Within seconds, her explosion threw the entire household into commotion. Everyone, from her sisters to her grandparents to distant family members, including males, females, parents, non-parents, adults, and children, clamored in tumultuous unison as if reading from the very same script, written by Natalie herself, demanding that I put the baby down. I complied just as Natalie's eyes began to well up with tears. This time she was not easily placated. Even after her trembling had subsided, she refused to be removed from my lap for the remainder of the visit. Not once have I ever seen a human being as angry as Natalie was on that day.

My daughter's three outbursts sparked numerous questions about the nature and meaning of such behavior. Through asking when, where, how, and why the young child is disturbed by maternal attention toward another child, this chapter seeks to inform understanding of child–caregiver and child–child relationships. Based on attention to these four questions, the final section seeks broadened understanding of jealousy itself. Toward this end, we close by offering refined definitions of jealousy and a theoretical model of its development.

When Is Jealousy Displayed?

For many parents, especially those of only one child, the arrival of a newborn infant sibling marks their first encounter with child jealousy. Almost unequivocally, a sibling's arrival has been found stressful to older children (Dunn, Kendrick, & MacNamee, 1981; Field & Reite, 1984; Gottlieb & Mendelson, 1990; Legg, Sherick, & Wadland, 1974; Nadelman & Begun, 1982; Stewart, Mobley, Van Tuyl, & Salvador, 1987; Volling, 2005). In light of wide individual differences in older siblings' adjustment and out of concern for those who become highly disturbed, the transition to older sibling is a period that has received considerable attention in popular literature and empirical works, as both clinicians and researchers seek to explain and remedy children's disturbances (Campbell, 2006; Kramer & Ramsburg, 2002; Volling, 2005).

These efforts have brought to light three types of circumstances that contribute to older siblings' distress. The first pertains to maternal separation during hospitalization for childbirth. During maternal absence, Field and Reite (1984) observed increases in toddlers' heart rate, negative affect, night walking, and crying. Trause et al. (1981) found that distress during maternal hospitalization was mitigated among toddlers who were permitted to visit their mothers during hospitalization. The second type of contributor pertains to the quality of interactive experiences with mother. As mothers become burdened by the increased physical and emotional demands of pregnancy, childbirth, and caring for several young children, the quality of interactions with their firstborn children is diminished (Baydar, Greek, & Brooks-Gun, 1997; Dunn & Kendrick, 1981; Feiring, Lewis, & Jaskir, 1983; Stewart et al., 1987; Taylor & Kogan, 1973). Others (Teti, Sakin, Kucera, Corns, & Das Eiden, 1996; Touris, Kromelow, & Harding, 1995) have noted destabilization in the quality of attachment security, which for some dyads entails transition from secure to insecure.

Although it seems clear that firstborn children are disturbed by separation from mother and by reduced quality of mother–child interactions, it is unlikely that either of these sorts of adversities can ever fully account for child difficulties during the transition to older sibling. One limitation is the implicit assumption that jealousy is an externally driven phenomenon that is attributable entirely to environmental influences, particularly those involving the mother. If this were true, we would expect to find children displaying lesser distress in situations where the arrival of a newborn sibling does *not* coincide with separation from mother or lowered quality of mother–child interactions. However, support for this prediction is lacking. In fact, it is markedly absent in research on experimentally induced jealousy (Draghi-Lorenz, 1998; Hart, this volume, Chapter 4; Hart & Carrington, 2002; Hart, Field, del Valle, & Letourneau, 1998a; Masciuch & Kienapple, 1993), in which the object of maternal attention is manipulated (see Chapter 4 for more detail on jealousy evocation) and in which mothers generally had *not* been pregnant, and so these children had *not* been systematically exposed to maternal separation or diminished quality of mother–child interactions. Nonetheless, they were most upset when the object of their mothers' attention was another child.

A third type of explanation for child disturbances upon a sibling's arrival has been derived from observations that confrontations between mother and first-born child are increased during situations in which mothers are preoccupied with the newborn infant. The older child is then faced with having to cope with maternal attention that is reduced in absolute quantity and in amounts relative to another child (Bryant & Crockenberg, 1980; Dunn, 1985). This situation has been interpreted as representing differential treatment or favoritism, a triadic inter-active context that can spark rivalry (Dunn, 1985; Miller, Volling, & McElwain, 2000; Teti & Ablard, 1989; Volling, Kennedy, & Jackey, this volume, Chapter 17; Volling, McElwain, & Miller, 2002; Vandell & Bailey, 1992).

One problem with reliance on differential treatment as an explanation for child disturbances on a sibling's arrival is that it leads to difficulty explaining reactivity to experimentally induced jealousy by children who are firstborn. The consistent finding (Hart, this volume; Hart & Carrington, 2002; Hart et al., 1998a) that infants who are onlies do not differ from those who have siblings despite their lesser history of exposure to differential treatment is perplexing.

Another difficulty with reliance on differential treatment as an explanation for child disturbances on a sibling's arrival stems from the short latency with which infants react to jealousy evocation. In laboratory studies, observations are conducted within episodes that are only 60 seconds in duration. Often, mood deterioration is noticeable within a matter of seconds, and so, even the 60-second episode is too long for some infants, and must be terminated early. In the anecdotal account of Natalie at the opening of this chapter, jealousy was induced twice in succession by me, and each time, her response was sudden, as if turned on by the flip of a switch. As illustrated by Nathan, the firstborn, 1-year-old male depicted in Figures 15.1 and 15.2, heightened vigilance can be triggered by even fleeting exposure to differential treatment. This particular child froze within seconds of noticing his mother turn toward a toy baby (actually a lifelike doll handled like a real infant). A similar pattern of reactivity could be noted in Victoria, the 6-month-old female presented in Figure 15.3. When her mother attended to a storybook, she was "impassive and a little bored" (Wingert & Brant, 2005, August 15, p. 33), but when faced with maternal attention being turned toward a toy baby, her response prompted the description, "soon she's beet red and crying so hard it looks like she might spit up" (Wingert & Brant, 2005, August 15, p. 33). Notably, this child's acute reaction was forecasted by the expression of wariness, illustrated in Figure 15.3, which she displayed *before* her mother even touched the toy baby. These anecdotal and empirical accounts uphold Bowlby's observation that "the mere sight" of another child in mother's arms is "enough" (1969, p. 260) to provoke child disturbances.

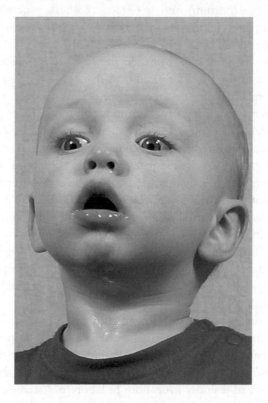

Figure 15.1

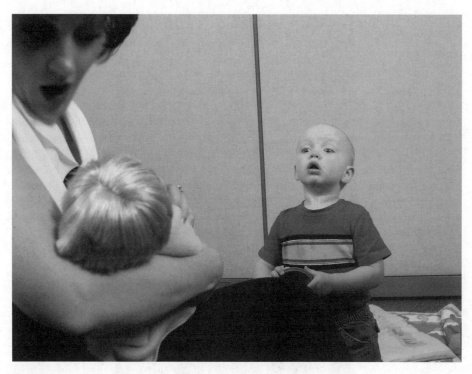

Figure 15.2
Caption for figure 15.1–15.2   Nathan, a firstborn 1-year-old, displays heightened vigilance as his mother turns her attention toward a toy baby
Source: Photos by Kenny Braun, courtesy of Sybil L. Hart, Texas Tech University

We would submit that the speed of an infant's negative reaction to jealousy evocation, and the fact that it is displayed equivalently by onlies and non-onlies, mark exquisite sensitivity to loss exclusivity, or what is referred to here as jealousy. Moreover, we argue that when exposure to loss of exclusivity in a valued relationship elicits jealousy, it does so independently of other types of elicitors, such as differential treatment. We propose that sensitivity to loss of exclusivity arises from the child's active involvement in generating the interpretation that the context in which another child receives mother's attention is one that represents threat. We hold that this stimulus is disturbing *prior* to experiences of differential treatment because the perception of exclusivity within a valued relationship is of inherent value, and so its loss is inherently painful.

Because infant jealousy usually does not present until the arrival of a newborn sibling, it is rarely considered in advance of this juncture. This is unfortunate since a sibling's arrival coincides with a constellation of changes and adversities, resulting in difficulty capturing the independent effects of any single factor. While there have been some attempts to unravel the interwoven effects of various

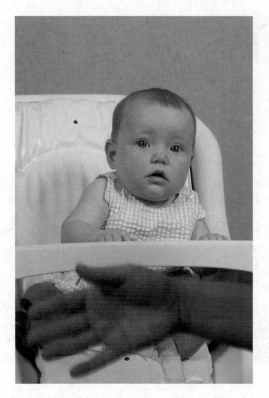

Figure 15.3   Victoria, a 6-month-old female, exhibits wariness as her mother turns toward a toy baby

Source: Photos by Kenny Braun, courtesy of Sybil L. Hart, Texas Tech University

environmental stressors, child characteristics have received limited attention, and these rare efforts have consisted of attention to more diffuse dimensions of temperament, such as irritability, thus far only tenuously linked with jealousy. Others have employed longitudinal approaches which explore change trajectories following a newborn's arrival. Though important toward establishing continuity across age, these have rarely separated environmental factors from child characteristics. Further, by starting around the time of a newborn's arrival, early types of sensitivities and experiences which could be pivotal toward the differentiation of early jealousy, such as those involved in molding expectancies of receiving preferential treatment, cannot receive proper investigative attention since the dyadic contexts in which they emerged no longer exist.

Insight into the nature of disturbances upon a sibling's arrival may be advanced by attention to the child's active role in precipitating negative reactivity. In addition to an innately based sensitivity to loss of exclusivity in concert with other, more diffuse dimensions of temperament, child factors may be found to differ with perceptions, expectations, or working models of exclusivity. Importantly, productive approaches toward this end should include longitudinal designs in which the period surrounding a newborn sibling's arrival represents an end point, or perhaps a turning point, rather than a starting point. By directing investigative attention to processes that take place well before a sibling's arrival, it may be possible to isolate child characteristics that contribute to reactions to a sibling's arrival so that these can later be parsed from external stressors with which they inevitably become confounded. Especially productive longitudinal approaches may be those in which the newborn's arrival is cast as a stressor in and of itself. As in research on infant reactions to other types of constitutionally based stressors, such as inoculation, insight into reactivity to a newborn sibling's arrival may be informed through models in which it too is understood as a response to a stimulus that is inherently painful. Moreover, it may be another in which parental behavior in the immediate situation is not found to be directly linked with child reactivity (De Wolf & van IJzendoorn, 1997; Lewis & Ramsay, 1999). In articulating the manner through which parental behavior drives infant stress responses, Lewis and Ramsay (1999) point to the impact of a child's general well-being. They note that while qualities of distress responses are poorly predicted by parental behavior in the immediate setting, they do appear to be consistent with a history of everyday interactions with caregivers which engender positive emotionality in the face of adversity.

In sum, not only do we propose that an early form of jealousy is evident before the arrival of a sibling, we argue that it is discernible prior to exposure to differential treatment. This contention leads to suggesting that disturbances associated with loss of exclusivity are organized independently of those associated with another known elicitor of jealousy, that is, differential treatment. Clarity in understanding jealousy as an outcome of expectancies of exclusivity is greatly needed in order to shed light on jealousy in its most fundamental form.

Where Is Jealousy Displayed?

The context most frequently associated with jealousy in the young child is the familial setting which includes parents and siblings. Concepts of sibling rivalry and displacement, and their universality and inevitability within the family system, are themes that have been elaborated on by psychodynamic and neo-Freudian theorists (Adler, 1959; Dreikurs, 1964; Levy, 1934; S. Freud, 1920), and have become firmly entrenched in modern Western tradition. Yet, the familial context is not the sole arena in which child jealousy is displayed.

Accounts of jealousy among institutionalized peers over nurses and non-parent caregivers have been recorded in a number of works, including several that have been exceptionally influential (Bowlby, 1973; Bridges, 1932; A. Freud & Dann, 1947; Gesell, 1906). Bridges' account of peer rivalry among orphans in Canada contributed to the foundation of a hierarchical theory of emotion which served as a basis for later models of emotional development. With greater attention to detailing the manner in which early jealousy is displayed, Gesell (1906) reported a number of cases, including an account of a 4-year-old female who had been hospitalized for over a year. In situations where her nurse turned attention toward a rival, presumably another patient, the girl engaged in four types of behaviors: (1) efforts, such as talking and coaxing, to redirect attention from the rival toward herself; (2) sulking; (3) adopting bizarre and uncomfortable physical postures, perhaps to attract sympathetic attention; and (4) outbursts of self-injurious behaviors that without adult intervention could be life-threatening.

Possibly the most influential account of jealousy was that reported by Freud and Dann (A. Freud & Dann, 1947) within their classic account of 6 German-Jewish children who were relocated to an English orphanage during the Nazi Holocaust. These cases would later receive considerable attention from Bowlby. The first volume of his *Attachment and Loss* trilogy opened by citing these cases among, "observations to be explained" (1969, p. 24). The second volume opened, once again, with attention to jealousy in these children:

> the children became strongly possessive of their nurse and acutely jealous whenever she gave attention to another child. (Bowlby, 1973, p. 3)

Setting the tone for the volume's formulations on *Separation: Anxiety and Anger,* Bowlby called attention to the importance of understanding the basis of jealousy's emergence by reflecting on the origins of acute jealousy:

> Why, it may be asked, should these children have become so strongly possessive of their nurse and so deeply distressed whenever she was missing? Was it, as some traditionalists might suppose, that they had been spoiled by having been given too much attention and allowed too much their own way? Or was it, by contrast, that since leaving home they had been subjected to too many changes of mother figure and/or had too limited access to whoever in the nursery was acting temporarily as their mother figure? (1973, pp. 3–4)

Since these reports of jealousy were based on orphans who, in addition to having endured parental death and abandonment, had suffered trauma through exposure to war, relocation, and institutionalization, and who exhibited atypical behaviors suggesting severe disturbance (Bowlby, 1969, 1973), it may not be surprising that Bowlby entertained the notion, and also contributed to growing consensus (Clanton, 2001; Stearns, 1989), that acute jealousy in a child's relationship with a caregiver marks atypical development.

Perhaps due to the enormous weight of these exceptionally compelling cases, lesser attention has been directed to reports of jealousy among non-siblings under circumstances that are more normative. According to one such account, by

Brazelton (1983), 11-month-old Laura demonstrated an intense emotional outburst in response to observing her mother attend to a friend's infant:

> Laura became frantic, whimpering and pulling on the baby's cloths and extremities to dislodge him. After he was put down, Laura sat huddled in her mother's lap, sucking her fingers, as if she did not dare leave her lap again. (Brazelton, 1983, p. 255)

It is notable that this anecdote was mentioned within a detailed, month-by-month account of development across the first year, in which the frantically jealous Laura was featured as the prototypic example of development in the infant who, like the normally placid Natalie, is mild tempered. Further evidence that jealousy, even intense jealousy, is normative in young children may be drawn from reports of its expression by infants receiving care in Israeli communal childrearing settings, known as *kibbutzim*. In this setting, jealousy over caregivers, or *metaplot*, has been described as "widespread" (Faigin, 1957), and for the most part, these are typical infants who are *not* orphans, refugees, or children suffering from illnesses that entail extended hospitalization and separation from parents (Maital & Bornstein, 2003; Sagi et al., 1995; van IJzendoorn & Sagi, 1999).

Reports such as these lead to suggesting that in some form, jealousy's presentation outside familial settings is normative. Some support for this suggestion may be derived from recent research on social interaction within childcare centers among triads consisting of a target infant, a same-age peer, and a caregiver (Roetzel & Hart, 2007). Each target infant in this study was ignored briefly while his childcare worker directed positive vocal affect exclusively toward either a child or a storybook from which she read aloud. As in similar work (Bauminger, this volume, Chapter 12) in which the caregiver was the infant's mother (instead of a childcare worker), infants were more distressed when the object of caregiver attention was a child. Interestingly, evidence of jealousy emerged only among the infants who were enrolled in higher-quality childcare. Why infants in lower-quality childcare failed to display evidence of jealousy is unclear. One possibility is that within these centers, infant–caregiver relationships were of lesser value and thus, differential treatment may have represented lesser cause for disturbance, much as has been found in instances where differential treatment has occurred at the hands of depressed mothers and strangers (Hart et al., 1998a; Hart, Field, Letourneau, & del Valle, 1998b; Hart, Jones, & Field, 2003). It is also reminiscent of findings on inversed affect sharing (Hart, this volume, Chapter 4) which revealed that infants are less upset by their mothers' attention to another child if the mother was exhibiting neutral rather than positive affect.

Given the endurance of classic reports on rivalry among institutionalized children, it is puzzling that jealousy's presentation within non-familial settings has received so little investigative attention. Some reluctance may have arisen from concerns that attention to jealousy within non-parental relationships could detract from monotropic views of attachment, in which the mother is regarded as the principal attachment figure (Lewis, this volume, Chapter 2). Indeed, as I left my infant daughter looking exceptionally contented as she nestled comfortably into the loving embrace of the childcare worker over whom she had exploded with jealousy, a thought that crossed my mind was: Does the expectancy of receiving exclusive attention in one relationship preclude such an expectancy within another? The answer arrived 3 months later, when Natalie erupted with jealousy which this time was elicited by me; and confirmed eventually by findings that children expect exclusive attention from both mothers and fathers (Miller et al., 2000; Volling et al., 2002). Apparently, the answer is no. The possibility that having an expectancy of receiving exclusive attention in one relationship does not preclude such an expectancy within another begs numerous questions. Some pertain to whether expectancies of exclusivity across multiple relationships progress independently, sequentially, or hierarchically. Others pertain to qualitative differences across various concurrent relationships. In addition to advancing insight into jealousy, answers to these questions may help inform understanding of the concept of monotropism, and yield insight into the integral role of exclusivity and fidelity in love relationships beyond infancy. What is more, inquiry into jealousy in multiple relationships might reveal that jealousy is not limited to attachment relationships. Following social network systems models of relationships, wherein children's various needs for care, protection, play, and education are met by an array of persons (Lewis, 2005), each of whom can distribute these resources among an array of children, future studies may show that some of these individuals may too hold potential for evoking jealousy (Dyck, this volume, Chapter 21). Though valued, some of these individuals may *not* serve as a secure base.

In sum, by a large margin, developmental research on child jealousy has focused on the mother–child–sibling triad. The narrowness of this focus is striking when considering what most would agree is jealousy's broad presence throughout the fabric of interpersonal functioning. Given the extraordinary endurance of classic accounts of rivalry among non-siblings, and in light of newly emerging empirical works which probe jealousy as an intra- and extra-familial phenomenon, it would appear that inquiry into triads beyond the parent–child–sibling triad are both feasible and potentially illuminating. Thus, we call for attention to jealousy in broader, and possibly quite numerous, types of contexts, and in the presence as well as the absence of attachment figures.

How Is Jealousy Displayed?

Numerous depictions of jealousy's structural features comment on the prominence of contacts that are parent-directed. For example, Bowlby (1969) noted:

In most young children the mere sight of mother holding another baby in her arms
is enough to elicit strong attachment behavior. (p. 260)

He noted further that an "older child insists on remaining close to his mother, or
on climbing on her lap" (1969, p. 260), an observation that he found reminiscent of
"clinging" to the mother, as had previously been recognized by Levy (1937). The
interpretation of a child's jealous behavior as a presentation of attachment behavior is being upheld by a growing body of work on the manner in which jealousy is
displayed by infants and young children (Fearon et al., this volume, Chapter 16).

Toddlers' proximal responses toward parents have been considered central
within various types of global measures of protest. To index rivalry, Teti and
Ablard (1989) coded rates of *distract*, a response consisting of verbal responses,
such as calling for the mother's attention, as well as physical behaviors, such as
placing oneself between mother and rival, hence drawing maternal attention
away from the rival and toward the self. Masciuch and Kienapple's (1993)
qualitative data noted the child's calling to the mother, trying to climb onto the
mother's lap, and verbalizing phrases, such as, "Me too, I come too." In research
on children's reactions to observing their parents display affection toward each
other, the investigators (Cummings, Zahn-Waxler, & Radke-Yarrow, 1981) coded
jealous affection, a response denoted by a child interrupting the parents and
behaving affectionately toward only one parent while attempting to divert all of
that parent's affectionate attention toward herself.

The predictability of observing parent-directed proximity-seeking behavior as a
response to jealousy evocation is further illustrated by our own work in which
these types of responses were coded separately from those pertaining to affect.
When exposed to a jealousy evocation episode in which their mothers' exclusive
attention was being directed toward a toy baby, we found that 1-year-olds
maintained proximity to their mothers during approximately 60% of the episode,
while in a control condition in which maternal attention was directed toward a
book, proximal behavior was displayed for only about half that amount of time
(Hart et al., 1998a, 1998b). Perhaps due to the more troublesome nature of
jealousy's negative affectivity, components of response, such as proximity seeking,
have been somewhat overlooked. Despite being overshadowed by more obvious
and compelling elements of affective response, data suggest that the most
predictable form of response to jealousy evocation involves the child seeking
proximal contact with a caregiver.

This being the case, and in line with Bowlby's interpretation, we maintain that
while jealousy is expressed via a wide range of behaviors, including clinging,
calling, distracting, and jealous affection, a central feature is proximity seeking, a
response which suggests activation of the attachment system. Further support for
this conceptualization of jealousy may be derived from newly emerging reports
from the field of neuropsychology which identify compatible patterns of response
in terms of neurological activity. During exposure to jealousy evocation, both

adults (Harmon-Jones, Peterson, & Harris, 2009) and infants (Jones & Mize, 2009) exhibit greater left frontal cortical activation, a pattern of brain activation that is consistent with approach motivation.

Despite the regularity with which attachment behavior is displayed by infants in these types of situations, it is exhibited in many different ways, and so difficulties arise in the matter of discerning whether or not a particular type of response represents psychopathology. Even Bowlby seemed perplexed by this quandary. Having placed considerable emphasis on jealousy as an outcome of maternal deprivation, suggesting origins in psychopathology, he nevertheless acknowledged that jealousy arises even under conditions that are benign. Tellingly, his willingness to consider jealousy as having *non*-pathological origins is reflected in the comment,

> It is possible that this well-known behavior is only a special case of a child reacting to mother's lack of attention and lack of responsiveness to him. The fact, however, that an older child often reacts in this way even when his mother makes a point of having been attentive and responsive suggests that more is involved. (1969, pp. 260–261)

Such conjecture notwithstanding, jealousy's development under benign conditions has received scant attention. Some insight into normative versus atypical jealousy can be derived from efforts to explore whether presentations of jealousy differ with risk and protective influences, such as those associated with attachment security and maternal responsivity. In a work on experimentally induced jealousy among siblings, Teti and Ablard (1989) found that 18-month-olds with secure (versus insecure) attachment displayed less protest and aggression, suggesting reduced jealousy. Yet, laboratory research by Hart and associates (Hart, Carrington, Tronick, & Carroll, 2004; Hart et al., 1998b) reported that mothers who had displayed greater sensitivity and reciprocity in dyadic interactions, and who had reported fewer symptoms of depression, had infants who responded to jealousy evocation with heightened protest, proximity seeking, and negative affectivity.

Why would protective influences predict attenuated jealousy in one line of work and acute jealousy in another? One possibility relates to methodological differences, especially those stemming from use of a sibling versus non-sibling to induce jealousy. Use of a sibling could tap patterns of response that are habitual, and so responses elicited during a laboratory procedure may have reflected patterns that had been established and regulated through prior experience. A second, and not incompatible, possibility is that the relationship between protective influences and the magnitude of jealousy's expression is curvilinear, in which case, acute *and* attenuated responses can represent abnormality if they are sufficiently extreme. It may be that an acute presentation of jealousy, such as that of the hospitalized girl who displayed self-injurious behavior (Gesell, 1906), is as rare as the less obvious case of a depressed mother's child in one of our studies

(Hart et al., 1998b) who displayed no sign of disturbance whatsoever. According to this formulation, protective influences should be associated with levels of distress that are moderate, while risk factors should be found associated with both acute *and* attenuated levels of distress. This prediction contrasts with popular uni-polar views and disease models of jealousy in which risk factors are generally associated only with acute jealousy.

To address this prediction, ongoing research (Hart & Behrens, 2008) has been exploring whether presentations of jealousy differ with quality of attachment security. In this study, a sample of 10-month-olds and their mothers participated in several interaction episodes including one involving jealousy evocation, in which the mother focused affectionate attention toward a toy baby. This procedure was followed 2 months later by a second lab visit during which the Strange Situation Procedure (SSP; Ainsworth, Blehar, Waters, & Wall, 1978; Ainsworth & Wittig, 1969) was administered (by K. Behrens) for assessing quality of attachment security. Results were based on cluster analyses in which durations of infants' displays of touching mother, proximity to mother, clinging and grabbing, and vocalizing, and a score for intensity of distress were used to group infants into three categories of jealous reactivity: Low, Moderate, and High. Comparisons across attachment classifications revealed that infants later identified as secure were more likely to fall within the Moderate group; infants later classified as insecure were more likely to be included in the Low or High clusters. While the generally high rates of mother-directed behaviors lend support for Bowlby's characterization of jealousy evocation as an elicitor of attachment behavior as well as findings of our previous laboratory research with 12-month-olds (Hart et al., 1998a), findings that insecure attachment is associated with both dampened *and* heightened reactivity appear to support the prediction that secure attachment is better described as an elicitor of moderate, rather than lesser, jealousy.

In sum, following Bowlby's observations and growing empirical evidence of the regularity with which maternal attention to another child evokes parent-directed proximal contact by her own child, we have suggested that protest behavior that is displayed in response to jealousy evocation may be construed as attachment behavior. The manner in which caregiver-directed proximal responses are expressed can differ widely and levels of accompanying distress can be severe, while foundations of individual differences are poorly understood. In line with views in the emerging tradition of developmental psychopathology (Achenbach & Edelbrock, 1978; Cicchetti, 1984), we hold that if we are to gain insight into the development of pathological forms of jealousy a key goal of research will entail some integration with basic understanding of early jealousy's ontogenesis under conditions that are normative. This balanced approach may be advanced by work in which normativity is established empirically through associations with protective influences and on the basis of statistical norms which recognize deviations that are both acute and attenuated. Moreover, measurement of the magnitude of global indices of distress will be overly simplistic without considering the range of continua on which differences might lie. Surely these are numerous, but at the very least, it may not be premature to recognize that by parsing attention to the child's approach responses from that toward negative affectivity, it may be possible to identify some of the processes responsible for findings that by as early as 10 months, jealousy's developmental trajectory shows signs of divergence along normative and atypical pathways.

Why Is Jealousy Displayed?

Bowlby observed that the individual with potential to evoke jealousy is the one to whom attachment behavior is directed in general:

> There is strong bias for attachment behavior to become directed mainly toward one particular person and for a child to become strongly possessive of that person. (Bowlby, 1969, p. 308)

Given that attachment behaviors that are elicited in the context of jealousy evocation share structural features with those evoked in other eliciting contexts, one is led to consider: Could the phenomenon of jealousy and other instances of attachment behavior also share a common fundamental basis? Having tapped behavioral interaction research in order to approach factors involved in jealousy's proximate causation, insight into underlying mechanisms may be informed by attention to the issue of ultimate causation.

Bowlby elaborated considerably on the phylogenetic origins of attachment behavior. Drawing on Darwinian principles regarding the adaptive function of behavioral responses which appear to exist universally, and tapping the literatures on ethology and biology, he espoused the view that by ensuring increased contact with a caregiver, attachment propensities evolved due to having served to increase a child's chances of survival. Thus, signaling behaviors, ranging from vocalizing and crying, as well as following and clinging, have been understood as maximizing proximity between the vulnerable child and her caregiver, thus promoting survival (Belsky & Cassidy, 1994; Tooby & Cosmides, 1992). From this standpoint it seems reasonable to extrapolate that caregiver-directed proximity seeking that occurs in the context of jealousy evocation may also serve to enhance chances of survival.

This interpretation requires reconciling some distinctions between conditions that elicit jealousy and those responsible for evoking other instances of attachment behavior. According to Bowlby (1969), the attachment system is triggered by natural cues to danger. Being alone and the presence of predators are cues that have often been construed as central to attachment theory, but there were others, such as loud noises, sudden movements, darkness, and looming objects. Sensitivity to these harbingers of danger is believed to have evolved, and to remain deeply entrenched, due to conditions of the ancestral environment, or Environment of Evolutionary Adaptedness (EEA). In this environment, they were associated with life-threatening events, and mother's role was that of providing a safe haven for the vulnerable child in need of protection from injury and predation.

Since jealousy is triggered in contexts where maternal attention is directed toward a rival, it is logical to posit that this context too may represent a cue to danger. In line with thought that there may be features of the *social* EEA that could represent threat to survival (Simpson, 1999), we submit that infants are genetically programmed to respond to the context in which caregiver attention is directed to another child much as they do when faced with other types of threat. Although threat posed by a rival has not received substantive attention in the literature on attachment, it has been a central topic in the fields of behavioral ecology and evolutionary psychology. Work using animal models has established that interests of parents and offspring are not isomorphic (Hamilton, 1964; Trivers, 1974). A newborn child's arrival can advance parents' chances of passing on their genes, yet its effect on a sibling can be less benign. Parent–offspring conflict ensues from the reality that parental resources are a finite resource, and those which are diverted toward the benefit of one child can come at some cost to another (Forbes, this volume, Chapter 7; Panksepp, this volume, Chapter 6). In addition to draining parental resources, a rival can even display sibling-directed aggression. Drawing on observations of maternal and offspring behavior in birds, Hrdy (1999) commented:

> The same mother who bravely drove away a predator from her nest would not intervene to protect the last-hatched chick from a less ferocious but more lethal enemy, its own older sib. (p. 31)

Certainly, sibling aggression is not unknown among human children (Steinmetz, 1977). Whether it can also be construed as having ever represented threat greater than that posed by a predator is an open question. It can be argued, however, that in the environment inhabited by our human ancestors and as reflected in our current genetic endowment (Bjorklund & Pellegrini, 2002; Eibl-Eibesfeldt, 1989), children were a relatively stable presence. Because humans inhabited a broad variety of geographical and climatic environments, the physical environment of the EEA is believed to have included numerous types of threats. Besides predation, these involved disease, starvation, and harsh climatic conditions. In contrast with the large degree of diversity in physical environments (Simpson, 1999; Simpson & Belsky, 2008), hence instability in the types of threats to which humans became adapted, the social environment may have been relatively static. Thus, threat posed by other children is more likely to have been universal, hence highly likely to have resulted in biological adaptation. Within the small clans where humans are believed to have lived for thousands of generations during human evolutionary history and where some continue to live until this day, most people were related to each other (Bjorklund & Pellegrini, 2002; Devore & Konner, 1974; Tronick, Morelli, & Ivey, 1992), and inevitably, children would have had exposure to other children. Siblings may have been most prominent, but the extended family units are likely to have also included half-siblings, step-siblings, adoptive siblings, and cousins; and to varying degrees, multiple caregiving would have been the norm. In the harsh environment of the EEA, parental resources are likely to have been scarce and so, as among nonhumans, parental investment in one child, either sibling or peer, is likely to have posed real and continuous threat to another child's survival (Buss, 2004; Chisholm, 1996; Lamb, Thompson, Gardner, & Charnov, 1985; Mock & Parker, 1997).

As an evolutionary adaptation to this type of threat, selection fashioned "adaptations in children to manipulate parents toward the children's optimum resource allocation" (Buss, 2004, p. 213). This adaptation yields affectively charged behavioral displays which biologists refer to as parent–offspring conflict. When exhibited by young humans, where they are commonly known as sibling rivalry, these displays may be best understood in terms of their communicative function and goal (Barrett & Campos, 1987; Frijda, 1986; Saarni et al., 2006) toward reallocation of parental resources. Though troublesome, jealousy may be deeply rooted in psychological mechanisms which evolved due to their adaptive function.

Without a doubt, conditions that spark rivalry in modern Western culture are numerous, and most assuredly, many differ from those found in the EEA. Yet, faced with mother's attention being directed toward a sibling or peer, the young child's expression of jealousy through presentation of attachment behavior may have changed little. It is interesting that even in settings far from modern Western tradition, maternal attention to another child has been depicted as sparking attachment behavior, such as that of the Indonesian child presented in Figure 15.4. Described as "a native drawing showing sibling rivalry" by Bateson and Mead (1942; p. 195) in their anthropological study of Balinese culture, this drawing portrays a toddler clinging to his nursing mother as she holds a suckling infant to her breast. Prior to the relatively recent advent of formula feeding, weaning from the breast may have been among the most universal triggers of rivalry across culture and history (Fouts, Hewlett, & Lamb, 2005) as it has been across a range of species (Trivers, 1974). More recently, Japanese mothers reported that their children responded to the birth of a sibling with mother-directed bids for closeness known as *amae* (Behrens, 2004).

One intriguing question pertains to whether rivalry continues to serve an adaptive function among children in modern times. It may be noteworthy that when epidemiological data on child mortality rates are documented by health organizations, including the World Health Organization (WHO, 2006), the United Nations Children's Fund (UNICEF, 2008), and the Centers for Disease Control (CDC, 2009), they are reported according to known risk factors, one of which is maternal fertility rates. Especially in developing nations, the association between mothers' greater number of pregnancies and higher death rates among

Figure 15.4 In their anthropological study of Balinese culture, Bateson and Mead (1942) present a Balinese artist's depiction of sibling rivalry. Reprinted with the permission of the New York Academy of Sciences

children under the age of 5 years has been well established. A related risk factor is close birth spacing. These data suggest that the type of child rival that is most threatening is one that is similar in age. Illustrating the magnitude of this threat to infants in developing countries, a CDC report noted that, "on average, babies born less than 2 years after the previous birth in the family are about twice as likely to die in the first year as babies born after at least a 2-year interval" (CDC, 2000, p. 10). Negative outcomes associated with these risk factors arise often as consequences of their contribution to environmental conditions that impact negatively on breastfeeding (Wachs, Black, & Engle, 2009). This particular pathway to child mortality is tellingly illustrated by estimations that in the developing world, "an infant is 4 times more likely to die if a mother stops any breastfeeding at 2 to 3 months of age than an infant who continues to breastfeed. At 9–12 months, if an infant is not breastfed, the risk of death is 2.3 times greater" (Lawrence & Lawrence, 2005, p. 14). In industrialized nations, large family size is also recognized as compounding risks for poor child outcomes in terms of social and cognitive development (Baydar, Greek, & Brooks-Gun, 1997; Petterson & Albers, 2001; Sameroff, Seifer, & Zax, 1982; Waldrop & Bell, 1966; Zajonc,

1976). In combination with close age spacing, child health may be compromised (Colletto, Segre, Rielli, & Rosario, 2003; Luke & Brown, 2008; Tas, 1990). Added risk factors, especially poverty (Lee et al., 2005; Mitra, Khoury, Hinton, & Carothers, 2004; Radecki, & Beckman, 1992), contribute to negative child outcomes that are associated with impeded access to benefits entailed by breast-feeding (Hart, Boylan, Carroll, Musick, & Lampe, 2003; Hart, Boylan, Border, Carroll, McGunegle, & Lampe, 2004; Hart et al., 2006; Hart, Jackson, & Boylan, forthcoming; Feldman & Eidelman, 2003).

Overall, the very fact that child mortality rates are still routinely accounted for in terms of birth spacing and maternal fertility rates provides compelling evidence that even today, and even in industrialized nations, threats posed by other children are neither inconsequential nor rare. Further, by highlighting risks posed by a child who is close in age, these data point to the *kind* of rival that may be most threatening to young children, hence the type that is most likely to trigger jealousy in children. Adaptation resulting in sensitivity to this type of trigger in particular may help account for findings (Draghi-Lorenz, 1998) that infants are more disturbed by loss of mothers' exclusive attention if the rival is a child rather than an adult.

Finally, it is important to note that within this model of jealousy's phylogenetic origins, the caregiver's role as safe haven from threat is not easily reconciled with that of safe haven *to another child*. Resolution of these seemingly incompatible roles may be advanced by efforts to define maternal sensitivity within contexts of caregiving that are not exclusively dyadic (Fearon et al., this volume). Cost–benefit analyses of behavior that have been used productively by evolutionary theorists, biologists, and behavioral ecologists may provide some useful models for use in future efforts by developmental psychologists and attachment researchers. Indeed, a realistic approach may be one that is willing to concede that in supra-dyadic contexts, optimal caregiving involves trade-offs. Productive works might include investigative attention to parenting strategies of multiparas (Crockenberg & Smith, 1982; Lewis & Kreitzberg, 1979), work grounded in diverse cultural contexts where multiple caregiving is more normative (Keller & Lamm, this volume, Chapter 20; Parkinson, Fischer, & Manstead, 2005), and through use of creative sorts of measures, such as *group-related sensitivity* (Ahnert, Pinquart, & Lamb, 2006). As LeVine and Norman (2008) point out, Bowlby's concept of maternal sensitivity is a moral ideal rooted in Western, child-centered ideology with respect to child rearing. These views, which have sometimes been challenged by cross-cultural research, may be challenged further or perhaps transformed entirely by research in which maternal sensitivity is detailed within contexts that are supra-dyadic.

In sum, by recasting infant jealousy as an expression of attachment behavior, Bowlby's theoretical model of attachment offers an evolutionary rationale for child disturbances that arise when maternal attention is turned toward another child. By prompting caregiver-directed proximity seeking, and thereby protecting a relationship that is vital to survival, these disturbances may be understood as operating much like parent–offspring conflict, toward an adaptive function. The integration of this construal of jealousy within attachment theory rests on widened understanding of cues to danger so as to incorporate threat posed by a rival, especially one that is a close-in-age child, and revised constructions of sensitive caregiving, in which service as a safe haven is extended to more than one child.

A Theoretical Model of the Development of Jealousy

To conclude, we turn to the thought that affective experiences and behavioral expressions of jealousy change with age, and suggest that by exploring jealousy's evolving forms and the timing of changes it may be possible to unearth more fundamental issues which pertain to the processes that are responsible for its development. As Campos and associates (this volume, Chapter 14) point out, jealousy is not the same at different points in life, nor is it clear that any early feature is continuous with later ones. Rather, each early step overlaps with adjacent steps, and so, efforts to track the progression of these steps opens potential to establish the contribution of early features, and possibly to predict or even change developmental outcomes.

Steps associated with changes in jealousy may be based on two types of criteria. The first pertains to differences in function (Campos et al., this volume). Goals may be classed broadly as differing with the degree to which jealousy serves toward preserving survival of the self versus one's genetic endowment and potential offspring. This distinction parallels differences in the type of valued relationships being protected. A second basis of change pertains to conditions under which jealousy is elicited. Here we build on our earlier discussion of jealousy as a response to different kinds of eliciting conditions. We have suggested that endogenously organized sensitivities to exclusivity that are present at birth (Hart, this volume, Chapter 4) are sculpted by social conditions that, at first, involve the shaping of expectancies of exclusivity, and later are elaborated further by exposure to conditions involving differential treatment. In the model being advanced (Figure 15.5), where development is organized according to jealousy's function and conditions responsible for its occurrence, four stages emerge.

(i)   The first stage entails a dimension of temperament that we refer to simply as *jealousy*, and define as a constitutionally based sensitivity to loss of exclusivity in a valued relationship. As we proposed in an earlier chapter (this volume, Chapter 4), temperamental jealousy is endogenously organized but separate from other dimensions of temperament. In the present chapter, we extend this point further by suggesting that as a type of sensitivity that is evident early in development, across multiple valued relationships, and which arises even in the absence of

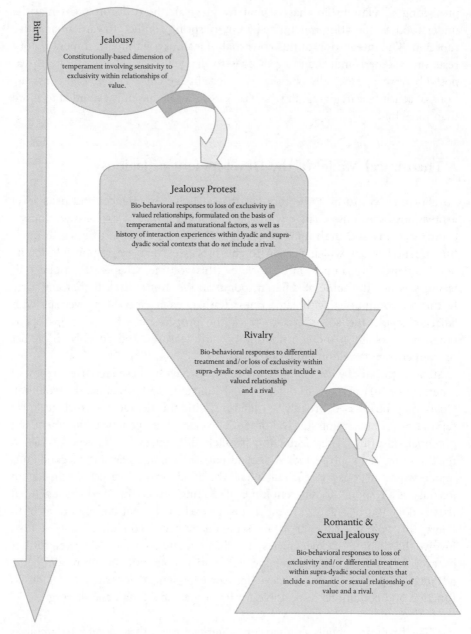

Figure 15.5 Theoretical model of the development of jealousy.

direct experience necessary for learning that exposure to jealousy evocation is an aversive event, jealousy is a robust phenomenon. Its robustness, we propose, is attributable to its being rooted in an evolutionary process comparable to that which is thought to account for parent–offspring conflict since it too is triggered by threat posed by a rival for access to a pool of caregiver resources that is both finite and vital to survival, especially that which is posed by a close-in-age child. In line with this reasoning, jealousy is understood as a mechanism that exists for the purpose of ensuring survival of the self.

(ii)   The second stage entails *jealousy protest* (Hart, del Valle, & Letourneau, 1994) which is defined as a negatively valenced response to loss of a valued person's exclusive attention. It involves bio-behavioral responses that are organized through processes involving endogenous influences that are interwoven with exogenous influences which emerge through the development of expectancies, or internal working models, of receiving exclusive or preferential treatment (Hart et al., 1998a). In light of findings of research on triadic social interaction among caregivers and in line with Bowlby's formulation of jealousy, jealousy protest is exhibited among caregivers by young infants through presentation of attachment behavior. It is also interpreted, like other presentations of attachment behavior, as behavior that is directed toward preserving access to the caregiver, thus functioning toward the aim of ensuring survival of the self.

Infants' expressions of jealousy protest differ widely, and abnormality encompasses atypical presentations that can be displayed as both acute and attenuated reactivity. What governs variation is far from clear, but in all likelihood, variability stems from both child characteristics and external influences. In addition to the exquisiteness of temperamental jealousy, child factors may involve other, more diffuse dimensions of temperament, as well as factors associated with gender (Hart et al., 2004), and concepts of the self as driven by cognitive advances (Hobson, this volume, Chapter 13; Lewis, this volume). External influences appear to relate to social interaction experiences in both dyadic and supra-dyadic types of contexts that impact working models of exclusivity. The importance of a history of dyadic social interaction with caregivers is supported by findings that presentations of jealousy protest differ with maternal characteristics, such as sensitivity, intrusiveness, and depression, as well as quality of attachment security (Hart et al., 1998b; Hart, Jones, & Field, 2003; Hart & Behrens, 2008), and follow from early affectivity which suggests the emotion of love (Hart, this volume, Chapter 4). The importance of supra-dyadic social interaction is suggested by findings on individual differences in the expression of induced jealousy among infants in higher- versus lower-quality childcare (Roetzel & Hart, 2007). It may also be inferred from the growing body of work on the infant's myriad social entry and interactive skills, some more charming than others, that are deployed as the child negotiates social inclusion among caregivers, strangers, and peers, and within families marked by different levels of functioning and different types of dynamics (Bradley, this volume, Chapter 10; Brown, Neff, Shigeto, & Mangelsdorf, 2009; Draghi-Lorenz, this volume, Chapter 11; Fivaz-Depeursinge, Favez, Lavanchy Scaiola, & Lopes, this volume, Chapter 19; Fivaz-Depeursinge & Corboz-Warnery, 1999; Ishikawa & Hay, 2006; Nadel & Tremblay-Leveau, 1999; Nash & Hay, 1993; Striano & Rochat, 1999).

(iii) The third stage involves *rivalry*, in which a valued and formerly exclusive relationship is shared with another child, either sibling or non-sibling. Typically, a display of rivalry is prompted by the awareness of a sibling's presence, and is maintained in familial contexts which include siblings, where differential treatment is, to some extent, inevitable. Elaborating on the previous stage, in which jealousy occurred in situations involving loss of exclusivity, rivalry occurs also in response to differential treatment. We have argued that these two types of precipitating events can, and often do, coexist, but they are not equivalent to each other. In a similar vein, Reddy (this volume, Chapter 8) points out that jealousy can be construed as arising from two distinct types of eliciting events. One involves a sense of equality, in which case, one insists that one's rival receives a fair share of the resources being distributed. The other involves a sense of possessiveness or rights of ownership, a notion that is quite antithetical to ideas of fairness and sharing. In asking which is more fundamental, a sense of fairness or a sense of ownership, she raises a provocative question. It is also one which we believe can be approached through investigative efforts toward parsing effects of *rivalry, defined as sensitivity to differential treatment*, which may relate primarily to the sense of fairness, from those stemming from *jealousy, defined as sensitivity to loss of exclusivity*, which may relate primarily to a sense of ownership. We believe that inquiry of this nature stands to yield insight into perplexing observations, such as those raised by findings that a child can be disturbed when parental attention is directed toward her sibling even though the absolute amount of attention that she herself receives is undiminished, or findings that differential treatment can be disturbing, not only to the child being disfavored, but to the one being favored as well (Bryant & Crockenberg, 1980; Fearon et al., this volume). Perhaps these situations are upsetting because they are an affront to a child's sense of fairness. Alternatively, it may be shown that they are offensive due to serving as bitter reminders that access to a caregiver, though fair or even marked by privilege, is still non-exclusive.

The function of rivalry is not clear cut. As a phenomenon that is apparent within intra-familial relationships, it seems, like jealousy protest, related to protection of the attachment relationship, and survival of the self. However, this type of goal seems less relevant within extra-familial relationships. It is interesting that work on rivalry among friends (Parker et al., this volume, Chapter 22) focuses on loss of exclusiveness, rather than differential treatment, as the eliciting event. In that sense, the body of research on peer rivalry seems to draw on traditions in the literature on romantic jealousy in adults rather than the body of work on sibling rivalry where differential treatment is more prominent (Volling et al., this volume; Hart, this volume, Chapter 18). With increases in the capacity to articulate mixed emotions (Harter & Buddin, 1987), older children and adolescents provide vivid portrayals of rivalry as an affectively painful event and one that emerges in a range of settings that do not include caregivers (Dyck, this volume; Parker et al., this volume). Hopefully, these verbal capacities will be tapped toward productive work on continuity across age and eliciting contexts (Hart, in press; Pike & Atzaba-Poria, 2003) that may help identify conditions and features of rivalry which resemble earlier expressions of jealousy protest, and those which appear more related to jealousy in later sexual relationships. Clues to understanding continuity or parallel processes should help yield insight into rivalry as a stage marked by important transitions.

(iv)   The final stage entails *romantic and sexual jealousy.* This form of jealousy is distinguished by the degree to which it is dedicated to preserving survival of one's genetic endowment via future offspring (Buss, 2000, 2004; Hill & Buss, 2008), and so it is often clear that at this stage, the relationship being protected is that with a romantic or sexual partner rather than an attachment figure. Affects, behaviors, and ideology associated with romantic jealousy have received considerable attention (Ben-Ze'ev, this volume, Chapter 3; Harris & Darby, this volume, Chapter 23; Pines, 1998) in works where the eliciting event is usually framed in terms of loss of exclusivity rather than differential treatment. Roots in earlier stages of development are poorly understood. Thus, little is known about early events that may be played out only later, and beyond the familial setting, as a different form of jealousy (Clanton & Kosins, 1991), nor the steps in between that may bridge earlier and later stages (Campos et al., this volume). Nor is it clear whether romantic jealousy precludes, parallels, or operates independently or co-dependently of co-occurring rivalries, such as those among siblings, friends, lovers, or other types of competitors. Cross-context comparisons should also be helpful not only toward parsing jealousy from rivalry but also toward distinguishing these from related affective experiences within supra-dyadic conditions, such those entailing frustrated expectations of social inclusion, shame, envy, and *schadenfreude* (joy in another's misfortune).

The working model that is offered here is presented humbly, and with hopes that it will be of some heuristic value toward advancing productive work in a startlingly under-researched field of inquiry. At the very least, we hope to have conveyed the notion that the development of jealousy is a researchable issue. Moreover, it is one that we believe is an area of enormous importance, as Bowlby concluded after questioning the origins of the young child's protests over his mother's attention to another child, and offering the alluring prediction, "On how we answer these questions turn all our practices of child-rearing" (Bowlby, 1973, p. 4).

References

Achenbach, T. M., & Edelbrock, C. S. (1978). The classification of child psychopathology: A review and analysis of empirical efforts. *Psychological Bulletin, 85,* 1275–1301.

Adler, A. (1959). *Understanding human nature.* New York: Premier Books.

Ahnert, L., Pinquart, M., & Lamb, M. E. (2006). Security of children's relationships with nonparental care providers: A meta-analysis. *Child Development, 74,* 664–679.

Ainsworth, M. D. S., Blehar, M. C., Waters, E., & Wall, S. (1978). *Patterns of attachment: A psychological study of the strange situation.* Hillsdale, NJ: Erlbaum.

Ainsworth, M. D. S., & Wittig, B. A. (1969). Attachment and exploratory behavior of one-year-olds in a strange situation. In B. M. Foss (Ed.), *Determinants of infant behavior* (Vol. 4, pp. 129–173). London: Methuen.

Barrett, K., & Campos, J. J. (1987). Perspectives on emotional development, Vol. 2. A functionalist approach to emotions. In J. Osofsky (Ed.), *Handbook of infant development* (2nd ed., pp. 555–578). New York: Wiley.

Bateson, G., & Mead, M. (1942). *Balinese character: A photographic analysis.* New York: New York Academy of Sciences.

Bauminger, N. (this volume). Jealousy in children with autism spectrum disorder (ASD). In S. L. Hart & M. Legerstee (Eds.), *Handbook of jealousy: Theory, research, and multidisciplinary approaches.* Malden, MA: Wiley-Blackwell.

Baydar, N., Greek, A., & Brooks-Gun, J. (1997). A longitudinal study of the effects of the birth of a sibling during the first 6 years of life. *Journal of Marriage and Family, 59,* 939–956.

Behrens, K. Y. (2004). A multifaceted view of the concept of amae: Reconsidering the indigenous Japanese concept of relatedness. *Human Development, 47,* 1–27.

Belsky, J., & Cassidy, J. (1994). Attachment: Theory and evidence. In M. Rutter & D. Hay (Eds.), *Development through life: A handbook for clinicians* (pp. 373–402). Oxford: Blackwell.

Ben-Ze'ev, A. (this volume). Jealousy and romantic love. In S. L. Hart & M. Legerstee (Eds.), *Handbook of jealousy: Theory, research, and multidisciplinary approaches.* Malden, MA: Wiley-Blackwell.

Bjorklund, D. F., & Pellegrini, A. D. (2002). *The origins of human nature.* Washington, DC: American Psychological Association.

Bowlby, J. (1969). *Attachment and loss: Vol. 1. Attachment* (1st ed.). New York: Basic Books.

Bowlby, J. (1973). *Attachment and loss: Vol. 2. Separation.* New York: Basic Books.

Bradley, B. S. (this volume). Jealousy in infant–peer trios: From narcissism to culture. In S. L. Hart & M. Legerstee (Eds.), *Handbook of jealousy: Theory, research, and multidisciplinary approaches.* Malden, MA: Wiley-Blackwell.

Brazelton, T. B. (1983). *Infants and mothers: Differences in development.* New York: Delacorte.

Bridges, K. M. B. (1932). Emotional development in early infancy. *Child Development, 3,* 324–341.

Brown, G. L., Neff, C., Shigeto, A., & Mangelsdorf, S. C. (2009). *Dyadic relationships and triadic family interaction: Linkages between attachment concordance and family dynamics.* Paper presented at the Society for Research in Child Development, Denver, CO.

Bryant, B. K., & Crockenberg, S. B. (1980). Correlates and dimensions of prosocial behavior: A study of female siblings with their mothers. *Child Development, 51,* 529–544.

Buss, D. M. (2000). *The dangerous passion: Why jealousy is as necessary as love and sex.* New York: Free Press.

Buss, D. M. (2004). *Evolutionary psychology.* Boston: Pearson.

Campbell, S. B. (2006). Maladjustment in preschool children: A developmental psycho-pathology perspective. In K. McCartney & D. Phillips (Eds.), *Blackwell handbook of early childhood development* (pp. 358–377). Malden, MA: Blackwell.

Campos, J.J., Walle, E.A., & Dahl, A. (this volume). What is missing in the study of the development of jealousy? In S. L. Hart & M. Legerstee (Eds.), *Handbook of jealousy: Theory, research and multidisciplinary approchaes*. Malden, MA: Wiley-Blackwell.

Centers for Disease Control and Prevention (CDC). (2000). *Family planning methods and practice: Africa* (2nd ed.). Atlanta, GA: United States Department of Health and Human Services.

Centers for Disease Control and Prevention (CDC). (2009). www.cdc.gov/reproductive-health/Products&Pubs/Africa/Chap_1.pdf

Chisholm, J. (1996). The evolutionary ecology of attachment organization. *Human Nature, 7*, 1–38.

Cicchetti, D. (1984). The emergence of developmental psychopathology. *Child Development, 55*, 1–7.

Clanton, G. (2001). Jealousy in American culture, 1945–1985. In A. Branaman (Ed.), *Self and society* (pp. 156–166). Malden, MA: Blackwell.

Clanton, G., & Kosins, D. J. (1991). Developmental correlates of jealousy. In P. Salovey (Ed.), *The psychology of jealousy and envy* (pp. 132–145). New York: Guilford Press.

Colletto, G. M., Segre, C. A., Rielli, S. T., & Rosario, H. (2003). Multiple birth rates according to different socioeconomic levels: An analysis of four hospitals from the city of Sao Paulo, Brazil. *Twin Research, 6*, 177–182.

Crockenberg, S. B., & Smith, P. (1982). Antecedents of mother–infant interaction and infant irritability in the first three months of life. *Infant Behavior and Development, 5*, 105–119.

Cummings, E. M., Zahn-Waxler, C., & Radke-Yarrow, M. (1981). Young children's responses to expressions of anger and affection by others in the family. *Child Development, 52*, 1274–1282.

De Wolf, M. S., & van IJzendoorn, M. H. (1997). Sensitivity and attachment: A meta-analysis on parental antecedents of infant attachment. *Child Development, 68*, 571–591.

Devore, I., & Konner, M. J. (1974). Infancy in hunter-gatherer life: An ethological perspective. In *Ethology and psychiatry: From the Clarence M. Hincks Memorial Lectures, held at McMaster University, 1970*. Oxford: University of Toronto Press.

Draghi-Lorenz, R. (1998, April). *Young infants can be jealous*. Paper presented at the 11th Biennial International Conference on Infant Studies (ICIS), Atlanta, GA.

Draghi-Lorenz, R. (this volume). Parental reports of jealousy in early infancy: Growing tensions between evidence and theory. In S. L. Hart & M. Legerstee (Eds.), *Handbook of jealousy: Theory, research, and multidisciplinary approaches*. Malden, MA: Wiley-Blackwell.

Dreikurs, R. (1964). *Children, the challenge*. New York: Hawthorne.

Dunn, J. (1985). *Sisters and brothers*. Cambridge, MA: Harvard University Press.

Dunn, J., & Kendrick, C. (1981). The arrival of a sibling: Changes in patterns of interaction between mother and first-born child. *Annual Progress in Child Psychiatry and Child Development*, 362–379.

Dunn, J., Kendrick, C., & MacNamee, R. (1981). The reaction of first-born children to the birth of a sibling: Mothers' reports. *Journal of Child Psychology and Psychiatry, 22*, 1–18.

Dyck, N. (this volume). Social class, competition, and parental jealousy in children's sports. In S. L. Hart & M. Legerstee (Eds.), *Handbook of jealousy: Theory, research, and multidisciplinary approaches*. Malden, MA: Wiley-Blackwell.

Eibl-Eibesfeldt, I. (1989). *Human ethology.* New York: Aldine de Gruyter.

Faigin, H. (1957). Observation of babies' social behavior in the kibbutz. *Ofakim, 11,* 485–507.

Fearon, R. M. P., Bakermans-Kranenburg, M. J., & van IJzendoorn, M. H. (this volume). Jealousy and attachment: The case of twins. In S. L. Hart & M. Legerstee (Eds.), *Handbook of jealousy: Theory, research, and multidisciplinary approaches.* Malden, MA: Wiley-Blackwell.

Feiring, C., Lewis, M., & Jaskir, J. (1983). Birth of a sibling: Effect on mother–first born child interaction. *Journal of Developmental and Behavioral Pediatrics, 4,* 190–195.

Feldman, R., & Eidelman, A. I. (2003). Direct and indirect effects of breast milk on the neurobehavioral and cognitive development of premature infants. *Developmental Psychobiology, 43,* 109–119.

Field, T. M., & Reite, M. (1984). Children's responses to separation from mother during the birth of another child. *Child Development, 55,* 1308–1316.

Fivaz-Depeursinge, E., & Corboz-Warnery, A. (1999). *The primary triangle: A developmental systems view of mothers, fathers, and infants.* New York: Basic Books.

Fivaz-Depeursinge, E., Favez, N., Lavanchy Scaiola, C., & Lopes, F. (this volume). Family triangular interactions in infancy: A context for the development of jealousy? In S. L. Hart & M. Legerstee (Eds.), *Handbook of jealousy: Theory, research, and multidisciplinary approaches.* Malden, MA: Wiley-Blackwell.

Forbes, S. (this volume). Sibling rivalry in the birds and the bees. In S. L. Hart & M. Legerstee (Eds.), *Handbook of jealousy: Theory, research, and multidisciplinary approaches.* Malden, MA: Wiley-Blackwell.

Fouts, H. N., Hewlett, B. S., & Lamb, M. E. (2005). Parent–offspring weaning conflicts among the Bofi farmers and foragers of central Africa. *Current Anthropology, 46,* 29–50.

Freud, A., & Dann, S. (1947). An experiment in group upbringing. In A. Freud & H. Hartmann (Eds.), *Psychoanalytic study of the child* (Vol. 3/4, pp. 127–168). Oxford: International Universities Press.

Freud, S. (1920). *A general introduction to psycho-analysis.* New York: Liveright.

Frijda, N. H. (1986). *The emotions.* New York: Cambridge University Press.

Gesell, A. L. (1906). Jealousy. *American Journal of Psychology, 17,* 437–496.

Gottlieb, L. N., & Mendelson, M. J. (1990). Parental support and firstborn girls' adaptation to the birth of a sibling. *Journal of Applied Developmental Psychology, 11,* 29–48.

Hamilton, W. D. (1964). The genetic evolution of social behavior. *Journal of Theoretical Biology, 7,* 1–52.

Harmon-Jones, E., Peterson, C. K., & Harris, C. R. (2009). Jealousy: Novel methods and neural correlates. *Emotion, 9,* 113–117.

Harris, C., R., & Darby, R. S. (this volume). Jealousy in adulthood. In S. L. Hart & M. Legerstee (Eds.), *Handbook of jealousy: Theory, research, and multidisciplinary approaches.* Malden, MA: Wiley-Blackwell.

Hart, S. L. (in press). Siblings and peers in the adult–child–child triadic context. In L. C. Mayes & M. Lewis (Eds.), *A developmental environmental measurement handbook.* New York: Cambridge University Press.

Hart, S. L. (this volume). The ontogenesis of jealousy in the first year of life: A theory of jealousy as a biologically-based dimension of temperament. In S. L. Hart & M. Legerstee (Eds.), *Handbook of jealousy: Theory, research, and multidisciplinary approaches.* Malden, MA: Wiley-Blackwell.

Hart, S. L. (this volume). The socialization of sibling rivalry: What's love got to do? In S. L. Hart & M. Legerstee (Eds.), *Handbook of jealousy: Theory, research, and multidisciplinary approaches*. Malden, MA: Wiley-Blackwell.

Hart, S. L., & Behrens, K. L. (2008). *Loss and recovery of exclusivity: Responses of dyads with secure and insecure attachment relationships*. Paper presented at the International Conference on Infant Studies, Vancouver, Canada.

Hart, S., Boylan, L. M., Border, B., Carroll, S. R., McGunegle, D., & Lampe, R. M. (2004). Breast milk levels of cortisol and Secretory Immunoglobulin A (SIgA) differ with maternal mood and infant neuro-behavioral functioning. *Infant Behavior and Development, 27*, 101–106.

Hart, S. L., Boylan, L. M., Carroll, S. R., Musick, Y. A., Kuratko, C., Border, B. G., et al. (2006). Newborn behavior differs with decosahexaenoic acid levels in breast milk. *Journal of Pediatric Psychology, 31*, 221–226.

Hart, S., Boylan, L. M., Carroll, S., Musick, Y., & Lampe, R. M. (2003). Breast-fed one-week-olds demonstrate superior neurobehavioral organization. *Journal of Pediatric Psychology, 28*, 529–534.

Hart, S., & Carrington, H. A. (2002). Jealousy in 6-month-old infants. *Infancy, 3*, 395–402.

Hart, S. L., Carrington, H. A., Tronick, E. Z., & Carroll, S. R. (2004). When infants lose exclusive maternal attention: Is it jealousy? *Infancy, 6*, 57–78.

Hart, S., del Valle, C., & Letourneau, M. (1994, June). *Jealousy protest*. Paper presented at the meeting of the 9th Biennial International Conference for Infant Studies, Paris, France.

Hart, S., Field, T., del Valle, C., & Letourneau, M. (1998a). Infants protest their mothers' attending to an infant-size doll. *Social Development, 7*, 54–61.

Hart, S., Field, T., Letourneau, M., & del Valle, C. (1998b). Jealousy protests in infants of depressed mothers. *Infant Behavior and Development, 21*, 137–148.

Hart, S. L., Jackson, S. T., & Boylan, L. M. (forthcoming). The breastfed infant's neurobehavioral organization: Implications for child health and cognitive development. In V. R. Preedy (Ed.), *Handbook of behavior, diet and nutrition*. New York: Springer.

Hart, S., Jones, N. A., & Field, T. (2003). Atypical expressions of jealousy in infants of intrusive- and withdrawn-depressed mothers. *Child Psychiatry and Human Development, 33*, 193–207.

Harter, S., & Buddin, B. (1987). Children's understanding of the simultaneity of two emotions: A five-stage developmental acquisition sequence. *Developmental Psychology, 23*, 388–399.

Hill, S. E., & Buss, D. M. (2008). The evolutionary psychology of envy. In R. H. Smith (Ed.), *Envy: Theory and research* (pp. 60–70). New York: Oxford University Press.

Hobson, R. P. (this volume). Is jealousy a complex emotion? In S. L. Hart & M. Legerstee (Eds.), *Handbook of jealousy: Theory, research, and multidisciplinary approaches*. Malden, MA: Wiley-Blackwell.

Hrdy, S. B. (1999). *Mother nature: A history of mothers, infants, and natural selection*. New York: Pantheon.

Ishikawa, F., & Hay, D. F. (2006). Triadic interaction among newly acquainted 2-year-olds. *Social Development, 15*, 145–168.

Jones, N. A., & Mize, K. D. (2009). *Infants with left anterior EEG asymmetry demonstrate more jealousy behaviors during loss of exclusive maternal attention*. Paper presented at the Society for Research in Child Development, Denver, CO.

Keller, H., & Lamm, B. (this volume). Culture, parenting, and the development of jealousy. In S. L. Hart & M. Legerstee (Eds.), *Handbook of jealousy: Theory, research, and multidisciplinary approaches*. Malden, MA: Wiley-Blackwell.

Kramer, L., & Ramsburg, D. (2002). Advice given to parents on welcoming a second child: A critical review. *Family Relations, 51*, 2–14.

Lamb, M. E., Thompson, R. A., Gardner, W., & Charnov, E. (1985). *Infant–mother attachment*. Hillsdale, NJ: Erlbaum.

Lawrence, R. A., & Lawrence, R. M. (2005). *Breastfeeding: A guide for the medical profession*. Philadelphia, PA: Mosby.

Lee, H. J., Rubio, M. R., Elo, I. T., McCollum, K. F., Chung, E. K., & Culhane, J. F. (2005). Factors associated with intention to breastfeed among low-income, inner-city pregnant women. *Maternal and Child Health Journal, 9*, 253–261.

Legg, C., Sherick, I., & Wadland, W. (1974). Reaction of preschool children to the birth of a sibling. *Child Psychiatry and Human Development, 5*, 3–39.

LeVine, R. A., & Norman, K. (2008). Attachment in anthropological perspective. In R. A. LeVine & R. S. New (Eds.), *Anthropology and child development: A cross-cultural reader* (pp. 127–142). Malden: Wiley-Blackwell.

Levy, D. M. (1934). Rivalry between children in the same family. *Child Study, 11*, 233–239.

Levy, D. M. (1937). Studies in sibling rivalry. *Research Monographs of the American Orthopsychiatric Association* (No. 2), 1–96.

Lewis, M. (2005). The child and its family: The social network model. *Human Development, 48*, 8–27.

Lewis, M. (this volume). Loss, protest, and emotional development. In S. L. Hart & M. Legerstee (Eds.), *Handbook of jealousy: Theory, research, and multidisciplinary approaches*. Malden, MA: Wiley-Blackwell.

Lewis, M., & Kreitzberg, V. S. (1979). Effect of birth order and spacing on mother–infant interactions. *Developmental Psychology, 15*, 617–625.

Lewis, M., & Ramsay, D. (1999). Environments and stress reduction. In *Soothing and stress* (pp. 171–192). Mahwah, NJ: Erlbaum.

Luke, B., & Brown, M. B. (2008). Maternal morbidity and infant death in twin vs triplet and quadruplet pregnancies. *American Journal of Obstetrics and Gynecology, 198*, 401. e1–401.e10.

Maital, S. L., & Bornstein, M. H. (2003). The ecology of collaborative child rearing: A systems approach to child care on the kibbutz. *Ethos, 31*, 274–306.

Masciuch, S., & Kienapple, K. (1993). The emergence of jealousy in children 4 months to 7 years of age. *Journal of Social and Personal Relationships, 10*, 421–435.

Miller, A. L., Volling, B. L., & McElwain, N. L. (2000). Sibling jealousy in a triadic context with mothers and fathers. *Social Development, 9*, 433–457.

Mitra, A. K., Khoury, A. J., Hinton, A. W., & Carothers, C. (2004). Predictors of breastfeeding intention among low-income women. *Maternal and Child Health Journal, 8*, 65–70.

Mock, D. W., & Parker, G. A. (1997). *The evolution of sibling rivalry*. New York: Oxford University Press.

Nadel, J., & Tremblay-Leveau, H. (1999). Early perception of social contingencies and interpersonal intentionality: Dyadic and triadic paradigms. In P. Rochat (Ed.), *Early* social cognition: Understanding others in the first months of life (pp. 189–212). Mahwah, NJ: Erlbaum.

Nadelman, L., & Begun, A. (1982). The effects of the newborn on the older sibling: Mothers' questionnaires. In M. E. Lamb & B. Sutton-Smith (Eds.), *Sibling relationships: Their nature and significance across the lifespan* (pp. 13–38). Hillsdale, NJ: Erlbaum.

Nash, A., & Hay, D. F. (1993). Relationships in infancy as precursors and causes of later relationships and psychopathology In D. F. Hay & A. Angold (Eds.), *Precursors and causes in development and psychopathology* (pp. 199–232). Chichester: Wiley.

Panksepp, J. (this volume). The evolutionary sources of jealousy: Cross-species approaches to fundamental issues. In S. L. Hart & M. Legerstee (Eds.), *Handbook of jealousy: Theory, research, and multidisciplinary approaches*. Malden, MA: Wiley-Blackwell.

Parker, J. G., Kruse, S. M., & Aikins, J. W. (this volume). When friends have other friends: Friendship jealousy in childhood and early adolescence. In S. L. Hart & M. Legerstee (Eds.), *Handbook of jealousy: Theory, research, and multidisciplinary approaches*. Malden, MA: Wiley-Blackwell.

Parkinson, B., Fischer, A. H., & Manstead, A. S. R. (2005). *Emotion in social relations: Cultural, group, and interpersonal processes*. New York: Psychology Press.

Petterson, S. M., & Albers, A. B. (2001). Effects of poverty and maternal depression on early child development. *Child Development, 72*, 1794–1813.

Pike, A., & Atzaba-Poria, N. (2003). Do sibling and friend relationships share the same temperamental origins? A twin study. *Journal of Child Psychology and Psychiatry, 44*, 598–611.

Pines, A. M. (1998). *Romantic jealousy: Causes, symptoms, cures*. New York: Routledge.

Radecki, S. E., & Beckman, L. J. (1992). Determinants of child-bearing intentions of low-income women: Attitudes versus life circumstances. *Journal of Biosocial Science, 24*, 157–166.

Reddy, V. (this volume). Green eyes in bio-cultural frames. In S. L. Hart & M. Legerstee (Eds.), *Handbook of jealousy: Theory, research, and multidisciplinary approaches*. Malden, MA: Wiley-Blackwell.

Roetzel, A. C., & Hart, S. L. (2007). *The infant's reactions to loss of a caregiver's exclusive attention in childcare settings*. Paper presented at the Society for Research in Child Development, Boston, MA.

Saarni, C., Campos, J. J., Camras, L. A., & Witherington, D. (2006). Emotional development: Action, communication, and understanding. In N. Eisenberg (Ed.), *Handbook of child psychology: Vol. 3. Social, emotional, and personality development* (6th ed., pp. 226–299). Hoboken, NJ: Wiley.

Sagi, A., van IJzendoorn, M. H., Aviezer, O., Donnell, F., Koren-Karie, N., Joels, T., et al. (1995). Attachments in a multiple-caregiver and multiple-infant environment: The case of the Israeli kibbutzim. *Monographs of the Society for Research in Child Development, 60*, 71–91.

Sameroff, A. J., Seifer, R., & Zax, M. (1982). Early development of children at risk for emotional disorder. *Monographs of the Society for Research in Child Development, 47*, 1–82.

Simpson, J. A. (1999). Attachment theory in modern evolutionary perspective. In J. Cassidy & P. R. Shaver (Eds.), *Handbook of attachment: Theory, research, and clinical applications* (pp. 115–140). New York: Guilford Press.

Simpson, J. A., & Belsky, J. (2008). Attachment theory within a modern evolutionary framework. In J. Cassidy & P. R. Shaver (Eds.), *Handbook of attachment: Theory, research, and clinical applications* (2nd ed.). New York: Guilford Press.

Stearns, P. (1989). *Jealousy: The evolution of an emotion in American history.* New York: New York University Press.

Steinmetz, S. K. (1977). The use of force for resolving family conflict: The training ground for abuse. *The Family Coordinator, 26,* 19–26.

Stewart, R. B., Mobley, L. A., Van Tuyl, S. S., & Salvador, M. A. (1987). The firstborn's adjustment to the birth of a sibling: A longitudinal assessment. *Child Development, 58,* 341–355.

Striano, T., & Rochat, P. (1999). Developmental links between dyadic and triadic social competence. *British Journal of Developmental Psychology, 17,* 551–562.

Tas, R. F. (1990). [Multiple births in The Netherlands, 1900–1988]. *Ned Tijdschr Geneeskd, 134,* 2189–2195.

Taylor, M., & Kogan, K. (1973). Effects of birth of a sibling on mother–child interactions. *Child Psychiatry and Human Development, 4,* 53– 58.

Teti, D. M., & Ablard, K. E. (1989). Security of attachment and infant–sibling relationships: A laboratory study. *Child Development, 60,* 1519–1528.

Teti, D. M., Sakin, J. W., Kucera, E., Corns, K. M., & Das Eiden, R. (1996). And baby makes four: Predictors of attachment security among preschool-age firstborns during the transition to siblinghood. *Child Development, 67,* 579–596.

Tooby, J., & Cosmides, L. (1992). Psychological foundations of culture. In J. Barkow, L. Cosmides, & J. Tooby (Eds.), *The adapted mind* (pp. 19–136). New York: Oxford University Press.

Touris, M., Kromelow, S., & Harding, C. (1995). Mother–firstborn attachment and the birth of a sibling. *American Journal of Orthopsychiatry, 65,* 293–297.

Trause, M. A., Voos, D., Rudd, C., Klaus, M., Kennell, J., & Boslett, M. (1981). Separation for childbirth: The effect on the sibling. *Child Psychiatry and Human Development, 12,* 32–39.

Trivers, R. L. (1974). Parent–offspring conflict. *American Zoologist, 14,* 249–264.

Tronick, E. Z., Morelli, G. A., & Ivey, P. K. (1992). The Efe forager infant and toddler's pattern of social relationships: Multiple and simultaneous. *Developmental Psychology, 28,* 568–577.

United Nations Children's Fund (UNICEF). (2008). The state of the world's children: Maternal and newborn health. New York: UNICEF.

van IJzendoorn, M. H., & Sagi, A. (1999). Cross-cultural patterns of attachment: Universals and contextual determinants. In J. Cassidy & P. R. Shaver (Eds.), *Handbook of attachment: Theory, research, and clinical applications* (pp. 713–734). New York: Guilford Press.

Vandell, D. L., & Bailey, M. D. (1992). Conflicts between siblings. In C. U. Shantz & W. W. Hartup (Eds.), *Conflict in child and adolescent development* (pp. 242–269). New York: Cambridge University Press.

Volling, B. L. (2005). The transition to siblinghood: A developmental ecological systems perspective and directions for future research. *Journal of Family Psychology, 19,* 542–549.

Volling, B. L., Kennedy, D. E., & Jackey, L. M. H. (this volume). The development of sibling jealousy. In S. L. Hart & M. Legerstee (Eds.), *Handbook of jealousy: Theory, research, and multidisciplinary approaches.* Malden, MA: Wiley-Blackwell.

Volling, B. L., McElwain, N. L., & Miller, A. L. (2002). Emotion regulation in context: The jealousy complex between young siblings and its relations with child and family characteristics. *Child Development, 73*, 581–600.

Wachs, T. D., Black, M. M., & Engle, P. L. (2009). Maternal depression: A global threat to children's health, development, and behavior and to human rights. *Child Development Perspectives, 3*, 51–59.

Waldrop, M. F., & Bell, R. Q. (1966). Effects of family size and density on newborn characteristics. *American Journal of Orthopsychiatry, 36*, 544–550.

Wingert, P., & Brant, M. (2005, August 15). Reading your baby's mind. *Newsweek, 146*, 32–39.

World Health Organization (WHO). (2006). Report of a WHO technical consultation on birth spacing. Department of Making Pregnancy Safer (MPS) and Department of Reproductive Health and Research (RHR). Geneva, Switzerland, June 13–15, 2005.

Zajonc, R. B. (1976). Family configuration and intelligence: Variations in scholastic aptitude scores parallel trends in family size and the spacing of children. *Science, 192*, 227–236.

16

Jealousy and Attachment
The Case of Twins

R. M. Pasco Fearon, Marian J. Bakermans-Kranenburg, and Marinus H. van IJzendoorn

Introduction

When John Bowlby completed his project to develop a scientific account of attachment, he had achieved something quite new (Bowlby, 1969). In particular, the first volume of his trilogy represents a remarkable synthesis of ideas, research findings, and principles that was truly interdisciplinary. In binding this synthetic enterprise together, considerations of evolutionary pressures and processes were fundamental because in light of evolutionary arguments, the functions of child–parent attachment became obvious and compelling. From this perspective, attachment represents a biobehavioral system shaped by evolution for the purpose of maximizing survival and eventual reproduction. The way the attachment system efficiently supports survival in immature infants and children is by actively monitoring the whereabouts and availability of selected individuals, and to signal to, and directly seek out, those individuals when there are "natural clues" to threat in the environment (Bowlby, 1969). In that sense, the caregiver acts as a "secure base" for the infant, by providing a haven of safety in times of threat, which should, in turn, support the child's effective exploration of the environment. It was with this secure base concept in mind, and with Bowlby's biobehavioral theory as backdrop, that Mary Ainsworth conducted her pioneering longitudinal Baltimore study on a small number of mother–infant dyads intensively observed at home during the first year after birth, resulting in the construction of the now-famous Strange Situation Procedure as a means of observing attachment behavior in infants in controlled, naturalistic conditions (Ainsworth, Blehar, Waters, & Wall., 1978).

Given that there were strong reasons for thinking that attachment serves a primary biological function, the discovery that some infants did not apparently demonstrate attachment behavior, even when strong natural clues to danger

Handbook of Jealousy: Theory, Research and Multidisciplinary Approaches, First Edition.
Edited by Sybil L. Hart and Maria Legerstee.
© 2013 Blackwell Publishing Ltd. Published 2013 by Blackwell Publishing Ltd.

were present, was a dramatic discovery and a puzzle (Main, 1999). Some infants, later to be described as avoidant, showed limited expression of attachment behavior when separated and reunited with a caregiver, and later research confirmed that this was not simply because the procedure was not stressful for these infants (Spangler & Grossmann, 1993). Other infants, labeled resistant, showed intense attention to, or preoccupation with, the parent and were angry and inconsolable upon reunion. Mary Ainsworth was convinced that the explanation for these differences in attachment behavior could be found in the patterns of interaction that took place between mother and infant during the daily routine. Extensive observational studies of interactions in the home appeared to confirm this by identifying features of parental sensitivity as crucial factors (Ainsworth et al., 1978). Parents who were attentive to their child's needs, responsive to their child's attachment cues, and provided timely and appropriate responses to those cues appeared to have babies who were more likely to be secure in the Strange Situation Procedure. Extensive research has now amply replicated this basic and important finding (De Wolff & van IJzendoorn, 1997), and, compared to associations found in other (behavioral or medical) areas of investigation, the combined effect size of the pertinent studies (combined $r = .24$) should be considered substantial (McCartney & Rosenthal, 2000).

While indicating associations with parental sensitivity, at least as currently measured, this body of evidence also clearly shows that sensitivity does not account for all the systematic variance in attachment security. Nor is it sufficient in magnitude to help explain the so-called "transmission gap" (van IJzendoorn, 1995). This refers to observations that an impressive amount of variance in children's attachment security is explained as having been transmitted by their parents through their representations of their own childhood attachment experiences, yet the actual process responsible for this intergenerational transmission of attachment is unclear. Moreover, it remains unbridgeable even when accounting for parental sensitivity. Over the years since Ainsworth's original work, many different formulations of parental sensitivity and reformulations of the relevant features of maternal behavior that might give rise to different attachment patterns have been considered (De Wolff & van IJzendoorn, 1997), but the effect size for the correlation between parental behavior and pattern of attachment has not substantially increased. It could be argued that one fundamental limitation of this approach toward illuminating variance in attachment security is its exclusive focus on the interactions that occur between one parent and one child (Cowan, 1997).

For some time now, attachment researchers have been thinking about the possibility that dyadic relationships, such as the mother–child relationship, might be affected by interactions that take place in other relationships (Marvin & Stewart, 1990; Hinde, 1987) or by "higher-order" family interactions. In the past, one could reasonably say that attachment theory was primarily focused on the mother–child relationship (in the early stages of the field) and on other dyadic relationships (in later work), such as attachment to fathers and to other significant providers of care (such as in Israeli kibbutzim; see Sagi et al., 1995). Perhaps as a result of the emphasis on dyadic interaction, developmentally oriented attachment research tended not to consider triadic processes, and rarely even considered the more general issue of how having one or more siblings might affect how infants and children feel about and behave toward their shared primary caregivers. Of course, the kibbutz studies provide examples of how the relationships of one child to various caregivers are shaped independently, as well as of the ways in which two different children relate to the same caregiver (Sagi et al., 1995; see also van IJzendoorn et al., 2000). Yet, this approach, in which the number of dyads is increased but still regarded independently of other dyads, represents only a first step toward a genuinely systemic approach which can explore the effects of one relationship on another, and can consider processes from the perspective of jealousy.

A major initiative was undertaken in the 1990s to change this, and to directly consider the interplay between different attachment relationships within a family in a more systematic way. Ideas from systems theory were artfully applied to attachment theory by several authors as a way of trying to impose some conceptual structure on what might otherwise be an exponentially complex set of interrelationships to understand and study (Hinde, 1987; Marvin & Stewart, 1990; Cowan, 1997). However, despite extensive effort having been invested in laying the conceptual foundations, it seems fair to say that the promise of a systems account of the development of attachment has fallen short of expectations. There may be several reasons for this. Two immediately strike us as significant, and they bear directly on the topic of jealousy that is the focus of this book. First, despite the apparently obvious benefits, the number of attachment studies that have looked at the development of more than one child in the same family is remarkably modest, even though strong calls for this kind of work started to be heard nearly two decades ago. Of course, the time-consuming nature of observational attachment studies did not help much to enhance the number of triadic investigations, because it inevitably multiplies the investment needed to collect valid data. Part of the explanation for the "failure to launch" of systems-oriented attachment research may thus represent a problem of inertia. Without an accumulation of empirical data and novel findings it may be that we have not seen a sufficient number of new phenomena for researchers to get their teeth into, and so their energies have, to a large extent, been directed elsewhere.

The second reason is more subtle, but may in fact be more significant. While systems theory is a very useful set of guiding principles for thinking about how complex self-organizing systems typically behave, it is not an explanation of attachment. Indeed, existing attempts to formulate systems applications of attachment theory tend not to produce very clear or easily testable hypotheses. Systems theory lacks a critical ingredient necessary for it to be a generative force in attachment research. Because it is a framework rather than a theory, it lacks an account of the psychological and motivational processes that make attachment sensitive to events that happen in other relationships. Right now, we need a theory of attachment that might give prominence to these kinds of processes. Arguably, without one, this branch of attachment research may remain in the slow lane.

In this chapter, we aim to make a small contribution to the understanding of variation in attachment security by describing our research on attachment in twins. This work has produced some interesting and surprising findings that suggest that attachment may be shaped by processes that reflect sibling competition; processes that may indeed be akin to jealousy. These findings have, in turn, led us to think more seriously about systemic influences on the development of attachment, and to question some basic assumptions of attachment research. To see how we arrived at these conclusions it is necessary to first go back a few steps and review the historical and theoretical background of twin research in developmental psychology, particularly as it pertains to attachment. So, to that end we begin by explaining why we first started studying attachment in twins. It was not in order to understand how the attachment of one child to one parent might be affected by the relationship that the other sibling, or co-twin, has with that parent. Rather, we were interested in the relative contribution of genes and environment to attachment security and insecurity. Studying twins was, in a sense, a means to that end. However, just as in other areas of developmental research (e.g. Dunn & Plomin, 1990), a consideration of genetics led us, unexpectedly, to think about the interplay between siblings' relationships with their parents.

Attachment in Behavioral Genetic Perspective

Behavior genetic studies have had a major impact on the way that scientists think about the kinds of influences that impinge on children's development (Plomin, DeFries, McClearn, & McGuffin, 2001). The first wave of challenges that behavior genetics studies posed for developmentalists centered on the potential for confounding the environment with genetics. In other words, for many years developmental psychologists had studied the social environments of young infants and children and inferred that these environments causally influenced children's development, but they did so in the absence of any information about the children's genes, or the genes that children share with their parents. Studying one child per family meant that researchers necessarily confounded genetic and environmental influences on child development that can only be disentangled by studying genetically unrelated (adoptive) children or by examining the development of more than one child per family.

At the time, attachment theory represented a typical example of the limitations of this approach. A great deal of work had been done to identify the social determinants of individual differences in attachment security, and parenting sensitivity had emerged as a crucial factor (Ainsworth et al., 1978; De Wolff &

van IJzendoorn, 1997). Theorizing on this topic had therefore largely assumed that individual differences in attachment security represented the action of environmental influences emanating from the parent. It was believed that a parent who consistently and appropriately responded to a child's attachment cues encouraged the development of expectations in the child that the parent would be available and responsive when called upon. These expectations, or internal working models, were, in turn, thought to guide the child's attachment behavior, and explained the striking differences in the expression of attachment behavior that are observed in Ainsworth's Strange Situation Procedure, as well as related separation–reunion procedures. However, relatively little consideration had been given to the possibility that these variations actually reflected genetically based dispositions. Because of the emergence of the transmission gap, it became even more urgent to examine the possible genetic bridge between parental and infant attachment.

It was with this crucial question in mind that we set about studying attachment in twins. The London–Leiden twin study was a collaborative effort to conduct attachment assessments using the gold-standard measurement procedure, Ainsworth's Strange Situation, in a sample of monozygotic (MZ) and dizygotic (DZ) twins at 12 months of age and to conduct direct observations of parental sensitivity in the home. The two sites followed identical procedures and the pooled data set consisted of 57 pairs of MZ twins and 81 pairs of DZ twins. The results of the study were remarkable. Although the vast majority of behavior genetic studies of children's development reveal evidence of strong genetic influence, and minimal influence of the shared environment, our study indicated the reverse. Using genetic modeling procedures, we estimated that 52% of the variance in attachment security was attributable to common environmental influences and that genetic effects were essentially zero (Bokhorst et al., 2003). Put simply, regardless of whether they shared all their genes with each other, or only half their genes, twins often had the same attachment classification (around 60% of them), suggesting some common environmental influence that impinged on them equally. This finding has recently been replicated in a larger twin study using a different method for assessing attachment (Roisman & Fraley, 2006) and is consistent with the results of several other twin and sibling studies (see Belsky & Fearon, 2008; Bakermans-Kranenburg & van IJzendoorn, 2007). These results were a rather resounding confirmation of some basic assumptions of attachment theory. Not only did attachment security appear to be a strongly, possibly exclusively, environmental variable, it also appeared to be strongly influenced by the shared environment.

It is worth dwelling for a moment on this latter point. Until the field of behavior genetics brought the non-shared environment to our attention, attachment researchers had not given much thought to whether or not children in the same family should have the same attachment classification to a given parent. However, strong similarities in siblings' attachments were clearly implied by a considerable body of theorizing and empirical work, such as the discovery that a singular classification derived from an interview concerning an adult's own early attachment experiences, the Adult Attachment Interview (AAI), could reliably predict infant attachment security (van IJzendoorn, 1995). This implies sibling resemblance for attachment because if a parent has only one fixed representation or "state of mind with respect to attachment," and the research in question measures the attachment security of one child chosen at random from a population of siblings, then correlations between the parent and child ought also to represent family-wide associations. At the level of theory, the predominant explanation for the transmission of attachment across generations made the same implication. Contemporary accounts of the transmission of attachment held that a parent's representation of early attachment experiences exert an organizing influence on their caregiving behavior (Bretherton & Mulholland, 1999), which in turn shapes the development of the infant's own representation of attachment. The child's internal working models were then thought to control the expression of attachment behavior and come to play an important role in the child's functioning later in life (Weinfield, Sroufe, Egeland, & Carlson, 1999).

This account of the development of attachment made strong predictions about shared environmental influences on attachment security. Because adult attachment is conceived of as a relatively stable psychological disposition it follows that it should exert similar influences on the parenting of different children within the same family. Furthermore, parental sensitivity, being influenced by parental attachment representations, should be experienced similarly by different children in the same family and should not, presumably, be directed differently to different children within the family. Studies showing that the Adult Attachment Interview can predict infant attachment security even when conducted before the birth of the child (e.g. Fonagy, Steele, & Steele, 1991; Ward & Carlson, 1995) provide a particularly striking illustration of the possibility that the relevant aspects of parental behavior might emerge from a trait-like feature of the parent, and may not be specific to the particular child in question.

This strong claim was rather at odds with a large body of evidence that emerged from behavior genetic studies which consistently showed that once genetic factors were taken into account, siblings tend to be no more similar to each other than children reared in entirely different families (Plomin & Daniels, 1987). As noted already, the results of our twin study partially supported the strong claim for the effects of a shared environment. Having said that, nearly 50% of the variance in attachment security was nevertheless estimated to be non-shared. In other words, half the variance in attachment varies *within* families, not between them, and oftentimes twins do not share the same attachment classification. It is worth noting that this finding has also been replicated, and is quite consistent with data coming from several studies of siblings too (van IJzendoorn et al., 2000). Even if one bears in mind that some or even a large part of the apparently non-shared variance in attachment may actually be measurement error, one is still forced to accept that substantial differences in children's attachments to the same parent may exist.

This clearly poses a significant challenge for attachment theory, which has little in the way of explanatory tools for conceptualizing how children within the same family could have such different relationships with the same parent. Furthermore, the finding raised the question of whether all the existing studies that had observed mother–infant interaction in the home, and then related the observed sensitivity of the mother to that child's attachment security (and there are many, see De Wolff & van IJzendoorn, 1997), had actually been picking up on dyadic-specific associations, rather than on processes that generalized across the family, as many had assumed. In other words, given that half the variance in attachment security is non-shared, and half shared, which half is the part that seems to relate to parental sensitivity? Theory would seem to suggest that sensitivity should predict (and causally give rise to) the shared environmental variance in attachment security. However, given what we knew about the non-shared aspects of attachment, we were also intrigued by the possibility that differences in how sensitive a parent was with one twin, compared to the other, might provide the first clues regarding the causes of differences in security within the family.

To address these questions we (Fearon et al., 2006) conducted 1.5- to 2-hour unobtrusive in-home observations with the mothers of the twins in our samples when they were 10 months old, and separate coders rated the sensitivity of the parent to one twin and the other from videotapes using Ainsworth's scales of maternal sensitivity (it was never the same observer who rated the mother's sensitivity to both twins). We deliberately conducted observations in such a way that they were as naturalistic as possible and involved both twins being present, because we reasoned that this was the typical state of affairs for baby twins and should therefore be most likely to pick up on processes most relevant to their development.

The results both confirmed our expectations and confounded them. In order to understand these results and their interpretation it is necessary to consider what pattern of correlations one might expect given the two theoretical positions we were considering. If parental sensitivity is a truly shared environment for infant twins, and only influences their attachment security via this shared pathway, then one would expect (a) a strong correlation between sensitivity as measured for one twin and sensitivity as measured for the other, (b) a significant correlation between sensitivity as measured for one twin and that twin's attachment security, and critically (c) a similar degree of predictability from one twin's sensitivity measurement to the other twin's attachment security. In other words, because in this model sensitivity is shared, measures of maternal sensitivity with each twin should reflect the same underlying process, and it should not matter whose attachment security one is predicting.

In the statistical analyses that we adopted, which are commonly employed in behavior genetic research, this "common environmental influences" pathway is represented by two latent variables, one for maternal sensitivity and one for attachment, that are allowed to correlate freely. The statistical estimate for the correlation between these two environmental factors tells us the extent to which the link between sensitivity and attachment is carried by common environmental factors (see Figure 16.1; genetic variables are omitted as they were estimated to be zero on the basis of the univariate analyses). If, on the other hand, the association between sensitivity and attachment is essentially unique to a specific mother–infant dyad then maternal sensitivity with "Twin X" should be a strong predictor of attachment in "Twin X," but a weak predictor of attachment in "Twin Y." So, when the within-twin correlation between sensitivity and attachment differs from the cross-twin correlation this indicates a dyad-specific pathway at work, and the correlations between the unique terms in Figure 16.1 would be estimated to be non-zero.

When the analyses were done, the results provided evidence for both these kinds of processes. Firstly, maternal sensitivity was quite strongly consistent between twins. The correlation between the observed degree of sensitivity a mother showed toward one twin and the other (coded by separate observers) was .65, which is high. There was also clear overlap in the common environmental

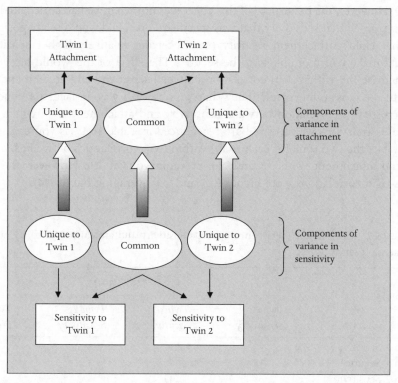

Figure 16.1 Schematic diagram of path model for estimating shared and non-shared components of the correlation between sensitivity and attachment

aspects of maternal sensitivity and infant attachment security. The model estimated the correlation between them to be .58. From this correlation, it was possible to calculate that commonalities in the experience of maternal sensitivity accounted for about a third of the observed similarity between twins in their attachment security. This finding fit well with formulations of attachment theory that emphasize parental working models of attachment and was also consistent with findings from siblings presented by van IJzendoorn et al. (2000). In their study, the authors also found that similarities in sibling attachments could be partially explained by similarities in parental sensitivity. In that sense, the findings of our study, considered against a background of research showing the predictive power of the AAI, provided rather convincing evidence that the emphasis in attachment theory on the shared family environment is, at least to a degree, well placed. Not only are there shared environmental influences on attachment, they can also be related to consistencies in how sensitive a parent is to the child's attachment cues, precisely as predicted by theory.

However, there was a wrinkle in this storyline. As well as pointing to a common environment pathway between attachment and parental sensitivity, the data also indicated that parental sensitivity and attachment could be linked with each other in ways that were dyad-specific (the Unique pathways in Figure 16.1). However, the patterning of this effect was not what we had anticipated. We had imagined that sensitivity that was specific to one child would relate positively to that child's attachment security (i.e., receiving relatively higher sensitivity should make you more likely to be secure). The effect of this would have been to increase the within-twin correlation between sensitivity and attachment relative to the cross-twin correlation. What we observed was, in fact, the opposite: the cross-twin correlation between sensitivity and attachment was higher. The actual correlations we observed are reproduced in Table 16.1. As you can see in this table, the two (one for each twin) within-twin correlations between sensitivity and attachment were .15 and .26, averaging out at .20. However, the two cross-twin correlations were higher (.25 and .43, averaging out at .34).

Table 16.1 Correlations between maternal sensitivity and attachment security, within and across twins

	Correlations			
	Twin 1 Sensitivity	Twin 1 Security	Twin 2 Sensitivity	Twin 2 Security
Twin 1 Sensitivity	–			
Twin 1 Security	.15	–		
Twin 2 Sensitivity	.63	.43	–	
Twin 2 Security	.25	.56	.26	–

In the standard statistical method for working with this kind of twin data, this pattern of results yields a negative non-shared pathway. In other words, when maternal sensitivity differs between twins, sensitivity winds up having the opposite effect to what happens when there is consistency (the Common path in Figure 16.1 is positive, while the Unique path is negative). How does this result relate to the observed correlations? The statistical model, in effect, infers that a non-shared process must have lowered the within-twin correlation (relative to the cross-twin correlation). This would happen if *sensitivity expressed to one twin, but not to the other, actually leads to insecurity in the twin who is the recipient of the greater sensitivity.* This seemed to us to be intriguing, to say the least, but also perplexing.

In our original paper, we made several tentative suggestions about how this result could have occurred. One way of thinking about it was to imagine that when attachment outcomes are discordant, mothers try to compensate by increasing their sensitivity to the insecure child. This would tend to lower the correlation between sensitivity and attachment within a dyad. However, it seems unlikely that parents are particularly aware of their child's attachment security in a systematic way, although one could certainly test this empirically (the limited validity of parent-ratings of attachment using the Attachment Q-Set (AQS) could be interpreted as evidence of this lack of awareness, see van IJzendoorn et al., 2003).

Another way of thinking about the effect is to note that the pattern of correlations could just as easily be generated by a process that raises the cross-twin correlation (rather than lowering the within-twin one). In other words, perhaps the sensitivity expressed toward one twin is having an effect on the attachment security of the other. The pattern of correlations could suggest that insensitive parenting expressed to one twin (but not expressed to the other) leads to decreases in the other twin's security. This, to our minds, seems a more plausible explanation, although precisely how such an effect might occur is unclear. The only suggestion we could make at the time was that perhaps observing insensitivity toward one's sibling reduces one's own feelings of security, regardless of its effects on the sibling to which the parenting is directed. Certainly, interpreting this effect as a positive cross-twin effect (one twin's relationship affecting the other's) rather than a negative within-twin effect seems to make more sense here, and suggests that it might be important to consider the potential dependencies between siblings' relationships within a family even at this young age.

However one conceptualizes it, the result certainly emphasized the need to think about how parenting behaviors could potentially have opposite effects depending on whether they are shared or non-shared, or on how they are perceived by a co-twin or sibling. Superimposed on a background of predominantly shared environmental connections between siblings' attachments and maternal behavior, the non-shared environment seemed to be creating rather complex interrelationships between different members of the family.

The challenge was to develop a clear model of how such contrasting effects could occur.

A New Approach

It must be said that none of the explanations that we mooted seem entirely satisfactory. Does it really make sense to argue that observing one's sibling being the subject of insensitivity makes one feel insecure, even though it may not have such an effect on the twin who is the subject of the insensitivity? Or, to put it another way, does it really make sense that relative sensitivity in favor of the co-twin makes twins feel secure? It must be acknowledged that this result was counterintuitive and a straightforward explanation did not leap out of the data. However, one possible reason why the finding is so difficult to come to grips with may really have more to do with what we understand security and sensitivity to be, rather than the data itself. Because the terms sensitivity and security have somewhat value-laden connotations it is hard to imagine how sensitivity shown to one's twin sibling/co-twin enhances one's own security.

However, if we adopt an evolutionary perspective, then explanations begin to present themselves. Maternal sensitivity is probably best conceived of as a resource that is (or has been in the evolutionary past) critical for infant survival, and attachment behavior is, arguably, a behavioral strategy that makes use of these parental resources. A secure child *demands* maternal resources (by calling, crying, clinging, maintaining contact) and may even actively compete to secure them. Cast in those terms, it becomes easy to see why observing resources being given preferentially to one's sibling may stimulate attachment behavior. If we assume that what we are seeing in our twin study is the situation where, in response to perceived inequalities in the allocation of maternal resources, there is a shift from minimized expressions of attachment behavior, characteristic of insecure-avoidant attachment, to strong expressions of attachment behavior, typical of secure attachment, then the finding suddenly starts to make sense. Infants who might otherwise have been avoidant detect that maternal resources are being allocated to the co-twin, and begin expressing attachment behavior as a means of competing for those resources, thus demonstrating behavior that is more consistent with secure, rather than insecure, attachment.

Another way of looking at this is to focus on the twin receiving the relatively greater allocation of maternal resources. In this case, the findings of our study could be understood by assuming that insecure attachment behavior represents a strategy to hold on to those resources. Indeed, it was notable that a considerable number of the insecure infants in our sample were insecure-resistant (more than is typical), and it is not hard to imagine that insecure-resistant behavior, characterized as it is by intense crying, anger, and an apparent active attempt to maintain a prolonged state of distress, might be "designed" to maintain maternal attention and other resources (cf. Cassidy & Berlin, 1994). Thus, we could imagine that the child who receives differentially greater parental resources adopts a strategy of expressing very intense and prolonged attachment behavior in order to keep a hold of them. Thus, the overall pattern of findings regarding the non-shared environment, as well as the excess of resistant infants seen in our twin sample as a whole, could be quite elegantly explained by assuming that infants who see maternal resources being preferentially allocated to the co-twin shift toward expressing greater, or stronger, attachment behavior, resulting in a shift from avoidance to security. At the same time, infants who are the recipients of relatively greater of maternal resources also increase attachment behavior, resulting in a shift from secure attachment toward insecure resistance as a means of maintaining those resources and out-competing their sibling.

One might argue that being sensitive to what happens between two other people and able to compute "differential resource allocation" requires greater cognitive sophistication than a 1-year-old is capable of. However, we know that there is good experimental evidence that infants of this age are capable of this. Hart, Field, del Valle, and Letourneau (1998), for example, found that infants were more likely to protest, look at mother, and seek the mother's proximity when she attended to a toy baby than when she was attending to a book, suggesting some degree of monitoring by the infant of the parent's attention toward other infants. Not only that, but the behaviors that were associated with maternal (in)attention were, on the face of it, attachment behaviors. These findings have even been replicated in 6-month-old infants (Hart & Carrington, 2002; see also Hart, this volume, Chapter 4). So, experimental data show quite clearly that infants are affected by interactions their parents have with third parties, and this opens the way for a model of the development of attachment that is sensitive to systemic processes.

Not only does this way of looking at our data help make sense of what at first seemed a quite counterintuitive set of findings, it also paints a rather different picture of what attachment behavior is, or at least might be. It suggests that attachment is influenced by the extent to which parental resources, of which maternal sensitivity may represent a good indicator, are allocated equally within the family. Furthermore, the findings suggest that this within-family, competitive, process operates independently of the "across-the-family" allocation of sensitivity, which from the point of view of our results seemed to behave in a more predictable fashion. Mothers who were *generally* more sensitive had babies who were more likely to be secure. Thus, one might speculate that the causal factors involved in these two processes are quite different. On the one hand, the mother's overall level of sensitivity may reflect what other studies focusing on only one child have found, namely that sensitivity is, to a significant extent, linked to the parent's own, singular, state of mind with respect to attachment. The effect of early attachment experiences, and more crucially the representation of these experiences, may influence a parent's overall level of "attachment resources," with adults who are insecure having fewer attachment or caregiving resources to deploy (either because they are generally limited, or because they are allocated in other domains—like adult–adult relationships, or other important life tasks). And on the other hand, entirely separate from this longer-term developmental process (arguably one that could be understood in terms of evolutionary life-history theory; see Simpson & Belsky, 2008), a set of emerging interactive processes may also come into play, when several children compete for the same parental resources. These processes may have as much to do with the personalities of the children, their interactions with each other, and most importantly their perceptions of the interactions between their parent and the other sibling as they have with the parent's attachment history.

A hint that the temperament of the infants might play a role in these processes emerged from an analysis of temperament that was conducted on a subset of the London sample (52 twin pairs). In this analysis, we looked at whether or not similarity of temperament could help explain why some twins had discordant patterns of attachment. For two of the three scales of temperament we had collected, significant links were found between temperament and concordance. What emerged also seemed to at least indirectly speak to possible competitive processes: If one twin was rated as highly emotional, for example, increasing emotionality in the co-twin tended to increase twin differences in attachment security (see Figure 16.2). Conversely, if the other twin was low on emotionality, increasing emotionality in the other twin tended to increase the likelihood of concordance. The sociability dimension of the temperament measure closely mirrored this picture, with the substantive interpretation being precisely the same: Increasing "distance" between twins in their temperament led to an

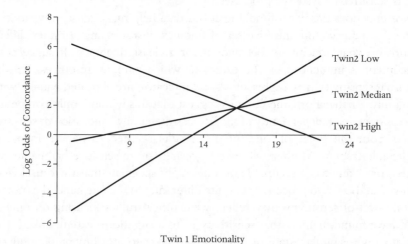

Figure 16.2 Interaction effect of twin emotionality (from the EAS Questionnaire, Buss & Plomin, 1984) and probability of concordance in attachment security

increased probability of concordance. Although this was a small sample, these effects were quite strong and highly statistically significant. There might be several ways of explaining these effects (such as attachment-related differences in parental *perceptions* of temperament), but one seemingly plausible account is that they represent a kind of "niche-competition" effect. One might speculate that infants with similar temperaments are more likely to come into direct competition with each other because they share similar interests, tempos, and needs, and as a result they compete more intensely for the same parental resources. It is not hard to imagine that it would be more difficult to deal with two infants when they make the same demands on parents than when they make quite different—and perhaps more complementary—demands. It is also possible that, quite apart from the effects on parental sensitivity, competition could go on directly between twins with similar temperaments, which could set in motion patterns of sibling and triadic interaction that lead to greater discordances in attachment.

Differential parental preference for one or the other infant might also come into play, even if this preference is not expressed in differential sensitivity. Instead, it may be picked up by the infants through more subtle communicative signals. Mothers of more than one child always have to divide their attention and mothers may prefer one of the two children because of, for example, slight differences in (projected) appearance or temperament. The preferred child may receive more caregiving, but when preference is based on perceived easiness of the child, the preferred child may also receive less attention than the child who is perceived as more difficult. Minde, Corter, Goldberg, and Jeffers (1990) found in their small twin study that mothers seemed to prefer the stronger, medically healthier twin. Allen, Pollin, and Hoffer (1971), however, reported that in their sample most mothers preferred the smaller and neurologically inferior child.

As another example, in the subset of Leiden twins ($n = 76$ pairs), Bokhorst et al. (unpublished data) used the Scale for Individual Differences, consisting of 10 positive and 10 negative child characteristics (based on Elphick, Slotboom, & Kohnstamm, 1996). For each item, the mother had to choose which child was described most adequately by the characteristic. The 10 most positive and the 10 most negative characteristics were used. An example of a positive item is: "Is very sweet" and an example of a negative item is: "Wants to play with different toys after a short time." To create an overall preference score the frequency of negative characteristics was subtracted from the frequency of positive characteristics. To their surprise, Bokhorst et al. found that in comparison with mothers of twins who were discordant in terms of attachment security, mothers of twins who were concordant differed more in their preferences toward the children ($d = .36$). Contrary to the authors' expectations, mothers showed more differences in preference toward the twins concordant in security than toward twins discordant in security. However, if we re-cast these findings in light of the temperament results from the London sample then they may be less counterintuitive than previously thought. If parental preference is related to temperament (and is not a direct index of differential resource allocation), then the two sets of results come into alignment: greater differences in maternal preference reflect the fact that the twins present distinctive and less similar temperaments and needs, which in turn creates less niche-competition between the siblings.

Our tentative conclusion, then, is that competitive processes that take place between siblings may be quite important in the development of attachment in certain circumstances, in ways that have not hitherto been anticipated. Thinking about these processes in terms of competition for maternal resources helped us make sense of a complex set of findings. Sibling competition and parental resource allocation are both central concepts in evolutionary models of parent–offspring relations. In view of the origins of attachment theory, it is surprising that these concepts have not been more widely adopted in empirical studies on attachment. Nevertheless, several authors have developed contemporary Darwinian accounts of the evolutionary functions of "secure" and "insecure" attachment that are helpful in fleshing out our emerging understanding of sibling competition.

Evolutionary Models of Attachment Security and Insecurity

While Bowlby's original thinking about the development and functions of attachment behavior were based on solid evolutionary principles, the science of evolution has changed considerably since that time, and as Simpson and Belsky (2008) note, this has important implications for our understanding of attachment. In particular, relatively recent advances in evolutionary thinking point to at least three critical issues that were not appreciated in Bowlby's day, that are particularly pertinent to this discussion: (a) The environments in which attachment behavior evolved are likely to have been much less predictable, static and benign than originally thought, (b) natural selection favors adaptations that promote survival and reproduction of an individual's genes, not those of a species, and (c) family members do not share all their genes, and hence cooperation between them (e.g., a mother supporting a baby's needs, siblings helping each other) may vary under different conditions and the interests of one may not coincide with those of another.

According to modern evolutionary theory, organisms are selected to maximize their overall reproductive output across the entirety of their lives and in order to do so they must solve a complex and uncertain set of problems. Parents have to decide, as it were, how to best expend their resources between several competing options. On the one hand, they could dedicate their resources to reproduction (including child rearing) in the here and now, or they could invest for the uncertain, but partially predictable, future (in one's own growth and other future-oriented resources, like coalition-building, learning). Furthermore, even in the here and now there is a choice between caring for existing offspring and focusing on mating (finding suitable mates, retaining them). The actuarial problem that all organisms face is how to balance these various constraints, which may take on different costs and benefits under differing ecological circumstances and over different time frames. In some conditions, it may be beneficial for the organism, for example, to shift investment away from current reproductive efforts toward future reproduction, or from investing heavily in current offspring to securing high-quality mates (Simpson & Belsky, 2008). In effect, what this means is that what is apparently best for the parent, in the evolutionary sense, may not be what is best for an individual child. This is most clearly illustrated in Triver's model of parent–offspring conflict (Trivers, 1974). Because parents share only 50% of their genes with their offspring, there is an intrinsic potential for conflict, because offspring may want more resources than their parents will have been selected to provide. In theory, parents may maximize their overall reproductive success by investing more in a different child, or in other areas of life that may enhance their personal reproductive success. Early on in a child's life, having already invested heavily in gestation, parental investment should be relatively low-cost from the point of view of the parent. However, there will come a point, as the child matures, when the parent may wish to divert resources elsewhere, and the child should be motivated (again in the evolutionary sense) to resist this as long as possible, assuming there are no significant costs attached to this (such as parental rejection or actual harm). As Simpson and Belsky (2008) point out, a large number of factors could affect how these costs and benefits are calculated by the parent, but particular features of the child, such as physical health, or indeed any sign that might forecast future survival and reproductive success, could lead to differences in how much a parent invests in different children in the same family. Critically, because a child also shares only half their genes with their siblings, they will be selected to not share parental resources equally. Thus, the level of parental resources a child actually receives may be a complex function of the investment strategies the parent has adopted (either affecting the overall level directed toward child-rearing or to particular children), the child's success in winning and retaining those resources (e.g., struggling to delay weaning), and their ability to compete for them against siblings.

Simpson and Belsky (2008) suggest that these models help solve the evolutionary puzzle of individual differences in attachment. Resistant attachment, for example, may have evolved as a means of securing parenting resources from parents who are over-burdened, naïve, under-involved, or in other ways unable to provide the infant with these resources. As such, these behavioral patterns may be designed to elicit care from an adult who is unable, rather than unwilling, to provide them (Simpson & Belsky, 2008; Chisholm, 1996). Our data fit quite well with this idea, if one assumes that what "unable" really means is that resources exist and their accessibility is potentially modifiable. In other words, the critical issue from the baby's point of view is not the parent's competence per se, but whether the resource is "extractable" from its current state of unavailability by strong, active efforts. Differential allocation of parenting resources would arguably represent a very strong signal of "extractability" because the infant witnesses the clear presence of a relevant resource that the subject is not currently benefiting from, because it is being expended on a sibling. In that sense, differential parental sensitivity may indicate to the less favored sibling that there are clearly untapped resources around that are "up for grabs," and may be worth competing for. Avoidant attachment, in contrast, may represent a circumstance in which the parent is essentially unwilling rather than unable to invest heavily in parenting (Chisholm, 1996), or perhaps one in which the degree of investment appears to be unmodifiable for any other reason from the point of view of the infant. In this case, avoidant attachment may represent parent–offspring conflict that was resolved far earlier in development. Presumably, the parent signaled clearly and unstintingly at an early stage in the lifespan that resource allocation to the infant was limited and non-negotiable. As a consequence, the infant is forced to adjust his or her attachment signaling in line with the availability of the resource that those signals typically call for (see Main, 1981).

Thus, from the point of view of evolutionary theory, several apparent paradoxes make sense. First of all, within-family differences in attachment security may emerge because (a) the parent chooses to invest more heavily in one child than another, (b) the parent's strategy changes over time as a function of local circumstances (for children spaced apart in age), or (c) the child out-competes a sibling for finite parental resources. We would argue that sibling competition may be an important circumstance that attachment behavior evolved to be responsive to, and may lead infants to shift their estimation of the various costs and benefits in favor of more strongly signaling for parental resources.

Findings from Sibling Studies

It is unfortunate that there have been few studies that have specifically attempted to identify siblings who have discordant attachment classifications and examine the extent to which they yield evidence of differential allocation of maternal resources, such as sensitivity. We are thus forced to look for clues from more indirect sources. Our hypothesis concerning the impact of sibling competition on attachment would find at least indirect support from any studies that indicated that discordant attachment relationships (where we assume there is greater sibling competition) are associated with a greater, and stronger, expression of attachment behavior (shift from avoidance to security or resistance, more clinging, crying, and proximity-seeking). Further indirect evidence could be found if conditions that lead to a change in the allocation of maternal resources from one child to another lead to increases in attachment behavior. The studies by Hart and colleagues (Hart et al., 1998; Hart & Carrington 2002; Hart, this volume, Chapter 4), mentioned above, represent an experimental example of this kind of evidence. Studies that have looked at children's reactions to the birth of a new sibling provide a non-experimental counterpart to this work.

The transition to siblinghood has been investigated in a number of published studies, starting with the seminal work of Judy Dunn and colleagues (Dunn & Kendrick, 1980). What Dunn and her colleagues established very clearly was that the birth of a sibling is a time of great family upheaval and brings with it a significant and consistent change in the quantity and quality of parent–child interactions for the older sibling. In Dunn and Kendrick's study, for example, observational assessments before and after the birth of a sibling revealed that older siblings received less maternal positive attention and more control, disciplining, and restraint after the birth of a sibling (although some of these changes may have been developmental rather than a direct response to the birth of a sibling). Notably, many of the episodes of discipline and control were observed to take place in response to difficult or demanding behavior of the sibling during periods when the mother was preoccupied with the newborn (e.g., feeding, changing). The birth of a sibling is also accompanied by increased clinginess, night waking, demands for bottles, and various displays of anxiety (see also Stewart, Mobley, Van Tuyl, & Salvador, 1987).

In a recent unpublished study, Hamilton, Ramadhan, Burke, and Fearon (unpublished data) found similar increases in anxious behavior in a small ($N = 31$) sample of toddlers with a newborn sibling. Interestingly, in younger toddlers (2 years and under) attachment security measured prior to the newborn's birth (using the AQS) was *positively* associated with increases in anxious behavior (pre- to post-birth of the sibling). One interpretation of this finding is that these infants had previously enjoyed substantial sensitivity from their parent, and therefore experienced a more dramatic relative loss of parental attention, which in turn heightened their attachment behavior (as evidenced in their mother's reports of anxious behavior, such as clinginess). Interestingly, apparently similar effects have been reported by Hart and colleagues in an experimental setting (Hart, Carrington, Tronick, & Carroll, 2004). In a sample of 96 six-month-old infants, Hart and colleagues found that negative affect displayed by infants in a "jealousy context" (maternal attention to a realistic doll) *positively* correlated with maternal sensitivity, as observed in a separate face-to-face play situation. Thus, infants who receive relatively greater maternal resources appear to be more sensitive to losing maternal attention to another child, and this stimulates what could be considered more intense attachment behavior.

Teti and colleagues have conducted a number of important studies regarding the transition to siblinghood. In one investigation, Teti et al. (1996) found that sibling birth was associated with decreases in attachment security, as indexed by the Attachment Q-Set (an assessment of attachment derived from home observations, see Waters & Deane, 1985). However, because studies using the

AQS do not routinely distinguish between types of insecurity it is not possible to determine whether these changes represent changes in the direction of resistance or avoidance. According to our tentative hypothesis, the net change in security that results from a decrease in maternal attention (and therefore greater differential allocation of parental resources) will depend on the original distribution of attachment patterns. If there are relatively large numbers of insecure-avoidant (A) infants, and few insecure-resistant (C) infants, then this shift in attention could lead to increases (e.g., the As becoming Bs) or decreases (Bs becoming Cs) in net security. Thus, it is unclear whether this study can be taken to be consistent with our hypothesis or not. We would predict that the decreases in security largely reflected changes from security to a more resistant-type presentation. Having said that, this argument is based on the assumption that the changes in security observed by Teti and associates (1996) actually reflect changes in the sibling's perception of differential sensitivity, either because there has been a decline in sensitivity, or because it is being shared. While this may change for some children, there are many other changes that occur in the transition to siblinghood that significantly complicate the picture (see for example Baydar, Hyle, & Brooks-Gunn, 1997).

One study has actually used the strange situation to assess attachment security before and after sibling birth (Touris, Kromelow, & Harding, 1995). Touris and associates (1995) also collected parallel data on a comparison sample that was not having a new baby. What was observed in this albeit small study ($n = 20$ in each group) was clear evidence of substantial change in attachment patterns, although there was no clear evidence of a systematic direction in that change (e.g., from avoidance to security, or security to resistance). The authors point out that the birth of a sibling is not always accompanied by negative changes in parental sensitivity, which of course is an inherent problem for any study that does not measure differential maternal sensitivity directly. Broadly speaking then, studies of the transition to siblinghood indicate that attachment may be affected by the changes in parental resources that accompany this period, but they say little about the extent to which this is a result of changes in parental attention and sensitivity, or more crucially still, the older sibling's perception of the interactions that take place between the parent and new baby.

Concurrent studies of siblings outside the newborn period may also be useful in ascertaining whether differential treatment results in heightened attachment behavior in infants and young children. Tentative evidence for our hypotheses is apparent in a trend finding from Teti and Ablard (1989). In their study, in which attachment was assessed in both older (using the AQS) and younger (using the SSP) siblings, insecure infants cried more when the parent left the room (leaving the siblings together) when their older sibling was secure than when their older sibling was insecure. The numbers of discordant sib pairs were small, so statistical power for this comparison was very low. Nevertheless, the study hints at the possibility that there may be some link between discordant sibling attachment status and the heightened expression of attachment behavior. More direct support comes from a study by Volling and Belsky (1992), who found that secure firstborn children were more sensitive to differential parenting than insecure firstborns. Specifically, the authors found a stronger correlation between maternal differential treatment and sibling conflict in firstborn siblings who had been secure (versus insecure) in Ainsworth's strange situation prior to the birth of the younger sibling (a finding which echoes Hart et al., 2004). Results of our small sibling study (Hamilton et al., unpublished data) pointed in the same direction when one of the authors (Ronan Burke) followed the families up when the new sibling was 5 months old. This follow-up revealed that when mothers were instructed to play with the 5-month-old sibling to the exclusion of the older sibling, the more secure older siblings (measured prior to siblinghood) tended to compete more for parental attention.

A very interesting example of a similar set of findings to our twin results, which were interpreted in similar terms, comes from a behavior genetic study of parenting and social competence in toddlers. Knafo (2009) found that twins who received relatively lower quality parenting than their co-twin showed higher social competence. The author interpreted this as a competitive process in which the less favored twin seeks to win back parental attention through heightened prosociality.

There is at least one study that appears to directly contradict the proposal we have outlined in this chapter. This study, by Roisman and Fraley (2008), conducted essentially identical analyses of attachment and sensitivity to those we conducted in our twin paper. Using twin data from the Early Childhood Longitudinal Study, they analyzed the extent to which shared and non-shared influences on attachment might be linked to shared and non-shared aspects of sensitivity. Just as in our study, they found that common environmental influences on attachment were linked to common environmental influences on attachment (and there were no significant genetic effects). However, whereas we found a negative non-shared pathway, they found a positive one. In other words, where there was differential sensitivity, the twin who received relatively more sensitivity was *more* likely to be secure. Roisman and Fraley's study involved a substantially larger sample of twins than ours and hence one could reasonably assign greater confidence in their finding. On the other hand, there are important differences between the two studies. First of all, the AQS, as we mentioned earlier, does not discriminate between different forms of insecurity so it is not possible to determine the relative preponderance of avoidance and resistance in the sample. Furthermore, the study involved a modified version of the AQS, with somewhat uncertain validity. It is also conceivable that differences in the populations may have had an impact. In particular, our twin study involved predominantly middle- to upper-class families, while Roisman and Fraley's sample covered a broader spectrum of social circumstances. Given the experimental data described earlier (Hart et al., 2004), it is conceivable that the effects we found were contingent upon the fact that the average level of sensitivity in our study was quite high. As Hart and associates indicate, competitive responses to maternal differential attention appear to be more readily triggered in infants who have experienced higher levels of maternal sensitivity in the first place. In that respect, it would be interesting to revisit Roisman and Fraley's data separately for families where the average sensitivity is above and below the sample mean. There is one further study that may be inconsistent with our proposals that we are aware of. This study (van IJzendoorn et al., 2000) examined maternal sensitivity in relation to attachment security in several modestly sized samples of fraternal siblings. As in our twin study, this sibling study found evidence consistent with the notion that commonalities in sensitivity between siblings account for similarities in their attachment security. However, unlike our study, but like Roisman and Fraley's (2008) report, these authors found that attachment was more likely to be concordant between siblings if maternal sensitivity increased from the time it was assessed in the older sibling to when it was assessed in the younger one. It is unclear how this finding fits with the framework we are proposing here. However, it must be noted that on average maternal sensitivity assessed with the 1-year-old second child was lower than it had been with the firstborn child at age 1, so concordance of attachment security might have been dependent on sensitivity with the second child. Furthermore, sensitivity was not measured for both siblings simultaneously so this study does not elucidate *differential* parenting at the same point in time. Because attachment and sensitivity were only measured once for each child it is not possible to determine, for example, whether increases in sensitivity shown to the younger sibling led to changes in the older sibling's attachment behavior, as we might predict.

Conclusions

Broadly speaking then, there are circumstantial findings and direct experimental studies that indicate that infants are sensitive to the degree to which their parent's attention and caregiving resources are deployed toward another infant, and that this may trigger a range of affective behaviors potentially identifiable as attachment behaviors. One interpretation of our twin data leads to similar conclusions, and some studies of siblings provide some further indirect support for this view. However, it is clear that there is a fair way to go before we can conclude definitively that differential parenting in triadic contexts truly affects the expression of precisely defined attachment behavior or affects the longer-term development of attachment. Nevertheless, it is an intriguing possibility and a potentially fruitful area for future research.

It is important to note that no study has yet examined the developmental consequences of discordant attachment relationships within a family, or the specific contribution that sibling–sibling competition for attachment resources might make for later development. A critical question to be addressed by future research thus also concerns the extent to which the long-term predictive significance of attachment insecurity is the same when it is concordant between siblings as when it is discordant. One could imagine that the apparent shifts in attachment strategy that our study seems to imply represent short-term functional adaptations to the relatively intense competition for maternal resources of the twin situation, or perhaps in closely spaced siblings.

Extensive evidence nevertheless indicates that maternal differential treatment, defined much more generally, is often quite stable over time (McGuire, Dunn, & Plomin, 1995) and has consistent negative effects. For example, Dunn, Stocker, and Plomin (1990) found that differential maternal control and affection were associated with worrying, anxiety, and depression in 7-year-olds. In particular, the sibling who reported experiencing more control and less affection was more likely to feel anxious or depressed. Differences in self-reported maternal differential behavior have also been linked to sibling self-esteem (Beardsall & Dunn, 1992). Furthermore, differential parental behavior appears to be linked to the quality of the relationship that siblings have with each other (Brody & Stoneman, 1994). Future research on the long-term outcomes of secure and insecure attachment may thus also benefit from a consideration of the possibility that differential parental sensitivity may be an important proximal influence on children's attachments. Further research is clearly needed to understand the processes that give rise to differential sensitivity, the possible role of other family relationships, particularly fathers, and the possibly active contribution that children themselves make in eliciting different patterns of care within the family. It may also prove to be important to consider the possibility that all secure attachments are not equal, and may have heterogeneous predictive power for future development, depending on the functional circumstances that gave rise to them.

References

Ainsworth, M. D. S., Blehar, M. C., Waters, E., & Wall, S. (1978). *Patterns of attachment: A psychological study of the Strange Situation*. Hillsdale, NJ: Erlbaum.

Allen, M. G., Pollin, W. & Hoffer, A. (1971). Parental, birth and infancy factors in infant twin development. *American Journal of Psychiatry, 127*, 33–39.

Bakermans-Kranenburg, M. J., & van IJzendoorn, M. H. (2007). Research Review: Genetic vulnerability or differential susceptibility in child development: The case of attachment. *Journal of Child Psychology and Psychiatry, 48*, 1160–1173.

Baydar, N., Hyle, P., & Brooks-Gunn, J. (1997). A longitudinal study of the effects of the birth of a sibling during the preschool and early grade school years. *Journal of Marriage and Family, 59*, 957–965.

Beardsall, L., & Dunn, J. (1992). Adversities in childhood: Siblings' experiences, and their relations to self-esteem. *Journal of Child Psychology and Psychiatry, 33*, 349–359.

Belsky, J., & Fearon, R. M. P. (2008). Precursors of attachment security. In J. Cassidy & P. R. Shaver (Eds.), *Handbook of attachment: Theory, research and clinical applications* (2nd ed., pp. 295–316). New York: Guilford Press.

Bokhorst, C. L., Bakermans-Kranenburg, M. J., Fearon, R. M. P., van IJzendoorn, M. H., Fonagy, P. & Schuengel, C. (2003). The importance of shared environment in mother–infant attachment security: A behavioral genetic study. *Child Development, 74*, 769–782.

Bowlby, J. (1969). *Attachment and loss: Vol. 1. Attachment*. London: Hogarth Press and the Institute of Psycho-Analysis.

Bretherton, I., & Mulholland, K. A. (1999). Internal working models in attachment relationships: A construct revisited. In J. Cassidy & P. R. Shaver (Eds.), *Handbook of attachment* (pp. 89–111). New York: Guilford Press.

Brody, G., & Stoneman, Z. (1994). Sibling relationships and their association with parental differential treatment. In E. M. Hetherington & D. Reiss (Eds.), *Separate social worlds of siblings: The impact of nonshared environment on development* (Vol. iii, pp. 129–142). Hillsdale, NJ: Erlbaum.

Buss, A. H., & Plomin, R. (1984). *Temperament: Early developing personality traits*. Hillsdale, NJ: Erlbaum.

Cassidy, J., & Berlin, L. J. (1994). The insecure/ambivalent pattern of attachment: Theory and research. *Child Development, 65*, 971–981.

Chisholm, J. S. (1996). The evolutionary ecology of attachment organization. *Human Nature, 7*, 1–38.

Cowan, P. A. (1997). Beyond meta-analysis: A plea for a family systems view of attachment. *Child Development, 68*, 601–603.

De Wolff, M., & van IJzendoorn, M. H. (1997). Sensitivity and attachment: A meta-analysis on parental antecedents of infant attachment. *Child Development, 68*, 571–591.

Dunn, J., & Kendrick, D. (1980). The arrival of a sibling: Changes in patterns of interaction between mother and firstborn child. *Journal of Child Psychology and Psychiatry, 21*, 119–132.

Dunn, J., & Plomin, R. (1990). *Separate lives: Why siblings are so different* (Vol. xiii). New York: Basic Books.

Dunn, J., Stocker, C., & Plomin, R. (1990). Nonshared experiences within the family: Correlates of behavioral problems in middle childhood. *Development and Psychopathology, 2*, 113–126.

Elphick, E., Slotboom, A., & Kohnstamm, G. A. (1996). Parental expertise on individual differences between children: Construction of the questionnaire "Beoordelings-Lijst Individuele verschillen tussen Kinderen" [Assessment questionnaire for individual differences between children]. Unpublished manuscript.

Fearon, R. M. P., van IJzendoorn, M. H., Fonagy, P., Bakermans-Kranenburg, M. J., Schuengel, C., & Bokhorst, C. (2006). In search of shared and non-shared environmental factors in security of attachment: A behavior-genetic study of the association between sensitivity and attachment security. *Developmental Psychology, 6*, 1026–1040.

Fonagy, P., Steele, H., & Steele, M. (1991). Maternal representations of attachment during pregnancy predict the organization of infant–mother attachment at one year of age. *Child Development, 62*, 891–905.

Hart, S. L. (this volume). The ontogenesis of jealousy in the first year of life: A theory of jealousy as a biologically-based dimension of temperament. In S. L. Hart & M. Legerstee (Eds.), *Handbook of jealousy: Theory, research, and multidisciplinary approaches.* Malden, MA: Wiley-Blackwell.

Hart, S. L., & Carrington, H. (2002). Jealousy in 6-month-old infants. *Infancy, 3,* 395–402.

Hart, S., Carrington, H., Tronick, E. Z., & Carroll, S. (2004). When infants lose exclusive maternal attention: Is it jealousy? *Infancy, 6,* 57–78.

Hart, S., Field, T., del Valle, C., & Letourneau, M. (1998). Infants protest their mothers' attending to an infant-size doll. *Social Development, 7,* 54–61.

Hinde, R. A. (1987). *Individuals, relationships and culture: Links between ethology and the social sciences.* Cambridge: Cambridge University Press.

Knafo, A. (2009). *Prosocial development: The intertwined roles of children's genetics and their parental environment.* Invited Address, The Society for Research in Child Development Biennial Meeting, Denver, CO.

Main, M. (1981). Avoidance in the service of attachment: A working paper. In K. Immelmann, G. Barlow, & M. Main (Eds.), *Behavioral development: The Bielefeld interdisciplinary project* (pp. 651–693). New York: Cambridge University Press.

Main, M. (1999). Mary D. Salter Ainsworth: Tribute and portrait. *Psychoanalytic Inquiry, 19,* 682–736.

Marvin, R. S., & Stewart, R. B. (1990). A family systems framework for the study of attachment. In M. T. Greenberg & E. M. Cummings (Eds.), *Attachment in the preschool years: Theory, research and intervention.* Chicago: University of Chicago Press.

McCartney, K., & Rosenthal, R. (2000). Effect size, practical importance, and social policy for children. *Child Development, 71,* 173–180.

McGuire, S., Dunn, J., & Plomin, R. (1995). Maternal differential treatment of siblings and children's behavioral problems: A longitudinal study. *Development and Psychopathology, 7,* 515–528.

Minde, K., Corter, C., Goldberg, S., & Jeffers, D. (1990). Maternal preference between premature twins up to age four. *Journal of the American Academy of Child and Adolescent Psychiatry, 29,* 367–374.

Plomin, R., & Daniels, D. (1987). Why are children in the same family so different from one another? *Behavioral and Brain Sciences, 10,* 1–16.

Plomin, R., DeFries, J. C., McClearn, G. E., & McGuffin, P. (2001). *Behavioral genetics.* New York: Worth.

Roisman, G. I., & Fraley, R. C. (2006). The limits of genetic influence: A behavior-genetic analysis of infant–caregiver relationship quality and temperament. *Child Development, 77,* 1656–1667.

Roisman, G. I., & Fraley, R. C. (2008). A behavior-genetic study of parenting quality, infant attachment security, and their covariation in a nationally representative sample. *Developmental Psychology, 44,* 831–839.

Sagi A., van IJzendoorn M. H., Aviezer O., Donnell F., et al. (1995). Attachments in a multiple-caregiver and multiple-infant environment: The case of the Israeli kibbutzim. *Monographs of the Society for Research in Child Development, 60,* 71–91.

Simpson, J., & Belsky, J. (2008). Attachment theory within a modern evolutionary framework. In J. Cassidy & P. R. Shaver (Eds.), *Handbook of attachment: Theory, research and clinical applications* (2nd ed., pp. 131–157). New York: Guilford Press.

Spangler, G., & Grossmann, K. E. (1993). Biobehavioral organization in securely and insecurely attached infants. *Child Development, 64,* 1439–1450.

Stewart, R. B., Mobley, L. A., Van Tuyl, S. S., & Salvador, M. A. (1987). The firstborn's adjustment to the birth of a sibling. *Child Development, 58,* 341–355.

Teti, D. M., & Ablard, K. E. (1989). Security of attachment and infant–sibling relationships: A laboratory study. *Child Development, 60,* 1519–1528.

Teti, D. M., Sakin, J. W., Kucera, E., Corns, K. M., et al. (1996). And baby makes four: Predictors of attachment security among preschool-age firstborns during the transition to siblinghood. *Child Development, 67,* 579–596.

Trivers, R. L. (1974). Parent–offspring conflict. *American Zoologist, 14,* 249–264.

Touris, M., Kromelow, S., & Harding, C. (1995). Mother–firstborn attachment and the birth of a sibling. *American Journal of Orthopsychiatry, 65,* 293–297.

van IJzendoorn, M. H. (1995). Adult attachment representations, parental responsiveness, and infant attachment: A meta-analysis on the predictive validity of the Adult Attachment Interview. *Psychological Bulletin, 117,* 387–403.

van IJzendoorn, M., Moran, G., Belsky, J., Pederson, D., Bakermans-Kranenburg, M., & Kneppers, K. (2000). The similarity of siblings' attachments to their mother. *Child Development, 71,* 1086–1098.

van IJzendoorn, M. H., Vereijken, C. M. J. L., Bakermans-Kranenburg, M. J., & Riksen-Walraven, M. J. (2003). Assessing attachment security with the Attachment Q Sort: Meta-analytic evidence for the validity of the observer AQS. *Child Development, 75,* 1188–1213.

Volling B. L., & Belsky J. (1992). The contribution of mother–child and father–child relationships to the quality of sibling interaction: A longitudinal study. *Child Development, 63,* 1209–1222.

Ward, M. J., & Carlson, E. A. (1995). Associations among adult attachment representations, maternal sensitivity, and infant–mother attachment in a sample of adolescent mothers. *Child Development, 66,* 69–79.

Waters E., & Deane, K. E. (1985). Defining and assessing individual differences in attachment relationships: Q-methodology and the organization of behavior in infancy and early childhood. *Monographs of the Society for Research in Child Development, 50,* 41–65.

Weinfield, N. S., Sroufe, L. A., Egeland, B., & Carlson, E. (1999). The nature of individual differences in infant–caregiver attachment. In J. Cassidy & P. R. Shaver (Eds.), *Handbook of attachment: Theory, research, and clinical applications* (pp. 64–86). New York: Guilford Press.

17

The Development of Sibling Jealousy

Brenda L. Volling, Denise E. Kennedy, and Lisa M. H. Jackey

Concerns about sibling rivalry and jealousy have been voiced by clinicians and parents for quite some time (Griffin & De La Torre, 1983; Leung & Robson, 1991; Levy, 1934; Podolsky, 1954; Ross, 1931). Consider, for instance, that violence between siblings is the most frequently occurring type of family violence, affecting about 70% of homes in the United States (Hoffman & Edwards, 2004; Steinmetz, 1977; Straus & Moore, 1990). Aggressive and violent sibling behavior may often be motivated by jealousy (Brody, 1998). Siblings also spend more time in the company of one another during childhood than with parents or even peers (Dunn, 2007; Volling, 2003) so sibling jealousy may occur frequently in many families (Thompson & Halberstadt, 2008). Further, hostile, destructive sibling interaction has been linked to children's behavior problems (e.g., Garcia, Shaw, Winslow, & Yaggi, 2000), whereas cooperative and prosocial sibling interactions have been related to children's constructive conflict resolution, social cognitive understanding, and successful relationships with peers (e.g., Herrera & Dunn, 1997; Ross, Ross, Stein, & Trabasso, 2006). What is clear from the literature on sibling relationships is that children spend a considerable amount of time with their siblings, during which they may encounter frequent opportunities to experience and cope with sibling jealousy, and this jealousy can influence the affective nature of the sibling relationship and, in turn, have significant developmental consequences for children's and adolescents' well-being. Despite the relevance of sibling jealousy, it is striking to see how little research has actually been conducted in this area.

Sibling rivalry refers to the feelings of envy, jealousy, and competitiveness that exist between brothers and sisters within the family. Rivalry can take many forms: the tug-of-war over a valued possession, the playful competition between brothers on the soccer field, the striving for academic success over one's sibling, and the intense feelings of hatred and envy over the personal accomplishments of one's sibling in comparison to one's self. In addition to the competition for status, objects, and

Handbook of Jealousy: Theory, Research and Multidisciplinary Approaches, First Edition.
Edited by Sybil L. Hart and Maria Legerstee.
© 2013 Blackwell Publishing Ltd. Published 2013 by Blackwell Publishing Ltd.

achievement, siblings also compete for the love and attention of their parents. Any competition between siblings may reflect rivalry, but when the rivalry involves the love and attention of parents and the sibling rival, we speak of jealousy and the feelings of sadness and anger experienced when one believes the beloved relationship with the parent is lost to a sibling rival. In the current chapter, we start by providing some theoretical background on sibling rivalry and particularly the jealousy that arises when children compete for their parents' love and attention. We then present a model of jealousy that we have used to guide our research on the development of sibling jealousy and the family correlates of children's jealousy. Next, we provide a brief review of the extant research conducted on sibling jealousy across childhood, adolescence, and into adulthood. We also present some recent findings from our research program examining sibling jealousy in a sample of toddler and preschool siblings during a triadic laboratory paradigm. The final part of the chapter focuses on future directions for research examining sibling jealousy across the lifespan.

Theoretical Background

There appears to be a multitude of ways in which jealousy has been measured in research to date and we will refrain from engaging in the theoretical battles endemic among researchers about the definition of what jealousy is or is not (see Salovey, 1991). Theoretical formulations are critical for understanding how researchers define jealousy because such formulations provide the basis for the researcher's conceptualization of jealousy and they also provide readers with an understanding of how jealousy was operationalized and assessed for a particular research program. Our work over the years has focused on sibling jealousy and the relationships that young children form with parents and their siblings. Our research is also informed by a developmental perspective and an understanding that jealousy responses may change over time. Our definition is couched within a family system's perspective as well, because parents and siblings are part of a larger family system and cannot be understood in isolation of other contextual forces (Cox & Paley, 2003). Further, our definition and view of jealousy are heavily influenced by the writings of Gregory White and Paul Mullen (1989) in their presentation of romantic jealousy. Yet, we do not believe that the jealousy we are studying between siblings in early childhood is the same as the jealousy that others have examined between adult lovers in romantic relationships. Although White and Mullen chose to focus on romantic jealousy between adults, their transactional perspective is inherently applicable to the development of sibling jealousy in the context of a wider family system (see White & Mullen, 1989, for a detailed and complete description of their theoretical approach).

Rather than searching for *the* single emotional expression or blend of emotions that constitutes jealousy, White and Mullen propose that jealousy is actually a complex of emotions, behaviors, and thoughts that arise in a very specific interpersonal context, in this case, the social triangle that consists of the jealous individual, the beloved (in our case, the parent), and the rival (here, one's sibling). For present purposes, we propose that jealousy is a complex of affects (A), behaviors (B), and cognitions (C) that an individual experiences following the perceived loss or threat to self-esteem and/or the loss of or threat to a valued relationship to a rival (see Figure 17.1). Figure 17.1 shows that each individual in the triad may have their own ABC complex of how they would react in a jealousy situation, and these differences among the three individuals can influence the dynamics within the social triangle. Because siblings in the family are often different ages (unless they are twins), the jealousy complex for an older sibling may be very different than the jealousy complex for a younger sibling, simply because of the cognitive advances that coincide with maturation and age changes. The jealousy *complex* is a patterned set of emotional, cognitive, and behavioral responses expressed by the jealous person in the *interpersonal jealousy system*, which is the system of interpersonal relationships among the three individuals involved, i.e., jealous person, beloved, and rival (see Figure 17.1). For instance, the jealous individual can cognitively interpret the beloved's affectionate behavior toward a rival as betrayal, feel anger as a result, and behave accordingly with aggression. In contrast, if the jealous person interprets the threat as a loss of the relationship, he or she may report feelings of sadness, and consequently,

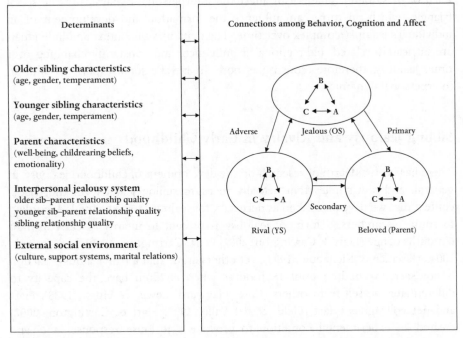

Figure 17.1 Transactional model of sibling jealousy based on White and Mullen (1989)

withdraw from social interaction. Each of these potential patterns of affective, behavioral, and cognitive responses constitutes a jealousy complex and is no more or less valid than the other.

Three dyadic relationships, as well as the social triangle, make up the inter-personal jealousy system. The primary relationship is the relationship between the jealous person and the beloved, the secondary relationship is the relationship between the rival and the beloved, and the adverse relationship is the relationship between the jealous person and the rival. Of course, the quality and closeness of each of these relationships may influence the jealousy complex of any single individual involved in the triangle, and indeed, may play an influential role in what form the jealousy complex takes or how often an individual may experience jealousy. Should a parent, for example, have a preference for one child over the other (i.e., favoritism), and express more frequent affection toward that child than his or her sibling, then naturally, the sibling experiences a different inter-personal context and is exposed differentially to displays of affection than is the other child. As Figure 17.1 also denotes, the social triangle is influenced by a larger social and cultural context and the dynamics of the interpersonal jealousy system can be influenced by characteristics of the three individuals, as well as the quality of other relationships that exist within the immediate family system (e.g., marriage) or by factors outside the family (e.g., social network of kin). The determinants, in this case, consist of the age, gender, and temperament of each of the siblings, as well as the emotional state and personality of the parent. Each of these determinants can affect the interpersonal dynamics of the social triangle, which, in turn, can influence the formation and development of an individual's jealousy complex over time. The dynamics of context and individuals are intricately related, bidirectional in influence, and constantly changing over time. Jealousy, therefore, constitutes both an intrapersonal experience and an interpersonal dynamic.

Sibling Jealousy and Rivalry in Early Childhood

There has been a dearth of research on the development of childhood jealousy, in general, and few studies that actually measure sibling jealousy in the triadic context that we have prescribed as necessary for jealousy to be elicited. According to some researchers, a form of jealousy is present in infants as early as 5 to 6 months of age (Hart & Carrington, 2002; Hart, Carrington, Tronick, & Carroll, 2004; Masciuch & Kienapple, 1993), yet others argue that a true jealousy reaction is not seen in children until 18 months when children have the capacity to differentiate the self from others (Case, Hayward, Lewis, & Hurst, 1988). Hart and her colleagues (Hart, Field, & del Valle, 1998; Hart & Carrington, 2002) created an experimental condition to provoke a jealousy response in 6- and 12-month-old infants by having mothers attend to and affectionately interact with an infant doll. Infants expressed sadness, anger, and protested their mothers' interactions with the doll, inhibited their play, expressed negative vocalizations, and approached the mother repeatedly, indicating that they were sensitive to the loss of maternal attention. Masciuch and Kienapple (1993) also found that infants as young as 8 months old responded with similar negative behaviors (e.g., frowns, crying, ceasing play, physical closeness, and physical intrusion) to a jealousy-provoking experimental condition where mothers attended to another infant and a peer. Early research on sibling interaction bears out the significance of parental attention for the emergence of jealousy. Corter, Abramovitch, and Pepler (1983) compared the rate of sibling conflict in the home when mothers were present with the siblings and when mothers left the two siblings alone. Siblings engaged in more agonistic interaction when mothers were present than when they were absent, suggesting that siblings were most likely jealous and competing for their mother's attention when she was present.

The birth of a sibling

The firstborn child's reactions to the birth of a baby sibling have often been interpreted as jealousy by clinicians and parents alike (Griffin & De La Torre, 1983; Legg, Sherick, & Wadland, 1974). Older children react to the arrival of the rival sibling by attempting to disrupt the mother–infant interaction, drawing attention to one's self, or directing aggression toward the mother and/or newborn (Field & Reite, 1984; Legg et al., 1974; Nadelman & Begun, 1982; Stewart, Mobley, Van Tuyl, & Salvador, 1987). Parents also report instances of regression in the older child's self-care skills (e.g., toileting accidents, requesting to drink from a bottle), increases in problem behavior, and sleep disturbances soon after the baby is brought home (Dunn & Kendrick, 1982; Field & Reite, 1984). Dunn and Kendrick (1981) followed 40 British families longitudinally from shortly after the sibling's birth to 14 months later and found that firstborn girls directed less positive behaviors toward their 14-month-old younger siblings if the mothers had engaged in more joint play and joint attention, and fewer prohibitions with the firstborn shortly after the baby's birth. One possible explanation for these findings is that firstborn daughters were more jealous of their baby sibling because of the disruption of the close relationship the girl had with her mother before the birth, and consequently, she directed less positive and potentially more conflict behaviors at the sibling almost a year later. Similar findings were not found for firstborn boys, however, and it is not clear why this would be the case. Perhaps boys would have displayed more jealousy if their relationship with their fathers had been disrupted instead, but because fathers were not observed in this study, future research is still needed to bear this out.

Given all the changes that are occurring in the family after the birth of a second child, it is difficult to ascertain whether these reactions of the firstborn are due to jealousy and the loss of exclusive attention from the mother or if the problematic behaviors are indeed due to other changes in the family that coincide with the second child's birth (e.g., postpartum maternal depression and fatigue, marital conflict, or increases in harsh discipline). More research is needed to tease apart which of these behavioral and emotional reactions are due to jealousy of the new baby and which are a direct result of the changes that are ongoing in the family once the baby arrives.

Attachment and jealousy

Most children experience the birth of a baby sibling somewhere between their second and third year (Baydar, Greek, & Brooks-Gunn, 1997) and have formed an attachment to their primary caregiver by this time. For young children, the threat to the primary relationship in the jealousy triangle is equivalent to the threat to or loss of an attachment relationship (Bowlby, 1980). As Bowlby (1980) explained:

> Many of the most intense emotions arise during the formation, the maintenance, the disruption and the renewal of attachment relationships. The formation of a bond is described as falling in love, maintaining a bond as loving someone, and losing a partner as grieving over someone. Similarly, threat of loss arouses anxiety and actual loss gives rise to sorrow; while each of these situations is likely to arouse anger. The unchallenged maintenance of a bond is experienced as a source of security and the renewal of a bond as a source of joy. Because such emotions are usually a reflection of the state of a person's affectional bonds, the psychology and psychopathology of emotion is found to be in large part the psychology and psychopathology of affectional bonds. (p. 40)

Disruption of the attachment or affectional bond to one's primary caregiver during a jealousy evocation should lead to similar behaviors that infants/toddlers use to maintain their attachment to the caregiver (i.e., clinging, approach to the mother, crying, protests). It should come as no surprise, then, to see that many of these same behaviors have been the focus of jealousy research with infants and toddlers (e.g., Hart & Carrington, 2002; Masciuch & Kienapple, 1993; Teti & Ablard, 1989; Volling, McElwain, & Miller, 2002).

A perceived threat to the self and the attachment relationship may activate the infant's internal working model and because the quality of the infant–mother attachment plays a role in the development of the infant's internal working model of self and relationships, infants with different attachment histories may react to jealousy-inducing situations differently (i.e., develop different jealousy complexes). Hart and Behrens (2008) recently reported that during a jealousy evocation, 1-year-olds with an insecure-resistant attachment to their mother were more likely to touch the mother, cling and grab the mother, and seek proximity to the mother than securely attached infants and avoidantly attached infants. Further, insecure-avoidant infants were less likely to touch their mother, vocalize to mother, and show distress than secure infants. Sharpsteen and Kirkpatrick (1997) in their research on adult attachment and romantic jealousy also found that the affective, behavioral, and cognitive components of romantic jealousy were related to different attachment styles. Specifically, securely attached individuals were inclined to express anger toward their partner as well as make attempts to maintain their relationships, avoidant individuals were far more likely to direct their anger at and blame the rival, and anxious individuals were more likely to repress their anger. Although research on childhood jealousy is just beginning to emerge, researchers may want to take a close look at the role of attachment theory in explaining children's emotional and behavioral reactions to the potential disruption to and loss of the primary relationship with the beloved.

Observational research on triadic interaction

If the model we are proposing is correct, observations of *triadic* parent–sibling interaction would provide stronger support for our model than research relying on child or parent reports of sibling rivalry or even observations of two siblings engaged in dyadic conflict. There are few observational studies available that have examined triadic interactions between a parent and two children in the family, so there is little information from which to draw strong conclusions about sibling jealousy. We start with the research of Teti and Ablard (1989) because the triadic laboratory paradigm we use was adapted from the 8-episode laboratory paradigm they designed to assess both sibling rivalry and sibling caregiving with toddler and preschool siblings. Sibling rivalry was assessed by having the mother play with one child for 3 min while telling the sibling to play alone and then switching these roles, where she played with the sibling and told the child to play alone. The target child's (i.e., the one playing alone) behaviors were coded for distraction, cry/protest, and aggression toward mother or sibling. The results examining whether insecurely attached children reacted differently from securely attached children when mothers played with their sibling was confirmed for the toddlers, who averaged 1.5 years, but not for their older siblings, who were on average 4 years old. Specifically, insecure toddlers cried and protested their mothers' interactions with their older sibling more than secure toddlers, and used more aggression toward mother and sibling than secure toddlers. Because the paradigm was triadic and involved the mother switching her attention from one sibling to the other, we believe Teti and Ablard were among the first researchers to successfully measure sibling jealousy.

In a study by Miller, Volling, and McElwain (2000), sibling jealousy was also observed in a triadic context with 16-month-old toddlers, their preschool-aged siblings, and a parent, either mother or father. They used a paradigm similar to that of Teti and Ablard (1989) and had parents alter their attention from one sibling to the other for 3-min episodes. While the parent was playing with one sibling, the other sibling was told to play with other toys in the room. Miller et al. found that both older and younger siblings were far more likely to display anger, sadness, and distress when they were told to play alone, while the parent was playing with the sibling, than when they were the focus of their parent's attention during parent–child play. Further, Volling et al. (2002) reported that older siblings displayed more jealous behaviors (e.g., distraction, aggression to mother and sibling) during mother–sibling triadic interaction when children were insecurely attached to their mother and father, had angry temperaments, had lower scores on a battery assessing emotional understanding, and spouses reported more marital conflict and less positive marital relationships. In line with the transactional model we proposed earlier, these findings highlight how characteristics of the children, their parents, and the family context play a role in the development of young children's jealousy.

As we have already noted, research on sibling jealousy in triadic contexts is scarce, so we now turn to a presentation of some of our most recent research on sibling jealousy that was designed to replicate the findings reported by Volling and her colleagues. The replication study included 57 families consisting of a biological mother and father, a 2-year-old child, and an older sibling between the ages of 4 and 6. All participating families were invited to the research laboratory to participate in a series of family interaction tasks, including mother–sibling and father–sibling triadic sessions, which were adapted from Teti and Ablard (1989), to induce jealousy. Each session consisted of three, 3-min triadic episodes. In the first 3-min segment, the parent was given an attractive toy and asked to play with one of the siblings (involved sibling) while attempting to get the other sibling (challenged sibling) to play with other toys in the laboratory playroom. For the second 3-min session, parents were asked to switch roles so that the involved sibling now became the challenged sibling. Parents were instructed during the last 3 min to play with both siblings in order to minimize any distress that may have been elicited during the prior two segments. This triadic paradigm is considered a jealousy-inducing situation for young children because it requires that the "challenged" sibling regulate his or her emotions in response to the beloved parent's exclusive focus on the sibling rival. Specifically, in the involved condition, the parent and target child were involved in *dyadic* free-play with a toy. The other child or "challenged sibling" was redirected by the parent to play with other toys in the lab while the parent played with the involved sibling. These roles were then reversed so that the challenged sibling now was involved in dyadic play with the parent while the other sibling, now the challenged sibling, was directed to play with other toys in the room. All triadic interaction sessions were videotaped and later coded for *child emotional displays* (sadness, anger, happiness rated globally on a 7-point scale for the involved and challenge session), *parenting behaviors* in response to the challenged child (supportive, control, unresponsive; 15-s interval coding), and *challenged child behaviors* (distracting parent, negativity toward parent, sibling, or object, touching the toy during parent–child interaction, seeking comfort from parent, monitoring parent–child interaction from a distance and up close, and sophistication of play: 15-s interval coding).

A comparison of each sibling's affect across the involved and challenged sessions (within-subject) compares the children's affect when interacting in dyadic free-play with a parent with the affect expressed when the parent's attention is directed at their sibling rival. We conducted 2×3 (context: involved versus challenged $\times$ emotion: happiness, sadness, anger) repeated measures ANOVAs for older and younger siblings' emotion displays. For both siblings across both the mother and father sessions, significant context by emotion interactions emerged, $F(2, 53) = 23.33$, $p < .001$, $\eta_p^2 = .30$ for younger siblings with mother, $F(2, 53) = 10.65$, $p < .001$, $\eta_p^2 = .17$ for older siblings with mother, $F(2, 53) = 13.74$, $p < .001$, $\eta_p^2 = .34$ for younger siblings with father, and $F(2, 53) = 14.68$, $p < .001$, $\eta_p^2 = .36$ for older siblings with father. Figures 17.2 and 17.3 present the means of children's affect across the involved and challenged contexts for older and younger siblings, respectively. There were significant changes for the three emotions when children were involved in dyadic parent–child free-play and the recipient of parental

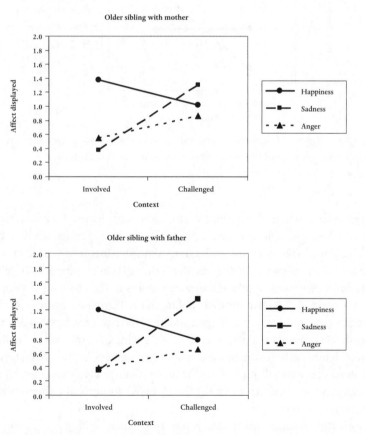

Figure 17.2 Means of jealous affect for older siblings across the involved and challenged sessions of jealousy induction with mothers and with fathers

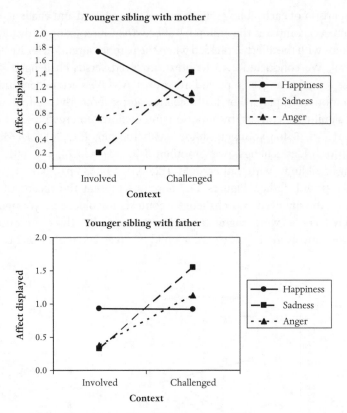

Figure 17.3 Means of jealous affect for younger siblings across the involved and challenged sessions of jealousy induction with mothers and fathers

attention versus when the parent's attention was focused exclusively on the sibling rival. Younger siblings expressed significantly more sadness and less happiness in the challenged (i.e., jealousy induction) than the involved (i.e., dyadic parent–child interaction) session during mother–sibling triadic interaction (p's < .001). Older siblings expressed significantly more sadness in the challenged as opposed to involved context (p < .001) in mother–sibling triads. Happiness decreased and anger - increased as expected across challenged and involved contexts, but this difference was not significant. Younger siblings and older siblings in the father–sibling triads expressed significantly less happiness and more sadness in the challenged than in the involved contexts (all p's < .001). Younger siblings also expressed significantly more anger in the challenged than in the involved sessions of father–sibling triadic interaction (p < .001).

In sum, the findings from this replication study with very young children indicated, in line with our model, that 2-year-old children and their older siblings expressed significantly more negative affect and less positive affect in the challenged than in the involved condition, and this occurred in both the mother–sibling and father–sibling triads. These findings, in combination with our earlier results, confirm that the triadic jealousy paradigm elicited greater negative affect and less positive affect when siblings received more attention than did children and this finding was found in four separate instances (i.e., older sibling with mother, older sibling with father, younger sibling with mother, and younger sibling with father).

As part of the developmental perspective guiding our work, we also proposed that children's jealousy responses may differ as a function of age such that older children may have more advanced abilities to regulate jealous affect and may use different coping behaviors as a result. To examine this possibility, we used children's behaviors during the challenge context and conducted a principal components analysis that resulted in three behavioral composites for the older sibling: *Interference* (consisting of touching toy, physical intrusion on parent–child interaction); *seeking comfort* (monitoring close, seeking comfort) and *attention seeking* (monitors from a distance, distracts parent); and two composites for the younger sibling: *interference* and *seeking comfort*. Attention seeking was not found for the younger siblings, which we believe is due to the developmental differences between the two children. Monitoring the interaction between the beloved and rival, and then using distracting behavior (e.g., asking mother if she would like a cup of tea from the tea set) that draws attention to the self is far more sophisticated than simply pushing oneself into the parent's lap to get attention. These differences between older and younger siblings in the strategies they used to get their parent's attention were noted repeatedly by the coders watching the videotaped observations and also appear to be borne out in our analyses.

We examined developmental differences in older and younger siblings' behavioral coping by conducting 2 (parent) × 2 (sibling) repeated measures ANCOVAs (controlling for order of counterbalancing). A significant parent × sibling interaction for comfort-seeking behavior, $F(1, 52) = 4.83$, $p < .05$, $\eta_p^2 = .09$, indicated that younger, toddler siblings were more likely to seek comfort from their mothers when they were challenged ($M = .62$) than were older siblings ($M = .47$), and younger siblings sought more comfort from mothers during the challenge session than they sought from fathers ($M = .49$).

One might argue that the reason older and younger siblings differ in their behavior might be due to the fact that parents are more or less involved with older and younger siblings during the dyadic play and these different involvement levels elicit different levels of jealous behavior. To test this possibility, we conducted 2 × 2 ANCOVAs looking at the involvement level between the parent and the target sibling. The findings were all nonsignficant, indicating that any differences in the challenged siblings' behaviors to parent–target sibling interaction were not due to differences in the parent's dyadic involvement with older and younger siblings.

Sibling Jealousy and Rivalry in Middle Childhood

Similar to the period of early childhood, there is very little research chronicling sibling jealousy with children in middle childhood. Even though research on sibling interaction in this age period focuses on a number of negative behaviors labeled agonistic, hostile, aggressive, or conflict, we do not automatically include these studies as a reflection of sibling jealousy because there must be evidence that the behaviors were elicited in a triadic context consistent with our theoretical framework. Sibling conflict, jealousy, and rivalry are most likely related and may mutually influence one another, but they are still different concepts and the motivations behind each may differ considerably. Conflict is a normal aspect of social relationships and is defined by the mutual opposition between two individuals (Cicirelli, 1995; Vandell, Bailey, Shantz, & Hartup, 1992); it may be based solely on dyadic exchanges (e.g., possession of a toy). Sibling conflict is not unusual and high levels of conflict can set a negative tone to family life. Again, whereas much of what is currently labeled conflict or aggression in sibling studies could be motivated by jealous affect, until research clearly distinguishes between negative sibling exchanges in dyadic contexts from those behaviors occurring in a social triangle where children's behavior can be directly linked to differences in parental attention to one or the other sibling, we cannot know for certain what is or is not jealousy. Therefore, only studies that were obviously conducted in a triadic context or were formulated to specifically address jealousy are included here.

Much of the extant research in middle childhood focuses on the negative features of sibling relationships such as conflict, competition, hostility, envy, and jealousy. Boer (1990) tried to identify the different dimensions of sibling rivalry and proposed that sibling rivalry and competition referred to *actions* while sibling jealousy and envy referred to *emotions*. According to Boer (1990), sibling rivalry during middle childhood stems from competition for parental approval and parental social comparisons between siblings, which appears to find support in the research of Prochaska and Prochaska (1985), who found that 5th and 6th grade children reported that fighting for parents' attention was one potential cause of sibling rivalry.

In a recent study, Thompson and Halberstadt (2008) developed a sibling jealousy interview looking at the frequency, duration, and intensity of sibling jealousy, as well as the cognitive, behavioral, and affective responses of childhood jealousy. Interviews from 5th and 6th grade children revealed that sibling jealousy was reported in an astonishing 98% of the families and occurred often (once per month on average). Children also reported that the primary causes for their jealousy were diverted parental attention and parental favoritism.

Although not specifically designed to assess sibling jealousy, several studies have used triadic parent–sibling observational paradigms to assess negative sibling interaction and, as such, are probably capturing some aspect of sibling jealousy.

Prominent among these studies is the research conducted with school-age children by Brody and his colleagues (e.g., Brody, Stoneman, & Burke, 1987; Brody, Stoneman, & McCoy, 1992, 1994). In one of these studies, mother–sibling and father–sibling triads were observed at home interacting with either a small hand-held computer or a Viewmaster projector. Negative sibling behaviors that were coded from the videotaped interactions included teasing, insults, quarrels, name calling, protesting, negative facial expressions, and aggression; behaviors that are very similar to those expressed by younger children during jealousy evocation. Parents' behaviors were also coded and difference scores reflecting the difference between the amount of interaction the parent had with the older and younger sibling were calculated to form differential positive and differential negative parental behavior composites. In several instances, mothers' and fathers' differential negative and controlling behavior was correlated with less positive and more negative sibling interaction. These significant associations between differential parental behavior directed at one child over the other and the children's negative interactions once again underscores the relevance of parental attention in jealousy expression. Stocker, Dunn, and Plomin (1989) also observed mother–sibling triads and found that in unstructured observation sessions, maternal differential behavior was positively correlated with more conflict in the sibling relationship, as well as with competition and control between siblings. In another study, more conflict and less prosocial sibling relationships were reported when maternal differential treatment was present (Bryant & Crockenberg, 1980).

In one interesting approach, Robey, Cohen, and Epstein (1988) asked children (8–12 years) to view vignettes portraying two individuals in competition for the attention of a third (i.e., a jealousy-inducing situation) and then asked them to report on how each individual in the story was feeling. The vignettes used included one instance of sibling jealousy (two siblings competing for a parent's attention) and three other triadic configurations. Unfortunately, the sibling vignette was not assessed separately from the other types, but overall, firstborn and later-born children did not differ in the emotions they ascribed to the characters, but children with divorced parents did attribute more unhappiness to an individual not receiving attention than did children whose parents were still married. Collectively, these studies in middle childhood indicate that sibling jealousy appears to be a significant experience in the familial life of children and deserves more attention by researchers in the future.

Sibling Jealousy and Rivalry in Adolescence

During adolescence, sibling jealousy continues to be studied extremely rarely. Studies of sibling relationships during this period frequently focus on the overall quality of the relationship, or may separate positive and negative aspects of sibling relationship quality, but do not examine jealousy specifically. Rivalry is sometimes examined, either on its own or as a component of sibling negativity or conflict more broadly. For example, in Furman and Buhrmester's (1985) examination of older children's sibling relationships, a dimension of sibling rivalry was iden- tified, which was comprised primarily of reports of parental partiality toward the self or the sibling. Tseung and Schott (2004) have operationalized rivalry only as feelings of being in competition or comparing oneself with one's sibling, and used perceptions of parental partiality as a predictor of these feelings. Still other investigators have allowed participants to interpret the concept of rivalry on their own or have used it interchangeably with terms such as conflict. For example, Cicirelli (1989) asked the question: "To what extent do you feel a sense of rivalry (conflict, bad feelings) with your sibling?"

Tseung and Schott (2004) examined late adolescents' responses to structured interviews regarding their sibling relationships and found a factor they referred to as rivalry, which included adolescents' perceptions of themselves as competing for approval with their siblings and making comparisons between their siblings and themselves. Across studies, rivalry appears to be an independent dimension of the sibling relationship, but it is positively correlated with hostility and negatively correlated with affection among siblings (Boer, Westenberg, & McHale, 1997; Tseung & Schott, 2004).

Among a group of adolescents and young adults in Israel, rivalry was oper- ationalized as parental favoritism of one sibling over the other. Mothers in the study actually reported higher levels of rivalry between sibling pairs than the siblings themselves reported (Scharf, Shulman, & Avigad-Spitz, 2005).

A reduction in the overall amount of contact between siblings during adoles- cence is thought to account for decreasing opportunities for both positive and negative interactions with one's siblings (e.g., Brody et al., 1994; Tseung & Schott, 2004). Jealousy, however, involves an inherent focus on gaining the parent's attention, and as such, is not necessarily dependent on actual contact with the brother or sister. Nevertheless, Buhrmester and Furman (1990) did find in a cross- sectional analysis that feelings of competition with an older sibling were lower among adolescents (9th and 12th grade) than among school-age children (3rd grade), with 6th grade students scores falling between those of 3rd and 9th graders, and not differing significantly from either.

Parental differential treatment continues to be associated with the rivalry that siblings experience once they reach adolescence, with late adolescents who felt that their fathers had expressed more affection for their sibling than for them reporting higher levels of rivalry than adolescents who did not report this relative lack of paternal affection (Tseung & Schott, 2004). Interestingly, differential affection by mothers was not associated with reported sibling rivalry, nor was differential control by either parent. Furthermore, rivalry was the only dimension of the adolescent sibling relationship associated with any aspect of perceived differential treatment by parents, indicating that to the extent that perceptions of differential treatment by parents may have an effect on the sibling relationship for adolescents, it serves to enhance a sense of rivalry or competition between siblings, but not to increase overall hostility or decrease affection for the sibling (Tseung & Schott, 2004).

Sibling Jealousy and Rivalry in Adulthood

The adult sibling relationship is structurally different than that in childhood and adolescence, as adults are typically no longer sharing living space with siblings or dependent on parents. During adulthood, sibling relationships are typically voluntary, but often there is a shared obligation to care for aging parents. Perhaps for this reason, adult sibling relationships, in general, are infrequently studied, and most extant studies focus primarily on the amount of contact or closeness with siblings, rather than jealousy over the attention of a parent with whom neither is likely to live. However, sibling relationships in adulthood are thought to be based, at least in part, on the history of the relationship, and when conflict or hostility in adult sibling relationships is studied, it is often hypothesized to be rooted in childhood rivalry over parental attention (Ross & Milgram, 1982). Moreover, when conflicts arise over care for the parents, they may reignite old rivalries about parental affections and which sibling may have been favored by the aging parent during their childhoods.

Descriptions of the prevalence of adult sibling jealousy are difficult to find. Although Cicirelli (1982) found that nearly 90% of middle-aged adults reported "rarely" or "never" arguing or feeling competitive with a sibling, Ross and Milgram (1982) found that nearly half of the adults they studied felt a sense of rivalry toward a sibling. Among studies of undergraduate students, two studies have shown that for those just transitioning into adulthood, feelings of rivalry with a sibling over parental attention is common (Bevan & Stetzenbach, 2007; Stocker, Lanthier, & Furman, 1997). Similar to adolescents, reports of rivalry were minimally related to reports of sibling warmth, but were modestly related to reports of sibling hostility. Sibling pairs generally agreed on the extent to which parents favored one sibling over the other, but were less consistent in their reports of rivalry than other aspects of the sibling relationship, such as warmth and general conflict (Stocker, Lanthier, & Furman, 1997). A cross-sectional study compared reports of rivalry (operationalized as parental favoritism) by adolescent and young adult sibling pairs, and found that the adolescents reported higher levels of rivalry than the young adults did (Scharf, Shulman, & Avigad-Spitz, 2005). In general, the literature on sibling jealousy is not abundant across any stage of the life course, and even when siblings have been the focus of empirical study there are instances in which it is not clear whether the conflict or negative sibling interactions are a reflection of jealousy, competition, or some other motivation that leads to hostility between siblings.

Child and Family Correlates of Sibling Jealousy

The transactional model presented in Figure 17.1 not only underscores the interpersonal dynamic of jealousy and the social triad that consists of the jealous person, the beloved, and the rival, but it also points to the different social and contextual factors that may influence the experience of jealousy within the triad. Characteristics of the individuals involved such as personality or temperament, the quality of the interpersonal relationships in the jealousy triangle, and the broader social context in which the triad is embedded will affect the manner in which the jealous individual will interpret the beloved's behavior toward a rival, the affect experienced, and the behaviors displayed toward the beloved and the rival. Here, we briefly review some of the research that has examined the individual and family correlates of sibling conflict/rivalry in childhood to see if there is evidence supporting the model presented in Figure 17.1. First, we should note that there are subtle distinctions as to what constitutes jealousy, envy, and rivalry between siblings (Neubauer, 1982). Often, a single measure of sibling conflict is the only source of information available in a sibling study and it is not entirely clear if this conflict is motivated by jealousy (e.g., loss of parental attention or differential parental treatment), envy (e.g., one sibling wants and forcefully takes something from the other), or rivalry (e.g., competition to be better than the sibling). As such, our review takes into account how individual and family factors have been related to sibling conflict, in general, with an understanding that these same factors may play a role in determining sibling jealousy as well. Given space limitations, we do not present an exhaustive review of studies in each of the areas, but instead, examine whether there is any preliminary evidence that supports our model. We will then present recent findings from our own research program examining the child and family correlates of sibling jealousy in early childhood.

Children's temperament

The temperament of the children should determine, in part, the intensity of jealousy experienced. Numerous studies have documented associations between the temperament of the two siblings and the conflict between them (e.g., Brody et al., 1987, 1994; Dunn & Kendrick, 1982; Munn & Dunn, 1989; Stocker, Dunn, & Plomin, 1989; Stoneman & Brody, 1993). In general, more active, irritable, emotionally intense, and persistent children engage in more sibling conflict (Munn & Dunn, 1989; Stoneman & Brody, 1993). Volling et al.'s (2002) study looking at sibling jealousy in early childhood found that angry temperament was positively associated with the toddler siblings' jealous affect and the older sibling's behavioral dysregulation during mother–sibling triads, providing at least limited support that temperamental characteristics are related to children's jealousy responses.

Differential parental treatment

One of the most consistent findings in the sibling relationship literature is the association found between sibling conflict and the preferential or differential treatment of siblings. Differential treatment reflects the difference in either parental control or parental affection directed to one sibling relative to the other. In most studies, when one sibling receives more affection and less control from their parent compared to their brother or sister, he or she is often referred to as the "favored" sibling. The concept of differential parental treatment is actually a reflection of the social dynamic inherent in a jealousy-inducing situation. More parental affection directed at your sibling than to you may be perceived as a threat to your own relationship with the parent and to your self-esteem (Rauer & Volling, 2007). Therefore, differential parental affection in which the parent shows more affection to one sibling than the other should be associated with more sibling conflict and/or jealousy. Indeed, there is consistent evidence across early childhood (Volling, 1997; Volling & Elins, 1998), middle childhood (McGuire, Dunn, & Plomin, 1995; Richmond, Stocker, & Rienks, 2005), adolescence (Brody et al., 1992; Kowal, Kramer, Krull, & Crick, 2002; Shebloski, Conger, & Widaman, 2005), and even into adulthood (Rauer & Volling, 2007) that differential parental affection is related to more conflict between siblings and to lower self-esteem for the less favored child (i.e., the one receiving less affection).

Marital relationship functioning

The quality of the marital relationship has also been implicated in the development of sibling conflict and is also considered as one of the social-contextual factors in Figure 17.1 that should be linked to sibling jealousy. Numerous studies have found links between marital conflict and sibling conflict (e.g., Brody et al., 1994; Erel, Margolin, & John, 1998; Hetherington, Clarke-Stewart, & Dunn, 2006; Stocker & Youngblade, 1999; Volling & Belsky, 1992; Volling, McElwain, & Miller, 2002). In our previous study looking at sibling jealousy in our triadic paradigm, we found that negative marital relationship quality (i.e., conflict and feelings of ambivalence) was positively correlated and positive marital relationship quality (i.e., feelings of love, efforts to maintain the relationship) was inversely related to the older siblings' jealous behaviors (e.g., distraction, aggression) with mothers (Volling et al., 2002). Indeed, positive marital relationship quality was a unique predictor of the older siblings' jealousy even after controlling for the order of the session, mother's behavior during the session, children's temperament, and marital conflict.

Emotion socialization

In addition to how parents treat each of the two siblings, the degree of jealous affect expressed may be associated with the manner in which parents cope with their children's negative affect and the emotion socialization strategies that parents use. Eisenberg and her colleagues (Eisenberg, Fabes, & Murphy, 1996; Eisenberg et al., 1999) have focused on the supportive (i.e., emotion-focused, comforting, and problem-focused reactions) and non-supportive (e.g., punitive, dismissing, or minimizing reactions) emotion socialization strategies parents use in response to children's negative emotions. Whether or not parents attempt to punish or minimize the child's jealous emotions or actually try to comfort the child or encourage the child to express jealousy probably has some effect on how the child will choose to express jealousy in future situations. To our knowledge, no study has examined the links between supportive or non-supportive emotion socialization practices and sibling inter-actions, including conflict, rivalry, and jealousy. Because of the lack of research in this area, it is not clear what associations to expect. Perhaps parents who punish their children for expressing jealousy actually diminish future incidents of sibling jealousy. On the other hand, because jealousy may actually reflect a normative response to the threat to the love relationship between jealous children and their beloved parent, being punished for objecting to the potential loss of parental love may actually escalate into more intense emotional expressions in the future as children attempt to restore their lost love. Simi-larly, encouraging the expression of jealousy might actually reward children and result in more frequent objections later or it may allow children to work through their jealous feelings with the help and support of their beloved parents, letting children see that mother's attention to a younger sibling does not equate to less love for them. The difficulty in making straightforward predictions about the relations between emotion socialization and jealousy is due to the complex interpersonal nature of the jealousy-inducing situation. Unlike most developmental research to date focusing on a single mother–child dyad, the jealousy-inducing triangle requires that one mother–child attachment relationship be considered in relation to a second mother–child attachment rela-tionship. Sensitively responding to one child may result in inconsistent responding to the other. Our research on jealousy highlights the limited application of most extant developmental perspectives relying on the direct effect of dyadic inter-action between mother and child to explain the complexity of social emotions such as jealousy. Family influence on children's socio-emotional development is far more complicated than most current developmental theories can explain.

A Study of the Family and Child Correlates of Sibling Jealousy

In this section we briefly present analyses examining the family and child correlates of children's jealousy in the challenge sessions of our triadic laboratory paradigm. For these analyses, we summed each child's angry and sad emotion when in the challenged situation to form a composite of *jealous affect*, and also used the behavioral composites of *interference, attention seeking,* and *comfort seeking* we introduced earlier. As measures of the child and family correlates, we focus on parental reports of (1) the marital relationship using the love and conflict scales of Braiker and Kelley's (1979) Intimate Relations Questionnaire, (2) sibling relationship quality using the rivalry and positive involvement scales of the Sibling Inventory of Behavior for older siblings (SIB; Hetherington & Cling-empeel, 1992) and the Sibling Relationships in Early Childhood questionnaire for the younger sibling (SREC; Volling & Elins, 1998), (3) parental differential treatment using the differential affection and differential control scales of the Sibling Inventory of Differential Experience (SIDE; Daniels & Plomin, 1985), (4) children's angry temperament using the anger subscale of the Child Behavior Questionnaire for older siblings (Rothbart, Ahadi, Hersey, & Fisher, 2001) and the Toddler Behavior Questionnaire for toddler siblings (Goldsmith, Riesser-Danner, & Briggs, 1991), and (5) parents' supportive and unsupportive reactions to children's negative emotions using the Coping with Children's Negative Emotions Scale (CCNES; Fabes, Poulin, Eisenberg, & Madden-Derdich, 2002). In the case of the marital relationship, the sibling relationship, and the children's angry temperament, we summed across mothers' and fathers' scores to create more robust composites. High scores on all scales indicated higher values for marital relationship and sibling relationship quality, angry temperament, and supportive/unsupportive emotion socialization. The differential treatment scales of the SIDE were scored such that 1 indicated the parent did the behavior more with the older sibling than the younger sibling, 5 more with the younger than the older sibling, and 3 equally with both siblings. For the sake of brevity, we present only the correlations between these factors and children's jealous affect and behavior during mother–sibling and father–sibling triads.

Older siblings with their fathers

Older siblings interfered more with father–younger sibling interaction when parents reported more marital conflict ($r=.29$, $p<.05$), less marital love ($r=-.30$, $p<.05$), less positive sibling involvement ($r=-.26$, $p=.06$), and more differential paternal control where fathers controlled older siblings more than younger siblings ($r=-.28$, $p<.05$). Older siblings sought more comfort from fathers when parents reported more marital conflict ($r=.32$, $p<.05$) and less positive sibling involvement ($r=-.31$, $p<.05$). Older siblings also expressed more jealous affect when parents reported greater temperamental anger ($r=.29$, $p<.05$). Older siblings' attention seeking with the father was actually positively correlated with mothers' reports of unsupportive reactions to negative emotions ($r=.31$, $p<.05$) and to mothers' differential control ($r=.34$, $p<.01$) such that more attention seeking was related to more control of the younger sibling compared to the older sibling.

Older siblings with their mothers

During the mother–sibling triadic interactions, older siblings' interference was positively associated with parent reports of angry temperament ($r = .30$, $p < .05$) and when mothers and fathers reported more differential control directed toward the older sibling relative to the younger sibling ($r = -.25$ and $-.24$, $p < .10$, for mothers and fathers, respectively). Older siblings' comfort seeking was positively correlated with fathers' reports of unsupportive reactions to the older child's negative emotions ($r = -.27$, $p < .05$), whereas the older siblings' expressions of jealous affect were positively correlated with parents' reports of positive sibling involvement ($r = .27$, $p < .05$). Attention seeking of older siblings with their mothers was negatively correlated with differential paternal affection ($r = -.28$, $p < .05$) as well as with differential paternal and maternal control ($r = -.23$ for mothers and fathers, $p < .10$). In other words, older siblings sought more attention from mothers during mother–younger sibling interaction when fathers used more affection and control with them, and mothers used more control with them, compared to the younger sibling.

Younger siblings with their fathers

The younger sibling's interference with father–older sibling interaction was marginally related to mothers' differential control ($r = .26$, $p = .06$) such that interference was related to mother's use of more control with the younger sibling relative to the older sibling. Differential paternal affection was negatively associated with more comfort seeking behavior ($r = -.31$, $p < .05$) such that younger siblings were more likely to seek comfort from their fathers when fathers reported they were more affectionate with the older sibling than with the younger sibling (i.e., favoritism). Finally, a marginal association indicated that younger sibling's jealous affect was positively correlated with parents' reports of the younger siblings' rivalry with the older sibling ($r = .27$, $p = .06$).

Younger siblings with their mothers

The younger siblings' attempts to interfere with mother–older sibling interaction were positively associated with fathers' reports of differential affection ($r = .33$, $p < .05$) such that younger siblings were more likely to interfere with mothers and older siblings when the fathers reported they favored the younger sibling by directing more affection toward them relative to their older siblings. The younger siblings' expressions of jealous affect were negatively related to fathers' differential control ($r = -.23$, $p < .10$) such that more jealousy was related to fathers' use of more control and discipline with older siblings relative to younger siblings. Finally, younger siblings' comfort seeking with mothers during mother–older sibling interaction was positively related to parent reports of marital conflict ($r = .33$, $p < .05$) and inversely to marital love ($r = -.31$, $p < .05$).

There are several consistencies in the results we report here on a sample of 2-year-olds and their older siblings with the findings we reported earlier with 16-month-old toddlers and their preschool siblings (Volling et al., 2002). In both studies, parents' reports of the children's angry temperament and the quality of the marital relationship consistently related to children's jealous affect and behaviors. In our replication study presented here, older siblings with more angry temperaments were more likely to express jealous affect when fathers interacted with their younger siblings and they interfered more in interaction between mothers and the younger siblings. Volling et al. (2002) also found that older siblings with angry temperaments displayed more hostility and used more distraction when mothers and fathers were interacting with their younger siblings, and younger siblings with angry temperaments expressed more jealous affect during mother–sibling triadic interaction. The consistency in findings across studies indicates that some part of how children react emotionally in jealousy situations is due to temperamental predispositions.

One of the strongest predictors of the older siblings' jealous affect with mothers in the Volling et al. (2002) study was the quality of the marital relationship, particularly parents' reports of less positive marital relationships. The current correlations also revealed that spouses' reports of marital conflict were positively related and their reports of marital love negatively related to the older siblings' interference in father–younger sibling interaction and to more comfort seeking of the younger sibling during mother–older sibling interaction. Davies, Harold, Goeke-Morey, and Cummings (2002) have proposed that exposure to marital conflict can result in children's feelings of emotional insecurity. This may explain why toddlers sought more comfort from their mothers when mothers' attention was focused on the older sibling. More emotionally insecure toddlers from homes high in marital conflict may also feel insecure if their attachment with their mother is threatened, even if that threat is coming from an older brother or sister. Older siblings, in contrast, may be more likely to physically interfere in interaction between fathers and their younger siblings. This interference might also reflect some form of seeking physical contact and comfort. However, we see comfort seeking and physical intrusion as less mature tactics for getting the parent's attention than distraction ("Hey, look at what I made!") or verbal strategies ("Mom, I really love you") that draw attention to the self and away from the rival. Thus, the interference on the part of the older siblings from homes with marital conflict could be seen as immature. Moreover, if children are exposed to marital conflict and verbal aggression between spouses, these children may also be more comfortable forcefully intruding on the interaction between their mothers and younger siblings. Certainly, additional research will allow us to tease apart the reasons why marital conflict is consistently associated with jealousy between siblings across the two studies we've conducted. But, in any case, these consistent links between marital relationship quality and young children's expressions of jealousy support the interpersonal dynamics inherent within the family system.

If jealousy is a product of one child's desire to maintain the attention and love of their parent in relation to their sibling, then we would expect an association between differential parental treatment and children's jealousy responses. We found that the older siblings' interference with mother–younger sibling and father–younger sibling interaction was associated with differential maternal and paternal control. In all cases, older siblings were more likely to interfere if mothers and fathers reported they controlled and disciplined older siblings more than younger siblings. We do not know if older siblings interfere more because their parents are more controlling with them than their younger siblings, or if the reason parents use more control and discipline with these children is because they are more likely to physically intrude and interfere, and thus require more discipline. A similar explanation may be used to explain the consistent relations between differential paternal and maternal control, and the older siblings' attention seeking with mothers. In one case, the younger siblings were more likely to seek comfort from their fathers when fathers reported more differential affection favoring the older sibling. Perhaps younger siblings have learned that if they want affection and love from fathers who favor their older brothers and sisters, the best way to get it is to interfere directly in father–older sibling interaction.

Finally, there was some evidence that the children's jealousy was also related to the quality of the sibling relationship, although these findings were not abundant and sometimes only marginal in their significance. In this case, the older siblings' interference in father–younger sibling interaction was negatively related to parent reports of the child's positive involvement with the younger sibling and the younger siblings' jealous affect with mothers was positively associated with parents' reports of the younger siblings' rivalry with the older sibling at home. In any event, the preliminary findings reported here provide some support that child and family factors contribute to the affective and behavioral responses of young siblings in a triadic paradigm designed specifically to elicit jealousy, and, in turn, the transactional model of sibling jealousy we have proposed.

Conclusions and Directions for Future Research on Sibling Jealousy

Parents often view the jealousy, rivalry, and conflict between siblings as a major child-rearing concern (McDermott, 1980; Ram & Ross, 2001). Only recently, though, have developmental scientists started to seriously study children's jealousy. At this point, children's jealousy has been assessed in a multitude of ways, including observations of mothers interacting with a doll and/or peer (e.g., Robey, Cohen, & Epstein, 1988; Hart & Carrington, 2002; Mascuich & Kienapple, 1993), vignettes depicting triadic interactions (e.g., Bauminger, 2004; Robey et al., 1988), and questionnaires asking children to report on how jealous they are of their friends' interactions with others (Parker, Low, & Walker, 2005).

Research focused on siblings has spanned a wide range of topics, including sibling aggression and physical violence, sibling conflict, which is often defined as dyadic opposition and/or verbal disagreements, and rivalry, which is often viewed as sibling competitions around resources, prestige, and status. If we define jealousy as involving a triadic social situation that involves a rival, a beloved, and the jealous individual, there is little in the way of research that has actually utilized such a model to inform research in the area of sibling jealousy, and to distinguish it from other forms of aggression, conflict, and rivalry. In our review, we found it necessary to draw from all these areas in order to provide some picture of what we currently know about the development of sibling jealousy. What we can conclude with certainty is that there is considerable room for additional research on sibling jealousy. Having offered such a conclusion, we now make several recommendations for future research in this area.

Research on sibling jealousy must be theory driven or at least based on some conceptual framework that allows one to distinguish between jealousy and other negative dimensions of sibling interaction. In all likelihood, sibling jealousy, conflict, and rivalry are intricately linked such that an incident starting out as a conflict over a prized possession can subsequently turn into jealousy when the mother steps in to pronounce that one child should relinquish the toy to the other, particularly if the child doing the relinquishing perceives or interprets the mother's actions to reflect favoritism. Our research has focused specifically on sibling jealousy in early childhood and was based on a family system's perspective and the triadic model of jealousy we presented in Figure 17.1. Based on earlier research on romantic jealousy and the notion of the social triangle, we designed a laboratory-based triadic paradigm that allowed us to test specifically whether or not more negative emotions such as anger and sadness were generated during parent–sibling triadic interaction. Also, because our samples have included predominantly toddler and preschool-age children, we chose to start with observationally based paradigms because of these young children's limited verbal and cognitive abilities for completing interviews and self-report measures. We have now designed several studies using triadic parent–sibling observational paradigms where parents are asked to alter their attention from one sibling to the other and, in line with our triadic model, young children do express significantly more negative emotions, both sadness and anger, when their parents, either mother or father, are attending more to their sibling than they are to them. Thus, we have empirical evidence to suggest that altering the dynamics of the social triangle results in a jealous child when the beloved parent attends more to the rival sibling than to the child.

Is it possible that we are also tapping into some other relationship dynamics or rivalry over the toy rather than the loss of parental attention and love? Certainly it is possible that the young children's negative emotions in this contrived situation are elicited because of their desire to play with the attractive toy and not necessarily strictly due to the loss of parental attention. We are currently devising methods that will allow us to disentangle the jealousy and feelings of loss of the primary love relationship from the rivalry or competition over the "beloved" toy. One way we are attempting to do so is by developing different triadic scenarios or vignettes involving different family members and then acting out these vignettes using dolls as props. Children pick the dolls to represent each member of their family and the experimenter then proceeds to act out the vignettes, some designed to elicit jealousy (e.g., your mother is playing and hugging your brother, but not you) and some that do not (e.g., the family goes out for ice cream together). Children, who are approximately 4 to 6 years of age, are shown a number of felt faces and asked to pick how they would feel in this situation and are then handed the dolls and asked to show the experimenter what they would do next. Each jealousy interview is videotaped and subsequently transcribed. Independent coders will eventually code the transcripts for the children's verbal behaviors and the videotapes for the actions with the dolls and the affect displayed. Anecdotal accounts from experimenters and initial viewings of the videotapes indicate that some children become extremely anxious at the possibility that a parent would prefer their sibling over them, whereas others engage in aggressive behaviors and actually hit the mother or sibling doll, and some children offer suggestions for ways of joining prosocially in the interaction between parent and sibling. Individual differences in these children's affect and behavior are apparent and the challenge for future research, our own included, will be to design multiple methods that are sensitive to these individual differences in children's jealousy of a sibling and how these differences are related to other contextual and individual characteristics.

As noted earlier, some sibling research has indeed relied on triadic observational paradigms with older children and it is quite possible that some of the negative affect and behaviors they have coded are a reflection of sibling jealousy. Thus, it is not surprising that in many such studies, differential parental behavior observed during triadic interaction is actually correlated with negative sibling behaviors. In the course of naturalistic triadic interactions between a parent and two siblings, there will be moments where the parent shifts attention from one child to the other, creating the triadic dynamic that elicits jealousy responses and the desire to reestablish the parent's love and attention to one's self. Until studies are actually designed with jealousy in mind, we are left to speculate which of the "negative" affect and behaviors observed in these triadic situations can be labeled jealousy. One challenge for researchers will involve the creative development of observationally based paradigms that are age-appropriate for the children involved. Toddlers and preschoolers may be easily engaged with a toy from Fisher-Price, but this is unlikely to be the case with children in middle-school and certainly not the case with adolescents. One recommendation, then, for future research is the need to utilize larger samples of children from more diverse backgrounds and across a wider age range, including middle childhood and adolescence. Other than the research of Teti and Ablard (1989) and now our own, we are not aware of any other studies that have used triadic observational paradigms to assess sibling jealousy. Because jealousy is evoked within the social triangle that involves the jealous individual, the beloved, and the rival, developmental researchers need to design more studies using triadic observations, and not rely solely on self- or parent-reports of sibling rivalry, conflict, and aggression.

Our triadic model also underscores that the jealousy complex is composed of affective, behavioral, and cognitive dimensions (the ABCs of Figure 17.1) that are elicited within the social triangle. Consider that conflict between toddler and preschool siblings occurs 6 to 7 times an hour (Dunn & Munn, 1986; Perlman & Ross, 1997) and many of these conflict episodes may be incidents of sibling jealousy resulting from differential parental attention. If jealousy responses are elicited this often on a daily basis whenever the beloved's attention is directed to the rival, then the pattern of the affective, behavioral, and cognitive components may be highly organized and practiced over repeated exposures to jealousy-eliciting situations. The cognitive appraisals of the situation (mom loves him more), the displays of intense affect (sadness), and the behavioral responses to regain the parent's attention (crying) may be so automatic that they occur outside conscious awareness. Our research has been conducted primarily with toddlers and preschoolers so we had no choice but to use observational methods in order to capture the complexities of jealous reactions in parent–sibling triads. Toddlers are simply too young to interview and do not have the cognitive understanding to grasp the information portrayed in vignettes that are often given to older children. Due to the children's young ages, our research also focused only on the behavioral and affective dimensions of the jealousy complex and we have not looked fully at the cognitive appraisals that children make when their relationships are threatened by a rival, and how these are related to their behavior and emotions. The interviews and vignettes depicting jealousy-inducing situations that we described earlier are one possibility for assessing the cognitive aspects of the jealousy complex when used with older children and we would recommend that these types of measures be used in addition to triadic observational protocols if researchers wish to gain a better understanding of the different jealousy complexes that may exist and how individual and social factors play a role in their development.

Finally, the model we proposed acknowledges that the interpersonal jealousy system is affected by and affects the individuals involved. In our research, we have focused on the temperamental characteristics of the children as one such factor and have found that children with angry temperaments, based on their parents' reports, appear to have more intense emotional reactions in our observational paradigm. The parent–sibling triad is not isolated from other social, contextual, and familial factors and, as Figure 17.1 denotes, characteristics of the social environment such as marital relationship quality and differential parental treatment should predict children's jealousy responses. Indeed, we have found consistent relations between parents' reports of the quality of the marital relationship and observations of young children's jealousy in both studies we have conducted to date. In addition, there is now a consistent line of research linking marital conflict with sibling conflict (e.g., Brody et al., 1992; Ingoldsby, Shaw, Owens, & Winslow, 1999; Stocker & Youngblade, 1999; Volling & Elins, 1998), and this research, in line with our own work on jealousy, supports our model underscoring the complex interconnections between individuals, the family system, and the interpersonal jealousy system. There is definitely a need for many more studies examining sibling jealousy and room for the development of multiple methods to do so. Nonetheless, we believe that the research we have reported here provides preliminary support that sibling jealousy can be elicited in observational triadic paradigms, even with very young children, and that individual, relational, and familial characteristics play some part in the development of young children's jealousy. We look forward to future studies that can explore the complexities of the interpersonal jealousy system in more detail.

Acknowledgment

The research reported in this chapter was supported by a grant from the John E. Fetzer Institute. Volling was also supported by an Independent Scientist Award (K02HD047423) from the National Institute of Child Health and Human Development during the writing of this chapter.

References

Bauminger, N. (2004). The expression and understanding of jealousy in children with autism. *Development and Psychopathology, 16,* 157–177.

Baydar, N., Greek, A., & Brooks-Gunn, J. (1997). A longitudinal study of the effects of the birth of a sibling during the first 6 years of life. *Journal of Marriage and Family, 59,* 939–956.

Bevan, J. L., & Stetzenbach, K. A. (2007). Jealousy expression and communication satisfaction in adult sibling relationships. *Communication Research Reports, 24,* 71–77.

Boer, F. (1990). *Sibling relationships in middle childhood: An empirical study.* Leiden: DSWO Press.

Boer, F., Westenberg, P. M., & McHale, S. M. (1997). The factorial structure of the Sibling Relationship Inventory (SRI) in American and Dutch samples. *Journal of Social and Personal Relationships, 14,* 851–859.

Bowlby, J. (1980). *Attachment and loss.* New York: Basic Books.

Braiker, H. B., & Kelley, H.K. (1979). Conflict in the development of close relationships. In R. L. Burgess & T. L. Huston (Eds.), *Social exchange in developing relationships* (pp. 135–168). New York: Academic Press.

Brody, G. H. (1998). Sibling relationship quality: Its causes and consequences. *Annual Review of Psychology, 49,* 1–24.

Brody, G. H., Stoneman, Z., & Burke, M. (1987). Child temperaments, maternal differential behavior, and sibling relationships. *Developmental Psychology, 23,* 354–362.

Brody, G. H., Stoneman, Z., & McCoy, J. K. (1992). Associations of maternal and paternal direct and differential behavior with sibling relationships: Contemporaneous and longitudinal analyses. *Child Development, 63,* 82–92.

Brody, G. H., Stoneman, Z., & McCoy, J. K. (1994). Forecasting sibling relationships in early adolescence from child temperaments and family processes in middle childhood. *Child Development, 65,* 771–784.

Bryant, B. K., & Crockenberg, S. B. (1980). Correlates and dimensions of prosocial behavior: A study of female siblings with their mothers. *Child Development, 51,* 529–544.

Buhrmester, D., & Furman, W. (1990). Perceptions of sibling relationships during middle childhood and adolescence. *Child Development, 61,* 1387–1398.

Case, R., Hayward, S., Lewis, M., & Hurst, P. (1988). Toward a neo-Piagetian theory of cognitive and emotional development. *Developmental Review 8,* 1–51.

Cicirelli, V. C. (1982). Sibling influence throughout the lifespan. In M. E. Lamb & B. Sutton-Smith (Eds.), *Sibling relationships: Their nature and significance across the lifespan* (pp. 267–284). Hillsdale, NJ: Erlbaum.

Cicirelli, V. G. (1989). Feelings of attachment to siblings and well-being in later life. *Psychology and Aging, 4,* 211–216.

Cicirelli, V. G. (1995). *Sibling relationships across the life span.* New York: Plenum.

Corter, C., Abramovitch, R., & Pepler, D. (1983). The role of mother in sibling inter-action. *Child Development, 54,* 1599–1605.

Cox, M., & Paley, B. (2003). Understanding families as systems. *Current Directions in Psychological Science, 12,* 193–196.

Daniels, D., & Plomin, R. (1985). Differential experience of siblings in the same family. *Developmental Psychology, 21,* 747–760.

Davies, P. T., Harold, G. T., Goeke-Morey, M. C., & Cummings, E. M. (2002). Child emotional security and interparental conflict. *Monographs of the Society for Research in Child Development, 67*(3, Serial No. 270).

Dunn, J. (2007). Siblings and socialization. In J. E. Grusec & P. D. Hastings (Eds.), *Handbook of socialization* (pp. 309–327). New York: Guilford Press.

Dunn, J., & Kendrick, C. (1981). Interaction between young siblings: Association with the interaction between mother and firstborn child. *Developmental Psychology, 17,* 336–343.

Dunn, J., & Kendrick, C. (1982). *Siblings: Love, envy, and understanding.* Cambridge, MA: Harvard University Press.

Dunn, J., & Munn, P. (1986). Sibling quarrels and maternal intervention: Individual differences in understanding and aggression. *Journal of Child Psychology and Psychiatry, 27,* 583–595.

Eisenberg, N., Fabes, R. A., & Murphy, B. C. (1996). Parents' reactions to children's negative emotions: Relations to children's social competence and comforting behavior. *Child Development, 67,* 2227–2247.

Eisenberg, N., Fabes, R. A., Shepard, S. A., Guthrie, I. K., Murphy, B. C., & Reiser, M. (1999). Parental reactions to children's negative emotions: Longitudinal relations to quality of children's social functioning. *Child Development, 70,* 513–534.

Erel, O., Margolin, G., & John, R. S. (1998). Observed sibling interaction: Links with the marital relationship and the mother–child relationship. *Developmental Psychology, 34,* 288–298.

Fabes, R. A., Poulin, R. E., Eisenberg, N., & Madden-Derdich, D. A. (2002). The Coping with Children's Negative Emotions Scale (CCNES): Psychometric properties and relations with children's emotional competence. *Marriage and Family Review, 34,* 285–310.

Field, T., & Reite, M. (1984). Children's responses to separation from mother during the birth of another child. *Child Development, 55,* 1308–1316.

Furman, W., & Buhrmester, D. (1985). Children's perceptions of the qualities of sibling relationships. *Child Development, 56,* 448–461.

Garcia, M. M., Shaw, D. S., Winslow, E. B., & Yaggi, E. (2000). Destructive sibling conflict and development of conduct problems in young boys. *Developmental Psychology, 36,* 44–53.

Goldsmith, H. H., Riesser-Danner, L. A., & Briggs, S. (1991). Evaluating convergent and discriminant validity of temperament questionnaires for preschoolers, toddlers, and infants. *Developmental Psychology, 27,* 566–579.

Griffin, E. W., & De La Torre, C. (1983). Sibling jealousy: The family with a new baby. *American Family Physician, 28,* 143–146.

Hart, S., & Behrens, K. (2008). *Loss and recovery of exclusivity: Responses of dyads with secure and insecure attachment relationships.* Poster presented at the International Conference on Infant Studies, Vancouver, BC.

Hart, S., & Carrington, H. (2002). Jealousy in 6-month-old infants. *Infancy 3,* 395–402.

Hart, S. L., Carrington, H. A., Tronick, E. Z., & Carroll, S. R. (2004). When infants lose exclusive maternal attention: Is it jealousy? *Infancy 6,* 57–78.

Hart, S. Field, T., & del Valle, C. (1998). Infants protest their mothers' attending to an infant-size doll. *Social Development, 7,* 54–61.

Herrera, C., & Dunn, J. (1997). Early experiences with family conflict: Implications for arguments with a close friend. *Developmental Psychology, 33,* 869–881.

Hetherington, E. M., & Clingempeel, W. G. (1992). Coping with marital transitions: A family systems perspective. *Monographs of the Society for Research in Child Development, 57*(2–3, Serial No. 227).

Hetherington, E. M., Clarke-Stewart, A., & Dunn, J. (2006). The influence of conflict, marital problem solving and parenting on children's adjustment in nondivorced, divorced and remarried families. In *Families count: Effects on child and adolescent development* (pp. 203–237). New York: Cambridge University Press.

Hoffman, K. L., & Edwards, J. N., (2004). An integrated theoretical model of sibling violence and abuse. *Journal of Family Violence, 19,* 185–197.

Ingoldsby, E. M., Shaw, D. S., Owens, E. B., & Winslow, E. B. (1999). A longitudinal study of interparental conflict, emotional and behavioral reactivity in preschoolers' adjustment problems among low-income families. *Journal of Abnormal Psychology, 27,* 343–356.

Kowal, A., Kramer, L., Krull, J. L., & Crick, N. (2002). Children's perceptions of the fairness of parental preferential treatment and their socioemotional well-being. *Journal of Family Psychology, 16,* 297–306.

Legg, C., Sherick, I., & Wadland, W. (1974). Reaction of preschool children to the birth of a sibling. *Child Psychiatry and Human Development, 5,* 3–39.

Leung, A. K., & Robson, W. L. (1991). Sibling rivalry. *Clinical Pediatrics, 30,* 314–317.

Levy, D. (1934). Rivalry between children in the same family. *Child Study, 11,* 233–239.

Masciuch, S., & Kienapple, K. (1993). The emergence of jealousy in children 4 months to 7 years of age. *Journal of Social and Personal Relationships, 10,* 421–435.

McDermott, J. F. (1980). *Raising Cain (and Abel too)*. New York: Wyden Books.

McGuire, S., Dunn, J., & Plomin, R. (1995). Maternal differential treatment of siblings and children's behavioral problems: A longitudinal study. *Development and Psychopathology, 7*, 515–528.

Miller, A. L., Volling, B. L., & McElwain, N. L. (2000). Sibling jealousy in a triadic context with mothers and fathers. *Social Development, 9*, 433–457.

Munn, P., & Dunn, J. (1989). Temperament and the developing relationship between siblings. *International Journal of Behavioral Development, 12*, 433–451.

Nadelman, L., & Begun, A. (1982). The effect of the newborn on the older sibling: Mothers' questionnaires. In M. E. Lamb & B. Sutton-Smith (Eds.), *Sibling relationships: Their nature and significance across the lifespan* (pp. 13–38). Hillsdale, NJ: Erlbaum.

Neubauer, P. B. (1982). Rivalry, envy, and jealousy. *The Psychoanalytic Study of the Child, 37*, 121–142.

Parker, J. G., Low, C. M., & Walker, A. R. (2005). Friendship jealousy in young adolescents: Individual differences and links to sex, self-esteem, aggression, and social adjustment. *Developmental Psychology, 40*, 235–250.

Perlman, M., & Ross, H. S. (1997). The benefits of parent intervention in children's disputes: An examination of concurrent changes in children's fighting styles. *Child Development, 64*, 690–700.

Podolsky, E. (1954). The jealous child. *Archives of Pediatrics, 71*, 54–56.

Prochaska, J. M., & Prochaska, J. O. (1985). Children's view of the causes and cures of sibling rivalry. *Child Welfare, 64*, 427–433.

Ram, A., & Ross, H. (2001). Problem-solving, contention, and struggle: How siblings resolve a conflict of interests. *Child Development, 72*, 1710–1722.

Rauer, A. J., & Volling, B. L. (2007). Differential parenting and sibling jealousy: Developmental correlates of self-esteem, attachment, and jealousy in young adults' romantic relationships. *Personal Relationships, 14*, 495–511.

Richmond, M. K., Stocker, C. M., & Rienks, S. L. (2005). Longitudinal associations between sibling relationship quality, parental differential treatment, and children's adjustment. *Journal of Family Psychology, Special Issue: Sibling relationship contributions to individual and family well-being, 19*, 550–559.

Robey, K. L., Cohen, B. D., & Epstein, Y. M. (1988). The child's response to affection given to someone else: Effects of parental divorce, sex of child, and sibling position. *Journal of Clinical Child Psychology, 17*, 2–7.

Ross, B. M. (1931). Some traits associated with sibling jealousy in problem children. *Smith College Studies of Social Work, 1*, 364–376.

Ross, H., Ross, M., Stein, N., & Trabasso, T. (2006). How siblings resolve their conflicts: The importance of first offers, planning, and limited opposition. *Child Development, 77*, 1730–1745.

Ross, H. G., & Milgram, J. I. (1982). Important variables in adult sibling relationships: A qualitative study. In M. E. Lamb & B. Sutton-Smith (Eds.), *Sibling relationships: Their significance across the lifespan* (pp. 225–249). Hillsdale, NJ: Erlbaum.

Rothbart, M. K., Ahadi, S. A., Hersey, K. L., & Fisher, P. (2001). Investigations of temperament at three to seven years: The Children's Behavior Questionnaire. *Child Development, 72*, 1394–1408.

Salovey, P. (1991). *The psychology of jealousy and envy.* New York: Guilford Press.

Scharf, M., Shulman, S., & Avigad-Spitz, L. (2005). Sibling relationships in emerging adulthood and in adolescence. *Journal of Adolescent Research, 20,* 64–90.

Sharpsteen, D. J., & Kirkpatrick, L. A. (1997). Romantic jealousy and adult romantic attachment. *Journal of Personality and Social Psychology, 72,* 627–640.

Shebloski, B., Conger, K. J., & Widaman, K. F. (2005). Reciprocal links among differential parenting, perceived partiality, and self-worth: A three-wave longitudinal study. *Journal of Family Psychology, Special Issue: Sibling relationship contributions to individual and family well-being, 19,* 550–559.

Steinmetz, S. K. (1977). The use of force for resolving family conflict: The training ground for abuse. *The Family Coordinator 26,* 19–26.

Stewart, R. B., Mobley, L. A., Van Tuyl, S. S., & Salvador, M. A. (1987). The firstborn's adjustment to the birth of a sibling: A longitudinal assessment. *Child Development, 58,* 341–355.

Stocker, C. M., Dunn, J., & Plomin, R. (1989). Sibling relationships: Links with child temperament, maternal behavior, and family structure. *Child Development, 60,* 715–727.

Stocker, C. M., Lanthier, R. P., & Furman, W. (1997). Sibling relationships in early adulthood. *Journal of Family Psychology, 11,* 210–221.

Stocker, C. M., & Youngblade, L. (1999). Marital conflict and parental hostility: Links with children's sibling and peer relationships. *Journal of Family Psychology, 13,* 598–609.

Stoneman, Z., & Brody, G. H. (1993). Sibling temperaments, conflict, warmth, and role asymmetry. *Child Development, 64,* 1786–1800.

Straus, M. A., & Moore, D. W. (1990). Differences among states in child abuse rates and programs. In D. J. Besharov (Ed.), *Family violence: Research and public policy issues* (pp. 150–163). Washington, DC: AEI Press.

Teti, D. M., & Ablard, K. E. (1989). Security of attachment and infant–sibling relationships: A laboratory study. *Child Development 60,* 1519–1528.

Thompson, J. A., & Halberstadt, A.G. (2008). Children's accounts of sibling jealousy and their implicit theories about relationships. *Social Development, 17,* 488–511.

Tseung, C. N., & Schott, G. (2004). The quality of sibling relationship during late adolescence: Are there links with other significant relationships? *Psychological Studies, 49,* 20–30.

Vandell, D. L., Bailey, M. D., Shantz, C. U., & Hartup, W. W. (1992). Conflicts between siblings. *Conflict in child and adolescent development* (pp. 242–269). New York: Cambridge University Press.

Volling, B. L. (1997). The family correlates of maternal and paternal perceptions of differential treatment in early childhood. *Family Relations, 46,* 1–9.

Volling, B. L. (2003). Sibling relationships. In M. Bornstein, L. Davidson, C. Keyes, & K. A. Moore (Eds.), *Well-being: Positive development across the life course* (pp. 205–220). Mahwah, NJ: Erlbaum.

Volling, B. L., & Belsky, J. (1992). The contribution of mother–child and father–child relationships to the quality of sibling interaction: A longitudinal study. *Child Development, 63,* 1209–1222.

Volling, B. L., & Elins, J. (1998). Family relationships and children's emotional adjustment as correlates of maternal and paternal differential treatment: A replication with toddler and preschool siblings. *Child Development, 69,* 1640–1656.

Volling, B. L., McElwain, N. L., & Miller, A. L. (2002). Emotion regulation in context: The jealousy complex between young siblings and its relations with child and family characteristics. *Child Development, 73,* 581–600.

White, G. L., & Mullen, P. E. (1989). *Jealousy: Theory, research, and clinical strategies.* New York: Guilford Press.

18

The Socialization of Sibling Rivalry
What's Love Got to Do?

Sybil L. Hart

Satisfaction that can be derived from family harmony is rarely underrated and most would agree that an important ingredient is the presence of children who get along with each other. Under any circumstances, children's misbehavior is disturbing to parents but that which arises from jealousy can be especially troubling (Eisenberg et al., 1999; Kramer, Perozynski, & Chung, 1999; Perlman & Ross, 1997; Volling, 2005; Volling & Blandon, 2005). Numerous works in which sibling conflict has been documented (Dunn, 1986; Field & Reite, 1984; Stewart, Mobley, Van Tuyl, & Salvador, 1987) support widely held views that it is ubiquitous, potentially serious, and can lead to poor sibling relations which can be highly stable over time (G. H. Brody, Stoneman, McCoy, & Forehand, 1992; L. R. Brody, Copeland, Sutton, Richardson, & Guyer, 1998; Dunn & Kendrick, 1982; Goodwin & Roscoe, 1990; Miner & Clarke-Stewart, 2008; Steinmetz, 1977; Stillwell & Dunn, 1985). It has also been noted that parental concerns run deep (Vandell & Bailey, 1992), reverberating with emotional intensity which, to some extent, stems from accounts of sibling rivalry as a recurring theme in religion and literature. It is noteworthy that perhaps the first written account of murder was a case of fratricide. According to both the Book of Genesis and the Koran, it involved Cain and Abel, the very first pair of siblings to walk the face of the earth. In line with its status as possibly the most longstanding parenting problem in recorded history, still today, sibling rivalry poses challenges to family harmony, is a leading factor prompting parents to seek counseling, and is a prominent topic of discussion in parenting classes (Buhrmester, 1992; Campbell, 1990; Furman & Lanthier, 2002; Vandell & Bailey, 1992).

This chapter seeks to help shed light on the issue of sibling rivalry by exploring adults' attitudes toward conflict that arises due to parents' differential treatment of siblings. We begin by discussing parental attitudes and handling of child misbehavior in general, and then present some of our own work which explores these in situations where child misbehavior is motivated specifically by parents' differential treatment. In a concluding section we speculate on these findings

Handbook of Jealousy: Theory, Research and Multidisciplinary Approaches, First Edition.
Edited by Sybil L. Hart and Maria Legerstee.
© 2013 Blackwell Publishing Ltd. Published 2013 by Blackwell Publishing Ltd.

as they pertain to the socialization of sibling rivalry and suggest directions for future research.

Contextual Determinants of Adults' Perceptions of Child Misconduct

Adults' reactions to children's misbehaviors have long been explored in contexts involving sibling conflict (Adler, 1931; Levy, 1937). Generally, these find that when parents decide to respond to these disputes they do so with the aim of modulating negativity, but the methods they utilize differ widely (Kramer, 2004). Child-centered approaches have been adopted with the aim of helping siblings communicate, empathize, compromise, and problem-solve, and have generally involved discussion and reasoning. A contrasting approach that involves power assertion has been seen as more singly and immediately aimed toward eliminating conflict, and entails greater use of disciplinary tactics and consequences, such as punishment, threats, or withholding privileges. Despite the obvious differences between these types of approaches, both power assertion (Allison & Allison, 1971; Furman & McQuaid, 1992; Olson & Roberts, 1987) and child-centered methods (Dunn & Munn, 1986; Kramer, 2004; Smith & Ross, 2007) have at times been found effective, leaving little consensus as to the optimal method for reducing conflict. Perhaps due to these seemingly contradictory results and despite the fact that parents are of the opinion that intervention is more effective than nonintervention, the tactic that is most typically adopted by parents of squabbling siblings is nonintervention. Tellingly, the practice of nonintervention has been associated with feelings of inadequacy in enacting disciplinary measures and low confidence in their effectiveness even if attempted (Perozynski & Kramer, 1999). Thus, further inquiry is warranted in order to gain some clarity with respect to issues which underlie this quandary.

Sibling conflict can ensue from disagreement over a broad range of issues, only one of which involves rivalry over parents' distribution of attention, praise, privileges, and possessions. Although the term rivalry has sometimes been reserved for conflict arising from favoritism, distinctions between differential treatment and favoritism are not always meaningful. What may seem fair to a parent and perhaps one child may not appear so to another child or even to a supposedly objective outside observer (Kowal, Krull, & Kramer, 2006; Vandell, Owen, Wilson, & Henderson, 1988; Volling, 1997). Fair or not, perceptions of inequitable treatment have a long history of being considered pivotal to triggering child misconduct. More recently, these observations have been well substantiated in empirical research with children of varying ages (Boll, Ferring, & Filipp, 2003; G. H. Brody, Stoneman, & Burke, 1987; Bryant & Crockenberg, 1980; Hetherington, 1988; Levy, 1937; Stocker, Dunn, & Plomin, 1989), and confirmed in experimental work which shows that even at the toddler stage, children are disturbed by inequality in parents' distribution of attention (Hart, Field, del Valle, & Letourneau, 1998; A. L. Miller, Volling, & McElwain, 2000; Teti & Ablard, 1989).

Despite the rare degree of regularity with which rivalry has been documented in contexts of parents' differential treatment, the manner in which parents respond to and manage sibling rivalry is poorly understood. Investigative attention has been hampered by a number of barriers. One difficulty is the likelihood that adults are poor judges when it comes to evaluating the equity with which their favors are distributed among children (Vandell & Bailey, 1992). Even if parents are willing to accept responsibility for their own culpability in precipitating rivalry, a sense of guilt may be involved, and this can be the case even when parents consider unequal treatment to be fair (Glasberg, Martins, & Harris, 2006), leading to biased responses. Finally, investigative attention is further complicated by the fact that not unlike the varied emotional responses that are elicited in other types of evocative situations (Lewis, 1997; Saarni, 2008), rivalry is indistinguishable from misbehavior which surfaces in other conflict situations. This poses difficulties because instances of differential treatment can co-occur with other types of inflammatory situations, such as disagreement over property, and so it is often unclear to parents whether or not rivalry played a role in precipitating their children's agonistic behavior. Given these obstacles, it may not be surprising that within the literature on sibling relationships, an area that has itself been described as understudied (Kramer & Ramsburg, 2002; Schachter & Stone, 1987), findings on management of rivalry have generally been obscured by attention to the broader topic of sibling conflict.

Nevertheless, a number of useful observations may be found in the literature on contextual factors and their role in determining parents' handling of child misbehavior. It has been observed, for example, that in the process of deciding on an appropriate disciplinary measure, parents typically call on their children to explain the circumstances in which conflict occurred (Perlman & Ross, 1997). Research on maternal responses to children's transgressions (Smetana, 1989) found that a mother's manner of responding to children's lapses depended on her insight into whether an infraction represented a moral versus conventional type of infraction. An especially insightful study by Martin and Ross (1996) explored parental responses to siblings' physical aggression by considering whether and how parent responses differed with contextual circumstances. Find-ings revealed that if committed under mitigating circumstances, such as lack of aggressive intent, consent of the victim, restitution, and having been preceded by provocation, child aggression was followed by lesser parental attention and fewer expressed prohibitions. Leniency toward mitigated (versus unmitigated) aggres-sion was attributed to parental opinions that in certain contexts, aggression can be considered justified and excusable. Notably, this pattern of showing leniency was apparent even in cases involving more severe levels of aggression. Although this study did not explore differential treatment as a mitigating factor, it unveils a number of interrelated clues that may be relevant. First, it illustrates the fact that parental involvement in sibling conflict is not based solely on absolute levels of aggression. Second, it highlights parental sensitivity to circumstantial events or contextual influences. Third, it indicates that under some conditions, some amount of aggression can be considered excusable.

The importance of circumstantial factors to parents' interpretation of child conflict has also been explored in social contexts that involve peers. Some particularly insightful work in this area has involved laboratory research using experimental designs in which children's problematic behaviors have been standardized by being presented either through a story in text, or in video format. In a study where parents were provided with text depictions of children demonstrating aggressive and socially withdrawn behaviors, Mills and Rubin (1990) found that in comparison with children's shy behaviors, aggressive behaviors elicited mothers' greater endorsements for interventions involving power assertion (Mills & Rubin, 1990). Using a paradigm in which mothers were presented with videotaped vignettes of preschoolers involved in common peer relationship problems, Colwell and associates (Colwell, Mize, Pettit, & Laird, 2002) found that when a child had been presented as the instigator, rather than victim, of aggression, mothers reported greater approval of management strategies involving power assertion. A third study (Werner, Senich, & Przepyszny, 2006), which explored maternal reactions to text depictions of preschoolers in problematic situations with peers which involved physical and relational aggression, found that children's physical aggression was again associated with mothers' greater endorsements for power assertion.

As in naturalistic work conducted in home settings (Martin & Ross, 1996; Perlman & Ross, 1997; Smetana, 1989), these experimental works highlight the salience of contextual information to parental reactions to child misbehavior. In particular, they highlight the importance of context to interpretations of child anger and aggression (Mills & Rubin, 1990). Reactions to child anger depended further on whether anger was expressed within contexts of physical or relational aggression, and whether it was exhibited by a child who participated as victim or victimizer (Colwell et al., 2002; Werner et al., 2006). It would appear that parents are so attuned to anger that they distinguish not only between situations that do and do not involve anger, but also within different kinds of anger-inducing contexts. Perhaps due to its ubiquity, or perhaps because it has been identified as a precursor of extra-familial aggression and as representing risk for poor child outcomes, it seems that parents are keenly aware of negative emotionality and place emphasis on its resolution (Arsenio & Lover, 1997; Carson & Parke, 1996; Denham, Mitchell-Copeland, Strandberg, Auerbach, & Blair, 1997; Putallaz & Sheppard, 1992; Steinmetz, 1977).

Child Gender as a Contributor to Adults' Perceptions

Especially when child misbehavior entails expressions of anger, parental reactions have often been found to differ with child gender. Some have noted that anger is tolerated to greater degrees when it is displayed by boys. For example, in their analysis of maternal responses to peer conflict, Ross and associates (Ross, Tesla, Kenyon, & Lollis, 1990) found that in instances where rights of ownership had been violated, mothers were more inclined to support their sons than daughters. A naturalistic study of conflict among preschool-age siblings (Martin & Ross, 2005) reported that even though aggression was more frequent and severe when exhibited by sons, parents were more likely to prohibit aggression, grabbing, and property damage by daughters, and show more tolerance of mild physical aggression among sons. When mothers did intervene, they were more likely to settle disputes in favor of sons. These studies suggest some greater lenience toward anger in boys, at least in instances of mild aggression, possibly because male anger and aggression are considered more normative and more consistent with societal, sex-stereotyped norms for appropriate behavior, and thus considered less deviant.

On the other hand, when parents do intervene in children's misdeeds, boys are more likely than girls to receive power assertive treatment (Maccoby & Jacklin, 1974; Ostrov, Crick, & Keating, 2005; Ostrov, Woods, Jansen, Casas, & Crick, 2004). Harsh discipline has been found more often directed toward sons than daughters (McKee et al., 2007), and research on child exposure to marital discord (J. P. McHale, 1995) reported that sons were more likely to be the object of hostile parenting. Smetana (1989) reported that mothers of boys were more likely to use punishment, while mothers of girls used child-centered approaches involving perspective taking and encouragement for showing concern for others. Others (Dunn & Kendrick, 1982; Miner & Clarke-Stewart, 2008) have found that in comparison with mothers of girls, mothers of boys are more consistent in their use of prohibitive and punitive treatment.

Laboratory research on adults' attitudes toward child misbehavior suggests that opinions, like actual behaviors, can differ with child gender (Bacon & Ashmore, 1985). Gender biases were highlighted in a classic study on gender labeling (Condry & Condry, 1976) in which adults were shown video footage of an infant who cried during exposure to a jack-in-the-box as it was repeatedly opened, suddenly and loudly, while being moved closer to the infant. Findings revealed that if the infant had been labeled male, infant negative affectivity was perceived by viewers as expressing greater anger. When labeled female, however, the infant was regarded as expressing fear. In their work on parental opinions about children who were depicted in text as expressing aggression, Mills and Rubin (1990) found that parents showed greater acceptance of anger expressions in boys. However, other work on parental attitudes toward children's misbehavior in problematic situations (Colwell et al., 2002; Werner et al., 2006) did not find differences with child gender. Overall, findings of research on adults' responses to children's expressions of anger are quite mixed though there appears a pattern, whereby boys' anger is treated with greater acceptance, yet harsher methods of discipline (Kerig, Cowan, & Cowan, 1993; Radke-Yarrow & Kochanska, 1990).

Differential treatment of siblings may not be as uncommon as some would imagine (Conley, 2005). In developmental research, however, rates of occurrence have rarely been found to differ systematically with child gender (Furman, 1995). So it follows that little is known about the manner in which parents handle rivalry, nor whether it differs with child gender.

In sum, findings of research on adults' interpretation and handling of child conflict highlight sensitivity to contextual information and child gender. In addition, laboratory studies on peer conflict suggest methodology for inquiry into sibling conflict arising from differential treatment. Importantly, these methods may have the potential to investigate rivalry in a manner that overcomes some of the barriers that are inherent in work in this area. Drawing on these conclusions, the pair of studies detailed below explored adults' opinions of sibling rivalry by having respondents report on child misbehavior that was presented on videotape.

In our first study, some participants were informed that child misbehavior was prompted by mother's differential treatment toward a newborn infant. Others were told that it was prompted by deprivation of a desired toy. This contrasting scenario was selected for inclusion because it is a situation that is widely known to be an elicitor of frustration and can trigger behaviors that are structurally indistinguishable from rivalry. Also, to some participants the child was portrayed as a male child and to others as a female child. In an effort to overcome a limitation that has been noted in previous work in which different instances of negativity were presented using different segments of videotape (Colwell et al., 2002), in the present study, the display of anger, whether attributed to rivalry or frustration by a girl or boy, was actually the very same footage. Thus, use of video was advantageous, not only to standardizing within-condition variability, but also to controlling for cross-context variation and potential confounds stemming from factors such as differences in child characteristics and quality or intensity of negative emotionality. Through this manipulation of context and child gender we sought insights into adults' perceptions of sibling rivalry and their opinions about appropriate interventions.

Participants

Participants were 167 females, 21.02 (SD = 2.33) years of age, and 85.63% Caucasian who were enrolled in a course on child development for students majoring in early childhood education. They were in four groups, each from a different section of the course which was given in similar time blocks over several semesters. The groups did not differ from each other in size or with respect to participant age, ethnicity, years in college, and status as parents. None of these demographic variables were associated with outcome measures.

Procedure

Each group was shown the exact same segment of videotape within a class lecture on the topic of methods of conducting child observations. Before viewing the tape, groups were provided with information about the situation that had taken place immediately prior to the behavioral display that was about to be seen. The two groups in the Frustration Context condition were told that the mother was holding a toy on her lap just after having taken it away from her child because it was time to stop playing and go home. In one group, the child was referred to as "he," and in the other group as "she."

The two groups in the two Jealousy Context conditions were informed that the mother was holding a newborn baby sibling who had just awakened from a nap; child gender was indicated as for participants in the Frustration Context groups. The four groups are referred to according to the contextual information that was provided: *Frustration-Female, Frustration-Male, Rivalry-Female,* and *Rivalry-Male.*

To help ensure that participants were fully engaged in watching the video, they were asked to take notes on the child's behavior while watching the video. Immediately after viewing the videotape, they were asked to write a brief narrative account of the behavior they had just observed. Finally, they were asked to answer a brief questionnaire.

Stimulus videotape

The videotape, obtained from the author's collection, shows a toddler with short hair, and clothed in a tee shirt, overalls, and sneakers. Because this style of hair and attire is commonly worn by both males and females in the United States, there was little to indicate child gender. The fact that the toddler had been videotaped using black and white film that was somewhat grainy in quality further obscured some subtle clues to gender that may have existed. The vignette starts with the child standing in front of his or her mother who is seated in a chair with her back to the camera, holding an object on her lap and directing her attention to the object. The toddler is looking at his or her mother and starts to whine, at first softly and then with increasing volume and emotional intensity. Next he or she starts to stomp his or her feet and flail his or her arms. The toddler then grabs the corner of a small blanket that is close by and starts thrashing it on the floor repeatedly and with increasing force while vocalizing loudly and stomping noisily and wildly. Finally, he or she throws the blanket on the floor, flings him- or herself onto the blanket, and begins to kick his or her feet, pound the floor with his or her fists, and scream. This demonstration of escalating negativity, known in the United States as a full blown temper tantrum, is generally regarded as an expression of intense anger. It has been observed in toddlers by parents as well as clinicians in various contexts of distress, including those precipitated by both frustration and jealousy (Brazelton, 1983; Kramer & Baron, 1995; Spock & Parker, 1998; Stearns, 1989; Stifter & Grant, 1993).

Questionnaire items
Participants were presented with a list of 6 emotion terms: Surprise, Happiness, Disgust, Fear, Anger, and Sadness, and asked to select the one which best described the toddler's predominant emotion. Three questions followed. First, participants were asked to rate their perception of the child's level of distress on a Likert scale ranging from 1, for indicating Mild, to 7, for indicating Intense. Next, participants were asked to indicate, on Likert scales ranging from 1, for indicating Not Applicable, to 7, for indicating Highly Applicable, answers to two questions: *How much firmness and discipline (e.g., time out, prohibitions) would you consider an appropriate parental response? How much warmth and reassurance would you consider an appropriate parental response?*

Results

Verifying that the toddler's tantrum had indeed been seen as an expression of anger, 97% of participants chose Anger as the best emotion label for describing the toddler's affect. Chi square analyses revealed that rates of selecting Anger did not differ by group. To compare responses to the next three questions, a multivariate analysis of variance (MANOVA) was used to analyze the effects of Context (frustration/rivalry) and Gender on ratings for the three questions. Significant main effects for Context $F(3, 155) = 26.26$, $p < .001$, Gender $F(3, 155) = 6.48$, $p < .001$, and the interaction of Context by Gender $F(3, 155) = 2.77$, $p < .05$ were followed by univariate analyses for each item.

Perceived level of child distress
The main effect of Context $F(1,157) = 7.75$, $p < .01$ and the interaction of Context by Gender $F(1, 157) = 7.73$, $p < .01$ were significant. Post hoc analyses revealed that if the toddler's attributed sex was female, perceived levels of distress did not differ with context. However, if the toddler had been labeled as male, anger in the context of frustration was perceived as lower than that for females, while anger in the context of rivalry was perceived as greater than that for females. (See Figure 18.1.)

Parental firmness and discipline
Endorsements for firm treatment were found to differ with both Context $F(1,157) = 56.42$, $p < .001$, and Gender $F(1,157) = 11.73$, $p < .001$. These main effects revealed that firmness was considered more appropriate in the context of frustration than rivalry, and when displayed by a child who was labeled male rather than female. (See Figure 18.2.)

Parental warmth and reassurance
Main effects were again found for Context $F(1,157) = 5.09$, $p < .05$, and Gender $F(1,157) = 4.31$, $p < .05$. These revealed that endorsements for

warmth were greater in the context of rivalry than frustration, and when attributed sex was female rather than male. (See Figure 18.3.)

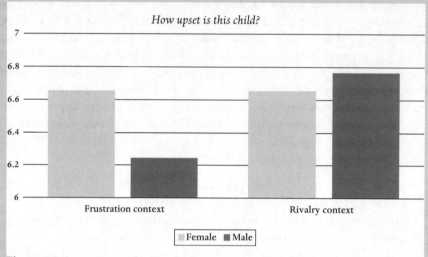

Figure 18.1

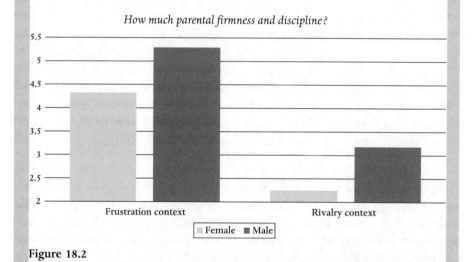

Figure 18.2

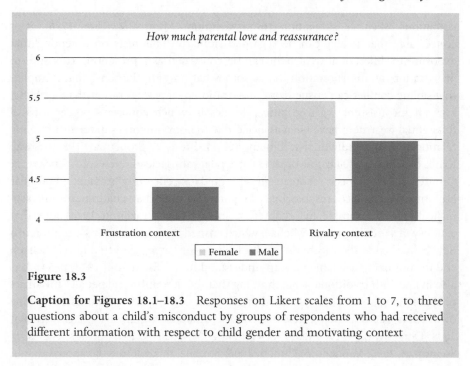

Figure 18.3

Caption for Figures 18.1–18.3 Responses on Likert scales from 1 to 7, to three questions about a child's misconduct by groups of respondents who had received different information with respect to child gender and motivating context

In line with earlier observations that when handling children's misbehavior, parents are more likely to use power assertion with boys and child-centered approaches with girls (Maccoby & Jacklin, 1974; J. P. McHale, 1995; McKee et al., 2007; Smetana, 1989), findings revealed that firmness and disciplinary tactics were viewed as more appropriate if the child in the video had been depicted as male. Correspondingly, support for providing warmth and reassurances was greater among participants who had been informed that the child was female. Endorsements for both types of treatment differed dramatically with context. Since the child behavior itself was actually identical across conditions, this result upholds findings of studies in naturalistic (Martin & Ross, 1996; Smetana, 1989) and laboratory studies (Colwell et al., 2002; Grusec & Kuczynski, 1980; Martin & Ross, 1996; Mills & Rubin, 1990; Werner et al., 2006) which point to the importance of contextual information to adults' interpretations of child misbehavior. Most intriguing, however, were findings on the direction of effects for context. These revealed that, regardless of child gender, anger was seen as warranting greater levels of warmth and lower levels of firm discipline if it had been attributed to sibling rivalry rather than frustration.

Why does rivalry generate weaker endorsements for consequences involving firm discipline? One possible explanation for such leniency is that as a response to differential treatment, an expression of rivalry may be construed as occurring under mitigating circumstances. Much as other conditions of sibling aggression have been considered to some degree legitimate if exhibited under mitigating conditions, such as subjection to provocation (Martin & Ross, 1996), it is conceivable that rivalry can be regarded similarly. This rests on accepting that exposure to differential treatment can be construed as representing exposure to provocation, an interpretation that is somewhat novel in the sense that it implies that sibling conflict can ensue from provocation by a parent, rather than a sibling, but not inconsistent with empirical studies in which children's perceptions of differential treatment have been associated with poor outcomes in terms of sibling relationships and individual well-being (G. H. Brody & Stoneman, 1987; Kowal, Krull, & Kramer, 2004; S. M. McHale, Updegraff, Jackson-Newsom, Tucker, & Crouter, 2000). Nor is it inconsistent with guidance currently provided in popular literature which places responsibility on parents, rather than children, for unleashing jealousy. For example, in a chapter on sibling rivalry, Brazelton (1974) notes that jealousy in a toddler named Michael which ensued from his mother's attention to a new baby elicited the mother's "guilty feelings for having deserted him [Michael] and for not being available now to understand him" (Brazelton, 1974, p. 54). It is also in line with traditional legal thinking that the definition and penalty for an act of aggression should be determined on the basis of motivating circumstances, one of which is jealousy (Ben-Ze'ev, this volume, Chapter 3; Ben-Ze'ev & Goussinsky, 2008; Dershowitz, 1997; Puente & Cohen, 2003; Stearns, 1989; Straus, Gelles, & Steinmetz, 2003; Vandello & Cohen, 2008; Stearns, this volume, Chapter 1).

The finding that, as an expression of rivalry, anger calls for parents responding with greater warmth and reassurance is less clear. In the same vein as findings on lesser endorsements for firm treatment of rivalry, it is possible that respondents have been influenced by guidance from authors in the popular press who endorse acquiescence. For example, on being confronted by a young child's jealous aggression toward a baby sibling, Spock and Parker (1998) advise that, "As a parent in this situation, you have three jobs: to protect the baby, to show the older child that he is not permitted to put his mean feelings into action, and to reassure him that you still love him and that he is really a good boy" (Spock & Parker, 1998, p. 482). To our knowledge, no research is available to substantiate recommendations to provide warmth and reassurance under these conditions. Support for child-centered approaches can be derived from work in which an older child's adjustment to the arrival of a newborn child was found enhanced by parents providing support (Dunn & Kendrick, 1982; Gottlieb & Mendelson, 1990), but it is far from clear that support in these studies included offers of reassurance directly in response to jealousy-motivated aggression.

Finally, findings on perceived levels of child distress were most perplexing. Whereas perceptions of anger levels in a female child were rated equivalently across context, perhaps suggesting that adults' perceptions of anger may be more objective with respect to girls, perceptions of the intensity of male anger differed with context. The bias toward perceiving a boy's angry expression of rivalry as more intense than a girl's could be considered consistent with reports on gender labeling (Condry & Condry, 1976), but it still remains far from clear why this would be the case only in the context of rivalry.

Adults' Intrapersonal Reactions to Sibling Rivalry

While illuminating the importance of contextual information and child gender to parental opinions about appropriate intervention strategies, research on parental responses to child conflict has also shown that parents react intrapersonally, with affective reactions of their own. Laboratory research in which parents commented on depictions of children's aggressive and shy behaviors among peers (Mills & Rubin, 1990) revealed that in comparison with children's shy behaviors, aggressive behaviors elicited mothers' heightened affective reactions of anger and disappointment. When mothers were presented with videotaped vignettes of preschoolers involved in relationship problems with peers (Colwell et al., 2002), situations in which a child was involved as the instigator, rather than the victim, of aggression were associated with mothers reporting greater feelings of disapproval and being upset. Maternal reactions to depictions of peers involved in cases of physical and relational aggression (Werner et al., 2006) revealed that children's physical aggression was associated with mothers' heightened affective responses of anger. Together, these studies indicate that parents react emotionally, and they do so with feelings of anger, disappointment, disapproval, and distress. Following numerous works which have shown that parents are disturbed by their children's misbehavior (Bugental, Blue, & Lewis, 1990; Colwell et al., 2002; Dix, Ruble, Grusec, & Nixon, 1986; Grusec, Dix, & Mills, 1982), these studies underscore the importance of contextual information, not only to parents' perceptions of children, but also, suggesting bidirectionality of influences (Lewis & Rosenblum, 1974), to parental affect in response to child affect.

Although it is well known that parents of siblings, like those of peers, are troubled by child conflict (Shantz & Hobart, 1989; Steinmetz & Lystad, 1986), less is known about their intrapersonal reactions to child misbehavior in situations that involve rivalry. In adult romantic relationships, jealousy has often been received with some ambivalence (Ben Ze'ev, this volume; Clanton, 1998; Stearns, 1989, this volume). While being deplored for reasons that are obvious, romantic jealousy has also had positive connotations through being construed as "proof of love." Notions that heightened levels of jealousy signify greater love, while diminished levels mark lesser love, have waxed and waned over time, and in recent years these notions have come to be seen as somewhat dated. Nevertheless, signs of positive interpretations of jealousy are still apparent when probed with subtlety, as in research in which heightened jealousy has been found characteristic of relationships that were more satisfying or longer-lasting (Barelds & Barelds-Dijkstra, 2007; Mathes, 1986).

Whether positive interpretations of rivalry can be applied in situations involving children is unknown. Thus, to follow up on our first study's finding which suggested parents' leniency toward sibling rivalry, the present study was designed with the aim of determining whether adults interpret heightened levels of a child's rivalry, not unlike heightened jealousy in adult romantic relationships, as an indication of greater love. Groups of participants viewed two segments of videotape. In one, a child displayed mild distress and in the other, intense distress. To some groups, the presentations were explained as having been prompted by maternal differential treatment toward another child. To others, they were explained as having been prompted by deprivation of a desired toy. Through this manipulation of motivating context and intensity of child distress, we explored adults' constructions of child rivalry as an index of parental love.

Participants

Participants were 140 females, 21.10 years (SD = 2.98) years of age, 90.00% Caucasian who were enrolled in a course on child development for students majoring in early childhood education. They were in four groups, each from a different section of the course which was given in similar time blocks over several semesters. The groups did not differ from each other in size or with respect to participant age, ethnicity, years in college, and status as parents. None of these demographic variables were associated with outcome measures.

Procedure

Participants in all 4 groups viewed the exact same videotapes, one showed a toddler displaying mild negative affect and the other showed a child displaying intense negative affect. Half of the groups were first shown the mildly distressed child, and half were first shown the highly distressed child. The two segments were shown on different days within class lectures on the topic of methods of conducting child observations. Prior to viewing the two videotape segments, participants in the two Rivalry Context groups were told that the mother was directing her attention toward a newborn sibling. Those in the Frustration Context groups were informed that the mother was focusing attention on a toy which had just been taken away from the toddler because play time was over and it was time to go home. Thus, the four groups were *Mild-Frustration*, *Mild-Rivalry*, *Intense-Frustration*, and *Intense-Rivalry*. To help ensure that participants were fully engaged in watching the video, they were asked to take notes on the child's behavior while watching the video. Immediately after viewing the videotape, they were asked to write a brief narrative account of the behavior they had just observed. Finally, they were asked to answer a brief questionnaire.

Stimulus videotapes
The two segments of videotape were obtained from the author's collection. In one, a toddler is seated on a carpeted area, facing his mother and the

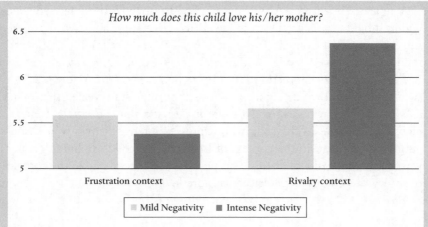

Figure 18.4   Responses on Likert scales from 1 to 7 by groups of respondents who had received different information with respect to the motivating contexts responsible for eliciting a child's mild or intense level of distress

camera, while the mother is seated in a chair with her back to the camera and focusing on an object located on her lap. Selected to represent a toddler demonstrating mild distress, the segment depicts the toddler approaching and then moving away from his mother, briefly whining and pestering her each time. In the other segment of videotape, a toddler and his mother are situated in a comparable setting. However, the toddler remains seated on the carpet and explosively emits a loud wail. He throws his head back, covers his eyes with his hands, and continues to cry and shed tears. Both of the stimulus toddlers were, in reality, male, although little information in the grainy black-and-white film drew attention to infant sex, and both of the toddlers wore trousers and were referred to by the experimenter using gender neutral terms.

Questionnaire items
Immediately after viewing each videotape, participants were asked to use a Likert scale ranging from 1, for indicating Mild, to 7, for indicating Intense, to answer two questions: *How upset is this child? How much do you think this child loves his or her mother?*

Results

Comparisons between ratings of distress in the toddler who exhibited mild pestering (M = 4.13, SD = 1.47) and crying (M = 6.42, SD = .73) differed from each other $F(1,76) = 191.43$, $p < .001$, suggesting that the study's manipulation of distress levels was valid.

A repeated measures ANOVA was used to analyze the effects of one within-subjects variable, Distress Level (mild/intense), and two between-subjects variables, Context (frustration/rivalry), and Order on participants' ratings of perceived levels of Maternal Love. Results revealed a Distress Level × Context interaction $F(1, 136) = 30.73$, $p < .001$. Order was not significant. As shown in Figure 18.4, post hoc analyses revealed that opinions of the child who expressed mild distress did not differ with context. However, opinions of the child who expressed intense distress were distinguished by context. In the context of frustration, a child exhibiting greater versus lesser intensity of distress was perceived as less loving. In the context of rivalry this child was perceived as more loving.

As in numerous works that have documented bidirectionality of affective responding, we found that adults' affective responses to a child's negative affect depended on its level of intensity (Perlman & Ross, 1997; Steinmetz, 1977). Whereas opinions of a child exhibiting mild negative affect were unchanged by context, those of a child exhibiting intense negative affect differed dramatically with motivating context. In the context of frustration, the toddler's heightened negativity was associated with perceptions of the child as being less loving, an expression of reproof that may not be inconsistent with reactions of disappointment, disapproval, and distress that have been noted in adults when faced with other instances of child negativity (Colwell et al., 2002; Mills & Rubin, 1990; Werner et al., 2006). In the context of rivalry, however, heightened negative affectivity was associated with perceptions of the child as being more loving. These diametrically opposed opinions are especially striking when recalling that respondents were commenting on the very same behavioral display. The respondents' positive spin on negative affectivity as an expression of rivalry is reminiscent of reports in the literature on adult romantic relationships which have noted that despite its obviously negative impact, hostile behavior that is attributable to jealousy can be construed favorably as "proof of love" (Clanton, 1998; Puente & Cohen, 2003; Stearns, 1989). Interestingly, in various anecdotal accounts, child jealousy has also been tacitly construed as an expression of love (Darwin, 1877). In a baby biography in which Darwin recounted his son Doddy's psychological development, jealousy received treatment not within a section on *anger*, but rather within a section on *affection* among indices of love, such as smiles and kisses.

Implications for the Socialization of Sibling Rivalry

Certainly, it is far from clear that a toddler's greater rivalry actually represents greater love. Still, as illustrated by the tender-hearted interpretations that jealousy evoked in Darwin, Brazelton, and Spock, this may be of little consequence.

As Malatesta and Haviland (1985) point out, "Although some psychologists are reluctant to believe that there is an isomorphism between an infant's affective state and its affective expression, the argument is almost irrelevant when considered pragmatically, as the caregiver will respond as if the expression were indeed isomorphic with the state" (Malatesta & Haviland, 1985, p. 90). To the extent that this is the case, and in light of theory and evidence that parenting behavior can be influenced by parents' perceptions of children (Darley & Fazio, 1980; Field et al., 1996; D. T. Miller & Turnbull, 1986; Stern, Karraker, McIntosh, Moritzen, & Olexa, 2006), impressions reported in these two studies are notable in terms of the socialization practices they portend.

Some speculation pertains first to quantitative differences in managing rivalry. We discovered that adults are more keenly aware of child anger if it is displayed by a male who is motivated by rivalry. Given that parental involvement in children's disputes is more likely to occur when conflict is more intense (Dunn & Munn, 1986; Perlman & Ross, 1997; Vandell & Bailey, 1992), it is possible that conflict which involves rivalry in a male child elicits parental over-involvement. Studies noting greater recognition of anger in males have associated it with boys receiving greater affirmation and attention for anger, possibly resulting in its greater reinforcement (Condry & Condry, 1976; Eisenberg & Fabes, 1994; Radke-Yarrow & Kochanska, 1990). How such judgments might pertain to anger motivated specifically by jealousy is unclear, though it does lead to predictions that it might represent greater acceptance, validation, or reinforcement for venting of male jealousy.

Once parents become involved, the quality of treatment called forth by jealousy may too differ from that elicited by other conflict situations. Indeed, we discovered that as an expression of rivalry, anger calls for parents providing greater warmth and reassurance, and lesser firmness and discipline. This may not be surprising in light of the subsequent finding that a more intensely distressed child was viewed as a more loving child if the outburst had been attributed to rivalry. These findings on warmth and love lead to predicting acquiescence and lenient treatment of rivalry, a management strategy that in other conflict situations has been found associated with the adoption of overly-permissive disciplinary practices which, among a number of other risk factors, have then been found predictive of increased aggression (Hartup, 2005; Parke & Slaby, 1983; Shaw, 2006). It is also noteworthy that research with adults (Puente & Cohen, 2003) has shown that while being regarded as reprehensible, jealousy-related violence is also considered "understandable" rather than cold-blooded, and less worthy of condemnation. Indeed, Puente and Cohen argue that jealousy's positive subtext can negate the meaning of aggression, if not entirely then at least considerably, a sentiment that was illustrated in a chilling comment by O. J. Simpson (Farber, 1998, February) on his possible culpability for the murder of his former wife, Nicole Brown Simpson, "Let's say I committed this crime ... Even if I did do this, it would have to have been because I loved her so much, right?" (p. 58). Aggression in children has also been legitimized substantially by mitigating circumstances (Perlman & Ross, 1997), and according to various clinical reports, these can include differential treatment. For example, in his interpretation of young Michael's aggression toward his infant brother Tom, Brazelton (1974) noted, "If Michael did indeed hurt Tom, he [Michael] is probably more deeply upset [than Tom]." Brazelton then goes on to recommend that the proper response to Michael's suffering would be a mother who "rushes to comfort the aggressor as well as the victim" (p. 48). This charitable interpretation may not be surprising given that adults show high regard for children expressing love and affection through demonstrations of positive behaviors, such as smiles (Sroufe, 1979), but it may be problematic when applied to rivalry. Faced with child misbehavior that is perceived to be coupled with an affective subtext which communicates love, parents may find themselves confronted with what we would argue lies at the heart of the challenge posed by sibling rivalry – dilemma over wishing to modulate overtly negative behavior but not at the risk of dismissing signal of love. Fearful of encouraging hostile behavior while at the very same time rejecting love, it is possible that parents find themselves so torn between jealousy's conflicting messages that they adopt disciplinary practices marked not only by over-involvement and leniency, but also, as depicted by popular guidance material (e.g., Spock & Parker, 1998), lack of conviction as suggested by inconsistency and ambivalence.

Future Research

It is unknown whether future research will bear out any of these predictions, but hopefully these may at least serve as a starting point. Concepts worthy of further investigation might be adapted from suggestions (Grusec & Goodnow, 1994) that parental socialization strategies are determined on the basis of characteristics of the problem situation, the child, and parents themselves. In accord with these recommendations, we chose to focus on a situation, maternal attention to a newborn infant, known to be difficult. We opted to explore child characteristics of gender and intensity of distress based on evidence of their relevance to socialization practices in other sorts of problem situations involving children and also to adult jealousy (Buss, 2000; Daly & Wilson, 1988; Wilson & Daly, 1992). Finally, we chose to focus on younger adults due to our observations, across a decade of conducting research on infant jealousy, that younger mothers are more vulnerable to differences in their children's presentations of jealousy (Hart, 2001). This was especially apparent in cases where infant jealousy had been expressed through attenuated negativity, an instance of objectively "good" behavior that under other circumstances would be considered optimal but in the context involving rivalry seemed to leave mothers, especially younger mothers, looking crushed. Whether heightened vulnerability to rivalry's positive message can be explained as arising from lack of parenting experience

(Condry & Condry, 1976; Whiteman, McHale, & Crouter, 2003), lesser confidence in an infant's love, or heightened romantic ideology (Ben Ze'ev, this volume), is an issue worthy of investigative attention. The fact that the study was conducted in Texas, an area of the United States which is known to be more conservative, may have contributed to effects of gender stereotyping (Bell & Carver, 1980). For the most part, the young adult participants in these studies were not parents, and this could be either a limitation or an advantage. Because those of our respondents who were non-parents did not differ from those who were parents, nor from past findings on parents' endorsements for use of firm and warm treatment, and since our results on biases associated with child gender also seemed consistent with the literature using parents, our reliance on non-parents may not have been a serious limitation. The extent to which it could have been an advantage depends on the extent to which parents in general might feel guilty or responsible for engendering children's disturbances and the extent to which this could bias responses. In the process of commenting on children's reactions to differential treatment, parents may be more biased than non-parents due to feeling that they are implicitly being asked to report on their own ineptitude as parents. Whether this is, in fact, the case remains to be verified. Also, due in part to younger adults' lesser experience with children, we chose to use video rather than text depictions of child behavior. Because of being less vivid, it is unclear whether vignettes in text would have evoked similarly dramatic findings on intense distress. Finally, it may be helpful to note that participants were given few questions to answer. This was done in hopes of stirring candid responses by prompting spontaneity while disclosing few clues that might serve to override tacit approval of jealousy which is overtly considered undesirable, and so kept secret. As Stearns (this volume) points out, adults are uncomfortable with jealousy and likely to believe that jealous feelings must be kept secret. Although this phenomenon may be more pronounced in the United States, parents in Canada, the United Kingdom, and Germany do not freely confess to jealousy, tend to under-report its occurrence in their children, and take steps to shield children from situations in which it is elicited (Draghi-Lorenz, this volume, Chapter 11; Dyck, this volume, Chapter 21; Keller & Lamm, this volume, Chapter 20), suggesting that secrecy is probably not limited to the United States.

We conclude with an ardent call for investigative attention to the process responsible for the socialization of sibling rivalry. In light of widely held views that it is among the most volatile factors responsible for inciting intra-familial conflict, and concern that intra-familial conflict, in turn, serves as a *training ground* for extra-familial aggression (Criss & Shaw, 2005; G. H. Brody, 1998; Garcia, Shaw, Winslow, & Yaggi, 2000; Steinmetz, 1977), inattention to rivalry should no longer be excused. Nor should it continue to be obscured by attention to broader issues of sibling conflict or child misconduct. Indeed, it may be worth recalling that the first case of murder in recorded history was a case of fratricide, and it was triggered by conflict arising from differential treatment. Given the numerous barriers to conducting research on rivalry, the current dearth of empirically derived knowledge is understandable. However, as we hope to have illustrated, experimental methods can be applied productively toward inquiry into this under-researched topic. In light of the present studies' findings, preliminary as they may be, that in children, as in adults, negative emotionality that is attributed to jealousy is interpreted distinctively and more favorably than other instances of misbehavior, it seems likely that while jealousy's socialization will be found to differ with known predictors (Grusec & Goodnow, 1994), the ways in which these predictors operate in contexts involving sibling rivalry stand to be quite unlike those operating in other problem situations. We believe that through research which is open to such possibilities it may be possible to learn how best to respond to jealousy's mixed messages, and perhaps be of some help to parents wishing to dampen rivalry while treating children with compassion.

References

Adler, A. (1931). *What life should mean to you.* Boston: Little, Brown.

Allison, T., & Allison, S. (1971). Time-out from reinforcement: Effect on sibling aggression. *The Psychological Record, 21,* 81–86.

Arsenio, W. F., & Lover, A. (1997). Emotions, conflicts and aggression during preschoolers' freeplay. *British Journal of Developmental Psychology, 15,* 531–542.

Bacon, M. K., & Ashmore, R. D. (1985). How mothers and fathers categorize descriptions of social behavior attributed to daughters and sons. *Social Cognition, 3,* 193–217.

Barelds, D. P. H., & Barelds-Dijkstra, P. (2007). Relations between different types of jealousy and self and partner perceptions of relationship quality. *Clinical Psychology and Psychotherapy, 14,* 176–188.

Bell, N. J., & Carver, W. (1980). A reevaluation of gender label effects: Expectant mothers' responses to infants. *Child Development, 51,* 925–927.

Ben-Ze'ev, A. (this volume). Jealousy and romantic love. In S. L. Hart & M. Legerstee (Eds.), *Handbook of jealousy: Theory, research, and multidisciplinary approaches.* Malden, MA: Wiley-Blackwell.

Ben-Ze'ev, A., & Goussinsky, R. (2008). *In the name of love: Romantic ideology and its victims.* New York: Oxford.

Boll, T., Ferring, D., & Filipp, S. H. (2003). Perceived parental differential treatment in middle adulthood: Curvilinear relations with individuals' experienced relationship quality to sibling and parents. *Journal of Family Psychology, 17,* 472–487.

Brazelton, T. B. (1974). *Toddlers and parents.* New York: Dell Publishing.

Brazelton, T. B. (1983). *Infants and mothers: Differences in development.* New York: Delacorte.

Brody, G. H. (1998). Sibling relationship quality: Its causes and consequences. *Annual Review of Psychology, 49,* 1–24.

Brody, G. H., & Stoneman, Z. (1987). Sibling conflict: Contributions of the sibling themselves, the parent–sibling relationship, and the broader family system. *Journal of Children in Contemporary Society, 19,* 39–53.

Brody, G. H., Stoneman, Z., & Burke, M. (1987). Child temperaments, maternal differential behavior, and sibling relationships. *Developmental Psychology, 23*, 354–362.

Brody, G. H., Stoneman, Z., McCoy, J. K., & Forehand, R. (1992). Contemporaneous and longitudinal associations of sibling conflict with family relationship assessments and family discussions about siblings problems. *Child Development, 63*, 391–400.

Brody, L. R., Copeland, A. P., Sutton, L. S., Richardson, D. R., & Guyer, M. (1998). Mommy and daddy like you best: Perceived family favouritism in relation to affect, adjustment and family process. *Journal of Family Therapy, 20*, 269–291.

Bryant, B. K., & Crockenberg, S. B. (1980). Correlates and dimensions of prosocial behavior: A study of female siblings with their mothers. *Child Development, 51*, 529–544.

Bugental, D. B., Blue, J., & Lewis, J. (1990). Caregiver beliefs and dysphoric affect directed to difficult children. *Developmental Psychology, 26*, 631–638.

Buhrmester, D. (1992). The developmental courses of sibling and peer relationships. In F. Boer & J. Dunn (Eds.), *Children's sibling relationships: Developmental and clinical issues* (pp. 19–40). Hillsdale, NJ: Erlbaum.

Buss, D. M. (2000). *The dangerous passion: Why jealousy is as necessary as love and sex.* New York: Free Press.

Campbell, S. B. (1990). *Behavior problems in preschool children.* New York: Guilford Press.

Carson, J. L., & Parke, R. D. (1996). Reciprocal negative affect in parent–child interactions and children's peer competency. *Child Development, 67*, 2217–2226.

Clanton, G. (1998). A sociology of jealousy. In G. Clanton & L. G. Smith (Eds.), *Jealousy* (3rd ed., pp. 297–314). Lanham, MD: University Press of America.

Colwell, M. J., Mize, J., Pettit, G. S., & Laird, R. D. (2002). Contextual determinants of mothers' interventions in young children's peer interactions. *Developmental Psychology, 38*, 492–502.

Condry, J., & Condry, S. (1976). Sex differences: A study of the eye of the beholder. *Child Development, 47*, 812–819.

Conley, D. (2005). *The pecking order* New York: Knopf.

Criss, M. M., & Shaw, D. S. (2005). Sibling relationships as contexts for delinquency training in low-income families. *Journal of Family Psychology, 19*, 592–600.

Daly, M., & Wilson, M. (1988). *Homicide.* Hawthorne, NY: Aldine de Gruyter.

Darley, J. M., & Fazio, R. H. (1980). Expectancy confirmation processes arising in the social interaction sequence. *American Psychologist, 35*, 867–881.

Darwin, C. (1877). A biographical sketch of an infant. *Mind, 7*, 285–294.

Denham, S. A., Mitchell-Copeland, J., Strandberg, K., Auerbach, S., & Blair, K. (1997). Parental contributions to preschoolers' emotional competence: Direct and indirect effects. *Motivation and Emotion, 21*, 65–86.

Dershowitz, A. M. (1997). *Reasonable doubts: The criminal justice system and the O. J. Simpson case.* New York: Simon & Schuster.

Dix, T., Ruble, D. N., Grusec, J. E., & Nixon, S. (1986). Social cognition in parents: Inferential and affective reactions to children of three age levels. *Child Development, 57*, 879–894.

Draghi-Lorenz, R. (this volume). Parental reports of jealousy in early infancy: Growing tensions between evidence and theory. In S. L. Hart & M. Legerstee (Eds.),

Handbook of jealousy: Theory, research, and multidisciplinary approaches. Malden, MA: Wiley-Blackwell.

Dunn, J. (1986). Stress, development, and family interaction. In M. Rutter, C. E. Izard, & P. B. Read (Eds.), *Depression in young people* (pp. 479–489). New York: Guilford Press.

Dunn, J., & Kendrick, C. (1982). *Siblings: Love, envy, and understanding.* Cambridge, MA: Harvard University Press.

Dunn, J., & Munn, P. (1986). Siblings and the development of prosocial behaviour. *International Journal of Behavioral Development, 9,* 265–284.

Dyck, N. (this volume). Social class, competition and parental jealousy in children's sports. In S. L. Hart & M. Legerstee (Eds.), *Handbook of jealousy: Theory, research, and multidisciplinary approaches.* Malden, MA: Wiley-Blackwell.

Eisenberg, N., & Fabes, R. A. (1994). Mothers' reactions to children's negative emotions: Relations to children's temperament and anger behavior. *Merrill-Palmer Quarterly, 40,* 138–156.

Eisenberg, N., Fabes, R. A., Shepard, S. A., Guthrie, I. K., Murphy, B. C., & Reiser, M. (1999). Parental reactions to children's negative emotions: Longitudinal relations to quality of children's social functioning. *Child Development, 70,* 513–534.

Farber, C. (1998, February). Whistling in the dark. *Esquire, 129,* 54–64, 119–120.

Field, T. M., Estroff, D. B., Yando, R., del Valle, C., Malphurs, J., & Hart, S. (1996). 'Depressed' mothers' perceptions of infant vulnerability are related to later development. *Child Psychiatry and Human Development, 27,* 43–53.

Field, T. M., & Reite, M. (1984). Children's responses to separation from mother during the birth of another child. *Child Development, 55,* 1308–1316.

Furman, W. (1995). Parenting siblings. In M. H. Bornstein (Ed.), *Handbook of parenting: Vol. 1. Children and parenting* (pp. 143–162). Hillsdale, NJ: Erlbaum.

Furman, W., & Lanthier, R. (2002). Parenting siblings. In M. H. Bornstein (Ed.), *Handbook of parenting: Vol. 1. Children and parenting* (2nd ed., pp. 165–188). Mahwah, NJ: Erlbaum.

Furman, W., & McQuaid, E. L. (1992). Intervention programs for the management of conflict. In C. U. Shantz & W. W. Hartup (Eds.), *Conflict in child and adolescent development* (pp. 402–429). New York: Cambridge University Press.

Garcia, M. M., Shaw, D. S., Winslow, E. B., & Yaggi, K. E. (2000). Destructive sibling conflict and the development of conduct problems in young boys. *Developmental Psychology, 36,* 44–53.

Glasberg, B. A., Martins, M., & Harris, S. L. (2006). Stress and coping among family members of individuals with autism. In M. G. Baron, J. Groden, G. Groden, & L. Lipsitt (Eds.), *Stress and coping in autism* (pp. 277–301). New York: Oxford University Press.

Goodwin, M. P., & Roscoe, B. (1990). Sibling violence and agonistic interactions among middle adolescents. *Adolescence, 25,* 451–467.

Gottlieb, L. N., & Mendelson, M. J. (1990). Parental support and firstborn girls' adaptation to the birth of a sibling. *Journal of Applied Developmental Psychology, 11,* 29–48.

Grusec, J. E., Dix, T., & Mills, R. (1982). The effects of type, severity, and victim of children's transgressions on maternal discipline. *Canadian Journal of Behavioural Science/Revue canadienne des Sciences du comportement, 14,* 276–289.

Grusec, J. E., & Goodnow, J. J. (1994). Impact of parental discipline methods on the child's internalization of values: A reconceptualization of current points of view. *Developmental Psychology, 30,* 4–19.

Grusec, J. E., & Kuczynski, L. (1980). Direction of effect in socialization: A comparison of the parent's versus the child's behavior as determinants of disciplinary techniques. *Developmental Psychology, 16,* 1–9.

Hart, S. L. (2001). *Preventing sibling rivalry.* New York: Simon & Schuster.

Hart, S. L., Field, T., del Valle, C., & Letourneau, M. (1998). Infants protest their mothers' attending to an infant-size doll. *Social Development, 7,* 54–61.

Hartup, W. W. (2005). The development of aggression: Where do we stand? In R. E. Tremblay & J. Archer (Eds.), *Developmental origins of aggression* (pp. 3–22). New York: Guilford Press.

Hetherington, E. M. (1988). Parents, children, and siblings: Six years after divorce. In R. A. Hinde & J. Stevenson-Hinde (Eds.), *Relationships within families: Mutual influences* (pp. 311–331). Oxford: Oxford University Press.

Keller, H., & Lamm, B. (this volume). Culture, parenting, and the development of jealousy. In S. L. Hart & M. Legerstee (Eds.), *Handbook of jealousy: Theory, research, and multidisciplinary approaches.* Malden, MA: Wiley-Blackwell.

Kerig, P., Cowan, P., & Cowan, C. (1993). Marital quality and gender differences in parent–child interaction. *Developmental Psychology, 29,* 931–939.

Kowal, A. K., Krull, J. L., & Kramer, L. (2004). How the differential treatment of siblings is linked with parent–child relationship quality. *Journal of Family Psychology, 18,* 658–665.

Kowal, A. K., Krull, J. L., & Kramer, L. (2006). Shared understanding of parental differential treatment in families. *Social Development, 15,* 276–295.

Kramer, L. (2004). Experimental interventions in sibling relationships. In R. D. Conger, F. O. Lorenz, & K. A. S. Wickrama (Eds.), *Continuity and change in family relations: Theory, methods, and empirical findings* (pp. 345–380). Mahwah, NJ: Erlbaum.

Kramer, L., & Baron, L. A. (1995). Parental perceptions of children's sibling relationships. *Family Relations, 44,* 95–103.

Kramer, L., Perozynski, L. A., & Chung, T. Y. (1999). Parental responses to sibling conflict: The effects of development and parent gender. *Child Development, 70,* 1401–1414.

Kramer, L., & Ramsburg, D. (2002). Advice given to parents on welcoming a second child: A critical review. *Family Relations, 51,* 2–14.

Levy, D. M. (1937). Studies in sibling rivalry. *Research Monographs of the American Orthopsychiatric Association*(2), 1–96.

Lewis, M. (1997). *Altering fate: Why the past does not predict the future.* New York: Guilford Press.

Lewis, M., & Rosenblum, L. A. (1974). *The effect of the infant on its caregiver.* Oxford: Wiley-Interscience.

Maccoby, E. E., & Jacklin, C. N. (1974). *The psychology of sex differences.* Stanford, CA: Stanford University Press.

Malatesta, C., & Haviland, J. (1985). Signals, symbols, and socialization: The modification of emotional expression in human development. In M. Lewis & C. Saarni (Eds.), *The socialization of emotion* (pp. 89–116). New York: Plenum.

Martin, J. L., & Ross, H. S. (1996). Do mitigating circumstances influence family reactions to physical aggression? *Child Development, 67,* 1455–1466.

Martin, J. L., & Ross, H. S. (2005). Sibling aggression: Sex differences and parents' reactions. *International Journal of Behavioral Development, 29,* 129–138.

Mathes, E. W. (1986). Jealousy and romantic love: A longitudinal study. *Psychological Reports, 58,* 885–886.

McHale, J. P. (1995). Coparenting and triadic interactions during infancy: The roles of marital distress and child gender. *Developmental Psychology, 31,* 985–996.

McHale, S. M., Updegraff, K. A., Jackson-Newsom, J., Tucker, C. J., & Crouter, A. C. (2000). When does parents' differential treatment have negative implications for siblings? *Social Development, 9,* 149–172.

McKee, L., Roland, E., Coffelt, N., Olson, A. L., Forehand, R., Massari, C., et al. (2007). Harsh discipline and child problem behaviors: The roles of positive parenting and gender. *Journal of Family Violence, 22,* 187–196.

Miller, A. L., Volling, B. L., & McElwain, N. L. (2000). Sibling jealousy in a triadic context with mothers and fathers. *Social Development, 9,* 433–457.

Miller, D. T., & Turnbull, W. (1986). Expectancies and interpersonal processes. *Annual Review of Psychology, 37,* 233–256.

Mills, R., & Rubin, K. (1990). Parental beliefs about problematic social behaviors in early childhood. *Child Development, 61,* 138–151.

Miner, J. L., & Clarke-Stewart, K. A. (2008). Trajectories of externalizing behavior from age 2 to age 9: Relations with gender, temperament, ethnicity, parenting, and rater. *Developmental Psychology, 44,* 771–786.

Olson, R. L., & Roberts, M. W. (1987). Alternative treatments for sibling aggression. *Behavior Therapy, 18,* 243–250.

Ostrov, J. M., Crick, N. R., & Keating, C. F. (2005). Gender-biased perceptions of preschoolers' behavior: How much is aggression and prosocial behavior in the eye of the beholder? *Sex Roles, 52,* 393–398.

Ostrov, J. M., Woods, K. E., Jansen, E. A., Casas, J. F., & Crick, N. R. (2004). An observational study of delivered and received aggression, gender, and social-psychological adjustment in preschool: 'This white crayon doesn't work . . .'. *Early Childhood Research Quarterly, 19,* 355–371.

Parke, R., & Slaby, R. (1983). The development of aggression. In E. M. Heatherington (Ed.), *Handbook of child psychology: Vol. 4. Socialization, personality, and development* (pp. 547–641). New York: Wiley.

Perlman, M., & Ross, H. S. (1997). The benefits of parent intervention in children's disputes: An examination of concurrent changes in children's fighting styles. *Child Development, 68,* 690–700.

Perozynski, L., & Kramer, L. (1999). Parental beliefs about managing sibling conflict. *Developmental Psychology, 35,* 489–499.

Puente, S., & Cohen, D. (2003). Jealousy and the meaning (or nonmeaning) of violence. *Personality and Social Psychology Bulletin, 29,* 449–460.

Putallaz, M., & Sheppard, B. H. (1992). Conflict management and social competence. In C. U. Shantz & W. W. Hartup (Eds.), *Conflict in child and adolescent development* (pp. 330–355). New York: Cambridge University Press.

Radke-Yarrow, M., & Kochanska, G. (1990). Anger in young children. In L. Stein, B. Leventhal, & T. Trabasso (Eds.), *Psychological and biological approaches to emotion* (pp. 297–310). Hillsdale, NJ: Erlbaum.

Ross, H. S., Tesla, C., Kenyon, B., & Lollis, S. (1990). Maternal intervention in toddler peer conflict: The socialization of principles of justice. *Developmental Psychology, 26*, 994–1003.

Saarni, C. (2008). The interface of emotional development with social context. In M. Lewis, J. M. Haviland-Jones, & L. F. Barrett (Eds.), *Handbook of emotions* (3rd ed., pp. 332–347). New York: Guilford Press.

Schachter, F. F., & Stone, R. K. (1987). *Practical concerns about siblings: Bridging the research gap.* New York: Haworth.

Shantz, C. U., & Hobart, C. J. (1989). Social conflict and development: Peers and siblings. In T. J. Berndt & G. W. Ladd (Eds.), *Peer relationships in child development* (pp. 71–94). Oxford: John Wiley & Sons.

Shaw, D. S. (2006). The development of aggression in early childhood. In H. E. Fitzgerald, B. M. Lester, & B. Zuckerman (Eds.), *The crisis in youth mental health: Critical issues and effective programs: Vol. 1. Childhood disorders* (pp. 183–203). Westport, CT: Praeger/Greenwood.

Smetana, J. (1989). Toddlers' social interactions in the context of moral and conventional transgressions in the home. *Developmental Psychology, 25*, 499–508.

Smith, J., & Ross, H. (2007). Training parents to mediate sibling disputes affects children's negotiation and conflict understanding. *Child Development, 78*, 790–805.

Spock, B., & Parker, S. (1998). *Dr. Spock's baby and child care.* New York: Simon & Schuster.

Sroufe, A. (1979). Socioemotional development. In J. Osofsky (Ed.), *Handbook of infant development* (pp. 462–516). New York: Wiley.

Stearns, P. N. (1989). *Jealousy: The evolution of an emotion in American history.* New York: New York University Press.

Stearns, P. N. (this volume). Jealousy in Western history: From past toward present. In S. L. Hart & M. Legerstee (Eds.), *Handbook of jealousy: Theory, research, and multidisciplinary approaches.* Malden, MA: Wiley-Blackwell.

Steinmetz, S. K. (1977). The use of force for resolving family conflict: The training ground for abuse. *The Family Coordinator, 26*, 19–26.

Steinmetz, S. K., & Lystad, M. (1986). The violent family. In *Violence in the home: Interdisciplinary perspectives* (pp. 51–67). Philadelphia, PA: Brunner/Mazel.

Stern, M., Karraker, K., McIntosh, B., Moritzen, S., & Olexa, M. (2006). Prematurity stereotyping and mothers' interactions with their premature and full-term infants during the first year. *Journal of Pediatric Psychology, 31*, 597–607.

Stewart, R. B., Mobley, L. A., Van Tuyl, S. S., & Salvador, M. A. (1987). The firstborn's adjustment to the birth of a sibling: A longitudinal assessment. *Child Development, 58*, 341–355.

Stifter, C., & Grant, W. (1993). Infant responses to frustration: Individual differences in the expression of negative affect. *Journal of Nonverbal Behavior, 17*, 187–204.

Stillwell, R., & Dunn, J. (1985). Continuities in sibling relationships: Patterns of aggression and friendliness. *Journal of Child Psychology and Psychiatry, 26*, 627–637.

Stocker, C., Dunn, J., & Plomin, R. (1989). Sibling relationships: Links with child temperament, maternal behavior, and family structure. *Child Development, 60*, 715–727.

Straus, M. A., Gelles, R. J., & Steinmetz, S. K. (2003). The marriage license as a hitting license. In M. Silberman (Ed.), *Violence and society: A reader* (pp. 125–135). Upper Saddle River, NJ: Prentice Hall/Pearson Education.

Teti, D. M., & Ablard, K. E. (1989). Security of attachment and infant–sibling relationships: A laboratory study. *Child Development, 60,* 1519–1528.

Vandell, D. L., & Bailey, M. D. (1992). Conflicts between siblings. In C. U. Shantz & W. W. Hartup (Eds.), *Conflict in child and adolescent development* (pp. 242–269). New York: Cambridge University Press.

Vandell, D. L., Owen, M. T., Wilson, K. S., & Henderson, V. K. (1988). Social development in infant twins: Peer and mother–child relationships. *Child Development, 59,* 168–177.

Vandello, J. A., & Cohen, D. (2008). Culture, gender, and men's intimate partner violence. *Social and Personality Psychology Compass, 2,* 652–667.

Volling, B. L. (1997). The family correlates of maternal and paternal perceptions of differential treatment in early childhood. *Family Relations, 46,* 1–9.

Volling, B. L. (2005). The transition to siblinghood: A developmental ecological systems perspective and directions for future research. *Journal of Family Psychology, 19,* 542–549.

Volling, B. L., & Blandon, A. Y. (2005). Positive indicators of sibling relationship quality: The sibling inventory of behavior. In K. A. Moore & L. H. Lippman (Eds.), *What do children need to flourish? Conceptualizing and measuring indicators of positive development* (pp. 203–219). New York: Springer Science + Business Media.

Werner, N. E., Senich, S., & Przepyszny, K. A. (2006). Mothers' responses to preschoolers' relational and physical aggression. *Journal of Applied Developmental Psychology, 27,* 193–208.

Whiteman, S. D., McHale, S. M., & Crouter, A. C. (2003). What parents learn from experience: The first child as a first draft? *Journal of Marriage and Family, 65,* 608–621.

Wilson, M., & Daly, M. (1992). The man who mistook his wife for a chattel. In J. H. Barkow, L. Cosmides, & J. Tooby (Eds.), *The adapted mind: Evolutionary psychology and the generation of culture* (pp. 289–322). New York: Oxford University Press.

Part V

Socio-Emotional Foundations within Other Eliciting Contexts

19

Family Triangular Interactions in Infancy

A Context for the Development of Jealousy?

Elisabeth Fivaz-Depeursinge, Nicolas Favez,
Chloé Lavanchy Scaiola, and Francesco Lopes

A naïve student trying to grasp what jealousy is will soon find out two things. On the one hand, jealousy is difficult to define. On the other, developmentalists disagree on its age of emergence. Many authors define jealousy as a complex social emotion; it occurs in a social triangle and cannot be understood without reference to this context (Volling, McElwain, & Miller, 2002). Jealousy is experienced when a subject perceives that a valued relationship is threatened, or that he might lose "formative attention," namely the attention that sustains one's self-concept (Tov-Ruach, 1980). It includes a range of emotions, depending on the focus of the subject: sadness when the focus is the loss of the relationship, anger when it is the betrayal of it, and fear or anxiety when the subject feels abandoned. Jealousy should not be confused with envy; envy concerns a property possessed by the person one envies rather than a relationship. As for the age of emergence of jealousy, developmentalists generally accept that complex emotions require self–other differentiation, but for mainstream developmental theorists, self–other differentiation must be conceptual; hence jealousy cannot appear before the advent of conceptual thought, during the second year at the earliest. In contrast, a growing number of developmentalists consider that interpersonal awareness is available to young infants (e.g., Legerstee, 2005; Markova & Legerstee, 2006; Meltzoff & Moore, 1992; Stern, 1985, 2004; Trevarthen, 1984). They see self–other awareness as a continuous process rather than emerging at a given point in time. Referring to Neisser (1994), Draghi-Lorenz, Reddy, and Costall (2001) state that in infancy, "the differentiation between self and other is directly perceived in the course of social interaction" (p. 296). Thus complex emotions such as jealousy, guilt, or shame may begin by being of a perceptual, non-reflective kind.

Recent findings relating to jealousy support this notion. Experimental paradigms designed to evoke jealousy show specific responses that are apparent

Handbook of Jealousy: Theory, Research and Multidisciplinary Approaches, First Edition.
Edited by Sybil L. Hart and Maria Legerstee.
© 2013 Blackwell Publishing Ltd. Published 2013 by Blackwell Publishing Ltd.

already in young infants. When exposed to her mother giving exclusive attention to a lifelike doll, the 6-month-old not only is as perturbed as she is when her mother poses a still-face; she manifests a specific response mixing sadness—more than in the still-face—and approach toward her mother—more than in regular play (Hart, Carrington, Tronick, & Carroll, 2004; Hart, Field, del Valle, & Letourneau, 1998a). Results of particular importance to this chapter showed that typical 12-month-olds responded more intensively to jealousy evocation than atypical ones living with depressed mothers (Hart, Field, Letourneau, & del Valle, 1998b; Hart, Jones, & Field, 2003). Moreover, jealousy protests were not differentiated by the sibling's status as first- or later-born. Thus, Hart and colleagues suggest that a history of triadic interactions is not necessary for the emergence of jealousy. We will discuss this important point below. Be that as it may, jealousy not only manifests itself early on in development, but it appears as a normative response to the loss of maternal exclusive attention rather than a sign of disturbance. This is clearly beyond the grasp of mainstream developmental theory. Other experimental triadic paradigms also challenge mainstream theory. They document that 3-month-olds discriminate among their partners' motives or intentions when the latter do not communicate with them. For instance, whereas young infants are markedly perturbed when their mothers pose a still-face, they are hardly so when their mothers stop playing with them to drink from a bottle; nor are they disturbed when their mother is being interrupted by a stranger who talks to her, as shown first by Murray and Trevarthen (1985). However, as shown by Legerstee, Ellenbogen, Nienhuis, and Marsh (this volume, Chapter 9), when the mother engages in a conversation with this stranger, the infants increase their vocalizations and the intensity of their signals to the mother, as if to attract her attention. Finally, another triadic paradigm has documented that 3-month-olds are able to coordinate their attention with two adult strangers conversing together and to initiate socially directed behaviors to gain inclusion in their conversation (Tremblay & Rovira, 2007).

These findings also challenge our ordinary understanding of jealousy as something mostly negative and often problematic. At this point, two notions may help us: first, the word "jealous" derives etymologically from "zealous"; this emphasizes a proactive, positive aspect of jealousy that we may come to feel pertinent after some reflection. Second, and in the same line, the evolutionary perspective affords jealousy a protective function which has survival value (Buss, 2000). In particular, jealousy in couples would serve as an alarm signal when the relationship is threatened. It would trigger specific behaviors, such as the re-affirmation of the couple's bond, or ostensive signals like an alliance, or speaking ill of the rival, and in extreme cases, violence toward the rival or the "guilty" spouse. In this view, the adaptive value for the male spouse is to minimize his uncertainty about paternity, ensuring the transmission of his own genes. For the female spouse, jealousy has the same protective function, but the goal is to ensure the provision of resources (Buss, 2000). Sibling rivalry may also serve the function of protecting a primordial relationship with a parent, especially regarding formative attention (Tov-Ruach, 1980). Young children are observed to cope with it by attempts to interfere between parent and sibling, by directing hostility to the parents, and by focusing their attention on alternative pleasurable activities (Volling et al., 2002).

As systems-oriented developmentalists studying family triangular relationships in infancy, we are familiar with one of the key characteristics of jealousy, namely three-person interactions. Hence we view jealousy as a particular emotional scenario taking place in the context of the triangular interaction system. All triangular systems have the following characteristics. First, they present four ways of arranging their elements, or four configurations: one in which all partners are actively engaged ("3-together") and three in which two partners are actively engaged and one is the third party ("2 + 1s"). Second, the four configurations tend to alternate flexibly. Third, the third party is as full a participant as the active partners, albeit in a different role. Being in the third party position entails components other than just playing second fiddle. It allows for pausing, to take a perspective on the relationship between the two others, and to have more autonomy. Being free from the constraints associated with active engagement, an individual has time to decide which actions to deploy in order to regain an active part in the trio. It is only when the third party feels threatened by the involvement between the two others that a jealousy scenario comes into play. Jealousy would be but one among various motives toward striving to regain an active role within the triad. Whether it then entails exchanging the third party position with another member of the trio or reconstituting a threesome depends on whether the challenged party feels that the relationship which is threatened is a dyadic one within the triad or is itself the triadic one.

Aims of the study: There is presently an interest in the ability of young infants to engage in interactions with two or more individuals at the same time; the body of data documenting the infant's general relational competence (Nash & Hay, 1993) or triangular competence (Fivaz-Depeursinge & Corboz-Warnery, 1999) is growing. Our first goal in this chapter is to present an observational paradigm for examining the infant's handling of the triangular system in the father–mother–infant primary triangle. As an example, we will report on a study of the 4-month-old's triangular competence under a still-face condition (Tronick, Als, Adamson, Wise, & Brazelton, 1978) using both parents, and then illustrate it with a case description. Our second goal comes closer to the emotional scenario of jealousy. Indeed, our acquaintance with the field of jealousy studies brought a new perspective to our view and interpretation of the infant's behaviors in our paradigm. This new perspective arose from similarity between paradigms designed to study the infant's response to intentional instances of inattention, and the observational paradigm we designed to systematically observe role permutations in the triad, namely the Lausanne Trilogue Play. The latter logically requires that each partner takes, in turn, each possible position in the triangular system.

Thus, it requires that the infant also takes the third party position. In practice, this moment comes after a part where the three partners play together. Then the parents are asked to actively engage with each other in a dialogue and to leave their child in the third party position. The infant is thus exposed to their inattention and she deploys, among other behaviors, strategies to regain her parents' attention. This situation bears similarities with responses to inattention paradigms rather than to jealousy-inducing ones. Thus, in the second study reported in this chapter, we focus on the 3- and 9-month-olds' triangular competence as onlookers of their parents' dialogue. Finally we discuss a question suggested by our findings: Are early family triangular interactions a context for the development of jealousy?

A Functional Perspective on Emotion in Triangular Contexts

The evolutionary and systems views accord well with the functional perspective on emotion. The functional perspective presents a unitary approach to emotion, emotional regulation, and emotional expression as being intrinsically relational and communicative (Campos, Frankel, & Camras, 2004; Campos, Mumme, Kermoian, & Campos, 1994). This view has important methodological implications since it advances the notion that "one cannot understand emotion by examining either the person or environmental events as separate entities. Person and event constitute an inseparable whole" (Campos et al., 1994, p. 285). Thus, it calls for the study of patterns of behavior as well as for interpreting behavior in context (Camras et al., 2002). In a similar perspective, Weinberg and Tronick (1994) suggest that each configuration of the infant's engagement with her mother has a specific message value such as: "I want to continue this interaction" for the social engagement configuration; or "change this" for the active protest configuration. Thus, affect signals that are addressed toward partners function as bids to share a particular experience and to influence the course of the interaction.

Triadic Paradigms

To date, there are two main types of triadic paradigms in infancy: experimental paradigms and semi-naturalistic ones. A growing number of experimental paradigms mentioned in our introduction examine the infant's sensitivity to triadic settings. They compare the infant's dyadic interactions with her mother under different conditions, such as jealousy evocation, the still-face perturbation, and diverse "modified still-face" situations (Hart et al., 2004; Legerstee et al., this volume). According to these authors, the results of these studies make a case for the early emergence of jealousy and its development, challenging the mainstream view that jealousy is a complex emotion appearing only with a conceptual sense of self. The infant's responses to the mother's inattention suggest the presence of attachment and self–other differentiation already between 3 and 6 months. While these paradigms have the advantage of careful experimental control, they stop short of investigating the infant's triangular communication and of affording insight into the infant as an active influence on the context.

A few semi-standardized paradigms, where jealousy was not intentionally induced, focus on the infant's triangular interactions, namely her capacity to communicate with two persons at a time. The degree to which they afford the infant with the opportunity to change the context varies. To date, three paradigms have been developed: the "exclusion" paradigm, for non-family adult–infant triads (Nadel & Tremblay-Leveau, 1999), the "infants-only trios" (Selby & Bradley, 2003) and the "Lausanne Trilogue Play" (LTP for short), for father–mother–infant triads (Corboz-Warnery, Fivaz-Depeursinge, Gertsch-Bettens, & Favez, 1993; Fivaz-Depeursinge & Corboz-Warnery, 1999). Nadel and Tremblay-Leveau looked at signs of active infant contribution to social interaction and at their understanding of the different positions in a triad using an exclusion paradigm with children aged 11–18 months. Exploring precursors of this capacity in toddlers, Tremblay and Rovira (2007) designed another situation to document 3- and 6-month-olds' ability to show joint attention, as well as to show 3-month-olds' capacity to produce socially directed behaviors in a three-person setting. While engaged in play with the infant, an adult turned to face another person and converse with her. Moreover, the adults responded to the socially directed behavior of the infant by turning back to her, affording her a degree of agency. The results showed that infants followed the gaze of the adults, gazed backwards and forwards between them, and produced socially directed behaviors toward them. Interestingly, the comparison between the three-person condition (PPP) and one which included two persons and an object (PPO) showed that infants expressed twice as many smiles, vocalizations, and hand movements in the PPP condition as in the PPO condition. It is of note that in parallel, recent experiments on the precursors of joint attention toward objects have made a case for the much earlier appearance of person–person–object interactions than previously thought (for a review, see Striano & Stahl, 2005).

A breakthrough was made when Selby and Bradley (2003) presented evidence of the "infant's relational capacity" in infants-only triads. They showed that 6- to 10-month-olds used double addresses, namely different expressive modalities, to interact with two partners at a time. These entailed touching one while looking at another, vocalizing, and smiling for the benefit of both. The authors argued that the infants-only paradigm, as applied in the absence of adult scaffolding, was the best route to show infants' general relational capacities (see also Markova, Stieben, & Legerstee, this volume, Chapter 5).

This pertinent objection notwithstanding, it remains crucial to examine the infant's triangular communication within the family, if only because it is its first natural developmental context. As noted above, the LTP paradigm was designed to systematically observe how a family of three handles the triangular system of interactions in play as they move through the four possible configurations. This semi-standardized situation allows us not only to assess how parents coordinate communication in order to jointly scaffold the infant's communication, but also to assess whether and when an infant is able to relate to both of her parents at the same time in each configuration. In the three-together configuration, she does so by sharing her attention and affects with both parents. In a 2 + 1, when playing with one parent while the other is the third party, she engages the active parent while showing an awareness of the third party parent's presence. Finally, as the third party during her parents' dialogue, she regulates her emotions in this mildly stressful situation while attending to her parents' exchange.

A more controlled version of the LTP, the *LTP with still-face* (LTP/SF), was designed to further test this triangular communication capacity within a configuration where one parent poses a still-face while the other is in the third party position. It has been established that in the dyadic still-face, typically developing infants work hard to regulate their affects by self-soothing and distraction strategies on the one hand; and on the other, by using protest or charm as if to try to modify the context (for a review: Adamson & Frick, 2003). In the LTP/SF, the infant might add triangular strategies to the interactive agenda, by turning or referring to the third party parent.

Study 1: The 4-Month-Old's Triangular Competence under a Still-Face Condition

This report is part of a larger study on the infant's triangular competence in the *LTP with still-face*, which included three regular play episodes in addition to a still-face part. It has been fully described in Fivaz-Depeursinge, Favez, Lavanchy, de Noni, and Frascarolo (2005). In this chapter, we specifically report on the infant's triangular competence within the still-face condition. This occurs in a 2 + 1 formation: one of the parents poses a still-face while the other parent remains in the third party position. We use, as a baseline, the regular 2 + 1 play episode which preceded it, with one parent engaged in play with the infant and the other one as the third party.

Method

Participants
The sample was derived from 40 couples volunteering to participate in a prospective longitudinal family study. All infants were healthy firstborns. Nine families were excluded because the infants were crying and/or the parents didn't follow the instructions. The remainder consisted of 31 sixteen-week-olds (18 boys) of middle to high SES.

Setting
The setting was designed to facilitate trilogue play according to intuitive interactive rules with infants (Papousek, 2007). The three partners were seated in a triangular formation which preserved the peripheral vision of each participant throughout and allowed them to face each other when active at dialogue distance. The infant's seat inclination and size were adjustable according to the infant's postural development; its orientation was also adjustable according to whether she had one or two active partners. Two video-recordings were made: one of the parents and one of the baby; the two recordings were combined and a digital timer was added.

Procedure
Once seated, the parents were given instructions about the successive contexts of play, each one lasting 2 minutes. They were invited to try to play without toys. Specific instructions were given for the 2 + 1s: The third party parent was to remain present and inactive, apart from the instances where the infant would turn to him or her. In this case, he or she was to acknowledge the infant and turn to the active parent to redirect the infant's gaze toward him or her. In the 2 + 1 with still-face, the previously active parent was to present a still-face to the infant, abstaining from talking and touching, while the third party parent was to respond to the infant as in the previous part. Beforehand, the parents were helped to enact the positions required for each context, such as the active parent leaning forward at dialogue distance versus the third party leaning back. The games they might play were also discussed.

Data coding and reduction
A half-second interval was used for coding from the videotape. Coding was performed separately for infant's gaze and affect configurations.

Gaze: Time spent looking at partners' faces and elsewhere was used as a measure of the infant's capacity to distinguish between contexts (Table 19.1 provides a summary description of the codes). Rapid transitions were then detected and were defined as shifts of gaze occurring within a 0.5 s interval. This time window was chosen after examining many shifts. Seventy-three percent of the shifts occurred within 1 s, 18% within 2–3 s and 9% within 4–5 s.

Affect: Coding of affect was conducted during periods of gazing at either parent, using Tronick's monadic phases where all modalities of expression (vocal, facial, body postures) are integrated into a coding system (Tronick, Als, & Brazelton, 1980; Weinberg & Tronick, 1994). Codes were mutually exclusive and included the following: social engagement (engagement for short), social monitoring (monitoring for short), tense monitoring (tension), active protest (protest). Social engagement covered positive signals like open-mouthed smiles and/or happy vocalizations, while monitoring covered interest. Protest

Table 19.1   Summary description of codes

1. Gaze:
    At mother's face, at father's face, elsewhere, un-codable

2. Affects:
    Social engagement: infant bids parent with facial and vocal expressions of joy (smiles, coos, positive vocalizing, laughing)
    Social monitoring: infant bids parent with a neutral or interested facial expression; may vocalize
    Tense monitoring: infant bids parent with attention colored by weariness or fear, yet not distress or protest
    Active Protest: infant bids parent with facial expressions of anger, grimaces and/or with crying, and/or with negative moves such as pick me up, arching the back.
    Non-engagement: infant does not address a parent

3. Triangular Bids – see text:
    Triangular engagement (social engagement at both parents)
    Triangular monitoring (social monitoring at both parents)
    Triangular tension (tense monitoring at both parents)
    Triangular protest (protest at both parents)

corresponded to signals of anger, grimaces, distress vocalizations, and/or arching back or pick-me-up gestures (see Table 19.1 for complete definitions).

Triangular bids: Comparison of the affect signals addressed at the two parents during rapid transitions showed that 92% had been coded in the same category. The affect coded in different categories were, with few exceptions, in contiguous categories. Thus, four categories of triangular bids were defined, which corresponded to the different affective configurations: triangular engagement, triangular monitoring, triangular tension, triangular protest.

Inter-rater reliability: One observer coded all the sessions, while a second observer, unaware of the hypotheses of the study, coded 40% of randomly selected material to assess reliability. Kappas were .85 for gazes and .83 for affective configurations, considered to be good to excellent (Bakeman & Gottman, 1986).

Measures

All measures were computed by episode. We consider the following in this report: time spent looking at partners, number of rapid transitions, time spent in each affect addressed at partners.

Overview of findings

The analyses of the infant's triangular engagement showed that 4-month-olds discriminated between the two contexts and that they shared their attention and affects with both parents in a context-sensitive way. Individual variations were large. Infants looked significantly longer at the active parent than at the third party in the regular as well as in the SF 2 + 1s. All but 5 infants made rapid transitions, namely rapid shifts of gaze between the parents, in one or both 2 + 1s, on average 1.55 (SD = 2.17) times in the regular 2 + 1 and 2.52 (SD = 3.79) in the still-face one; the difference failed to reach significance (*p* = .08). Although this was a low rate compared to the one in the 3-togethers (M = 7.03, SD = 6.26), it was still remarkable given that in the 2 + 1 context, rapid transitions were initiated by the infant in the absence of parental stimulation. The affects associated with rapid transitions were consistent across parents in more than 90% of the cases in both conditions; thus it was plausible that they signaled the same affective experience to both. The most frequent affects both throughout the play part and during rapid transitions were first monitoring, then engagement, followed by tension and protest. In contrast, there was a specific effect of the SF on affects, namely that compared to the normal 2 + 1, there was less social engagement, more monitoring of parents, more protest and tension addressed to the parents than in the play part. This effect was also reflected in the triangular bids, namely the affects associated with rapid transitions, though not significantly.

In sum, what stood out from these findings, in addition to confirming the 4-month-olds' sensitivity to triangular settings, was their capacity to handle triangular interactions, namely to coordinate their attention and affects with both parents at the same time. This was borne out in particular by the fact that the regular 2 + 1 play elicited more social engagement and less protest and tension than the still-face one. Likewise, infants initiated triangular bids in the concurrent absence of solicitation from the third party. Finally, infants tended to turn more often to the third party than to the active parent under stress, when the active parent posed a still-face.

Case illustration

The following description is a fairly representative case of a 4-month-old in the triangular still-face condition.

During the regular 2 + 1 where she played with her mother, Lucie had turned several times to address her father too, as if surprised that he didn't engage with her. Then she had appeared to understand that her mother was her play partner and had settled to play with her.

Lucie's still-face part may be divided into four episodes:

1 *Discovering and checking the still-faced parent: dyadic bids.* Lucie reacted to her mother's still-face within a split second; having checked her face, she looked down, focusing on her feet, raised her head, sat back, looked down at her feet again; within 16 seconds she was slowly raising her eyes again to stare at

mother with a stern expression. She checked three more times over the next 12 seconds, every time with a more negative expression, from frowning, to sighing, to pouting. For the next 25 seconds, she distracted herself by focusing on her feet, on her seat, averting her eyes and turning back to her feet.

2   *Recourse to third party parent: social monitoring triangular bid.* The next look at the mother initiated a triangular bid. It was at first only a sideways stare with a pout at her mother. Within 2 seconds, she was turning toward her father, glancing at him, looking down and then slowly raising her eyes up to his face with a stern expression, long enough for her to see him greeting her. Then she rapidly turned toward her mother, looking at her from below and down again. This 2-step triangular bid lasted 10 seconds.

3   *Attempt to change the context: dyadic bids.* Having focused again on her seat and feet for the next 10 seconds, she resorted to the well-established dyadic strategies: protesting to her mother with a grimace and, after distracting herself, turning back to her mother and smiling at her—but with a somewhat mitigated smile.

4   *Second recourse to the third party parent and returning to normal: tense monitoring triangular bid.* Finally, she repeated her triangular bid, this time colored with tension, with a stern look at her mother from below, shifting to her father with a frown and then looking down.

Comment: Lucie was not only able to use the known dyadic strategies but to also have recourse to the third party parent, presumably for some kind of help. One may see in this the precursor of the social referencing process appearing in full at the end of the first year when the infant, uncertain, uses the information from her parents' affective expression to guide her behavior.

In conclusion, these results speak for an early triangular competence of the infant. They find support in recent studies on family triangular communication. McHale, Fivaz-Depeursinge, Dickstein, Robertson, and Daley (2008) provided a replication of the results on rapid gaze transitions in a large sample of 3-month-olds ($N = 110$) in the LTP as well as the LTP/SF recorded at home. Their findings confirm that young infants make rapid transitions, single (from one parent to the other) as well as multiple (several in a row).

Study 2: The Infant as Third Party to her Parents' Dialogue at 3 and 9 Months

In this study, we examined the infant's triangular competence at 3 and 9 months in the parents' dialogue part of the regular LTP, in order to compare the infant's response to her parents' inattention to findings in other contexts of inattention. We used the 3-together play part as a baseline (see Figure 19.1a and b). Portions

(a)

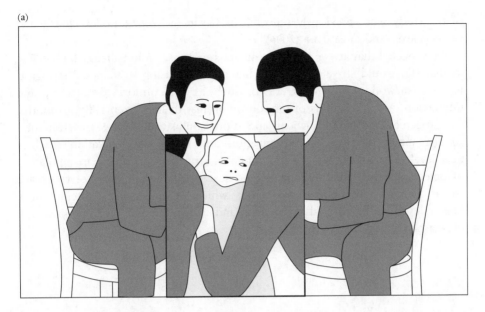

(b)

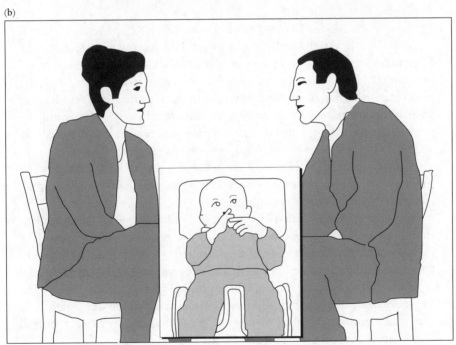

Figure 19.1 Father–mother–infant formations: a) in the 3-together; b) in the parents' dialogue

of the study were previously reported in Lavanchy (2002), Koller (2002), and Lopes, Favez, and Frascarolo (2006).

We expected that at 3 months, the infant's response would already be specific, in that she would strive to regulate her affect by using strategies (Braungart-Rieker, Garwood, & Powers, 1998), such as self-comfort, distraction, and interaction, in making bids of tension or protest to her parents. By 9 months, we expected to observe a wider and more sophisticated range of strategies. As the infant develops, communication and emotional regulation reach a new level. The infant has a wider range of strategies, involving manipulation of objects (in this situation, mainly the seat belt or other parts of the seat); she is acquiring the intentional stance which organizes her strategies at a higher level: setting a goal in advance and using different means to reach it (Tomasello, 1999).

Method

Participants

The sample was derived from the same $N = 40$ sample of families as in study 1. To control for the possibility that the observed differences would depend on the LTP contexts rather than on family relational difficulties, the sample retained only the 22 families that had demonstrated average to high family alliance (coordination during play) throughout the longitudinal study. These families were identified using cluster analysis of the alliance trajectories from the prenatal stage to 18 months (for more details, see Favez et al., 2006). The 22 infants (13 boys) were observed at 3 and 9 months.

The apparatus and setting were the same as in study 1. Once seated, the parents were given instructions about the LTP parts (for details, see Frascarolo, Favez, Carneiro, & Fivaz-Depeursinge, 2004).

Data coding and reduction, measures, and reliability were the same as in study 1, with the following exceptions: affect was coded also during periods of gazing away from the parents (withdrawal, interest for objects). In addition to the other measures, a rate of positive affect toward parents (positive/positive + negative affect) was computed, where positive affect included engagement and monitoring and negative affect included protest and tension. Taking age into consideration (Tremblay & Rovira, 2007), the time interval for rapid transitions at 9 months was decreased from 5 to 3 seconds.

In addition, a qualitative analysis was conducted to examine whether the "approach responses" reported by Hart and colleagues (2004) in response to jealousy evocation would also be observed in the LTP. We defined these as moments when the infant made a special attempt to draw the parents' attention. They were marked by gazing at one or both parents. They could also be

Table 19.2 Means and standard deviations of 3-month-olds' time spent looking at parents, expressing affects, rapid transitions, and consistency of affects during rapid transitions (*N* = 22)

Variables	PART III		PART IV	
	M	*SD*	*M*	*SD*
Time spent looking (%)				
Toward both parents	54.20	25.18	53.75	29.84
Toward mother	38.04	24.43	25.93	29.51
Toward father	16.16	13.47	27.83	28.76
Elsewhere	45.80	25.18	46.25	29.84
Time spent expressing (%)				
Active protest	7.16	17.19	8.98	16.06
Tense monitoring	10.17	13.54	13.51	17.33
Social monitoring	36.95	23.46	36.01	27.00
Social engagement	9.22	10.67	1.25	2.53
Positive affect (social monitoring + social engagement)	46.17	28.02	37.26	28.10
Negative affect (active protest + tense monitoring)	17.33	21.02	22.51	25.84
Withdrawal	21.14	14.01	29.18	27.92
Interest for object	13.70	15.80	11.06	19.81
Rate of positive affect	.73	.32	.69	.33
Rapid transitions (% per two mins)	12.36	9.96	4.68	4.26
High affect consistency (%)	90.68	12.17	88.41	17.60
Average affect consistency (%)	8.12	11.52	9.16	16.72
Low affect consistency (%)	1.20	3.27	2.41	8.07

simply physical, such as pick-me-up gestures and touching the parent's legs, or either screaming at them or expressing modulated moaning. Approach responses could also be more sophisticated, such as reproducing gestures that appeared to refer to a game that had been successfully played during the play episodes.

Findings on 3-month-olds

Data at 3 months were normally distributed for all variables except for protest and withdrawal. T tests were conducted for all normally distributed variables and a Wilcoxon test was used for the others.

Table 19.2 shows the means and standard deviations for gaze and affect measures in the parts of 3-together play and parents' dialogue. These descriptive results show that infants looked at their parents about half the time in both parts (3-together: *M* = 54; parents' dialogue: *M* = 54). All infants looked at both parents. However, they tended to look more at their mothers than at their fathers in the 3-together (gazing at mother: $M = 38$; gazing at father: $M = 16$); this difference reached significance (t (21) $= 3.38, p < .005$). This was not the case in the parents' dialogue (gazing at mother: $M = 26$; gazing at father: $M = 28$; t tests $=$ ns).

Among affects addressed to parents, social monitoring was dominant in both contexts, with no difference between the contexts (3-together: $M = 37$; parents' dialogue: $M = 36$). Social engagement was significantly more frequent in the 3-together ($M = 9$) than in the parents' dialogue ($M = 1$); Wilcoxon Signed Ranks Test: $z = 3.024, p < .005$. In the negative range, tension (3-together: $M = 10$; parents' dialogue: $M = 14$) and protest (3-together: $M = 7$; parents' dialogue: $M = 9$) had low frequencies in both parts.

Affects not addressed to the parents took somewhat more than a third of the time, with withdrawal more frequent (3-together: $M = 21$; parents' dialogue: $M = 29$) than interest for objects (3-together: $M = 14$; parents' dialogue: $M = 11$). There were no significant differences between the two parts.

Infants maintained about the same rate of positive affect in both contexts (3-together: $M = .73$; parents' dialogue: $M = .69$).

All but one infant made triangular bids in the 3-together and all but four in the parents' dialogue. The number of triangular bids was larger in the 3-together ($M = 12.36$ per 2 minutes) than in the parents' dialogue ($M = 4.68$ per 2 minutes). The difference was significant (t (21) $= 3.61, p < .005$). Ninety-one percent of the triangular bids had high affective consistency and a very small proportion of them had low affective consistency (1%).

Thus the only differences reaching significance for gaze and affect measures between the 3-together and the parents' dialogue concerned gazes at the mother and social engagement during the 3-together.

In sum, the infants maintained the same level of attention toward their parents in the parents' dialogue as in the 3-together play. They actively participated as onlookers by turning toward their parents and monitoring their dialogue. Not surprisingly, their level of social engagement was lower during the parents' dialogue than during play. But they also expressed their frustration in response to inattention, as if trying to change the context by means of triangular as well as dyadic bids which signaled their tension, protest, or attempts to charm. They maintained a balanced orientation toward their parents during their dialogue, but looked more at the mother during play.

Qualitative descriptions of cases involving approach responses

In this section, we describe a 3-together and a parents' dialogue sequence and illustrate the types of approach responses observed in 3-month-olds as onlookers of their parents' dialogue. The following interaction is that of Andrew, a 12-week-old.

Andrew at play

This brief episode of about one and a half minutes can be divided into four episodes:

1 *Three-way greetings (8 s)*: The episode began with the parents drawing close to each other and to Andrew, smiling at him. Andrew was looking at his mother who was addressing him: "Now we are both here, do you realize how spoiled you are to have both of us here …" Andrew smiled at his mother, turned to his father, smiling at him too; the father laughed, and Andrew turned back to his mother, who continued to speak to him with enthusiasm. Thus the play began with an episode of the threesome sharing of pleasure.

2 *Vocalizing at both parents (21 s)*: Andrew went on looking at his mother; bringing his hands to his mouth, he began to vocalize at her. Having glanced at his father, who responded verbally, he turned back to his mother. The mother pretended to eat his feet, while the father commented: "Oh, it is Andrew who is telling stories to-day!" Mother: "Yes, plenty!" Andrew switched from vocalizing at his mother to his father, who responded: "All that?" Mother: "… and this do you know what this is?" as she began tickling him, from the leg up to his torso. Meanwhile, Andrew continued vocalizing. The father began tickling his side.

3 *Pausing (9 s)*: Andrew brought his hands to his mouth again and looked away for 2 seconds. He glanced at his father, turned to his mother with a tense expression and looked ahead between his parents. A few seconds later, he resumed vocalizing, looking up, back and forth at his parents.

4 *Vocalizing in dyads (12 s)*: For the next two episodes, Andrew focused on his father, then on his mother.

5 *Vocalizing to both parents (45 s)*: Then he resumed his gazing and vocalizing back and forth between his parents, while they went on tickling him softly and commenting: "But you are telling us so many stories that we don't have time to tell any … you are doing the entertainment today … it is a feast!"

In sum, the almost uninterrupted succession of triangular bids was realized in a threesome exchange of positive affect: smiling at each other, sustaining a continuous dialogue through Andrew's vocalizations and the parents' comments.

The parents' dialogue

The parents conducted carefully the transition from the 3-together to their dialogue. The part was brief (one and a half minutes) and was divided into three parts:

1 *Monitoring parents*: During the first half-minute, Andrew was mostly focused on his parents, looking back and forth at them, oscillating between slightly whining and bringing his fists to his mouth and watching them with interest.

2 *Trying to get father's attention*: During the next half-minute, he oscillated more widely: his looking at his father and his imploring vocalization progressively

turned into humming. Interestingly, at some point, he noticed that his father was looking at him from the corner of his eye; he quieted down and slowly turned with a smile toward his mother, turned back to his father—who was engaged with his mother, only to begin wriggling his arms again a few seconds later.

3 *Protesting to both parents and succeeding in getting their attention back*: During the last half-minute, Andrew raised his voice to direct protest at both parents several times, punctuated by moments of self-soothing—sucking on his fists, closing his eyes, until the parents turned back to him. He brightened up, having finally won them back.

Comment: At no time was Andrew overloaded by negative affect. He monitored his parents' dialogue with interest mitigated by tension and directly communicated to them his need for change by means of dyadic and triangular bids. The latter were spontaneous in that at no time did the parents directly address signals to him; they were also consistent: interest or protest was directed at both parents.

Approaches

Interestingly, at some point, many 3-month-olds made clear-cut approaches to gain attention, in addition to or in combination with triangular bids. The following are representative examples.

As Alice's parents changed their body's orientation to face each other, laughing, Alice observed them intently. She caught her father looking at her, and responded with a wide smile. The father did not resist smiling back, to which she responded by widening her smile, sticking out her tongue, and extending her right arm on his side in a gracefully inviting posture. Delighted, the father responded in an animated tone. As he turned toward mother to finally engage with her, Alice sobered, looked down at her hands. Then came the approach: a few seconds later, she looked up at him again with bright eyes, with a hint of the previous inviting gesture and making little breathing sounds, as if to repeat the previous episode. Yet this time she was not successful at getting her father's attention. She followed her father's gaze toward her mother and spent the rest of the time quietly attending to their exchange, looking back and forth between them.

Many infants were quite emphatic in their seeking of attention. For instance, looking intently at a parent, an infant repeatedly hit his seat (on the parent's side) while vocalizing at him; or moaned at the parent very expressively on different tunes. Another infant resonated to the parents' laughs with an animated expression and laughter, or suddenly made a loud yell. Or, having sneezed and failed to obtain the predictable "cheers" from the parents, an infant engaged in a bout of energetic protest bids at both parents.

In sum, there were several methods that 3-month-olds used, presumably to draw their parents' attention and attempt to change the context. These were definitely more forceful and more frequent than those observed in the constricted situation of the still-face.

Results on 9-month-olds

Table 19.3 shows the means and standard deviations for gaze and affect measures in the 3-together and parents' dialogue episodes. Data at 9 months were normally distributed for all variables except for protest, and for social engagement and interest for objects in the parents' dialogue. Thus t tests were conducted for all normally distributed variables and Wilcoxon tests were used for the others.

As shown in Table 19.3, 9-month-olds looked at their parents about a third of the time in both episodes (3-together: $M = 33$; parents' dialogue: $M = 34$). They looked on average half of the orientation time at each parent (3-together: gazing at mother: $M = 16$; gaze at father: $M = 17$; parents' dialogue: gazing at mother: $M = 19$; gazing at father: $M = 15$).

Table 19.3 Means and standard deviations of 9-month-olds' time spent looking at parents, expressing affects, rapid transitions, and consistency of affects during rapid transitions ($N = 22$)

Variables	PART III		PART IV	
	M	SD	M	SD
Time spent looking (%)				
Toward parents	33.34	18.22	33.90	22.22
Toward mother	16.32	11.33	18.69	19.09
Toward father	17.02	13.03	15.21	14.04
Elsewhere	66.66	18.22	66.10	22.22
Time spent expressing (%)				
Active protest	4.40	6.72	5.44	10.38
Tense monitoring	11.43	10.63	14.97	15.18
Social monitoring	24.29	13.25	20.79	15.79
Social engagement	15.68	12.84	8.96	12.72
Positive affect (social monitoring + social engagement)	39.97	19.08	29.74	22.68
Negative affect (active protest + tense monitoring	15.83	14.23	20.42	19.03
Withdrawal	2.00	5.50	2.42	6.56
Interest for object	39.77	22.51	47.42	22.35
Rate of positive affect	.72	.23	.59	.35
Rapid transitions (per two mins)	4.88	3.56	3.22	2.64
High affect consistency (%)	78.62	24.86	77.17	27.40
Average affect consistency (%)	19.12	24.87	17.39	24.94
Little affect consistency (%)	2.26	6.19	5.44	11.40

Among positive affects toward parents, social monitoring was most frequent (3-together: $M = 24$; parents' dialogue: $M = 21$). Social engagement came next, and tended to be more frequent in 3-together ($M = 16$) than in parents' dialogue ($M = 9$; $t (21) = 1.96$, $p = .06$). In the negative range, tension was most frequent (3-together: $M = 11$; parents' dialogue: $M = 15$), with protest the least frequent (3-together: $M = 4$; parents' dialogue: $M = 5$); none of the other differences between contexts reached significance.

Among the affects not addressed at parents, interest for objects was dominant (3-together: $M = 40$; parents dialogue: $M = 47$); withdrawal had a very low frequency (3-together: $M = 2$; parents' dialogue: $M = 2$).

Nine-month-olds showed no significant differences in the rates of positive affect in both episodes (respectively $M = .72$ and $M = .59$).

All infants but two made triangular bids in the 3-together and all but three in the parents' dialogue. The number of triangular bids tended to be larger in the 3-together ($M = 4.88$ per 2 minutes) than in the parents' dialogue ($M = 3.22$ per 2 minutes), but the difference was not significant. Almost 80% of the triangular bids had high affective consistency (3-together: $M = 79$; parents' dialogue: $M = 77$), and a very small proportion of them had low affective consistency (3-together: $M = 2$; parents' dialogue: $M = 5$).

In sum, the 9-month-olds as third parties maintained the same level of attention toward their parents, on the one hand, and toward objects, on the other, in the parents' dialogue as well as in the 3-together play. They actively participated in their parents' interaction by monitoring their dialogue and by communicating to them—signaling their tension, protesting to either or both parents, sometimes also by charming—presumably to try to change the context. A majority maintained a balanced orientation to both parents.

Comparison between 3- and 9-month-olds' responses

As a means of determining differences between ages and contexts, we examined the time spent looking at both parents, the rate of positive affect addressed at the parents, and the number of triangular bids in both contexts and both ages. Thus a 2×2 (age $\times$ context) MANOVA was conducted with age and context as within-subjects factors. The results showed an effect of age but not of context on the time spent looking at the parents. Infants looked at their parents significantly more at 3 than at 9 months ($F(1, 21) = 9.45$, $p < .01$). There was no difference between the time spent looking at parents between episodes.

There was no effect of age or context on the rate of positive affect. The comparison of age and context for the number of rapid transitions showed an effect of age ($F(1, 21) = 12.07$, $p < .005$) and of context ($F(1, 21) = 12.71$, $p < .005$) on the number of rapid transitions. The 3-month-olds made significantly more rapid transitions than 9-month-olds. Three- and nine-month-olds made more numerous rapid transitions in the 3-together than in the parents' dialogue. Moreover, there was an interaction effect between age and context: 3-month-olds made more rapid transitions in the 3-together ($F(1, 21) = 9.92$, $p < .005$). Finally, there was an effect of age on interest in objects ($F(1, 21) = 27.99$, $p < .001$). Nine-month-olds manifested more interest for objects than 3-month-olds. There was an interaction effect between age and context for interest in object ($F(1, 21) = 5.13$, $p < .05$). Nine-month-olds were more interested in objects during the parents' dialogue than during the 3-together.

Qualitative description of case involving approach responses

The following case is representative of the upper range of triangular communication because of the richness of the infant's style. Also, it illustrates in a particularly dramatic way a 9-month-old's response to her parents' manifestation of affection.

1   *Three-together play.* At the beginning of the 3-together play, each parent took one of Lea's hands. Mother: "Do you want to dance?" The parents began to rock themselves and Lea joined them, staring at them with a very attentive expression, while the father repeated the question.

2   *The real belt versus the symbolic belt.* As the father began to sing, Lea switched to leaning on her side to examine the leather belt. Mother: "Oh she is interested in the belt . . ." as she presented it to Lea, exclaiming: "The tail!" Father: "Yes, you are interested!" Mother: "This is our dog!" And she swung the "tail" toward father: "Hello daddy!" The parents played mostly variations of this game during the 3-together: passing the belt around from the mother to the father and sometimes to Lea, pretending it was their dog's tail. Lea, intrigued and fascinated, followed their moves, looked up alternatively at her father, at her mother, and at their hands. Yet she switched several times to lean out to look at the other end of the belt (it was attached to the table below her seat)—as if it were another belt.

3   *Working hard at participating in the symbolic game.* As Lea grasped the mother's end of the belt, the mother exclaimed: "Are you taking Ola's tail?" (Ola was

the name of their dog). The parents playfully barked. Lea smiled animatedly at them, but then leaned down on the other side, perhaps looking for the end of the other side of the belt; but as she did so, she also rocked herself. Mother: "How does she do, Ola?" Lea looked up at father and "barked," making a long vocalization at him, then at her mother, while the parents echoed (triangular bid, sharing pleasure).

4 *Taking a break.* Lea paused. Having seized the belt, she examined it at length, brought it to her mouth, took it out, examined it again; her parents watched her; mother: "You have discovered something haven't you?" Lea looked at it, made an exclamation of enthusiasm and rocked herself while looking at the belt.

5 *Play with the real belt.* When the mother finally initiated a kissing game, Lea protested, seized the real belt, clearly indicating her own interest. The parents joined her and she showed her satisfaction by rocking herself again.

Comment. The smooth cooperation between the parents and their creativity allowed for a complex interaction to emerge. It coordinated four poles of attention, combining triangular (person–person–person) and triadic (person–person–object) interactions. Lea followed her parents throughout. To be sure, much of the symbolic meaning of the game was beyond her zone of proximal development. But she had a parallel agenda of her own: exploring and possessing the "real" belt; she never gave up on it, inviting her parents to participate in it too. She seemed to be able to handle the two agendas without too much difficulty.

The parents' dialogue episode
The parents initiated the transition while Lea was absorbed in trying to catch the seat's belt. Interestingly, the mother had forgotten about this last episode and was about to call for the experimenter. The father reminded her of the instructions and, as she laughed at herself, their dialogue started. In the meantime, they had leaned back and turned their heads and shoulders toward each other. Thanks to the active support of the mother by the father, neither turned to look at or address Lea, even when after about a minute, she experienced some trouble, having pushed the belt in her mouth a bit too deep. The father then held the mother's hand. While the episode was short, their dialogue was playful, affectionate, reflecting a deep connection between them.

Its course may be divided into four episodes according to Lea's communicative strategies:

1 *Discovering the new context and building up animation with the parents along with object manipulation (45s).* As Lea straightened up, holding the leather belt in one hand, she caught sight of her mother's changed orientation and looked at her with a surprised expression (dyadic social-referencing bid). She alternated several times between attending to the belt, examining it and

bringing it to her mouth, and following her mother's moves (mother's laughs, adjusting her hair, gesturing). Then she shifted her orientation toward her father, first by extending her leg toward him, then by straightening up, looking up at him and addressing him with an exclamation of enthusiasm (approach). After a new episode of careful exploration of the belt, she looked up at her father again, rocking herself several times, as during play. Then she turned back to the belt, looked up at her mother, eyes wide open, turned her head toward her father, still looking at her mother, then looked up at her father with the same wide-eyed expression, and vocalizing with enthusiasm (social engagement triangular bid). After refocusing on the belt for a few seconds, she straightened up and rocked herself, looking at her father and making wild exclamations (approach). After a brief glance at the belt, she looked up again at her mother (who was laughing with her father), then at her father, with wide eyes and more exclamations of enthusiasm (approach). She repeated this episode with minor variations two more times, repeating her approach with her foot too: extending her foot in her father's direction.

2 *Exploring the seat belt, slightly choking herself and signaling discomfort to parents (20s)*: Lea refocused on the belt, vocalizing with enthusiasm, but pushed the belt too far into her mouth; she coughed a bit and made faces of disgust in the direction of her mother, fussing slightly, culminating in a show of disgust toward each parent (triangular protest bid) and screaming at them.

3 *Sadness contemplating her parents holding hands (18s)*: as her father took her mother's hand, Lea looked at her parents' joined hands with an expression which progressively shifted from sternness to sadness, then to a pout for two long stretches of time, punctuated only by a few social referencing looks at her mother (see Figure 19.2a and b). As they let go, Lea went on contemplating her mother's hands, then her own, joined on the multicolored belt.

4 *Activation and shift to protest (25s)*: Lea progressively activated herself by focusing on the belt, but within a few seconds became agitated, shifting from the belt to the back of the seat and to the table without being able to focus. She made an aborted pick-me-up gesture without looking up at her parents (approach) and kept her eyes averted from them until they decided to terminate the episode and call her. She responded immediately by looking up at both of them.

Comment. Lea appeared again to have two agendas in parallel. On the one hand, she focused on objects and on the other hand, she followed her parents' interaction, experiencing it in different successive ways: discovering it, partaking in their animation, apparently feeling excluded, finally protesting and attempting to regulate her state by means of distraction and being rescued by her parents. Throughout the sequence, she made dyadic and triangular bids and approaches. This example illustrates how, as they grow, infants become more active and differentiated in their communication with their parents.

(a)

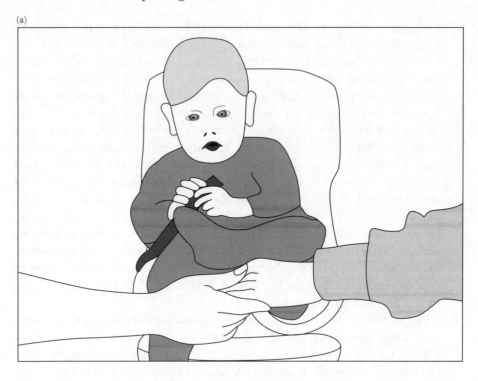

(b)

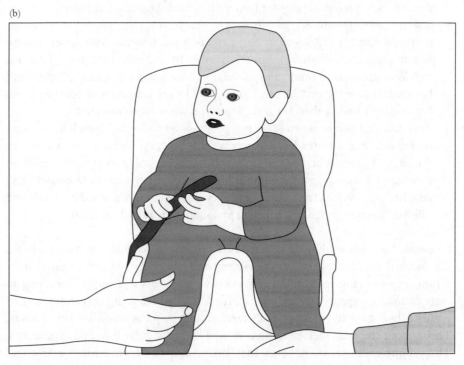

Figure 19.2   a) Lea looks at her parents holding hands with a sad expression; b) Lea looks up at her mother with an interrogative expression (social referencing bid)

Approach responses

The 9-month-olds' approach responses were more powerful than those of the 3-month-olds. Their motor development allowed for physical proximity. Likewise, their socio-affective development allowed for a more differentiated interest in their parents' interaction and for a wider variety of strategies and more deliberate ways to reach their goal of regaining parents' attention.

In practice, some infants simply tried to physically connect with their parents by leaning out and touching a parent's leg, or making a pick-me-up gesture with a tense vocalization. Request vocalizations were successively modulated in various ways, from fussy to quasi-playful to loud, imperative yells. An infant alternated several times between leaning out toward a parent, begging, and laughing along with the parents.

Several infants made approach responses at moments that were sensitive for their parents. For instance, as his parents turned toward each other as his mother said somewhat shyly, "we don't know what to say to each other," and the father responded with, "it is difficult …," an infant broke in animatedly, looking at his mother, mouth wide open, smiling, vocalizing with enthusiasm, his arms and legs wriggling. Or, as his parents came to discuss a disagreement and their voices became tense, another infant suddenly made enthusiastic gestures and vocalizations, as if to draw their attention.

Typical of the 9-month-olds' emerging intentional stance, several approach behaviors appeared to be references to previous games played with the parents, especially the ones that had been most fun, as if more likely to attract the parents' attention because they were high points. For instance, one infant held out a cookie to his father, with which he had just played give-and-take-a-cookie. Another infant scratched her head rest, looking at her mother and at her father, apparently hoping to draw their attention with this interesting noise as she had so successfully done before. Another one made specific gestures with his hands, gestures that had previously been part of a "puppet" game with his parents. In a more provocative vein, another infant looked up at his father with a smile and wide open eyes, very aroused. He was sucking on the seat belt noisily, as if to provoke them, "See, now I am sucking on the belt!" His parents had repeatedly taken it away from him during the 3-together play.

In sum, on the one hand, 9-month-olds had recourse to a variety of ingenious approach responses to attract their parents' attention and to effect change in the context. Most noteworthy was their intentional stance as manifested by using previously successful games to this end. On the other hand, the frustration generated by their parents' inattention did not prevent them from attending to their dialogue, not only by monitoring it and presumably trying to grasp their exchange, but also by trying to actively participate in it. Finally, they also found at times alternative pleasurable activities by focusing on objects.

Comment on differences between 3 and 9 months

The results of the comparison between 3- and 9-month-olds make sense insofar as the 3-month-olds' interest is mainly focused on persons rather than shared between persons and objects as it is in 9-month-olds. This explains why 3-month-olds looked more at their parents during their dialogue and made more triangular bids to them in both contexts. Yet it must be stressed that given that joint attention on objects has not been measured, the lower frequency of gaze at parents during play at 9 months underestimates the engagement with the parents. A portion of the looks directed at the parents might have been coordinated with looks at objects and been references to them. Likewise, references to objects may have been realized through joint gestures and voice, so that gaze alone does not account for engagement toward parents as fully as it did at 3 months. That the rate of positive affect was not different at 9 and 3 months is more surprising, given the growth in emotional regulation. In play, however, it may have been counterbalanced by the increase in conflict with the parents. Typically the 9-month-old wanted not only to play with the seat belt but to bring it to her mouth, which itself triggered more tension and protest than at 3 months.

Discussion

Our first goal in this chapter was to document the young infant's triangular capacity in the primary triangle. Toward this end, we reported on the 4-month-old and her two parents in a still-face condition. Our second goal was to describe the infant as onlooker of her parents' dialogue at 3 and 9 months as a new instance of the infant's response to inattention and to discuss our observations in the light of the results of inattention and jealousy evocation paradigms. Finally, we wanted to discuss whether one may consider family triangular interactions as a context for the development of jealousy.

The infant's triangular competence in the 2 + 1 still-face

Using as a baseline a regular 2 + 1 play, we showed that 4-month-olds placed in the paradoxical still-face situation with a parent posing a still-face and the other one as third party discriminated the two contexts. In particular, their affect signals were more positive during play and they tended to turn more often toward the third party parent during the still-face. Not only did they use the strategies described in the dyadic still-face, such as bids of protest or charm to the parent posing a still-face, but they also used triangular bids including the third party parent without any solicitation on his/her part. From a functional perspective, triangular protest appeared to indicate a request for change, whereas triangular monitoring, and more so triangular tension, seemed possible precursors of triangular social referencing bids observed later in development under conditions of uncertainty. Note that in the classical experiments on social referencing done at the end of the first year, the ultimate test is whether the infant, having checked on the parent's affective expression, actually guides her behavior according to this expression: a positive, encouraging one versus a negative, discouraging one (Klinnert, Campos, Sorce, Emde, & Svejda, 1983). This test is not applicable in the still-face situation, given that these affective expressions are not part of it. Yet one may presume that the infant's bids manifest her uncertainty in the face of a paradoxical situation. A longitudinal study is required to explore this issue.

The presence of the third party parent provided the infant with another strategy to initiate change, namely to recruit the third person to help deal with the situation. In general, triangular bids constituted an as yet little described prosocial behavior, pointing to the ability of a young infant to make connections with two other different people concurrently.

It is worth mentioning that documentation on individual differences in the infant's triangular interaction is also available, which was not presented in this chapter for the sake of space. McHale et al.'s study (2008) on rapid gaze transitions in a large sample observed in the still-face and regular LTP has confirmed that young infants make rapid transitions. These authors follow Lavanchy (2002), who had found that 3-month-olds make more rapid transitions under conditions of functional family alliances (with high cooperation between the parents) than of problematic ones (with low cooperation). They found that this capacity could be linked to co-parenting process and to co-parenting risk beyond the LTP situation. We will return to this important issue below.

Together, these findings constitute a new argument in favor of an early awareness of self and other and of the importance of the parents' attunement in this development (Legerstee, 2005). They indicate that the relationships infants engage in when interacting in three-person settings are based on a capacity for relating to two—and presumably more—others simultaneously. In other words, there is the possibility that infants are biologically prepared for relationships in general rather than specifically for attachments (Nash & Hay, 1993).

The infant as third party

In the second report, we compared the responses of typical 3- and 9-month-olds to their parents' inattention with their responses to playing with both parents. Understandably, there was a difference between the two conditions concerning social engagement, which was observed almost only in play. But the main quantitative result was that, at both ages, gaze, interest, and rate of positive affect did not change when infants shifted from play to third party. In other words, their overall attention was as sustained and their overall affect as positive during their parents' dialogue as during play.

These results may seem surprising insofar as during 3-together play, the parents jointly used finely attuned intuitive parenting behaviors (Papousek, 2007) to stimulate their child; this style stood in contrast to the low-key adult style of their dialogue.

Yet the infant's arousal during the parents' play stimulations did not outweigh her arousal during their adult dialogue. This doesn't mean that the infants did not discriminate between the two contexts. It is known that infants distinguish between the intentions of their partners (Legerstee et al., this volume), notably on the basis of orientations and distances between bodies (Stern, 1981; Fivaz-Depeursinge, 1991). Moreover, that the overall results yielded the same rate of attention and of positive over negative affect in both situations does not mean that the function these behaviors served was the same, given that the context was different (Volling et al., 2002). The 3-together play served the function of interacting together to reach moments of delight, whereas the parents' dialogue served the function of allowing the parental-marital team to engage together and the infant to be onlooker.

In play, the infants alternated between episodes of engagement with their parents and brief episodes of confrontation; during engagement, they reached twosome and threesome moments of delight marked by their dyadic or triangular bids of pleasure and interest; during confrontation, they attempted to impose their own agenda—such as playing with the belt or sucking on it—marked by dyadic and triangular bids of tension and protest. Their orientation and positive affects were mainly in the service of engaging jointly with their parents. Their negative affects served to regulate the play interaction, to better adjust it to their own goals.

As third parties, infants alternated between three coping strategies: interest, as if trying to capture the meaning of their parents' behaviors and relationship; pauses, at 3 months mainly by withdrawing and at 9 months mainly by focusing on objects, namely using distraction; finally, approach behaviors addressed to one or both parents, as if trying to modify the context. Approaches were varied and ingenious. Infants signaled tension and protest to one or both parents, manifesting their fear of loss or anger at losing the parents' attention. Approach behaviors grew more varied and sophisticated with age. By 9 months, some appeared as attempts to participate in the parents' relationship by resonating, echoing, animating, and offering. The infants' interest in objects had increased at the expense of withdrawal and interest in the parents. In other words, they had found new ways of coping, by focusing on alternative pleasurable activities. Yet, it is of note that a non-measured portion of their interest in objects might have been part of a strategy to recapture their parents' interest. These were manifested by looks at parents following or preceding interest in objects, seemingly to refer to games successfully played during the previous episodes with the parents. These actions denoted the 9-month-old's intentional stance.

It appears that the driving forces behind the infants' high attention and positive affect as third parties were, first of all, the surprise of seeing the parents turn away from them and thus of being shifted from the center of attention to the periphery. Secondly, it involved the intriguing experience of observing the parents' dialogue. Last but not least, there was the challenge of regaining parents' attention.

Insofar as they showed no differences in attention and rate of positive affect between the two conditions, our results do not indicate that the third party position was more disturbing for the infant than play. In this regard, they do not point to a jealousy response as observed in the experimental condition of Hart et al.'s paradigm (1998a). The baby as third party situation comes closer to Hart's control conditions, Legerstee's modified still-face paradigm (Legerstee et al., this volume), or Tremblay and Rovira's (2007) exclusion paradigm in that these conditions all involve inattention to the infant. They also correspond with natural situations, namely they include salient reasons why contact is broken: a stranger interrupting the mother to talk with her, a partner stopping play to drink from a bottle (Legerstee et al., this volume), turning to the other adult or to an object (Tremblay & Rovira, 2007), or the parents talking together, in our situation.

Moreover, at least in the exclusion and in the LTP paradigms, some degree of control over the situation was afforded the infant. Inherent in the exclusion paradigm was the possibility for the infant to recover contact by addressing the adults. This experience was bound to reinforce the infant's sense of agency and might have thus stimulated her triangular communication by means of socially directed behaviors, the equivalents of triangular bids in the LTP. This possibility was only implicit in the LTP paradigm. The parents were in a position to intuitively modulate the form of their dialogue (intensity, animation) to help the child regulate her affect. This was easy to perceive for infants who were comfortable with their parents. Moreover, given flexibility with the duration of the episode, the parents tended to terminate a session at an appropriate time, like after a particularly brilliant approach by their child, thus providing her with a sense of agency. It would be advantageous to develop this aspect in the still-face paradigm too. Providing the infant with the opportunity to change the context following her triangular bids would further inform us about the infant's expectations (E. Tronick, pers. comm., October 2008).

In Legerstee's and in Tremblay's studies, responses in the conditions of inattention were contrasted with those in regular play and/or the still-face perturbation, and with a triadic, person–person–object situation. According to the authors, the results showing the 3- and 6-month-olds' ability to discriminate between these conditions, as well as their quiet interest during inattention, suggest an awareness of the reason why contact was broken; in other words, discrimination between various communicative intentions. However, it is of note that in the modified still-face situation with a stranger addressing the mother, a response reminiscent of Hart's findings on the infant's approach responses was observed, but only when the mother engaged in a dialogue with the stranger (Legerstee et al., this volume). Then, the infant's vocalizations increased as did the intensity of their signals. Our findings on approach appear to come close to this response. In this sense, they speak for a mild jealousy response.

Thus, we suggest that the triangular interactions observed in the primary triangle prepare the infant not only to handle triangular dynamics in general, but also to develop jealousy responses in particular, before the possible confrontation with the birth of a sibling.

From an evolutionary perspective on jealousy, we could interpret our findings in the following way: faced with the inattention of her parents, the infant might have been motivated to protect these important relationships for her survival. We envision several possible scenarios. Depending on her temperament and her present disposition, she could have felt compelled to protect her relationship with her mother or with her father, and by actively trying to engage her or him and to relegate the other parent to a third party position. This could be the case in instances where the infant maintains attention to only one of the parents during their dialogue. But alternatively, she could have felt compelled to protect her relationship with her co-parenting party and strive to reengage in the threesome. This could be the case when the infant distributes attention between both parents, making multiple triangular bids, as demonstrated by Andrew at 3 months.

One might also ask, along with other authors, whether this struggle to reestablish the relationship might be motivated by attachment (for a review, see Hart et al., 1998b). This might have been the case with Lea. The incident where she hurt herself slightly with the belt, and which led her to direct disgust and distress bids to her parents, might have activated her attachment system. But in general, given that the LTP is a play context where the goal is to share delight, it is more likely that the activated motivational system would be intersubjectivity (Trevarthen & Hubley, 1978; Stern, 2004). In the inattention condition, the infant might experience an interruption of the intersubjective contact with her parent(s). For instance, at 3 months, Andrew vocalized almost continuously to both his parents during play. The interruption of direct contact with them led him to address protest bids to both of them, as if to reestablish contact with them. In this perspective, an investigation of the association between jealousy responses and measures of attachment versus measures of intersubjectivity, in a large sample, is in order.

Finally, on the basis of Lavanchy (2002) and McHale and associates' (2008) findings that triangular bids differentiate family and co-parenting alliances, it is to be expected that jealousy protests of the infant as third party might also differentiate them, adding to the list of disturbed relationships which differentiate jealousy protests (Hart et al., 1998b). Our observations of the parents in problematic alliances during their dialogue show that they tend to avoid confrontation by remaining focused on the infant (inclusion) or by turning away from him (exclusion) rather than maintaining a clear but flexible boundary between the infant and their unit. The infant would then respond with overuse of approach responses that would normally be used in functional alliances as animation or confrontation strategies to distract the parents from the tension between them. Indeed, he would use them to serve the function of regulating his parents' conflicted relationship rather than for his own sake, or he would withdraw, excluding himself from the triangle (Fivaz-Depeursinge, Frascarolo, Lopes, Dimitrova, & Favez, 2007; Phillip, Fivaz-Depeursinge, Corboz-Warnery, & Favez, 2009). In other words, inclusion/exclusion dominate over "clusion," a neologism coined by

D. Stern (pers. comm., October 2008) to refer to the very existential fact that we have to live with the reality of our partners having other relationships too.

Overall, assuming that the present findings on the infant's triangular capacity are confirmed, it appears that triangular or multiple interactions are an inherent part of the infant's ordinary experience, and this before a firstborn becomes a sibling. Returning to Hart and colleagues' conclusion that "direct experience in triadic contexts is not a necessary precondition for the emergence of jealousy" (Hart et al., 1998a, p. 138), we suggest that the experience with two or more adult caretakers might be. This is one of the main issues open to investigation at this point. Note that one may envision using the LTP situation in different versions in this regard: as a three-person situation involving one parent and two siblings, as in the Volling, McElwain, and Miller studies (2002); or a situation with four or more people involving a family with two or more siblings (Fivaz-Depeursinge & Corboz-Warnery, 1999).

In conclusion, triangular interactions create a dynamic not present in dyadic ones, given the social feedback provided by the third party and the increased number of possible interactive contexts. Therefore they multiply the possibilities for understanding self–other differentiation, for developing reciprocity and for awareness of shareable feelings, contributing in turn to the normative development of jealousy.

Authors' Note

This research was supported by the Swiss National Scientific Research Found grant No 32-52508.97.

The authors wish to express their gratitude to Roland Fivaz for his skillful drawings and Gabriela Quoex-Gelsinius for reviewing and editing the English version of this paper.

References

Adamson, L., & Frick, J. (2003). The still-face: A history of a shared paradigm. *Infancy, 4,* 451–473.

Bakeman, R., & Gottman, J. M. (1986). *Observing interaction: An introduction to sequential analysis.* Cambridge: Cambridge University Press.

Braungart-Rieker, J., Garwood, M., & Powers, B. P. (1998). Infant affect and affect regulation during the still-face paradigm with mothers and fathers: The role of infant characteristics and parental sensitivity. *Developmental Psychology, 34,* 1428–1437.

Buss, D. (2000). *The dangerous passion: Why jealousy is as necessary as love and sex.* New York: Free Press.

Campos, J., Frankel, C., & Camras, L. (2004). On the nature of emotion regulation. *Child Development, 75,* 377–394.

Campos, J., Mumme, D., Kermoian, R., & Campos, R. (1994). A functionalist perspective on the nature of emotion. In N. Fox (Ed.), The development of emotion regulation:

Biological and behavioral considerations. *Monographs of the Society for Research in Child Development, 59*(2–3, Serial No. 240), 284–303.

Camras, L., Meng, Z., Ujiie, T., Dharamsi, S., Miyake, K., Oster, H., et al. (2002). Observing emotions in infants: Facial expression, body behavior, and rater judgments of responses to an expectancy-violating event. *Emotion, 2,* 179–193.

Corboz-Warnery, A., Fivaz-Depeursinge, E., Gertsch-Bettens, C., & Favez, N. (1993). Systemic analysis of father–mother–baby interaction: The Lausanne triadic play. *Infant Mental Health Journal, 14,* 298–316.

Draghi-Lorenz, R., Reddy, V., & Costall, A. (2001). Rethinking the development of "nonbasic" emotions: A critical review of existing theories. *Developmental Review, 21,* 263–304.

Favez, N., Frascarolo, F., Carneiro, C., Montfort, V., Corboz-Warnery, A., & Fivaz-Depeursinge, E. (2006). The development of the family alliance from pregnancy to toddlerhood and children outcomes at 18 months. *Infant and Child Development, 15,* 59–73.

Fivaz-Depeursinge, E. (1991). Documenting a time-bound, circular view of hierarchies: A microanalysis of parent–infant dyadic interaction. *Family Process, 30,* 101–120.

Fivaz-Depeursinge, E., & Corboz-Warnery, A. (1999). *The primary triangle. A developmental systems view of mothers, fathers and infants.* New York: Basic Books.

Fivaz-Depeursinge, E., Favez, N., Lavanchy, C., de Noni, S., & Frascarolo, F. (2005). Four-month-olds make triangular bids to father and mother during trilogue play with still-face. *Social Development, 14,* 361–378.

Fivaz-Depeursinge, E., Frascarolo, F., Lopes, F., Dimitrova, N., & Favez, N. (2007). Parents–child role reversal in trilogue play. Case studies of trajectories from pregnancy to toddlerhood. *Attachment and Human Development, 9,* 17–31.

Frascarolo, F., Favez, N., Carneiro, C., & Fivaz-Depeursinge, E. (2004). Hierarchy of interactive functions in father–mother–baby three-way games. *Infant and Child Development, 13,* 301–322.

Hart, S.L., Carrington, H., Tronick, E., & Carroll, S. (2004). When infants lose exclusive maternal attention: Is it jealousy? *Infancy, 6,* 57–78.

Hart, S., Field, T., del Valle, C., & Letourneau, M. (1998a). Infants protest their mothers' attending to an infant-size doll. *Social Development, 7,* 54–61.

Hart, S., Field, T., Letourneau, M., & del Valle, C. (1998b). Jealousy protests in infants of depressed mothers. *Infant Behavior and Development, 21,* 137–148.

Hart, S., Jones, N., & Field, T. (2003). Atypical expressions of jealousy in infants of intrusive and withdrawn-depressed mothers. *Child Psychiatry and Human Development, 33,* 193–207.

Klinnert, M. D., Campos, J. J., Sorce, J. F., Emde, R. N., & Svejda, M. (1983). Emotions as behavior regulators: Social referencing in infancy. In R. Plutchik & H. Kellerman (Eds.), *Emotion. Theory, research and experience* (pp. 57–86). New York: Academic Press.

Koller, R. (2002). *Les affects de l'enfant de trois mois dans l'interaction avec ses deux parents* [The affects of the 3-month old infant during interaction with both parents]. Unpublished manuscript. Switzerland: University of Lausanne, Center for Family Studies.

Lavanchy, C. (2002). *L'interaction visuelle de l'enfant de trois mois* [Gaze interaction of the three-month old infant]. Unpublished manuscript. University of Lausanne, Center for Family Studies.

Legerstee, M. (2005). *Infants' sense of people: Precursors to a theory of mind.* New York: Cambridge University Press.

Legerstee, M., Ellenbogen, B., Nienhuis, T. & Marsh, H. (this volume). Social bonds, triadic relationships, and goals: Preconditions for the emergence of human jealousy. In S. L. Hart & M. Legerstee (Eds.), *Handbook of jealousy: Theory, research, and multidisciplinary approaches*. Malden, MA: Wiley-Blackwell.

Lopes, F., Favez, N., & Frascarolo, F. (2006, July). *How does an infant react when mommy and daddy speak to each other and how is it related to family alliance?* Poster presented at the World Association of Infant Mental Health, Paris.

Markova, G., & Legerstee, M. (2006). Contingency, imitation, and affect sharing: Foundations of infants' social awareness. *Developmental Psychology, 42*, 132–141.

Markova, G., Stieben, J., & Legerstee, M. (this volume). Neural structures of jealousy: Infants' experience of social exclusion with caregivers and peers. In S. L. Hart & M. Legerstee (Eds.), *Handbook of jealousy: Theory, research, and multidisciplinary approaches*. Malden, MA: Wiley-Blackwell.

McHale, J., Fivaz-Depeursinge, E., Dickstein, S., Robertson, J., & Daley, M. (2008). New evidence for the social embeddedness of infant's early triangular capacities. *Family Process, 47*, 445–463.

Meltzoff, A. N., & Moore, M. K. (1992). Early imitation within a functional framework: The importance of person identity, movement and development. *Infant Behavior and Development, 15*, 479–505.

Murray, L., & Trevarthen, C. (1985). Emotional regulation of interaction between two-month-olds and their mothers. In. T. Field & N. Fox (Eds.), *Social perception in infants* (pp. 177–197). Norwood, NJ: Ablex.

Nadel, J., & Tremblay-Leveau, H. (1999). Early perception of social contingencies and interpersonal intentionality: Dyadic and triadic paradigms. In P. Rochat (Ed.), *Early social cognition* (pp. 189–212). Hillsdale, NJ: Erlbaum.

Nash, A., & Hay, D. (1993). Relationships in infancy as precursors and causes of later relationships and psychopathology. In D. F. Hay & A. Angold (Eds.), *Precursors, causes and psychopathology* (pp.199–232). Chichester: Wiley.

Neisser, U. (1994). *Self-perception and self-knowledge* (pp. 3–21). New York: Cambridge University Press.

Papousek, M. (2007). Communication in early infancy: An area of intersubjective learning. *Infant Behavior and Development, 30*, 258–266.

Phillip, D., Fivaz-Depeursinge, E., Corboz-Warnery, A., & Favez, N. (2009). Young infants' triangular communication with their parents in the context of maternal post-partum breakdown. Four case studies on impact of psychopathology. *Infant Mental Health Journal, 30*, 341–365.

Selby, J. M., & Bradley, B.S. (2003). Infants in groups: A paradigm for the study of early social experience. *Human Development, 46*, 197–221.

Stern, D.N. (1981). The development of biologically determined signals of readiness to communicate which are language "resistant." In R. E. Staerk (Ed.), *Language behavior in infancy and early childhood* (pp. 45–62). Amsterdam: Elsevier.

Stern, D. N. (1985). *The interpersonal world of the infant*. New York: Basic Books.

Stern, D. N. (2004). *The present moment in psychotherapy and everyday life*. New York: Norton.

Striano, T., & Stahl, D. (2005). Sensitivity to triadic attention in early infancy. *Developmental Science, 8*, 333–343.

Tomasello, M. (1999). Having intentions, understanding intentions and understanding com-
    municative intentions. In P. D. Zelazo, J. W. Astington, & D. R. Olsen (Eds.), *Developing
    theories of intention: Social understanding and self-control* (pp. 63–75). Mahwah, NJ: Erlbaum.

Tov-Ruach, L. (1980). Jealousy, attention, and loss. In A. O. Rorty (Ed.), *Explaining emotions*
    (pp. 465–488). Berkeley, CA: University of California.

Tremblay, H., & Rovira, K. (2007). Joint visual attention and social triangular engagement
    at 3 and 6 months. *Infant Behavior and Development, 30,* 366–379.

Trevarthen, C. (1984). Emotions in infancy: Regulators of contact and relationships with
    persons. In K. R. Scherer & P. Ekman (Eds.), *Approaches to emotion* (pp. 129–157).
    Hillsdale, NJ: Erlbaum.

Trevarthen, C., & Hubley, P. (1978). Secondary intersubjectivity: Confidence, confiding
    and acts of meaning in the first year. In A. Lock (Ed.), *Action, gesture and symbol. The
    emergence of language* (pp. 183–229). New York: Academic Press.

Tronick, E. Z., Als, H., Adamson, L., Wise, S., & Brazelton, T. B. (1978). The infant's
    response to entrapment between contradictory messages in face-to-face interaction.
    Journal of the American Academy of Child Psychiatry, 17, 1–13.

Tronick, E. Z., Als, H., & Brazelton, T. B. (1980). Monadic phases: A structural description
    analysis of infant–mother face-to-face interaction. *Merrill Palmer Quarterly, 26,* 3–24.

Volling, B., McElwain, N., & Miller, A. (2002). Emotion regulation in context: The
    jealousy complex between young siblings and its relation with child and family
    characteristics. *Child Development, 73,* 581–600.

Weinberg, M., & Tronick, E. (1994). Beyond the face: An empirical study of infant affective
    configurations of facial, vocal, gestural and regulatory behaviors. *Child Development,
    65,* 1495–1507.

20

Culture, Parenting, and the Development of Jealousy

Heidi Keller and Bettina Lamm

Defined as an individual's reaction to the actual or potential loss of a loved one to a real or imagined rival, jealousy is widely assumed to be a universal phenomenon (Hupka, 1981). It is already apparent in infants as young as 5 to 6 months of age, according to research (Draghi-Lorenz, 2000; Hart, Field, del Valle, & Letourneau, 1998; Hart & Carrington, 2002) in which early expressions of jealousy were inferred from observations that infants become distressed when their mothers ignore them, especially when the mother is attending to another infant or a baby-like doll. Contrastingly, infants are less distressed when their mothers' attention is directed to other adults or books. The context in which infant jealousy is displayed appears to be quite specific to the mother–infant relationship. While suggesting an interpersonal awareness of the attention distribution of an infant's major social resource, that is, the caregiving mother, it can also be considered an evolutionary-shaped strategy toward ensuring resource acquisition and maximization. Yet, jealousy and its regulation are embedded within an interactional process to which both mother and infant contribute. In this chapter we will seek to shed some light on the evolutionary basis of jealousy before turning to a discussion of cultural conditions that influence the manner in which jealousy develops and is expressed.

Jealousy as an Evolutionary-Based Phenomenon

Human infants are characterized by a level of helplessness that is unparalleled in nature. Widely understood as an outcome of physical immaturity at birth (Prechtl, 1984), this neonatal condition stems from the obstetrical dilemma (Washburn, 1960), the extreme brain growth that evolved during human phylogeny. By 2 months before birth the human brain is already more developed than that of a newborn macaque (Clancy, Darlington, & Finlay, 2001). Human neonatal brain growth then continues in a rapid, fetal-like trajectory for the next year

Handbook of Jealousy: Theory, Research and Multidisciplinary Approaches, First Edition.
Edited by Sybil L. Hart and Maria Legerstee.
© 2013 Blackwell Publishing Ltd. Published 2013 by Blackwell Publishing Ltd.

(Martin, 1983). Highly altricial, that is, born helpless and requiring nourishment and protection from parents, human infants are able to see, but their vision is still imperfect since convergence and acuity have not yet been mastered (Kaufmann-Hayoz & van Leeuwen, 1997). Furthermore, vision and movement are not yet coordinated, and the memory span covers only about 1 s. As a consequence of their immaturity, infants are dependent on a special co-designed caregiving environment which can compensate for their behavioral shortcomings and deficits. In "normal" cases, the caregiving environment will consist of the biological parents. However, due to the importance of social support to survival, human infants accept support from any caregiver if it is attuned to their needs. Help of non-parental caregivers is viewed as part of an evolutionary-shaped social system (Hrdy, 1999).

Yet, the helplessness of the infant can be seen as part of an "egoistic" reproductive strategy that drives the infant to invest all available resources in growth and development (Alexander, 1979). This inevitably leads to conflict between parents' and infants' reproductive interests. Parents and children as well as siblings share 50% of their genes. According to evolutionary perspectives, there is enough room for competition due to the assumption of genetic egoism (Dawkins, 1976). Parent–offspring conflict (Trivers, 1974) stems from sibling competition for the limited resources that parents can invest in a child's survival. The firstborn child, on the one hand, wants exclusive parental attention for as long as possible. The parents, on the other hand, are interested in maximizing their reproductive success by having more children. Later-born children, in turn, take an interest in getting as much as possible of the remaining parental care and resources. Since children compete for parental attention and resources irrespective of birth order, it is not surprising to find that both first- and later-born children react in the same way to jealousy evocation (Hart, Carrington, Tronick, & Carroll, 2004).

It is important to stress at this point that, even if behaviors are evolutionary based and inborn, this does not mean that behavioral expressions emerge automatically. To the contrary, there is substantial evidence that biology is expressed differently according to contextual demands (Greenfield, 2002; Keller, 2002; Bjorklund & Pellegrini, 2002), and so they differ with respect to frequency and intensity across culture. Cultures define display rules (Ekman, 1973) that prescribe the appropriateness or inappropriateness of facial expressions and emotional behavior. In one of our studies (Keller et al., 2006), mothers of different cultural communities were interviewed about their socialization goals. In research on parents' opinions about desirable developmental achievements, mothers of small children were asked whether they thought that children should learn to control their emotions during the first 3 years of life. The results revealed substantial differences between mothers from different cultural backgrounds (Figure 20.1). Whereas mothers from Western middle-class families did not emphasize the control of emotions as a developmental goal, mothers from

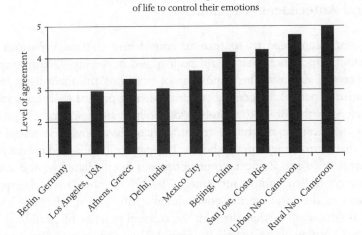

Children should learn during their first three years
of life to control their emotions

Figure 20.1 Mothers' agreement with the socialization goal of "learning to control emotions"

communities with a traditional cultural heritage, especially those from rural farming communities, placed high value on the control of emotions as a socialization goal.

Cultures also differ in terms of beliefs about the appropriateness of experiencing particular emotions and how these can depend on place, time, occasion, and intensity of feeling (Ellsworth, 1994). Thus, not only the expression or display of emotions, but also the actual experience itself is influenced by cultural norms. For example, a study comparing Euro-Americans and Minangkabau from West Sumatra reported remarkable cultural differences in the subjective experience of emotion despite the fact that their physiological responses were not dissimilar (Levenson, Ekman, Heider, & Friesen, 1992). When asked to pose the face so as to mimic certain emotional expressions, participants from both cultural backgrounds showed systematic autonomous changes. However, Euro-Americans also reported corresponding changes in the subjective feeling which were not reported as being experienced by the Minangkabau. The distinctive patterns of response were explained by Levenson and colleagues (1992) as stemming from the absence of meaningful involvement by another individual, a factor that is considered critical to emotional experience among the Minangkabau. These results suggest the involvement of prewired and largely culture-free physiological and neurochemical processes in emotions, although the actual experience of emotion depends nonetheless on cultural norms and customs. With respect to jealousy, we might posit a similar process in which a universal genetic heritage may enable all human beings to experience jealousy. However, the motive for being jealous, the contextual parameters that trigger jealousy, as well as the mode of expressing jealousy are acquired through learning (Hupka, 1991).

Cultural Antecedents of Jealousy

These conclusions lead us to turn to considering cultural variations in early socialization experiences that might be involved in driving differing experiences and displays of jealousy. The acquisition of emotions and their display rules can be regarded as part of the general cultural learning process that starts at birth, or even before birth (Brazelton, Robey, & Collier, 1969; Greenfield, 2002). For example, Zinacantec newborns from Mexico show lower levels of physical activity than Euro-American newborns. The pattern of subdued motor responses that characterize the Zinacantec newborn has been related to the Zinacantec woman's controlled motor movements which restrain prenatal exposure to movement in the intra-uterine environment. After birth, relatively low motor activity is reinforced further through the cultural practice of swaddling.

Cultural learning occurs mainly through children's active participation in socially structured activities (Rogoff, Mistry, Göncü, & Mosier, 1993). The concept of guided participation focuses simultaneously on individual, interpersonal, and cultural processes. Thus, children develop through their participation in various practices of their community while guided and supported by more skilled members of the society. It is assumed that children become more responsible actors in the practices of their communities as they participate and thereby enhance their understanding in a co-constructed process (Rogoff et al., 1993). Since culture itself is not static, it is also influenced by the shared activities of the people, living and acting so that culture becomes both internal and external to the individual (Greenfield, 1997). Observation and imitation serve major roles toward learning through participation. This style of learning is especially prioritized in contexts that do not exhibit strict segregation between environments of adults and children (Keller, 2007a). Hence, observation- and imitation-based learning have been identified and described in numerous traditional cultural contexts (e.g., Crago, 1992; Greenfield & Childs, 1991; Maynard, Greenfield, & Childs, 1999; Ochs, 1988; Rogoff et al., 1993). Western theorists are also aware of the relevance of imitation (e.g., Bandura, 1986). Considering the universality of imitating persons of higher status and age, an evolutionary disposition seems indicated (Keller, 2007a). This pattern also becomes obvious in the sibling context. Younger siblings imitate their older brothers and sisters more often than they are imitated by their older siblings (Pepler, Abramovich, & Corter, 1981).

Emotional development is strongly influenced by observational learning. Empirical evidence suggests that socialization of affect expression occurs during the first year of life (Malatesta & Haviland, 1982). Even newborns imitate facial expressions (Meltzoff & Moore, 1989, 1994). Malatesta and Haviland's (1982) observations revealed that mother–infant dyads were highly correlated in presenting certain expressions and in using particular parts of the face expressively. The analysis of contingency patterns revealed imitation in both directions. Three- to six-month-old infants in their research imitated their mothers' expression, but the mothers also imitated their children's expression. The mothers' selectivity in responding to their infants' emotional expressions was interpreted as fostering the child's learning of appropriate display rules (Malatesta & Haviland, 1982). Furthermore, the infants demonstrated "brow flashes." This rapid raising of the brows is regarded as a greeting gesture (Eibl-Eibesfeldt, 1979) and had previously been observed only in adults. Infants used this gesture in the same context as do adults; they showed brow flashes when attending to maternal speech and social play, or when their mothers returned after a separation phase (Malatesta & Haviland, 1982). Thus, infants not only reproduced the muscle configurations associated with various discrete emotional expressions, but also demonstrated an appropriate application of the observed expressions.

As in the preceding example, early caregiver–infant interactions generally form the first learning context for cultural learning. Learning is based on experiences within early family contexts. Early conceptions of the self as well as the relationships with social partners are developed through decoding of information from the significant social partners (Keller, 2002). The expression of infant jealousy has been related to the distribution of maternal attention. Jealousy is presented when the mother does not give her infant her undivided attention. Apparently, mothers are aware of this interactive pattern. In addition to other normative events, Gusii mothers from Kenya avoid eye contact with their infants because they think that it is overly exciting for the child and raises expectations, which will later be frustrated when a sibling is born (LeVine et al., 1994). Thus, right from the outset, Gusii mothers try to minimize the children's desire and expectation of exclusive maternal attention in order to avoid conflict driven by jealousy.

Culturally Shaped Strategies for the Distribution of Parental Attention

Cultures can differ substantially with respect to norms and strategies for distributing parental attention. According to much of the literature on parent–child interaction that has been conducted with Western middle-class societies, high quality parenting is defined by a number of factors, one of which pertains to the availability of a parent's undivided or exclusive attention within dyadic contexts where mothers and infants spend most of their time during the day. Among the most central criteria for evaluating quality of parenting is the concept of sensitivity which is construed largely as parental attention to infants' signals (Ainsworth, Blehar, Waters, & Wall, 1978). According to this definition, the highly sensitive mother is able to see things from her infant's point of view. She knows what the infant wants and she responds even to her infant's most subtle, minimal, and understated cues. This responsiveness to infant signals is inextricably connected with parental attention. Awareness of an infant's subtle signals is not possible without directing full and exclusive attention toward the infant.

In line with empirically determined definitions of parental sensitivity, Western mothers consider exclusive attention to an infant as absolutely essential to optimal child development. When asked to comment on videotaped mother–infant interactions being presented by dyads from their own and other cultural backgrounds, German middle-class women reacted with criticism when viewing Cameroonian Nso farming mothers directing their attention too frequently to targets other than their 3-month-olds, and felt that the mothers should be completely involved with their infants (Keller, Völker, & Yovsi, 2005). Despite the popularity of such views in Western societies, in most of the world's child-rearing contexts exclusive attention is a resource that caregivers cannot afford to provide to large degrees. In much of the world (Kagitçibasi, 1996), shared attention is the more typical attentional pattern of caregiving (Rogoff et al., 1993). In these contexts, caregiving is conceptualized as a co-occurring activity (Saraswathi, 1994). Caregivers attend to extra-dyadic activities as well as infants who are carried on the caregiver's body. While enabling the caregiver to engage in household or subsistence work which contributes to family sustenance, these caregivers provide their infants with constant physical proximity. This manner of distributing attention is considered as an appropriate method of caregiving in rural non-Western subsistence-based communities. Analyses of early socialization environments and early social interaction patterns in India revealed that rural Gujarati infants experience less exclusive attention than their counterparts from urban educated middle-class families (Abels et al., 2005). Whereas the urban infants received exclusive attention about half of the time, the rural infants received exclusive attention only approximately 20% of the time. In the same vein, focus groups with rural Cameroonian Nso women revealed preferences for shared attentional strategies (Keller, Völker, & Yovsi, 2005). Even Nso sibling caregivers emphasized this strategy of providing co-occurring care (Lamm, 2008). In interviews, approximately 10% of 4- to 8-year-old Nso children spontaneously mentioned that it is important to accomplish household tasks (e.g., fetching water or firewood) while caring for a baby. When faced with the dilemma of having to choose between caring for a baby or playing with friends, as many as 70% of the Nso children resolved the problem by opting for the shared attention solution, while only 20% of a German comparison group chose this type of solution.

Attentional patterns that differ with culture are also apparent in styles of communication. Overlapping or parallel conversations which rarely enable an individual to take center stage appear to be related to shared attentional patterns. Turn taking, on the other hand, demands one-to-one attention. These contrasting communication styles have also been found to vary with mothers' cultural backgrounds. A comparison between rural Cameroonian Nso mothers and German middle-class mothers revealed a tendency for Nso mothers to parallel greater proportions of their infants' vocalizations (Keller, Otto, Lamm, Yovsi, & Kärtner, 2008). Similarly, Gratier (2003) reported cultural differences in the vocal interactions of French, Indian, and Indian immigrant mother–infant dyads. Her microanalysis of vocal turn taking and speech overlap time revealed that in comparison with Indian immigrant and French dyads, Indian mother–infant pairs had shorter intervals between vocal turns and greater overlap. Typical conversational patterns of Japanese mother–infant pairs have also been characterized as highly overlapping in comparison with those of Euro-Americans which were found consisting largely of turn taking (Kajikawa, Amano, & Kondo, 2004). Overlapping conversations are also found to be typical among African Efe communities (Verhoef, Morelli, & Anderson, in prep.). In sum, synchronous verbal/vocal interaction has been found to be more characteristic of families who favor parent–infant exchanges which involve co-occurring attentional patterns or shared focus of attention and relatedness rather than emphasis on autonomy.

Parental attention strategies are maintained as children increase in age. In a comparison of African foragers (Efe) and Euro-American middle-class (Salt Lake City) mother–toddler pairs, Verhoef et al. (in prep.) observed that Efe caregivers rarely interrupted conversation with the interviewer in order to attend explicitly to their children. Instead, they tended to handle the requirements of maintaining the ongoing adult-directed conversation while attending to the needs of their children who were working on a difficult task. Salt Lake City mothers, on the contrary, were more likely to interrupt their conversations in order to respond to their children's bids for assistance and attention. In addition to differences in the way mothers from these two cultures preferred to distribute attention, toddlers had adopted different strategies for seeking attention (Verhoef et al., in prep.). Whereas Salt Lake City toddlers repeatedly tried to fully occupy their mothers' attentional resources, Efe children rarely competed for their mothers' exclusive attention. Rather, they employed non-disruptive methods to make their needs and desires known, doing so without drawing attention exclusively to themselves and without overtaking the conversation. Often, these children tried to gain attention through nonverbal means and without disrupting the adult conversation.

A cultural community's normative style of attention management is acquired very early in life. By toddlerhood, Guatemalan Mayan children from San Pedro attended to several events simultaneously, showing the same pattern of attention as their caregivers (Chavajay & Rogoff, 1999; Rogoff et al., 1993). For example, they worked with their caregiver on a task while monitoring another ongoing conversation. The skill with which these 12- to 24-month-olds attended simultaneously to several events is remarkable (Rogoff et al., 1993). In comparison, Euro-American toddlers from Salt Lake City were less likely to attend to several events simultaneously. In general, they focused on one event at a time by alternating attention between two. Their pattern of exclusive or alternating attention was also compatible with that of their caregivers who showed a comparable pattern of deploying attention. It is unlikely that cultural differences in the deployment of attention signify differences in the ability to attend simultaneously to several events. Nor does it seem likely that the differences are a reflection of current family circumstances, such as the presence of a sibling or the prevalence of competing events (Chavajay & Rogoff, 1999). It has been argued (LeVine, 1980) that cultural patterns of managing attention are reflections of family circumstances, such as large family size, that evolved over time and are thus considered to reflect historical rather than immediate characteristics of family structure.

Children reared with co-occurring attention seldom experience being the center of attention, but they are never alone. The cultural practice of co-occurring care during day and night (co-sleeping) fosters a sense of closeness that is a strong contributor to the formation of strong and loyal family bonds. Within these bonds, every member accepts the place that has been assigned to him or her by tradition (Nsamenang & Lamb, 1994, for the Cameroonian Nso; Greenfield, 1999, for Zinacantecan Mayan; Rabinovich, 1998, for Brazilians; Rothbaum, Pott, Azuma, Miyake, & Weisz, 2000, and Rothbaum, Weisz, Pott, Miyake, & Morelli, 2000, for Japanese). The shared attention strategy entails expectations that children learn from a very early age to integrate themselves within their surrounding relational network. The fact that caregivers do not respond to children's bids by attending to them exclusively serves also to convey information with respect to status and differences between those of adults and children. These imply that the importance of children's requests is subordinate to those of adults (Verhoef et al., in prep.). Through emphasis on respect for and obedience to elders children learn that they are co-agents in a community. Shared attention appears also to be related to sharing of other resources. Cultural communities that apply the shared attention pattern mostly emphasize give-and-take routines as efforts to stay socially connected (Verhoef et al., in prep.). Furthermore, sharing is an important strategy to ensure economic survival in environments of scarce resources. Evidence suggests that mothers from cultural contexts such as these expect their children to learn to share at an earlier age than mothers of (Western) middle-class families (see Figures 20.2a and 20.2b). Whereas middle-class mothers from Berlin expected sharing to be evident by approximately 2 years of age, Nso mothers expected that by the age of approximately 1 year or even less, children should be able to share objects and food with others. These maternal expectations of children are also reflected in children's actual behavior. When we (Keller, Borke, Yovsi, & Kleis, in prep.) tested 19-month-old toddlers' sharing behavior by giving them an attractive snack we found, as expected, that rural Cameroonian Nso toddlers were more likely to share spontaneously than their German counterparts from Berlin, although many Nso mothers immediately requested sharing so that the children had no chance to share spontaneously. Moreover, all children who did not share on their own were asked to share, and even on demand, only two-thirds of the German toddlers shared whereas nearly all Nso toddlers complied.

When a child is awarded exclusive attention it encourages the development of the sense of being a distinct individual and a unique agent. Children who find that

(a)

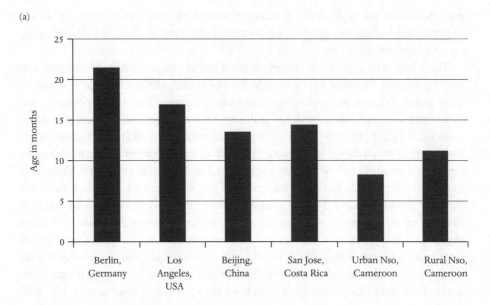

(b)

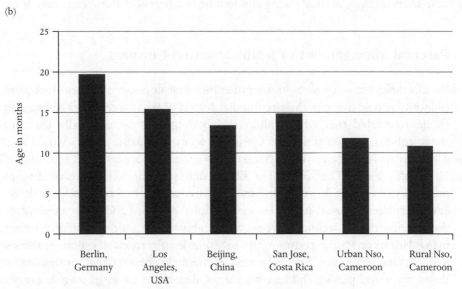

Figure 20.2 Mothers' expectations with respect to the age children are able to share (a) objects and (b) food

adults comply with their requests for exclusive attention by attending to them and interrupting an ongoing activity, such as adult conversation, learn that their presence deserves exclusive adult recognition (Verhoef et al., in prep.). Events of this nature also convey information about children's status. In Verhoef and colleagues' research, toddlers from Salt Lake City often appeared to make bids for the sole purpose of drawing attention to themselves and accentuating their presence in the social situation, behavior that may be interpreted as an outgrowth of maternal behaviors which had conveyed the importance of distinguishing oneself from others in social situations.

These different caregiving strategies with respect to attention distribution and sharing suggest different types of influences on the development of jealousy in infants and toddlers. It can be expected that a focus on sharing of attention and other resources will not encourage jealousy. This assumption may seem counter-intuitive in light of the evolutionary disposition of jealousy. If jealousy is a strategy that is aimed at maximizing resource acquisition, the experience of lesser access to key shared resources should lead to intensified jealousy. However, it appears that the discrepancy with formerly experienced exclusive attention rather than the absolute amount received is the critical element in the development of jealousy. Perhaps by heightening expectancies of receiving exclusive attention, extensive experience of exclusivity makes its loss all the more threatening and, thus, precipitates more jealousy. Although, so far, there is no empirical evidence for this notion it has been upheld by ethnographic descriptions and reports about parental eth-notheories. With this possibility in mind, we turn to considering parents' handling of nascent jealousy in their young children from different cultural communities.

Parental Management of Jealousy across Cultures

Parents differ across cultures in their tolerance of jealousy. A comparison of Sami (minority people living in the circumpolar region of Scandinavia) and Norwegian children revealed that while children in both groups were equally likely to show jealousy when a sibling or friend got a new toy, Sami parents would stop such displays significantly more often than Norwegian parents (Javo, Ronning, & Heyerdahl, 2004). The birth of a sibling and weaning as a consequence of pregnancy or childbirth are among the most frequently cited reasons for jealousy among children across cultures. However, adults' reactions and understanding for the weaned child's feelings differs considerably across cultures. Reports from many African or Pacific communities reveal little tolerance for jealous reactions (e.g., LeVine & LeVine, 1963; Maretzki & Maretzki, 1963). Gusii mothers from Kenya train and punish children who show dependent or aggressive behaviors upon the birth of a sibling (LeVine & LeVine, 1963). Although displaced children often do not easily accept the decrease in maternal attention and display disturbances, the crying of an older child while his or her mother is holding or carrying a newborn baby is interpreted by the Gusii as murderous jealousy ("okoema"), i.e., crying that is believed to mean that the older child wishes the death of the younger sibling (LeVine & LeVine, 1963). In many cases, bitterly crying older children are beaten because such aggressive intentions are condemned.

Taira toddlers from the Pacific island of Okinawa also do not give up the indulgences of infancy without stormy protests (Maretzki & Maretzki, 1963).

Weaning from the breast and from the back, which often occur at the same time, frequently result in temper tantrums and incessant whining. Nevertheless, despite the short interval between weaning and a sibling's arrival, aggression toward a newborn sibling is almost unheard of among Taira children (Maretzki & Maretzki, 1963). If at all, hostility is expressed toward the mother. Prosocial behavior toward the newborn may be attributable to early role training in which 2-year-olds are encouraged to imitate older boys and girls, especially in their roles as caregivers. Dolls made of rolled blankets or jackets are strapped on the toddlers' backs, and they receive praise for being such fine caregivers. In addition to such benefits along with the new status of being an older brother or sister, the transition is softened by support and nurturance that is provided by other family members, particularly grandmothers and older siblings who continue to indulge and comfort the child (Maretzki & Maretzki, 1963). It is interesting that, unlike the Gusii, Taira children are allowed to express jealousy, at least in terms of aggression against the mother, and grandmothers even encourage such behavior.

Middle-class families deal with the birth of a sibling and upcoming jealousy in an entirely different way. They consider jealousy an inescapable concomitant phenomenon and natural component of sibling relationships. Children are not punished consistently for expressing jealousy, and parents tend to feel ambivalent because they do not want to neglect the needs of an older sibling or appear to show favoritism toward one child over another. Therefore, Euro-American parents try to avoid situations in which one sibling receives more parental attention than another (Fischer & Fischer, 1963). Although there is much sympathy for feelings of jealousy, its expression, particularly in terms of aggressive behavior, is considered undesirable. Therefore, sibling rivalry has historically been the most studied aspect of sibling relationships (Dunn, 1993) and there is a large market for popular literature and guidebooks.

Jealousy is present as a topic in parenting ideas and beliefs. In one of our studies assessing parenting ethnotheories about early infant care, many mothers spontaneously raised the issue of jealousy even though we did not specifically ask for it. Some expressed their ideas about reasons for jealousy or strategies for its prevention much as the 32-year-old mother of two children from New Delhi who describes her older daughter,

> She is very, very fond of her younger brother, which I feel is because we have brought her up in such a loving manner and she is equally loving with her sibling, which I feel that lots of my friends are having problems of sibling rivalry and all that stuff. Fortunately it doesn't exist in my house. So I feel that if you give a lot of love to your child the child will grow up to be a much more secure individual rather than being someone who is always sort of lost and all.

Another New Delhi mother (37 years old) of two children emphasized the nature of sibling interactions which help reduce jealousy,

... one to develop a bond between them and also for the older sibling because most of the times it is the older sibling who has a problem more than the younger one. So it's important that they are in contact and the older sibling is very much in tune with the younger one and keeps in touch with the younger one and not as in don't touch because then the older one gets a little insecure so if the older sibling is more active in the interaction with the younger child then it is good for both.

As in the Taira practice of early role training, New Delhi mothers feel that jealousy is inhibited by the involvement of an older child in care activities with the infant. The strategy is elaborated by a 27-year-old mother of a 3-month-old daughter,

The elder one is also getting involved in whatever you are doing with the little one so that he also feels a part of the new child, that is in case of the babies who are second. Like in our case, this is my first baby but this is very important because I have mostly heard and seen in my sister's family. Mumma always says that it is very important to keep the first one involved in every activity of the baby even if you are giving a shower to the baby. So you should take the elder one also along that come we will give him a shower. So that he doesn't feel neglected in any way. He is as welcoming as the younger one. So he should also like we are welcoming the younger one, he should not develop any kind of jealousy that we are giving more importance to the younger one because any ways the parents will have to take care of the little one more but in the same case if they are trying to involve the elder one also it will also have a better bonding with the brother also, the brother, sister or whatever.

The same mother continues by considering the benefits to the younger child,

He will also know that he is also a part of my family. There is not just mom and dad and grandmom and grandpa but there is someone of my age also. One or two years older, my brother or my sister who play with me. I have seen children are more comfortable with children.

The interview excerpts from the Delhi mothers maintain the attitude that jealousy is something that has to be averted because it disturbs social harmony, which is considered very important, especially in extended families. Western middle-class mothers also do not want jealousy among their children. They too strive for the ideal of having siblings that are intimate friends. However, the relationship is seen more as a free choice. A 40-year-old mother of three children from Berlin explains vividly,

But I think, when I allow her (the older sister) to decide on her own, she won't come to the point of petty jealousy at all. That would probably arise, when I would say: "No, you are not allowed to do that" or "you have to do that". Yes.

In her further elaborations it becomes clear that she thoroughly cares about fulfilling the individual needs of each child and is very interested in avoiding any animosity of one child against the other. Yet, the relationship between the siblings is not mentioned at all.

> The baby is carried in the sling almost the whole day. That means, I can undertake a lot with Anna all the same. Sure, she has to accept constraints sometimes. I am not able to run or bike with her as before. But at least, I'm always engaged with her. And the baby, he does not miss out anyway, because he is hanging on me anyway. So, nevertheless he has his body contact, even though I actually do more with Anna.

This interview excerpt also highlights the inner conflict of the mother who tries to achieve the unachievable standard of providing one hundred percent attention for both children. This marks an interesting difference in the focus of managing changes in the distribution of attention. Whereas the children of the rural communities are left alone or with little assistance in coping with the loss of maternal attention after the birth of a sibling, middle-class mothers from New Delhi help their firstborns adapt to the new family situation while mothers from Berlin take the full responsibility and perceive it as their duty to minimize the decrease in attention to an older child despite the additional requirements of the new baby.

Conclusion: Cultural Models of Socialization

In summary, in spite of the evolutionary basis of jealousy the reported findings suggest substantial differences across cultures. Cultural communities differ in their attention management strategies, and these, we believe, may be associated with the development of jealousy, as well as the management of situations that evoke jealous responses. Attentional patterns vary between the extremes of exclusive dyadic attention and shared attention as well as any combinations or shifts between these strategies. The interpretation of jealous behavior and tolerance toward jealous responses also vary tremendously between cultural communities, with empathic understanding on the one hand and rigorous punishment on the other.

These differences are by no means arbitrary. Rather than varying randomly across contexts or locations, these differences are related to cultural models in a systematic manner and can be regarded as expressions of these cultural models. In this section, we briefly consider these cultural models. We differentiate between two prototypical cultural models that are defined by specific eco-cultural conditions that are associated with different conceptions of the self (Keller, 2007b). It is important to mention here that we do not address countries or societies as units of cultural and cross-cultural analysis, but rather our basis for comparison focuses on particular sociocultural environments of communities within societies.

The goal of achieving social harmony and accordingly, the suppression of jealousy, is associated with an interdependent cultural model. The interdependent model is typically represented by the eco-cultural context of the traditional village community. This context is characterized by a dense social network with person-to-person interactions as the familiar mode of social exchange. The economy is usually subsistence-based and formal education is basic, if available at all. Strict age and gender hierarchies influence the way of living together in extended families and clans. Reproduction starts early and having many children is the cultural norm. Children are of high value to the family in terms of psycho-logical as well as economic perspectives (Kagitçibasi, 1996). The interdependent self (Kagitçibasi, 1996; Keller, 2003b; Markus & Kitayama, 1991) pertains to a self-construal within which the individual is defined as part of a social system (mainly the family). An individual's role within the social environment provides the basis for establishing identity. Harmonious relationships, cooperation, and conformity are highly valued. The interdependent self-construal emphasizes perceptions of an individual as an interrelated co-agent with others who is fluidly defined depending on the social context (Keller, 2003a).

The independent model is typically represented in the eco-cultural context of highly industrialized or post-industrialized Western societies (Keller, 2003a). Large-scale social life is characterized by anonymity. The economy is based on money and income varies substantially on individual levels. Personal achievement influences lifestyle. The level of formal education is usually high. Reproduction starts late and only a few children are born to a family; parental investment is more individualized (Keller, 2003a; Belsky, Steinberg, & Draper, 1991). Children are of high psychological but not economic value to parents (Kagitçibasi, 1996). The independent self (Kagitçibasi, 1996; Markus & Kitayama, 1991) refers to a self-construal that is conceptualized on the assumption of an independent (or individualistic, autonomous) individual. Such an individual is considered self-contained, competitive, separate, unique, assertive, and self-reliant (Markus & Kitayama, 1994). Self-enhancement, self-expression, and self-maximization are highly emphasized. The self is defined by means of personal traits that are timeless and do not change across situations (Keller, 2007b).

These two environments and their respective associated cultural models form prototypes that should be considered as extreme patterns from which many varieties may arise. Proposing these two prototypes, we do not pursue a one-dimensional conception. Rather, independence and interdependence are built on two separate dimensions, which are agency (with the poles autonomy and heteronomy) and interpersonal distance (with poles of relatedness and separate-ness) (Kagitçibasi, 2005). According to Kagitçibasi (2005), interdependence is defined as embodying heteronomy and relatedness. Heteronomy means being governed from the outside or depending on another person for action. Related-ness refers to including others within the boundaries of the self. Thus, the relationship with others becomes the central feature of the self-concept (Keller,

2007b). Independence, on the other hand, is characterized by autonomy and separateness (Kagitçibasi, 2005). The self as an autonomous entity does not depend on others (Markus & Kitayama, 1991). In applying these prototypes we do not mean to simplify the world's complexity along any dichotomy. It is important to keep in mind that there are infinite combinations along the dimensions of agency and interpersonal distance that generate great variety on cultural as well as individual levels.

The social world of infants differs substantially according to the eco-cultural environment. Since parents and other caregivers all over the world try to socialize their children in a way that allows them to successfully manage adult life in their respective cultural communities (LeVine, 1980), these prototypes also differ with respect to parenting models. Infants in prototypically interdependent communities experience multiple care arrangements. Mostly in extended households, they are surrounded by several members of the family and are never alone. Infants in prototypically independent families, in contrast, spend most of the time during the first months of their life exclusively with the mother and also spend a remarkable amount of time alone. Using the method of spot observations, we found that German middle-class infants spent about 40% of their day time without anyone within viewing distance (Keller, Abels, et al., 2005). In comparison, we found that infants born in a rural Cameroonian Nso community or a rural community in Gujarat, India experienced being alone less than 10% of the daytime. These rural infants were usually in close physical proximity to their caregivers. Nso infants, for example, experienced body contact more than 80% of their waking time (Keller, Völker, et al., 2005). Therefore, the parenting style of rural communities has been described as proximal, and characterized by focus on primary care, body contact, and body stimulation (Keller, 2007b). The parenting style that is typical in urban middle-class contexts has been identified as distal parenting. This style emphasizes object stimulation, face-to-face interaction, and vocal interaction. These parenting behaviors are related to different patterns of attention, which were discussed previously in some detail. Evidently, body contact or nursing allows the caregiver to attend to other persons or other activities, while active engagement in verbal or vocal exchange or eye contact requires full attention.

These parenting styles also differ immensely in terms of the importance that is attached to emotion. Whereas parents' proximal behaviors are aimed at minimizing or preventing negative affect, distal parenting tends to elicit excitement, thus maximizing positive emotions. Emotions are an essential constituent of autonomous agency. To express oneself, that is, to express one's emotions, is an important characteristic of the autonomous individual. Such self-expression is facilitated from the very beginning of life. Contingent responses to infants' signals provide a basis for driving the child's sense of uniqueness and separateness. The infant learns that he or she has feelings that are independent of those of others and that their expression causes reactions in the social environment. In accord

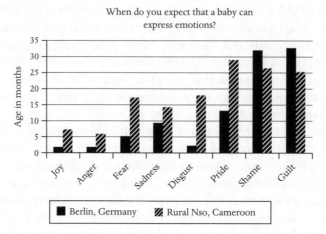

Figure 20.3   Mothers' expectations of the age at which children express emotions

with this early training, expectations about the development of emotions vary between cultural communities. When we asked rural Cameroonian Nso mothers and German middle-class mothers from Berlin at what age they expected infants to express various emotions (Keller, Lamm, Abels, & Yovsi, in prep.), we found that German mothers expected basic emotions to be expressed at significantly earlier ages. (See Figure 20.3.) The same was true for the complex emotion of pride, which is closely related to valuing self-enhancement. Interestingly, the reverse picture, in which earlier expectations were held by rural Cameroonian mothers, applied to the expressions of shame and guilt. These emotions pertain heavily to interpersonal relations and status, and are thus more deeply valued in this interdependent community.

The expression of emotion for the purpose of self-expression is not encouraged, actually not tolerated, in traditional rural communities. Especially the expression of negative feelings is considered inappropriate. Cameroonian Nso infants are trained not to show negative emotions (Otto, 2008). When Otto observed Nso toddlers' behaviors while being approached by a stranger, only one-third of the children showed any emotions in this situation that is known to activate the attachment system and is expected to provoke fear. The Nso mothers viewed this behavior very positively. In the same vein, LeVine and LeVine (1963) described the opinion of Gusii mothers from Nyansongo in Kenya:

> Nothing annoys a Nyansongo mother more than a child who cries "for nothing," that is, a child who cries when he does not want food and has not been hurt. (LeVine & LeVine, 1963, p. 153)

In this context, emotions, especially negative emotions, are interpreted as signals rather than expressions of mental states. The crying of an infant serves to signal the mother that health and survival of the infant are at risk and mothers are expected to respond immediately. This rapid soothing strategy contributes to reduced caloric expenditure because crying is minimized (LeVine et al., 1994). Furthermore, this strategy is a first step toward raising an acquiescent child that acquires respect and obedience. Already the infant is seen as a participant in the domestic hierarchy and is required to integrate the self within the community without trouble (LeVine et al., 1994).

In this chapter we have attempted to demonstrate that jealousy is an evolved emotion and belongs to the pan-human behavioral repertoire. However, an evolutionary origin by no means implies that the behavioral expression is the same across different contexts. We have partly equated context with culture, since sociodemographic characteristics are strongly related to shared ideas about autonomy and relatedness, and their respective interplay. Cultural models inform parental socialization goals, which frame their ethnotheories and finally fine-tune the behavioral contexts and interactional strategies. We have described two consistent patterns associated with two extremely different cultural models, the model of independence and the model of interdependence.

Finally, we would like to share some ideas for future research. First of all, we recognize that there are numerous facets of society that contribute to differences between cultures. These as well as varying quantities and qualities of different combinations of autonomy and relatedness need to be addressed in future research on jealousy and culture. It would be especially interesting to verify the proposed relation between parental attentional patterns and the development of jealousy. Longitudinal observations of different cultural communities could help confirm our hypothesis that exclusivity fosters jealousy. Another potential area of further research could be gender differences. Our studies did not reveal any differential socialization strategies for boys and girls. However, this could have resulted from the types of cultural communities or age ranges that we studied. Finally, in order to tease apart the separate influences of cultural heritage and socioeconomic status on parenting and development, future research needs to explore samples who have similar cultural backgrounds but different socioeconomic status. Investigative attention to this issue is of particular importance in view of rapid changes that are taking place in numerous village societies and increasing rates of migration. We hope that this chapter has contributed to awareness of development as a cultural solution of universal tasks and will spark research on the development of jealousy from cross-cultural perspectives.

References

Abels, M., Keller, H., Mohite, P., Mankodi, H., Shastri, J., Bhargava, S., Jasrai, S., & Lakhani, A. (2005). Early socialization contexts and social experiences of infants in rural and urban Gujarat, India. *Journal of Cross-Cultural Psychology, 36*, 717–738.

Ainsworth, M. D. S., Blehar, M. C., Waters, E., & Wall, S. (1978). *Patterns of attachment: A psychological study of the strange situation*. Hillsdale, NJ: Erlbaum.

Alexander, R. D. (1979). *Darwinism and human affairs*. Seattle, WA: University of Washington Press.

Bandura, A. (1986). *Social foundations of thought and action: A social cognitive theory*. Englewood Cliffs, NJ: Prentice-Hall.

Belsky, J., Steinberg, L., & Draper, P. (1991). Childhood experience, interpersonal development, and reproductive strategy: An evolutionary theory of socialization. *Child Development, 62*, 647–670.

Bjorklund, D. F., & Pellegrini, A. D. (2002). *The origins of human nature: Evolutionary developmental psychology*. Washington, DC: American Psychological Association.

Brazelton, T. B., Robey, J. S., & Collier, G. (1969). Infant development in the Zinacanteco Indians of Southern Mexico. *Pediatrics, 44*, 274–283.

Chavajay, P., & Rogoff, B. (1999). Cultural variation in management of attention by children and their caregivers. *Developmental Psychology, 35*, 1079–1090.

Clancy, B., Darlington, R. B., & Finlay, B. L. (2001). Translating developmental time across mammalian species. *Neuroscience, 105*, 7–17.

Crago, M. B. (1992). Communicative interaction and second language acquisition: An Inuit example. *TESOL Q, 26*, 487–505.

Dawkins, R. (1976). *The selfish gene*. New York: Oxford University Press.

Draghi-Lorenz, R. (2000). *Five-month-old infants can be jealous: Against cognitivist solipsism*. Paper presented in a symposium convened for the XIIth Biennial International Conference on Infant Studies (ICIS), 16–19 July, Brighton, UK.

Dunn, J. (1993). *Young children's close relationships: Beyond attachment*. Newbury Park, CA: Sage.

Eibl-Eibesfeldt, I. (1979). Human ethology concepts and implications for the sciences of man. *Behavioral and Brain Sciences, 2*, 1–57.

Ekman, P. (1973). Cross-cultural studies of facial expression. In P. Ekman (Ed.), *Darwin and facial expression* (pp. 169–222). New York: Academic Press.

Ellsworth, P. C. (1994). Sense, culture, and sensibility. In S. Kitayama & H. R. Markus (Eds.), *Emotion and culture: Empirical studies of mutual influence* (pp. 23–50). Washington, DC: American Psychological Association.

Fischer, J. L., & Fischer, A. (1963). The New Englanders of Orchard Town, U.S.A. In: B. B. Whiting (Ed.), *Six cultures: Studies of child rearing* (pp. 869–1010). New York: John Wiley and Sons.

Gratier, M. (2003). Expressive timing and interactional synchrony between mothers and infants: Cultural similarities, cultural differences, and the immigration experience. *Cognitive Development, 18*, 533–554.

Greenfield, P. M. (1997). Culture as process: Empirical methods for cultural psychology. In J. W. Berry, Y. H. Poortinga, & J. Pandey (Eds.), *Handbook of cross-cultural psychology: Vol. 1. Theory and method* (2nd ed., pp. 301–346). Needham Heights, MA: Allyn & Bacon.

Greenfield, P. M. (1999). Historical change and cognitive change: A two-decade follow-up study in Zinacantecan, a Maya community in Chiapas, Mexico. *Mind, Culture, and Activity, 6*, 92–108.

Greenfield, P. M. (2002). The mutual definition of culture and biology in development. In H. Keller, Y. H. Poortinga, & A. Schölmerich (Eds.), *Between culture and biology* (pp. 57–76). London: Cambridge University Press.

Greenfield, P. M., & Childs, C. P. (1991). Developmental continuity in biocultural context. In R. Cohen & A. W. Siegel (Eds.), *Context and development* (pp. 135–159). Hillsdale, NJ: Erlbaum.

Hart, S., & Carrington, H. (2002). Jealousy in 6-month-old infants. *Infancy, 3,* 395–402.

Hart, S. L., Carrington, H. A., Tronick, E. Z., & Carroll, S. R. (2004). When infants lose exclusive maternal attention: Is it jealousy? *Infancy, 6,* 57–78.

Hart, S., Field, T., del Valle, C., & Letourneau, M. (1998). Infants protest their mothers' attending to an infant-size doll. *Social Development, 7,* 54–61.

Hrdy, S. B. (1999). *Mother nature: A history of mothers, infants, and natural selection.* New York: Pantheon books.

Hupka, R. B. (1981). Cultural determinants of jealousy. *Alternative Lifestyles, 4,* 310–356.

Hupka, R. B. (1991). The motive for the arousal of romantic jealousy: Its cultural origin. In P. Salovey (Ed.), *The psychology of jealousy and envy* (pp. 252–270). New York: Guilford Press.

Javo, C., Ronning, J. A., & Heyerdahl, S. (2004). Child-rearing in an indigenous Sami population in Norway: A cross-cultural comparison of parental attitudes and expectations. *Scandinavian Journal of Psychology, 45,* 67–78.

Kagitçibasi, C. (1996). *Family and human development across cultures: A view from the other side.* Mahwah, NJ: Erlbaum.

Kagitçibasi, C. (2005). Autonomy and relatedness in cultural context: Implications for self and family. *Journal of Cross-Cultural Psychology, 36,* 403–422.

Kajikawa, S., Amano, S., & Kondo, T. (2004). Speech overlap in Japanese mother–child conversations. *Journal of Child Language, 31,* 215–230.

Kaufmann-Hayoz, R., & van Leeuwen, L. (1997). Entwicklung der Wahrnehmung [Perceptual development]. In H. Keller (Ed.), *Handbuch der Kleinkindforschung* [Handbook of infancy research] (2nd ed., pp. 483–507). Bern: Huber.

Keller, H. (2002). Development as the interface between biology and culture: A conceptualization of early ontogenetic experiences. In H. Keller, Y. H. Poortinga, & A. Schölmerich (Eds.), *Between culture and biology* (pp. 215–240). London: Cambridge University Press.

Keller, H. (2003a). Socialization for competence: Cultural models of infancy. *Human Development, 46,* 288–311.

Keller, H. (2003b). Ontogeny as the interface between biology and culture: Evolutionary considerations. In T. S. Saraswathi (Ed.), *Cross-cultural perspectives in human development: Theory, research and applications* (pp. 102–127). New Delhi, India: Sage.

Keller, H. (2007a). Die soziokulturelle Konstruktion impliziten Wissens in der Kindheit [The sociocultural construction of implicit knowledge during childhood]. In G. Trommsdorff & H.-J. Kornadt (Eds.), *Enzyklopädie der Psychologie, Band C/VII: Theorien und Methoden der kulturvergleichenden Psychologie* [Encyclopedia of Psychology, Vol. C/VII: Theories and methods of cultural psychology] (pp. 703–734). Göttingen: Hogrefe.

Keller, H. (2007b). *Cultures of infancy.* Hillsdale, NJ: Erlbaum.

Keller, H., Abels, M., Lamm, B., Yovsi, R. D., Voelker, S., & Lakhani, A. (2005). Ecocultural effects on early infant care: A study in Cameroon, India, and Germany. *Ethos, 33*, 512–541.

Keller, H., Borke, J., Yovsi, R. D., & Kleis, A. (in prep.). *Parenting strategies in early infancy and sharing behavior.*

Keller, H., Lamm, B., Abels, M., & Yovsi, R. D. (in prep.). *Developmental timetables concerning the expression of emotions.*

Keller, H., Lamm, B., Abels, M., Yovsi, R. D., Borke, J., Jensen, H., Papaligoura, Z., Holub, C., Lo, W., Tomiyama, A. J., Su, Y., Wang, Y., & Chaudhary, N. (2006). Cultural models, socialization goals, and parenting ethnotheories. A multi-cultural analysis. *Journal of Cross-Cultural Psychology, 37*, 155–172.

Keller, H., Otto, H., Lamm, B., Yovsi, R. D., & Kärtner, J. (2008). The timing of verbal/vocal communications between mothers and their infants: A longitudinal cross-cultural comparison. *Infant Behavior and Development, 31*, 217–226.

Keller, H., Völker, S., & Yovsi, R. D. (2005). Conceptions of parenting in different cultural communities: The case of West African Nso and Northern German women. *Social Development, 14*, 158–180.

Lamm, B. (2008). *Children's ideas about infant care: A comparison of rural Nso children from Cameroon and German middle class children.* Doctoral dissertation, University of Osnabrück. http://elib.ub.uni-osnabrueck.de/publications/diss/E-Diss808_thesis.pdf

Levenson, R. W., Ekman, P., Heider, K., & Friesen, W. V. (1992). Emotion and autonomic nervous system activity in the Minangkabau of West Sumatra. *Journal of Personality and Social Psychology, 62*, 972–988.

LeVine, R. A. (1980). A cross-cultural perspective on parenting. In M. D. Fantini & R. Cardenas (Eds.), *Parenting in a multicultural society* (pp. 17–26). New York: Longman.

LeVine, R. A., Dixon, S., LeVine, S., Richman, A., Leiderman, P. H., Keefer, C. H., & Brazelton, T. B. (1994). *Child care and culture: Lessons from Africa.* Cambridge: Cambridge University Press.

LeVine, R. A. & LeVine, B. B. (1963). Nyansongo: A Gusii community in Kenya. In: B. B. Whiting (Ed.), *Six cultures: Studies of child rearing* (pp. 15–202). New York: John Wiley and Sons.

Malatesta, C. Z., & Haviland, J. M. (1982). Learning display rules: The socialization of emotion expression in infancy. *Child Development, 53*, 991–1003.

Maretzki, T. W., & Maretzki, H. (1963). Taira: An Okinawan village. In B. B. Whiting (Ed.), *Six cultures: Studies of child rearing* (pp. 363–539). New York: John Wiley and Sons.

Markus, H. R., & Kitayama, S. (1991). Culture and the self: Implications for cognition, emotion, and motivation. *Psychological Review, 98*, 224–253.

Markus, H. R., & Kitayama, S. (1994). The cultural construction of self and emotion: Implications for social behavior. In S. Kitayama & H. R. Markus (Eds.), *Emotion and culture: Empirical studies of mutual influence* (pp. 89–130). Washington, DC: American Psychological Association.

Martin, R. D. (1983). *Human brain evolution in an ecological context: Fifty-second James Arthur lecture.* New York: American Museum of Natural History.

Maynard, A. E., Greenfield, P. M., & Childs, C. P. (1999). Culture, history, biology, and body: Naive and non naive acquisition of technological skill. *Ethos, 27*, 379–402.

Meltzoff, A. N., & Moore, M. K. (1989). Imitation in newborn infants: Exploring the range of gestures imitated and the underlying mechanisms. *Developmental Psychology, 25*, 954–962.

Meltzoff, A. N., & Moore, M. K. (1994). Imitation, memory, and the representation of persons. *Infant Behavior, 17*, 83–100.

Nsamenang, A. B., & Lamb, M. E. (1994). Socialization of Nso children in the Bamenda grassfields of northwest Cameroon. In P. M. Greenfield & R. R. Cocking (Eds.), *Cross-cultural roots of minority child development* (pp. 133–146). Hillsdale, NJ: Erlbaum.

Ochs, E. (1988). *Culture and language development: Language acquisition and socialization in a Samoan village.* Cambridge: Cambridge University Press.

Otto, H. (2008). *Culture-specific attachment strategies in the Cameroonian Nso: Homogeneity and variability of a universal developmental task within an ethnic community in Africa.* Unpublished doctoral dissertation, University of Osnabrück.

Pepler, D. J., Abramovich, R., & Corter, C. (1981). Sibling interactions in the home: A longitudinal study. *Child Development, 52*, 1344–1347.

Prechtl, H. (1984). *Continuity of neural functions from prenatal to postnatal life.* London: Spastics International Medical Publications.

Rabinovich, E. P. (1998, August). *Comparative study of sleeping arrangements and breastfeeding in Brazilian children.* Paper presented at the 14th IACCP Congress, Bellingham, WA.

Rogoff, B., Mistry, J., Göncü, A. & Mosier, C. (1993). Guided participation in cultural activity by toddlers and caregivers. *Monographs of the Society for Research in Child Development, 58*(8), v-179.

Rothbaum, F., Pott, M., Azuma, H., Miyake, K., & Weisz, J. (2000). The development of close relationships in Japan and the United States: Paths of symbiotic harmony and generative tension. *Child Development, 71*, 1121–1142.

Rothbaum, F., Weisz, J., Pott, M., Miyake, K., & Morelli, G. (2000). Attachment and culture: Security in the United States and Japan. *American Psychologist, 55*, 1093–1104.

Saraswathi, T. S. (1994). Women in poverty context: Balancing economic and child care needs. In R. Borooah, K. Cloud, S. Seshadri, T. S. Saraswathi, J. T. Peterson, & A. Verma (Eds.), *Capturing complexity: An interdisciplinary look at women, households and development* (pp. 162–178). New Delhi, India: Sage.

Trivers, R. L. (1974). Parent–offspring conflict. *American Zoologist, 14*, 249–264.

Verhoef, H., Morelli, G. A., & Anderson, C. (in prep.). *"Please don't interrupt me, I'm talking": Cultural variation in toddlers' attention-seeking efforts and caregivers' responses.*

Washburn, S. L. (1960). Tools and human evolution. *Scientific American, 203*, 63–75.

21

Social Class, Competition, and Parental Jealousy in Children's Sports

Noel Dyck

Introduction

Jealousy and competition intersect in complex ways in community sport activities for children in Canada, not least among the parents of child and youth athletes. Watching from the sidelines of community sport competitions, mothers and fathers keep track not only of scores and results that reveal a child's athletic prowess (or limitations) but also forms of behavior that might be read as indicators of his or her emerging character and future social prospects. Youthful accomplishments and disappointments revealed on the fields of play can be recounted and compared in minute detail by parents, coaches, and other adults who search for "telling signs" not only of a child's current status within a team or club but also of the implications of on-field performances for "who" and "what" individual girls and boys might one day become as adults—assuming, of course, that athletic accomplishments and social deportment within sports activities can be relied upon to provide plausible bases for making such predictions.

But parents, too, in their capacities *as* parents of young athletes can become part of what is being assessed. Community sports, which operate outside the realm of school athletic programs, typically rely heavily upon parental support to sustain the existence of the ubiquitous teams, clubs, and leagues that dot the urban and suburban landscape in Canada. Fathers and mothers are expected to become more or less dutiful sponsors of and participants in the organization and sometimes even the coaching of these sports. Thus, community sports for children and youths gather together not only boys and girls, but also mothers and fathers who exhibit varying measures of enthusiasm and/or aptitude for supporting and helping out with the local team. Parents of child and youth athletes also differ in terms of their willingness to make such involvement in a son's or daughter's sports a more or less prominent and central part of their own childrearing strategies and duties.

Handbook of Jealousy: Theory, Research and Multidisciplinary Approaches, First Edition.
Edited by Sybil L. Hart and Maria Legerstee.
© 2013 Blackwell Publishing Ltd. Published 2013 by Blackwell Publishing Ltd.

Accordingly, diverse forms of athletic and social performance are enacted publicly by children, youths, parents, and other adults at the fields, pools, gymnasia, and rinks that host children's sports. Since forms of competition essential to organized sport ultimately anchor these activities, they extend countless opportunities for winning and losing, for accomplishment and disappointment, for celebration and humiliation. The potential rewards and inherent risks proffered by different forms of participation within these arenas render community sports especially apt settings within which to investigate the interplay of class, competition, and parental jealousy.

This chapter presents an ethnographic account and anthropological analysis of the dynamics of parental jealousy within community sports for children and youths in Canadian cities and suburbs.[1] The first section identifies some distinctive features of an anthropological approach to the study of emotions such as jealousy and outlines certain difficulties that ensue when childrearing and competitive sport are conjoined within the confines of community sports. The second examines the organization of community sport activities in Canada, noting different forms of participation possible within these activities and specifying their attractions. The third section investigates a set of ethnographic cases that elucidate some of the practical difficulties of reconciling and accommodating varying modes of participation in community sports and demonstrates how the inability to do so may serve to trigger jealousy among parents of young athletes. The final section summarizes the challenges posed by the interplay of competition and jealousy in children's sports.

Anthropological Approaches to Jealousy in Children's Sports

In recent decades anthropologists have displayed a growing interest in what Lutz and White (1986, p. 405) have depicted as "the emotional" within social and cultural life. An essential first step in moving beyond a traditional disciplinary reluctance to trespass into the realm of "the psychological" has been for anthropologists to acknowledge, if not resolve, underlying differences and tensions that exist between, on the one hand, universalist and positivist approaches to the conceptualization and investigation of the emotions and, on the other, relativist and interpretive approaches that tend to be preferred within anthropology. Although a comprehensive review of work conducted by anthropologists on the emotions is beyond the scope of this chapter,[2] it is important to highlight some distinctive aspects of anthropologically preferred approaches to the study of emotions in general as well as to jealousy in particular.

Reliance upon ethnography, both as a means of description and mode of analysis, along with an appreciation of the insights that may be afforded by cross-cultural comparison, comprise definitive aspects of anthropological inquiry. Ethnographically based studies characteristically seek to document and comprehend what people say and do in given social settings, paying careful attention to the manner in which stated cultural categories and expectations may not always answer for what actually transpires in social life. Specifying the arrangements and workings of social contexts and cultural systems within which everyday lives are lived remains a primary anthropological concern. In studying the emotions, therefore, the "core of the [anthropological] attempt to understand the relation between emotion and culture lies in ethnographic description of the emotional lives of persons in their social contexts" (Lutz & White, 1986, p. 427). This emphasis upon observation and contextualization dovetails with the comparative and cross-cultural aims and capacities of anthropology.[3]

Anthropologists have interpreted the concept of emotion as a master Western cultural category that rests upon assumptions that become discernible when encountered through cross-cultural comparisons. Lutz explains the approach thus:

> Exploration of the cultural schema with which any anthropological observer begins fieldwork provides a methodological key, as translating between two cultural systems requires explication of the relevant meaning systems on both sides of the cultural divide. The [Western] cultural meaning system that constitutes the concept of emotion has been invisible because we have assumed that it is possible to identify the essence of emotion, that the emotions are universal, and that they are separable from both their personal and social contexts. (Lutz 1986, p. 288)

Studies conducted by anthropologists—for instance, Dunham's (2002) account of complex and variable manifestations of love and jealousy in the "space of death" among the Herero of Botswana—often take issue with that approach and argue instead that emotions may be understood and experienced in differing ways both between and within given cultural contexts. The proposal that it might, therefore, be imperative to distinguish between emotion, defined as "private feelings that are usually not culturally motivated or socially articulated," and sentiment, defined as "socially articulated symbols and behavioral expectations," has received a mixed reception within the discipline (Lutz & White, 1986, p. 409). Yet, there remains a strong inclination among anthropologists to treat emotions as being both socially shaped and shaping.

Jealousy, according to the *Oxford English Dictionary*, designates "the quality of being jealous" which refers variously to an "anxiety for preservation or well-being of something," "vigilance in guarding a possession from loss or damage," and a "state of mind arising from the suspicion, apprehension or knowledge of rivalry" either in love or in respect of success or advantage. Although jealousy and envy are sometimes treated as being synonymous, they can and should, argues Foster (1972), be clearly distinguished from one another:

> Envy stems from the desire to acquire something possessed by another person, while jealousy is rooted in the fear of losing something already possessed. In

schematic form both emotions involve a dyad, a pair of individuals whose relationship is mediated, or structured, by an intervening property or object. The intervening object may take innumerable forms, such as wealth, a material good, the love and affection of a human being, or it may be intangible, such as fame or good reputation. The mediating property is possessed by one member of the dyad; the other member does not possess it, but wishes to. It is this desire that creates the feeling of envy in the latter person, making him what I shall call an "envier" … In contrast to envy, however, in which the emotion is directed at the other person of the dyad, jealousy is centered on the valued possession. A jealous person is not jealous of the envier; he is jealous of what he possesses, and fears he may lose. (Foster 1972, p. 168)

Within arenas of community sport neither jealousy nor envy is likely to be self-attributed or freely confessed even when rumors of the susceptibility of others to these might abound. The public display and acknowledgment of emotions remain ambivalent and complicated matters within children's sports, in no small part due to the manner in which these types of sport activities seek to combine two otherwise separate and diverging fields of social endeavor. Rearing children rests at the heart of domesticity and family life.[4] Mothers and fathers are expected to establish a family home as a private setting within which intimate responsibilities for ensuring the well-being and guiding the appropriate socialization of infant, child, and adolescent sons and daughters can be undertaken. In contrast, sport typically occupies and resides within public venues. Sport entails diverse forms of rule-governed physical and athletic performance that are performed not merely for the personal satisfaction of athletes but also for the enjoyment of spectators or fans who need not be personally connected or known to the athletes. Indeed, the anticipated presence of an audience comprises an essential factor in the social construction of selected physical activities and informal games into organized sports (Dyck, 2000a, p. 29).

Concerns about the appropriate management and display of emotions that surface within community sports provide a vantage point from which to trace certain complications that result from connecting childrearing to competitive sports. Family life is commonly taken as the primary locus within which children are supposed to receive the loving care, guidance, and security needed for them to develop their emotions and to learn how to manage and express these in healthy ways. Although some degree of tolerance and patience with youthful misbehavior or inappropriate and untimely displays of emotions might be held out in various extra-domestic settings, nonetheless, boys and girls who are deemed to be unduly fearful, angry, envious, or jealous in behavior are regarded as requiring further emotional care and attention either from their parents or, if mother and/or father are unwilling or unable to do so, from others. Children who appear to fit relatively easily into formally or informally organized activities outside the immediate bounds of family life are judged to have developed (or to be developing) an ability to get along with others, a capacity especially valued in sport activities organized by adults for children. Suitably behaved children, in turn, imply conscientious and effective parenting.

But the enrolment of sons and daughters in community sport activities involves them not merely spending time more or less companionably (or at least peaceably) with other children, coaches, and officials but doing so while engaging in one or another form of competitive contest. Calibrated to distinguish the athletically proficient, the more determined, the better coached, or simply the more fortunate of competitors from others, organized sports relentlessly function to register wins, losses, ties, records, championships, triumphs, and failures. Competition is meant to be taken seriously; athletes are enjoined to do their very best to win or at least to improve their competitive performances and standing. The prospects of perennially losing in athletic contests or, even worse, of not particularly minding doing so are deeply problematic within organized sport.[5] Athletes, whatever their age, are expected to care about their performances and to commit themselves to improving these in whatever ways they can. Indeed, Canadian children are regularly implored to "show some emotion" when participating in sports. Giving vent to anger over the outcome of a game or race, an off-target shot at net, or an unsuccessful at-bat may not only be tolerated by many adults but may even become preferred behaviors that are seen as testifying to an athlete's desire and personal commitment to win. The cultivation and tactical manipulation of emotion is a longstanding preoccupation within competitive sport that is pursued in various ways at different levels. This includes community sports where children may become members of teams and clubs even before they enter elementary school.

In an ideal world, childrearing and organized sports for children might be engineered in ways that sustain a nuanced and balanced reconciliation of the principal objectives of both spheres. Within this scenario, parents would prepare their daughters and sons to become socially adept, emotionally adroit, and highly "coachable" individuals. For their part, coaches and other officials would endorse and observe the values and objectives of parents while augmenting the physical and athletic capabilities and competitive spirit possessed by boys and girls under their charge. Yet no matter how often parents and coaches might declare their commitment to fostering one or another rendering of this preferred state of affairs, the taken-for-granted priorities and purposes that they fall back upon when participating in community sports for children are not always compatible and thus collide in sometimes pivotal ways. Resulting frustrations and conflicts tend to inflate the currency of stereotypical claims about the motivations of particular "types" of parents and/or coaches who are implicitly held responsible for such outcomes.[6] But clichés can't explain the complex ways in which relatively inconspicuous yet tangible forms of jealousy contribute to these consequences. To grasp these matters it is necessary to specify both the types of factors that so powerfully attract parents and coaches to children's sports as well as certain underlying social dynamics that can threaten their enjoyment of these activities.

The Attractions of Community Sport

Community sports constitute familiar features of urban, suburban, and small-town life in Canada. When asked to identify the enticements that promote participation in community sports, Canadians normally draw from a predictable list. Thus, sport is said variously to offer fun and excitement, to develop athletic skills, to increase physical fitness, to build self-esteem, and to afford opportunities for making new friends, winning awards, or pursuing an athletic scholarship or even a career as a professional athlete (Dyck, 2000b, pp. 141–142). So widely propagated are these claims that even those with little or no interest, let alone experience, in sports can, if pressed to do so, ordinarily recite at least one or another of these alleged charms. That being the case, one must look beyond the promotional rhetoric of sport to appreciate why, though some individuals and families who venture into community sports drop out even before the end of their first full season of participation, others opt to remain involved for many years. What types of experiences and outcomes prompt some individuals and families to invest themselves personally in community sport and to make this a continuing aspect of their lives?

Viewed as sets of patterned activities that generate roughly standardized types of roles and relationships, community sports for children and youths possess certain salient properties. To begin with, these are voluntary activities; participation is not compulsory and, indeed, may not in practice be accessible to everyone who might wish to play a given sport or belong to a particular club or team. Community sports also depend significantly upon unpaid volunteers to perform many, and sometimes all, of the requisite tasks of arranging, scheduling, coaching, and refereeing the games, meets, and tournaments that make up competitive sports.[7] For the want of volunteers who are more or less willing and able to attend to these and other chores, community sport organizations would—and sometimes do—cease to exist. The organizational demands and coaching duties that must be seen to, week in and week out, season after season, in order to build and maintain sport teams, clubs, and leagues make the recruiting and retention of adult volunteers, as well as of child and youth athletes, vital matters.

Concomitantly, the institutional structures erected and operational procedures devised to sustain child and youth sports create myriad opportunities for those individuals who assume these volunteer positions to develop—should they care to do so—organizational "careers" within community sports. Though occupying mainly unpaid positions, officials and coaches—many of whom are parents themselves—can over time come to exercise considerable power in directing child and youth sports. Mothers and fathers who are not entirely new to the community sport scene but who have neither the time nor inclination to serve in these roles are often cautious about expressing too openly any disagreement they might have with the way a team or club is organized lest they be faced with an ultimatum along the lines of "if you don't like how this team is being coached, then coach it yourself!"

While community sports are designed to serve the needs of children and youths, the girls and boys who participate in them remain subject to adult direction and reliant upon parental support. These are not informal sports activities organized and conducted by children for children.[8] Community sports for the most part operate upon the assumption that child and youth athletes will enjoy the financial, logistical, and personal backing of their parents or, in exceptional circumstances, of other family members. Young athletes cannot readily participate in community sports without parental subsidization of fees and equipment, provision of transportation to and from sport practices and competitions, and the furnishing of other forms of support and assistance.[9] Not surprisingly, then, community sport clubs and teams reflect parental purposes and preferences. Yet since the young athletes drawn to community sports differ in terms of social class as well as other criteria, the parental objectives and inclinations that inevitably tag along when they join a club or team are neither singular in nature nor necessarily simple to accommodate.

Games, matches, and competitive events stand at the center of sport, showcasing the movements and performances that exemplify athletic endeavor. Routine plays along with sometimes-exceptional feats accomplished by individual athletes and teams remain focal matters for spectators and athletes alike. But the social behavior exhibited both on and alongside the fields of play by children, youths, and adults acting in various capacities can also be observed at close hand. Whether community sports ought to be approached strictly *as sports* and enjoyed and valued in their own right or, conversely, be treated as pliable social activities that can be harnessed to more fundamental projects of childrearing marks a basic cleavage. An ongoing tug-of-war between these two positions percolates within the operations of many community sport associations. How individuals perform socially within the ambit of community sports may be construed as being at least as important as the athletic outcomes totted up on scoreboards.

But what are the attractions of different forms of participation that one might pursue within community sports? Reasonably similar sets of activities and role repertoires exist across a broad range of sports. Athletes take part in games and competitions and dedicate themselves more or less zealously to enhancing their athletic abilities in order to attain competitive success. Coaches provide training and direction for athletes and may devote as much time and energy as they can muster to improving their teaching of skills, understanding of athletic tactics and strategy, and proficiency in managing and motivating athletes to prevail over their competitors. Referees and umpires preside over the officiating of athletic events; their knowledge of the written and unwritten rules of a sport and the finesse with which they interpret and apply these during games and meets are essential to the formal composition of competitive sports. Other sport officials register athletes and coaches, arrange the use of athletic facilities, and schedule competitive events—mundane but necessary tasks that serve to build and maintain the structures and infrastructures of sport. Parents and whoever else happens to show up to watch community sports events provide an invaluable audience whose presence helps to transform running, jumping, and throwing into athletic events.

Of course, each of these forms of involvement can be realized in various ways, thereby offering some scope for realizing personal styles and preferences. Girls and boys might join teams simply to spend time with friends playing games that are fun to play; alternately, they might wish to work towards one day competing at the Olympics. The coach of a youth soccer team might be a father or mother conscripted just before the beginning of the season so that there could be a team for his or her child to join; long after that child has stopped playing soccer, the now veteran coach might still be working to complete the higher levels of the national coach training program[10] in order to be eligible to mentor an elite youth team that represents an entire league or city in regional or national competitions. Those who agree to serve as club or league officials might approach this rather like jury duty—just taking their turn to help out for a season or two. But officials who discover that they enjoy these activities may transform this sport involvement into a veritable calling that becomes the equivalent of an unpaid second job. Spectators who attend children's sports events may spend this time chatting sociably with other onlookers or can make it their mission to provide professional-caliber cheerleading in support of "our team."

Audiences at community sports events tend to be made up largely of parents and other family members. In contrast to the social distance that separates athletes and spectators in professional sports, boys and girls who compete at the community level are not just financed, transported, and accompanied to their sports events by mom and/or dad, but may also at some point be coached by their own (or a teammate's) parent. The athletic successes or failures chalked up as well as the shows of social aplomb or immaturity evinced by young athletes are not those of distant figures but of girls and boys whose parents might well be standing or sitting along with all of the other parents on the sidelines. Whose child is who can, if this is not already known, usually be worked out easily enough. In the absence of anonymity, there is a propensity for the deeds of children and youths to be linked discursively to observed styles of parenting.

Community sports provide mothers and fathers with venues where their performances of parenting can be witnessed and validated by other parents. The responsibility that Canadian parents are increasingly expected to shoulder for the eventual outcomes of their sons and daughters as adults makes child-rearing a long-term and challenging undertaking. What is more, the efficacy of their efforts cannot be known with any certainty until their children reach adulthood. In the meantime, whether or not fathers and mothers are making the right choices and doing what will be best for their child over the long run must remain matters to be determined.

What community sports offer is a set of structured events and activities that accommodate and valorize publicly performed acts of parenting in ways that schools, for example, generally do not. By doing what parents are asked to do in community sports, mothers and fathers can tangibly demonstrate their care and concern for their child. Implicit and explicit recognition by other parents of the conscientiousness and effectiveness of one's efforts is more or less immediately forthcoming, especially when a daughter's or son's enjoyment and success in sport are plainly evident to other dads and moms who are looking on. While this might be taken as prima facie evidence of an underlying instrumentality that guides parental involvement in community sports, it should not lead us to lose sight of either the hazards and risks that parents might also encounter within these settings (which are discussed below) or the existence of other kinds of attractions.

The pleasures that sport can generate take many forms. To begin with, community sports may provide a welcome release from the everyday demands and rigors of adult employment as well as of child and youth schooling. These predictably scheduled events permit parents to allocate a certain amount of time each week to accompanying their children to recreational activities. The minutes and hours spent driving to practices, games, and tournaments may represent not only a shared journey to pleasurably anticipated occasions but also a significant proportion of the overall time that parents and children might actually spend discussing how they are and what they have been up to. "Karen",[11] a mother of two pre-teenaged boys, sums up the attractions of spending time with her sons in community sports as follows:

> It's also a way for us to spend time with them because, from what I have observed, when kids get to be teenagers—and I see it happening now with our older son—they think we're stupid and they don't want to be around us. So if they want to join track or hockey or football, we all join because we're the people [i.e., parents] that have to sell the hotdogs and line the playing field [before games]. So like it or not—and they may not like it!—we get to share some of their life where ordinarily they would turn their back ... [on us].

Once at the field, pool, or rink, girls and boys come under the supervision of coaches while fathers and mothers get to sit back and watch the action with other parents. Although parents and children remain mostly within sight of each other, they may also interact not just with their generational counterparts but also with adults who are not their parents or with girls and boys who are not their children. Thus, family members are able to spend extended periods being more or less together without being constantly on top of one another. As was explained to me by "Kate," a mother whose two children belonged to a track and field club that competed in weekend meets throughout the summer, "Our family really only happens on the weekends, at track meets."

Community sports are regularly utilized to host larger and smaller undertakings that range from the pursuit of personal dreams to family projects to enterprises that enlist the support of entire teams, clubs, or leagues. A child or youth athlete's wish to excel within a sport can be nourished, supported, and even initiated by a coach or parent. Alternately, a mother or father might wish to ensure that the competitive imperatives of sport won't be permitted to threaten a son's or daughter's satisfaction of simply being a member of a team and playing a sport as well as they can without worrying too much about winning or losing. Amateur coaches might seek to emulate the exploits and win the recognition that leading coaches and managers receive within professional sports. So too can ambitious club and league officials give free rein to previously hidden organizational and planning skills by mounting campaigns to increase the membership of a club or to pressure municipal politicians into providing more and better athletic facilities.

These and other attractions draw child and youth athletes, their parents, and other adults to ensconce themselves in varying ways and to differing degrees in the activities of community sport. The levels of gratification that such involvement can yield stretch from reasonable satisfaction to moments of intense joy to the realization of deeply held goals and dreams. Yet no matter how pleasing the prospects for and the actual experience of these may be, their attainment and continuation remain utterly contingent and dependent upon what others may seek and decide to do within these settings. In short, what parents and others involved in community sports come to love and depend upon within this sector can be threatened and perhaps even destroyed by the enthusiasms and objectives of others. The vulnerabilities that participation in community sports can expose frequently unleash acute feelings of jealousy that complicate and corrode activities and pastimes that are meant to bring health and happiness.

Inequalities and Jealousy in Community Sport

Jealousy arises when that which is particularly valued is damaged or threatened not by accident but because of the known or suspected interventions of a rival. Thus, the loss or impairment of any of the various types of attractions afforded by community sport can stoke up the anxiety, vigilance, and suspicion commonly associated with jealousy. Unlike envy, this does not stem from "the desire to acquire something possessed by another"; instead, it is rooted "in the fear of losing something already possessed" (Foster, 1972, p. 168). Because parents are well positioned to appreciate the benefits that community sports bestow upon not only their children but also themselves, mothers and fathers may be doubly susceptible to experiencing jealousy when they fear that the operations of a team or club may be shifting in ways that will negatively impact their daughter or son and, thereby, them.

To enroll one's child in a team or club is to assume that he or she will receive instruction on how to play the sport and sufficient opportunities to do so. But disputes about unequal allocation of playing time during games and competitions are endemic within community sport. This may be less of an issue on teams established to introduce young children to a sport. Coaches of novice teams who adopt a policy of providing every athlete under their charge with more or less equal playing time or opportunities to compete explain it in terms of their chosen priorities: typically, that primary consideration is to be given not to competitive results, but to "letting the kids have fun" and "letting them get to know the sport." Proceeding in this manner, at least at the outset, can serve to nurture a sense of camaraderie and "being in this together," both for children and for parents.

But some children develop proficiency in a sport more rapidly and fulsomely than do others, and sooner or later someone will question the wisdom of always providing teammates with equal amounts of playing time. When a team is not winning more games than it loses, then a coach's abilities and/or methods are especially subject to criticism, often initially expressed behind his or her back. Rationales for making changes of one sort or another begin to circulate tentatively along the sidelines. Thus, it may be contended that "always losing is no fun," that kids have to find out about the "hard facts of competition" sometime, or that it is unfair to "hold back the development of the more talented kids." Provisions implemented by leagues or sport associations for streaming or separating child and youth athletes according to their athletic abilities are intended to resolve the difficulties of allowing all kids who wish to play sport to do so while also permitting the more talented among them to enhance their skills by joining elite teams or programs. But even measures such as these cannot prevent the unequal treatment of child and youth athletes—most frequently in the form of differential amounts of "playing time"—from reemerging again and again as a divisive issue within clubs and teams, whether these are situated at elite levels or consigned to lowly "recreational" or "house" leagues that are supposed to ensure that less talented players' opportunities to play a sport will be protected from the ravages of untrammeled competition.

These issues can be illustrated with the use of two ethnographic examples. In the first, a 12-year-old girl who was the leading scorer on a championship soccer team was surreptitiously recruited by the coach of the championship team at the next highest age-level to join his squad the following season so she could improve her game by playing with and against slightly older players. Her parents, who were interested in boosting her prospects of eventually winning an athletic scholarship to a large university in the United States, agreed with this proposal, and she switched teams. Her previous coach was initially quite disappointed by her departure. Nevertheless, he moved on to design and implement a rather different style of play for his team that made better use of the talents of his remaining players. That season his team once again captured the championship in its division, largely as a result of the new tactics that showcased the abilities of several players who had previously been viewed primarily as "hard workers" who had provided a solid "supporting cast" for the erstwhile scoring star.

As it happened, the team to which she bolted recorded a "decent" season but did not repeat as division champion. Shortly after their daughter's former team won its second consecutive championship, the parents of the player in question contacted her former coach to inquire delicately about the possibility of her rejoining his team for the coming season. The parents of the girls who had "remained loyal" to the team and who had shone in the absence of the former leading scorer now contemplated the prospect that the gains their daughters had individually and collectively achieved might be undermined and devalued by the return of a player whose preferred style of play would most likely lead to a turning back of the clock for the team, both on and off the field. The impact upon team parents when the coach opted to let the prodigal star return was visceral. While the player subsequently made a sustained effort to accommodate herself to the team's new style of play, she again became the leading scorer. There was a discernible discomfort and stiffness among the familiar figures along the sidelines when her parents took up their place there at the beginning of the next season.

A second example comes from a championship match in football for 10-year-olds. To ensure that all team members would, in fact, be allowed to have an active part in this match, league rules require that every player must take the field for a minimum of 10 plays. One of the teams dressed all of its players for this prestigious final game and made certain that each of them got into the game for at least 10 plays. The opposing team, which in the end triumphed, similarly observed the formal rule. But it did so by dressing a roster of players from which 6 boys—who, though team members, were identified by those familiar with the team as being among its weakest players—were absent. When questioned about their absence, the winning head coach produced signed notes indicating that each of them was either injured or ill that day and, hence, unable to take part in the game. Parents from the losing team were furious with what they interpreted as a cynical fabrication and unsporting stratagem on the part of the opposing coaches. Some of them felt that by honoring the letter but not the spirit of the league's regulations, the opposing team had stolen their sons' chance to engage in a "fair and square" competition for the league championship. But a number of them also wondered aloud just how those 6 young boys whose contribution to the championship victory had been to be declared sick or injured might have felt about their place on the winning team. One might also wonder about how the boys' parents viewed this episode.

Complications sparked by the recognition or collision of social class differences can also compromise and erode one's enjoyment of community sport activities. Teams and clubs often draw participants from different neighborhoods and from varying income and occupational categories. In recognition of the potential sensitivity of these differences, care is often exercised informally within clubs and teams to under-communicate or simply steer clear of discussions or situations that might touch upon explicit recognition or discussion of social class, religion, or politics. Yet, considerations of social class remain pertinent, if problematic, aspects of community sports.

Evidence of concern on the part of middle-class mothers and fathers regarding the social prospects of their children and the chances of them being able to reproduce, if not surpass, their parents' class status (Fussell, 1983; Newman, 1988, 1993) is not hard to find within community sports. Thus, "Janet," an immigrant mother whose teenage son and daughter belong to a sport club that she views as being solidly middle-class in its membership, cheerfully identifies as its most attractive feature the fact that it brings together "kids who are going somewhere in their lives." In a similar vein, "Quentin," a track and field coach whose daughter had recently graduated from the club, observes that among the boys and girls he mentors, "it is not a matter of them asking each other, 'Are you going to university?' Instead, they're asking, 'Which university will you be going to?'"

But the assumption that young athletes who are seen to be developing self-discipline and an ability to set goals for themselves within sport are the types who are also most likely to be upwardly mobile in their adult lives is not the only way of interpreting middle-class styles of participation in sport. "Steve," a self-identified "working man" who stepped down from a successful "career" in coaching boys' hockey in a region that spanned both working-class and middle-class neighborhoods, explains that a large part of the frustration he had run into was caused by "kids from families with a lot of money" who came to practices or skipped them as they wished. In Steve's view, kids from families that haven't much money tend to make hockey much more of a priority in their lives. Interestingly, "Eric," a "dad coach"[12] of a girls' soccer team in an upper-middle-class neighborhood in another city, substantially corroborates this observation, albeit approaching it from a rather different perspective. Speaking about the "special challenges" of coaching a team such as his, Eric explains:

> Our kids all come from families that have money, so these kids could be doing a lot of other things besides kicking a soccer ball. Most of their folks go skiing or have cottages, so many weekends it's not easy to ensure that we have a full team.

Eric goes on to cite the affluence of children on a team such as his as a rationale for streaming soccer players into elite programs at a much earlier age than is permitted by league rules. This, he argues, would make it possible to identify and recruit the best athletes to elite soccer programs in a timely manner, thereby permitting this sport to compete more effectively with others in the drive to corral superior athletes.

Unanticipated sources of friction may be generated when taken-for-granted social practices stumble over class differences that can scuttle the best-laid plans for "getting everyone to pull together" on a team or in a club. "Lorraine," a mother whose two children clearly enjoyed taking up track and field, was dismayed to learn midway through the season that each family with a child in the club would be required to "sell" two small advertisements for the printed program that would be distributed at the club's annual meet. A member of the club's executive explained to those present at a parents' meeting that "it should be no problem to ask your lawyer or accountant to make a contribution in return for a bit of advertising." Families that neglected to "sell their ads" would, he advised, be expected to contribute the $100 advertisement charge themselves. But as Lorraine confided to one of the other parents she had befriended at the club, she didn't know any lawyers or accountants and the family's budget was already fully accounted for. She worried that this might force her kids to drop out of the club. A behind-the-scenes intervention initiated by that other parent with the club executive resulted in an unannounced exception being made in the case of Lorraine, but she and her children did not return to the club the following season.

No less awkward was the situation created when the coaches and parents of a girls' soccer team drawn from a socioeconomically mixed suburb decided that purchasing warm-up jackets in team colors (with the name and playing number of each girl on her jacket) would give a much-needed boost to team morale. To offset the cost of jackets, team parents organized a "bottle drive",[13] but the returns realized from this fundraising effort still left half the cost of each jacket to be covered individually by parents. On the prearranged afternoon when the jackets were brought to the field for distribution, one member of the team, "Sylvie," was missing. All of the parents present were reminded that they would have to pay the team manager the balance of the cost of their daughter's jacket.

When Sylvie missed also the following week's practice and game, the team manager telephoned her mother to advise her about the time and place of the next scheduled game and to remind her about the payment owing for Sylvie's as yet unclaimed team jacket. The mother replied that her daughter did not need the jacket since the family had already purchased winter-wear for her and her siblings. Since the team had accepted delivery of the jacket and could not return it, the team manager, wishing to avoid a situation in which Sylvie would be the only player without a team jacket, made an on-the-spot "executive decision" to "forget" the outstanding payment. When Sylvie appeared at the next team practice, one of the coaches took her father aside to explain that the team had never wanted the jackets to be a problem. Sylvie's father, however, insisted on paying the amount owing on the jacket. He and his wife had decided to get the jacket for their daughter "as her Christmas present." He went on to detail just how much his daughter seemed to have benefited from playing soccer that season. Sylvie's teacher had identified her as a "discipline problem" the previous year, but this year the same teacher had asked her parents what had led to the startling and positive change in her classroom deportment. Although he and his wife credited Sylvie's participation in soccer for much of the responsibility for this change, from that point on neither of them came to watch Sylvie's games.

Even when social class differences are not especially salient factors, any formal or implied recognition of disparities in the status of young athletes or of their parents within a team or a club can cause grief. Awards ceremonies are often rather tense occasions, for these oblige coaches (or whoever is called upon to determine who will receive which awards or honors) to make decisions and draw distinctions that might thrill winners but that may be seen as invidious and possibly even experienced as being injurious by those who feel themselves spurned or slighted. For instance, during the awards ceremony at the year-end banquet of a swim club, the parents seated at one table started the evening in good spirits. They had become friendly with one another over several seasons and all had made substantial contributions to the operations of the club. When the daughter of one of the couples at the table won the club award for her event specialty, hearty agreement was expressed. But when the son of another couple seated there was overlooked for an award in his event, the bonhomie that had engulfed the table began to deflate.

The disappointed father, "Brad," turned his attention directly to another parent, a father who was part of the group of coaches that had decided the awards. Brad cited the seven first-place finishes that his son had recorded that season and argued that his results were at least as impressive as those of the award winner. He turned then to his own—highly successful and well-known—efforts to raise funds on behalf of the club, the assistance that he had rendered in organizing several of the club's meets, and his wife's work as a coach who had filled in as an instructor at the novice level the previous year. It was, in Brad's view, unlikely that either he or she would play very active parts in the club in the future.

Conclusions

Jealousy is not, as noted earlier, an emotion freely confessed within the realm of community sports—unless it takes the form of an obviously jocular declaration meant to serve as a feigned compliment or ironic comment. Lacking easy access to parents' self-declarations of jealousy, not to mention candid accounts of the fears and anxieties that this emotion can fuel, anthropologists must rely upon contextualized observation and analysis of what can be seen to unfold within particular types of events and situations. The examples presented above illustrate what may be gained by looking ethnographically into matters that, although spoken of indirectly and in an intentionally guarded manner, nonetheless, warrant study in a field such as this. Fathers and mothers often take great care to frame and present as "normal" or "obvious" arrangements to which, in fact, they may as individuals have highly visceral but not fully declared or clearly articulated commitments. To note this is to underline the advantages of paying attention to the dynamics of larger and smaller disagreements, disputes, disappointments, and conflicts that unfold within community sport clubs and teams. It is within these junctures and patches of turbulence that forms of jealousy, which befall parents who accompany their children to community sports, are to be found and understood.

Community sports in Canada tend to convene socially mixed constituencies and to be conducted in settings where people who differ in various respects encounter one another at close hand and recurrently. Passionately pursued individual, family, and group objectives and styles invariably bump into the counterpart predispositions and projects of others. Social class distinctions may come into play with respect to the costs, conditions, and styles of participation that are favored. The immediate and longer-term objectives that some parents may seek to put into place in community sports for the benefit of their children do not always fit well with those of others, not to mention those of coaches or other volunteer officials. Yet the diverse forms of satisfaction and pleasure that can be sought and that are often achieved by children, youth, and adults through involvement in community sport continue to draw willing participants to this field.

Once there, however, parents, coaches, and sport officials must confront the possibility of being obliged to surrender or compromise their own values and ventures by virtue of being overwhelmed by and/or assimilated into those of others. Scenarios that sketch out such possibilities can reach far beyond that of having to put up with the personal foibles and penchants of one or another individual for an afternoon or two. The prospect of having to grit one's teeth and endure an unabating stream of assumptions, comments, and undertakings that appeal strongly to some, but not all, class tastes for an entire season is entirely another matter. In consequence, parental camaraderie and jealousy rest cheek by jowl in community sport, standing uneasily alongside one another, supporting and shaping the direction of child and youth sport activities as well as family life.

Notes

1 The data for this chapter were collected through ethnographic research conducted by the author in various urban and suburban communities in Canada since the early 1990s. See Dyck (2000c) for a discussion of the manner in which this research was undertaken.
2 See Lutz and White (1986) for an earlier review of this literature.
3 Simply put, the comparative approach embodies an ongoing search for pertinent and illustrative similarities in the differences—as well as differences in the similarities—between the ways in which social life may be constructed in different times, locations, and settings.
4 See James (1998) on how the presence of children is symbolically required in order to transform a "married couple" into a "family."
5 See Dyck (2000a, pp. 22–25) for a discussion of informal versions of sports organized for children by children that violate the rules of organized sports.
6 Such stereotypes include: the parent who lives vicariously through the achievements of their child; the unscrupulous coach who will do anything to win; the "dad coach" who runs his team primarily to develop and showcase the talents of his kid; the "stuck-up" parent who doesn't want to help out with fund-raising; the out-of-control parent, kid, or coach who can be expected to "lose it" sooner or later in closely contested games or situations; and the parent who is determined to see a given sport team or club organized to suit "my kid's schedule" and interests.

7 In several community sports—including, notably, competitive swimming and gymnastics—coaches are paid for their services. In sports such as soccer or track and field a community league or club might provide some modest form of remuneration to a few elite coaches or "consultants," but most coaches serve on an unpaid basis. But even within leagues or clubs where some coaches may receive some level of compensation for their services, there often remain other team, club, and league executive positions that are held by volunteers.

8 See also Dyck (2003) on the manner in which child-organized sport activities such as "pond hockey" may be elided into rationales for adult-organized sports for children.

9 In some inner city areas there exist fully subsidized leagues for underprivileged children and youths that require minimal or no registration fees and that provide free transportation and personal equipment for players. Within non-subsidized leagues and community sport organizations, there may also sometimes be formal or informal provision for participation by a small number of children and youths who would not otherwise be able to afford the full fees or to get to and from games without assistance. But these sorts of exceptions are, in practice, often reserved for gifted athletes.

10 The National Coaching Certification Program (NCCP) is a coach training and certification program for 65 different sports in Canada.

11 All names have been replaced with pseudonyms to protect the confidentiality of subjects.

12 A "dad coach" coaches a team on which his son or daughter plays.

13 A bottle drive is a familiar although not especially lucrative means of fundraising for sports and youth groups that involves children (accompanied by their parents in cars and trucks) going door to door asking for empty soft-drink and beer bottles and cans that are subsequently returned by the team for the compulsory deposit charges that are charged at the time of sale and refunded upon return by retailers.

References

Dunham, D. (2002). Love and jealousy in the space of death. *Ethnos, 67*, 155–180.

Dyck, N. (2000a). Games, bodies, celebrations and boundaries: Anthropological perspectives on sport. In N. Dyck (Ed.), *Games, sports and cultures* (pp. 13–42). New York: Berg.

Dyck, N. (2000b). Parents, kids and coaches: Constructing sport and childhood in Canada. . In N. Dyck (Ed.), *Games, sports and cultures* (pp. 137–161). New York: Berg.

Dyck, N. (2000c). Home field advantage? Exploring the social construction of children's sports. In V. Amit (Ed.), *Constructing the field: Ethnographic fieldwork in the contemporary world* (pp. 32–53). New York: Routledge.

Dyck, N. (2003). Embodying success: Identity and performance in children's sport. In N. Dyck & E. P. Archetti (Eds.), *Sport, dance and embodied identities* (pp. 55–73). New York: Berg.

Foster, G. M. (1972). The anatomy of envy: A study in symbolic behavior. *Current Anthropology, 13*, 165–186.

Fussell, P. (1983). *Class: A guide through the American status system*. New York: Summit Books.

James, A. (1998). Imaging children 'at home', 'in the family' and 'at school': Movement between the spatial and temporal markers of childhood identity in Britain. In N. Rapport & A. Dawson (Eds.), *Migrants of identity: Perceptions of home in a world of movement* (pp. 139–160). New York: Berg.

Lutz, C. (1986). Emotion, thought, and estrangement: Emotion as a cultural category. *Cultural Anthropology,* 1, 287–309.

Lutz, C., & White, G. M. (1986). The anthropology of emotions. *Annual Review of Anthropology,* 15, 405–436.

Newman, K. S. (1988). *Falling from grace: The experience of downward mobility in the American middle class.* New York: Free Press.

Newman, K. S. (1993). *Declining fortunes: The withering of the American Dream.* New York: Basic Books.

22

When Friends Have Other Friends
Friendship Jealousy in Childhood and Early Adolescence

Jeffrey G. Parker, Sara A. Kruse, and Julie Wargo Aikins

Children rarely have their friends to themselves. At all ages, but especially in late childhood and early adolescence, friendship experiences are normally embedded in the wider relational context of group interaction and networks of peer relationships (Cairns, Xie, & Leung, 1998; Fletcher, Hunter, & Eanes, 2006; Sabongui, Bukowski, & Newcomb, 1998; South & Haynie, 2004). For example, studies employing diaries, observations, surveys, or other techniques that assess time use indicate that children's opportunities for interaction with their friends are almost overwhelmingly public in that other children are present and interacting as well (e.g., Crockett, Losoff, & Petersen, 1984; Larson & Richards, 1991; Montemayor & Van-Komen, 1985; see Brown, Larson, & Saraswathi, 2002). In addition, most children have several friends and are aware that their specific friends like or have friendships with other, outside children (e.g., George & Hartmann, 1996; Parker & Seal, 1996). Isolated friendships, it seems, are the exception not the rule.

The public nature of friendship in late childhood and early adolescence is a potentially important but often underappreciated consideration in understanding why these relationships form, have certain qualities, and take specific directions. In particular, by serving as the broader context in which friendship experiences unfold, outsiders and outside relationships shape children's experiences within friendships in important ways. At times, outsiders have a positive influence on specific friendships (see Milardo & Helms-Erikson, 2000). For example, when third parties and other friends recognize and respond to pairs of children as friends, this can have an important "audience effect" that cements the partners' identification with and commitment to one another (McCall, 1988). Outsiders can also positively influence friendships in more direct ways. For example, if motivated to do so, outsiders can be effective at helping members resolve disputes or rectify perceived injustices (e.g., Simmons, 2002).

Handbook of Jealousy: Theory, Research and Multidisciplinary Approaches, First Edition.
Edited by Sybil L. Hart and Maria Legerstee.
© 2013 Blackwell Publishing Ltd. Published 2013 by Blackwell Publishing Ltd.

However, outsiders are not invariably welcomed in friendships and can also be significant sources of tension and conflict between friends (Asher, Parker, & Walker, 1996; Kless, 1992). For example, the presence of outsiders may preempt opportunities for frank discussion between friends, and the coordination of social activities may be more complicated and less satisfying in groups larger than two persons (e.g., Benenson et al., 2002; Lansford & Parker, 1999). In addition, children with several friends can become squeezed between their loyalty to specific friends and the obligations to others, leaving no one satisfied (Asher et al., 1996; Selman, 1980). Finally, and of specific interest here, consider the sentiment expressed by Nichole, a 6th grade girl in one of our studies:

> One of the things I like best with Jessica is that we hang out together—you know, at the mall or after school. We don't do anything special—but that's when we usually talk about stuff. I'd didn't mind at first when Tara came along. But then she came *every* time. She'd even call our house, and if my Mom said we were at the mall or something, she would go find us. She and Jess have a class together, and when they get together all they do is talk about the boys in that class. I don't have a thing to say, and feel, like, stupid and left out. And I also don't get to talk privately to Jess anymore. She's wrecking our friendship.

Nichole's complaint illustrates that feelings of jealousy and other negative emotions and attributions can arise when others introduce competing demands on the time and emotional commitments of one or both partners or when members perceive their partner's activities with others as an infringement on the quality or sovereignty of the relationship (Asher et al., 1996; Lavallee & Parker, in press; Parker & Gamm, 2003; Parker, Low, Walker, & Gamm, 2005; Roth & Parker, 2001).

To date, developmental researchers have a very poor understanding of the forces exerted on friendship dyads by outsiders and outside friendships, including the jealousy that seems to be compromising Nichole's relationship with Jessica. This is true despite the fact that references to jealousy or outside interference in friendship surface almost invariably whenever children are queried in open-ended ways about the interpersonal difficulties they face or the friendship issues that concern them (e.g., Bigelow, Tesson, & Lewko, 1996; Silverman, La Greca, & Wasserstein, 1995; Kuttler, Parker, & La Greca, 2002). The difficulty is that, although research on children's friendships has flourished recently (e.g., Berndt, 2007; Nangle & Erdley, 2001; Rubin, Bukowski, & Parker, 2006), this work is dominated by a focus on friendships as discrete units, isolated from other relationships and individuals. For example, observational researchers have produced a rich understanding of the processes of friendship support and conflict, and how these vary for children of different genders, ages, or backgrounds (e.g., Gottman, 1983; Fonzi, Schneider, Tani, & Tomada, 1997; Hartup, French, Laursen, Johnston, & Ogawa, 1993; Parker & Herrera, 1996; Simpkins & Parke, 2002). However, when these researchers observe dyads of friends they almost always do so without others present. In other research, investigators examine individual children's reports of the features of their friendships (see Berndt, 2002, 2007; Furman, 1996). These studies provide information on the support and satisfaction that children receive from specific friends or sets of friends, but they seldom ask children about the dynamics of how their several friends get along with each other or their vulnerability to jealousy when friends have other friends.

Observation and survey studies of pairs of friends are useful, but these strategies will have difficulty accounting for variance in children's friendship experiences that stems from influences that are not strictly dyadic or individual. Consider again Nichole and Jessica. This pair is unlikely to appear much different to observers from other pairs of friends their age, unless and until Tara is also present. In fact, Nichole does not appear to have many complaints about her relationship with Jessica—until the conversation turns toward Tara. Nichole's difficulty is not that she and Jessica are not close; her complaint is that Jessica is also close to someone else. Indeed, Nichole might feel less strongly about Jessica's relationship with Tara if her own relationship with Jessica was less close. By studying children's friendship in isolation, researchers have arguably underestimated the challenges to relational competence that children face in friendships and missed an opportunity to refine potential targets of interventions aimed at increasing the quality or stability of children's friendship participation.

In the present chapter, we provide an overview of emerging research on the nature, significance, and origins of the type of friendship jealousy that is experienced and expressed by children like Nichole during late childhood and early adolescence. As noted, researchers have seldom considered outsiders' influence on friendships and therefore work on children's friendship jealousy is particularly scant. An exception is research by Selman (e.g., 1980; Selman & Schultz, 1990). Selman explored children's possessiveness over friends in the context of his broader investigation into developmental changes in social perspective taking and the nature of friendships. According to Selman, children's vulnerability to friendship jealousy waxes and wanes over development, reflecting changes in children's underlying ability to coordinate multiple perspectives in relationships. In Selman's view, younger children rarely express jealousy over friends' activities with others unless this extra-dyadic involvement has obvious and immediate negative effects on their own welfare. However, several factors subsequently conspire to alter children's reactions to third parties from almost benign disinterest in the early years to suspicion and jealousy. In particular, as children become more capable of understanding how specific activities between individuals contribute to broader feelings of affection and commitment, they are likely to see (correctly or incorrectly) their friend's specific activities with others as part of a broader pattern of attachment, and thus more likely to feel threatened by this involvement. Older children, too, are more likely to make social comparisons with the third party, and thus are more likely to react more negatively to third parties because a friend's interest in someone else implies a personal failure in oneself. In Selman's view, jealousy over friends remains a problem for most individuals until middle or late adolescence and then abates as subsequent social cognitive advances help older children take a more balanced view in which they recognize that no single relationship, no matter its quality, can meet all the interpersonal needs of an individual.

Selman's account of children's friendship jealousy, while descriptively rich, was based largely on semi-formal interviews with children and must be considered speculative. However, recently we have conducted several interrelated studies on this topic. Accordingly, we draw heavily on these published and unpublished data for our presentation in this chapter. In addition, a rich theoretical and empirical literature exists within communication studies and social psychology on adult romantic jealousy. We pull selectively from these frameworks for our presentation as well.

The chapter organization is as follows. We start by providing a framework for conceptualizing friendship jealousy at this age. The study of romantic jealousy in adults provides a point of departure for this discussion, but we provide a definition specific to children and friendship contexts and subsequently offer insights from our recent studies on the multifaceted affective, cognitive, and behavioral aspects of friendship jealousy.

Following this, we turn to individual differences. Although all children can grow jealous in certain, warranted circumstances, in this section we address whether some children are more vulnerable to jealousy than others. We illustrate two broad methods for identifying jealousy-prone children and adolescents, one based on the individuals' self-reports and the other based on the judgments of close friends and other peers. We also present data on potential sex and age differences in vulnerability to friendship jealousy.

For the balance of the chapter, we take up the origins and significance of these differences. Specifically, we initially review the limited information that exists on the personal characteristics of children that are associated with a proneness to friendship jealousy and presumably contribute to it. These include various aspects of self-esteem as well as certain attitudes toward peers and family. Next, we consider how the disposition to friendship jealousy is associated with the quality of children and young adolescents' friendship adjustment, and with broader difficulties in getting along with peers. The chapter concludes with a summary and some brief thoughts on potentially interesting directions for further research.

Toward Conceptualizing Friendship Jealousy in Childhood and Adolescence

With adults, jealousy is commonly conceptualized as a negative cognitive, emotional, and behavioral reaction triggered by a valued partner's actual or anticipated interest in or relationship with another person, regarded as an interloper (e.g., Guerrero & Andersen, 1998; Salovey & Rodin, 1989; Sharpsteen & Kirkpatrick, 1997). Generally, jealousy results when individuals feel that a partner's relationship with someone else threatens their own, existing relationship with the partner. Individuals who are jealous may feel that they are in danger of being replaced in the relationship by the interloper, thereby losing it entirely. However, even when they understand that their own relationship with the partner can continue, jealous individuals may be distressed at the expected diminution of the quality of the relationship arising from the need to share the relationship rewards or privileged access to a partner with others (Mathes, Adams, & Davies, 1985).

In corresponding fashion, Parker, Low, et al. (2005) recently proposed that friendship jealousy in late childhood and adolescence be defined as *a negative reaction triggered by a close friend's actual or anticipated interest in or relationship with another peer and based upon the target's perception that the partner's relationship with someone else threatens their own, existing relationship with him or her.* According to this definition, jealousy arises only when individuals perceive that a partner's relationship or contact with another person threatens their own valued friendship with the partner. One would not expect jealousy to result from all forms of contact that friends have with others—only those that suggest to the perceiver that his or her status with the friend is in jeopardy because the friend's interest in the relationship is flagging or the friend is starting a competing friendship with another peer. Additionally, like adults in parallel romantic circumstances, children and adolescents who are jealous over a friend may fear that they are in danger of being replaced in the friendship by the interloper and risk losing it entirely. However, even when they understand that their friendship will continue, they may be nonetheless distressed over the prospect of an anticipated diminution of the quality or exclusivity of the relationship.

In short, a triangle of interpersonal relationships is always at the heart of friendship jealousy and essential to the conceptual clarity of this construct. Jealousy begins with an established close, emotional relationship between two parties—the jealous individual and his or her friend. When a third person, an "interloper," is introduced into this relationship by establishing a potential friendship with the partner, jealousy may result. Presumably, it is this triangle of relationships that gives jealous circumstances their potency. It is one thing to realize that one is not getting along with a friend, perhaps not meeting her needs, but quite another to realize that someone else is. And, of course, because three people are involved, jealous individuals have a wider range of possible responses, including some aimed at the third party as well as the friend.

Multifaceted responses to friendship jealousy

Children's jealous responses around friends, like those of adults in romantic contexts, may be characterized along several simultaneous and related affective, cognitive, and behavioral facets.

Affect

Adults experiencing jealousy display psychophysiological stress and arousal (Buss, Larson, Weston, & Semmelroth, 1992; Harris, 2000) and typically report strong, but blended, emotions involving anger, sadness, and some anxiety and embarrassment (e.g., Bringle & Buunk, 1985; Pfeiffer & Wong, 1989; Salovey & Rodin, 1989; Sharpsteen, 1993). The character of the emotional experience of jealousy is probably fluid and influenced, among other things, by the individuals' focus of attention and attributions. When jealous individuals dwell on the gloomy prospects for the relationship, they may experience sadness and anxiety (Levine, 1995). When they perceive negligent or intentional insensitivity or betrayal by the partner and inter-loper, they may experience concurrent anger (Canary, Spitzberg, & Semic, 1998).

Like adults, children experience a strong blend of negative emotions when they become jealous over friends. Of course, children experience negative emotions around other friendship disappointments, but there is evidence that friendship disappointments resulting from third party interference are especially acute and have a unique emotional character. This conclusion stems from several studies in which children are presented with hypothetical vignettes depicting themselves, their current best friend, and a fictitious, attractive, same-sex third peer (e.g., Parker, Ramich, & Roth, 2009; Roth & Parker, 2001). In some vignettes, the participating children were asked to imagine being disappointed when their plans for a special activity with their friend were frustrated because a third peer interfered in the relationship by monopolizing the friend's time at an important point or by encroach-ing on a previously exclusive aspect of the relationship, For example, in one vignette the subject's hope to enter a talent contest with the best friend is frustrated when the third peer teams up with the friend first. In other vignettes, the participant's plans for the friend also fall through, but the third peer plays only a tangential role (e.g., the talent contest is canceled by officials). After each vignette, participants are asked to provide their anticipated emotional reactions. By introducing several different types of friendship disappointments and carefully counterbalancing over subjects, a variety of friendship disappointments can be presented while systematically varying whether the disappointment occurs with versus without the complicity of an interloper.

Figure 22.1 presents results of a representative study using this design (Parker, Ramich, et al., 2009). Seventy-two preadolescents were asked to consider three relevant potential emotional reactions—jealousy, anger, and sadness. In addition, as a point of comparison, we asked participants about their feelings of guilt. Although also a negative emotion, guilt normally applies to the perpetrators, not the victims, of relational transgressions (Guerrero & Andersen, 2000; Tangney & Salovey, 1999). Therefore, in these circumstances it should be inappropriate. In the figure, emotions that were anticipated in response to friendship disappointments involving a third peer as an interloper were compared with similar disappointments which featured a third peer whose role was strictly tangential to events.

As shown, participants anticipated strong and mixed emotional responses to friendship disappointments involving interlopers. Naturally, they expected to feel

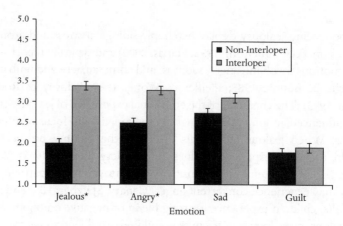

Figure 22.1   Preadolescents' anticipated jealous, angry, sad, and guilty responses when third peers play an interloper verses non-interloper role in friendship disappointments. Note: Sets of bars with asterisks indicate significant post hoc differences between interloper and non-interloper

jealous in these circumstances, but they also expected a good deal of sadness and anger. They did not expect to feel guilty, however, suggesting that they were not indiscriminately reporting negative emotions. Of course, sadness and anger are emotions that children experience around negative friendship events that do not involve interlopers. A comparison of the bars representing interloper vignettes to control vignettes provides insights into which emotions are relatively specific to third party interference. As shown, participants' feelings of jealousy and anger were more tempered when the third peer's role was tangential to events and the threat to the relationship was reduced. Interestingly, as Figure 22.1 shows, sadness was high regardless of the role of the third peer.

Why should the same disappointing events be experienced so much more negatively when they feature third party interference? In vignettes without interlopers, preadolescents were no doubt frustrated that their plans for an interesting activity with their friend fell through. In fact, it is reasonable to infer that this failure accounts for the sadness they reported in this circumstance (see Levine, 1995). Presumably, however, whatever doubts might have arisen about the relationship's future were slight and abstract. Indeed, preadolescents might have reasonably perceived that their friends were just as disappointed as they were by the turn of events. In contrast, in vignettes featuring interlopers, preadolescents' concerns presumably shifted from disappointment over missed opportunity to enjoy a shared experience with a close friend, to a sense of relationship threat inherent in the situation. Put differently, although the manifest outcome for the individual was the same in both conditions, the presence of an interloper introduced the prospect of the partner's starting a competing friendship with a rival. In other words, it created jealousy.

Cognition

Jealous children and adolescents are in a state of high uncertainty regarding their friend's commitment to them and report preoccupying and ruminative thought over the future or quality of the relationship (Lavallee & Parker, in press). However, cognitive processes probably play even broader roles in jealousy responses. For example, children's understanding of others' motives and the meaning of events to others are likely important to their conclusions about whether their relationship is at risk. To grow jealous a child must infer that her friend finds her social interaction with the interloper rewarding and is considering pursuing a deeper relationship. In addition, children presumably take stock of their existing friendships: What are their own and their friend's relative investments, commitment, and alternatives to the relationship? Obviously there is quite a bit of ambiguity in these aspects of others' behavior, and thus the potential for misunderstanding is great.

Children's perceptions of rivals are also likely to play a role. For example, in a pair of recent studies involving 200 later adolescents (Parker, Ebrahimi, & Libber, 2005) and 353 middle school students (Parker, Campbell, Kollat, & Lucas, 2008) we examined how physical attractiveness of a same-sex peer alters an individual's response when that peer interferes in another friendship. Coming to terms with the biological changes of puberty is a central task of adolescence, but made more difficult by increased social comparison with peers and the premium placed on physical attractiveness and popularity with the opposite sex at this age. We reasoned that, compared with unattractive peers, attractive peers who are interlopers should be more threatening to existing friends and generate stronger jealous reactions. However, attractiveness should not be important when a peer does not represent a relationship threat. The apparent attractiveness of the third peer was varied systematically across conditions through the introduction of independently judged full-body photographs in the later adolescents study and simple verbal descriptions in the middle school students study. As expected, results revealed that, for both sexes, attractive interlopers generated greater jealousy than did unattractive interlopers. However, this was particularly true for female participants.

Finally, appraisals of threat and their responses to interlopers probably depend in refined but important ways on the conclusions they reach about the circumstances of their friend's outside involvement, including the motives of the friend and the interloper. In fact, recent, broader conceptual models of social cognitive processing in children (e.g., Crick & Dodge, 1994; Halberstadt, Denham, & Dunsmore, 2001; Lemerise & Arsenio, 2000) suggest that even if these conclusions are not accurate, they will dictate the goals children pursue and behaviors they show under the circumstances. If children reach benign conclusions, their responses are likely to be less intense and more adaptive. On the other hand, stronger and less adaptive responses are likely if children blame themselves, perceive intentional rejection by their partner, or judge the interloper's behavior as insensitive and assume he or she might have foreseen the negative consequences for the existing friendship.

At present, children's interpretations of others' motives in circumstances involving interloper interference are poorly understood and this represents an important gap in our understanding. Without a firm understanding of how children reach conclusions about themselves and others in these circumstances it is likely to be difficult to anticipate their emotions and behavior. However, the above study by Parker, Ramich, et al. (2009) provides a beginning to understanding of how preadolescents view others' insensitivity and responsibility for interloper interference. In the study using vignettes which featured third party interference versus simple disappointment, we asked preadolescents to rate degree of insensitivity as perceived in the best friend, the third peer, and themselves. Figures 22.2a and 22.2b present results of a significant three-way interaction that emerged from this analysis. This interaction indicated that male and female subjects differed somewhat in the relative culpability they assigned to the friend, the peer, and themselves in situations involving third party interference. In particular, Figure 22.2a presents girls' views of the insensitivity of the best friend, the third peer, and themselves in vignettes featuring bystanders versus interlopers. As shown, when friendship disappointment involved an interloper, girls' opinions of the insensitivity of their friend and the third peer rose sharply relative to circumstances in which this peer acted only as a bystander. Recall that, apart from the complicity of the third peer, the disappointment is the same in both conditions. Yet, without the threat to the relationship, girls did not regard their friends and the third peers as insensitive.

Figure 22.2b presents the insensitivity ratings given by boys to the best friend, peer, and self for vignettes featuring bystanders versus interlopers. Like girls, boys' ratings of friends in the interloper condition were significantly higher than their ratings of friends in the bystander condition. Unlike girls, however, boys' ratings of the insensitivity of the third peer seemed unaffected by his role as an interloper versus bystander. Finally, overall, boys' insensitivity ratings of both the best friend and the outside child (but not themselves) in the interloper condition were significantly lower than those of girls under the same circumstance. Overall, it seems that boys, compared with girls, found everyone less blameworthy.

Taken together, the results of this preliminary study illustrate the potential utility of considering children's interpretations and expectations of others in circumstances involving interloper interference. When their plans and expectations for privileged access to a best friend were disrupted by a third peer, preadolescents of both sexes perceived their best friends as insensitive. Children's judgments of responsibility and culpability are important because knowledge of which actors preadolescents see as insensitive, which owe them an apology, and how strongly those expectations are held will presumably provide a better understanding of preadolescents' behavioral responses to the friend and the interloper. These behaviors, in turn, may dictate ramifications of outside interference for the friendship. For example, partners who do not receive apologies from the

(a)

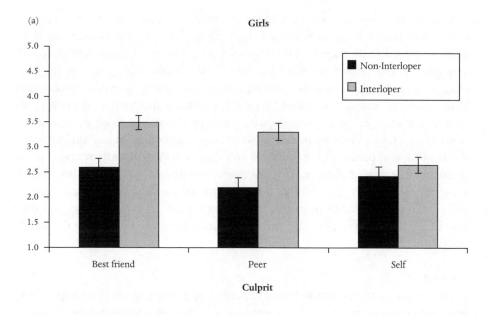

(b)

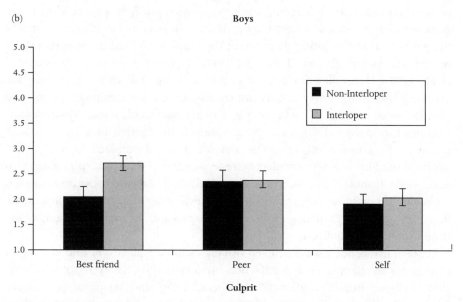

Figure 22.2   Preadolescents girls' (a) and boys' (b) judgments of insensitivity in them-selves and others when third peers play an interloper versus non-interloper role in friendship disappointments

appropriate party may respond aggressively to the friend or outsider, or may decide to leave the relationship. Interloper situations, like most others, undoubt-edly have multiple layers of meaning that are open to interpretation and merit better understanding.

Girls' perceptions of the third peer in interloper contexts are particularly interesting. Unlike boys, girls judged third parties harshly, essentially as harshly as they judged their friends. This implies that girls expect third parties to be sensitive to and respect an implicit, but shared social rule: One should not engage in normally exclusive activities (e.g., discussing personal problems) with a girl who already has a best friend. Undoubtedly, this attitude is the source of much conflict in girls' groups, particularly at transitions (e.g., transitioning from elementary school to middle school), when girls may be unfamiliar with the landscape of preexisting friendships and cannot always be certain about who is already friends with whom. At these times, it is probably especially important for girls to carefully understand the network of existing social relationships before making friendship overtures to others in order to avoid stepping on the toes of existing friends. Boys, on the other hand, do not seem to have the same obligation.

Behavior

No necessary relation exists between experiencing jealousy and expressing it, but how one responds behaviorally to jealousy is critical to understanding its interpersonal consequences (Guerrero, Andersen, Jorgensen, Spitzberg, & Eloy, 1995). Behavioral expressions of jealousy are goal-directed attempts to influence the self, the partner, or the situation to preserve the relationship, reduce uncertainty, or restore self-esteem (Buunk & Bringle, 1987; Guerrero & Afifi, 1999; Guerrero et al., 1995). Depending upon their nature and the skill with which they are executed, these efforts may or may not contribute to relationship satisfaction and broader social success and adjustment. On the one hand, research with adults indicates that many individuals respond positively to experiences of jealousy with enhanced communication, compensatory interest and outreach to others, and efforts at self-improvement or adaptive renegotiation of relational rules (Guerrero et al., 1995; Rusbult & Buunk, 1993). Indeed, skillfully executed positive responses probably do not strike partners or others as evidence of jealousy at all; instead, they may appear as evidence of interest or expressions of caring, closeness, and commitment (see Guerrero et al. 1995).

Yet jealousy is not always or even usually expressed positively, and is a major contributor to relationship dissatisfaction (Andersen, Eloy, Guerrero, & Spitzberg, 1995; Bringle, Roach, Andier, & Evenbeck, 1979) and relationship violence (Hansen 1991; Stets & Pirog-Good, 1987). Typical negative responses may include abandoning the relationship entirely (e.g., Buunk, 1982) or various forms of passive (e.g., sarcasm, sulking, threats to end the relationship, guilt induction, giving the "silent treatment"), direct (e.g., verbal or physical assault, humiliation), or indirect (e.g., derogating interlopers through gossip, manipulating social circumstances to exclude others) aggression (see Guerrero et al., 1995). Negative behavioral responses to jealousy are likely to be recognized by partners and others, and, when habitual, may earn individuals reputations for jealousy.

The emphasis placed on indirect or passive aggression as behavioral expressions of jealousy may in part reflect the communicative dilemmas faced by jealous individuals. Individuals who feel jealous may need to avoid obvious aggression against a partner because normally it is incompatible with relationship ideals, and can endanger their maintenance. Moreover, jealousy normally carries some degree of negative social stigma (White & Mullen, 1989). Thus, jealous individuals may avoid obvious forms of aggression and retaliation to avoid appearing even less desirable to the partner. Likewise, patent aggression against a rival that is regarded as undeserved can engender sympathy for the victim in the partner or among others in the social network. By relying more on indirect forms of aggression, jealous individuals may hope to escape some of the social accountability of direct aggression while achieving the same retaliatory or coercive ends (Björkqvist, 1994). Women and girls may be inclined to employ indirect or passive forms of aggression since social disapproval for direct aggression may be stronger for females than for males (Brown, Way, & Duff, 1999).

Children in our studies endorse a sweeping array of behavioral responses, particularly when given an open-ended opportunity to do so. For example, in one early study (Giltenboth, 2001), we conducted a content analysis of the open-ended responses of a large sample of pilot subjects to vignettes involving third party interference. This analysis produced no fewer than 64 distinct categories of behavioral responses, ranging from "Act hurt next time you see them" to "Spend time with other friends" to "Spread rumors [about the rival]" to "Make [the friend] something special to show him/her how much they mean to you." Many of these responses were endorsed by only a few subjects, however. Our subsequent work (e.g., Parker, Campbell, & Lucas, 2007) suggests that behavioral reactions tend to take one or several of 10 distinct forms: (1) Asking the best friend to clarify their intentions and actions, (2) Giving the best friend the "cold shoulder," (3) Aggressing physically to the best friend or rival, (4) Ending the friendship by breaking up, (5) Talking to the best friend to resolve the hurt feelings, (6) Ignoring the issue altogether, (7) Acting sarcastic toward the best friend, (8) Spreading negative rumors about the best friend or rival to hurt their reputations, (9) Conducting "surveillance" to learn more about the threat the rival poses, and (10) Shunning the best friend or rival and excluding them from the larger peer group. Obviously some of these responses are adaptive but others are more problematic.

Figures 22.3a and 22.3b display the degree to which these 10 behavioral responses are endorsed by boys and girls, respectively. These data were obtained in a recent study involving 244 female and 237 male 7th and 8th grade adolescents who anticipated their responses to hypothetical vignettes involving friendship disappointments that did and did not involve interlopers (Parker et al., 2007). As shown, adolescents of both sexes had significantly stronger behavioral reactions and were significantly less likely to ignore the disappointment when the peer's role was that of an interloper rather than of a bystander. However, boys were more likely than girls to ignore the disappointment when the peer was an

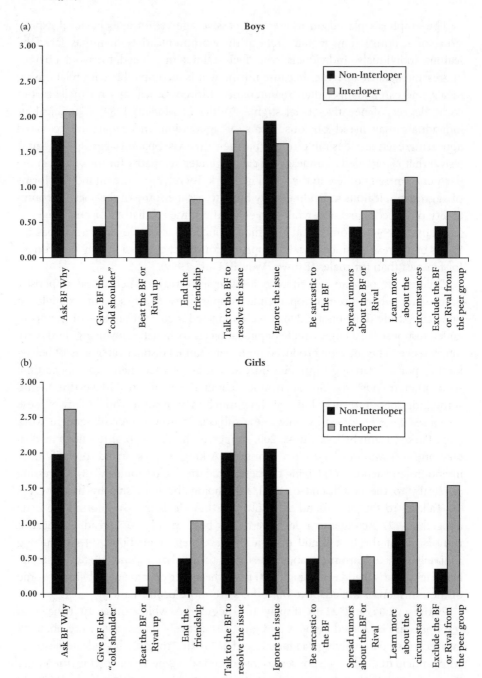

Figure 22.3   Boys' (a) and girls' (b) responses to friendship disappointments resulting from interloper versus non-interloper interference

interloper versus a bystander. Girls were less likely to attack others physically than were boys, although neither group strongly endorsed this response. Compared with boys, girls were more likely to talk to their friend about their disappointment, especially when the third peer was an interloper versus bystander. However, girls were also more likely than boys to give their friend the cold shoulder or exclude them from the group when the third peer was an interloper versus bystander.

It is important to note that the children in this study were not especially prone to friendship jealousy. We can assume that children who are habitually prone to friendship jealousy are more prone to behave negatively than others. This raises the potentially important topic of individual difference, to which we turn next.

Individual Differences in Proneness to Friendship Jealousy

Although the experience and expression of jealousy depend to some extent upon situational factors, research with adults in romantic contexts indicates that robust individual differences in the vulnerability to jealousy also exist, such that some individuals display extreme and counterproductive reactions to the outside activities and relationships of their partners whereas others are relatively immune. These individual differences have proven relatively stable with time and across specific contexts (Bringle, Renner, Terry, & Davis, 1983) and bear a relation to individuals' behavior in real-world as well as contrived, analogue settings involving relationship threat (Mathes, Phillips, Skowran, & Dick, 1982).

In this section, we explore whether corresponding individual differences exist for children's vulnerability to jealousy surrounding their friends. Are some children and adolescents more disposed than others to routinely perceive their friend's outside relationships as threatening and react in unwarranted or excessively negative ways? We first outline two broad strategies for assessing children's and adolescents' disposition to jealousy. The first of these relies on children's and adolescents' self-reports and therefore taps their subjective perceptions of their vulnerability to this experience. The second utilizes peer behavioral nominations to ascertain which children or adolescents have widely shared peer reputations for expressing jealousy. Following this, we present data on potential sex and age differences in the vulnerability to friendship jealousy.

Children's and adolescents' self-reports

Little attention has focused on the important question of whether young adolescents display stable differences in their tendencies to react with jealousy to their friends' activities with others. With adults, a number of effective self-report scales have been developed to identify individuals who are more readily jealous than others in romantic contexts (see Bringle & Buunk, 1985; Pfeiffer & Wong, 1989). In these assessments, respondents are asked to imagine their partners in a variety of semi-intimate social circumstances with other potential partners (e.g., a business trip, a luncheon, at work, etc.) and indicate the extent to which the situation makes them feel jealous. The short vignettes allow for benign interpretation of the behavior of the partner and others, but individuals disposed to jealousy perceive relationship threat and report greater jealousy and subjective distress than typical individuals do.

In parallel fashion, we recently developed the *Friendship Jealousy Questionnaire* (FJQ; Parker, Low, et al., 2005). The FJQ consists of 27 short vignettes in which subjects are presented with hypothetical social situations involving a specific best friend and are asked to imagine and report their emotional reactions. Fifteen items are primary items, which also feature one or more hypothetical potential interlopers who are described as peer acquaintances. In these items, events in the vignettes unfold in such a way that the actions or presence of the other same-sex individual or individuals pose a threat to the exclusivity of the established best friendship. The behavior of the best friend in all vignettes is ambiguous. That is, although there is no overt rejection of the target by the best friend, it is possible for the respondent to interpret events as rejection by the friend or at least to view the friend as receptive to the interloper's advances. Subjects are then asked to indicate the level of jealousy they would feel using a 5-point scale ranging from "not at all true of me" (0) to "really true of me" (4). Jealousy scores are computed by averaging responses across primary items. The remaining 12 vignettes do not portray the involvement of a third child. These items are included to discourage an acquiescent or contrarian response set. Like primary items, distracter items involve social situations (i.e., an interdependence of the target with their best friend). However, the events portrayed in distracter items are otherwise quite diverse, and were chosen to pull for a variety of specific emotions other than jealousy (e.g., sadness, happiness, and anger). Each of these items is also worded as a declarative statement. The participant is asked to indicate how likely it is that they would feel the emotion presented in the scenario using a 5-point scale, ranging from "not at all true of me" (0) to "really true of me" (4).

We have employed the FJQ in 10 published or unpublished studies involving over 2,500 children or teens from grades 5 to 12 as well as college-age students. Factor analyses of this scale confirm the presence of a single dimension underlying the primary items, and estimates of internal consistency have ranged between .92 and .94 across all studies, ages, and both sexes. The test–retest stability of individual differences in self-reported vulnerability to jealousy over 2–3 weeks is quite high, $r = .86$, and is nearly identical for boys and girls (Parker, Low, et al., 2005). Over one year's time, stability has been shown to be .41 for girls and .37 for boys (Parker, Wargo, & Aikins, 2009). In this instance, jealousy was assessed first during the 6th grade and again one year later, following a transition to junior high school. Because considerable turnover in friendships took place

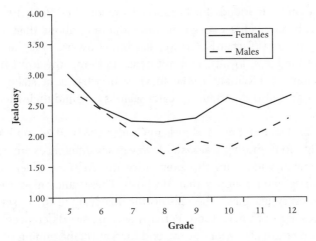

Figure 22.4   Grade differences in boys' and girls' friendship jealousy

over this transition, most individuals in this sample were reporting on their jealousy in different relationships across the two time points. With this in mind, even consistency in this range is particularly impressive. In ordinary usage, especially with adults, feelings of jealousy may carry stigma, and individuals can be motivated to minimize this experience or present themselves in the most favorable light (White & Mullen, 1989). However, children and adolescents' reports of their vulnerability to jealousy on this scale do not appear to be strongly influenced by their concerns about presenting themselves in a favorable light (Parker, Low, et al., 2005). It is also important to note that FJQ scores are also unrelated to children's general verbal intelligence (Lavallee, 2002).

Figure 22.4 presents information on grade differences in boys' and girls' self-reports of vulnerability to jealousy using data aggregated over 5 representative studies that included the FJQ (Lavallee & Parker, in press; Parker, Low, et al., 2005; Parker et al., 2007; Parker, Ramich, et al., 2009; Parker & Wargo Aikins, 2009). In all, 1,899 individuals are included in this figure, representing grades 5 through 12. Recall that Selman (1980) proposed that cognitive advances from preadolescence to adolescence will contribute to steady decreases in youth's proneness to jealousy. As shown in Figure 22.4, children of both sexes do appear to decline in their disposition to jealousy in the period from 5th to 8th grade, as Selman proposed. However, contrary to Selman's proposal, this decline does not continue into the later grades. In fact, vulnerability to friendship jealousy increases somewhat from 8th to 12th grade. This curvilinear trend is highly significant by formal statistical curve estimation tests. Selman's theory, it would appear, offers, at best, only a partially accurate account of how and why jealousy changes with development.

Figure 22.4 also presents information on sex differences in friendship jealousy at various grades. Beginning in preadolescence, girls have more open and self-disclosing relationships with their friends than do boys, and they rely more heavily on their friends for emotional support (see Beal, 1994). Likewise, compared with boys, girls engage in more thinking about their friends when separated from them (Richards, Crowe, Larson, & Swarr, 1998), and expect and receive more kindness, loyalty, commitment, and empathy from friends (Sharabany, Gershoni, & Hofman, 1981). In view of what is at stake, it might be expected that girls also experience greater jealousy around their friendships than do boys.

As Figure 22.4 shows, boys and girls in Grades 5, 6, and 7 report similar levels of vulnerability to friendship jealousy. However, sex differences emerge about 8th grade and remain wide from this point forward. At these older ages, girls on average report greater jealousy than do boys. These differences are statistically significant in every instance. The reasons for this delay in the onset of expected sex differences are not understood. Perhaps because sex differences in the intimacy of friendships are also wider at the end than at the beginning of adolescence (Berndt, 2007; McNelles & Connolly, 1999), differences in jealousy grow wider with age as well. Broader factors may be at work as well, however. Most of the children in the samples represented by the graph made a transition to middle or junior high about the 7th grade. Sex differences, therefore, appear to emerge soon after this transition. Perhaps it is some factor associated with the social setting at school—not the quality of friendships—that contributes to widening sex differences in the vulnerability to jealousy.

Peer reputations for friendship jealousy

Peer behavioral assessment can also be used to learn which children are vulnerable to friendship jealousy. Peer behavioral assessment involves polling all or a portion of the age-mates who know an individual well to ascertain whether that individual displays a particular behavior of interest (Rubin et al., 2006). This technique enjoys widespread use among researchers interested in children's social adjustment, in part because it taps the collective wisdom of a group of individuals with deep and extended experience with those being evaluated, namely, the child's peers. As such, it is particularly well suited for the assessment of behaviors, like jealousy, that occur with relatively low frequency but are psychologically salient. Also, peer assessments represent the perspectives of many observers with whom the target child has had a variety of personal relationships. Thus, the chance that error will be introduced by some idiosyncratic aspect of any single reporter's experience with the target is correspondingly reduced.

We have employed peer behavioral assessments on occasion to understand young adolescents' reputations for friendship jealousy among their friends and other peers. In one recent study with 485 children in Grades 5 to 9, we gave children four descriptions of characteristically jealous children and asked them to nominate from a list of random classmates others who fit these profiles (Parker, Low, et al., 2005). These included: "Students who are possessive of their friends,"

"Students who try to keep their friends to themselves," "Students who get really jealous if you do something cool or fun with their friend," and "Students who get really jealous if you try to be friends with their friend." The number of nominations received from same-sex mutual friends and from other, non-friend peers were subsequently tallied for individual children and standardized. We distinguished reports of mutual friends from those of peers who were not friends with the individual in the belief that these sources might not have completely consistent views of whether someone is prone to jealousy. One the one hand, compared to non-friends, friends presumably have a deeper understanding of their partners and a wider context for judging their behavior. They might, therefore, recognize jealousy in individuals that went unrecognized by non-friends. On the other hand, as the likely target of their consternation, non-friends may see the possessiveness of jealous individuals in clearer relief and may be less charitable than friends when interpreting it. Perhaps non-friends, then, are more objective when deciding which peers are and are not prone to jealousy.

Results demonstrated that peers can indeed provide reliable information on young adolescents' jealousy. The internal consistency of the four jealousy items, regardless of source, was excellent, alpha = .93. Results also highlighted the importance of considering the source's vantage point in the use of peer assessments of behavior, at least when considering behaviors as complex as jealousy. Reports of friends and non-friends were only modestly correlated among girls ($r = .45$) and among boys ($r = .34$). Moreover, structural equation modeling indicated a sex difference in the transparency of jealousy to peers. Boys' self-reported jealousy predicted a reputation for jealousy among both friends and non-friends, as we expected. But, as we expected, friends and non-friends did not strongly agree on whether specific boys were highly jealous. Peer reputations in these two groups seem to arise somewhat independently. Like boys, girls who reported being prone to jealousy also had a reputation for jealousy among their friends. However, unlike boys, girls did not develop a reputation for jealousy outside their circle of friends unless they also had a reputation for jealousy among friends.

There are many possible ways to interpret this pattern of findings, but among the interesting ones is that, unlike among boys, the difficulties that girls have with their friends over jealousy are highly transparent to the broader peer group, and outside peers base their judgments of who is jealous directly on this knowledge. More generally, this research raises the question of how friends and non-friends come by their impressions of who is jealous. Presumably the task of judging others' jealousy depends on making inferences about others' motivations (i.e., their disposition to be insecure about their friend's other friends and social activities) in complex situations involving subtle cues. For example, bragging and boasting may represent just an irksome personality trait when it occurs frequently, indiscriminately, and unpredictably; but it could be a sign of jealousy when it occurs selectively, following a close friend's choice of another, high-status peer as an activity partner.

In sum, self-reports and peer behavioral assessments can be used to produce hierarchies of individual differences in friendship jealousy. Girls report a higher vulnerability to jealousy than do boys and, although jealousy appears to decline somewhat from childhood to early adolescence, it rises somewhat at older ages. Self-reports and peer reports are overlapping, but they are not redundant, precisely as we might expect if children and teens do not always express the jealousy they may be experiencing. Children's reputation for jealousy also depends somewhat on who is asked. When girls have a reputation for jealousy among their close friends they also tend to have a reputation for jealousy among their broader peer group of non-friends. Boys, too, can develop a broader reputation for jealousy among peers, but this reputation is not as directly linked to their friends' perceptions as it is among girls. How do these differences arise and is there cause for concern for children or teens who are especially prone to jealousy? These questions relate to the origins and significance of individual differences in friendship jealousy and are taken up next.

Origins of Individual Differences in Friendship Jealousy

Why do some individuals react so strongly and habitually negatively when their friends have other friends? Given the intricacies of jealousy, a simple theory that adequately captures the origins of individual differences in jealousy is unlikely. For example, as a response triggered by perceptions of environmental threat, temperamental and other presumably biologically based factors that govern emotional arousal and regulation are likely to play a role (Hart, this volume, Chapter 4; Hart & Carrington, 2002). Likewise, factors that foster dependency on the relationship, such as few relationship alternatives and low social skills, may also be important. Exchange and interdependence theories of relationship development, in particular, would predict that a high level of dependency on the relationship will be accompanied by a stronger desire to preserve the quality and stability of the current relationship and resulting higher levels of jealousy (Buunk & Dijkstra, 2002; Rusbult, 1983). Feelings of jealousy may be especially intense if individuals who are highly dependent on particular friends also perceive that their dependence on the relationships exceeds the dependence and commitment of their partner (e.g., White, 1981b).

Additionally, both theoretical arguments (e.g., Salovey & Rodin, 1988; White, 1981a; White & Mullen, 1989) and empirical data (e.g., Bers & Rodin, 1984; DeSteno & Salovey, 1996; Mathes et al., 1985; Salovey & Rodin, 1984; Sharpsteen, 1995) support the assertion that what jealous individuals find particularly distressing is not only the interloper's infringement on the relationship, but also the implied unfavorable social comparison to the interloper and inferred rejection by the partner. As Guerrero et al. (1995, p. 274) aptly note, "jealous individuals believe that their partners have compared them to the rival and that they have somehow failed to 'measure up'."

One interesting implication of the fact that jealous situations necessarily involve social comparison and prompt self-evaluation is that it suggests that individuals with chronically low self-esteem will habitually overestimate their partner's attraction to others and be prone to experience threat and jealousy when it is otherwise unwarranted. By comparison, individuals with higher self-regard are presumably less likely to feel competitive with their friends' other friends and, in the absence of evidence to the contrary, more likely to offer benign interpretations of their friends' activities with others. Consistent with this view, we have obtained negative correlations between vulnerability to jealousy and preadolescents' global self-esteem in several past studies (Ebrahimi, Parker, Lavallee, & Seiffke-Krenke, 2005; Lavallee & Parker, in press; Parker, Low, et al., 2005; Parker, McGuire, Rosen, & Underwood, 2009).

Although statistically significant, these correlations have been generally modest in magnitude. To some degree, this relation is not more robust because a good deal of dyad-to-dyad variability in jealousy exists (Parker, McGuire, et al., 2009). That is, even children prone to jealousy do not report high jealousy in each of their friendships (see Parker, McGuire, et al., 2009). Factors other than personality traits like self-esteem probably also contribute to whether an individual, even a vulnerable one, feels jealous around a specific friend. If a good deal of jealousy is relationship specific, it will be difficult to use individual factors, such as the target's level of self-esteem, to make highly accurate predictions about jealousy in specific relationships. Nonetheless, evidence suggests that prediction is further improved when more specific aspects of self-perception are examined. For example, according to Tesser's self-evaluation maintenance theory (Salovey & Rodin, 1989), negative social comparisons are more likely to have insidious effects when they involve issues and domains that are central rather than peripheral to an individual's self-definition. Because coming to terms with the biological changes of puberty is a central task of adolescence, it is not surprising that variability in body image among late adolescents is a stronger predictor of jealousy than is global self-worth (Parker, Ebrahimi, et al., 2005). Likewise, another aspect of self-esteem that seems to be related to jealousy and improves its prediction is the degree to which self-esteem is socially contingent (Kollat & Parker, 2005, 2007; Parker et al., 2008). Individuals with highly contingent self-esteem can maintain positive self-views only if they perceive that they are meeting social expectations and held in high esteem by peers. Highly contingent individuals appear to regard their friends' enjoyable activities with others as a sign of their own slipping prestige in the group, are highly sensitive to it, and react with jealousy even if they have generally positive self-views.

Children's conceptions of friendships also seem to play a role. Children that approach their friendships in a relatively flexible way that allows them to appreciate their friends without being overly dependent on them are better prepared for the minor disappointments that inevitably occur in friendships when a partner is unavailable or busy with someone else. On the other hand, children and adolescents that construe friendship rigidly, insisting that only specific other individuals can fulfill the interpersonal functions of friendships, are likely to perceive greater threat when, inevitably, outsiders encroach on their friendship activities. As a result, their experience and expression of jealousy are commensurately stronger (Lavallee & Parker, in press).

Finally, because feelings of jealousy are rooted in perceptions of relationship threat, defection, and loss, extensions of developmental attachment theory appear to be useful in the search for insights into the basis of friendship jealousy (Buunk, 1997; Radecki-Bush, Farrell, & Bush, 1993; Sharpsteen & Kirkpatrick, 1997). According to Bowlby (1969), the attachment system evolved to protect infants from harm by keeping them close to caregivers and to provide children with a secure base that enables them to engage their environment confidently. In the expectable family environment, caregivers are responsive, skilled, self-validating, and available, and their developing children form secure cognitive schemas (internal working models) of both their own competence and attractiveness and the accessibility and responsiveness of significant others. These internal representations generalize to other close relationships. Thus, individuals with secure views of self and others are expected to be comfortable with closeness, confident in their relationship skills, and handle relationship separations and conflict with more constructive attributions and behaviors. However, when caregivers are rejecting, unresponsive, or inconsistent, their offspring adapt with predictable patterns of avoidance or preoccupation. The internal working models these insecure individuals possess may exaggerate their self-importance and minimize their dependence on others (anxious-avoidant style) or they may belie excessive dependence on others coupled with intrinsic doubts about their own attractiveness and others' faithfulness and commitment (anxious-preoccupied style).

Consistent with this theoretical perspective, adults with insecure views of themselves or others have been found to more readily interpret negative events in close relationships as rejection and abandonment and therefore to have a lower threshold for jealousy in their romantic relationships (Radecki-Bush et al., 1993; Sharpsteen & Kirkpatrick, 1997; White, 1981c). Limited available evidence suggests that is the case with young adolescents in friendship contexts as well. In particular, as part of a larger study of 121 young adolescents followed for one year as they made the transition from elementary school to junior high school (Parker & Wargo Aikins, 2009), we observed that, compared with other adolescents, adolescents who expressed insecurity in their relationships with family members also reported an increased vulnerability to friendship jealousy. This relation was obtained concurrently, in 6th grade, as well as one year later, when the participants were in their new school.

Friendship Jealousy and Intra- and Interpersonal Adjustment

Children and adolescents who admit to being vulnerable to jealousy express greater loneliness and dissatisfaction with their peer experiences in general, are more depressed, and report spending more time ruminating in unhealthy ways over the prospects for their friendships (Lavallee & Parker, in press; Parker, Low, et al., 2005). The "gloom and doom" that jealous children express over their friendships and broader social lives might be dismissed as just one further manifestation of their insecurity around peers, except that there is evidence that their friendships are in fact compromised. This conclusion stems from studies in which children or their friendship partners are asked to report on the levels of closeness and conflict they experience in their friendship (Lavallee & Parker, in press; Parker, McGuire, et al., 2009; Parker & Wargo Aikins, 2009). Children or young teens who are highly prone to jealousy report greater conflict and less closeness with their friends than do other children. More importantly, when children are prone to jealousy, their friendship partners also indicate that the relationship has more conflict and less closeness. Indeed, a recent social relations analysis using multilevel modeling indicates that a primary reason that different children who are friends with the same individual report different levels of conflict in their relationship with that partner is because that target partner is not equally jealous in each relationship (Parker, McGuire, et al., 2009). When a target is more jealous toward one friend than another, those friends have different social experiences with the target.

The conflict that jealous children have with their friends is not surprising. Because little consensus exists on the norms of exclusivity in friendship, substantial opportunity presumably exists in this context for disagreement on behaviors that constitute infidelity and betrayal. Negative jealous responses can be flattering to partners, at least for a time. Eventually, however, partners will find this behavior difficult. Coercive efforts to keep partners dependent on the relationship or relationally aggressive attempts to keep others away are likely to be received negatively by partners, for example. Threats to end the relationship, or passive aggressive pouting or use of "silent treatment," while perhaps immediately effective, can become tiresome to even a committed partner. Jealousy can therefore contribute to conflict between the friends and, via this route, ultimately undercuts the closeness and more positive features of these relationships. Ironically, then, jealous individuals may compromise the very relationships they are so concerned with preserving.

Although negative jealous behavior is likely to have its strongest impact on relationship partners, it may also influence social adjustment beyond the context of the immediate relationship. Over time, habitually jealous individuals may build a retinue of disgruntled past friends within the group, lowering their overall social standing and acceptance. Likewise, even if their friends remain patient with them,

Table 22.1   Correlations among friends' and non-friends' reports of jealousy and several forms of aggression

	JF	JO	DA	PA	IA
Jealousy—friend reported (JF)		.45	.41	.42	.44
Jealousy—non-friend reported (JO)	.34		.77	.87	.91
Direct aggression (DA)	.09	.49		.82	.80
Passive aggression (PA)	.38	.71	.55		.88
Indirect aggression (IA)	.29	.70	.74	.64	

Note: Correlations for girls appear above the diagonal and those for boys appear below the diagonal. Correlations that appear in bold are $p < .05$ or greater.

individuals who habitually behave in overprotective ways around friends, particularly if they direct aggression toward outsiders, may exhaust the goodwill of the peer group and develop enemies. Further, peers may perceive unwarranted jealousy as a sign of insecurity, immaturity, and weakness, leaving habitually jealous children at risk for being victimized by more powerful and successful peers.

These hypotheses have been supported to some extent in several of our past studies. In particular, children with peer reputations for friendship jealousy also are less accepted by peers in general, have more mutual enemies, and are victimized by their peers (Parker & Gamm, 2003; Parker, Low, et al. 2005). Additionally, our past work supports the presence of a reliable link between jealousy and aggression. Table 22.1, for example, presents simple correlations from one of our recent studies (Parker, Low, et al., 2005) in which children's peer reputation for several forms of aggression were found to be related with their best friends' and other non-friend peers' reports of their vulnerability to jealousy over friends. Direct aggression refers to acts of physical assault or intimidation. Passive aggression includes whining, giving the silent treatment, or threats to break off the friendship. Indirect aggression includes excluding others or spreading rumors and gossip. As shown, jealousy is positively and significantly associated with passive and indirect aggression in boys and with every form of aggression in girls. The magnitude of these associations is generally quite high, particularly with regard to indirect aggression in girls.

Summary and Conclusions

It might be difficult to discern from the way researchers have approached friendships in the past, but children's friendship experiences are very public affairs. Typically children have many friends, spending time with these friends at the same time, and are aware that their friends have other friends. Friendship interaction in groups can be rewarding in specific ways and extra-dyadic network members can cement dyadic partners' commitments to one another, mitigate friendship disputes, and introduce innovation and variety into relationships (Milardo & Helms-Erikson, 2000). However, the time and emotional commitments that friendship partners make to outside peers can limit that available within the relationship, diminish its perceived uniqueness, and lead to feelings of jealousy.

The experience of jealousy is a blend of strong negative emotions, much stronger than those that accompany other types of friendship disappointments. In addition, jealousy is based on perceptions of threat, although very little is confidently known about the appraisals and attributions children and teens make in jealous circumstances. Our research does seem to indicate that both boys and girls judge their friends harshly in jealous circumstances, regarding them as insensitive. This presumably has important consequences for the relationship. In addition, girls also seem to hold harsh views of the culpability of interlopers in jealous circumstances. No doubt, this is a source of great tension in groups of girls, particularly if all members are not already friends or if envy and rivalry already exist within specific pairs of group members. Additionally, some support exists for the conclusion that what jealous individuals find particularly distressing is not only the interloper's infringement on the relationship, but also the implied unfavorable social comparison to the interloper and inferred rejection by the partner. Finally, children's behavioral responses to jealousy are quite varied, and include some adaptive and positive responses. However, jealousy is emotionally disquieting, and it is therefore not surprising that children also respond problematically to jealousy, including with subterfuge and aggression. The emotions, attributions, and behavioral responses of jealous individuals are presumably linked, but little about these linkages is well understood at present.

Although all children experience jealousy from time to time, there is good evidence that some children are highly prone to this experience. Peers, friends, and the children themselves can all provide meaningful data on this point, although these sources understandably don't always agree completely. These differences are highly reliable and generally stable, even over lengthy periods. Chronically jealous children appear to have several personality or other traits that leave them vulnerable. They tend to have lower global self-esteem, for example, and more negative views of their physical appearance at an age when physical attractiveness is an important form of social capital in the peer group. Their self-esteem also appears to be more closely tied to social recognition and approval than that of other children. And they have less faith that peers and their parents accept and value them. Presumably, children with insecure views of themselves or others may more readily interpret negative events in close relationships as rejection and abandonment and therefore to have a lower threshold for jealousy in their relationships. It is important to extend understanding of the psychological roots of the disposition to friendship jealousy by considering other self-perceptions, family climate variables, and patterns of parent–child discourse that may play a role, however.

When individuals report being or are perceived by friends and others as being prone to friendship jealousy they are lonely, unhappy, and ruminative. Moreover, while a good deal remains to be understood regarding how characteristically jealous children differ behaviorally from their non-jealous peers, our research supports the conclusion that their friendships suffer. This link between jealousy and friendship adjustment is significant in light of other research indicating that children who are unable to form and maintain friendships are at relative risk for a variety of subsequent negative interpersonal and intrapersonal outcomes (Parker & Asher, 1987). Over the past decade, progress has been made in understanding the social skills underlying successful peer involvement in childhood and adolescence (Asher, Parker, & Walker, 1996; Parker, Saxon, Asher, & Kovacs, 1999). An assumption of this approach is that some individuals encounter difficulties with friends or potential friends because they fail to handle various friendship challenges effectively. For example, to form and maintain friendships, individuals must manage disagreements effectively, possess skills for participating in self-disclosure, recognize and respect norms of equality between partners, and be able to express caring, concern, and affection in appropriate ways (Asher et al., 1996; Rose & Asher, 2000). However, few of these frameworks acknowledge that even when individuals treat their friendship partners well directly, problems can surface when they engage in interesting activities with others or have outside relationships.

Our findings suggest that it might be helpful to social skills oriented friendship interventions to prepare friendship members to be sensitive to the circumstances that can sometimes lead partners to feel abandoned, excluded, or jealous, particularly if those partners are vulnerable to this. On the other hand, it would seem that some individuals could be helped by greater attention in these interventions to promoting the social and cognitive skills that prepare individuals to expect disappointment due to outside interference at times, interpret group friendship involvement benignly and even benefit from it, and assist adolescents and children with taking a more balanced view in which they recognize that no single relationship, no matter its quality, can meet all the interpersonal needs of an individual (Selman, 1980).

However, problems of jealousy are not just issues for the dyads in which they arise; jealousy appears to have broader implications for adjustment and may become entrenched through a spiraling and self-fulfilling cycle. Jealous individuals are poorly liked, have more enemies, and are more victimized in the peer group. Moreover, habitually jealous individuals are among the most notoriously aggressive individuals in their classroom or group. Furthermore, jealousy is a strong predictor of children's reputations for forms of subtle aggression, such as spreading rumors and excluding others. This is particularly notable because these so-called relational forms of aggression have been difficult to account for in traditional models developed to explain physical aggression and emphasizing social skills deficits. Perhaps the perpetrators of relational aggression are not so much incompetent as they are insecure and self-doubting.

Acknowledgments

We would like to acknowledge the numerous colleagues, graduate students, and undergraduate honors students whose research and theses contributed to the findings described in this chapter, including: Cynthia Campbell, Joanna Chango, Nassim Ebrahimi, Bridget Gamm, Kaelyn Giltenboth, Sarah Kollat, Kristen Lavallee, Karen Libber, Christine Low, Alysa Lucas, Amanda Lukens, Jessica McGuire, Christine Ramich, Melanie Roth, Kathryn Stump, Sarah Tarquini, Alisha Walker, Erica Wampold, and Emily Wills. The research reported in this chapter was supported by National Science Foundation grant BCS0451261, awarded to the first author.

References

Andersen, P. A., Eloy, S. V., Guerrero, L. K., & Spitzberg, B. H. (1995). Romantic jealousy and relational satisfaction: A look at the impact of jealousy experience and expression. *Communication Reports, 8*, 77–85.

Asher, S. R., Parker, J. G., & Walker, D. (1996). Distinguishing friendship from acceptance: Implications for intervention and assessment. In W. M. Bukowski, A. F. Newcomb, & W. W. Hartup (Eds.), *The company they keep: Friendships in childhood and adolescence* (pp. 366–405). Cambridge: Cambridge University Press.

Beal, C. R. (1994). *Boys and girls: The development of gender roles.* New York: McGraw-Hill.

Benenson, J. F., Maiese, R., Dolenszky, E., Dolenszky, E., Sinclair, N., & Simpson, A. (2002). Group size regulates self-assertive versus self-deprecating responses to interpersonal competition. *Child Development, 73*, 1818–1829.

Berndt, T. J. (2002). Friendship quality and social development. *Current Directions in Psychological Science, 11*, 7–10.

Berndt, T. J. (2007). Children's friendships: Shifts over a half-century in perspectives on their development and their effects. In G. W. Ladd (Ed.), *Appraising the human developmental sciences: Essays in honor of Merrill-Palmer Quarterly* (pp. 138–155). Detroit, MI: Wayne State University Press.

Bers, S. A., & Rodin, J. (1984). Social-comparison jealousy: A developmental and motivational study. *Journal of Personality and Social Psychology, 47*, 766–779.

Bigelow, B. J., Tesson, G., & Lewko, J. H. (1996). *Learning the rules: The anatomy of children's relationships.* New York: Guildford Press.

Björkqvist, K. (1994). Sex differences in physical, verbal, and indirect aggression: A review of recent research. *Sex Roles, 30*, 177–188.

Bowlby, J. (1969). *Attachment and loss: Attachment.* New York: Basic Books.

Bringle, R. G. & Buunk, B. (1985). Jealousy and social behavior: A review of person, relationship and situational determinants. In P. Shaver (Ed.), *Review of Personality and Social Psychology* (Vol. 6, pp. 241–264). Beverly Hills, CA: Sage.

Bringle, R. G., Renner, P., Terry, R. L., & Davis, S. (1983). An analysis of situation and person components of jealousy. *Journal of Research in Personality, 17*, 354–368.

Bringle, R. G., Roach, S., Andier, C., & Evenbeck, S. (1979). Measuring the intensity of jealous reactions. *JSAS Catalog of Selected Documents in Psychology, 9*, 23–24 (Ms. No. 1832).

Brown, B. B., Larson, R. W., & Saraswathi, T. S. (2002). *The world's youth: Adolescence in eight regions of the globe.* Cambridge: Cambridge University Press.

Brown, L. M., Way, N., & Duff, J. L. (1999). The others in my I: Adolescent girls' friendships and peer relations. In N. G. Johnson, M. C. Roberts, & J. Worell (Eds.), *Beyond Appearance: A new look at adolescent girls* (pp. 205–226). Washington, DC: American Psychological Association.

Buss, D. M., Larson, R. J., Weston, D., & Semmelroth, J. (1992). Sex differences in jealousy: Evolution, physiology, and psychology. *Psychological Science, 3,* 251–255.

Buunk, B. (1982). Strategies of jealousy: Styles of coping with extramarital involvement of the spouse. *Family Relations, 31,* 13–18.

Buunk, B. P. (1997). Personality, birth order, and attachment styles as related to various types of jealousy. *Personality and Individual Differences, 23,* 997–1006.

Buunk, B. P. & Bringle, R.G. (1987). Jealousy in love relationships. In D. Perlman & S. Duck (Eds.), *Intimate relationships: Development, dynamics, and deterioration* (pp. 123–147). Thousand Oaks, CA: Sage.

Buunk, B. P., & Dijkstra, P. (2002). Extradyadic relationships and jealousy. In C. Hendrick & S. S. Hendrick (Eds.), *Close relationships: A sourcebook* (pp. 317–330). Thousand Oaks, CA: Sage.

Cairns, R., Xie, H., & Leung, M. (1998). The popularity of friendship and the neglect of social networks: Toward a new balance. In W. M. Bukowski & A. H. Cillessen (Eds.), *Sociometry then and now: Building on six decades of measuring children's experiences with the peer group* (pp. 25–53). San Francisco: Jossey-Bass.

Canary, D. J., Spitzberg, B. H., & Semic, B. A. (1998). The experience and expression of anger in interpersonal settings. In P. A. Andersen & L. K. Guerrero (Eds.), *Handbook of communication and emotion: Theory, research, and applications* (pp. 189–213). San Diego, CA: Academic Press.

Crick, N. R., & Dodge, K. A. (1994). A review and reformulation of social information processing mechanisms in children's social adjustment. *Psychological Bulletin, 115,* 74–101.

Crockett, L., Losoff, M. & Petersen, A.C. (1984). Perceptions of the peer group and friendship in early adolescence. *Journal of Early Adolescence, 4,* 155–181.

DeSteno, D. A. & Salovey, P. (1996). Jealousy and the characteristics of one's rival: A self-evaluation maintenance perspective. *Personality and Social Psychology Bulletin, 22,* 920–932.

Ebrahimi, N., Parker, J. G., Lavallee, K., & Seiffke-Krenke, I. (April, 2005). *Adolescent self-esteem and jealousy's reciprocal relations over time.* Paper presented at the biennial meetings of the Society for Research in Child Development, Atlanta, GA.

Fletcher, A. C., Hunter, A. G., & Eanes, A. Y. (2006). Links between social network closure and child well-being: The organizing role of friendship context. *Developmental Psychology, 42,* 1057–1068.

Fonzi, A., Schneider, B. H., Tani, F., & Tomada, G. (1997). Predicting children's friendship status from their dyadic interaction in structured situations of potential conflict. *Child Development, 68,* 496–506.

Furman, W. (1996). The measurement of friendship perceptions: Conceptual and methodological issues. In W. M. Bukowski, A. F. Newcomb, & W. W. Hartup (Eds.), *The company they keep: Friendship in childhood and adolescence* (pp. 41–65). Cambridge: Cambridge University Press.

George, T. P. & Hartmann, D. P. (1996). Friendship networks of unpopular, average, and popular children. *Child Development, 67,* 2301–2316.

Giltenboth, K. J. (2001). *Expressions of jealousy in friendships and romantic relationships: Influence of gender and type of rival.* Unpublished honors thesis. Pennsylvania State University, PA.

Gottman, J. M. (1983). How children become friends. *Monographs of the Society for Research in Child Development, 48*(3, Serial No. 201), 1–86.

Guerrero, L. K., & Afifi, W. A. (1999). Toward a goal-oriented approach for understanding communicative responses to jealousy. *Western Journal of Communication, 63*, 216–248.

Guerrero, L. K., & Andersen, P. A. (1998). The dark side of jealously and envy: Desire, delusion, desperation, and destructive communication. In B. H. Spitzberg & W. R. Cupach, (Eds.), *The dark side of close relationships* (pp. 33–70). Mahwah, NJ: Erlbaum.

Guerrero, L. K., & Andersen, P. A. (2000). Emotions in close relationships. In C. Hendrick & S. S. Hendrick (Eds.), *Close relationships: A sourcebook* (pp. 171–184). Thousand Oaks, CA: Sage.

Guerrero, L. K., Andersen, P. A., Jorgensen, P. F., Spitzberg, B. H., Eloy, S. V. (1995). Friendship jealousy in junior high school coping with the green-eyed monster: Conceptualizing and measuring communicative responses to romantic jealousy. *Western Journal of Communication, 59*(4), 270–304.

Halberstadt, A.G., Denham, S.A., & Dunsmore, J.C. (2001). Affective social competence. *Social Development, 10*, 79–119.

Hansen, G. L. (1991). Jealousy: Its conceptualization, measurement, and integration within family stress theory. In P. Salovey (Ed.), *The psychology of jealousy and envy* (pp. 252– 272). New York: Guilford Press.

Harris, C. R. (2000). Psychophysiological responses to imagined infidelity: The specific innate modular view of jealousy reconsidered. *Journal of Personality and Social Psychology, 78*, 1082–1091.

Hart, S. L. (this volume). The ontogenesis of jealousy in the first year of life: A theory of jealousy as a biologically-based dimension of temperament. In S. L. Hart & M. Legerstee (Eds.), *Handbook of jealousy: Theory, research, and multidisciplinary approaches.* Malden, MA: Wiley-Blackwell.

Hart, S. L., & Carrington, H. (2002). Jealousy in 6-month-old infants. *Infancy, 3*, 395–402.

Hartup, W. W., French, D. C., Laursen, B., Johnston, M. K., & Ogawa, J. R. (1993). Conflict and friendship relations in middle childhood: Behavior in a closed-field situation. *Child Development, 64*, 445–454.

Kless, S. J. (1992). The attainment of peer status: Gender and power relationships in the elementary school. *Sociological Studies of Child Development, 5*, 115–148.

Kollat, S. H., & Parker, J. G. (April, 2005). *What me jealous? Social sensitivity, emotion regulation, and young adolescents' aggressive responses to jealous threats.* Paper presented at the biennial meetings of the Society for Research in Child Development, Atlanta, GA.

Kollat, S. H., & Parker, J. G. (April, 2007). *It's all in the outcome: The role of contingent parental communication in children's development of contingent self-esteem and aggression.* Paper presented at the biennial meetings of the Society for Research in Child Development, Boston, MA.

Kuttler, A. F., Parker, J. G., & La Greca, A. M. (2002). Developmental and gender differences in preadolescents' judgments of the veracity of gossip. *Merrill-Palmer Quarterly, 48*, 105– 132.

Lansford, J., & Parker, J. G. (1999). Children's interactions in triads: Behavioral profiles and effects of gender and patterns of friendships among members. *Developmental Psychology, 35*, 80–93.

Larson, R., & Richards, M. H. (1991). Daily companionship in late childhood and early adolescence: Changing developmental contexts. *Child Development, 62*, 284–300.

Lavallee, K. L. (2002). *Just the two of us: The role of social inflexibility in young adolescents' friendship jealousy and social-emotional adjustment*. Unpublished master's thesis, Pennsylvania State University, PA.

Lavallee, K. L, & Parker, J. G. (in press). The role of inflexible friendship beliefs, rumination, and low self-worth in preadolescents' friendship jealousy and adjustment. *Journal of Abnormal Child Psychology*.

Lemerise, E. A., & Arsenio, W. F. (2000). An integrated model of emotion processes and cognition in social information processing. *Child Development, 71*, 107–118.

Levine, L. J. (1995). Young children's understanding of the causes of anger and sadness. *Child Development, 66*, 697–709.

Mathes, E. W., Adams, H., E., & Davies, R. M. (1985). Jealousy: Loss of relationship rewards, loss of self-esteem, depression, anxiety, and anger. *Journal of Personality and Social Psychology, 48*, 1552–1561.

Mathes, E. W., Phillips, J. T., Skowran, J., & Dick, W. E. (1982). Behavioral correlates of the Interpersonal Jealousy Scale. *Educational and Psychological Measurement, 42*, 1227– 1231.

McCall, G. J. (1988). The organizational life cycle of relationships. In S. Duck (Ed.), *Handbook of personal relationships* (pp. 467–484). Chichester: Wiley.

McNelles, L., & Connolly, J. (1999). Intimacy between adolescent friends: Age and gender differences in shared affect and behavioral form. *Journal of Research on Adolescence, 9*, 143–159.

Milardo, R. M., & Helms-Erikson, H. (2000). Network overlap and third-party influence in close relationships. In C. Hendrick & S. S. Hendrick (Eds.), *Close relationships: A sourcebook* (pp. 33–46). Thousand Oaks, CA: Sage.

Montemayor, R., & Van-Komen, R. (1985). The development of sex differences in friendship patterns and peer group structure during adolescence. *Journal of Early Adolescence, 5*, 285–294.

Nangle, D. W., & Erdley, C. A. (2001). *The role of friendship in psychological adjustment*. San Francisco: Jossey-Bass.

Parker, J. G. & Asher, S. R. (1987). Peer relations and later personal adjustment: Are low-accepted children at risk? *Psychological Bulletin, 102*, 357–389.

Parker, J. G., Campbell, C., Kollat, S., & Lucas, A. (July, 2008). *The role of contingent self-esteem in adolescents' jealous and aggressive responses to friendship interference*. Paper presented at the annual meetings of the International Association of Relationship Researchers, Providence, RI.

Parker, J. G., Campbell, C., Lucas, A. (April, 2007). *Individual differences in adolescents' behavioral and cognitive responses to jealousy and rival attractiveness among same-sex friends*. Paper presented at the biennial meetings of the Society for Research in Child Development, Boston, MA.

Parker, J. G., Ebrahimi, N., & Libber, K. (April, 2005). *Body image insecurity and rival's physical attractiveness in adolescents' jealousy surrounding friends and romantic partners*. Paper presented at the biennial meetings of the Society for Research in Child Development, Atlanta, GA.

Parker, J. G., & Gamm, B. K. (2003). Describing the dark side of preadolescents' peer experiences: Four questions (and data) on preadolescents' enemies. *New Directions for Child and Adolescent Development, 2003*(102), 55–72.

Parker, J. G., & Herrera, C. (1996). Interpersonal processes in friendship: A comparison of maltreated and nonmaltreated children's experiences. *Developmental Psychology, 32,* 1025–1038.

Parker, J. G., Low, C., Walker, A. R., & Gamm, B. A. (2005). Friendship jealousy in young adolescents: Individual differences and links to sex, self-esteem, aggression, and social adjustment. *Developmental Psychology, 41,* 235–250.

Parker, J. G., McGuire, J. E., Rosen, L., & Underwood, M. K. (April, 2009). *Actor, partner, and relationship contributions to early adolescents' expressions of jealousy surrounding close friends.* Paper presented at the biennial meetings of the Society for Research in Child Development, Denver, CO.

Parker, J. G., Ramich, C., & Roth, M. (2009). *Third party peers as interlopers: Role of outside peer interference in preadolescents' feelings and thoughts surrounding friendship disappointments.* Unpublished manuscript: University of Alabama, AL.

Parker, J. G., Saxon, J. L., Asher, S. R., & Kovacs, D. M. (1999). Dimensions of children's friendship adjustment: Implications for understanding loneliness. In K. J. Rotenberg & S. Hymel (Eds.), *Loneliness in childhood and adolescence* (pp. 201–221). New York: Cambridge University Press.

Parker, J. G., & Seal, J. (1996). Forming, losing, renewing, and replacing friendships: Applying temporal parameters to the assessment of children's friendship experiences. *Child Development, 67,* 2248–2268.

Parker, J. G., & Wargo Aikins, J. (2009). *Understanding the antecedents, relationship implications, and perpetuation of the disposition to friendship jealousy at the transition to junior high school.* Unpublished manuscript. University of Alabama, AL.

Pfeiffer, S. M., & Wong, P. T. (1989). Multidimensional jealousy. *Journal of Social and Personal Relationships, 6,* 181–196.

Radecki-Bush, C., Farrell, A. D., & Bush, J. P. (1993). Predicting jealous responses: The influence of adult attachment and depression on threat appraisal. *Journal of Social and Personal Relationships, 10,* 569–588.

Richards, M. H., Crowe, P. A., Larson, R., & Swarr, A. (1998). Developmental patterns and gender differences in the experience of peer companionship during adolescence. *Child Development, 69,* 154–163.

Rose, A. J., & Asher, S. R. (2000). Children's friendships. In C. Hendrick & S. Hendrick (Eds.), *Close relationships* (pp. 47–58). Thousand Oaks, CA: Sage.

Roth, M. A., & Parker, J. G. (2001). Affective and behavioral responses to friends who neglect their friends for dating partners: Influences of gender, jealousy, and perspective. *Journal of Adolescence, 24,* 281–296.

Rubin, K., Bukowski, W. M., & Parker, J. G. (2006). Peer interactions, relationships, and groups. In W. Damon & R. M. Lerner (Series Eds.) & N. Eisenberg (Vol. Ed.), *Handbook of child psychology: Vol. 3. Social, emotional, and personality development* (6th ed., pp. 571–645). New York: Wiley.

Rusbult, C. (1983). A longitudinal test of the investment model: The development (and deterioration) of satisfaction and commitment in heterosexual involvements. *Journal of Personality and Social Psychology, 45,* 172–186.

Rusbult, C. E., & Buunk, B. P. (1993). Commitment processes in close relationships: An interdependence analysis. *Journal of Social and Personal Relationships, 10,* 175–204.

Sabongui, A. G., Bukowski, W. M., & Newcomb, A. F. (1998). The peer ecology of popularity: The network embeddedness of a child's friends predicts the child's subsequent popularity. In W. M. Bukowski & A. H. Cillessen (Eds.). *Sociometry then and now: Building on six decades of measuring children's experiences with the peer group* (pp. 83– 92). San Francisco: Jossey-Bass.

Salovey, P., & Rodin, J. (1984). Some antecedents and consequences of social-comparison jealousy. *Journal of Personality and Social Psychology, 47,* 780–792.

Salovey, P., & Rodin, J. (1988). Coping with envy and jealousy. *Journal of Social and Clinical Psychology, 7,* 15–33.

Salovey, P. & Rodin, J. (1989). Envy and jealousy in close relationships. In C. Hendrick (Ed.), *Close Relationships* (pp. 221–246). Newbury Park, CA: Sage.

Selman, R. L. (1980). *The growth of interpersonal understanding: Developmental and clinical analyses.* New York: Academic Press.

Selman, R. L., & Schultz, L. H. (1990). *Making a friend in youth: Developmental theory and pair therapy.* Chicago: University of Chicago Press.

Sharabany, R., Gershoni, R., & Hofman, J. E. (1981). Girlfriend, boyfriend: Age and sex differences in intimate friendship. *Developmental Psychology, 17,* 800–808.

Sharpsteen, D. J. (1993). Romantic jealousy as an emotion concept: A prototype analysis. *Journal of Social and Personal Relationships, 10,* 69–82.

Sharpsteen, D. J. (1995). The effects of relationship and self-esteem threats on the likelihood of romantic jealousy. *Journal of Social and Personal Relationships, 12,* 89–101.

Sharpsteen, D. J. & Kirkpatrick, L. A. (1997). Romantic jealousy and adult romantic attachment. *Journal of Personality and Social Psychology, 72,* 627–640.

Silverman, W. K., La Greca, A. M., & Wasserstein, S. B. (1995). What do children worry about? Worries and their relationship to anxiety. *Child Development, 66,* 671–686.

Simmons, R. (2002). *Odd girl out: The hidden culture of aggression in girls.* Harcourt: New York.

Simpkins, S. D., & Parke, R. D. (2002). Do friends and nonfriends behave differently? A social relations analysis of children's behavior. *Merrill-Palmer Quarterly, 48,* 263–283.

South, S. J., & Haynie, D. L. (2004). Social networks of mobile adolescents. *Social Forces, 83,* 315–350.

Stets, J. E., & Pirog-Good, M. A. (1987). Violence in dating relationships. *Social Psychology Quarterly, 50,* 237–246.

Tangney, J. P., & Salovey, P. (1999). Problematic social emotions: Shame, guilt, jealousy, and envy. In R. M. Kowalski, M. Robin, & M. R. Leary (Eds). *The social psychology of emotional and behavioral problems: Interfaces of social and clinical psychology* (pp. 167–195). Washington, DC: American Psychological Association.

White, G. L. (1981a). A model of romantic jealousy. *Motivation and Emotion, 5,* 295–310.

White, G. L. (1981b). Some correlates of romantic jealousy. *Journal of Personality and Social Psychology, 49,* 129–147.

White, G. L. (1981c). Relative involvement, inadequacy, and jealousy. *Alternative Lifestyles, 4,* 291–309.

White, G. L., & Mullen, P. E. (1989). *Jealousy: Theory, research, and clinical strategies.* New York: Guilford Press.

23

Jealousy in Adulthood

Christine R. Harris and Ryan S. Darby

If you have not experienced jealousy, you have not loved. (Saint Augustine)
Jealousy, that dragon which slays love under the pretence of keeping it alive.
(Havelock Ellis)

There is no doubt that jealousy is a source of great personal misery and an emotion with far-reaching social consequences. For example, jealousy is frequently implicated as a factor in relationship dissolution, spousal abuse and even murder (Daly & Wilson, 1988; Harris, 2003a). Despite its destructive side, jealousy also may have some positive effects for individuals and relationships. For example, it alerts one to relationship threats and can motivate behaviors that protect the relationship.

This chapter will focus on jealousy in adulthood, particularly as it occurs in romantic relationships, given that this is the area that has received the most empirical attention. We begin with a discussion of theoretical approaches and conceptual debates on the nature and function of jealousy. The next sections cover factors that impact the elicitation, experience, and expression of jealousy including adult attachment styles, relationship variables, attributional processes, rival characteristics, and gender. We also examine jealousy at its most dire, including jealousy-inspired homicide and pathological jealousy. We then discuss empirical challenges faced by the field and present some new studies that actively elicit jealousy in the laboratory.

Theoretical Approaches to Jealousy

Theories of jealousy are quite varied, with researchers focusing on different levels of analyses ranging from ultimate (Darwinian) function to psychological mechanisms and situational variables. These diverse approaches have resulted in many intriguing findings. However, such variation also makes it difficult to summarize

Handbook of Jealousy: Theory, Research and Multidisciplinary Approaches, First Edition.
Edited by Sybil L. Hart and Maria Legerstee.
© 2013 Blackwell Publishing Ltd. Published 2013 by Blackwell Publishing Ltd.

major theoretical ideas in the field since researchers use a number of different terminologies and often do not place their findings in any larger theoretical framework. In this chapter, we will describe some of the more prominent ideas and try to draw connections across different approaches where possible. The first few theoretical issues we will discuss are conceptual or definitional in nature.

Defining features

For most theorists, the most defining features of jealousy are that it requires a social triangle and occurs when someone perceives that another person (who may be real or imaginary) poses a potential threat to an important interpersonal relationship (e.g., Parrott & Smith, 1993; Mathes, 1991; Salovey & Rothman, 1991; White & Mullen, 1989). Rejection, or fear thereof, can also be integral in jealousy. The rejection that induces jealousy is proposed to be different from some other types of rejection in that one's interpersonal loss involves another's interpersonal gain (Parrott, 1991; Mathes, Adams, & Davies, 1985).

Jealousy is generally agreed to be an emotion that serves to motivate behaviors that protect one's relationship from potential usurpers. As we will see, some theorists have focused on immediate consequences of jealousy-induced behaviors for individuals and relationships, whereas others have theorized about possible (Darwinian) functions in remote human ancestral past.

Most of the work on jealousy in adults has focused on jealousy in romantic relationships. However, several theorists have argued that the same basic process that produces jealous feelings in sexual relationships also leads to jealousy that arises in other kinds of relationships such as friendships or between siblings for a parent's favor (DeSteno, Valdesolo, & Bartlett, 2006; Harris, 2003a; Parrott, 1991; Salovey & Rodin, 1984). For many, the first pangs of jealousy may arise during competition with siblings for parental attention (Trivers, 1972; Volling, McElwain, & Miller, 2002).

Jealousy: A blended or specific emotion?

The exact nature of the emotional underpinnings of jealousy and the processes that give rise to it are debated. Some have suggested that jealousy involves different component emotions such as anger, fear, and sadness. One possibility is that all of these emotions are experienced simultaneously (Sharpsteen, 1991). Another hypothesis is that the specific emotion one feels changes over the course of a single jealous episode as appraisals of the situation change (Hupka, 1984). A third possibility is that jealousy is a term that encompasses any of a variety of thoughts and feelings that arise within a specific type of social situation, namely, a love triangle (White & Mullen, 1989). There seems little doubt that various emotions can occur in situations that invoke jealousy or as a result of attempting to cope with jealousy. However, others see jealousy as a distinct affective state with its own unique motivations, separate from other emotions.

One way researchers have tried to understand distinct emotions is by focusing on their ultimate functions (Frijda, 1986). From this perspective, emotions are motivational states that have been shaped by natural selection. Each emotion functions to motivate one to engage in certain behaviors that one might otherwise not engage in—behaviors that have, over phylogenetic history, tended to confer some adaptive advantage in some set of situations (Ekman, 1992; Frijda, 1986; Keltner & Haidt, 1999). Each emotional state is proposed to have its own distinct motivational tendencies or "urges" (Frijda, 1986) that are activated by particular appraisals. For example, fear is induced by the appraisal of threat, even if not conscious, and motivates escape from or avoidance of the dangerous stimuli.

One functional view proposes that jealousy evolved as a specific emotion to motivate behaviors that break up or prevent, either psychologically or physically, the threatening liaison that is perceived to exist between an important other and a rival, and thereby, protect the primary relationship (Harris, 2003a). Importantly, this motivational state would not be created automatically by other emotions that are frequently offered as the more essential emotional components of jealousy (namely, anger, fear, and sadness). Threats to usurp relationships likely had important consequences for one's Darwinian fitness given that relationships, whether romantic/sexual or not, provide a variety of important benefits to an individual (Baumeister & Leary, 1995; House, Landis, & Umberson, 1988). For example, jealousy over siblings may have ensured that one received one's necessary share of a parent's limited time, affection, food, etc. (Trivers, 1972).

As noted above, most researchers who take a specific emotions view of jealousy assume that it was selected for by natural selection. However, theories of jealousy as a blended emotion are also potentially compatible with the idea that jealousy is an evolved adaptation.

Appraisals in Jealousy

Some researchers who employ a specific emotions perspective focus on the appraisals that give rise to jealousy (Lazarus, 1991; Harris, 2003a). Although the appraisal and motivational approaches can be viewed as distinct, they are generally complementary and in practice often tend to differ only in a matter of which aspect of an emotional episode is emphasized (Lerner & Tiedens, 2006).

Primitive and elaborated jealousy

One possible model of jealousy is that it has a primitive or "core" form that can be elicited by a primary appraisal of threat that arises from input as simple as the perception that a loved one has turned their attention to a potential rival and away from the self (Harris, 2003a). The jealous state would then motivate behaviors designed to restore the loved one's attention to the self. Ontogenetic studies that find jealousy in infants as young as 6 months and cross-species work that documents behaviors resembling jealousy in nonhuman animals would be consistent with the view that minimal cognition, which need not be conscious, is necessary for the elicitation of jealousy (Cubiciotti & Mason, 1978; Hart & Carrington 2002; see also other chapters in this volume).

However, at least in humans, jealousy can also take on a more elaborate form. With cognitive development, triggers for jealousy become more sophisticated. For example, work by Masciuch and Kienapple (1993) finds that even by 4 years of age, the specifics of a social triangle influence whether jealousy arises. Children who were 4 or older expressed more jealousy over their mothers interacting with a similar-aged peer than with an infant. Jealousy in younger children was not affected by the age of the rival. One possibility is that in this situation, older children have learned that babies require special attention. Therefore, one's mother paying attention to an infant is perceived as less threatening relative to her appearing to favor a peer who is more similar to oneself. Thus, it seems that over the course of development, an individual's social and cognitive appraisals of the meaning of the interactions between the rival and the loved one become increasingly important in the evocation of jealousy.

Appraisals also play an important role in the progression of jealous affect. Extension of Richard Lazarus's (1991) theory of emotions may illuminate this progression. After the initial appraisal of threat to the relationship, one immediately engages in further cognitive assessments. These secondary appraisals include trying to determine the scope of the threat as well as attempts to cope with it (e.g., *I'll put a stop to this; Is my partner going to leave me?; It is my own fault that this happened?*). As one attempts to further assess and to deal with the jealous situation, other secondary emotions such as anger, fear, and sadness are likely to be elicited.

Social cognitive perspective

Given that many theorists have emphasized the importance of cognitive appraisals in the elicitation of emotion, it is not surprising that much of the work on jealousy in adults has employed a social cognitive framework. Research in this tradition has focused on two general features that make a partner's involvement with another particularly threatening. The first is the potential loss of relationship rewards. Many of the benefits that are obtained from interpersonal relationships are finite, such as money or resources. Even intangible rewards like affection and attention that may seem infinite are limited by time. Therefore, if a relationship partner is providing these benefits to someone else, it can be at a cost to oneself. This is likely one of the reasons why the arrival of a new sibling can be particularly difficult for a child—the exclusive attention and affection that were theirs are now shared. Interestingly, the same underlying process may also be responsible for the feelings that new fathers sometimes express when their wives' attention is consumed by a newborn.

A second factor that plays an important role in jealousy is threat to representations of the self. The existence of a rival can be particularly threatening because it challenges some aspect of a person's self-definition (Parrott, 1991), self-identity (Salovey & Rothman, 1991), or self-esteem (Mathes, 1991). Several theorists have noted the importance that relationships play in defining the self and self-worth. Therefore, rivals to relationships not only threaten relationship rewards, but also the very value of the self. For example, when faced with a partner's infidelity, people appraise the meaning of the betrayal in terms of the implications about the self (*Did she have sex with him because I'm a bad lover? Or because I am unattractive?*). The answers to such questions will impact the intensity of the distress. According to Salovey and colleagues' "domain relevance hypothesis," rivals who surpass an individual in domains that he or she finds important and relevant to his or her self-definition are most likely to evoke jealousy (Salovey & Rothman, 1991; Salovey & Rodin, 1984; Tesser, 1988). Research on this topic will be discussed in a later section. Jealousy may be particularly likely to occur when the threatened relationship involves a person to whom one is sexually attracted or involved with because of the special importance of romantic relationships in self-esteem and in providing relationship rewards (White & Mullen, 1989).

Attachment Style and Jealousy

Romantic relationships seem to be formed, at least partially, through attachment processes that are similar to those which occur between infants and their caregivers (Hazan & Shaver, 1987). Roughly defined, an attachment relationship is an emotional or affectionate bond with another individual. As discussed in John Bowlby's (1969) seminal work, infants are predisposed to form emotional connections with their caregivers. This encourages caregivers to remain close to infants in order to provide security and care. Work by Bowlby and others, however, has shown that attachment relationships differ qualitatively.

The primary caregiver is hypothesized to play an important role in creating attachment style differences. Although some caregivers will respond immediately to an infant's distress by holding and comforting the baby, other caregivers may be more distant or inconsistent in their responses. Over time, based on these experiences, an infant develops expectations of what to expect from others and therefore what to expect from the self (Bowlby, 1969). For example, if the primary caregiver is non-responsive to the needs of the child, the child learns that others are not to be depended upon and that he or she must depend upon the self, which is characteristic of some forms of the insecure-avoidant attachment style. If the mother is responsive to the child and fills the child's needs, the child adopts a positive view of others and self, which is characteristic of the secure attachment style (Bartholomew, 1990). Development of attachment style is also likely to be influenced by the infant's temperament as well as the interaction between temperament and the caregiver's ability or desire to respond appropriately to the particular physical and emotional needs of the infant. In childhood, the three most common attachment styles are secure, insecure-avoidant, and anxious (also commonly referred to as the ambivalent attachment style because of a tendency to draw caretakers in and then push them away). This early attachment process between the primary caregiver and the child acts as an archetype for future attachment relationships, such as romantic relationships (Hazan & Shaver, 1987).

In work with adults, Hazan and Shaver (1987) have found analogous attachment styles between adult romantic attachments and infant caregiver attachments. In adulthood, individuals with a secure attachment style tend to be more confident in themselves and in their partners. They also tend to view the attachment relationship as a positive source in their lives and find it easy to establish romantic relationships with little anxiety over possible abandonment. These appraisals and behaviors are markedly different than the anxious/ambivalent attachment style. Anxious individuals also view attachment relationships positively, yet they are anxious in the attachment relationship. They have a pervasive worry of abandonment because they fear they may not be deserving of love (Hazan & Shaver, 1987). The prototypical insecure-avoidant attachment style has a negative internal working model of others (Bartholomew, 1990). Individuals with this attachment style have little confidence in other people and as a result rarely find security in attachment relationships. Some modern theorists, such as Bartholomew (1990), separate the negative internal working model of others into two different attachment styles, fearful and dismissing. The former is characterized by a fear of attachment relationships, while the latter is characterized by a lack of need for attachment relationships. In this chapter, we will focus on the original Hazan and Shaver definition and include individuals with a negative others model under the umbrella of the insecure-avoidant attachment style.

Returning to the topic of jealousy, it is easy to imagine how attachment style and jealousy may be interrelated. At its simplest, jealousy is the feeling that arises when an attachment relationship is threatened by a third party. Given that attachment styles are associated with different expectations of relationships, it has been proposed that each style has a somewhat different reaction to possible relationship threats. As Sharpsteen and Kirkpatrick (1997) aptly point out, "because romantic relationships are likely to be attachment relationships, individual differences in jealousy are likely to parallel individual differences in attachment behavior" (p. 628). Although several studies have examined the relationship between adult attachment styles and jealousy, their findings, at least at first blush, appear inconsistent. For example, some studies suggest that jealousy is more common in insecurely attached individuals, and yet other studies suggest that securely attached individuals are more likely to show jealous anger

(Buunk, 1997; Sharpsteen & Kirkpatrick, 1997). In the next section, we will discuss such research and will present a model that may help shed light on these apparently discrepant findings.

Attachment and threat—a two-stage model

We propose that one important variable that is likely to moderate an attachment style's impact on jealous reactions is stage of threat. For example, is the threat merely a vague possibility or is it a definite reality? The first stage of this model, appraisal of a threat, occurs when an individual is just becoming cognizant of a possible rival. Not all social relationships between the partner and others will actually interfere with one's romantic relationship. In order for jealousy to be elicited, the individual must appraise that on some level the new presence is in fact vying for the attention of the partner or is a potential threat to the relationship. Individuals differ in their propensity toward appraising possible rival threat. Some have low thresholds resulting in almost any new presence being interpreted as a rival. Others have high thresholds and rarely appraise another as an interloper. Thus, the initial stage in the jealousy experience focuses on whether or not a threat from a rival subjectively exists.

The second stage of the jealousy experience is the reaction to the threat. Once a potential rival passes the threat threshold, he or she is determined to be a real rival. At this point, individuals engage in additional coping mechanisms, which include reacting to the threat. Determining how to respond to feelings of jealousy is an integral part of the jealousy experience. We now turn to discussing differences in attachment styles in these two stages of the jealousy experience.

Secure attachment style

People with a secure attachment style have positive mental models of themselves and others. They put value in relationships and tend to have longer-lasting and more successful relationships (Kirkpatrick & Hazan, 1994). The success of their relationships has led researchers to two seemingly contradictory hypotheses regarding their jealousy experiences. The secure/low reactive hypothesis proposes that secure individuals feel less jealousy. The thought is that since these people tend to have successful relationships in which both they and their partners are happy, there is probably little reason for them to fear threat from possible rivals. Thus, they should feel less jealousy. In contrast, the secure/high reactive hypothesis predicts that secure individuals should show at least similar levels or perhaps even greater jealousy compared to people with other attachment styles. In particular, they may be more prone to jealous anger or may engage in more overt actions in response to their jealousy (Sharpsteen & Kirkpatrick, 1997). As secure individuals especially value attachment relationships, they may be more prone to employ jealousy to protect their important relationships. On this view, jealousy may help maintain the relationship by motivating the individual to eliminate possible threats to the relationship. The secure/high reactive hypothesis is consistent with a functional approach that jealousy evolved to preserve attachment relationships.

Empirical work on secure attachment style and jealousy finds supportive evidence for both hypotheses. Studies that ask participants to anticipate their levels of jealousy tend to find that secure individuals anticipate feeling less jealous than insecurely attached individuals (Buunk, 1997). However, studies that ask participants to recall instances that made them jealous tend to find little difference in jealousy levels between securely attached individuals and insecurely attached individuals (Sharpsteen & Kirkpatrick, 1997).

We suggest a way to reconcile these apparently contradictory findings. Attachment style may differentially impact jealousy depending on the temporal aspect of jealousy, namely, whether the threat is in the process of being appraised or is already certain. We propose that in the first stage, the appraisal stage, securely attached individuals are likely to have a higher threshold for appraising potential threat and are therefore likely to have less frequent bouts of jealousy. In the second stage, after the threat is certain, secure individuals are more likely to react with jealous anger.

During the first stage of jealousy, secure individuals are probably less likely to appraise others as possible threats because secure individuals have a positive mental model of their partners and therefore do not expect betrayal. Across numerous dimensions of trust, including predictability, dependability, faith, and security, secure individuals rate their partners higher than insecurely attached individuals (Simpson, 1990), which most likely translates into trusting their partners to not betray them with potential rivals. Experimental studies examining threat perception seem to confirm this hypothesis. Radecki-Bush, Bush, and Jennings (1988) asked individuals to picture their partner in situations that had been rated as high threat (their partner growing close to an old girl/boyfriend), low threat (their partner commenting on the attractiveness of another person), or non-threat (their partner's phone line being busy for a half hour). Radicki-Bush and colleagues found, that regardless of scenario type, securely attached individuals viewed the scenarios as less threatening than insecurely attached individuals. Furthermore, appraisals of threat significantly predicted the intensity of jealousy. Thus, secure individuals reported feeling less jealousy overall, which supports the secure/low reactive hypothesis and the finding by Buunk (1997) that securely attached individuals anticipate feeling less jealousy.

Turning to the second stage of jealousy, reaction to the threat, securely attached individuals seem to behave quite differently under circumstances in which a threat is more certain. When their high threshold for threat is exceeded, secure individuals appear to have strong jealous reactions. Sharpsteen and Kirkpatrick (1997) asked participants to remember times when they had actually experienced jealousy and to report on their feelings and behaviors during these experiences. In terms of the severity of their actual jealousy experiences, secure individuals were not less jealous than insecure individuals. In fact, they reported feeling more intense anger than insecure-avoidant individuals and were more likely to direct that anger at their partner than either of the insecure attachment styles. These results lend support to the secure/high reactive hypothesis.

Directing anger at the partner is also consistent with the thought that for securely attached individuals, jealousy may have some beneficial effects. Anger that is directed at the partner may discourage the partner from encouraging interloper interest. Anger that is directed at the rival only discourages that specific rival from showing interest in the partner. Rivals generally come and go but partnerships tend to be more stable. Thus, discouraging the partner may have a longer-lasting impact on relationship maintenance than discouraging the rival. It may, therefore, be in the best interest of preserving the attachment relationship that one directs jealous anger toward the partner rather than the rival. Indeed, Sharpsteen and Kirkpatrick (1997) found that individuals with a secure attachment style were the only attachment style group to report that the jealousy experience brought the couple closer together. Thus, it appears that jealousy can, in some respects, preserve and protect the romantic relationship of secure individuals.

Insecure attachment styles

A strikingly different picture emerges for the insecure attachment styles. Anxiously attached individuals, unlike their securely attached counterparts, have little trust in their partners. They view themselves as unworthy of their partners' love or affection, and so expect their partners to abandon them at some point in their relationship. Simpson (1990) examined anxious attachment as a personality dimension and found that degree of anxious attachment is negatively correlated with the trust individuals have in their partner. Guerrero (1998) found further evidence for this negative correlation in her study in which participants endorsed the frequency of different types of jealous behaviors. Anxiously attached individuals reported that they often engaged in surveillance behavior like spying on their partner, keeping closer "tabs" on their partner, and searching for evidence of suspected infidelity in their partners' belongings.

The lack of trust that anxious individuals have in their partners may lead to a lower threshold for threat appraisal. When given potentially threatening scenarios, such as their partner dancing intimately with someone else, anxious individuals foresee themselves as being more jealous than more secure individuals. They are also more concerned over the possibility of their partner finding someone else (Buunk, 1997). In one experimental study (Powers, 2000), participants were assigned a partner and then shown video footage of their partner flirting with another person. Anxious individuals reported higher levels of jealousy than either secure or insecure-avoidant individuals. Across multiple studies, such as these, anxiously attached individuals appear to be more sensitive to possible threats from a rival. It appears that anxiously attached individuals have lower thresholds for threat, which make them prone to more frequent bouts of jealousy.

Reactions of anxious individuals when the threat is subjectively certain are slightly more complex. Anxious individuals tend to be low in self-regard and sometimes almost seem to expect betrayal from their partners. When betrayal does come, they often suppress overt anger toward their partner and rival (Sharpsteen & Kirkpatrick, 1997), possibly to avoid further rejection. Guerrero's (1998) examination of anxiously attached individuals' reactions to jealousy-provoking events found that they feel envy of their rivals and hurt at the possibility of separation from their partner. However, instead of attempting to heal the damage done by the interloper, they engage in behaviors like distancing themselves from their partner. Thus, their distancing reactions to threat appear to be more counterproductive than the jealousy expressions of the securely attached individuals.

Insecure-avoidant individuals, who put little stock in the relationship in the first place, appear to be the least threatened by a possible rival. Guerrero (1998) reported that individuals with negative other models (a key component of the insecure-avoidant attachment style) are the least fearful of possible rivals to their relationships. As they value attachment relationships less in general, it appears as if they are the least threatened by the possibility of the relationship ending. Simpson (1990) found that of the attachment styles, insecure-avoidant individuals showed the least remorse when the relationship ended, which is consistent with placing lower value on relationships.

When insecure-avoidant individuals do feel jealousy, they tend to direct their anger and blame at the rival rather than at their partner (Sharpsteen & Kirkpatrick, 1997). When given the opportunity to aggress against their rivals, they are amongst the most aggressive (Powers, 2000). However, even though they were aggressive to the rival, the aggression appeared to lack a strong subjective component, as these individuals reported feeling the least amount of anger and jealousy of all the attachment styles during the jealousy experience (Powers, 2000).

Jealousy and Relationship Factors

The jealousy experience likely influences aspects of the relationship such as satisfaction, quality, and security. Likewise, this influence is probably reciprocal with relationship factors contributing to jealousy. What follows is a brief review of the research that examines how jealousy influences and is influenced by relationship factors.

Satisfaction and relationship quality

One recent study on jealousy has taken the unique approach of studying jealousy from both sides of the dyad—the participant and the partner (Barelds & Barelds-Dijkstra, 2007). Of primary interest was the effect of relationship satisfaction and quality on jealousy. Using a mailed survey, the researchers were able to assess how the degree of satisfaction in a relationship relates to jealousy. They found that the higher the degree of suspicion and jealous perseveration over possible betrayal in either the participant or the partner, the less satisfied either partner was in the relationship and the lower the overall quality of the relationship. Given the relationship between insecurity and jealousy, the idea that rumination over the possibility of betrayal is harmful to a relationship is hardly a surprise. But interestingly, the degree of negative affect one felt in response to actual liaisons between a partner and a rival was positively correlated with both relationship satisfaction and quality. In other words, the better the quality of the relationship, the more jealousy one felt in response to actual betrayal. As this is a correlational study, it cannot be determined in which direction the causal arrow points. However, this finding is at least consistent with the idea that jealousy can have protecting and preserving effects on relationships.

One of the few longitudinal studies of jealousy adds more support to the view that jealousy may have some positive effects on relationship maintenance. Mathes (1986) published a 7-year longitudinal study of the long-term effects of jealousy on romantic relationships. In 1978, undergraduates in dating relationships completed jealousy measures pertaining to their current relationships. Seven years later those same participants were surveyed about the nature of their relationship with that 1978 partner, including the degree of love they currently felt toward that partner. Individuals who were high in jealousy in 1978 were more likely to be married, engaged, or living with that same partner in 1985. Participants who were lower on jealousy were less likely to be still involved with that person. Mathes postulated that jealousy may safeguard the relationship from potential relationship threats. This work suggests that jealousy may have positive effects on relationship duration. However, given that relationship satisfaction was not assessed, it remains an open question whether jealousy actually also increased positive emotional experiences.

Relationship uncertainty

Knobloch, Solomon, and Cruz (2001) examined different types of uncertainty in relation to jealousy. Participants were asked to rate their self-uncertainty, "How certain are you about your feelings for your partner?", their perceptions of their partner's uncertainty, "How certain are you about your partner's feelings for you?", and uncertainty of the relationship, "How certain are you about the future of this relationship?", and the degree to which they felt different aspects of jealousy (such as suspicion or anxiety regarding possible infidelity). Self, partner, and relationship uncertainty were all significantly correlated with suspicion and anxiety over possible threat. It appears that the more uncertain someone is about their feelings toward their partner, their partner's feelings toward them, or the future of their relationship, the more likely they are to be suspicious of possible threats.

The most likely explanation is that uncertainty may lower the threshold of subjective threat. This explanation seems consistent with what is seen in anxiously attached individuals. Indeed, Knobloch and colleagues also gave participants an attachment measure and found that anxious attachment was significantly correlated with anxiety and suspicion of betrayal. Thus, feelings of uncertainty, whether they arise from the relationship itself or from an individual's disposition, appear intricately tied with a lower threshold for appraising threat.

One factor that may influence relationship uncertainty is the existence of actual rivals. Support for rival threats affecting relationship uncertainty comes from work discussed earlier (Radecki-Bush, Bush, & Jennings, 1988) that used a jealousy-evoking imagery task to examine perception of threat. This study also asked participants in romantic relationships to rate the stability and security of their relationships while they imagined their partners in situations that were independently rated as threatening or non-threatening. Participants in the threat conditions reported more jealousy than the participants in the no threat condition. Further, the more intense the jealousy threats, the less secure the relationship felt to the participants. This finding seems consistent with the idea that feelings of jealousy are closely tied with feelings of uncertainty.

The combined results of these two studies offer us a glimpse of what may be the relationship between jealousy and relational uncertainty. It appears that the less one feels sure in a relationship, the more one appraises relationship threats in the world, which leads to more jealousy. The more jealous one feels, the more uncertain one becomes in the relationship, which in turn may feed the cycle of jealousy.

Jealousy and Attributions

Possibly the largest influence on the jealousy experience is the attributions drawn about a partner's actions. According to attribution theory (Weiner, 1985, 1995), people are constantly making appraisals about the actions of others. It is from these attributions that conclusions about others are drawn. When the outcome of an action is negative, these attributions also designate the proportion of blame the individual should receive. Recent revisions to this theory focus on three types of attributions: causality, controllability, and intent (Weiner, 1995). Causality refers to whether the action was personally caused or caused by some other force, such as fate. Controllability refers to the degree of control an actor has over the situation. An added element of control is responsibility. Take the example of John holding Martha's arm as they walk to class. If John's partner, Jane, saw this picture she would likely be jealous and blame John for his actions, as John is personally responsible for his actions and he has a high degree of control over this action. However, if Martha was having a hard time walking because of an injury, John's responsibility is much lower than previously assumed. This detail is a mitigating circumstance that allows Jane to attribute blame elsewhere, such as the lack of handicap-accessible classrooms on campus. Finally, intention of the actor plays a large role in the attributions one makes about the actor and the situation. In the example of John holding Martha's arm, one would draw different conclusions if John were holding Martha's arm to purposely make Jane jealous than if he did not realize helping her to class would make Jane upset.

The different attributions one makes about the actions of a partner play a large role in whether of not one feels jealousy. When participants were asked to rate scenarios that manipulate causality, controllability, responsibility, and intention, the results were clear and consistent. If the partner personally caused the action, has control over the action, is responsible for the action, and intentionally committed the action, the participant felt more jealousy. The opposite was also found. Actions that someone or something else causes, that the partner has no control over, was not responsible for, and does not intend to do elicited very little jealousy (Bauerle, Amirkhan, & Hupka, 2002). Thus, in a large part, it is the appraisals and attributions one makes about a partner's actions that produce jealousy, not necessarily the actions themselves.

The Rival and Jealousy

For most of this chapter, we have examined the jealousy experience as it relates to the dyad, the relationship between the individual and his or her partner. Jealousy, however, is a triadic relationship and cannot exist without the third person—the interloper. In this section we will examine this cloaked figure and what it is about him or her that can induce jealousy.

As reviewed earlier, the domain relevance hypothesis posits that one mechanism in jealousy is threat to the self-concept. When a threat to self appears, jealousy motivates one to end that threat, and thus helps to maintain the self-concept. Threats to the self are thought to be greatest in the areas that are critical to one's self-concept, i.e., the things about oneself that are valued and boost self-esteem.

Several studies have found support for this hypothesis. Early work examined individual differences in jealousy and envy over wealth, fame, popularity, and physical attractiveness (Salovey & Rodin, 1984). People reported the greatest jealousy in those domains that were most self-relevant. DeSteno and Salovey (1996a) further tested this theory by having participants read scenarios in which their partners conversed with a potential rival at a party. The scenarios depicted their partners as appearing attentive and interested in the rival. The rival was described as high in intelligence, popularity, or athleticism. Participants then rated their degree of jealousy. Later, participants were asked to rate themselves in each of these three domains. In support of the domain relevance hypothesis, participants felt the most relationship threat in reaction to rivals who had qualities that they valued most in themselves.

This effect may be due to the value placed on uniqueness. In forming one's self-concept, it often behooves one to draw distinctions between the self and others, thereby making oneself unique and special. Similar others may threaten that uniqueness, which may be especially threatening when that similar other is vying for the attention and interest of a beloved—the beloved that presumably fell for those unique, special qualities that are so valued by oneself in the first place (Broemer & Diehl, 2004). Thus, to know which rivals are going to inspire jealousy is sometimes as simple as looking in the mirror—they are a reflection of oneself.

Gender Differences in Jealousy

Is one gender more jealous than the other? Some studies find men to be more jealous than women, whereas other studies find the reverse. Thus, there seem to be no overall consistent differences in the intensity of jealousy in the two genders.

A controversial topic that has drawn a great deal of attention centers on whether men and women are jealous over different forms of infidelity. One theory hypothesizes that men should be particularly upset over a partner's sexual betrayal whereas women should be particularly upset over a partner's emotional betrayal (Buss, Larsen, Westen, & Semmelroth, 1992; Daly, Wilson, & Weghorst, 1982; Symons, 1979). This view (sometimes referred to as jealousy as a specific innate module or the JSIM hypothesis—see Harris, 2000) claims that such differences exist as a result of ancestral men and women having faced different threats to their rates of producing viable offspring (inclusive fitness). The problem that a man faced was that he could never know with 100% certainty that an offspring is genetically his own since fertilization occurs internally within women. Therefore, ancestral man needed a way to reduce this inclusive fitness threat by insuring that he spent his resources (food, time) only on children that were biologically his own. Supporting unrelated children supposedly would be quite costly to a man's inclusive fitness because it helped pass on another man's genes rather than his own. According to the JSIM hypothesis, sexual jealousy and its resulting behaviors emerged as a way for men to reduce the risk of being cuckolded. Thus, men in modern times are wired up to be jealous of sexual betrayal. Since women could always tell that an infant was indeed their own, they did not face the risk of cuckoldry. Therefore, they would not have needed to be specifically vigilant to a partner's sexual infidelity per se and would not have developed a jealousy mechanism tuned to sexual infidelity per se. However, according to the JSIM hypothesis, ancestral women did face a different inclusive fitness threat: preventing a mate from giving his resources to other women and their children, which would decrease the likelihood of the woman's own children surviving and reproducing. Thus, JSIM proposes that jealousy over emotional betrayal evolved in women as a solution to losing resources. Inherent in this proposal is the assumption that a man's emotional involvement is a strong cue to his spending resources on another. Thus, modern-day men and women should be differentially jealous over a mate's sexual vs. emotional infidelity.

Initial survey research seemed to offer support for gender differences in line with predictions of JSIM (Buss et al., 1992). People were asked to imagine that they had a partner who was engaging in either sexual or emotional infidelity and then were forced to predict which infidelity type would be more upsetting. Studies using this method almost always find that relative to men, more women chose emotional infidelity as worse (e.g., DeSteno & Salovey, 1996b; Geary, Rumsey, Bow-Thomas, & Hoard, 1995; Harris & Christenfeld, 1996; see Harris, 2003a, for a review).

However, several lines of new research with other types of measures and with participants who have actually experienced a loved one's betrayal do not support the JSIM hypothesis. Hypothetical forced-choice measures have failed to show convergent validity. Such responses usually show no relationship with other measures of jealousy over hypothetical infidelity, psychophysiological indices, or with people's recalled reactions to a mate's past infidelity (Grice & Seely, 2000; Harris, 2000, 2003b). Notably, studies examining people's feelings over real infidelity (as opposed to hypothetical infidelity) generally do not find gender differences in jealousy. For example, one study with adults of a wide age range found that men and women, regardless of sexual orientation, focused more on the emotional aspects of their partner's actual betrayal relative to the sexual aspects (Harris, 2002). Two other studies also found that men and women had similar reactions to their mates' infidelity (Berman & Frazier 2005; Harris, 2003b). Another study (Buunk, 1981) found, contrary to JSIM, that wives more than husbands had greater negative perceptions of their spouses' affairs and were specifically more upset by thinking about their mate having sexual intercourse with another person (although participants were a somewhat exotic sample, namely, people who were attempting to have sexually open relationships). It remains somewhat of a mystery why the forced-choice questions about infidelity produce gender differences when more face-valid measures have not. Findings from several studies suggest that the dubious validity of hypothetical measures in this domain may partially be due to the evocation of complex inferential thinking and presentational concerns rather than immediate emotional reactions (DeSteno & Salovey, 1996b; DeSteno, Bartlett, Braverman, & Salovey, 2002; Harris, 2000, 2003a; Harris & Christenfeld, 1996; Sabini & Green, 2004).

These findings raise the question of why evolution would have failed to produce gender differences in jealousy over infidelity. Two ideas, not mutually exclusive, have been suggested. First, there may have been no need for sexually dimorphic jealousy mechanisms—a more general jealousy mechanism may have addressed the inclusive fitness risks faced by either gender (Harris, 2003a), which could be the case even if the JSIM theory is correct in its description of the unique adaptive problems faced by ancestral man and woman. The best way to avoid the inclusive fitness risks of cuckoldry or resource loss is to prevent a mate from ever getting to the point of engaging in sexual *or* emotional infidelity. Humans, like other animals, have mating rituals that occur before intercourse (i.e., flirting). The same flirtatious behaviors (smiling, eye contact, glances back and forth) may signal sexual interest, emotional interest, or both. These usually occur well before sexual intercourse or emotional commitment in modern times, and presumably in the ancestral past. Perhaps the most successful way for both sexes to prevent a partner's betrayal would be to be watchful for any of these common early warning signs. Taking preventative steps as soon as such behaviors occur between a mate and potential rival could prevent both sexual and emotional infidelity. This type of general jealousy mechanism is consistent with the emerging evidence that men and women have similar emotional reactions to sexual and emotional infidelity.

Second, the ancestral past may have been significantly different than the one envisioned in the JSIM hypothesis. In fact, very little is known for certain regarding the sociocultural environment in which humans evolved. One possibility is that infidelity may not have occurred at high enough rates to require the evolution of specific jealousy mechanisms. Theorists such as Miller and Fishkin (1997) argue that since human infants have a particularly long period of dependency on caregivers relative to most other species, they likely required extensive paternal investment. Males who formed deep emotional attachments to their mates and offspring may have been more likely to produce viable offspring for a variety of reasons (e.g., such bonds might reduce a woman's desire for another; and if a mate died in childbirth, these men would be more likely to stick around and raise their children to maturity, etc.) (see also Zeifman & Hazan, 1997, for other possibilities). A very different hypothesis is that the ancestral past of humans may have been like many hunter-gatherer societies of the present, where sharing and cooperation are emphasized. Thus, individual males may not have been responsible for providing resources to their own offspring since the group shared food resources (White & Mullen, 1989). Therefore, a man's inclusive fitness would not be as disastrously affected by cuckoldry as suggested in the JSIM theory.

Abuse and homicide

Several studies suggest that jealousy is one of the contributing factors involved in many cases of domestic violence. For example, Mullen and Martin (1994) found that more than 15% of the men and women surveyed in a community sample reported that they had experienced physical aggression at the hands of a jealous lover. Women at shelters also often cite jealousy as the motive behind their partners' violence (Gayford, 1975). Jealousy can even lead individuals to kill the very people they love. It frequently ranks as the third or fourth most common motive in non-accidental homicides across cultures, including those as diverse as the Bhil of India, Basoga of Africa, as well as subcultures within the United States including Native Americans such as the Navajo (Betzig, 1989; Daly & Wilson, 1988; Felson, 1997; Harris, 2003a).

Early reports claimed that jealousy in men was a stronger motive for murder than in women (Daly et al., 1982). However, such work failed to take into account that men commit far more than their share of homicides of all types. Therefore, the difference in sheer numbers of jealousy-inspired murders could present a misleading picture. Two more recent studies have taken gender differences in overall murder rates into account and found a strikingly different pattern of results. Felson (1997) examined 2,060 homicides recorded in a database of 33 large urban U.S. counties and found that female murderers were significantly more likely to have been motivated by jealousy than were male murderers (approximately twice as likely). In a meta-analysis of murder motives in 20 cross-cultural samples (totaling 5,225 murders), Harris (2003a) found no overall sex difference. There was, however, a nonsignificant tendency for jealousy to be a more frequent motive for women murderers, which is consistent with Felson's findings. Thus, there is no reason to believe that jealousy is a disproportionate contributor to murder by males compared to females.

Pathological (morbid) jealousy

Sometimes jealousy takes such extreme characteristics that it is diagnosed as a clinical disorder referred to as "pathological jealousy" or "morbid jealousy" by psychiatrists (Shepherd, 1961). Jealousy in such patients is often due to delusional beliefs that a mate is cheating on them, although the diagnosis can also be given to individuals who exhibit an overly intense or exaggerated reaction to a real betrayal. People suffering from this disorder experience intensely negative feelings that are frequently accompanied by strong urges to spy on a partner. For example, an excerpt from a case study of jealousy by Wright (1994) illustrates how intense this state can be. "She exhibited a compulsion to ask her husband repeatedly if he had been unfaithful, and her day was dominated by behaviors to investigate this. For example, she would take all the phones out of the house when she was away to prevent her husband from calling another woman. She would mark his penis with a pen and examine it later to see if it had been touched. She would accompany her husband to work and stay in the car for hours at a time to stop any possible illicit liaison" (p. 431). Other case studies also vividly describe the extreme behaviors that patients with pathological jealousy will engage in. Stein, Hollander, and Josephson (1994) describe a patient who "made sure that all the blinds in the house were closed to prevent men from looking in at his wife and insisted that his wife go to the beach fully clothed" (p. 31). Pathological jealousy can also motivate violent behaviors.

There are gender differences in the prevalence of pathological jealousy. A review of several large samples of pathological jealousy suggests that approximately 64% of the diagnosed cases involved male patients while only 36% of the cases involved female patients. At least some cases of pathological jealousy appear to be a form of obsessive-compulsive disorder (OCD). Of interest, OCD with sexual obsessions occurs about twice as often in men as it does in women (Lensi et al., 1996; Roy, 1979). Thus, one possibility is that pathological jealousy is a form of sexual obsession. Three separate research groups have reported successfully treating some pathological jealousy cases with fluoxetine, a serotonin reuptake blocker, which has also been found to be helpful with other forms of OCD (Stein et al. 1994; Wing, Lee, Chiu, Ho, & Chen, 1994; Wright, 1994).

New Methodologies for the Study of Adult Jealousy

The jealousy researcher confronts a particularly challenging problem: how to elicit jealousy experimentally. This hurdle is not easily overcome given that jealousy requires complex interpersonal situations. It is also ethically challenging, because damage to existing relationships could occur as a result of the jealousy manipulation. Given these issues, the vast majority of research on adult jealousy has relied on either hypothetical scenarios in which participants try to imagine themselves in situations and then attempt to predict how they might feel or react, or retrospective recall of jealous experiences. These lines of research clearly offer insights into jealousy as discussed in the previous sections of this chapter. However, such approaches also have limitations.

Reactions to hypothetical scenarios, particularly ones that do little to engage the participant, can be poor proxies for how people will feel and react in more real emotional situations. For example, there is a large literature on emotional forecasting that suggests that people are often inaccurate in predicting emotional feelings in a variety of situations ranging from missing a subway train to failing to get tenure (e.g., Gilbert, Pinel, Wilson, Blumberg, & Wheatley, 1998; Wilson & Gilbert, 2005). Furthermore, as discussed previously, research specifically on jealousy suggests that people are particularly poor at predicting their emotions to completely hypothetical events involving infidelity.

The second method of studying jealousy, retrospective recall, has the virtue of being based on actual past emotional experiences, rather than participants' abilities to imagine people, relationships, and events that do not exist. However, recall is also subject to limitations such as potential memory failure or bias. Given the importance of jealousy, it is unfortunate that little research has experimentally manipulated it in controlled laboratory situations during adult interpersonal interactions.

Several methods have been developed to elicit jealousy in a real-time interactive way with infants and children as discussed in other chapters in this volume (see also Hart & Carrington, 2002; Hart, Carrington, Tronick, & Carroll, 2004; Hart, Field, del Valle, & Letourneau, 1998; Hart, Jones, & Field, 2003; Masciuch & Kienapple, 1993; Miller, Volling, & McElwain, 2000). However, very few studies exist that actively evoke jealousy among adults in real-time interactions due to logistical and ethical constraints. Fortunately, several new methods are being developed that may help enable researchers to actively elicit jealousy while minimizing potentially risky negative influences on the participant's actual relationships. Such methods range from intricately scripted face-to-face interactions to social rejection via computerized players.

DeSteno and colleagues (2006) have designed a sophisticated way of eliciting jealousy in the lab through orchestrated social encounters in which a participant is rejected by a partner (a confederate) in favor of a third person. (As noted earlier, rejection that triggers jealousy is proposed to be different from other forms of rejection in that it requires a social triangle and that one's interpersonal loss be another's gain.) The DeSteno and associates' experiments provided direct evidence that threats to self-esteem in a social triangle mediate jealousy. This work also found that participants who were rejected administered more unpleasant tastes (hot sauce) to both the rival and partner, which further documents the link between jealousy and interpersonal aggression.

Other recent work has also employed a rejection situation to induce jealousy in the lab (Harmon-Jones, Peterson, & Harris, 2009). In these studies, the participant played Cyberball—a cyber analogue of a ball-tossing game—with two computer-simulated players. Participants were able to select one of the two other players from a set of 8 female (or male) photos. They then played a Cyberball game while photographs of the selected player and another player of the same sex as the participant were displayed. After being included in the game for a few minutes, participants either continued to be included (control condition) or were ostracized (jealousy condition) by the player they had chosen earlier. When the ostracism occurred, the chosen partner's eyes, which were previously fixated on the participant, moved so that they now gazed at the third player. After the game, participants completed a questionnaire to assess emotions. Participants reported feeling the greatest amount of jealousy when ostracized rather than when included, and they felt more jealous when ostracized by an opposite sex partner as compared to a same-sex partner. A second study focused on the condition in which a male participant was rejected by the female partner in favor of another male to examine neural activity during the active experience of jealousy. Electroencephalograph (EEG) was recorded during the non-rejection and rejection periods and revealed that jealousy experiences were correlated with increased activity in the left frontal cortex.

Research on other emotions suggests that the brain's left hemisphere may play a particularly strong role in emotional states that lead to approach behaviors.

Although approach behaviors are often linked with positive emotions, they are also associated with the negative emotional state of anger, which can be contrasted with emotions associated with withdrawal behaviors such as fear or sadness. These data are consistent with the hypothesis that jealousy, at least initially, motivates one to engage in approach behaviors. Such behaviors might take the form of maintaining and reestablishing the relationship or may include active attempts at breaking up the threatening liaison. In work with infants, Hart and colleagues have also found that the most predictable response to jealousy evocation is approach behavior (Hart et al., 1998, 2004). Although infants show various types of negative affect (e.g., sadness, anger, fear), they show great consistency in mother-directed visual attention and proximity-seeking behaviors during jealousy evocation. Thus, several studies are consistent with the idea that jealousy is associated with action tendencies of approach.

A third new study (Harris, 2010) has focused on actively eliciting jealousy in romantic relationships that are already established. As noted above, inducing jealousy can be a potentially treacherous enterprise. If a participant witnesses a romantic partner flirting with a rival, then the effects of that flirtation on the primary relationship may last even after the experiment is over. The experimenter faces the challenge of how to elicit jealousy while ensuring that such manipulations do not have any long-lasting effects on the primary relationship. To overcome such obstacles, Harris has couples come in and then has one of them see a flirtatious computer dialogue that is purportedly occurring between the partner and another participant (a rival). In actuality, there is no rival and the partner merely types a script, which is supplied by the experimenter, into the computer. This paradigm has the advantage that jealousy is actively evoked yet potential harm to the primary relationship can be resolved at the end of the experiment. This is done by revealing that no third person actually existed and that the partner in no way engaged in flirtatious behaviors. A full debriefing at the end of the experiment as well as follow-up phone interviews later have disclosed no relationship harm. This experimental work has documented increases in physiological arousal during jealousy and has also shown that jealousy is often expressed by derogating the rival. These new interactive paradigms seem promising, although they too have limitations in the types and degree of jealousy that can be studied.

Concluding Remarks

In closing, this chapter has focused on theories, debates, and empirical research pertaining to adult relationships. Jealousy is a fundamentally social emotion with complicated underpinnings that can produce both functional and dysfunctional behaviors. At its most intense, it can have dire social and personal consequences as seen in the crime statistics and pathological jealousy cases. Even the less intense forms of jealousy can have undesirable effects, as discussed earlier. One issue that remains open is to what degree extreme cases reflect the same underlying mechanisms that give rise to more common forms of jealousy. However, both theory and research suggest that jealousy may not produce unitarily negative effects. One prominent theory of the origins of jealousy is that it evolved to promote the maintenance and restoration of relationships that are threatened by potential rivals. Some of the empirical work covered in this chapter is clearly consistent with such a view. For example, people report that jealousy led them to make themselves more attractive to their partners and to attempt to secure greater relationship commitment (Mullen & Martin, 1994). Moreover, higher initial levels of jealousy were associated with a greater propensity to be in the same relationship 7 years later (Mathes, 1986).

This chapter has covered several of the factors that are associated with propensity toward jealousy and differential behavioral reactions to jealousy. However, getting tighter control on precisely when jealousy will occur and what factors make it detrimental or beneficial has been partially hindered in the adult domain by methodological limitations. We are optimistic that some of these barriers will be overcome with recent innovations in paradigms that elicit jealousy actively in interpersonal situations in the laboratory.

References

Barelds, D. P., & Barelds-Dijkstra, P. (2007). Relations between different types of jealousy and self and partner perceptions of relationship quality. *Clinical Psychology and Psychotherapy, 14,* 176–188.

Bartholomew, K. (1990). Avoidance of intimacy: An attachment perspective. *Journal of Social and Personal Relationships, 7,* 147–178.

Bauerle, S. Y., Amirkhan, J. H., & Hupka, R. B. (2002). An attribution theory analysis of romantic jealousy. *Motivation and Emotion, 26,* 297–319.

Baumeister, R. F., & Leary, M. R. (1995). The need to belong: Desire for interpersonal attachments as a fundamental human motivation. *Psychological Bulletin, 117,* 497–529.

Berman, M. I., & Frazier, P. A. (2005). Relationship power and betrayal experience as predictors of reactions to infidelity. *Personality and Social Psychology Bulletin, 31,* 1617–1627.

Betzig, L. (1989). Causes of conjugal dissolution: A cross-cultural study. *Current Anthropology, 30,* 654–676.

Bowlby, J. (1969). *Attachment and loss: Vol. 1. Attachment.* New York: Basic Books.

Broemer, P., & Diehl, M. (2004). Romantic jealousy as a social comparison outcome: When similarity stings. *Journal of Experimental Social Psychology, 40,* 393–400.

Buss, D. M., Larsen, R. J., Westen, D., & Semmelroth, J. (1992). Sex differences in jealousy: Evolution, physiology, and psychology. *Psychological Science, 3,* 251–255.

Buunk, B. (1981). Jealousy in sexually open marriages. *Journal of Family and Economic Issues, 4,* 357–372.

Buunk, B. P. (1997). Personality, birth order and attachment styles as related to various types of jealousy. *Personality and Individual Differences, 23,* 997–1006.

Cubiciotti, D. D., & Mason, W. A. (1978). Comparative studies of social behavior in Callicebus and Saimiri: Heterosexual jealousy behavior. *Behavioral Ecology and Sociobiology, 3,* 311–322.

Daly, M., & Wilson, M. (1988). *Homicide.* Hawthorne, NY: Aldine de Gruyter.

Daly, M., Wilson, M., & Weghorst, S. J. (1982). Male sexual jealousy. *Ethology and Sociobiology, 3,* 11–27.

DeSteno, D., Bartlett, M. Y., Braverman, J., & Salovey, P. (2002). Sex differences in jealousy: Evolutionary mechanism or artifact of measurement. *Journal of Personality and Social Psychology, 83,* 1103–1116.

DeSteno, D. A., & Salovey, P. (1996a). Jealousy and the characteristics of one's rival: A self-evaluation maintenance perspective. *Personality and Social Psychology Bulletin, 22,* 920–932.

DeSteno, D. A., & Salovey, P. (1996b). Evolutionary origins of sex differences in jealousy? Questioning the "fitness" of the model. *Psychological Science, 7,* 367–372.

DeSteno, D., Valdesolo, P., & Bartlett, M. Y. (2006). Jealousy and the threatened self: Getting to the heart of the green-eyed monster. *Journal of Personality and Social Psychology, 91,* 626–641.

Ekman, P. (1992). Facial expression of emotion: New findings, new questions. *Psychological Science, 3,* 34–38.

Felson, R. B. (1997). Anger, aggression, and violence in love triangles. *Violence Victims, 12,* 345–362.

Frijda, N. (1986). *The emotions.* Cambridge: Cambridge University Press.

Gayford, J. J. (1975). Wife battering: A preliminary survey of 100 cases. *British Medical Journal, 1,* 194–197.

Geary, D. C., Rumsey, M., Bow-Thomas, C. C., & Hoard, M. K. (1995). Sexual jealousy as a facultative trait: Evidence from the pattern of sex differences in adults from China and the United States. *Ethology and Sociobiology, 16,* 355–383.

Gilbert, D. T., Pinel, E. C., Wilson, T. D., Blumberg, S. J., & Wheatley, T. P. (1998). Immune neglect: A source of durability bias in affective forecasting. *Journal of Personality and Social Psychology, 75,* 617–638.

Grice, J. W., & Seely, E. (2000). The evolution of sex differences in jealousy: Failure to replicate previous results. *Journal of Research in Personality, 34,* 348–356.

Guerrero, L. K. (1998). Attachment-style differences in the experience and expression of romantic jealousy. *Personal Relationships, 5,* 273–291.

Harmon-Jones, E., Peterson, C. K., & Harris, C. R. (2009). Jealousy: Novel methods and neural correlates. *Emotion, 9,* 113–117.

Harris, C. R. (2000). Psychophysiological responses to imagined infidelity: The specific innate modular view of jealousy reconsidered. *Journal of Psychology and Personal Psychology, 78,* 1082–1091.

Harris, C. R. (2002). Sexual and romantic jealousy in heterosexual and homosexual adults. *Psychological Science, 13,* 7–12.

Harris, C. R. (2003a). A review of sex differences in sexual jealousy, including self-report data, psychophysiological responses, interpersonal violence and morbid jealousy. *Personality and Social Psychology Review, 7,* 102–128.

Harris, C. R. (2003b). Factors associated with jealousy over real and imagined infidelity: An examination of the social-cognitive and evolutionary psychology perspectives. *Psychology of Women Quarterly, 27*, 319–329.

Harris, C. R. (2010). *Jealousy in couples: A new experimental paradigm.* Manuscript in preparation, University of California at San Diego.

Harris, C. R., & Christenfeld, N. (1996). Gender, jealousy, and reason. *Psychological Science, 7*, 364–366.

Hart, S., & Carrington, H. (2002). Jealousy in 6-month-old infants. *Infancy, 3*, 395–402.

Hart, S., Carrington, H., Tronick, E. Z., & Carroll, S. (2004). When infants lose exclusive maternal attention: Is it jealousy? *Infancy, 6*, 57–78.

Hart, S., Field, T., del Valle, C., & Letourneau, M. (1998). Infants protest their mothers' attending to an infant-size doll. *Social Development, 7*, 54–61.

Hart, S., Jones, N. A., & Field, T. (2003). Atypical jealousy in infants of intrusive- and withdrawn-depressed mothers. *Child Psychiatry and Human Development, 33*, 193–207.

Hazan, C., & Shaver, P. (1987). Romantic love conceptualized as an attachment process. *Interpersonal Relations and Group Processes, 52*, 511–524.

House, J. S., Landis, K. R., & Umberson, D. (1988). Social relationships and health. *Science, 241*, 540–545.

Hupka, R.B. (1984). Jealousy: Compound emotion or label for a particular situation? *Motivation and Emotion, 8*, 141–155.

Keltner, D., & Haidt, J. (1999). Social functions of emotions at four levels of analysis. *Cognition and Emotion, 13*, 505–521.

Kirkpatrick, L. A., & Hazan, C. (1994). Attachment styles and close relationships: A four-year prospective study. *Personal Relationships, 1*, 123–142.

Knobloch, L. K., Solomon, D. H., & Cruz, M. G. (2001). The role of relationship development and attachment in the experience of romantic jealousy. *Personal Relationships, 8*, 205–224.

Lazarus, R.S. (1991). *Emotion and adaptation.* New York: Oxford University Press.

Lensi, P., Cassano, G. B., Correddu, G., Ravagli, S., Kunovac, J. L., & Akiskal, H. S. (1996). Obsessive-compulsive disorder: Familial-development history, symptomatology, comorbidity and course with special reference to gender-related differences. *The British Journal of Psychiatry, 169*, 101–107.

Lerner, J. S., & Tiedens, L. Z. (2006). Portrait of the angry decision maker: How appraisal tendencies shape anger's influence on cognition. *Journal of Behavior Decision Making, 19*, 115–137.

Masciuch, S., & Kienapple, K. (1993). The emergence of jealousy in children 4 months to 7 years of age. *Journal of Social and Personal Relationships, 10*, 421–435.

Mathes, E. W. (1986). Jealousy and romantic love: A longitudinal study. *Psychological Reports, 58*, 885–886.

Mathes, E. W. (1991). A cognitive theory of jealousy. In P. Salovey (Ed.), *The psychology of jealousy and envy* (pp. 271–286). New York: Guilford Press.

Mathes, E. W., Adams, H. E., & Davies, R. M. (1985). Jealousy: Loss of relationship rewards, loss of self-esteem, depression, anxiety, and anger. *Journal of Personality and Social Psychology, 42*, 1552–1561.

Miller, A. L., Volling, B. L., & McElwain, N. L. (2000). Sibling jealousy in a triadic context with mothers and fathers. *Social Development, 9*, 433–457.

Miller, L. C., & Fishkin, S. A. (1997). On the dynamics of human bonding and reproductive success: Seeking windows on the adapted-for human–environmental interface. In J. A. Simpson & D. T. Kenrick (Eds.), *Evolutionary social psychology* (pp. 197–
236). Mahwah, NJ: Erlbaum.

Mullen, P. E., & Martin, J. (1994). Jealousy: A community study. *The British Journal of
Psychiatry, 164,* 35–43.

Parrott, W. G. (1991). The emotional experiences of envy and jealousy. In P. Salovey (Ed.),
The psychology of jealousy and envy (pp. 3–30). New York: Guilford Press.

Parrott, W. G., & Smith, R. H. (1993). Distinguishing the experiences of envy and
jealousy. *Journal of Personality and Social Psychology, 64,* 906–920.

Powers, A. M. (2000). The effects of attachment style and jealousy on aggressive behavior
against a partner and a rival. *Dissertation Abstracts International, 61,* 6-B, 3325.

Radecki-Bush, C., Bush, J.P., & Jennings, J. (1988). Effects of jealousy threats on
relationship perceptions and emotions. *Journal of Social and Personal Relationships,
5,* 285–303.

Roy A. (1979). Obsessive-compulsive neurosis: Phenomenology, outcome and a comparison with hysterical neurosis. *Comprehensive Psychiatry, 20,* 528–531.

Sabini, J., & Green, M.C. (2004). Emotional responses to sexual and emotional infidelity:
Constants and differences across genders, samples, and methods. *Personality and
Social Psychology Bulletin, 30,* 1375–1388.

Salovey, P., & Rodin, J. (1984). Some antecedents and consequences of social-comparison
jealousy. *Journal of Personality and Social Psychology, 47,* 780–792.

Salovey, P., & Rothman, A. (1991). Envy and jealousy: Self and society. In P. Salovey (Ed.),
The psychology of jealousy and envy (pp. 271–286). New York: Guilford Press.

Sharpsteen, D. J. (1991). The organization of jealousy knowledge: Romantic jealousy as a
blended emotion. In P. Salovey (Ed.), *The psychology of jealousy and envy* (pp. 31–51).
New York: Guilford Press.

Sharpsteen, D. J., & Kirkpatrick, L. A. (1997). Romantic jealousy and adult romantic
attachment. *Personality Processes and Individual Differences, 72,* 627–640.

Shepherd, M. (1961). Morbid jealousy: Some clinical and social aspects of a psychiatric
syndrome. *Journal of Mental Science, 107,* 687–753.

Simpson, J. A. (1990). Influence of attachment styles on romantic relationships. *Journal of
Personality and Social Psychology, 59,* 971–980.

Stein, D. J., Hollander, E., & Josephson, S. C. (1994). Serotonin reuptake blockers for the
treatment of obsessional jealousy. *Journal of Clinical Psychiatry, 55,* 30–33.

Symons, D. (1979). *The evolution of human sexuality.* New York: Oxford University Press.

Tesser, A. (1988). Toward a self-evaluation maintenance model of social behavior. In
L. Berkowitz (Ed.), *Advances in experimental social psychology* (Vol. 20, pp. 181–227).
New York: Academic Press.

Trivers, R.L. (1972). Parental investment and sexual selection. In B. Campbell (Ed.), *Sexual
selection and the descent of man, 1871–1971* (pp. 136–179). Chicago: Aldine.

Volling, B. L., McElwain, N. L., & Miller, A. L. (2002). Emotion regulation in context: The
jealousy complex between young siblings and its relations with child and family
characteristics. *Child Development, 73,* 581–600.

Weiner, B. (1985). An attributional theory of achievement motivation and emotion.
Psychological Review, 92, 548–573.

Weiner, B. (1995). *Judgments of responsibility: A foundation for theory of social conduct.* New York: Guilford Press.

White, G., & Mullen, P. E. (1989). *Jealousy: Theory, research, and clinical strategies.* New York: Guilford Press.

Wilson, T. D., & Gilbert, D. T. (2005). Affective forecasting: Knowing what to want. *Current Directions in Psychological Science, 14,* 131–134.

Wing, Y. K., Lee, S., Chiu, H. F., Ho, C. K., & Chen, C. N. (1994). A patient with coexisting narcolepsy and morbid jealousy showing favorable response to fluoxetine. *Postgraduate Medical Journal, 70,* 34–36.

Wright, S. (1994). Familial obsessive-compulsive disorder presenting as pathological jealousy successfully treated with fluoxetine. *Archives of General Psychiatry, 51,* 430–431.

Zeifman, D., & Hazan, C. (1997). Attachment: The bond in pair-bonds. In J. A. Simpson & D. T. Kenrick (Eds.), *Evolutionary social psychology* (pp. 237–263). Mahwah, NJ: Erlbaum.

Index

Handbook of Jealousy: Theory, Research and Multidisciplinary Approaches, First Edition.
Edited by Sybil L. Hart and Maria Legerstee.
© 2013 Blackwell Publishing Ltd. Published 2013 by Blackwell Publishing Ltd.